International Business Studies

B

International Business Studies

AN OVERVIEW

Peter J. Buckley and Michael Z. Brooke

Blackwell Publishers
108 Cowley Road
Oxford OX4 1JF
UK

Three Cambridge Center
Cambridge, Massachusetts 02142
USA

A CIP catalogue record for this book is available from the British Library.

Library of Congress Cataloging in Publication Data
Buckley, Peter J.
International business studies: an overview/Peter Buckley and Michael Brooke.
p.   cm.
Includes bibliographical references and index.
ISBN 0–631–15742–5 (alk. paper)
1. International economic relations.   2. International trade.   3. International business enterprises.   I. Brooke, Michael Z.   II. Title.
HF 1359.B83   1991   91–12915
338.8′8—dc20   CIP

Typeset in 10 on 12 pt Ehrhardt
by Graphicraft Typesetters Ltd., Hong Kong
Printed in Great Britain by TJ Press Ltd, Padstow, Cornwall

This book is printed on acid-free paper.

Contents

Preface

This book is written with the conviction that there is a body of intellectual knowledge that covers all aspects of business across frontiers, and that this body of knowledge can be brought together within a systematic volume. We have set out to identify the rich variety of thought and research that has gone into producing the theoretical and empirical work recorded here. Inevitably we have been selective – we have been compiling a book not a library – and some will find favourite themes omitted; but we have enlisted much help in using our judgement on the themes to include.

Many members of the Academy of International Business and other scholars have contributed to this work by writing to the authors with suggestions when the idea was first conceived, by sending us lists of publications and by drafting individual chapters. Both authors have played a part in all the chapters through discussion and editing and both accept responsibility for the whole. Within this general responsibility, Peter Buckley has written or commissioned Parts 1, 2, 4, 5 and 7, while Michael Brooke has written Parts 3 and 6 (apart from Chapter 3.4, Chapter 6.6, Chapter 6.8, Chapter 6.9, Chapter 6.11 and Chapter 6.12). Individual chapters have been written by Jeremy Clegg (Part 2); Hafiz Mirza (Chapter 3.4 and Chapter 4.4); Bob Pearce (Chapter 4.3); Eugen Jehle (Chapter 4.5); Bryan Lowes (Chapter 4.6, Chapter 6.6 and Chapter 6.12); Kate Prescott (Chapter 6.8); Alexander von Boehmer, Klaus Brockhaff and Alan Pearson (Chapter 6.9) and Peter Enderwick (Chapter 6.11). Jenny Woods contributed to Chapter 3.1, Bob Pearce to Chapter 1.3 and Brian Dawes to Part 7. Guy Lawson contributed to Part 3.

In attempting to summarize a body of knowledge of such breadth, the authors have accepted that different aspects demand different approaches. The statements of economic theory in Part 1, for instance, are treated differently from the more political issues at stake with the treaty organizations and the new international economic order that form the substance of Part 3. We hope that the reader will be as convinced as we are that we have portrayed the rich diversity of the subject in presentation as well as in content.

No one can survey the literature on international business without being impressed at the quality of so much research coming from so many sources and a range of disciplines; some of the research has developed in a relatively short space of time. However ancient studies of trade theory may be, the multinational as a management phenomenon is a much more recent topic, as are many aspects of a rapidly changing environment. A few bad habits have also crept into international business studies. Shared with other management writing is a tendency to dress up a little banal advice in grandiose phrases like 'a normative approach'; or there is an abuse of words like 'strategy', which finds itself employed to cover most management activities. This latter tendency is remarked in Chapter 6.1 in emphasizing the distinction between strategy and planning. These are minor blemishes in the forming of a body of knowledge whose codification we are proud to undertake.

This is designed as a reference book for the scholar. To any individual reader, some parts will be all too familiar; most of us are specialists and we have assumed there are gaps to be filled in the knowledge of all of us. So we have aimed at general statements accompanied by bibliographies that should be regarded as recommended reading. To make them truly comprehensive would have been to produce several volumes. Apart from publications considered seminal, or at least not so far replaced, our policy has been to restrict references to books and papers published in the 1980s.

We should like to thank Mrs Chris Barkby and Mrs Liz Hickson for their efficient word-processing of the many drafts of this volume.

Peter J. Buckley
Michael Z. Brooke
Bradford
Manchester
May 1991

Part 1

Theories Relevant to International Trade and Investment

Introduction

Part 1 introduces and summarizes the theories relevant to international business. Trade theory is examined in Chapter 1.1, the theories of international investment in Chapter 1.2, technology transfer in Chapter 1.3 and theories of the Multinational Enterprise in Chapter 1.4. Part 1 provides the background for the examination of international trade and its institutions in Parts 2 and 3; for national characteristics and international investment in Parts 4 and 5; for management aspects in Part 6 and for International Business Teaching and Research in Part 7.

Contents

1.1

Theories of International Trade

1.1.1 Introduction

The study of international trade has been a major element in economic theory for as long as (and perhaps before) the subject has existed. This chapter attempts a brief review of a voluminous and complicated literature. It concentrates on the positive theory of international trade with a brief examination of the normative theory.

Trade theory has developed from the evolution of successively dominant single models to a variety of models attempting to explain different aspects of international trade, within a coherent overall framework. Overviews of the subject include standard textbooks such as Grubel (1981), Lindert and Kindleberger (1982), Wilson (1986), shorter treatments such as Shone (1972), more detailed treatises such as Dixit and Norman (1980), and survey collections such as the two volumes edited by Jones and Kennen (1984) (single-volume summary edited by Jones (1986)). Trade policy and issues of money and the balance of payments are dealt with briefly in Section 1.1.8 and in Part 2 below.

Following a brief statement of the concept of absolute advantage, Section 1.1.2 considers the key notion of comparative advantage. Section 1.1.3 examines the Hecksher-Ohlin theorem and factor price equalization. Section 1.1.4 and Section 1.1.5 consider multi-level trade and multi-behavioural trade which attempt to encompass real world complications in single analytical models. Section 1.1.6 considers the relationship between growth and trade and Section 1.1.7 briefly examines normative trade theory. The conclusion reviews the relevance of trade theory to an understanding of modern international business.

Absolute advantage

The most obvious basis for international trade, usually traced back to Adam Smith (1776) but much older than that, is the concept of absolute advantage.

If country A can produce a good cheaper than country B, and country B can produce a second good more cheaply than country A, then it is to the advantage of both countries to specialize in the good in which their production is most efficient. International exchange thus facilitates specialization and the division of labour and enables an increase in welfare to occur in both countries.

A more important question, for analytical purposes, is: where country A can produce *both* goods in greater amount with the same cost of production as country B, will trade still be viable? The answer to this leads to the concept of comparative advantage and to the key issues in trade theory.

1.1.2   Comparative advantage

David Ricardo (1817) was concerned to show there could be welfare gains from international trade *even when* one country has an absolute advantage in all production of commodities. This is the case so long as each country has a comparative advantage, i.e. its advantage is greater in one commodity than in the other. It should then export the good where its relative cost of production is lower and import the good for which it has a comparative disadvantage.

The model of comparative advantage as developed by Ricardo implicitly assumed the only factor of production that determined cost was labour. Essentially, the value of output was proportional to the amount of labour-time involved in production. Other costs were ignored, perhaps for simplicity of exposition. Many other restrictive assumptions are involved in this model. Much of the development of international trade theory has been the progressive relaxation of these assumptions. Key limitations include: static conditions and given resources, two countries, two goods, one factor of production (labour, which is mobile nationally but not internationally), constant costs per unit, zero transportation costs, no role for demand and no distribution of income effects.

Despite this, the principle of comparative advantage is one of the most important and general concepts to have been developed in the economics literature.

1.1.3   The Hecksher-Ohlin approach and factor price equalization

A theory that might be termed the standard neoclassical approach to trade has been derived from classic works by Hecksher (1919) and Ohlin (1933), with later additions, and is known as the Hecksher-Ohlin model. Its basic explanation of trade is that different goods require different proportions of factors of production (land, labour, capital) and that different countries are endowed with unequal amounts of these factors. In countries well-endowed with particular factors, the production of goods that embody relatively large amounts of these abundant factors will result in lower prices. Countries will specialize in goods where they have this price advantage and will exchange them for goods where they are similarly disadvantaged. An increase in world welfare and efficiency will result from such specialized production and exchange.

This model requires a large number of highly restrictive assumptions to achieve determinancy. Among these are homogeneous products (no product differentiation), identical production functions in all countries (i.e. the proportions of the factors required to produce a certain good are invariant), equal access to the same body of technical knowledge, identical consumer preferences, factors of production perfectly mobile within countries but immobile between them and no transport costs or other barriers to trade, such as tariffs, are perfectly competitive markets.

A whole industry has arisen in generalizing the Hecksher-Ohlin model beyond its initial two-good, two-factor, two-country format and in relaxing the restrictions of its assumptions. Essentially, though, the model retains heuristic value in its powerful but simple explanation of trade patterns. An important corollary of the theory first expounded by Samuelson (1948) is the factor-price equalization theorem. This states that, if Hecksher-Ohlin conditions hold, then free trade between countries with different factor prices and therefore comparative costs will lead to a tendency towards the equalization of factor prices between countries.

An attempt to test the empirical validity of the Hecksher-Ohlin theorem is provided by Edward Leamer (1984). Leamer attempts to explain the pattern of trade and resource supplies of 59 countries in terms of the abundance of 11 key resources. Problems of aggregation, distinguishing one theory from a close rival, estimation and relating data to theory abound in the work but the quality of the explanation of the pattern of trade given by resource endowments is impressive.

1.1.4   Multi-level trade

This section introduces complications into the basic trade-model, examining the impact of specific factors of production, non-traded goods trade in intermediate goods and natural resources, trade in factors and technology trade.

It is apparent that international trade does not take place exclusively, even primarily, in final goods. Much trade takes place in raw materials, in intermediate goods and in factors of production (labour (including management), capital and technology).

Trade in technology is an important facet of modern international business. The essentially static nature of the basic trade models led to a search for adequate modelling of the impact of technological change on trade patterns. These include the models of Posner (1961), Hufbauer (1966) and Vernon (1966).

Posner's model examines the impact of an innovation in one country that diffuses to other countries with a time lag. This lag is of two parts – a reaction lag during which the impact of the technological advance reaches other countries as imports impinge on their markets, and an imitation lag during which foreign competitors assimilate the new product or process. At the end of the sum of these lags, foreign competitors succeed in imitating the innovation and imports begin to recede. This model is similar to Hufbauer's, except that he extends the possibilities by introducing long-run dynamic economies of scale arising from 'learning by doing'. Average costs fall as achieved volumes of production increase, giving innovators an important competitive advantage. Vernon's model is a programmatic analysis of technological innovation involving initially technology gap type trade, then a switch to foreign investment by innovators to tap foreign demand and choke off local competition and finally cost-reduction-orientated investment as the product traded becomes standardized. (Vernon's model is discussed in detail in Sections 1.2.3 and 6.8.4.) A review of technical change and international trade is provided by Dosi and Soete (1988).

1.1.5   Multi-behavioural trade

When allowance is made for imperfections in markets, then discretionary behaviour becomes possible for management although models of trade that allow for imperfect competition severely constrain the scope for variation in behaviour by restrictive assumptions. This limits the practical utility of the models but makes them determinate. It leads on to envisaging trade behaviour in a game-theoretic framework (Section 1.1.7 below). Further, when technological possibilities allow for economies of scale and increasing returns, outcomes are widened. Trade within an industry group and within a firm are further variants of multiple outcomes.

The Hecksher-Ohlin approach assumed that demand patterns (tastes) are identical in different countries. Thus trade is entirely supply-determined. However, if consumer preferences in different countries diverge, then relative prices could differ even if factor endowments are identical. The basis for trade would thus be that demand was greatest for a particular product. This provides the germ of an explanation for the preponderance of world trade being between advanced industrialized countries with similar factor endowments. Linder's theory (1961) was that overlapping demand leads to the possibility of countries of similar factor endowments, geographical proximity, cultural links and per capita income doing most trade with each other. This leads on to the explanation of intra-industry trade in differentiated products.

The demand-side explanation is strengthened when the empirical phenomenon of increasing returns to scale is incorporated into the explanation of trade patterns. The Hecksher-Ohlin theory assumed decreasing returns to scale (increasing average costs). However, many manufacturing industries exhibit decreasing average costs. This focuses attention on the length of runs and the tension between product variety and standardization.

Intra-industry trade

Intra-industry trade theory attempts to explain trade in differentiated products that are close substitutes, i.e. the simultaneous import and exports of goods and services with the same industry. (Grubel and Lloyd (1975), Greenaway and Milner (1986).) The theoretical developments stem from modelling of preference diversity and economies of scale and link closely with the impact on trade of imperfect competition models (Greenaway and Tharakan (1986)).

Vertical integration and world trade

A study of multinationals and world trade that concentrates on vertical integration and the nature of the division of labour in world industries suggests an interesting typology of industries (Casson (1988)) and their associated intra-industry trade. Type I new industry is product-based with intra-firm trade in final goods between advanced countries. Type II is mature product industries where technology is codified and transferable and where intra-firm exports of specialized components and capital equipment occurs while finished products are exported to final markets from parent or subsidiary. Type III industries are designated rationalized product industries where the intra-firm division of labour is developed so that component specialization takes place on an international basis. Offshore assembly is undertaken, also based on low-cost labour in the newly industrializing countries. In Type IV, resource-based industries, trade is dominated by the export of raw materials or some processed intermediate products from countries with large endowments of raw materials to more developed countries for finishing and marketing. Type V industries, 'trading services', are international wholesale and retail operations confined to advanced countries and newly industrializing countries. Finally, in Type VI, non-tradeable services, no trade in intermediate products takes place. This typology shows the richness of the modes of modern trade and highlights the importance of trade in intermediate goods and services.

Trade in services

The role of services as intermediate inputs suggests that such trade plays an important part in the process of economic growth. The efficient supply of key services is an important part of international competitiveness (Tucker and Sundberg (1988)). The internal trade of services such as management, engineering, marketing and financial services, along with the services of such assets as patents, trademarks and reputations form a major part of the activities of multinational enterprises. (Enderwick (1988) particularly Chapter 2: 'Service Trade by the Multinational Enterprise' by Markusen.)

Intra-firm trade

International trade that is also intra-firm is a rapidly growing phenomenon. An increased division of labour leads to pressure for vertical integration to control supplies of intermediate goods and services within the firm. The multinational enterprise as a device for the control of internal markets thus becomes a major factor in world trade. (Casson (1986), Buckley and Casson (1976).) As a single firm is both buyer and seller in these situations, a large proportion of world trade is carried out using internal transfer prices that may well differ from arm's-length market values.

1.1.6   Growth and trade

Trade and trade policy does not occur in a static world. The relationship between trade and growth has been a long-standing issue of importance, particularly with regard to causality. Models have variously assumed (often implicitly) that trade causes growth or that growth is the result of trade.

The inappropriateness of this argument has been suggested in particular with reference to the less-developed countries. Trade as an engine of growth for less-developed countries has been challenged in particular through the publications and policies of the United Nations Conference on Trade and Development (UNCTAD). The static nature of the gains from trade approach has been challenged, based on the view that free trade condemns the less-developed countries to specialize in primary products that have suffered a secular decline in their terms of trade (crudely, the ratio of their export prices index to an index of import prices). Evidence on terms of trade has been controversial (Spraos (1980)) but generally supports this hypothesis.

This third-world trade protest led to an increase in the numbers of countries following inward-looking protectionist policies. However, the success of outward-looking policies based on the creation of new islands of competitiveness in manufactures followed by countries such as South Korea, Taiwan and Singapore has led to a revision of views on the merits of outward-orientated development policies. The search for niches of comparative advantage in less-developed countries is by no means easy and demands for a fundamental restructuring of the world trading regime are still strong under the banner of the New International Economic Order (NIEO). This is fully covered in Section 1.3.4. For a review of trade theory as it applies to less-developed countries, see Greenaway and Milner (1987).

1.1.7   Normative trade theory

Recent developments in the international economics literature have placed trade policy back on the political agenda and brought the theory of international trade much closer to the theory of the multinational enterprise. The introduction of market imperfections leads to the possibility of oligopolistic actions and reactions or strategic behaviour. Arguments that parallel the optimum tariff have been reinvigorated to suggest that import restrictions might be welfare-improving for the protectionist nation. The concepts used to justify this approach provide scope for integration with the theory of the multinational enterprise in the theoretical arena.

Many of the earlier models took the internalization decision for granted (see 1.3 below) but the rapprochement between trade theory and the multinational enterprise is now proceeding apace (see Helpman and Krugman (1987), and Ethier (1986)).

Political economy aspects should not be ignored. In a short article, Frey (1987) shows that explicitly political considerations can be incorporated into the economic model to show that tariffs might still be chosen even in a democratic society where a small group, holding intense views, may dictate policy.

Customs union theory

The classic work of Jacob Viner (1950) moved the theory of customs union away from a general presumption that welfare would improve because the formation of such a union was a move towards free trade. Instead, Viner identified the fact that a union also involves the erection of a common external tariff; the consequence of this is trade diversion as well as trade creation. The net effect is thus dependent on the size of trade diversion, away from lower-cost sources to intra-union trade as well as the increase of trade within the union consequent on the disappearance of internal tariffs. To these static effects must be added the dynamic gains from forming the union. These arise from the advantages of the larger market allowing economies of scale to be exploited (Owen (1983)) and the effects of extra competition on domestic industry. As well as trade effects, investment effects will also occur – for a review see Buckley and Artisien (1987).

1.1.8 Money and the balance of payments

The pure theory of trade concerns real variables and relative prices rather than monetary values. International monetary theory concerns itself with values measured in currency units and includes the general price level, financial assets and exchange rates between different currencies. Thus macroeconomic policy variables such as inflation and unemployment are shown to be connected to international trade.

The balance-of-payment accounts are the record of all transactions between the residents of one country and the rest of the world over a given period. The accounts follow the principles of double entry book-keeping with each item appearing twice in the accounts – once as a debit, once as a credit. The principles underlying balance-of-payment accounts are outlined in the International Monetary Fund's Balance of Payments Manual (1977) which attempts to give individual national accounts international comparability. Details of the minutiae of the British accounts are given in Buckley and Pearce (1991). Particular difficulties arise in measuring and recording international financial flows, particularly those that are intra-firm. There is a growing concern that the global current-account balance (the sum of the individual countries' balance of payments) shows an increasing discrepancy because of major changes in the nature and speed of international financial transaction, notably new financial instruments. The increased liberalization of the international financial system and the closer integration of financial markets, together with rapid technological developments in the means of effecting these transaction, have outpaced statistical recording. An International Monetary Fund working party is currently examining these difficulties.

Balance-of-payment policies

While the balance of payments always balances in an accounting sense, policies need to be implemented to correct fundamental disequilibria that show up as persistent deficits (or surpluses) in the accounts. Automatic adjustment mechanisms such as fluctuations in the value of the currency are then inappropriate; longer-term, more sustained action must be taken. These actions are usually classified as expenditure changing (reducing demand to reduce imports, for instance), expenditure switching (not necessarily altering the level of demand but switching it away from imports, for instance), and direct controls. Within a general equilibrium framework, balance-of-payments policies must be maintained not only to keep the external balance stable but also the internal balance of the economy between inflationary conditions and unemployment. Attention must be paid to the trade-offs between these policy targets. (See Stern (1973), Grubel (1981).) Both monetarist (Williamson (1983)) and structuralist approaches (Thirlwall (1983)) to balance-of-payments adjustment policies are advocated. The latter are regarded as particularly appropriate to less-developed countries.

1.1.9   The relevance of international trade theories to international business

International trade theories are relevant to international business in two ways. First, trade theories are key components in understanding the means by which the international economy operates. Second, trade theories are a powerful influence on the policies of particularly national governments but also those of firms and international bodies.

At the beginning of the 1990s, trade theories are becoming much more relevant both to international business theory, through their emphasis on behaviour in imperfect markets, and to policy-making, through their emphasis on the presumed gains from strategic intervention in trade flows (Krugman (1986)). The possibility of a theoretical justification for subsidizing a high-return domestic industry both to give it a head start, as in the infant industry argument, or to sustain its competitive advantages, reopens the debate on free trade versus protectionism (Krugman (1988)). This rethinking of trade theory and policy seems set fair to reinvigorate this important branch of international business theory.

References

Buckley, Peter J. and Artisien, Patrick (1987): *North-South Direct Investment in the European Communities*. London: Macmillan.

Buckley, Peter J. and Casson, Mark (1976): *The Future of the Multinational Enterprise*. London: Macmillan.

Buckley, Peter J. and Casson, Mark (1985): *The Economic Analysis of the Multinational Enterprise*. London: Macmillan.

Buckley, Peter J. and Pearce, Robert D. (1991): *International Aspects of UK Economic Activities*. London: Chapman and Hall.

Casson, Mark and associates (1988): *Multinationals and World Trade*. London: George Allen & Unwin.

Dixit, A.K. and Norman, V. (1980): *Theory of International Trade*. Cambridge: Cambridge University Press.

Dosi, Giovanni and Soete, Luc (1988): 'Technical Change and International Trade' in G. Dosi, C. Freman, R. Nelson, G. Silverberg and L. Soete (eds): *Technical Change and Economic Theory*. London: Pinter Publishers.

Ederwick, Peter (1988): *Multinational Service Firms*. London: Routledge.

Ethier, Wilfred J. (1986): 'The Multinational Firm', *Quarterly Journal of Economics*, Vol. CI, No. 4, pp. 805–33.

Frey, Bruno S. (1987): 'The Political Economy of Tariffs', *The Economic Review*, May 1987, pp. 29–31.

Greenaway, David and Milner, Chris (1986): *The Economics of Intra-Industry Trade*. Oxford: Basil Blackwell.

Greenaway, David and Milner, Chris (1987): 'Trade Theory and the Less Developed Countries' in Norman Gemmell (ed.): *Surveys in Development Economics*. Oxford: Basil Blackwell.

Greenaway, David and Tharakan, P.K.M. (1986): *Imperfect Competition and International Trade*. Brighton: Wheatsheaf Books.

Grubel, Herbert G. and Lloyd P.J. (1975): *Intra-Industry Trade*. London: Macmillan.

Heckscher, Eli F. (1919): 'The Effects of Foreign Trade on the Distribution of Income', *Economics Tidskrift*. Reprinted in Howard S. Ellis and L.A. Metzler (eds): *Readings in the Theory of International Trade*. Homewood, Illinois: Richard D. Irwin.

Helpman, Elhanan and Krugman, Paul R. (1987): *Market Structure and Foreign Trade*. Cambridge, Mass: MIT Press.

Hufbauer, Gary (1966): *Synthetic Materials and the Theory of International Trade*. Cambridge, Mass: Harvard University Press.

International Monetary Fund (IMF) (1977): *Balance of Payments Manual* (revised version). Washington, DC: IMF.

Jones, Ronald W. (1986): *International Trade: Surveys of Theory and Policy*. Amsterdam: North-Holland.

Jones, Ronald W. and Kenen, Peter (1984): *The Handbook of International Economics*. Amsterdam: North-Holland.

Krugman, P. (ed.) (1986): *Strategic Trade Policy and the New International Economics*. Cambridge, Mass: MIT Press.

Krugman P. (1988): 'Rethinking International Trade', *Business Economics*, Vol. XXIII, No. 2, April, pp. 7–12.

Leamer, E.E. (1984): *Sources of International Comparative Advantage: Theory and Evidence*. Cambridge, Mass: MIT Press.

Linder, Staffan B. (1961): *An Essay on Trade and Transformation*. New York: John Wiley.

Lindert, Peter H. and Kindleberger, Charles P. (1982): *International Economics*, Homewood, Illinois: Richard D. Irwin.

Markusen, James R. (1989): 'Service Trade by the Multinational Enterprise' in Enderwick (ed.): *op. cit.*

Ohlin, Bertil (1933): *Interregional and International Trade*. Cambridge, Mass: Harvard University Press.

Owen, Nicholas (1983): *Economies of Scale, Competitiveness and Trade Patterns within the European Community*. Oxford: Clarendon Press.

Posner, Michael V. (1961): 'International Trade and Technical Change', *Oxford Economic Papers*, Vol. 13, pp. 323–41.

Ricardo, David (1817): *On the Principles of Political Economy and Taxation* edited by Piero Sraffa. Cambridge: Cambridge University Press. Published 1951.

Samuelson, Paul H. (1948): 'International Trade and the Equalisation of Factor Prices', *Economic Journal*, June.

Shone, R. (1972): *The Pure Theory of International Trade*. London: Macmillan.

Smith, Adam (1776): *An Inquiry into the Nature and Causes of the Wealth of Nations*, Cannan, Edwin (ed.). Chicago: University of Chicago Press, 1976.

Spraos, John (1980): 'The Statistical Debate on the Net Barter Terms of Trade Between Primary Commodities and Manufactures', *Economic Journal*, June.

Stern, Robert (1973): *The Balance of Payments: Theory and Economic Policy*. Chicago: Aldine.

Thirlwall, Anthony (1983): *Growth and Development*. London: Macmillan.

Tucker, K. and Sundberg, M. (1988): *International Trade in Services*. London: Routledge.

Vernon, Raymond (1966): 'International Investment and International Trade in the Product Cycle', *Quarterly Journal of Economics*, Vol. 80, May, pp. 190–207.

Viner, Jacob (1950): *The Customs Union Issue*. New York: Carnegie Endowment for International Peace.

Williamson, John (1983): *The Open Economy and the World Economy*. New York: Basic Books.

Wilson, P.R.D. (1986): *International Economics: Theory, Evidence and Practice*. Brighton: Wheatsheaf Books.

1.2

Foreign Investment

Foreign investment is a major strategic weapon in international business policy. This chapter examines the different theoretical approaches to this crucial policy decision.

An important distinction arises between direct foreign investment and portfolio foreign investment. Direct investment entails control over the management of the assets bought or established in the foreign country. Normally, the power of control will vary with the distribution of the equity in the venture, so that an investor holding 30 per cent of the voting equity in which no other investor holds more than 10 per cent is more likely to be able to exercise control than he would if he held 49 per cent with the other 51 per cent in one person's or company's hands. Management is clearly one such resource, but technical capability, marketing knowledge and other forms of transferable skills are also frequently involved. Indeed, in an extreme case, direct investment need not involve a flow of capital from one country to another at all. All the capital can be raised in the host country through local borrowing or retained earnings. Consequently, a concise definition of direct foreign investment is the creation of, or transfer of control over, income-generating assets by agents of one nationality in another nation's economy.

By contrast, portfolio investment is a pure form of capital movement. Control of the investment is not entailed. Portfolio in foreign investment is the purchase of one country's securities by nationals of another country. This form of foreign investment is analysed in Chapter 5.1.

The motives for direct foreign investment

The motives, the process of direct investment and the entry strategy into a particular foreign market vary greatly according to the characteristics of the entrant firm, its past relationship to the market and the nature of the foreign market. Attempts at generalization must be tempered by reference to these factors. An investment is rarely undertaken for a single motive. Moreover, the decision is not an instantaneous one but is the result of a process delineated below. The firm's objectives will have a great bearing on the motives for an investment; as such the contribution of the prospective investment to the firm's profitability and self-sustaining growth are vital constituents of the decision.

Three major types of foreign direct investment can, however, be identified:

(1) market-oriented investment;
(2) cost-oriented investment;
(3) raw-material-oriented vertical investment.

These broad categories each contain a wide variety of sub-types.

There will often be supporting motives, which may not be sufficient in themselves to induce firms to invest overseas, but give an extra stimulus or 'appeal' to the investment decision. Major categories of supporting motives are:

(1) the investment climate of the host country;
(2) an external approach to the investing firm;
(3) source-country factors causing a 'push' from the home country.

Theoretical approaches to the foreign direct investment decision have concentrated on developing a pure theory of foreign investment, international portfolio diversification, the timing of an initial foreign direct investment, the process of investment and the foreign direct investment behaviour of established firms.

The shift of emphasis away from the analysis of foreign direct investment towards a focus on multinational enterprises has left the former in something of an indeterminate and fragmented state. Despite attempts at integration (Calvet (1981)), the area is in need of restructuring, perhaps moving back towards the economic theory of investment itself. This arises because the theory of foreign direct investment is the logical intersection of the theory of international capital markets, the theory of the international firm (1.3 below) and the theory of international trade (1.1 above).

1.2.1   The pure theory of international investment

The pure theory of international investment dates from a classic article by MacDougall (1960). Using the marginal physical product of capital as the main analytical tool, MacDougall was able to show that an increment of foreign investment redistributes income from domestic capitalists to labour, benefiting the host country overall. In Figure 1.2.1 the initial capital stock is AC, of which AB is owned by local capitalists and BC by foreign investors. Under a set of restrictive assumptions, total profits are FEBA for locals and EDCB for the foreign investors. Output is GDCA and labour gets GDF. A marginal increase in foreign capital from BC to BL has the following effects: foreign profits now

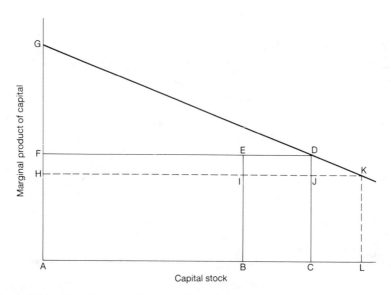

Figure 1.2.1   The MacDougall Model of Inward Foreign Investment.

are IKLB (new foreign capital earns JKLC and existing foreign investment loses EDJI) because the profit rate (= marginal product of capital) falls. Local capitalists lose FEIH and labour gains FDKH; thus overall the host country gains EDKI. The great bulk of labour's gain is redistribution from existing capitalists. Introducing taxation into the model allows the host country to gain tax on the net increase in foreign profits.

MacDougall's model was extended by Kemp (1962) who, by imposing the marginal productivity of capital in the lending country on that of the borrowing country, was able to demonstrate an international equilibrium in foreign investment and to draw out the meaning of an optimum tax on inward foreign investment. His basic analysis is shown in Figure 1.2.2. In equilibrium, the marginal product of capital in the lending country (total capital K_1) $M_1 M_1$ is equated with that in the borrowing country (total capital K_2) $M_2 M_2$ and the amount of foreign investment is AO_2.

This form of modelling has been extended by Casson (1985) who notes that the existence of international capital markets permits the functional separation of funding, ownership and utilization. Thus it is possible for one group of individuals (or national group) to fund international investment through debenture holding, another group to own the assets via control of equity and yet another to discharge the management function of utilizing the asset. This approach allows a rich variety of interpretation of the issues of international investment and links to the issue of optimally diversified portfolios internationally.

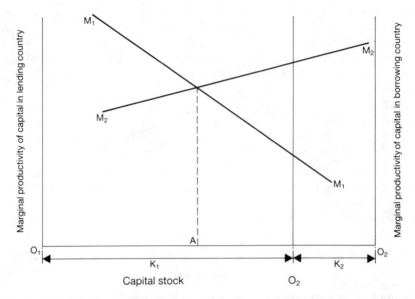

Figure 1.2.2   The Kemp Model of International Investment Equilibrium.

A further development of this basic model has been that of Svedberg (1981), (1982) who applies it to the analysis of colonialism.

1.2.2   International portfolio diversification

Risk diversification as a motive for foreign investment has long been recognized as important. Its applicability to direct foreign investment, however, has been a source of controversy. The choice of an optimal portfolio of foreign assets is a logical extension of the theory of portfolio choice as applied to domestic assets in an uncertain world.

This strand of research, beginning with Grubel (1968) shows that the risk on assets R_j consists of the rate of interest r plus a risk premium that will vary according to the particular conditions of individual investments such as cyclical economic influences, management skills, technology and taste factors and government regulations. Because the risks differ between assets, the risk of a portfolio of assets will be less than that of a typical security within the portfolio. Risk-averse investors will therefore hold diversified portfolio assets; see Grubel (1968). The degree to which international factors enter an optimal portfolio depends on the extent to which single-country portfolios display independence from each other. Empirical evidence has been provided by Levy and Sarnat (1978). Empirical evidence suggests the potential for risk reduction is greatest in a portfolio that includes assets from less-developed countries whose returns are uncorrelated with those of assets from advanced countries. The uncertainties surrounding these assets differ in kind and their capital markets are relatively unintegrated with those of the leading advanced countries, while within advanced countries intertrading and arbitrate mean assets have a low covariance internationally.

The relevance of this approach to direct foreign investment must be questioned (Buckley and Casson (1985)). First, shareholders can diversify as much as they wish by spreading their shareholdings over a number of different multinational firms. Only so far as there are obstacles to individual diversification is there a case for corporate diversification. Second, the essence of direct investment is that it involves control of the asset; in most cases this will require a fairly substantial proportion, if not a majority, of the equity. Consequently, only a sub-optimal degree of diversification will be possible. Third, the empirical evidence on the direction of direct investment shows it to be concentrated among advanced countries, thereby foregoing the benefits of the high covariance of assets in less-developed countries' assets *vis-à-vis* those of advanced countries. Empirical evidence suggests that the security price of multinationals does reflect the extent of diversification (see Rugman (1979)) and that managerial discretion may include diversification as a motive, for risk-aversion purposes.

1.2.3 The timing of a foreign direct investment

The timing of a firm's move abroad is a difficult management decision because it involves a great deal of uncertainty and is also difficult to model adequately. The product-cycle approach to foreign direct investment suggests that the switch to foreign investment should occur according to the following cost-based formulation (Vernon, 1966):

$$\text{Invest abroad when } MPC_X + TC > ACP_A$$

where MPC_X is marginal cost of production for export
  TC is transport cost
  ACP_A is average cost of production abroad

The argument here is that marginal costings are appropriate for exports because domestic production would be undertaken anyway while the foreign unit must bear the full average costs of production.

A fuller model of the switch to foreign investment is given by Buckley and Casson (1985). Essentially, two types of cost, fixed and variable, attach to the different forms of foreign-market servicing, licensing, exporting and foreign direct investment. As the market grows the variable cost declines and so the switch occurs from low-fixed to low-variable cost modes, typically from exporting to direct investment (see Figure 1.2.3). This model is complicated when set-up costs are also included. Key variables in the timing of the move abroad are, therefore, the costs of servicing the foreign market, demand conditions in that market and host-market growth.

A major complicating factor in the move abroad is the action of competitors. This oligopolistic reaction among large firms has been analysed as a major influence on foreign direct investment (Knickerbocker (1973)). Among the largest multinational firms Knickerbocker found that entry into particular host-country markets was grouped in time around a three-year peak. The important influences on this were (1) industry structure: the more concentrated the industry, the more leader-follower behaviour occurred; (2) industry stability: rivalistic investment behaviour was directly connected with the break-up of industry stability under pressure from new entrants; and (3) the smaller the number of alternatives open to the firm, the more likely they were to engage in oligopolistic reaction. Interestingly, low-technology firms are more active defensively than high-technology ones.

1.2.4 Foreign direct investment as a process

The approach of Yair Aharoni (1966), in a classic work, was to view the foreign investment decision as a process. This allows consideration of internal and market-transmitted pressures on the key decision-makers, of the influence of the organization's goals and of the crucial role of uncertainty. Viewing the decision as a process focuses attention on the role of time; it permits the decision to be resolved into a series of sub-decisions. The role of time, however, is not explicit and although the decision is broken into stages, there is no attempt to predict the timing of these discrete phases nor the crucial trigger variables that move the process along.

The foreign direct investment, in Aharoni's view, is begun by an initiating force that may come from within the organization or as an outside pressure. In response, the firm begins an investigation process, collecting the extra information it needs on a foreign investment and carrying out an on-the-spot survey of the foreign country. It then moves to the investment decision via the creation of individual and organization commitment. The investment is then reviewed and renegotiated among the power groups within the firm before finally going ahead. Aharani then adds a long-run stage: changes through repetition, to what has been a powerful description of short-run decision-making under uncertainty.

Later attempts to map the decision process concentrated on smaller firms: in one case on the firms' initial foreign direct investment (Buckley, Newbould and Thurwell (1988), Buckley, Berkova and Newbould (1983)). This approach attempts to evaluate the success of a foreign direct investment on a multiple variable scale and then to judge the effectiveness of sub-decisions according to their measured outcome. The management processes are resolved into a preliminary stage, a planning stage, an investment stage, an operating and control stage and an evaluation stage.

There is little integration of this managerial literature with the more strictly theoretical work. A complete theory of foreign direct investment needs to complete the task of integration.

1.2.5 The foreign direct investment behaviour of established firms

Many analyses of foreign direct investment have been concerned with the firm's *initial* foreign direct investment – its primary move in 'going international'. This section examines the foreign direct investment behaviour of established multinational enterprises.

The early literature on foreign direct investment was largely concerned with the investment pattern of firms and particularly its financing. The observed phenomenon of a large plough-back of profits into foreign subsidiaries, combined with a small initial investment, led eventually to a payment of dividends that was very large in relation to the initial sum invested (Penrose (1956), Barlow and Wender (1955)). Consequently, it was suggested that foreign investors behaved like compulsive gamblers – constantly putting their winnings back into the game until a real 'killing' was made. The essence of this 'Gamblers' Earnings Hypothesis' is that to some extent, the foreign subsidiary has a life of its own and its growth depends on subsidiary variables (its earnings, growth, opportunities) alone, without reference to factors influencing the parent or the rest of the firm. At the extreme this implies that the multinational enterprise will go on ploughing back profits into the subsidiary from whence they came, even if this is *not* justified by comparative rates of return. This supposition is dependent on either the independence of the foreign subsidiary arising from difficulties of control from the parent, the need for 'local judgement', or a lack of policy coordination in the firm or an ignorance of relative rates of return worldwide, which may be the result of a lack of knowledge of alternatives, myopia or the desire (for non-economic reasons) to reinvest.

For the multinationals of today, operating efficient internal financial markets and scanning international horizons for potentially profitable investments, such myopic behaviour cannot be supported. For 'first time' foreign investors the uncertainties surrounding a foreign environment are indeed great, but for a multinational with an existing worldwide network a further new environment must hold far fewer terrors. There is a learning process at work that will reduce the 'costs of doing business abroad' to a point where, except for particularly difficult exceptional environments, such costs begin to approximate to zero.

Two instruments of policy can be seen to be important for established multinational enterprises: a market-servicing policy and a 'sourcing' policy within a

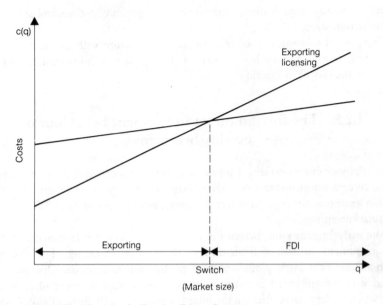

Figure 1.2.3   The Timing of a Foreign Direct Investment

corporate-planning framework. A market-servicing policy describes the set of decisions about which production units can service which foreign markets and the channel through which this is implemented. It thus covers the choice between exporting, foreign licensing and foreign direct investment (Buckley and Pearce (1984)). A sourcing policy describes the decisions about the origin of inputs purchased for production units. Consequently a multinational firm can be viewed as two networks, one linking outputs to markets, the other linking inputs to production. Foreign direct investment is thus a crucial weapon in building and maintaining these two networks.

The adoption of corporate-planning techniques on an international scale is gradually formalizing the approach of multinational enterprises to foreign direct investment appraisal. The 'biased search' approach described by Aharoni (1966) has largely been replaced by a more formal scanning of investment opportunities by at least the biggest multinational enterprises. The process of clarifying objectives, setting the corporate strategy, monitoring progress and obtaining forecasts of business conditions and success is now widely applied internationally.

The linked advantages of size, degree of integration, specialization of executives and international experience limit the 'extra' risks of foreign direct investment for established multinational firms. The emergence of international corporate-planning techniques and of a specialist cadre of executives has integrated foreign direct investment decisions with the overall strategy of the firm. The application of planning and forecasting techniques to the international level is now well established and documented (Brooke and van Beusekom (1979), Channon and Jalland (1979), Porter (1986)).

The influence of the competitive process

One of the elements that can only be built imperfectly into an international corporate strategy is the effect of moves made by competitors. The desire of competitors in oligopolistic or other highly concentrated industry structures to match each other's competitive moves is well known and has been adapted to provide insights into foreign direct investment behaviour.

The pioneering work by Knickerbocker (1973) suggested that the timing of foreign direct investment is largely determined by competitors' reaction to investments, resulting in a 'bunching' in time of multinational enterprise's investment entries into particular host countries. Oligopolistic reaction is hypothesis as a form of risk-minimizing behaviour employed by firms to reduce the perceived competitive threats of other members of the industry (Flowers (1976)). Oligopoly members are perceived to prefer the expense of such a strategy rather than allowing the 'leader' to control a particular host market. Alternative explanations have been provided to explain this behaviour – profit maximization (Stevens (1974)) and the imperfect dissemination of market information among firms (Buckley and Casson (1985)), but the competitive process does appear to play a role in the planning of foreign direct investment.

1.2.6 Foreign direct investment in the non-manufacturing sectors

Much of the above theory is implicitly concerned with foreign direct investment by manufacturing firms. Special categories of literature have grown around foreign direct investment made in other areas, notably (1) to control raw materials (vertical direct investment) and (2) in service industries. Examples of the former include Hennart (1986), (1988) and case-studies in Casson (1986), while work on service industries includes Enderwick (1989). A large section of the United Nations Centre on Transnational Corporations (UNCTCs) latest survey (1988) is also devoted to service industries.

1.2.7 International alliances

International alliances between multinational firms have attracted increasing attention, particularly in the establishment of the European Single Market. An alliance may be defined as an 'interfirm collaboration over given economic space and time for the attainment of mutually defined goals' (Buckley (1990)). A number of factors are conducive to the establishment of such alliances including (1) the possession of complementary assets; (2) similarity or congruence of goals (which may include the desire to reduce competition); and (3) barriers to full integration, economic, political or legal. Alliances have much in common with joint ventures, the theory of which is examined by Buckley and Casson (1988) and rests on internalization economies, indivisibilities and obstacles to merger. Alliances can be between firms linked in the value chain (vertical) so long as this is not a purely buyer–seller relationship. They can be between direct competitors producing essentially the same output (horizontal) or they can be cross-sectoral between unrelated companies (conglomerate). Each type of alliance has different implications for competition. Special cases of alliance arise in technology agreements between companies – Chesnais (1988) provides a review.

References

Aharoni, Yair (1966): *The Foreign Investment Decision Process*. Boston, Mass: Graduate School of Business Administration, Harvard University.

Barlow, E.R. and Wender, I.T. (1955): *Foreign Investment and Taxation*. Englewood Cliffs, NJ: Prentice Hall.

Brooke, Michael Z. and Beusekom, Mark van (1979): *International Corporate Planning*. London: Pitman.

Buckley, Peter J. (1990): 'Alliances, Technology and Markets'. University of Bradford *mimeo*.

Buckley, Peter J., Berkova Z. and Newbould, Gerald D. (1983): *Direct Investment in the United Kingdom by Smaller European Firms*. London: Macmillan.

Buckley, Peter J. and Casson, Mark (1985): *The Economic Theory of the Multinational Enterprise: Selected Essays*. London: Macmillan.

Buckley, Peter J. and Casson, Mark (1988): 'A Theory of Cooperation in International Business' in Farok J. Contractor and Peter Lorange (eds): *Cooperative Strategies in International Business*. Lexington, Mass: Lexington Books.

Buckley, Peter J., Newbould Gerald D. and Thurwell, Jane (1988): *Foreign Direct Investment by Smaller UK Firms* (2nd edn). London: Macmillan.

Calvet, A.L. (1981): 'A Synthesis of Foreign Direct Investment Theories and Theories of the Multinational Firm', *Journal of International Business Studies*, Vol. 12, No. 1, pp. 43–60.

Casson, Mark (1985): 'The Theory of Foreign Direct Investment' in Buckley and Casson: *op. cit.*

Casson Mark and associates (1986): *Multinationals and World Trade*. London: George Allen & Unwin.

Channon, Derek F. and Jalland, R.M. (1979): *Multinational Strategic Planning*. London: Macmillan.

Chesnais, François (1988): 'Technical Cooperation Agreements between Firms', *STI Review* (OECD, Paris), Vol. 4, December, pp. 51–120.

Enderwick, Peter (ed.) (1989): *Multinational Service Firms*. London: Routledge.

Flowers, E.B. (1976): 'Oligopolistic Reaction in European and Canadian Direct Investment in the United States', *Journal of International Business Studies*, Vol. 7, No. 1, pp. 43–55.

Grubel, H.G. (1968): 'Internationally Diversified Portfolios: Welfare Gains and Capital Flows', *American Economic Review*, Vol. 58, pp. 1299–314.

Hennart, Jean-François (1986): 'Internalisation in Practice: Foreign Direct Investment in Malaysian Tin Mining', *Journal of International Business Studies*, Vol. 17, No. 2, Summer, pp. 131–43.

Hennart, Jean-François (1988): 'The Tin Industry' in Casson associates: *op. cit.*

Kemp, M.C. (1962): 'The Benefits and Costs of Private Investment from Abroad: Comment', *Economic Record*, Vol. 38, pp. 108–10.

Knickerbocker, Frederick T. (1973): *Oligopolistic Reaction and the Multinational Enterprise*. Cambridge, Mass: Harvard University Press.

Levy, H. and Sarnat, M. (1978): *Capital Investment and Financial Decisions*. Englewood Cliffs, NJ: Prentice-Hall.

MacDougall, G.D.A. (1960): 'The Benefits and Costs of Private Investment from Abroad: A Theoretical Approach', *Economic Record*, Vol. 33, pp. 13–35

Penrose, Edith T. (1956): 'Foreign Investment and the Growth of the Firm', *Economic Journal*, Vol. 66, pp. 230–5.

Porter, Michael E. (ed.) (1986): *Competition in Global Industries*. Boston: Harvard Business School Press.

Rugman, Alan M. (1979): *International Diversification and the Multinational Enterprise*. Lexington, Mass: Lexington Books.

Stevens, G.V.G. (1974): 'The Detriments of Investment' in John H. Dunning (ed.): *Economic Analysis and the Multinational Enterprise*. London: George Allen & Unwin.

Svedberg, Peter (1981): 'Colonial Enforcement of Foreign Direct Investment', *The Manchester School*, Vol. 49, No. 1, March, pp. 21–38.

Svedberg, Peter (1982): 'The Profitability of UK Foreign Direct Investment under Colonialism', *Journal of Development Economics*, Vol. 11, pp. 273–86.

United Nations Centre on Transnational Corporations (1988): *Transnational Corporations in World Development Trends and Prospects*. New York: UNCTC.

Vernon, Raymond (1966): 'International Investment and International Trade in the Product Cycle', *Quarterly Journal of Economics*, Vol. 80, pp. 190–207.

1.3

Technology Transfer and Multinational Enterprises

Technology transfer is intimately bound up with the existence and *raison d'être* of the multinational firm as Chapter 1.4 shows. The multinational enterprise plays a major role in the creation, development and diffusion of technology, from which it derives much of its competitive strength. The interests of the multinational firm in appropriating the maximum returns from technological advances conflict with the interests of host countries in obtaining the results of technological development at the lowest possible cost. This conflict, and the associated bargaining positions that derive from this clash of interests, have focused most strongly on North–South issues (technology transfer to Third World countries) and on West–East issues (technology transfer to socialist countries). The North–South issues have mainly welfare implications with associated distribution consequences, while the West–East issues have been overlaid with implications for strategy and competition. This chapter analyses the role of technology transfer in the innovation process and examines technology transfer to the Third World, including the development of a new form of international technology transfer. A conclusion summarizes the state of the literature.

1.3.1 Technology transfer and the innovation process

It has long been conventional to distinguish between invention (the idea creating a new product or process) and innovation (the application of the idea in a commercial setting). Innovation and research and development is now viewed as a much more complex process, involving technical feasibility, commercial development and design, as well as other refinements. The performance of these processes within a firm require a sophisticated management style. Of crucial importance is the communication of information between the marketing-production function and other functions. Figure 1.3.1 illustrates the information inputs necessary.

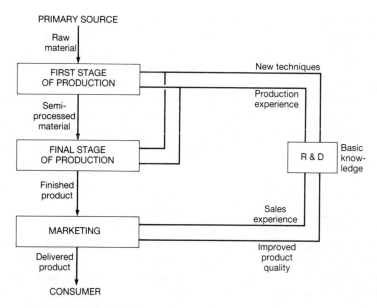

Figure 1.3.1 Information Flows in the Multinational Firm

Notes: Successive stages of production are linked by flows of semi-process materials. Production and marketing are linked by a flow of finished goods ready for distribution. Production and marketing on the one hand are linked to R & D on the other hand by two-way flows of information and expertise.

(Reproduced from Buckley and Casson (1976))

As the exploitation of a technological lead is a major competitive weapon and a major reason for foreign investment (Buckley and Casson (1976), Porter (1986), Dunning (1988)), it is in the interests of the firm to prevent diffusion from outside. As technological development is a continuous, dynamic process, constant investment in updating technology is essential. Thus the firm must strike a strategic balance between capitalizing its technological advances while slowing diffusion. This dilemma accounts for the centrality and sensitivity of technology transfer in the strategies of multinational firms and also for the care that enters the design of contracts for the external sale of technology (Casson (1979)).

The multinational firm plays a threefold role in the technology process (1) as a creator of new technology; (2) as an adopter of new technology into commercial products and processes – as an innovative risk taker; and (3) as a vehicle for transferring technology internationally.

From the host countries' viewpoint, a major concern is to obtain the use of technology. It is not necessary to produce the know-how in order to use it. In fact there are a variety of strategies open to the host country to obtain the use of know-how. It can (1) import the goods embodying the know-how; (2) import the producer goods embodying know-how in order to manufacture the final goods; (3) import the technology itself and carry out production; and (4) produce the know-how directly. It is a fallacy to believe that route (4), technology creation, is always optimal. Most host countries are constrained to adopt a mix of policies (1) to (3) because the resource of technology creation is too high for most countries, except possibly in a very narrow area. This raises the crucial issue in international technology transfer of the choice of other modes of transfer.

This issue is dealt with in detail below, but it is overlaid (particularly in the case of less-developed countries) by the controversy on the appropriate nature of technology. This concerns both the processes of production, the capital-intensity debate and the nature of the products. The capital-intensity and nature-of-products debates are dealt with in detail in Chapter 4.1. Both the capital-intensive nature of much Western technology is felt to be harmful to employment in (labour abundant), less developed countries, while the outputs of technology are felt to be aimed at an elite minority with harmful knock-on effects that include synthetics replacing natural exports and processed food replacing local production. Even in advanced countries, the form of technology import can generate a hostile political reaction. A particular sensitivity concerns the foreign takeover of indigenous technology-intensive firms.

It is commonly accepted that the ability to create and transfer technology is central to the competitive strength of many multinational enterprises. The manner in which multinational enterprises create technology tends to be similar to that of most large firms , though distinctive issues are now emerging in relation to the international dispersion of such research and development work in multinational enterprise groups (Pearce, 1990). Perhaps the most discussed issues in this area, therefore, relate to the ways in which technology is transferred within or by multinational enterprises. As an important part of the theory of multinational enterprises has made clear, a key issue is whether these companies make use of their technology-based productive assets overseas internally (by incorporating them in operations owned and controlled by the multinational enterprise) or externally (by isolating the productive asset in a marketable form and hiring it to an independent foreign firm). A large part of our discussion in fact relates to defining certain characteristics of the external routes for the transfer of technology and other knowledge assets. Nevertheless this fits into an important part of the discussion of multinational enterprises for two reasons.

First, the vast majority of the external transfer of technology to independent foreign firms is done by firms which either are multinational enterprise (companies that also have controlled subsidiaries overseas) or could be multinational enterprise (companies that have considered the possibility of having controlled subsidiaries overseas). Thus in the great majority of cases where technology is transferred overseas, the alternative route of foreign direct investment will have been considered. This makes analysis of these alternative external routes important to a full understanding of the behaviour of multinational enterprises.

A second reason why an understanding of the external ways of transferring technology is relevant in analysing multinational enterprises is that the terms of such transfers can often provide the multinational enterprise with some degree of control over the foreign company that receives the technology, at least with regard to how it uses it. This implies that when a multinational enterprise sells technology to a foreign firm, it may to some degree pull that firm into its own global network even without acquiring an ownership share.

In the context of this discussion it may be useful to distinguish between positive and negative control. In its most perfect form a positive control exists wherever a technology transferor is able to induce the receiving enterprise to behave in exactly the same way as it would if it were a majority-owned subsidiary of the seller: that is if the conditions attached to the transfer enable the buyer to be integrated into the multinational enterprise's international production and marketing network, even though the multinational enterprise has no ownership share in the technology buyer.

On the other hand, a negative control may be said to exist whenever the activities of the recipient firm have no effect on the international activities of the seller. In this case control is sought not so much to influence actively how the firm operates but to constrain its operational environment to one where it does not affect the profitability and growth of the multinational enterprise's own existing activity. How these types of control are implemented will emerge at various points in our discussion.

Analysis of technology transfer has tended to distinguish four areas of discussion:

(1) The defining of the distinctive characteristics of the particular mechanisms through which various types of technology and knowledge can be transferred internationally.

(2) The terms on which multinational enterprises transfer their technology to independent foreign firms. The issue of applying control is very much tied up with this.

(3) The factors that influence the choice of multinational enterprises between internal and external transfer routes.

(4) The appropriateness of multinational enterprise's technology to the countries to which it is transferred.

We distinguish four external mechanisms for the transfer of various elements of the multinational enterprises technology and skills: (1) licensing agreements, (2) technical assistance agreements, (3) management contracts, and (4) franchising. These are examined in Section 1.3.5 below.

1.3.2   The mode of international technology transfer

It has been traditional to see international technology-transfer modes in terms of a spectrum of depth of involvement of the multinational firm in the host country, running from a wholly-owned subsidiary at one extreme to loose time-limited arrangements such as sub-contracting at the other. It is useful, however, to isolate several dimensions of involvement before such a concept can be accepted. These dimensions include (i) the locus of control, (ii) the transfer of a (limited) set of rights and resources and the mode of transfer, internal to the firm or by the agency of a market transaction, (iii) time limitations, and (iv) space limitations.

The locus of control

The issue of control is central to the growth of new forms of international industrial cooperation. Recipient countries, notably the less-developed countries, wish to achieve the transfer of technology and skills without the necessity of accepting foreign control over the use of these resources. Many host countries feel the exercise of control and potential costs implied in the operation of a wholly-owned subsidiary of a foreign multinational are unacceptable; they restrict or prohibit such institutional arrangements by law.

Consequently, the desire for technology and skills on the part of host countries has to be matched to the profit-seeking desires of source-country firms through new arrangements. The equation of control with ownership is only part of the story. However, a frequent attempt to dilute foreign control is the creation of joint ventures whereby host-country interests share the equity. Many kinds of arrangements are implied by such a division of equity. For instance, a foreign investor holding 30 per cent of the voting equity in a company where no other investor holds more than 10 per cent is more likely to be able to exercise control, in spite of his minority holding, than he would if the held 49 per cent, with the other 51 per cent in one person's or company's hands (Buckley and Roberts (1982)). A further important distinction lies in the nature of the host-country's equity holding. If this is a single shareholder, a prominent host-country company or the host government, then it might be expected that host-country influence will be greater than if the holding is split or if the equity is traded on the host stock-market.

Definitions of joint ventures have centred on the issues of cooperation and control. Friedmann and Kalmanoff (1981, p. 6) define joint international-business ventures as 'a type of association which implies collaboration for more than a very transitory period'. Tomlinson (1970, p. 8) takes this further: a joint venture is 'a commitment for more than a very short duration, of funds, facilities and services, by two or more legally separate interests to an enterprise for their mutual benefit'. Lamers (1976, p. 138) suggests that to this must be added the sharing of control and risk. Sukijasovic (1970) states that joint ventures have four properties, 'a community of interests involving doing business in common, the sharing of business risk and losses and longevity of cooperation'.

The attractions of joint ventures for the multinational firm are time-unlimited access to the market and resources of the host country, possible political preferment and a measure of equity control. The host country, in theory at least, gains access to the full range of the skills and resource package of the foreign firm, while not sacrificing full equity control. (See also Paliwoda (1981), Weralski (1980)).

The limiting forms of joint ventures are minority holdings by foreign corporations where the foreign investor chooses a small equity stake (typically of the order of 5 to 12 per cent, Buckley (1981)) often in order to share research or marketing arrangements. In companies with diffuse shareholding, 5 to 12 per cent may give the foreign entrant the largest block of votes.

Resource transfer

A crucial distinction between types of international industrial cooperation is the nature of the combination of resources and rights that are transferred and the mode by which such transfer is effected.

The wholly-owned subsidiary here provides a polar extreme. A whole package or bundle of resources is transferred, consisting of capital, technology, skills and a wide range of rights, usually covering the rights to produce, market and develop products and to raise resources backed by the parent (Kindleberger (1969), Caves (1971), Dunning (1981), Balasubramanyam (1980)). The mode of this transfer is internal to the firm rather than through external markets. Thus internalization permits effective parent-company control, allows long-term planning, avoids market uncertainties, allows discriminatory pricing and may reduce external interference, notably by governments (Buckley and Casson (1976), Buckley (1989)). It is through the use of internal markets in capital, labour, management, technology and intermediate goods that effective control of foreign subsidiaries is exercised, rather than through equity ownership, although complete equity control means that no external influences are directly concerned in the management of these internal markets.

In cases where dilution of complete control occurs (joint ventures and minority holdings) this complete transfer may be reduced in order to prevent a leakage of secrets, competitive devices and new technology to outsiders (Parker (1978)). This cannot be completely protected in a fully internalized transaction because of quitting among key workers, in breakaways and through industrial espionage; the more outsiders are involved, the more restricted the transfer of resources and rights is likely to be.

Licensing agreements represent the market alternative to the internalized transfer of resources (including information) and rights (Davies (1977)). Licensing is a generic term that encompasses a wide variety of contractual agreements between a foreign firm and a local firm for effecting transfers of rights and resources. Balasubramanyam (1973) uses the term 'technical collaboration agreements' to cover the sale and purchase of technical information. Typically, licensing will also include certain rights to market the product that embodies the transferred information (a wider term than knowledge); many ancillary transfers of resources and rights are included.

The transfer process in licensing is complex and time-consuming. Hall and Johnson (1970) say:

> Technology can be transferred in two basic forms. One form embraces physical items such as drawings, tools, machinery, process information, specifications and patents. The other form is personal contact. Put simply, knowledge is always embodied in something or somebody, the form being important for determining the transfer process and cost.

The issue of effective transfer through the market route is crucial and will be taken up in Section 1.3.4.

Telesio (1979) states that 'Licensing of manufacturing technology can be defined as the sale of "intangible property rights, such as patents, secret processes or technical information".' To this transfer of technology must be added other forms of information transfer, including marketing and managerial aspects. The widest, and most terse, definition of a licence is 'a covenant not to sue' (Prasad (1981), quoting Finnegan (1976)), although the writer goes on to list the positive aspects of licensing. Later, we discuss the issues of just what is transferred in different licensing agreements.

One specialized but important type of licence agreement is franchising. Franchising is 'a form of marketing or distribution in which a parent company customarily grants an individual or a relatively small company the right or privilege to do business in a prescribed manner over a certain period of time in a specified place' (Vaughn (1979) pp. 1–2). The franchise contract usually has several elements:

(1) specification of the duration of the commercial relationship;
(2) grant of a set of rights to the 'franchisee' to offer, sell and distribute goods and services manufactured, processed, distributed or organized and directed by the 'franchisor';
(3) the franchisee as an independent business constitutes a component of the franchisor's distribution network;
(4) the franchisee's business is substantially associated with advertising or other commercial symbol designating the franchisor;
(5) the franchisee's operations are substantially reliant on the franchisor for the continued supply of goods or services;

(6) the franchisee will be geographically limited (Vaughn (1979), Izreali (1972)).

A large element of the franchise thus involves the carefully controlled transfer of managerial and marketing skills.

Usually, the franchisee will be an individual or a small independent business. Franchise systems may be of the manufacturer-retailer type (car distributorship, petrol dealership), manufacturer-wholesaler (soft drinks' bottlers), wholesaler-retailer or trademark licensor-retailer types. The most salient franchise relationships occur in fast-food chains and in hotels (see Dunning and McQueen (1981)). A key element of franchising is the ability to segment the market spatially between different franchisees in order to prevent competition between them. Grants of exclusive rights to these territories can then assure full market coverage without internal competition. Services are suitable for franchising.

The benefits to the host country from franchising are often thought to be high, because training and development of management skills are frequently integral to the franchising package (Wright (1981)). Management and technical training, assistance in locating, equipping and decorating as well as financial and advertising back-up are valuable imported components that are added to the franchisee's motivation to be his own boss to make franchising attractive to small businesses. For the franchisor, effective market penetration is often combined with minimal capital outlay. However, indigenous alternative products (soft drinks, restaurants and hotels, for instance) are often unable to compete with internationally known alternatives; charges of cultural imperialism are frequently aimed at franchisors.

Management contracts are a growing form of carrying out business abroad.

> The management contract is an arrangement under a certain degree of responsibility for the operations of one enterprise are vested in another. The latter undertakes the usual management functions, makes available a whole range of skills and resources and trains personnel. The contract covers payment to the company and the handing over of authority to the locals once trained. (Ellison (1977), p. 25).

Management contracts are rarely purely concerned with transferred management skills. Usually an infusion of technology is involved (Brooke (1985), Gabriel (1967), (1972)). Importantly, though, management contracts are less reliant on transferring information and skills to an already functioning enterprise; they can frequently build a new enterprise from scratch, relying little, if at all, on local experts. Ellison (1977, p. 26) lists the transfer of corporate capabilities as a unique element of such contracts. This is essentially a link with the transferring company, allowing the recipient, through the contract, to rely on the transferer's corporate skills in access to funds, general reputation and worldwide procurement capacity. Essentially, the contract involves access to inherited corporate skills. This implies an ongoing non-market relationship that is difficult to specify fully in a legal contract and that relies greatly on goodwill between the parties. Hence, management contracts can be highly rewarding or difficult to operate; it depends on the relationship between the parties, which cannot be written in to the contract.

Turnkey projects are arrangements where the process of constructing, making operative and usually initially running a facility are contracted to outside enterprise (or enterprises) in return for a fee. The facility is then handed over to local interests. Most usually the construction period is followed by a period covered by a management contract (and possibly a licensing arrangement) whereby continuing relationships with the outsiders provide for extended training and de-bugging. The customers are usually governments who have decreed that a given product or service must be produced locally and under local control (Wright (1981)).

Turnkey contracts that end when the physical plant and equipment has been set up by the supplier in the host country are referred to as light turnkey contracts; those with clauses providing for the extensive training of local personnel are heavy contracts. Contracts referred to as product-in-hand operations mean that the supplier's responsibility is not fulfilled until the installation is completely operational with local personnel. Extension of contracts to market-in-hand calls for the supplier to give assistance in, or in some cases take responsibility for, the sale of at least part of the operation's output. Under some circumstances, buy-back, counter-purchase or compensation agreements call for the supplier to take payment directly in the form of physical output (Oman (1980)).

Time limitations

Many market contracts have time limitations directly written into them – licence agreements will run for a specified time period with specified conditions for renewal; management contracts likewise. The essence of turnkey arrangements is the limited time-span of foreign control and the detail of the handover of control to local interests. However, equity ventures too can be time-limited as in fade-out arrangements.

Such fade-out or planned divestment agreements involve the multinational firm in liquidating its investment and selling its stake to locals, usually government (Hirshman (1972)). These fixed-term agreements (usually 5 to 10 years) were first suggested in order to reduce tension in economies where a high degree of foreign penetration is viewed as a political problem. The countries of Latin America are prime examples. Such arrangements involve a complex move from an internalized transfer of resources to market transfer, for they are usually followed by a licence agreement or a management contract or both. Problems arise over the issues of (1) the price at which the multinational firm is bought out, (2) specification of the exact nature of the continuing resource transfer, (3) the timing of the transfer, (4) the desire of the foreign corporation to reduce its time horizon to the period over which it exercises full control and to milk the project in that period, and (5) ensuring continuing viability.

Space limitations

Licence agreements usually include limitations on the economic space across which the licence is valid. This is most usual in the export-restriction clauses noted in most surveys of licensing (Buckley and Davies (1981), Casson (1979)). This provides the licensor with a means of segmenting his market effectively, reducing competition among multiple licensees and ensuring that his licensees do not become competitors. It also permits price discrimination by the licensor (Casson (1979)).

In internalized transactions, the same objective can be achieved by management fiat, dividing world markets between subsidiaries according to a market-servicing policy based on internal and external pressures (Buckley and Pearce (1979), (1981), (1984)).

Certain forms of internalized industrial cooperation are designed to be limited in space (most usually also in time). Important among these are contractual joint ventures. Wright (1981, p. 500) states that:

> the contractual joint venture is a risk-sharing venture in which no joint enterprise with a separate personality is formed. It is a partnership in which two or more companies (or a company and a government agency) share the cost of an investment, the risks and the long-term profit. The contractual joint venture may be formed for a particular project of limited duration, or for a longer term cooperative effort, and the contractual relationship may terminate once the project is complete.

Consortium ventures by banks to finance large loans and co-publishing agreements are examples. It was noted above that for the individual franchisor, space limitations were essential to segment the market and to prevent competition between franchisees.

A special form of contractual joint venture is Tripartite Industrial Cooperation where at least three firms or organizations domiciled in the East (centrally planned economy), in the West (industrialized market economy) and in the South (less developed country) join forces to carry out common activities in the host-developing country. Normally these activities would include one or more of (1) building-up of physical infrastructure, (2) prospecting for and extracting natural resources, (3) supply of industrial plant and assembly work and (4) marketing (joint importing or exporting) (Oman (1980)).

Finally, international sub-contracting is a clearly defined market relationship covering an agreement of a foreign firm to purchase from a local firm. Although such arrangements are, in ideal type, purely market-based, linking purchaser to producer, in practice there is often an input from the purchaser to ensure that quality standards meet specifications and to advise on methods of production. Such arrangements are limited in space. Such production-sharing agreements usually involve selling in the purchaser's home market. These arrangements are closely related to tariff regulations in the developed countries and to the proliferation of free-trade zones in less-developed countries.

1.3.3   Issues in international technology transfer

Table 1.3.1 provides a typology of modes of international industrial cooperation in five dimensions: equity versus non equity ventures, time limitations, space limitations, transfer of resources and rights, and mode of transfer (internal versus market) (Buckley (1985)). Although some of the entries in the table are contentious, the analysis shows that a simple spectrum running from wholly-owned foreign subsidiary to simple contracts is an inadequate representation of the nuances and complexities of the different arrangements. Many of the new forms are also linked to each other in particular circumstances, such as joint ventures and licensing agreements, turnkey operations and management contracts. The following section builds on this to provide an analytical framework for the consideration of these forms of cooperation.

Transfer of resources and rights

All forms of international industrial cooperation involve the transfer of resources and right either by the agency of the market or within the firm. Typically, the new forms represent an attempt to externalize transactions that had previously been intra-firm. The new forms are best understood as attempts to release the multinational firm's control of resource transfer by replacing such modes by contracts.

The transfer of physical resources between organizations and of intangible information both require a transferable property right. Casson (1979) distinguishes a right of access and a right of exclusion: the former is the right to use an asset, the latter the right to prevent others using it except at the holder's discretion. In the case of non-diffusable assets the first right necessarily implies the second: to give one person access to it automatically denies it to others. Where a diffusable asset is concerned the capacity to supply users is theoretically infinite, so the right of exclusion must be separately upheld (1979, p. 37). Information is a diffusable asset; a legally enforceable right of exclusion over it is known as a patent. A patent can be conferred free of charge or sold to the highest bidder.

Table 1.3.1 A Typology of International Technology Transfer

Form of cooperation	Equity or non-equity	Time limited or unlimited	Space limited	Transfer of resources and rights	Mode of transfer
1 Wholly-owned foreign subsidiaries	Equity	Unlimited	At discretion of MNE	Whole range	Internal
2 Joint ventures	Equity	Unlimited	Agreed	Whole range?	Internal
3 Foreign minority holdings	Equity	Unlimited	Limited	Whole range?	Internal
4 Fade-out agreements	Equity	Limited	Nature of agreement	Whole range? for limited period	Internal changing to market
5 Licensing	Non-equity	Limited by contract	May include limitation in contract	Limited range	Market
6 (Franchising)	Non-equity	Limited by contract	Yes	Limited + Support	Market
7 Management contracts	Non-equity	Limited by contract	May be specified	Limited	Market
8 Turnkey ventures	Non-equity	Limited	Not usually	Limited in time	Market
9 Contractual joint ventures	Non-equity	Limited	May by agreed	Specified by contract	Mixed
10 International sub-contracting	Non-equity	Limited	Yes	Small	Market

Source: Buckley (1983)

Where the transferred asset is easily identified and vested in exclusive and freely transferable property rights, market transfer through licensing can be optimal (Buckley and Davies (1981)). This is most easily the case when the asset to be transferred is embodied in a patent, a brand name, a machine or a separable process. If this condition is violated, it may be difficult or impossible to make the asset the subject of a transaction. In particular, difficulties may arise in negotiating the limits within which the asset can be used in economic space and time. In the face of fragmented markets with uncertain and changing boundaries, and given uncertainty about the life of an asset, companies rationally restrict their attention to specific markets and time periods. The potential licensor needs to be assured that the terms of the arrangement will be adhered to and the advantage will not be used in ways which have not been paid for. Consequently the enforcement of a contract gives rise to considerable policing costs. The licensor can use natural safeguards to protect himself. He may restrict supply of a secret ingredient or other essential part to control his licensee's output; or he may rely on technical progress to out-compete his licensee if necessary. If such safeguards are not available, contractual means must be sought with the resultant policing costs.

Rights of ownership are frequently ill-defined and difficult to enforce; to publicize possession is often to invite imitation, replication or to encourage rival claims. In such cases, possession is best maintained through secrecy. This gives rise to a severe problem: to sell the asset requires publicity, with the consequence that ownership may be lost. This problem is avoided by integrating forward into the use of the asset and so internalizing the market. The alternative is to offer a contingent contract, including insurance to the buyer that the asset will perform well. This method of avoiding buyer uncertainty (the buyer is unable to assess the worth of knowledge to him until he is in possession of it) is part of the reason for the search for new forms of cooperation that effectively transfer information without the necessity of foreign control.

Transaction costs

The minimization of transaction costs is central to theories of the existence of the multinational firm (Casson (1979), Buckley (1989), Buckley and Casson (1985)). The model in Casson (1981) shows that the tendency to internalize is greater, the higher the volume of trade between plants. But this depends on a large volume of trade being associated with a high frequency of transactions in the external market. The incentive to internalize is reduced if this frequency is diminished by long-term contracts, for instance, or by bulk-buying. Nevertheless, in many cases the most efficient institution for transferring technology internationally (that which minimizes transaction costs) will be the multinational enterprise. This is frequently true in less developed countries where markets are often imperfect in ways that favour an hierarchical solution to the allocation problems, the internalization of markets within the multinational firm.

There is a shortage of information on the relative size of transaction costs in the internal as against the external transfer of technology, but some information can be gleaned form extant empirical studies. Teece (1977) defines transfer costs as 'the costs of transmitting and absorbing all the relevant unembodied knowledge' (p. 247). Teece's survey of 26 international projects does not distinguish between internal and external transfer costs but an average figure of 19 per cent of the total project costs was found to represent transfer costs. The range is 2 per cent to 59 per cent. Interestingly in Teece's 26 cases the international component of transfer costs was negative in six cases and zero in four. In other words, domestic transfer would have been more expensive than international transfer in six cases.

Table 1.3.2 shows a complete breakdown of the costs of foreign licensing by Australian licensors. It shows that a quarter of total costs of foreign licensing

Table 1.3.2   Relative Cost of Licensing Overseas (Australian Licensors)

Breakdown of total costs of licensing overseas	%
Protection of industrial property	24.8
Establishment of licensing agreement	46.6
Maintenance of licensing agreement	29.0
	100.0
Breakdown of establishment costs	
Search for suitable licensee	22.8
Communication between involved parties	44.7
Adoption and testing of equipment for licensee	9.9
Training personnel for licensee	19.9
Other (additional marketing activity and legal expenses)	2.5
	100.0
Breakdown of Maintenance costs	
Audit of licensee	9.7
On-going market research in market of licensee	7.2
Back-up services for licensee	65.0
Defence of industrial property rights in licensee's territory	11.0
Other	7.1
	100.0

Reproduced from Carstairs & Welch (1981)

is represented by the protection of industrial property, nearly half the cost is represented by the costs of establishing a licensing agreement and over a quarter in maintenance costs of the agreement. In the breakdown of establishment and maintenance costs, the most significant items are communication between involved parties (20.8 per cent of total costs) and back-up services for licensees (18.9 per cent of total costs). Interestingly, search costs for potential licensees account for 10.6 per cent of total costs (Carstairs and Welch (1981)). It is not possible to suggest that magnitude of such costs for internal transfers, but it is reasonable to assume search costs to be zero and the policing element to be vastly reduced. A further problem of the external transfer of information is time lags. The lag in licensing on joint ventures has been shown to be longer than internal transfers (Mansfield, Romeo and Wagner (1979)).

It is, therefore, clear that licensing involves continuing expense on the part of the licensor to ensure successful transfer and police his rights. Several studies (including Behrman and Wallender (1976), Baranson (1978)) have emphasized the continuing transfer of skilled personnel in cementing the know-how. In other words, licensing is a relationship rather than an act. Interaction between recipient and seller is both essential to successful transfer and a continuing element of cost.

The importance of the provisions of individual contract should not be underestimated. The time and effort put into contract design is a testament to the central importance of the legal document.

Absorptive capacity in the host country

It is over-simplistic to place the types of cooperation on a spectrum from wholly-owned foreign subsidiaries to simple contracts in terms of the ease with which the information can be absorbed by the host country (internalized transactions easiest, simple-market contracts most difficult). Many multinational firms have found the absorptive capacity of host countries to be a major problem for activities they substantially control (Baranson (1967)); there may be an argument in some cases that absorptive capacity increases when local control is involved.

However, it is partly the desire to increase absorptive capacity that leads to a simple asset-transfer contract becoming more complicated because a larger onus is placed on the transferring firm to ensure effective transfer. The lack of expertise on the part of the host country will raise the costs of transfer (borne by the licensee) and increase the benefits of internalization, if this is allowed by host-country legislation.

The capacity to absorb a borrowed technology depends on (1) indigenous research efforts, (2) the skills and capabilities of recipient firms and (3) the transferor firm's commitment (Balasubramanyam (1973)). A distinction must be made between the ability to restructure, to adapt and to develop technologies to local conditions. The former needs an upgrading of managerial and labour skills at the plant level; the adapting and developing require investment in research and development. Balasubramanyam (based on Indian experiences) suggests that where the transferor has no equity stake in the recipient, the sale of knowledge will often be regarded as marginal; the transferor cannot be expected to evince any interest in restructuring the knowledge (often any improvements will have to be transmitted back to the licensor). Consequently he concludes that, where adapting is the objective, technical-collaboration agreements may be fruitful only in the case of large firms in the host country that can provide the resources to undertake the adaptation. Conversion personnel are extremely important internally as, externally, is the availability of high-quality inputs and sub-contractors (Baranson (1967)).

The effects of competition

Much of the analyses of licensing and other new forms of cooperation ignores the competitive process. This is clearly untenable in a world of large firms, proprietary knowledge and imperfect markets (Lall (1978), (1981)). The search for new forms of cooperation is in part due to a desire by the host country to reduce foreign control; it is also made possible by the willingness of multinational firms to compromise on total ownership. This compromise is often the result of competitive pressure.

New forms of cooperation often offer entry into markets that would otherwise be closed to multinational firms. They may be closed to wholly-owned subsidiaries because of government policy (and to exports by tariffs, quotas or other protective devices) but also because of the existing competitive structure. If the market is already oligopolistic, entry by means of setting-up a subsidiary may spoil the market for all firms, including the entrant. Some form of cooperation will be preferable. Hence, we observe cross-licensing in concentrated markets (Buckley and Davies (1981)).

Host-country firms may resort to entry-forestalling practices, reducing prices or taking political action to protect domestic industry from foreign investors (Kidron (1965)). The result will be to make cooperation more attractive. In terms of follow-the-leader behaviour, noted as typical among large firms in several industries (Knickerbocker (1973)) there comes a point, depending on the relation between the host-market size and scale economies, where followers will turn to licensing rather than head-to-head competition. This pattern of behaviour can be exploited by host-country interests and increase their bargaining power. For instance, where the competitive situation dictates a rapid response from following firms, the necessity for a quick entry may be exploited by the host country to dictate the mode of entry. The desire of oligopolistic multinationals not to allow particular host markets to be cornered by one of their number may provide opportunities for host countries to impose conditions on entry.

1.3.4   Issues raised by the new forms of international industrial cooperation

1   Effective transfer

The successful absorption of foreign technology into the host country's economic structure is the key to judging the success of any form of international industrial cooperation (Helleiner (1975)). However, international technology transfer can only be achieved at a cost. The minimization of this cost to the recipient country is a further criterion of success. There may be a trade-off between this objective of minimizing transfer costs and host-country political control of projects involving foreign technology. Given this degree of host control, transfer costs must be minimized. A careful match between the foreign firms and local interests is, therefore, essential. We see today a mushrooming of host-country investment authorities whose task is to cooperate with importers of technology and smooth these transfers. Politically, costs may be involved, as investment authorities often wield a great deal of power outside the normal political channels of control.

2   Bargaining

Any form of international industrial cooperation involves a continuous process of bargaining (Vaitsos (1974)). Casson points out, however, that the nature of buyers' ignorance and its effects on the bargaining process may have been widely misunderstood (1979, p. 113). He suggests it is the buyer's knowledge, not of the product or process itself, but of the other sources of supply or the availability of substitutes, which strengthens his bargaining power. Even when the buyer does not know what the product or process is, he may know what it *does* and hence be able to evaluate alternatives. The exception to this rule is where the seller intends to practise deception and the buyer is not suspicious. But once the buyer becomes suspicious, his valuation will decline. Vaitsos, however, acknowledges that a lack of the knowledge of alternatives is often a problem for less-developed countries and that an 'international search for knowledge and its alternative sources of supply could institutionally prove to be of the highest importance' (Vaitsos (1974) p. 131). Attempts to improve the host-country's bargaining power are detailed in United Nations Centre on Transnational Corporations (1979).

3   Are new forms competitive or complementary to direct foreign investment?

It has become fashionable to argue that the growth of non-direct investment forms of international involvement implies the decline of multinationals and the end of their subsidiaries as a primary means of international-technology transfer.

Superficially, this seems correct. However, it is pertinent to examine the argument more closely. There remain many areas where the necessity to control information within the corporate family permits little institutional innovation – computers and bio-engineering are perhaps examples. But the new forms present additional opportunities for multinationals to penetrate markets and countries that would otherwise be closed. New forms of arrangement also benefit multinationals in reducing risk, improving their sensitivity to local conditions and penetrating awkward market segments. A comparison of returns does not always favour the direct-investment route (Contractor (1981)); a judicious mix of forms of doing business abroad is an increasingly acceptable corporate objective (Wright and others (1982)). Many multinationals have developed dispersal skills, enabling complex higher-order activities such as research and development to be performed abroad (Behrman and Fisher (1980)). (See also Hennart (1989).)

4   Institution building: new intercompany relationships

Policy towards international-technology transfer to the Third World and Eastern bloc has often been negative. Policies on control of technology transfer by the United Nations Conference on Trade and Development, and others, seem likely to restrict rather than liberate the international flows of productive information. In many cases the restrictive practices adopted by multinationals are second-best attempts to extract return from diffusable knowledge in the absence of perfect information. Other strategies rest on the ability of firms and host nations to build satisfactory institutional forms, partially to reconcile competing interests. Transfer must be profitable for the multinational firm and effective for the host-country's objectives. If we accept the premise that technology creators and transferors must be rewarded for their efforts, then the design of institutions that effectively achieve these ends is as important for them as for the technology's recipients.

Summary

Modes of international industrial cooperation are changing under pressure from host countries to achieve greater political and economic control over their development, and from multinational firms to achieve a return on their investment in creating, developing and transferring knowledge. Given that the circumstances of individual firms and nations vary so much, it is not surprising that from this melting pot new institutional arrangements emerge. Rigidities in legal arrangements, in policies of firms, governments and international institutions, as well as peculiarities in the market for diffusable assets have meant the search for acceptable forms has not been easy. In policy-making areas, it is essential to keep in mind the peculiarities of the market for information and its relationship to the markets for final goods. Attempts at making policy that ignore these fundamental relationships are doomed to failure.

1.3.5   Types of technology transfer agreements

Licensing agreements

A licensing agreement can be defined as 'relating to a specific product and/or production process that incorporates inventions of the licensor (seller) that are made available to the licensee (buyer) in return for an agreed payment and on stipulated terms with regard to use'. Three types of licensing agreement may be distinguished: (1) patent licenses; (2) know-how licences; and (3) trademark licenses, though any licensing agreement usually includes two or more of these types in combination.

(1) A patent licence gives the buyer the right to produce a product, or use a process, patented by the licensor. The pure-patent licence does no more than pass over this permission. A case where this might work could be envisaged where firm A had independently created (or acquired) the ability to produce a product where firm B holds a patent relating to that product/process and

therefore can prevent A using its own ability with no need for further knowledge-transfer from B.

(2) A know-how licence is added where the buying firm does not know how to use the acquired patent and therefore needs to be provided with documentation before it can attempt to start production. This documentation may include the equipment required, optimal plant layout and design, blueprints and drawings relating to the design of the product and other information such as materials, standards and specifications.

Even with this documentation the recipient firm may find it hard to get effective production started. Where this occurs the licence may be augmented by a technical-assistance agreement where the firm owning the licensed technology commits some of its own engineers to the recipient company for a certain period to teach that firm how to use the technology.

(3) Trademark licences convey to the licensee (buyer) the right to use trademarks owned by the licensor (seller).

Turning to the terms involved in licences we need to distinguish between the financial terms and other conditions.

(1) Financial terms vary between agreements but usually involve a lump-sum payment at the start of the agreement and an annual payment of royalties related to the licencee's sales of the licenced product. There has tended to be controversy over the price set in licensing agreements, which reflects the inherent difficulty of putting a value on technology. Because the market for technology is highly imperfect, prices are rarely determined in a competitive situation; the most common situation is that the price is set as a result of a bilateral bargain between the buyer and seller. Less-developed countries, in particular, have argued that when their firms have bargained with multinational enterprises to buy technology they have been vulnerable, because of their lack of bargaining experience and knowledge, and have ended up paying too high a price.

(2) Restrictions on exports. Clauses in licensing agreements that restrict the exporting potential of the licensee are a major example of the exercise of negative control by the licensor, who does not attempt to draw the licensee into its operations, but seeks to prevent it affecting its own established activity.

(3) Tied-purchases of intermediate products, capital goods and spare parts oblige the licensee to buy these goods from the licensor (or a source designated by the licensor). The control given to a licensor as a result of tied-purchase clauses tends to serve the function of positive control by establishing some degree of sustained economic link between the licensor and licensee beyond the simple payment of royalties. In so far as the licensee plays a role in the worldwide sales programme of the licensor, for example by servicing certain specified markets in addition to its domestic market, restrictions on the sources of inputs may be necessary to guarantee the quality of output. This case, where to some degree the licensee has become a sub-contractor for the licensor, involves a strong degree of positive control. A weaker degree of positive control persists

where the tied-purchase provisions are aimed only at enhancing the market for the licensor's intermediate goods or plant and equipment, where the licensee might otherwise have opted for competitive sources. A dimension of this case, which particularly concerns less developed countries, is that once a monopoly position is obtained through those tied-purchase provisions, it may be exploited through increased prices.

(4) Provisions affecting the technological potential of technology purchasing countries. Considerable concern has been expressed lest certain provisions included in licensing agreements hold back the development of indigenous technology potential in host countries, especially less-developed countries, and thus prolong their 'technological dependency' on more industrialized countries. This type of dependency could benefit licensing multinational enterprises either by holding back potential independent competitors (negative control) or by locking the licensee into the technological set-up of the multinational enterprise, so that it can be integrated into the multinational enterprise's international network (positive control).

Three specific types of technologically restrictive provision were found in licensing agreements.

(a) Restrictions on 'own' research. Many licensing agreements include provisions prohibiting the licensee from undertaking research, either at all or at least of a type that would be in direct competition with that undertaken by the supplier. Such limitations might also cover adaptive research or the licensor's freedom to introduce changes in the technology acquired.

(b) Grant-back provisions. Agreements containing this type of clause oblige the technology buyer to grant back to the technology seller any improvements or adaptations it subsequently makes to the technology. This gives the licensor a degree of negative control by limiting the scope of the buyer to create an independent technical capability. Thus the existence of grant-back provisions may either inhibit the buyer from performing independent adaptive work, or if it does, it will mean that any distinctive improvements it makes are not its unique property and may be used more competitively by the multinational enterprise that gets them granted back.

(c) Requirements regarding the compulsory purchase of inventions or technological improvements. While discretionary access to improvements in licensed technology is clearly beneficial to a licensee, provision for the compulsory purchase of such developments is potentially damaging. For example, if a licensee is tied to a particular source of technology, it is unlikely to establish its own research and development facilities; thus the potential for the creation of technology more suitable to local conditions is diminished.

(5) Restrictions on production patterns. An agreement of this kind usually requires that a licensee manufactures a product covered by the licence only in the manner or form prescribed by the licensor. The resulting inability of the licensee to extend its product line or adjust to local market conditions (either in

its domestic or export markets) could conceivably prevent it from realizing its full market potential.

Analysis of the role of licensing in multinational enterprises (see Telsio (1979) Chapter 2) has permitted the delineation of their benefits and costs. Five types of potential benefit may be located.

(1) Through licensing a multinational enterprise can obtain royalty receipts from foreign markets that it could not otherwise profitably exploit directly. If a multinational enterprise is short of capital or management ability, or explicitly lacks management, manufacturing or marketing ability relevant to a particular host country, a licensee may provide these and provide the multinational enterprise licensor with returns not otherwise accessible to it.

(2) If a foreign market is too small for a full investment by a multinational enterprise in that it would yield an unsatisfactory return on investment, and if imports are restricted, licensing a local enterprise provides a means for local manufacturing operation. This may be especially feasible if the local firm is diversified and can add the multinational enterprise product to its range at relatively small marginal costs.

(3) Sometimes a multinational enterprise's access to a market is rendered difficult because of the presence of strong, established, competing companies in the host economy. In such a case a multinational enterprise might have an ownership advantage over local firms, but not one big enough to overcome the barriers to entry the local firms can erect. In such a case, licensing the technology to the local firms might be mutually profitable. However, this would be a particularly strong case where the multinational enterprise might seek to place export restrictions on the licensor to prevent that firm becoming a rival in third-country markets.

(4) Technologically dynamic firms may prefer to commit most of their resources to maximizing the income from their more profitable new innovations. However, rather than totally abandon their older lower-income, standardized technology products, they may continue to earn some income from these by licensing overseas producers in countries where they still have earning potential.

(5) Licensing also offers the possibility of achieving a low-profile presence in manufacturing in countries where the investment climate is unfavourable to foreign-owned operations. Firms using licensed multinational enterprise technology, but themselves locally-controlled, may be relatively less vulnerable to political pressure. Similarly, licensing may make it possible for a multinational enterprise to secure the manufacture of its products in countries that restrict foreign ownership in certain sectors.

On the other hand, three types of costs to licensing may be distinguished. (1) Many of the argued benefits of licensing are based on the licensed operations being import-substituting activity, aimed at serving the host-country market. With multinational enterprises becoming increasingly concerned with the creation of globally integrated networks of activity, such isolated host-market operations do not ideally suit multinational enterprises' needs for optimal global efficiency. Thus it is not easy to draw independent licensed firms into multinational enterprise networks as controllable sub-contractors. (2) There will be costs to the multinational enterprise of licensing its technology if the licensor does not use it as efficiently as the multinational enterprise would have done. At the least, this will cost the multinational enterprise in terms of financial return. Thus, if the licensor performs poorly in terms of sales, then sales-related royalties to the multinational enterprise may be less than it would have earned through an owned operation. Perhaps worse, as a longer-term concern, if the licensee is selling the product under the multinational enterprise's trade name and produces a sub-standard product, this may undermine the multinational enterprise's own credibility. (3) There is also a fear on the part of the licensor that the vital technology (a key ownership advantage) it transfers to a licensee might leak to other competitors in a way that could threaten the worldwide competitive position of the licensor. The licensee itself might also manage to become a competitor when the licensing agreement runs out.

Technical assistance agreements

These agreements seek to transfer more general technical skills and capabilities than those incorporated in the documentation of licensing agreements. Such technical assistance agreements often occur in conjunction with licensing agreements so that the buyer of the licensed technology can get it into effective, profitable operation. Thus they include skills like welding or casting of metal parts, machine maintenance and repair, quality control techniques and organization expertise like plant layout and personnel training. Agreements may also include some marketing knowledge.

Technical assistance agreements are usually implemented through face-to-face contacts, usually of the licensor's personnel visiting the operations of the licensee.

Though, technical-assistance agreements often occur in practice to assist recipient firms fully to implement licensed technology, the nature of the expertise transferred is unlikely to be specific to the licensed technology. Thus abilities learnt in technical assistance agreements may increase the recipient enterprise's technical and organizational abilities in parts of its operations not related to the more detailed licensed technology.

Management contracts

Management contracts may be defined (Gabriel (1967)) as 'arrangements under which operational control of an enterprise, which would normally be exercised by its own board of directors and managers, is performed under contract by a separate enterprise in return for a fee'. It has also been suggested (Gabriel (1967)) that 'the services rendered under a management agreement are approximately comparable to the administrative and technical functions which a foreign firm performs in operating a subsidiary established by direct investment'.

In carrying out a management contract the firm selling its ability will perform two functions:

(1) it will actually run the firm, make it competitively operative at a time when it could not otherwise be so;
(2) it will train local managers to take over the running of the firm at the end of the management-contract period.

As follows logically from this the most likely time for a management contract to be operative is when a new firm is starting up, or when it is taking on a major new dimension to its operations, perhaps through the use of a newly acquired license.

The obvious return to a multinational enterprise taking part in a management contract is that it can obtain a return on elements of its distinctive managerial capabilities from countries where it may not wish, or be permitted, to commit itself to a full-scale or longer-term investment. Another possible source of return to a multinational enterprise from a management contract is that by exercising positive control over the managed firm, that firm could contribute to the overall efficiency or profitability of the multinational enterprise while not being an owned part of it. Thus the decisions taken from the firm by the multinational enterprise during the management contract period may, in effect, tie that company into the multinational enterprise's global network as if it were an owned subsidiary. Though this need not inevitably be to the detriment of the company that is hiring management services from the multinational enterprise it is obviously a possibility that needs to be treated with suspicion.

Franchising

Franchising is predominantly a service-industry variation on the types of knowledge-transfer mechanisms discussed above. Essentially, local entrepreneurs own and run a business using the trade name of the franchisor. To provide the service associated worldwide with such trade names, the franchisor will receive information (e.g. recipes) and documentation relation to the style of service to be provided. The franchisor is then unlikely to be substantially involved in the running of the franchised restaurant, hotel or car rental other than monitoring it to make sure the service is up to expectations and is not undermining the global reputation of the trade name. This represents negative control only exercised by the franchisor over the franchisee.

1.3.6   Conclusion

The search for new institutional forms to minimize conflict between the technology transferor (usually a multinational firm) and transferee has led to a proliferation of new forms of conducting international business. This has led to a renaissance of interests in licensing, management contracts (Brooke (1985)) and joint ventures (Contractor and Lorange (1988)). The fundamental issue – that of obtaining a return on the costs of innovation – remains the same, as do the efficiency and equity implications of solutions to the problem. However, moves to alter the bargaining relationship by bodies such as the United Nations Conference on Trade and Development have created an atmosphere of flexibility of approach that promises to make the future design of technology-transfer arrangements one of the exciting areas of international business theory and practice.

There are two ways in which advanced foreign technology could be used appropriately in a host country: selection and adaptation. In the case of selection the multinational enterprise chooses a part of its technology and uses it in a situation that makes optimal use of host-country conditions. We may argue that selection might be best achieved by multinational enterprises in the context of their own investments. The fact that host countries seek to buy technology means they have limited knowledge of existing technology; this means they are unlikely to be able to select effectively the ideal technology to utilize their conditions. Multinational enterprises' detailed knowledge of their own technology, and their ability to research and assess local conditions, puts them in a stronger position to perform such selection. With regard to adaptation, again the multinational enterprise's in-depth knowledge of its existing technology, and its expertise in evolving technology and evaluating scope for changes, puts its in the best position to perform this function. These points underline the familiar view that when technology is transferred between countries at substantially different levels of development, licensing is only likely to be effective in the case of standardized technology.

References

Balasubramanyam, V.N. (1973): *International Transfer of Technology to India*. New York: Praeger.

Balasubramanyam, V.N. (1980): *Multinational Enterprises and the Third World*. Thames Essay No. 26. London: Trade Policy Research Centre.

Baranson, Jack (1967): *Manufacturing Problems in India*. Syracuse: Syracuse University Press.

Baranson, Jack (1978): *Technology and the Multinationals*. Lexington, Mass: D.C. Heath & Co.

Behrman, J.N. and Fischer, W.A. (1980): Overseas R & D Activities of Transnational Companies. Cambridge, Mass: Oelgeschlager.

Behrman, J.N. and Wallender, H.W. (1976): Transfer of Technology Within Multinational Enterprises. Cambridge, Mass: Ballinger.

Brooke, Michael Z. (1985): Selling Management Service Contracts in International Business London: Holt, Rinehart and Winston.

Buckley, Peter J. (1981): 'The Entry Strategy of Recent European Direct Investors in the USA', Journal of Comparative Law and Securities Regulation, Vol. 3, No. 2, pp. 169–91.

Buckley, Peter J. (1983): 'New Forms of International Industrial Cooperation: A Survey of the Literature', Aussenwirtschaft, Vol. 38, No. 2, June.

Buckley, Peter J. (1989): The Multinational Enterprise – Theory and Applications. London: Macmillan.

Buckley, Peter J. and Casson, Mark (1976): The Future of the Multinational Enterprise. London: Macmillan.

Buckley, Peter J. and Casson, Mark (1985): The Economic Theory of the Multinational Enterprise: Selected Essays. London: Macmillan.

Buckley, Peter J. and Davies, Howard (1981): 'Foreign Licensing in Overseas Operations: Theory and Evidence from the UK' in R.G. Hawkins and A.J. Prasad (eds): Technology Transfer and Economic Development. Greenwich, Conn: JAI Press.

Buckley, Peter J. and Pearce, Robert D. (1979): 'Overseas Production and Exporting by the World's Largest Enterprises – A Study in Sourcing Policy', Journal of International Business Studies, Vol. 10, No. 1, Spring, pp. 9–20.

Buckley, Peter J. and Pearce, Robert D. (1981): 'Market Servicing by Multinational Manufacturing Firms: Exporting versus Foreign Production', Managerial and Decision Economics, Vol. 2, No. 4, December, pp. 308–21.

Buckley, Peter J. and Pearce, Robert D. (1984): 'Exports in the Strategy of Multinational Firms', Journal of Business Research, Vol. 12, No. 2, pp. 209–26.

Buckley, Peter J. and Roberts, Brian R. (1982): European Direct Investment in the USA Before World War I. London: Macmillan.

Carstairs, R.T. and Welch, L.S. (1981): A Study of Outward Foreign Licensing of Technology by Australian Companies. Licensing Executives Society of Australia.

Casson, Mark (1979): Alternatives to the Multinational Enterprise. London: Macmillan.

Casson, Mark (1981): 'Foreword' to Rugman, Alan M.: Inside the Multinational. London: Croom Helm.

Caves, Richard E. (1971): 'International Corporations: The Industrial Economics of Foreign Investment', Economica (New Series), Vol. 38, pp. 1–27.

Contractor, Farok J. (1981): International Technology Licensing: Compensation, Costs and Negotiation. Lexington, Mass: D.C. Heath.

Contractor, Farok J. and Lorange Peter (eds) (1988): Cooperative Strategies in International Business. Lexington, Mass: D.C. Heath.

Davies, Howard (1977): 'Technology Transfer through Commercial Transactions', Journal of Industrial Economics, Vol. 26, December, pp. 161–75.

Dunning, John H. (1981): International Production and the Multinational Enterprise. London: George Allen & Unwin.

Dunning, John H. (1988): Multinationals, Technology and Competitiveness. London: George Allen & Unwin.

Dunning, John H. and McQueen, Matthew (1981): *Transnational Corporations in International Tourism*. New York: United Nations Commission on Transnational Corporations.

Ellison, R. (1977): 'Management Contracts' in Michael Z. Brooke and H. Lee Remmers *The International Firm*. London: Pitman.

Finnegan, M.B. (1976): *Current Trends in Domestic and International Licensing*. New York: Practising Law Institute.

Friedman, W.F. and Kalmanoff, G. (eds) (1981): *Joint International Business Ventures*. New York: Columbia University Press.

Gabriel P.P. (1967): *The International Transfer of Corporate Skills – Management Contracts in Less Developed Countries*. Cambridge, Mass: Harvard University Division of Research, Graduate School of Business Administration.

Gabriel, P.P. (1972): 'Multinationals in the Third World: Is Conflict Inevitable?', *Harvard Business Review*, Vol. 50, pp. 93–102.

Hall, G.R. and Johnson, R.E. (1970): 'Transfers of United States Aerospace Technology to Japan' in Raymond Vernon (ed.) *The Technology Factor in International Trade*. New York: National Bureau of Economic Research, Columbia University Press.

Helleiner, G.K. (1975): 'The Role of Multinational Corporations in the Less Developed Countries' in K. Kojima and M. Wionczek (eds) *Technology Transfer in Pacific Economic Development*. Tokyo: Japan Economic Record Centre.

Hennart, Jean-François (1989): 'Can the New Forms of Investment Substitute for the Old Forms? A Transactions Cost Perspective', *Journal of International Business Studies*, Vol. 20, No. 2, Summer, pp. 211–33.

Hirshman, A.O. (1972): 'How to Divest in Latin America and Why' in A. Kapoor and P.A. Grub (eds): *The Multinational Enterprise in Transition*. Princeton, New Jersey: Darwin Press.

Izraeli, Dov (1972): *Franchising and the Total Distribution System*. London: Longman.

Kidron, Michael (1965): *Foreign Investments in India*. Oxford: Oxford University Press.

Kindleberger, C.P. (1969): *American Business Abroad*. New Haven: Yale University Press.

Knickerbocker, Frederick T. (1973): *Oligopolistic Reaction and the Multinational Enterprise*. Cambridge, Mass: Harvard University Press.

Lall, Sanjaya (1978): 'Transnationals, Domestic Enterprises and Industrial Structure in Host LDCs: A Survey', *Oxford Economic Papers*, Vol. 30, pp. 217–48.

Lall, Sanjaya (1981): 'Technology and Developing Countries: A Review and an Agenda for Research', in Sanjaya Lal (ed.): *Developing Countries in the International Economy*. London: Macmillan.

Lamers, E.A.A.M. (1976): *Joint Ventures between Yugoslav and Foreign Enterprises*. Tilburg: Tilburg University Press.

Mansfield, E., Romeo, A. and Wagner, S. (1979): 'Foreign Trade and U.S. Research and Development', *Review of Economics and Statistics*, Vol. 61, No. 1, pp. 49–57.

Oman, Charles (1980): *The New Forms of Investment in Developing Countries*. Paris: OECD Development Centre.

Paliwoda, Stanley J. (1981): *Joint East–West Marketing and Production Ventures*. Farnborough: Gower Press.

Parker, J.E.S. (1978): *The Economics of Innovation: The National and Multinational Enterprise in Technology Change* (2nd edn). London: Longman.

Pearce, R.D. (1990): *The Internationalisation of Research and Development by Multinational Enterprises*. London: Macmillan.

Porter, Michael E. (ed.) (1986): *Competition in Global Industries*. Boston: Harvard Business School Press.

Prasad, S.J. (1981) 'Technology Transfer to Developing Countries through Multinational Corporations' in R.G. Hawkins and A.J. Prasad (eds): *Technology Transfer and Economic Development*. Greenwich, Conn: JAI Press.

Sukijasovic, M. (1970): 'Foreign Investment in Yugoslavia' in I.A. Litvak and C.J. Maule (eds): *Foreign Investment: The Experience of Host Countries*. New York: Praeger.

Teece, David J. (1977): 'Technology Transfer by Multinational Firms: The Resource Cost of Transferring Technological Know-how', *Economic Journal*, Vol. 87, pp. 242–61.

Telesio, P. (1979): *Technology Licensing and Multinational Enterprise*. New York: Praeger.

Tomlinson, J.W.C. (1970): *The Joint Venture Process in International Business: India and Pakistan*. Cambridge, Mass: MIT Press.

Vaitsos, Constantine V. (1974): *Intercountry Income Distribution and Transnational Enterprises*. Oxford: Oxford University Press.

Vaughn, C.L. (1979): *Franchising* (2nd edn). Lexington, Mass: D.C. Heath.

Weralski, M. (1980): 'The New Policies and Legislation Concerning Joint Ventures in Poland', *European Taxation*, Vol. 20, pp. 99–105.

Wright, P. et al. (1982): 'The Developing World to 1990: Trends and Implications for International Business', *Long Range Planning*, Vol. 15, pp. 116–25.

Wright, R.W. (1981): 'Evolving International Business Arrangements' in K.C. Dhawon, H. Etemad and R.W. Wright (eds): *International Business: A Canadian Perspective*. Don Mills, Ontario: Addison Wesley.

1.4

The Multinational Enterprise

The theory of the multinational enterprise has been developed to explain and predict the growth and pattern of multinational enterprise and in particular (1) the concentration patterns of multinationals, and (2) the important conceptual issues.

1.4.1 What the theory should explain

The concentration pattern of multinational enterprises

Multinationals are *concentrated* by (1) country of origin, (2) industry and (3) location of economic activity they control. This pattern of ownership, sector and distribution requires explanation with reference to a coherent theory of multinational firms.

1 Country of origin
In 1985, 35.1 per cent of all foreign direct investment stocks was owned by one country, the United States of America, 49.8 per cent by two countries (United States of America and United Kingdom) and 82.4 per cent by the largest six foreign investors, only slightly down from the 90.0 per cent recorded in 1970–2 (United Nations Centre on Transnational Corporations, 1988). Concentration of ownership has been recorded since the earliest days of foreign investment (Buckley and Casson (1985) pp. 199–200).

Effects attributed to foreignness or multinationality may in fact be due to the particular nationality of ownership of firms. These ownership effects are generally found to be highly significant in studies of the growth, profitability and policy decisions of multinationals. (For a summary of the evidence, see Buckley and Casson (1985).)

2 Concentration by industrial sector

Studies of the types of industries dominated by multinational firms show the following characteristics to be positively associated with foreign penetration:

(1) high wage rates;
(2) high salary levels;
(3) high ratio of staff to operatives;
(4) high ratio of royalty payments to net output;
(5) high industry concentration;
(6) high advertising expenditure as a percentage of net output.

(Buckley and Casson (1976).)

The concentration of multinationals in vertically integrated extractive or primary industries, in high-technology research-intensive industries, in capital-intensive industries and in skill, knowledge and communication-intensive services (banking, insurance) is well documented.

3 Location of activity of multinationals

Most of the activity of multinationals is in the advanced market economies; but 25 per cent of foreign direct investment went to developing countries and was highly concentrated in the largest six recipients (66.2 per cent in 1980). In 1980–5 86 per cent of all foreign investment flows to less-developed countries went to 18 developing countries. Stock figures reflect the some imbalance (United Nations Centre on Transnational Corporations (1988)).

Newly industrializing countries, oil-exporting countries and tax havens account for 64.5 per cent of investment in developing countries, while the least-developed countries receive 1.5 per cent of the total (United Nations Centre on Transnational Corporations (1983)).

There has, however, been an interesting difference in the pattern of Japanese foreign direct investment, which declined from 57 per cent in 1975 in developing countries to 33 per cent in 1986. This represents a large switch to investing in advanced-country markets. Several analysts have suggested that Japanese direct investment requires a separate approach (see Section 1.4.6 below).

Conceptual issues

In addition to giving an explanation of the above empirical phenomena, any theory of the multinational firm must explain three conceptual issues:

(1) The existence of *cross investment*, whereby firms from country A in industry I invest in country B's industry I at the same time as capital is flowing in the opposite direction. This is in contradiction to interest-rate explanations of capital movement: these predict that capital flows from capital-rich to capital-poor countries.

(2) Why *foreign firms*, not local ones, can service a given country's home market.

(3) Why firms choose to own and control income-generating assets abroad *in preference* to exporting or utilizing these assets by arms-length contracts in asset services such as technology licensing and management contracts.

This chapter analyses the development of theoretical approaches to the multinational enterprise. The several avenues of theoretical development are classified as (Section 1.4.3) the Hymer–Kindleberger tradition; (Section 1.4.4) the place of the multinational enterprise in the product cycle; (Section 1.4.5) the importance of the concept of internalization; (Section 1.4.6) diversification versus internationalization; (Section 1.4.7) location theory as applied to the multinational enterprise; and (Section 1.4.8) attempts at achieving a synthesis into a general theory.

1.4.2 The definition of a multinational enterprise

Whole papers have been devoted to the question of defining the multinational enterprise (Aharoni (1971)). Four alternative types of definition would seem to be:

an *operating* definition, one form of which is the ownership-threshold definition – a firm that owns or controls income-generating assets in more than one country;

a *structural* definition where multinationality is judged according to the organization of the company;

a *performance* criterion, incorporating some relative or absolute measure of international spread, such number of foreign subsidiaries or percentage of sales accounted for by foreign sales; and

a *behavioural* criterion based on the corporation's degree of geocentricity.

Definitions are not right or wrong, just more or less useful. Throughout this book, our definition is the simplest form of a threshold definition – a firm that owns outputs of goods or services originating in more than one country (Casson (1983a)). Consequently we avoid the issue of defining control and do not necessarily imply that the firm is a foreign direct investor. Thus we bring new forms of international involvement (see Chapter 1.3) within the ambit of the theory (Buckley (1985b)).

1.4.3 The Hymer–Kindleberger tradition

The initial core of modern theory of the multinational enterprise was a deceptively simple proposition: that in order to compete with indigenous firms, which possess innate strengths such as knowledge of the local environment, market and business conditions, foreign entrants must have some compensating advantage. This proposition took foreign direct investment away from the theory of capital movements into the theory of industrial organization. For, in a perfect market, foreign direct investment could not exist because local firms would always be able to out-compete foreign entrants.

The initial phase of the Hymer–Kindleberger approach was therefore the search for the compensating advantage that foreign investors possessed. Kindleberger's exposition (1969) examined four main areas of internationally transferable advantages. First, departures from perfect competition in goods markets, including product differentiation, marketing skills and administered pricing; secondly, departures from perfect competition in factor markets, including access to patented or proprietary knowledge, discrimination in access to capital and skill differences embodied in the firm (particularly its management); thirdly, internal and external economies of scale, including those arising from vertical integration; and finally, government intervention, particularly those forms restricting output or entry. Such advantages enable the foreign entrant to overcome its lack of knowledge of local conditions innate in the local firm, which the foreign firm can only acquire at a cost, and also serve to compensate for the foreigner's cost of operating at a distance.

The focus of investigation was thus placed firmly in the field of industrial organization and was more specifically related to the analysis of imperfect competition. Hymer had relied greatly on Bain's (1956) pioneering work on barriers to entry to an industry; this thread of analysis has been deepened and broadened by Caves (1971), (1982). Caves (1971) suggested that the critical Hymer–Kindleberger advantage was the ability to differentiate a product, thus enabling the firm to service simultaneously several international markets. Johnson (1970), (1975) suggested that the significant advantage must have the characteristic of a public good that can be exploited by a subsidiary at a cost that is low in relation to the acquisition costs facing a rival firm. Such an advantage strongly suggests special knowledge or skills.

We must, however, turn to a second critical element in the Hymer–Kindleberger approach. Given the special advantages that enable the firm to invest abroad successfully (the necessary condition), it remains to be proved that the direct investment is the preferred means of exploiting the advantage (the sufficient condition). The basis for the decision, according to Hymer–Kindleberger, is profitability. In many cases, direct investment will be preferred to either exporting or licensing the advantage to a host-country firm. Exporting will in many cases be excluded by tariff and transport-cost barriers; also, a local producer may be better placed to adapt his product to local conditions and a local presence may have demand-stimulating effects.

The arguments that firms will often prefer foreign direct investment to licensing are more subtle. Hymer (1976) argued that the advantage-possessor cannot appropriate the full return (or rent) from its utilization because of imperfections in the market for knowledge. Such imperfections arise from buyer uncertainty when the buyer is unable to assess the worth of the knowledge until he is in possession of it, lack of an institutionalized market for the knowledge and the dependence of the value of the knowledge on its secrecy. The seller thus cannot induce competitive bids in order to appropriate the full returns. Further factors that favour foreign direct investment over licensing the advantage to host-country firms are the desire for control by the advantage-possessor and the danger that the advantage-seller will create a competitor if the buyer uses the advantage in ways that have not been paid for. Licensing may incur heavy firm-to-firm transfer costs, including costs of policing the transferred property rights (Buckley and Davies (1980)) – costs that do not arise in the case of parent-to-subsidiary transfers.

In summary, therefore, this approach suggests that a multinational entrant must possess an internally transferable advantage, the possession of which gives it a quasi-monopolistic opportunity to enter host-country markets. Barriers to trade and barriers that prevent host-country firms from duplicating this advantage mean that foreign direct investment is frequently the preferred form of exploiting the advantage in foreign markets.

It is arguable, however, that the fundamental proposition of the Hymer–Kindleberger approach is not as easily applicable to established multinational firms as opposed to firms becoming multinational. How far do the barriers to entry to a foreign market decline as the international spread of the firm widens? Established multinational firms have gained worldwide dominance and developed techniques to learn in advance of local conditions; products, processes, management style and marketing techniques are continually adapted to local markets. The ability of a multinational to forecast and adapt is one of the major competitive skills. It is now the only entry into unusually isolated markets (such as the People's Republic of China) where the heavy costs of foreignness are still encountered. The advantages of locals in other instances can be discounted in advance by an experienced multinational firm.

The whole concept of firm-specific advantages must therefore be questioned (Buckley (1983a)). The concept is artificially attenuated at the point where the firm first crosses national boundaries, or at least has the potential to do so. Firm-specific advantage is a reflection of this cut-off point as a snapshot in time of a dynamic process. The existence of firm-specific advantages depends on a set of assertions on (a) the diffusion of technical and marketing know-how, (b) the comparative advantage of firms in particular locations, and (c) the existence of particular types of economies of scale.

The first set of assertions rests on the size and extent of barriers to the sale of information on the market that are increasingly open to challenge, as are the assumptions on the relatively costless nature of internal information transfer (Teece (1983)). The second set of assertions is under threat from the worldwide rise of multinational enterprises. Finally, empirical propositions on economies of scale in research and development, on which firm-specific advantages rest, remain to be proved empirically; there is no guarantee that those who undertake research and development are necessarily the optimum users of its output. Separation through the market of research and its implementation in production may be a better solution. Finally, multinational firms can become locked into outmoded technologies whose institutional rigidities may prevent the creation and absorption of new developments in established firms. This provides opportunities for new-generation products and processes outside existing multinationals that gives flexibility to growth paths and often leads to the emergence of new firms.

The notion of firm-specific advantage is thus short-run when endowments of proprietary knowledge are fixed. In the long run, investment policy is crucial and a dynamic reformulation of industry barriers to entry is necessary to bring about an approach integrating the life cycle of a firm to expansion paths over time (Buckley (1983a)).

The multinational enterprise as a currency area phenomenon

A variant of the Hymer–Kindleberger approach, particularly associated with Aliber (1970), deals with an advantage that is not specific to particular firms but to all firms based in a particular currency area. According to Aliber it is the international financial market in which multinational enterprises have an advantage over host-country firms. Consequently Aliber argues that foreign direct investment can take place *even if* the market for advantages (licensing) is perfect.

The analysis centres on the currency premium. The holder of debt denominated in a particular currency bears the risk that its returns will be reduced if that currency depreciates in value relative to other currencies. If there is no aversion to risk then, in a perfect market, the rate of interest on the debt denominated in a particular currency will exactly reflect its expected rate of depreciation. But investors are risk-averse and demand a premium for bearing the uncertainty of exchange risk. However, Aliber argues that the market is subject to a *bias* in the application of the currency premium. Investors are myopic – they treat *all* the assets of a multinational enterprise as if they were in the same currency areas as the parent firm. Consequently a United Kingdom factory is a sterling asset, but when the factory is owned by a United States company it is regarded by the market *as if* it were a dollar asset.

The effect of these propositions is that source-country firms are ones able to borrow at lower interest rates (those relating to hard-currency assets) and are more highly valued by the market because their earnings are all capitalized at the rate relevant to the source-country currency.

Several criticisms of Aliber's theory are in order (Buckley and Casson (1976)). First, it seems unlikely that as a long-term explanation, investor myopia can bear the weight placed on it. Could speculators not turn such a bias to their advantage and thereby eliminate the phenomenon? Surely the international market recognizes that multinational enterprises are multiple-currency earners and that such earnings are subject to exchange risk if converted back to source-country currency? Secondly, the theory fails to explain the industrial distribution of foreign direct investment and the phenomenon of simultaneous cross-investment within one industry between currency areas. However, in broad terms, the approach explains well the direction of multinational enterprise investment in the postwar world: United States' expansion followed by extensive German and Japanese outward investment and the invasion of the United States by European multinationals during the 1970s and early 1980s.

Oligopolistic reaction and the multinational enterprise

Although closely linked with product-cycle models (see Section 1.4.4) the work of Knickerbocker (1973) clearly belongs to the theme of industrial organization. In a carefully designed study using the Harvard Multinational Enterprise Study sample of 187 United States corporate giants, Knickerbocker found a close relationship between oligopolistic reaction (demonstrated by the bunching in the time of entry into a particular market by oligopolistic firms) and industry structure. Moreover, the greater the degree of seller concentration, the more closely was entry into a market by the leader matched by followers. Profitability was also related to intensity of oligopolistic reaction. Knickerbocker suggested that brisk defensive investment transplants profitable patterns of oligopolistic behaviour to foreign markets.

1.4.4 The product-cycle model

The product-cycle hypothesis chiefly associated with Raymond Vernon ((1966), (1974), (1979)) has yielded many insights into the development of the multinational enterprise. The models rest on four basic assumptions:

(1) products undergo predictable changes in production and marketing;
(2) restricted information is available on technology;
(3) production processes change over time and economies of scale are prevalent;
(4) tastes differ according to income and thus products can be standardized at various income levels.

The original model (Vernon (1966)) suggested that new products would appear first in the most advanced country (the United States of America) because demand arising from (a) discretionary spending on new products arising from high income and (b) substitution of new capital goods for expensive labour, would be most easily transmitted to local entrepreneurs. Consequently, the *new product stage*, where an unstandardized product with a low-price elasticity of demand is produced on an experimental basis, occurs in the United States of America. The second stage is the *maturing product*. The product begins to be standardized and the need for flexibility on both supply and demand sides declines. The possibilities of economies of scale lead to expansion in production; this is matched by increasing demand as the product becomes cheaper. The market begins to appear in other advanced countries and is initially satisfied by exports from the United States of America. Eventually cost factors begin to dictate that these foreign markets should be serviced by local production and the emergence of indigenous producers adds a defensive motive to the advantages of investment by United States producers. So other advanced countries are the first recipients of United States direct investment. In the third stage, a *standardized product* emerges that sells entirely on the basis of price competitiveness. The imperative now is to produce the product at the lowest possible cost. Consequently the labour-intensive stages of production are hived off and carried out, via foreign direct investment, in the less-developed countries, where labour is cheapest.

Vernon's initial model has the virtues of simplicity and directness. It explains United States investment in other advanced countries and the phenomenon of offshore production in cheap-labour countries. Despite its advantages in integrating supply-and-demand factors, it has been outdated by events. First, the United States is no longer totally dominant in foreign investment – European and Japanese multinational expansion also needs explanation. Secondly, multinational enterprises are now capable of developing, maturing and standardizing products almost simultaneously, differentiating the product to suit a variety of needs without significant time-lags.

It was to counter the first objection that Vernon adapted his model to deal with non-United-States multinational enterprises after virtually admitting the redundancy of the 'simple' model. The modified product cycle (1979) brings the hypothesis much closer to the Hymer–Kindleberger model outlined above, resting as it does on oligopoly and market behaviour. The hypothesis is now concerned to emphasize the oligopolistic structure in which most multinational enterprises operate and their attempts to forestall entry into the industry by new firms. The names of the stages tell the story of the competitive devices used to construct and maintain oligopoly – innovation-based oligopoly, mature oligopoly (price competition and scale economies) and senescent oligopoly (cartels, product differentiation and the essential breakdown of entry barriers).

The product-cycle model thus yields many interesting insights into the process of global competition. It has also led to several valuable empirical studies – notably Hufbauer (1966) and Hirsch (1967). However, its over-deterministic and programmatic nature are features that have to be modified in view of the increasing sophistication of global competition (Giddy (1978)). In its analysis of the strategy of established multinational firms, the product-cycle approach splits three interdependent decisions: (1) investment in product development; (2) the method of servicing a foreign market; and (3) the firm's competitive stance in relation to foreign firms. These elements need to be considered simultaneously by multinational enterprises. As the basis for a forward-planning model, the product-cycle hypothesis has been outdated by the existence of experienced firms facing worldwide competition. Modelling of the process by which a beginner becomes an established multinational firm represents a gap in the theoretical framework, despite several empirical studies. Whatever the defects of Vernon's models, their virtues serve to focus attention on a more truly dynamic version of the growth of (multinational) firms.

1.4.5 Internalization and the theory of the multinational enterprise

Attempts at integration of the various strands of the theory of the multinational firm have centered on the concept of internalization. The framework of analysis is derived from Coase (1937). It is pointed out in Casson (1985c) that two connotations of this concept exist. One aspect is the internalization of a market where an arm's length contractual relationship is replaced by unified ownership. The other concerns the internalization of an externality where a market is created where none existed before. Often, internalization of the second kind is a consequence of the first, but logically the two should be dissociated. The excessive generality ascribed to internalization has led to it being described as 'a concept in search of a theory' (Buckley (1983a, p. 42)), but careful distinctions between types of internalization and the incidence of costs and benefits on a firm-by-firm basis lead to concrete propositions on the optimal scope of the firm (Casson (1981), Teece (1983)).

The thrust of the concept of internalization is that the actions of firms can replace the market or alternatively augment it. The explanatory power of the concept rests on an analysis of the costs and benefits to the firm of internalizing markets, particularly markets in intermediate goods. The predictive power of the concept for the growth and pattern of multinational enterprises is given by a statement of the likelihood of the internalization of the various markets a company faces. The advantages of internalization (and therefore of control by the firm versus the market solution) are given by:

(1) the increased ability to control and plan production and in particular to coordinate flows of crucial inputs;
(2) the exploitation of market power by discriminatory pricing;
(3) the avoidance of bilateral market power;

(4) the avoidance of uncertainties in the transfer of knowledge between parties that may exist in an alternative (market) solution;
(5) the avoidance of potential government intervention by devices such as transfer prices.

Costs arise from communication, coordination and control difficulties, and the costs of foreignness (Buckley and Casson (1976)). Three cases of empirical importance are (a) the advantages of vertical integration; (b) the importance of situations where intermediate product flows in research-intensive industries; and (c) the internalization of human skills, particularly in areas with high returns to team cooperation such as marketing and financing.

Magee (1977) bases his explanation on the ease of appropriability of returns from the creation of information: that is, the ability of the private originators of ideas to obtain for themselves the pecuniary value of the ideas to society. This extension of Johnson's (1970) concept and Arrow's (1962) analysis of the public good nature of proprietary information is linked with an industry cycle to derive expectations on the nature of multinational enterprise development and its ability to transfer technology effectively (particularly to less-developed countries (Magee (1977)).

Underlying this internalization approach is the view that internal solutions will be sought where international market imperfections would impose costs on firms using those markets. Internalization of markets also imposes severe barriers on new entry. The multinational is thus seen as both responding to market imperfections and creating them. Clearly, strong links with the Hymer–Kindleberger approach and the product-cycle hypothesis are apparent. Attention to imperfections on intermediate markets should not obscure the role of imperfections in final-goods markets, leading to competitive devices such as product differentiation and administered pricing. Multinationals are not passive reactors to imperfections, and internalization decisions interact. The critical role of information as an intermediate product is an important synthesizing element.

The role of multinationals in creating imperfections has not yet been fully incorporated into the theory because more attention has been paid to multinational enterprises' reactions to market imperfections. What is required is a thorough-going theory of barriers to entry for industries and markets. Further, the concept of internalization is a difficult one to measure empirically. The use of internal exports and flows relating to research and development (Buckley and Pearce (1979), (1981), (1984)) do not always fully discriminate between this approach and others.

1.4.6 Diversification and internationalization

It is possible to regard the multinational enterprise not as an aggressive risk-taker, investing heavily in research and development, diffusing the fruits through an international network of subsidiaries and appropriating the returns, but as risk-averse, using its multinational spread to achieve stability of returns. Moreover, internalization may be regarded as an alternative to domestic diversification. Here we bring these two ideas together.

The typical multinational enterprise will be diversified in two ways: by its position in the product and in the market, and by earning its returns in a variety of currencies. It is argued that the advantages of international financial diversification have led to superior stock-market performance by multinational enterprises over domestic firms, even after allowing for size and industry influences (Rugman (1981)). Thus multinational enterprises are regarded as an alternative vehicle for international financial diversification to individual diversification by the purchase of shareholdings. This argument rests on imperfections in the world-capital market which prevent individuals from enjoying the benefits of diversification (see Chapter 1.2). Such imperfections must impede individuals from satisfactorily diversifying; they reduce the optimal diversification of intermediaries so that diversification through controlling interests is more efficient than a larger number of smaller shareholdings. Direct investment involves control; without some such supporting argument *control* would involve a sub-optimal amount of diversification relative to the amount of each holding.

The arguments adduced for such imperfections are that transaction costs exist in the equity market in the form of costs of acquiring and disseminating the relevant information; that this results in the application by the market of a premium to the equity valuation of diversified firms. It can also be argued that the divorce of ownership and control reinforces this tendency because managers in an imperfect capital market can pursue policies that enhance their own welfare, within the constraint that returns to shareholders do not fall below those that would make them liable to a takeover bid. Managers may be risk-averse (preferring the safeguarding of their jobs to extra returns) and may therefore prefer a widely diversified company with the hoped-for stability that goes with it. Diversification through foreign investment widens the scope of their discretion. However, this would presumably accord with a strategy of avoidance of high-risk research and development, which is not consistent with the evidence (Buckley and Casson (1976)).

A further theoretical avenue concerns the choice between domestic (product) diversification and internalization. The simplest answer is to regard the multinational enterprise as a bundle of sector-specific resources, facing high barriers to entry into other industries but with relatively easy investment-access to foreign markets (Kindleberger (1969)).

A more rigorous analysis of this choice has been carried out by Wolf ((1975), (1977)) following work by Horst ((1972a), (1972b)). Horst showed that it was *total* United States sales to the Canadian market (exports and investment sales) that were explained by the theoretically significant factors (research and development intensity and size). Wolf takes this further by suggesting that domestic diversification and internalization should be regarded as alternative expansion routes. Wolf's theoretical underpinning relies on the pioneering work by Penrose (1969), who suggested that under-utilized resources within the firm, particularly management (the development of an idea in Robinson (1934)) can be called into service at home or abroad as rent-yielding assets. The opportunity cost of such under-utilized resources is close to zero but will have positive marginal revenue when utilized. The difficulty in such an approach is represented in finding appropriate measures or proxies for under-utilized resources. Wolf uses average-firm size (by industry) to represent economies of scale and the proportion of scientists and engineers in total employment as a proxy for technological expertise.

This avenue of investigation leads us into the area of multinational enterprises as special cases of multiplant firms. The theory of multiplant firms is addressed to the question: why should firms operate several plants of sub-optimal size rather than a smaller number of plants that could be above the minimum efficient scale? This question is tackled by Scherer and others (1975); it is clear that the results are of direct relevance to multinational enterprises. Scherer brings together findings from location theory, optimal lot-size theory, monetary theory and physical-distribution theory to derive hypotheses concerning 'optimal unbalanced specialization paths' for firms. In the international sphere, it is clear that many markets are small and do not provide enough scope for even one optimal-size plant. Buyers' desires for choice and variety also dictate from the demand side that no one firm, let alone plant, shall dominate individual markets. Thirdly, in many industries, long-run unit-production cost is relatively flat and cost penalties are not severely imposed on less-than-optimal plant scales. Finally, multiplant operation is often a rational response to problems of manufacturing highly specialized products with volatile demand or other features requiring close managerial supervision of technologies well-suited to low-volume production. These findings can be integrated with the above theory and with location theory to yield a fruitful synthesis (Part 6). The interplay of *plant* level economies and *firm* level economies plays a major role in the market-servicing (exports versus direct investment) decisions of multinational enterprises (Dunning and Buckley (1977)) and represents central concepts around which the different theoretical perspectives can be integrated.

1.4.7 Multinational enterprises and location theory

It is fair to suggest that location-theory elements in the modern theory of the multinational enterprise have been neglected. Yet any viable explanation of the growth, pattern and operations (sourcing policies) of inputs and market-servicing policies must include elements of location theory. Under the general rubric above, the multinational enterprise can be seen simply as a major vehicle for the transfer of mobile resources (technology, capital and management skills) to areas with immobile (or fixed) complementary inputs (markets, raw materials and labour). Thus Ricardian endowments enter the theory.

The location-specific endowments of particular importance to multinational enterprises are (1) raw materials, leading to vertical foreign direct investment; (2) cheap labour, leading to offshore-production facilities; and (3) protected or fragmented markets leading to foreign direct investment as the preferred means of marketing servicing. Location factors therefore enter the theory not only in their own right, as an influence on the relative costs facing a multinational enterprise with a choice of locations, but may also provide the motives for international expansion.

The important connections between location factors and the (internal) organization of multinational enterprises should, however, be given due weight. First, the multinational enterprise will normally be a multistage, multifunction firm and the location of different stages and functions will be subject to different locational influences connected by (international) flows of intermediate products. Secondly, the internalization of markets will affect location in two important ways:

(1) The multinational enterprise will have an incentive to minimize government intervention through transfer pricing, for instance, to reduce the overall tax liability by the input of high mark-ups in the lowest tax countries and possibly by altering its location strategy completely to take in a low-intervention tax haven. (For evidence on the nature and amount of intra-company trade and its determinants, see Buckley and Pearce (1979), (1981), (1984)).

(2) The increased communication flows in an internal market may bias high communication-cost activities towards the centre – usually towards the source country where critical activities are focused on head office. (A forceful extension of this argument is given by Hymer (1976)).

In his restatement of the product-cycle hypothesis, Vernon (1974) gives a great deal of weight to the interplay between the stage of the industry's development and the relevant locational influences upon it. The location of research activities (in the centre) and the changing locational influences on production provide the dynamic for the theory.

Standard location theory can be shown to be of direct relevance to the strategy of multinational enterprises as illustrated by Dunning's paper on the location of multinational enterprises in an enlarged European Community (1972) (see also Casson (1985b) and Horst's work on the servicing of the Canadian market by United States multinational enterprises (1972)). The reduction, removal or increase of tariffs between nations will alter multinational enterprise market-servicing decisions and cause a restructuring of the location of multinational enterprise activities. This area leads into an interesting discussion centred on the relative comparative advantages of firms and nations and thence to relative bargaining capabilities (Vaitsos (1974), Casson (1979)).

1.4.8   Japanese direct investment: a distinct approach?

Some people believe that Japanese direct investment requires a special approach because of several alleged differences from Western European and United States investment (Ozawa (1979a), (1979b)). Among these differences are a later take-off of Japanese investment; a clustering in Latin America and Asia of such investments; the supposed greater labour-intensity of Japanese investment; its openness to joint ventures; and the existence of group-controlled investment (Buckley (1983b), (1985a)).

These characteristics have led Japanese analysts to propose alternative explanations specifically related to Japanese conditions. One of the most ingenious is the theoretical framework developed by Kiyoshi Kojima ((1978), (1982), Kojima and Ozawa (1984)). Kojima's approach is variously called a macroeconomic approach, a factor-endowments approach and a model of trade-oriented (Japanese-type) foreign investment, to distinguish it from anti-trade-oriented (American type) foreign direct investment. Kojima's aim is to integrate trade theory with direct-investment theory and to contrast Japanese-type investment with American-type.

Kojima (1978) begins with the standard two-country, two-factor, two-product Hecksher-Ohlin model of trade. He then introduces Mundell's demonstration that under rigorous Hecksher-Ohlin assumptions, the substitution for commodity-of-factor movements will be complete. The process for achieving this is that capital – homogeneous (money) capital – flows from the capital-rich to the capital-poor country, perhaps response to the imposition of a prohibitive tariff on capital-intensive exportables. As a result, the recipient country becomes more capital-abundant and reallocates its resources so that production of capital-intensive goods expands, and that of labour-intensive goods declines, until equilibrium is reached at a point exactly corresponding to the post-trade situation in the absence of the capital movement. This pattern of output change – that the recipient country's comparatively disadvantaged industry expands and its comparatively advantaged (in terms of its *original* factor-endowment) industry contracts – is posited in the Rybczynski theorem. Kojima views American foreign direct investment in this light, arguing that the basis for trade is eliminated by outflows of capital from the capital-exporting country's advantaged industry, so foreign direct investment is a substitute for trade.

In the Japanese case, however, Kojima's argument is that the host-country's production frontier expands in such a direction that the (pre-investment) comparatively advantaged industry expands and the comparatively disadvantaged industry contracts, thus enhancing the basis for trade.

This *complements* case is achieved by the Rybczynski line sloping in an opposite direction (the line linking the original production point and the post-capital inflow production point moves upward). This effect cannot occur if homogeneous money capital, perfectly re-allocable to any industry, is the norm. Therefore Kojima suggests at this point that direct investment capital is a package involving technical knowledge and human-skill components (including management skills); it is therefore, to some extent, industry specific. This capital moves to the host country because of comparative advantages in improving productivity in the host country; the resultant increase in profitability adds the motivation. Here Kojima introduces a crucial assumption: that productivity in the host country is increased *more* through direct investment in the labour-intensive industry than in the capital-intensive industry, because of the smaller technological gap and a greater spillover of technology to local firms' ((1978) p. 126). The same amount of output is produced with proportionately smaller inputs of labour and capital. Hicks-neutral technological change is deemed to have taken place.

The critical factor in this model is the disproportionate effect on productivity, when sector-specific capital moves into the host's comparatively advantaged industry. The implicit assumption is that industry-specific public goods have been transferred – the proof of this is Kojima's ((1978) p. 127) statement that the production frontier in the source country remains unchanged 'since the technology and managerial skills do not decrease even when they are applied abroad and since labour and capital are assumed unchanged' in the source country. For Kojima includes the assumption that direct foreign investment involves a negligible transfer of money capital.

The comparative advantage in improving productivity can thus be seen as the result of the combination of internationally mobile inputs transferred by the investing (Japanese) firm that include managerial and organization skills, with the vital addition of guaranteed access to (Japanese) markets and distributive networks, together with locationally immobile inputs, notably cheap labour. Kojima suggests that because of the sector-specific nature of these productivity-improving resources, it is easier for firms that possess such attributes to relocate abroad (outside Japan) rather than diversify into other domestic industries. Consequently there is no presumption (unlike product-cycle-type United States foreign direct investment) that the outward investors are the leading firms. Indeed, it is suggested that weaker firms, just exposed to exogenous shifts in comparative advantage, will be the most likely to be relocated in less-developed countries.

The crucial element in Kojima's explanation of Japanese foreign direct investment is the improvement in productivity in the host country brought about by the infusion of the package of resources involved in Japanese investment. Of key importance is the market access brought by the link with a Japanese distribution network, and the organization skills of Japanese management when working with relatively unskilled or semi-skilled labour. The host-country unit, when taken over or set up by Japanese foreign direct investment, becomes integrated with a marketing network guaranteeing market access. The addition of a Japanese imprint enhances the quality image of the product. Japanese ownership therefore confers immediate benefits.

The specialist skills infused include those developed by Japanese enterprises in response to the particular stimuli they have faced in Japan: notably a cooperative rather than competitive environment, a docile and relatively cheap workforce and skills in organizing high-quality, mass-production systems. The range of industries over which these skills are crucial is very different from those where United States and European firms have developed intra-industry specialisms; consequently the industrial structure of Japanese foreign direct investment is different to Western foreign direct investment. It has, however, been differentiated by Kojima more starkly than the version presented here by his concentration on a product-cycle interpretation of American-type foreign direct investment.

Japanese foreign direct investment represents a search for location-specific inputs (stable environment, low transport costs, but chiefly cheap labour) to complement the skills developed by Japanese enterprise. It corresponds to Western, chiefly United States, firms' offshore production and exhibits a similar industry structure.

Japanese outward investment must indeed be explained by reference to locational criteria: notably the relative labour costs in nearby less-developed countries as compared with Japan. The firm-specific skills of Japanese firms – access to a (worldwide) distribution network, organization ability and managerial skills – differ significantly from the typical United States or European multinational enterprise's strengths. Consequently the industrial distribution of Japanese foreign direct investment differs from these other industrialized countries. Differentiation of Japanese foreign direct investment has been exaggerated by its comparison with product-cycle-type United States foreign direct investment, which is at most only a sub-set of that country's outward investment – an explanation that has been outdated by events (Giddy (1978)).

1.4.9 Synthesis – a general theory of the multinational enterprise

There are now several candidates for a general theory of the multinational enterprise (see Casson (1987)). Among these are Dunning's eclectic theory (1981), (1988), which relies on the ownership/location/internalization paradigm: ownership-specific advantages, location endowments and internalization advantages. Several unresolved issues remain in this approach. First, the relationship between these three elements and their development over time is unclear and leaves a classification system bereft of a dynamic content. Secondly, the existence of separate (and separable) ownership advantages is doubtful and logically redundant because internalization explains why firms exist in the absence of such advantages.

Rugman (1981) claims that internalization in itself represents a general theory of the multinational enterprise. This is achieved partly by relegating location factors to a footnote by including spatial cost-saving as an internalized firm-specific advantage. Internalization requires restrictions on the relative sizes of internal and external transaction costs to have any empirical content; without a theory of this incidence, it remains tautological.

The markets and hierarchies approach associated with Oliver Williamson ((1975), (1981), (1985)) has also been advanced as a candidate for a general theory of the multinational enterprise (Calvet (1981)). Williamson suggests that his general theory of why firms exist explains the existence of the multinational firm as a special case. Without a theory of the conditions under which one ideal-type form (market or hierarchy) will be replaced by the other, only an arid, comparative, static framework remains. The transition from market to hierarchy may be explained by the minimization of transaction costs, once these have been carefully specified (Buckley and Casson (1985)). The concept of bounded rationality in management decision-making utilized by Williamson is useful but it sits awkwardly within an essentially neoclassical framework. Further, Rugman's (1981) identification of hierarchy with internal market may be unjustified because internal organization may more closely resemble a perfect market, with transfer prices approximating to shadow prices of a perfect allocation, than the hierarchical mode.

The theory of the multinational firm therefore requires development in several directions before it can be seen to be adequate. First, the fusion between institutional and neoclassical elements must be made more secure. Secondly, the general area of the economics of business strategy is in need of greater attention. Thirdly, the role of time must be more carefully defined in the relationship between the growth (and decline) of firms, technologies, products and industries. Finally, the formulation and testing of hypotheses from the theory is an urgent task (Buckley (1988)).

Recently, further integration has been achieved between the purportedly incompatible approaches of internalization and market structure theories after Hymer. Buckley (1990) has shown that the two approaches are complementary not competitive. Hymer himself, in a paper originally written in French (1968) and now republished (Casson (1990)), used Coase's framework; the synthesis of the two approaches represents a step forward in theorizing.

References

Aharoni, Yair (1971): 'On the definition of a Multinational Corporation', *Quarterly Review of Economics and Business*, Vol. 11, pp. 22–37.

Aliber, R.Z. (1970): 'A Theory of Foreign Direct Investment' in Kindleberger, C.P. (ed.): *The International Firm*. Cambridge, Mass: MIT Press.

Arrow, K.J. (1962): 'Economic Welfare and the Allocation of Resources for Invention' in *The Rate and Direction of Inventive Activity*. Princeton: National Bureau of Economic Research, Princeton University Press.

Bain, Joe S. (1956): *Barriers to New Competition*. Cambridge, Mass: Harvard University Press.

Buckley, Peter J. (1983a): 'New Theories of International Business: Some Unresolved Issues' in Casson, M.C. (ed.): *The Growth of International Business*. London: George Allen & Unwin.

Buckley, Peter J. (1983b): 'Macroeconomic versus the International Business Approach', *Hitotsubashi Journal of Economics*, 24, 1, June, pp. 95–100.

Buckley, Peter J. (1985a): 'The Economic Analysis of the Multinational Enterprise: Reading versus Japan?', *Hitotsubashi Journal of Economics*, 26, 2, December, pp. 117–24.

Buckley, Peter J. (1985b): 'New Forms of International Industrial Cooperation', Chap. 3 in Buckley and Casson (1985).

Buckley, Peter J. (1988): 'The Limits of Explanation', *Journal of International Business Studies*, XIX, 2, Summer, pp. 181–93.

Buckley, Peter J. (1990): 'Problems and Developments in the Core Theory of International Business', *Journal of International Business Studies* (forthcoming).

Buckley, Peter J. and Casson, Mark (1976): *The Future of the Multinational Enterprise*. London: Macmillan.

Buckley, Peter J. and Casson, Mark (1985): *The Economic Theory of the Multinational Enterprise: Selected Papers*. London: Macmillan.

Buckley, Peter J. and Davies, Howard (1980): 'Foreign Licensing in Overseas Operations: Theory and Evidence from the UK' in Hawkins, R.G. and Prasad, A.J. (eds): *Technology Transfer and Economic Development*. Greenwich, Conn: JAI Press.

Buckley, Peter J. and Pearce, R.D. (1979): 'Overseas Production and Exporting by the World's Largest Enterprises', *Journal of International Business Studies*, 10, 1, Spring, pp. 9–20.

Buckley, Peter J. and Pearce, R.D. (1981): 'Market Servicing by Multinational Manufacturing Firms: Exporting versus Foreign Production', *Managerial and Decision Economics*, 2, 14, December, pp. 220–46.

Buckley, Peter J. and Pearce, R.D. (1984): 'Exports in the Strategy of Multinational Firms', *Journal of Business Research*, 12, 2, June, pp. 209–26.

Calvet, A.L. (1981): 'A Synthesis of Foreign Direct Investment Theories and Theories of the Multinational Firm', *Journal of International Business Studies*, 12, pp. 43–60.

Casson, Mark (1979): *Alternatives to the Multinational Enterprise*. London: Macmillan.

Casson, Mark (1981): 'Foreword' to Rugman, A.M.: *Inside the Multinationals*. London: Croom Helm.

Casson, Mark (1985a): 'Transaction Costs and the Theory of the Multinational Enterprise' in Buckley and Casson (1985) *op. cit.*

Casson, Mark (1985b): 'Multinationals and Intermediate Product Trade' in Buckley and Casson (1985) *op cit.*

Casson, Mark (1987): 'General Theories of the Multinational Enterprise: A Critical Examination' in Mark Casson: *The Firm and the Market*. Oxford: Basil Blackwell.

Casson, Mark (1990) (ed.): *The Multinational Enterprise*. Cheltenham: Edward Elgar.

Caves, Richard E. (1971): 'International Corporations: The Industrial Economics of Foreign Investment', *Economica* (New Series), Vol. 38, pp. 1–27.

Caves, Richard E. (1982): *Multinational Enterprise and Economic Analysis*. Cambridge: Cambridge University Press.

Coase, R.H. (1937): 'The Nature of the Firm', *Economica* (New Series), Vol. 4, pp. 386–405.

Dunning, John H. (1972): *The Location of International Firms in an Enlarged EEC: An Exploratory Paper*. Manchester: Manchester Statistical Society.

Dunning, John H. (1981): *International Production and the Multinational Enterprise*. London: George Allen & Unwin.

Dunning, John H. (1981): *Explaining International Production*. London: Unwin Hyman.

Dunning, John H. and Buckley, Peter J. (1977): 'International Production and Alternative Models of Trade', *Manchester School*, Vol. 65, pp. 392–403.

Giddy, Ian H. (1978): 'The Demise of the Product Cycle Model in International Business Theory', *Columbia Journal of World Business*, Vol. 13, pp. 90–7.

Hirsh, Seev (1967): *The Location of Industry and International Competitiveness*. Oxford: Oxford University Press.

Horst, T.O. (1972a): 'Firm and Industry Determinants of the Decision to Invest Abroad: An Empirical Study', *Review of Economics and Statistics*, Vol. 54, pp. 258–66.

Horst, T.O. (1972b): 'The Industrial Composition of US Exports and Subsidiary Sales to the Canadian market', *American Economic Review*, Vol. 57, pp. 37–54.

Hufbauer, G.C. (1966): *Synthetic Materials and the Theory of International Trade*. London: Duckworth.

Hymer, Stephen H. (1968): 'The Large Multinational "Corporation": An Analysis of some Motives for the International Integration of Business' in Casson M. (ed.): (1990), *op cit.*

Hymer, Steven H. (1976): *The International Operations of National Firms*. Lexington, Mass: Lexington Books.

Johnson, H.G. (1970): 'The Efficiency and Welfare Implications of the International Corporation' in C.P. Kindleberger (ed.): *The International Corporation*. Cambridge, Mass: MIT Press.

Johnson, H.G. (1975): *Technology and Economic Independence*. London: Macmillan.

Kindleberger, C.P. (1969): *American Business Abroad*. New Haven: Yale University Press.

Knickerbocker, F.T. (1973): *Oligopolistic Reaction and Multinational Enterprise*. Cambridge, Mass: Harvard University Press.

Kojima, K. (1978): *Direct Foreign Investment: A Japanese Model of Multinational Business Operations*. London: Croom Helm.

Kojima, K. (1982): 'Macroeconomic versus International Business Approach to Direct Foreign Investment', *Hitotsubashi Journal of Economics*, 23, 2, June, pp. 1–19.

Kojima, K. and Ozawa, T. (1984): 'Micro- and Macro-Economic Models of Direct Foreign Investment', *Hitotsubashi Journal of Economics*, 23, 1, June, pp. 1–19.

Magee, S.P. (1977): 'Multinational Corporations, Industry Technology Cycle and Development', *Journal of World Trade Law*, 11, pp. 297–321.

Ozawa, T. (1979): *Mutlinationalism, Japanese Style: The Political Economy of Outward Dependency*. Princeton, N.J.: Princeton University Press.

Penrose, Edith T. (1969): *The Theory of the Growth of the Firm*. Oxford: Basil Blackwell.

Robinson, E.A.G. (1934): 'The Problem of Management and the Size of Firms', *Economic Journal*, Vol. 44, pp. 242–57.

Rugman, Alan M. (1981): *Inside the Multinationals*. London: Croom Helm.

Scherer, F.M. et al. (1975): *The Economics of Multi-Plant Operation – An International Comparisons Study*. Cambridge, Mass: Harvard University Press.

Teece, D.J. (1983): 'Technological and Organizational Factors in the Theory of the Multinational Enterprise' in Mark Casson (ed.): *The Growth of International Business*. London: George Allen & Unwin.

United Nations Centre on Transnational Corporations (1983): *Transnational Corporations in World Development: Third Survey*. New York: UNCTC.

United Nations Centre on Transnational Corporations (1988): *Transnational Corporations in World Development: Trends and Prospects*. New York: UNCTC.

Vaitsos, C.V. (1974): *Intercountry Income Distribution and Transnational Enterprises*. Oxford: Oxford University Press.

Vernon, R. (1966): 'International Investment and International Trade in the Product Cycle', *Quarterly Journal of Economics*, 80, pp. 190–207.

Vernon, R. (1974): 'The Location of Economic Activity' in John H. Dunning (ed.): *Economic Analysis and the Multinational Enterprise*. London: George Allen & Unwin.

Vernon, R. (1979): 'The Product Cycle Hypothesis in a New International Environment', *Oxford Bulletin of Economics and Statistics*, Vol. 41, pp. 255–67.

Williamson, Oliver, E. (1975): *Markets and Hierarchies: Analysis and Anti-Trust Implications*. New York: Free Press.

Williamson, Oliver, E. (1981): 'The Modern Corporation: Origins, Evolution, Attributes', *Journal of Economic Literature*, Vol. 19, pp. 1537–68.

Williamson, Oliver E. (1985): *The Economic Institutions of Capitalism*. New York: Collier Macmillan.

Wolf, Bernard, M. (1975): 'Size and Profitability among US Manufacturing Firms: Multinational versus Primarily Domestic Firms', *Journal of Economics and Business*, Vol. 28, pp. 15–22.

Wolf, Bernard, M. (1977): 'Industrial Diversification and Internationalization: Some Empirical Evidence', *Journal of Industrial Economics*, Vol. 26, pp. 177–91.

Part 2

The Framework of International Trade

Introduction

This part is concerned with both the pattern of trade and those established structures that influence its course, some by promoting and some by impeding it. The rapid growth of trade since the end of the Second World War has been remarkable, particularly in manufactured goods. Initially this growth was most pronounced between the developed countries. However, more recently and following the lead of Japan, exports from the newly industrializing countries to the developed countries of the West have attained a high degree of prominence.

The benefits accruing from the international exchange of goods and services, together with asset transactions, are well known: in practice, countries engaged in trade face a number of conflicts of objectives as well as barriers to trade imposed within the world economy.

The allegedly high costs of economic adjustment from old to new patterns of comparative advantage serve to highlight the divergence of producers' and consumers' interests within countries, and are used to justify impediments to trade; imperfections in the market structure of trade, resulting in market power on the parts of countries, also exert a brake on the pursuit of free trade in providing the temptation to exploit bargaining strength. Such issues are dealt with in the theory of protection. There are also the natural costs of doing business internationally, which act to impede trade while benefiting no one.

Novel types of threat to the growth of trade are not rare. The view, increasingly gaining ground, that a bilateral balance of trade should be a precondition for the expansion of trade is but a short step from protectionism; at times a similar argument has been applied to foreign direct investment. However, rising interest in service sector industries augurs well for their future role in international trade, though this will demand an innovative approach to liberalization.

Different aspects of the institutional framework of trade can be viewed as a multi-layered response to a diversity of trade barriers: in respect of artificial barriers the progressive reduction of tariffs under the auspices of the General Agreement on Tariffs and Trade is one example of progress which could only have been pursued through international cooperation on a multi-lateral basis. The movement towards economic integration on the part of a number of groups of countries establishes another layer of arrangements by those most likely to benefit.

The continued search for international monetary arrangements that stabilize exchange rates and so reduce the exchange risks inherent in the international monetary economy is also crucial to the expansion of trade, as are provisions to alleviate balance of payments imbalances. The need for solutions to the instability of international commodity markets is felt most by the developing countries, who urgently need a secure basis from which to participate in the growth of world trade.

The resurgence of countertrade arrangements provides an illustration of the response made by countries to political and economic distortions; in the cases of Eastern Bloc and certain developing countries this has often amounted to a palliative rather than a cure for more deep-seated problems. The same might be said of the increased incidence of managed trade, whereby countries are persuaded to limit their exports of products or groups of products. The controversy continues over such measures, and over the role of unfair trade practices in the rise of the new protectionism.

The framework of governance structures in trade has become further extended in the form of the international operations of firms. These developments are explained by the theory of the multinational enterprise, but are manifested in the rising levels of intra-firm trade between countries; the nature and behaviour of this trade is thought to be distinctive from trade between independent firms.

Opportunities for trade between the developed market economies and those of Eastern Europe may form a further impetus for growth; however, these highlight the predicament of the lower income developing economies, which have perhaps most to lose from the intensification of trade between the countries of the Northern Hemisphere, especially in the absence of further preferential trade concessions by the developed economies.

Contents

2.1

The Growth of World Trade

2.1.1 Introduction

Since the end of the Second World War international trade has grown at a faster rate than world output. From 1970 to the mid-1980s visible (or merchandise) exports have grown by an approximate factor of nine in terms of volume compared with around a factor of five for output. The trade sector of the world as a whole has therefore unquestionably become more important (see General Agreement on Tariffs and Trade 1987) and the world economy has become more integrated as a result.

There are two dimensions to this growth: the internationalization of consumption and the internationalization of production. The rise in the trade of final products for consumption has been most marked between the developed market economies or industrialized countries, and, as noted in Chapter 2.3 (Section 2.3.6), is characterized by intra-industry trade in final goods. One explanation for the growth of this type of trade is provided by the preference-similarity hypothesis: that similar countries (in terms of income per capita and tastes) will trade most intensively with each other (Linder (1961)). These products will typically be differentiated manufactured goods, with scale economies in production, naturally leading to an incentive to expand exports. Indeed, the facts support this reasoning: exports of manufactured goods have risen by over a factor of 16 since 1950 compared with an output growth of around seven.

This pro-trade bias of the manufacturing sector has also been responsible for the successive reductions in tariff barriers on manufactured goods under the General Agreement on Tariffs and Trade negotiations (see Section 2.4); these in turn have permitted further expansion in trade, while movements towards regional integration and free trade areas have also played a central part.

The internationalization of production has also characterized world trade. This involves the linking of production processes between countries and therefore an increase in the trade in intermediate products and services. This increase in the international division of labour has been a feature of trade between developed countries, but it has also included the less-developed countries and in particular the newly industrializing countries. International differences in the abundance of resources and factors of production retain much power to explain the inter-industry specialization of countries (see Leamer (1984)) where exported products are classified to a different product sector from those imported. However, the reduction in certain barriers to the coordination of production between countries has also led to specialization within industries (see Casson and Associates (1986)). Much of this increase in international vertical integration has occurred within the control of multinational firms (see Section 2.6.4). For this reason the growth of multinational production is now strongly identified with the trade of intermediate products and services as well as with that of final products.

The growth of trade can therefore partly be attributed to the breaking-up of production stages between countries. Where this involves the re-export of imported products after processing, it is evident that the growth of global trade will be overstated in terms of value as it is commonly recorded at gross output values. Other statistical problems exist and are discussed in General Agreement on Tariffs and Trade 1987, Appendix 1. International trade in services is poorly covered in most official publications on trade patterns, and often only in an aggregated form. This must represent a grey area in any appraisal of the growth of trade. The importance of services is overviewed in Section 2.3.3.

2.1.2   The growth of output and trade

Between 1980 and 1986, global real gross-domestic product rose by 17 per cent, world commodity output by 14 per cent and the volume of world exports by 19 per cent (Table 2.1.1). However, most of the growth in trade volume was the result of manufactured exports (which rose by 30 per cent). The recessionary period in the early 1980s left its mark on both trade volumes and the unit values of exports (used as a substitute for prices), though especially on the latter. The contrasts between the performance of manufactures as compared with agricultural products and minerals is evident in terms of trade volume, with manufactures the first to recover; however, the average price of minerals' trade (calculated to include fuels and non-ferrous metals) lags furthest behind.

The expansion of trade is therefore an uneven process between these three broad major product categories. Manufactures' trade tends to lead that of minerals because the latter comprise fuels and metals used in the manufacturing sector. This relationship has been weakened both because of the drive to reduce the degree of energy consumption in manufacturing through greater efficiency (following the oil crises of the 1970s) and because of the substitution of alternate materials, such as plastics for metals, which have most of their value added within the manufacturing sector.

Table 2.1.1 Development of World Merchandise Output and Exports, US $billion and indices

	1980	1981	1982	1983	1984	1985	1986	1987
WORLD EXPORTS								
Value (billion dollars)								
Total	1,990	1,963	1,844	1,809	1,907	1,924	2,119	...
Agricultural products	299	295	271	267	279	267	298	...
Minerals[a]	567	550	493	454	452	430	345	...
Manufactures	1,095	1,089	1,053	1,057	1,141	1,191	1,431	...
Unit Value								
Total	100	98	94	89	87	84	90	...
Agricultural products	100	95	88	85	87	83	93	...
Minerals[a]	100	108	102	95	93	89	67	...
Manufactures	100	96	94	90	87	86	101	...
Volume								
Total	100	101	99	102	111	115	119	123
Agricultural products	100	104	103	105	108	108	107	...
Minerals[a]	100	90	85	84	85	83	89	...
Manufactures	100	104	102	107	119	126	130	...
WORLD COMMODITY OUTPUT								
Total	100	101	99	101	108	111	114	117
Agricultural products	100	104	107	107	113	115	116	...
Mining	100	93	87	86	87	88	92	...
Manufactures	100	101	99	101	109	113	117	...
WORLD real GDP	100	103	103	106	110	114	117	...

Note: a) Including fuels and non-ferrous metals.
Source: GATT (1987)

Trade in agricultural products has grown more slowly than its world output, partly reflecting the fact that the degree of protection in agriculture remains higher than for other types of merchandise, with major producing countries limiting the process of specialization and trade and the exploitation of comparative advantage (see Chapter 2.5).

A salutary warning against placing too much confidence in the valuation of world exports is provided by Table 2.1.2. This serves to demonstrate that the currency in which trade flows are valued will sometimes significantly affect the trade recorded. The adoption of floating exchange rates, the difference in inflation rates between the United States and other countries and changes in the

Table 2.1.2   Unit Value of World Exports, Percentage Change over Preceding Year, 1976–86

	1976	1977	1978	1979	1980	1981	1982	1983	1984	1985	1986
In dollar terms	2	9	11	19	20	−2	−4	−5½	−3½	−1	7
In SDR terms	7	8	4	17	20	9	1	−2	2	−2½	−7½
In Ecu terms	13	7	0	10	18	23	8	4	10	0	−17

Source: GATT (1987)

Table 2.1.3   Growth of World Manufacturing Production, Annual Rates, 1963–85

	World	*Developed market economies*	*Developing countries*	*Centrally planned economies*
1963–1970	7.1	6.1	6.8	8.1
1971–1980	4.2	3.1	6.9	6.9
1980–1985	2.5	1.7	4.7	3.8

Source: United Nations, Department of International Economic and Social Affairs (1987)

Table 2.1.4   Growth of Exports of Manufactures by Country Groups, Annual Rates, 1965–85[a]

	1965–1970	*1970–1980*	*1980–1985*
Developed market economies	13.4	18.7	0.4
Developed countries	17.8	23.7	6.0
Centrally planned economies	8.2	16.4	1.1

Note: a) Growth of export values at current dollar prices.

Source: United Nations, Department of International Economic and Social Affairs (1987)

prices of commodities (particularly petroleum) priced in dollars all contribute to this problem (see General Agreement on Tariffs and Trade 1987, Appendix 1).

Tables 2.1.3 and 2.1.4 overview the growth in the production and export of manufactures respectively by economic classification of the exporting country. The deceleration in the production of manufactures has been a predominant feature of the developed economies as their industrial structures shifted towards services and a response to the oil crises and recession. The performance of manufactured exports from the developing countries is superior to that of the developed and centrally planned economies throughout the 20 years from 1965.

Table 2.1.5 Selected Groups of Countries: Elasticities of Real Imports to Output, 1965–85[a]

	1965–1985	1965–1973	1971–1979	1977–1985
Developed market economics	1.59	1.97	1.45	1.29
Germany, Federal Republic of	1.96	2.26	1.83	1.55
Japan	1.14	1.47	1.23	0.45
United States	1.88	2.77	1.68	1.76
European centrally planned economies	1.31	1.35	1.36	0.98
Energy-exporting developing countries	1.83	1.07	2.30	1.87
Energy-importing developing countries	1.02	1.23	1.06	0.53
10 large debtors[b]	1.03	1.27	1.21	-0.74

Notes:

a) All elasticities are the estimated parameters of a double-logarithmic regression of real imports on real GDP data (NMP for the centrally planned economies) for the periods specified. With the exception of two parameters (elasticities of energy-exporting developing countries and the 10 large debtors in 1977–1985), all coefficients are statistically significant.

b) The 10 largest debtors with private bank rescheduling: Argentina, Brazil, Chile, Mexico, Nigeria, Peru, Philippines, Turkey, Venezuela and Yugoslavia.

Source: United Nations, Department of International Economic and Social Affairs (1986)

This increase in less-developed countries' exports has been mainly directed towards the developed countries, which account for approximately two-thirds of less-developed-country exports and in which demand has grown substantially faster than within the less developed countries.

2.1.3   The openness of the world economy

The propensity of countries to trade depends fundamentally on their own economic size. The larger a country's internal economy in terms of the diversity of resources and size of population (and so the scope for the internal division of labour) the greater the degree of internal trade. In contrast, proximity to countries with large markets will tend to raise the degree of external trade, especially the existence of long borders with neighbouring states, as in the case of the United States and Canada.

The prospects for growth in external trade depend on the relationship between increases in internal consumption and production, and imports and exports. Tables 2.1.5 to 2.1.7 examine this relationship using the elasticity of trade volume (exports or imports) with respect to factors such as domestic output or the prices of goods. In the case of the output elasticity of demand for imports, for example,

Table 2.1.6   Apparent Elasticities of Trade under Different Definitions of Trade and Output, 1950–85[a]

	1950–1965	1965–1973	1971–1979	1977–1985
Change in world trade Change in world income	2.04	1.83	1.37	1.25
Change in trade in manufactures Change in world income	2.56	2.50	1.90	2.40

Note: a) Apparent elasticities measured as percentage change in merchandise trade divided by percentage change in output.

Source: United Nations, Department of International Economic and Social Affairs (1986) derived from GATT, *International Trade*.

Table 2.1.7   Export and Import Elasticities for Germany, Japan and the United States, 1977–86

| | | Price elasticity[a] ||
Trade volume by country	Income elasticity	Short-term[b]	Long-term[b]
Germany, Federal Republic of			
Exports	0.95	−0.04	−0.36
Imports	2.04	−0.21	−0.46
Japan			
Exports	1.75	−0.06	−1.35
Imports	0.75	−0.03	−0.49
United States			
Exports	1.00	−0.21	−0.93
Imports	2.19	−0.30	−1.20

Notes:

a) Relative price of exports: unit value of exports in dollars divided by that of the rest of the world; relative price of imports: unit value of imports in domestic currency divided by the country's wholesale prices.

b) Short-term: one quarter; long-term: eight quarters.

Source: United Nations, Department of International Economic and Social Affairs (1987)

this is calculated as the percentage change in the volume of imports induced by a 1 per cent increase in a country's output. An elasticity value of more than one (or an absolute value of one in the case of price elasticity) is described as elastic, and implies that trade is estimated to expand more than in its existing proportion (with respect to output, income or some other variable such as price). A value of less than one implies the opposite, while a value of exactly one would mean a precisely proportionate expansion of trade.

Between 1965 and 1985 there was a perceptible and general decline in world trade elasticities. One reason for this is the low performance of commodities' trade and trade in agricultural goods, noted earlier. During the 1950s the elasticity of world trade as a whole was put at around two, but in the 1980s it has been only a little over one. The lowest country elasticities are recorded by those in economic difficulties, such as the energy-importing less-developed countries, the ten largest debtor countries and the centrally planned economies. Clearly, the prospects for the growth of world trade depend on the alleviation of these difficulties through domestic economic progress. The low Japanese import elasticity reflects the composition of the Japanese visible account, where predominantly primary commodities are imported.

The decline in the responsiveness of world trade to the growth of output and income is also contributed to by the increasing importance of the service sector in developed economies' national incomes, while their overall recorded trade in services has remained relatively stagnant – no doubt partly due to problems of measurement (see Section 2.3.3). These developments do not necessarily result from the less-tradable nature of certain services, but may reflect rather more the higher degree of national protection common in the service sector (see Section 2.5) in which case the prospects for the growth of trade depend strongly on the progress of liberalization.

Disaggregating the trade elasticities for manufacturing at the global levels (Table 2.1.6) does indeed suggest that the elasticity of manufactures' trade remains high.

The prospects for trade growth also depend on countries satisfactorily being able to balance their external payments and receipts. When this is arduous, recourse is often made to trade-reducing deflationary (or protectionist) policies. For those countries with balance-of-trade deficits, one of the conditions required is that exports should grow proportionately faster than imports. For world adjustment to be expedited the reverse would need to be true for balance-of-trade surpluses.

In 1979 United States visible imports were 10 per cent in excess of United States exports; by 1986 this had risen to 65 per cent in excess, amounting to a difference of United States $145 billion. For Japan in 1986 visible exports were 65 per cent above imports, while in the Federal Republic of Germany the trade surplus was 30 per cent above the level of imports.

Table 2.1.7 reports estimates of income and price elasticities calculated by the

United Nations Secretariat. As noted earlier in the case of Japan, the income elasticities for imports are dependent on commodity composition. It is evident that the stimulation of domestic demand in Germany will reduce the trade surplus more readily than in Japan, while in the United States income growth is set to increase the trade deficit. As things stand, for the United States trade deficit to close, real imports by the rest of the world must grow by more than three times the growth of United States real domestic demand for the United States deficit to be reduced quickly (see United Nations Department of International Economic and Social Affairs (1987) Chapter 2).

Adjustment in the balance of trade also depends on the responsiveness of foreign and domestic demand to price changes; in particular, trade gaps will tend to close if the price elasticities of imports and exports sum to greater than unity (ignoring the negative sign). In a floating exchange-rate system, such price adjustments are affected by depreciations or appreciations in a currency's foreign exchange values. In the long term (two years) this condition is satisfied by the United States and Japan; however, the leading problem with exchange-rate adjustments is that they do not occur in response to the trade balance alone (on the current account) but can frequently be dominated by capital-account transactions. So a country with attractive domestic assets, perhaps because of high interest rates, may not obtain the required depreciation to bring an adjustment on its trade balance. This type of barrier to adjustment has occurred in the experiences of the United States and United Kingdom.

The growth of world trade depends crucially on countries' attitudes to free trade, which will in turn depend both on the arguments for protection in the home economies and therefore on their balance-of-payments position. Since the end of the Second World War the growth of trade in manufactures has been the dominant force. However, the internationalization of production, with manufactured exports increasingly originating in countries that do not themselves import manufactures in comparable quantities, has brought the need for structural adjustment in the developed countries. The growth of world trade also depends on liberalization in sectors other than manufacturing, in which respect the developed countries have the potential to lead further trade expansion.

2.2

Directions of World Trade

2.2.1 Introduction

In analysing the growth of world trade in Chapter 2.1, it transpired that the world economy has become increasingly integrated over the last 20 to 30 years. The movement towards regional integration is only partly responsible for this, as the importance of trade for almost all countries has grown appreciably. This chapter investigates the countries and country groups involved in this expansion of trade, both on a multilateral and a bilateral basis.

2.2.2 Major trading nations

The leading 25 countries in world visible trade are presented in Table 2.2.1. The top ten exporting nations in 1986, with the exception of the Union of Soviet Socialist Republics, were developed market economies. The Federal Republic of Germany is seen to occupy first place, followed by the United States and Japan. In terms of visible imports United States share is considerably higher than its export share, while the reverse is true for Japan; otherwise the ranks for exports and imports are identical.

Countries exporting less than United States $50 billions' worth, however, are more varied, with Taiwan the leader and a number of other newly industrializing countries exporting in excess of United States $20 billions' worth. Apart from European developed market economies, significant exporters from the Eastern bloc are the German Democratic Republic and Czechoslovakia, while China occupies sixth place in this group. The significance of Saudi Arabia is almost entirely due to its petroleum exports; it does not feature as a leading importer.

Chapter 2.1 noted that the most significant source of growth in world trade has been that of manufactured goods. Accordingly, the most important trading nations are those specializing in manufactures. The leading exporters in

Table 2.2.1 Merchandise Trade by Countries and Areas in 1986, US $billion and Percentage Distribution

	Exports (f.o.b.)			Imports (c.i.f.)	
	Value	Share		Value	Share
World	**2,119.00**	**100.0**		**2,200.00**	**100.0**
More than 50 billion					
Germany, Fed. Rep.	243.35	11.5	United States	387.10	17.6
United States	217.30	10.3	Germany, Fed. Rep.	191.10	8.7
Japan	210.75	9.9	France	129.40	5.9
France	124.95	5.9	Japan	127.55	5.8
United Kingdom	107.00	5.0	United Kingdom	126.35	5.7
Italy	97.80	4.6	Italy	99.45	4.5
USSR	97.30	4.6	USSR[a]	88.85	4.0
Canada	89.70	4.2	Canada	85.65	3.9
Netherlands	80.50	3.8	Netherlands	75.55	3.4
Belgium-Luxembourg	68.80	3.2	Belgium-Luxembourg	68.60	3.1
Total of 10 areas above	**1,337.45**	**63.1**	**Total of 10 areas above**	**1,379.60**	**62.7**
Between 20 and 50 billion					
Taiwan	39.80	1.9	China	43.15	2.0
Switzerland	37.45	1.8	Switzerland	41.05	1.9

Table 1

Sweden	37.25	1.8
Hong Kong[c]	35.45	1.7
Korea, Rep. of	34.70	1.6
China	31.15	1.5
Spain	27.20	1.3
German Dem. Rep.	25.50	1.2
Saudi Arabia[b]	23.50	1.1
Australia	22.65	1.1
Singapore[c]	22.50	1.1
Austria	22.50	1.1
Brazil	22.40	1.1
Denmark	21.25	1.0
Czechoslovakia	20.25	1.0
Total of 15 areas above	**423.55**	**20.0**
Total of 25 areas above	**1,761.00**	**83.1**

Table 2

Hong Kong[c]	35.35	1.6
Spain	35.05	1.6
Sweden	32.70	1.5
Korea, Rep. of	31.60	1.4
Austria	26.85	1.2
Australia	25.80	1.2
Singapore[c]	25.50	1.2
German Dem. Rep.[a]	25.20	1.1
Taiwan	24.15	1.1
Denmark	22.85	1.0
Czechoslovakia[a]	20.85	0.9
Norway	20.30	0.9
Total of 14 areas above	**410.40**	**18.7**
Total of 24 areas above	**1,790.00**	**81.4**

Notes:
a) Imports f.o.b.
b) Secretariat estimates
c) Includes re-exports and imports for re-exports

Source: GATT (1987) derived from IMF, *International Financial Statistics* and national statistics.

manufactured goods in Table 2.2.2 are therefore largely the same as those in Table 2.2.1.

The performance of a country as an exporter depends not only on the quantity exported but also on the value received per unit. The terms of a country's trade is given by the average price of its exports over the average price of its imports. The terms of trade of the developed countries were on the whole constant from 1960 to 1973, but fell thereafter as a consequence of the rise in the price of oil. As Table 2.2.2 shows, this led to a reduction in their share of world trade until 1982 when oil and other commodity prices began to fall. Despite a fall in their terms of trade after 1983, the newly industrializing countries sufficiently expanded the quantity of their exports to increase their share of exports. The terms of trade for the least-developed countries, which specialize in primary commodities as opposed to manufactures, have fallen since around 1977 (see Grimwade (1989) Chapter 2).

Between 1970 and 1986 the leading countries gaining share in world exports were Japan, Korea, Spain, China, Hong Kong, Singapore and Taiwan; the exports of the last three countries comprise a significant amount of re-exported goods which cannot be determined (see General Agreement on Tariffs and Trade 1987, Appendix 1). The leading losers-of-share were the United States, the United Kingdom, Belgium-Luxembourg, the Union of Soviet Socialist Republics and Poland.

Despite the perceptible shift in the source of manufactured exports from the established exporting countries of the West, the leading eight countries still accounted for 53.3 per cent of world exports (63.6 per cent in 1970), and with the inclusion of Japan, 67.4 per cent (73 per cent in 1970). The 30 countries listed exported 94.1 per cent of exports, demonstrating that the degree of concentration in manufactures' trade is still considerable. (See Geiger (1988) Chapters 2 and 3 for an overview of the aggregate pattern of trade.)

2.2.3 Major partners

The development of international trade is likely to involve an intensification of trade between certain areas and types of country (or individual countries) and a diminution with respect to others. One classification based on economic type is presented in Table 2.2.3, and covers the period 1963 to 1986.

Of the 67.3 per cent share of world visible exports enjoyed by the developed countries in 1963, 50.1 per cent was trade between the developed countries themselves, or nearly three-quarters of their total exports. By 1986 this overall proportion had risen to just over 77 per cent, representing an intensification of trade between the developed countries. Developed countries' exports outside the developed areas are still predominantly directed towards the less-developed countries, although some inroads into this share have been made by the Eastern bloc.

Table 2.2.4 examines the pattern and development of manufactures' trade in the same fashion as Table 2.2.3. Here it can be seen that the intensity of manufactures' trade between the developed countries in 1963 was a little lower, at 71 per cent of total developed-country exports, than for all developed areas' visible exports. However, by 1986 this had risen to just under 77 per cent, the same intensity attained for all visible trade. If anything, therefore, the orientation of the developed countries towards the markets (for manufactures) of other developed countries has increased.

The economic designation of countries in Tables 2.2.3 and 2.2.4 does not give a true picture of the concentration of world trade into trading blocs, which are said to exist when countries trade intensively with each other. Table 2.2.5 identifies four major trading blocs, of which by far the largest is the European Community. The concentration of trade is measured by the share of intra-bloc trade as a percentage of total trade, by which criterion the European Community is again the most significant trading bloc. Tariffs on internal trade within the European Community have already been abolished; however, the completion of the internal market through the objective of eliminating non-tariff barriers by 1992 will undoubtedly increase the degree of intra-bloc trade (see Chapter 2.5).

The Canada–United States free-trade agreement aims to abolish tariffs on trade between the two countries and, while it does not go as far as the economic integration of the European Community, the concentration of trade must clearly increase on the figure of 17 per cent recorded in Table 2.2.5. Trade between the United States and Canada is the largest bilateral trade flow in the world, together amounting to 2.6 per cent of world trade. However, this trade is more crucial for Canada than the United States, as in 1987 Canada received one-quarter of all United States exports while the United States was the market for three-quarters of all Canadian exports (see United Nations Department of International Economic and Social Affairs (1989)).

The European Free Trade Association, although smaller, nevertheless constitutes a bloc. Other preferential trading arrangements exist, which are noted in Chapter 2.4. The European centrally planned economies, in particular those in the Council for Mutual Economic Assistance, have a high degree of internal trade comparable to the European Community, although there are a number of reasons why this group of countries may wish to expand their trade relations with the developed market economies, noted later.

A sharper focus on the key bilateral trade relationships in international trade is provided by Table 2.2.6. Among the most significant bilateral trade relationships are those within the European Community and between Japan and the United States, Japan and the less-developed countries, the European Community and the United States, and the European Community and the less-developed countries. For the developing countries and South-East Asian countries, all trade with the developed countries is significant in addition to trade within their own groups. The dependence of Japan on the United States in trade as well as the

Table 2.2.2 The World's Leading Exporters of Manufactures, 1970–86, US $billion and Percentage Distribution

	1970		1973		1980		1985		1986	
	Value	*Share*	*Value*	*Share*	*Value*	*Share*	*Value*	*Share*	*Value*	*Share*
Germany, Fed. Rep.	29.9	15.7	59.0	17.0	162.1	14.8	157.9	13.3	213.0	14.9
Japan	17.9	9.4	34.6	9.9	122.7	11.2	169.4	14.2	201.9	14.1
United States	28.4	14.9	43.7	12.6	139.5	12.7	143.5	12.1	147.3	10.3
France	13.1	6.9	25.4	7.3	81.2	7.4	71.8	6.0	90.2	6.3
Italy	11.0	5.7	18.4	5.3	65.1	6.0	67.0	5.6	85.2	6.0
United Kingdom	15.5	8.1	24.3	7.0	81.8	7.5	66.0	5.5	77.7	5.4
Canada	8.2	4.3	12.0	3.5	30.4	2.8	51.0	4.3	53.1	3.7
Belgium–Luxembourg	8.6	4.5	17.0	4.9	44.4	4.1	37.8	3.2	50.1	3.5
Netherlands	6.6	3.5	13.4	3.9	37.0	3.4	34.8	2.9	45.6	3.2
Taiwan[a]	1.1	0.6	3.7	1.1	17.4	1.6	27.8	2.3	36.2	2.5
Switzerland	4.6	2.4	8.5	2.4	26.6	2.4	25.2	2.1	35.0	2.4
Hong Kong[a]	2.3	1.2	4.7	1.3	18.0	1.6	27.3	2.3	32.4	2.5
Korea, Rep. of	0.6	0.3	2.7	0.8	15.6	1.4	27.6	2.3	31.9	2.2
USSR	5.0	2.6	7.5	2.2	19.5	1.8	20.0	1.7	25.0	1.7
Sweden	5.1	2.7	9.2	2.6	24.0	2.2	24.3	2.0	30.8	2.2
German Dem. Rep.	3.7	1.9	6.0	1.7	13.6	1.2	18.0	1.5	…	…

Spain	1.3	0.7	3.2	0.9	14.9	1.4	16.8	1.4	20.5	1.4
Czechoslovakia	2.9	1.5	5.2	1.5	17.5	1.6	15.3	1.3	...	...
Austria	2.3	1.2	4.3	1.2	14.5	1.3	14.6	1.2	19.7	1.4
China	0.3	0.2	0.6	0.2	3.0	0.3	10.0	0.8	13.6	1.0
Singapore[a]	0.4	0.2	1.6	0.5	9.0	0.8	11.7	1.0	13.3	0.9
Finland	1.5	0.8	2.7	0.8	9.9	0.9	10.5	0.9	13.2	0.9
Denmark	1.8	0.9	3.3	1.0	9.1	0.8	9.5	0.8	12.2	0.9
Brazil	0.4	0.2	1.2	0.3	7.5	0.7	15.0	1.3	11.8	0.8
Hungary	1.6	0.8	3.0	0.9	7.5	0.7	8.7	0.7	9.6	0.7
Yugoslavia	1.0	0.5	1.9	0.5	6.5	0.6	8.4	0.7	8.3	0.6
Ireland	0.4	0.2	0.9	0.3	4.6	0.4	6.7	0.6	8.2	0.6
Poland	2.5	1.3	4.3	1.2	11.7	1.1	7.3	0.6	7.9	0.6
Romania	0.9	0.5	2.0	0.6	6.0	0.6	7.8	0.7	7.5	0.5
Norway	1.4	0.7	2.8	0.8	5.9	0.5	5.6	0.5	6.8	0.5
Total of above	180.2	94.5	327.1	94.2	1,026.5	93.7	1,117.3	93.9	1,347.0	94.1
World trade of manufactures	190.7	100.0	347.4	100.0	1,095.0	100.0	1,190.1	100.0	1,431.0	100.0

Note: a) Includes significant entrepôt trade.

Source: GATT (1987)

Table 2.2.3 World Merchandise Exports by Main Areas, 1963–86, US $billion and Percentage Distribution

Origin	Destination	Developed countries		Developing areas		Eastern trading area		World	
		Value	Share	Value	Share	Value	Share	Value	Share
Developed countries	1963	77	50.1	22	14.7	4	2.5	103	67.3
	1970	174	55.7	41	13.2	8	2.7	223	71.6
	1973	316	55.0	72	12.5	19	3.3	407	70.8
	1979	780	47.7	236	14.4	53	3.2	1,069	65.3
	1980	900	45.2	294	14.8	62	3.1	1,256	63.1
	1981	854	43.5	321	16.3	59	3.0	1,234	62.8
	1982	821	44.5	296	16.1	54	2.9	1,171	63.5
	1983	833	46.1	272	15.0	52	2.9	1,157	64.0
	1984	908	47.6	268	14.0	55	2.9	1,231	64.5
	1985	957	49.8	253	13.2	65	3.4	1,275	66.3
	1986	1,141	53.9	269	12.7	65	3.1	1,475	69.7
Developing areas	1963	23	15.1	7	4.4	2	1.1	32	20.6
	1970	42	13.4	11	3.5	3	1.0	56	17.9
	1973	82	14.3	23	4.0	5	0.9	110	19.2
	1979	300	18.4	98	6.0	16	1.0	414	25.4
	1980	397	20.0	137	6.9	21	1.1	555	27.9
	1981	373	19.0	149	7.6	22	1.1	544	27.8
	1982	317	17.2	140	7.6	22	1.2	479	26.0
	1983	295	16.3	128	7.1	23	1.3	446	24.7
	1984	315	16.5	125	6.6	26	1.4	466	24.5
	1985	295	15.3	116	6.0	30	1.6	441	22.9
	1986	278	13.1	108	5.1	28	1.3	414	19.5

Eastern trading area								
1963	4	2.3	3	1.7	12	8.1	19	12.1
1970	8	2.5	5	1.6	20	6.4	33	10.5
1973	16	2.7	9	1.5	32	5.7	57	10.0
1979	47	2.9	26	1.6	79	4.8	152	9.3
1980	58	2.9	31	1.6	89	4.5	178	9.0
1981	57	2.9	37	1.9	90	4.6	184	9.4
1982	58	3.1	40	2.2	95	5.1	193	10.5
1983	59	3.2	41	2.3	104	5.8	204	11.3
1984	62	3.3	41	2.2	107	5.6	210	11.0
1985	60	3.1	38	2.0	110	5.7	208	10.8
1986	59	2.8	43	2.0	127	6.0	230	10.8
World								
1963	104	67.5	32	20.8	18	11.7	154	100.0
1970	224	71.6	57	18.3	32	10.1	313	100.0
1973	414	72.0	104	18.1	57	9.9	574	100.0
1979	1,127	69.0	360	22.0	148	9.0	1,635	100.0
1980	1,355	68.1	462	23.3	172	8.7	1,989	100.0
1981	1,284	65.4	507	25.8	171	8.7	1,962	100.0
1982	1,196	64.9	476	25.9	171	9.2	1,843	100.0
1983	1,187	65.6	441	24.4	179	10.0	1,807	100.0
1984	1,286	67.4	434	22.7	188	9.9	1,907	100.0
1985	1,311	68.1	407	21.2	205	10.7	1,924	100.0
1986	1,478	69.8	420	19.8	221	10.4	2,119	100.0

Source: GATT (1987)

Table 2.2.4 World Exports of Manufactures by Main Areas, 1963–86, US $billion and Percentage Distribution

Origin	Destination	Developed countries		Developing areas		Eastern trading area		World	
		Value	Share	Value	Share	Value	Share	Value	Share
Developed countries	1963	47.7	58.8	16.9	20.8	2.2	2.7	66.8	82.3
	1970	121.9	63.9	32.1	16.8	6.3	3.3	160.3	84.0
	1973	221.5	63.8	54.5	15.7	12.7	3.6	288.7	83.1
	1979	551.6	58.4	186.9	19.8	38.0	4.0	776.5	82.2
	1980	623.8	57.0	229.7	21.0	42.4	3.9	895.9	81.8
	1981	591.7	54.3	250.7	23.0	38.3	3.5	880.7	80.9
	1982	571.6	54.3	235.3	22.4	36.5	3.5	843.4	80.1
	1983	584.6	55.3	211.2	20.0	37.4	3.5	833.2	78.8
	1984	646.5	56.7	204.5	17.9	38.7	3.4	889.7	78.0
	1985	695.1	58.4	195.2	16.4	50.0	4.2	940.3	79.0
	1986	874.6	61.1	211.9	14.8	52.2	3.6	1,138.7	79.6
Developing areas	1963	2.0	2.4	1.4	1.8	0.1	0.1	3.5	4.3
	1970	6.4	3.4	3.4	1.8	0.4	0.2	10.2	5.4
	1973	16.3	4.7	6.9	2.0	0.8	0.2	24.0	6.9
	1979	53.7	5.7	30.5	3.2	1.8	0.2	86.0	9.1
	1980	62.9	5.7	40.1	3.7	2.8	0.3	105.8	9.7
	1981	66.9	6.1	45.5	4.2	3.7	0.3	116.1	10.7
	1982	67.1	6.4	43.0	4.1	3.5	0.3	113.6	10.8
	1983	77.3	7.3	42.3	4.0	4.2	0.4	123.8	11.7
	1984	96.7	8.5	44.2	3.9	6.3	0.6	147.2	12.9
	1985	96.1	8.1	40.7	3.4	8.0	0.7	144.7	12.1
	1986	118.2	8.3	41.8	2.9	9.1	0.6	169.0	11.8

	Year								
Eastern trading area	1963	1.1	1.4	1.6	1.6	8.1	10.0	10.8	13.3
	1970	3.0	1.6	2.9	1.6	14.3	7.5	20.2	10.6
	1973	5.6	1.6	4.6	1.3	24.5	7.0	34.7	10.0
	1979	15.6	1.7	13.7	1.5	53.2	5.6	82.5	8.7
	1980	18.0	1.6	16.7	1.5	58.6	5.4	93.3	8.5
	1981	17.0	1.6	19.7	1.8	55.3	5.1	92.0	8.4
	1982	17.0	1.6	21.0	2.0	57.6	5.5	95.6	9.1
	1983	16.6	1.6	20.8	2.0	62.5	5.9	99.9	9.5
	1984	18.4	1.6	20.8	1.8	64.5	5.7	103.7	9.1
	1985	18.7	1.6	19.5	1.6	67.5	5.7	105.7	8.9
	1986	23.4	1.6	22.4	1.6	77.8	5.4	123.6	8.6
World	1963	50.8	62.7	19.9	24.6	10.4	12.8	81.1	100.0
	1970	131.3	68.8	38.4	20.1	21.0	11.0	190.7	100.0
	1973	243.4	70.1	66.0	19.0	38.0	10.9	347.4	100.0
	1979	620.9	65.7	231.1	24.5	93.0	9.8	945.0	100.0
	1980	704.7	64.4	286.5	26.2	103.8	9.5	1,095.0	100.0
	1981	675.6	62.0	315.8	29.0	97.4	8.9	1,088.8	100.0
	1982	655.7	62.3	299.3	28.4	97.6	9.3	1,052.6	100.0
	1983	678.5	64.2	274.3	25.9	104.1	9.8	1,056.9	100.0
	1984	761.7	66.8	269.5	23.6	109.5	9.6	1,140.6	100.0
	1985	809.9	68.0	255.4	21.4	125.5	10.5	1,190.7	100.0
	1986	1,016.1	71.0	276.0	19.3	139.1	9.7	1,431.3	100.0

Source: GATT (1987)

Table 2.2.5   Major Trading Blocs in World Trade, 1987[a]

	Value of intra-bloc trade (billions of dollars, 1987)	Share of world trade (percentage)	Share of intra-bloc trade in the bloc's total trade (percentage)
EEC	1,111	22.3	58.4
Canada–United States	127	2.6	17.0
EFTA	46	0.9	14.1
European centrally planned economies	275	5.5	53.0
Total	1,559	31.3	

Note: a) Trade is defined as exports plus imports.

Source: United Nations, Department of International Economic and Social Affairs (1989)

dependence of the less-developed countries and South-East Asian countries on the developed countries in general reveals the underlying asymmetry in the importance of trade to large and small economic partners. The imbalances in trade flows, evident in the contrast of export and import ratios, constitute a source of concern for the deficit countries. For countries with an overall balance-of payments deficit, even in a multilateral trading system, bilateral trade deficits become a focal point. This clearly applies to the United States, and, given the leading importance it holds for its trading partners, the trade policy it adopts is of great significance.

2.2.4   Key markets

In identifying the leading markets in international trade it is possible to make the case that no market should be overlooked. In this brief overview it is not possible to identify the attractions of all markets; the reader is referred to Section 5 in Brooke and Buckley (1988) which deals thoroughly with the world's regions.

A number of points are already evident from the discussion in the previous sections. The preeminent markets are unquestionably the developed countries, both for developed country exporters and for exporters from the newly industrializing countries and the developing countries. Japan, however, remains relatively under-exploited as a market compared with other developed countries, particularly in manufactures' trade.

Exports and imports of country or country group (1)	Trading partners (2)				Developing countries		Centrally planned economies
	United States	Japan	European Economic Community	Federal Republic of Germany	Total	Energy exporters	
United States[b]							
Exports	—	0.6	1.1	0.2	1.8	0.7	0.2
Imports	—	1.9	1.8	0.6	3.2	1.0	0.2
Japan[b]							
Exports	5.5	—	1.5	0.5	4.0	1.2	1.2
Imports	1.7	—	0.6	0.2	4.6	3.2	0.5
European Economic Community[c]							
Exports	2.5	0.3	13.2	3.2	3.8	1.8	1.0
Imports	2.0	0.9	13.0	3.5	4.3	2.5	1.3
Germany, Federal Republic of[b]							
Exports	3.2	0.4	14.8	—	5.4	1.7	—
Imports	1.7	1.1	13.0	—	5.0	1.6	—

Table 2.2.6 (*Cont.*)

Exports and imports of country or country group (1)	Trading partners (2)				Developing countries		Centrally planned economies
	United States	Japan	European Economic Community	Federal Republic of Germany	Total	Energy exporters	
Developing countries[d]							
Exports	7.2	3.6	5.4	1.8	6.8	—	1.6
Imports	4.1	3.1	5.3	2.0	6.9	—	2.0
South and East Asia							
Exports	12.0	6.2	4.3	—	11.4	—	2.6
Imports	5.5	7.3	4.4	—	11.5	—	3.1

Notes:

a) Trade in services is not included. The figures in each row represent bilateral merchandise exports and imports of the country or country group (1) *vis-à-vis* the countries or groups in each column (2) divided by the GNP of the row country (1). All figures are calculated from output and trade figures in 1985 prices and dollar exchange rates.

b) GNP data used.

c) Including the Federal Republic of Germany.

d) Including Asia but excluding China, which is included in the centrally planned economies group.

Source: United Nations, Department of International Economic and Social Affairs (1987) derived from GATT, IMF and OECD statistics.

The two principal attributes desired in a market are size (in terms of total annual sales) and growth. Strong indigenous or foreign competition within markets will clearly reduce its potential for export penetration, although the firm should consider employing alternative methods of competing abroad, such as joint ventures, foreign direct investment and contractual forms of collaboration (such as technology licensing) (see Brooke (1986), Brooke and Buckley (1988) Section 3).

The complex of factors influencing the attractiveness of a market commends an ex-post investigation of the performance of the leading world markets. Table 2.2.7 looks at the trend in the share of world imports accounted for by major countries and country groups, between 1971 and 1986.

During the 1970s the average growth of world imports was 5 per cent. The developing economies significantly exceeded this rate; however, this was entirely due to the high growth of imports to the capital-surplus developing countries (especially the oil-producing countries). Targeting these markets for exports in the 1980s, however, would have led to poor export results, as the fall in oil prices caused imports (year on year) to fall dramatically by between 10 and 21 per cent. The imports of the capital-importing less-developed countries also fell in 1985 and 1986, although their share of world imports remains substantial.

The economic problems of the Eastern bloc countries mean that the detailed knowledge of individual markets necessary in all trade matters is particularly crucial. As a group, these countries have performed consistently in terms of import growth until this was attenuated in 1986 by economic difficulties. The Chinese mainland market is itself highly volatile, given that its share of world imports is small.

The most consistent import-market growth has been the European Community, though not attaining the high growth rates of the United States. The importance of the European Community as a market can only be expected to rise, although a certain amount of external imports are likely to be replaced as firms from non-European-Community-member countries increase production within the market via joint ventures and foreign direct investment in subsidiaries. The United States remained a high but variable growth market, although it retained its steady appeal because of its considerable internal market size and share of world imports. Japanese imports are even more erratic; despite Japan's large internal market its share of world imports remains modest at 6 per cent.

2.2.5   East–West trade

Trade with the Eastern bloc countries is of relatively minor significance for the developed market economies. This, however, only applies in absolute terms, not

Table 2.2.7 World Imports: Geographical Composition and Volume Changes, 1971–86, Percentage Distribution and Annual Rate of Change

	Share in world trade^a 1985	Volume of imports (annual rate of change)			
		Trend 1971–1980	1984	1985	1986^b
Country or country group					
World	100.0	5.0	9.0	3.5	3.6
Developed market economies^c	68.8	4.8	11.1	5.5	8.0
United States	18.0	4.5	23.9	8.7	10.5
Western Europe	38.0	5.0	6.1	5.7	6.2
of which:					
Germany, Federal Republic of	(7.9)	(4.9)	(5.2)	(4.2)	(6.5)
Japan	6.0	5.0	10.8	-0.2	13.3
Developing economies	20.5	6.5	1.0	-5.0	-7.5
Capital-surplus countries	3.3	12.7	-10.6	-17.9	-21.0
Capital-importing countries	17.2	4.2	3.7	-2.3	-4.7
Centrally planned economies of Europe^d	8.5	4.8	5.0	4.8	0.0
China	2.2	–	29.2	50.3	-20.0
Memorandum item:	Billions of dollars				
Value of world trade	2,000	20.3	5.5	1.0	12.0
of which:					
Developing country imports	410	22.3	-2.0	-5.0	1.8

Notes:
a) Shares are based on merchandise imports valued in terms of United States dollars at current prices. Figures are rounded.
b) Preliminary estimates.
c) Including Australia, Canada, New Zealand and South Africa.
d) Eastern Europe and the USSR.

Source: United Nations, Department of International Economic and Social Affairs (1987) deried from GATT, IMF and OECD Statistics.

in terms of potential. Economic reforms, such as the granting of foreign-trade-enterprise status to firms other than the state monopolies, have already taken place in a number of countries' industrial sectors and more radical political reform leading to market-based economic systems clearly holds still further potential. Any future growth of trade must depend on the stability of economic progress in the Eastern bloc, with perhaps the greatest scope for growth lying in conjunction with local joint ventures and export-oriented production.

Tables 2.2.3 and 2.2.4 (in Section 2.2.3) detail the development of East–West trade. The share of Eastern bloc countries in total developed country imports has remained constant over the period 1963 to 1986 because of a fall in 1986. In manufactures' trade alone the expansion of share has been positive, rising from 2.3 per cent to 2.7 per cent.

The proportion of manufacturing trade in Eastern exports to the West has risen from just over 25 per cent to 40 per cent. In terms of the Eastern bloc's export orientation the developed markets have become more important, rising from 21 per cent of exports in 1963 to 26 per cent in 1986. A sharper rise still is evident for manufactures alone, from 10 per cent to 19 per cent in 1986. As Eastern countries' orientation towards the less-developed countries has also risen, it is clear that as a trading bloc the Council for Mutual Economic Assistance has become less dependent on intra-trade.

The share of developed countries' exports in Eastern-bloc imports has risen both for total trade and manufactures alone: from 3.9 and 3.3 per cent in 1963 to 4.4 and 4.6 per cent respectively in 1986. Nevertheless, this cannot yet be said to represent a significant intensification.

2.2.6 North–South trade

Trade between the developed market economies and the less-developed economies has undergone substantial changes since the early 1960s. In examining these it is important to distinguish between the developing economies, and in particular to identify the role of the newly industrializing countries in changing trade patterns. For an analysis of the principal institutional and economic dimensions of the countries of the South, see Mirza (1988).

Referring back to Tables 2.2.3 and 2.2.4 it can be seen that since 1982 the share of less-developed countries in total developed country imports has diminished, while the developed countries' share of world imports has risen. The fact that this has not occurred for manufactures alone makes it clear that the effect of falling commodity prices has dominated the flow of trade. In manufactures, developing countries accounted for 8.3 per cent within the 71.0 per cent share of developed countries in world imports, or just over 11.5 per cent of all developed imports of manufactures in 1986.

In the other direction, the importance of exports from developed countries has

Table 2.2.8 The Growth of Exports to the Developed Market Economies from the Leading Exporters of Manufactures among the Developing Countries, 1985–87, Percentage Change in Current Value Dollars

	1985	1986	1987[a]
Argentina	1.2	−9.1	−3.0
Brazil	0.6	−6.9	8.8
Hong Kong	−3.6	20.7	19.7
India	−4.1	3.9	19.7
Malaysia	−6.5	−1.5	17.5
Philippines	−11.0	−0.3	11.3
Republic of Korea	6.4	30.6	40.0
Singapore	0.4	6.7	30.8
Thailand	3.0	29.1	25.7
Yugoslavia	7.8	27.0	19.1
Total	−0.2	11.1	22.8

Note: a) January–October.

Source: United Nations, Department of International Economic and Social Affairs (1988)

fallen in developing countries' imports, from 68.8 per cent of total less-developed country imports in 1963 to 64.0 per cent in 1986. The figures for manufactures alone are 84.9 and 76.8 respectively. Evidently trade from within the less-developed-country economic sphere is replacing that from the developed countries, although most less-developed-country imports are still from the developed areas.

The rise of developed economies' imports from less-developed countries, and the loss of developed countries' shares of less-developed-country imports, particularly of manufactures, is largely the result of exports from the newly industrializing countries. Table 2.2.2 identified the world's leading exporters of manufactures, which featured the export-oriented economies of South-East Asia. Table 2.2.8 examines the more recent growth of exports to the developed markets originating from ten of the foremost exporting developing countries. Since 1985 the leading export-growth performances have been achieved by Hong Kong, Korea, Singapore and Thailand. Other less-developed country exporters are also clearly capable of significant trade expansion. The growth of exports from South to North will largely depend on the growth of income in the developed market economies. As already seen in Table 2.2.6, the South-East Asian countries have been the major beneficiaries among the less-developed countries from the growth in the developed markets. The further expansion of exports from these and other less-developed countries relies both on developed markets' growth and the degree of freedom from future protectionist measures.

2.3

The Industrial Structure of World Trade

2.3.1 Introduction

The structure of economic activity within developed countries has been shifting towards the service sector for some time (see Enderwick (1989) Chapter 1). The tendency for this to manifest itself in trade statistics has only been a modest one. The service transactions that characterize international trade and the balance of payments are strongly related to intermediate factor services: they are linked to the expansion of activities within other sectors such as manufacturing. Final output service industries (such as tourism) currently do not generate the same level of balance-of-payments income; however, liberalization in key service sectors, such as banking and finance, may change this situation.

Table 2.3.1 presents a breakdown of world trade in goods and services for 1985, which in terms of Special Drawing Rights amounted to SDR 2,550 billion. The relationships between the entries are often complex, devolving upon the behaviour of firms, including multinational firms, engaging in merchandise exports, foreign-technology licensing and other contractual arrangements (as well as foreign direct investment). Each of these activities generates balance-of-payments flows. The activities of firms engaged in international competition is, however, the usual starting point for analysing the structure of international trade.

2.3.2 Major industries

The major industries in international trade are those relating to visible or merchandise trade: according to Table 2.3.1 they collectively account for 68 per cent of all trade. The classification of trade by product group is rarely clear-cut, and an exposition on product categories is to be found in the General Agreement on Tariffs and Trade (1987) Appendix 1.

The Framework of International Trade

Table 2.3.1 World Exports of Goods and Services on a Balance of Payments Basis, Percentage Distribution

	Percentage share
Goods services and unrequited transfers	**100**
Merchandise f.o.b.	68
Other goods and services	29
Shipment	2
Other transportation	3
Travel	4
Investment income	13
Reinvested earnings on direct investment	2
Other direct investment income	1
Non-direct investment income	11
Other goods, services and income	7
Official	1
Private	6
Unrequited transfers	3

Source: GATT (1987) derived from IMF *Balance of Payments Statistics*

Table 2.3.2 presents the main products involved in international trade, together with a profile of their development from 1955 to 1986. In interpreting these statistics it should be remembered that a change in the share of a product group in trade may arise for either, or both, of two reasons: a change in quantity that is faster or slower than that of total trade, or a change in unit values that is faster than that of total trade. The importance of these distinctions is apparent on first sight of Table 2.3.2.

The marked variability in the share of trade in fuels reflects predominantly the instability in the price of petroleum, with the price falling after 1978. Other than fuels, over the long period a clear downward trend in the share of primary products can be discerned: from a share of nearly 50 per cent of trade in 1955, by 1986 this had fallen to just 30 per cent. This reflects both the falling price of primary products relative to manufactures and a slower growth in the quantity traded (for a more detailed account see Grimwade (1989) Chapter 2).

The tendency for the demand for primary food products to grow more slowly than income (that is, to be income inelastic) is a recognized factor; however, world agriculture is among the most protected industries and therefore is unlikely to record as large an expansion of trade as products in the manufacturing sector (see Chapter 2.5).

Table 2.3.2   The Commodity Composition of World Trade, 1955–86, US $billion and Percentage Distribution

	1955		*1978*		*1986*	
	value	*share*	*value*	*share*	*value*	*share*
Primary products						
Food	20.42	21.9	162.60	12.5	226.60	10.7
Raw materials	12.13	13.0	52.05	4.0	71.55	3.4
Ores and minerals	3.44	3.7	24.50	1.9	33.35	1.6
Fuels	10.26	11.0	223.60	17.2	272.05	12.8
Non-ferrous metals	3.62	3.9	27.80	2.1	39.60	1.9
Total	49.87	53.5	490.60	37.7	643.15	30.4
Manufactures						
Iron and steel	4.25	4.6	57.15	4.4	73.50	3.5
Chemicals	4.91	5.3	100.60	7.7	189.85	9.0
Other semi-manufactures	4.47	4.8	65.20	5.0	103.40	4.9
Engineering products:	19.59	21.0	439.05	33.7	820.90	38.8
Machinery specialized	6.43	6.9	117.45	9.0	183.80	8.7
Office and telecommunications	5.82	0.9	38.80	3.0	120.50	5.7
Road and motor vehicles	3.32	3.5	99.45	6.9	196.15	9.3
Other machinery and transport equipment	7.72	8.3	147.90	11.4	252.65	11.9
Household appliances	1.30	1.4	35.40	2.7	67.80	3.2
Textiles	4.72	5.1	40.70	3.1	66.25	3.1
Clothing	0.80	0.9	28.35	2.2	61.80	2.9
Other consumer goods	3.00	3.2	57.50	4.4	115.55	5.4
Total	41.73	44.7	788.50	60.5	1,431.25	67.6
Total exports	93.30	100.0	1,303.00	100.0	2,118.70	100.0

Source: GATT (1987)

As the share of primary goods in visible trade has declined, so the share of manufactured goods has necessarily risen, from 44.7 per cent in 1955 to 67.6 per cent by 1986. Within manufacturing the products gaining share tend to be in the technology-intensive category. The chief examples are chemicals, office and tele-communications equipment (including computers) and road and motor vehicles. Manufactures with declining shares are iron and steel products and textiles products. These industries tend to be in a state of decline within the developed economies and therefore to suffer from over-capacity. For this reason they are among the most highly protected of manufacturing activities, which itself acts as a brake on trade growth.

The increased share of clothing reflects the export drives of the developing countries, mainly towards the developed markets. The category of other consumer goods includes glassware, pottery, furniture, travel goods, building fitments and other manufactures. The increased share of this group is probably mainly due to the more differentiable nature of certain products in this category.

The major industries involved in international trade within manufacturing are also those identified with the activities of multinational firms and the transfer of technology. Consequently a sizeable amount of service transactions will be linked in some way with these sorts of activities. Furthermore, the growth of this type of trade is associated with intra-industry trade, examined in Section 2.3.6 and with intra-firm trade, the subject of Section 2.6.4.

2.3.3   Service flows

The coverage of service transactions in official statistics is considerably less detailed than that of merchandise trade. This partly derives from the acute difficulties encountered in measuring trade in services. A classification of three broad types of trade in services is presented in United Nations Department of International Economic and Social Affairs (1987). (See also Enderwick (1988).)

First, there are services whose border exchange is visible, such as shipping, passenger services (the transportation of persons), other transportation (mainly port services) and travel (mainly tourism). Each of these types involves transport and travel.

A second group comprises royalties and licence fees, which appear under the heading property income not included elsewhere in the International Monetary Fund Balance of Payments Statistics. The treatment of intellectual property is controversial because the monetary receipts generated can be viewed as payments for factor services. Because of this, and the crucial role they occupy in the theory of international trade and business, these transactions are analysed separately in Section 2.3.4.

The third group within service trade comprises 'other goods, services and incomes'. This very heterogeneous category in fact largely excludes goods other than those that are more properly embodied services, such as periodicals and probably recordings. Official and non-official trade can be distinguished here, where the former relates to the government and central bank, and which should be excluded for certain purposes. Other private services include communications, insurance and brokerage fees not included in merchandise (cost, insurance, freight), statistics, financial services, merchandising (excluding capital gains in transactions between residents of the same country), management and related services, legal services, franchise and similar rights, software and data services, research analyses, education services, construction and building design, leasing of structures' machinery and equipment (other than transport), leasing of recorded material, medical and related services, and other professional and technical services.

The quality of statistics varies markedly between reporting countries. Apart from the dangers of misclassification, the most widespread problem is of under-reporting and underestimation. In comparison with merchandise trade, the detail is poor: there is normally no information on costs and prices (unit values) and quantities, merely total transactions' values.

Using this classification Table 2.3.3 analyses the trade in non-factor services from 1975 to 1985 for both developed and less-developed economies. Here it can be seen that the share of service trade in the merchandise trade of developed economies is typically around, or a little above, 20 per cent. For the developing countries it is a higher proportion of imports at around 28 per cent in 1985, reflecting their collective deficit on these items. However, services are relatively high in less-developed countries' exports, due it would seem to passenger services and travel (tourism).

In the developed countries much growth has occurred in the other private services category. The growth elements vary between countries. For the United States the principal components are insurance, construction, health, education and computer software. For the United Kingdom the leading element is financial services, with other business consultancy services in second place.

The increase in international tourism has attracted much interest for its contribution to export earnings. Table 2.3.4 presents a summary of the development of travel for the United States since 1960. These date are recorded at current values, so the balance of transactions is the most revealing indicator of developments. The United States appears to be a net importer of travel services throughout the period, with the exception of 1980. By 1985 the growth of United States residents' travel abroad had again outstripped that of foreigners in the United States.

The situation for the United Kingdom is examined in Tables 2.3.5 and 2.3.6; it appears similar to the United States position of a deficit on travel. This amounted to £2,042 million in 1988. Using figures in Table 2.3.5 as a guide it would seem that this deficit is probably the result of a bilateral surplus with the United States being dominated by a bilateral deficit with other countries of Europe. Further detailed discussion of international tourism is to be found in Witt (1988).

2.3.4   Technology flows

Trade in technology is a focus of interest for both the developed and the less-developed countries. For developed economies the balance-of-technology trade is seen as an indicator of the relative international progress of home industry, while for less-developed countries technological inflows (in key industries) is viewed as desirable.

Table 2.3.3 International Trade in Services, 1975–85, US $million

| | | 1975 | 1980 | 1982 | 1984 | 1985 | Annual average rate of growth | |
							1985/1975	1985/1980
			Developed market economies					
Shipping	+	25.9	50.0	44.9	41.8	43.3	5.3	-2.8
	−	26.8	50.6	46.3	49.4	49.7	6.4	-0.4
	=	-0.9	-0.6	-1.4	-7.6	-6.4		
Passenger services	+	6.4	14.3	14.4	15.0	15.4	9.0	1.5
	−	6.5	13.3	14.1	15.8	16.6	9.8	4.5
	=	-0.1	+1.0	+0.3	-0.8	-1.2		
Other transportation	+	21.3	43.5	41.5	38.0	38.2	6.0	-2.6
	−	23.3	47.0	45.8	40.4	40.5	5.7	-2.9
	=	-2.0	-3.5	-4.3	-2.4	-2.3		
Travel	+	32.8	72.2	69.7	70.5	73.8	8.5	0.2
	−	35.5	76.7	71.5	71.6	75.3	7.8	-0.6
	=	-2.7	-4.5	-1.8	-1.1	-1.5		
Royalties and fees	+	6.3	11.5	9.5	10.2	10.8	5.5	-1.3
	−	5.0	9.3	9.3	10.2	10.8	7.7	3.0
	=	+1.3	+2.2	+0.2	0	0		

Other private services	+	41.6	88.9	89.6	86.5	91.3	8.2	0.5
	−	33.8	71.9	74.6	72.3	75.1	8.3	0.9
	=	+7.8	+17.0	+15.0	+14.2	+16.2		
Total non-factor services	+	134.3	280.4	269.6	262.0	272.8	7.3	−0.6
	−	130.9	268.8	261.6	259.7	268.0	7.4	−0.1
	=	+3.4	+11.6	+8.0	+2.3	+4.8		
Share in merchandise exports (per cent)		23.9	22.7	23.5	21.5	21.7		
Share in merchandise imports (per cent)		23.5	20.6	22.3	20.5	20.6		
Shipping	+	3.5	7.1	8.1	7.8	7.4	7.8	0.8
	−	14.3	32.9	33.7	28.5	23.8	5.2	−6.3
	=	−10.8	−25.8	−25.6	−26.7	−16.4		
Passenger services	+	1.1	3.8	4.4	4.2	4.3	14.6	2.5
	−	1.3	4.1	4.1	3.4	2.9	8.4	−6.7
	=	−0.2	−0.3	+0.3	+0.8	+1.4		
Other transportation	+	4.9	12.4	11.6	10.3	9.3	6.6	−5.6
	−	4.0	11.7	11.8	10.5	8.9	−8.3	−5.3
	=	+0.9	+0.7	−0.2	−0.2	−0.4		
Travel	+	4.6	24.2	21.9	21.4	20.7	16.3	−3.1
	−	6.9	21.7	21.0	18.3	18.0	10.1	−3.7
	=	−2.3	+2.5	+0.9	+2.8	+2.7		
Royalties and fees	+	0.2	0.5	1.1	0.2	0.1	−6.7	−14.9
	−	0.5	1.0	1.3	1.0	1.0	7.2	0
	=	−0.3	−1.0	−1.2	−0.8	−0.9		

(Cont.)

Table 2.3.3 (Cont.)

		1975	1980	1982	1984	1985	Annual average rate of growth	
							1985/1975	1985/1980
				Developing countries				
Other private services	+	6.7	17.1	26.4	22.1	20.0	11.6	3.2
	–	8.6	26.5	38.0	32.5	32.3	14.2	4.0
	=	–1.9	–9.4	–11.6	–10.4	–12.3		
Total non-factor services	+	20.8	64.6	72.4	65.5	61.7	11.5	–0.9
	–	35.6	97.9	109.9	94.2	86.9	9.3	–2.4
	=	–14.8	–33.3	–37.5	–28.7	–25.2		
Share in merchandise exports (per cent)		11.5	14.0	17.6	16.9	17.7		
Share in merchandise imports (per cent)		21.4	26.2	28.6	27.0	28.0		

Notes:
A plus sign (+) indicates an export or receipt.
A minus sign (–) indicates import or payment.

Source: United Nations, Department of International Economic and Social Affairs (1987) derived from IMF, *Balance of Payments Statistics*, partial data for 24 developed and 100 developing countries.

Table 2.3.4   United States International Travel, 1960–88, US $million

	1960	1965	1970	1975	1980	1985	1988
+	919	1,380	2,331	4,697	10,588	17,937	29,202
–	1,750	2,438	3,980	6,417	10,397	24,517	32,112
=	–831	–1,058	–1,649	–1,720	191	–6,580	–2,910

Notes:
A plus sign (+) indicates export or receipt.
A minus sign (–) indicates import or payment.
Source: US Department of Commerce (1989) *Survey of Current Business*, 69, No. 6, June.

Table 2.3.5   United Kingdom International Travel and Tourism, in Thousands

	Overseas visitors to the UK				Visits abroad by UK residents			
		Area of residence				Area visited		
	Total all visits	North America	Western Europe	Other areas	Total all visits	North America	Western Europe	Other areas
1984	13,644	3,330	7,551	2,763	22,072	919	19,371	1,781
1985	14,449	3,797	7,870	2,782	21,610	914	18,944	1,752
1986	13,897	2,843	8,355	2,699	24,949	1,167	21,877	1,905
1987	15,566	3,394	9,317	2,855	27,447	1,559	23,678	2,210
1988	15,798	3,272	9,668	2,859	28,828	1,823	24,519	2,486
% change 1988/1987	+1	–4	+4	–	+5	+17	+4	+11

Source: UK Department of Industry (1989) *British Business*, 14 July.

The causes of international transactions in technology fundamentally depend on the rate of creation of innovations. However, whether these innovations are exploited by domestic industry, ultimately generating exports of visible goods, or exported as trade in technology, is a central theme in the economic theory of the multinational enterprise and international business (see Part 1). Therefore a high level of technological exports could simply reflect a high propensity to export technology rather than a high degree of domestic technology generation, and vice versa.

The controversy over the inclusion of technology flows in service transactions concerns the debate over whether the sale of technology is that of a service or of a factor itself; indeed, in economic theory technology is often described as

Table 2.3.6   United Kingdom International Travel and Tourism, 1984–88

	Overseas visitors to the UK	UK residents going abroad	Balance (£m)
	Earnings (£m) current prices	Expenditure (£m) current prices	Current prices
1984	4,614	4,663	−49
1985	5,442	4,871	+571
1986	5,553	6,083	−530
1987	6,260	7,280	−1,020
1988	6,085	8,127	−2,042
% change 1988/1987	−3	+12	

Note: Figures exclude payments for air and sea travel to and from the UK.

Source: UK Department of Industry (1989) *British Business*, 14 July.

an intangible asset. For whatever precise reasons, technology trade is worthy of examination in its own right.

The payment for technology is normally in the form of royalties and licence fees, within which different schemes of payment are possible: remuneration may be based on a lump sum, or expressed as a proportion of output sales, value added, or profits (see Davies (1988)). Payment for technology may instead take the form of reciprocal licence rights (cross-licensing) or an equity interest in a foreign project. In these last two cases, technology trade figures will be under-valued as no monetary transaction will have occurred. A further reason why the value of technology trade may be underestimated or misrepresented in official statistics is that trade between affiliate firms (within a multinational enterprise) may intentionally over- or undervalue payment (see Section 2.6.4).

Tables 2.3.7 to 2.3.9 examine the development of technological trade of the United States, United Kingdom and Germany. The United States has a clear surplus on technological trade, which is understated in Table 2.3.7 because almost 60 per cent of payments in 1988 were not of a directly technological nature (including recorded material, trademarks, live broadcasting and record-ing, franchises and other). The United Kingdom's surplus is more modest, while Germany records a consistent deficit.

The breakdown between affiliated and non-affiliated transactions in the most recent year available is, for affiliated receipts: 77 per cent (United States), 55 per cent (United Kingdom) and 15 per cent (Federal Republic of Germany); and for affiliated payments: 47 per cent (United States), 84 per cent (United Kingdom) and 80 per cent (Federal Republic of Germany). This pattern could result from both national firms operating abroad and foreign firms operating locally in

Table 2.3.7 United States International Transactions in Technology: Royalties, Licence and Other Fees, 1960–88, US $million

	1960	1965	1970	1975	1980	1985	1988ᵃ
+	837	1,534	2,331	4,300	7,085	5,995	10,735
−	74	135	224	472	724	891	2,048
=	763	1,399	2,017	3,828	6,361	5,104	8,687

Notes:
A plus sign (+) indicates an export or receipt.
A minus sign (−) indicates an import or payment.
a) Until 1987 certain management fees were included. The proportions of pure technological receipts and payments in 1988 were 74.5 per cent and 41.8 per cent respectively.

Source: US Department of Commerce (1989) *Survey of Current Business*, 69, No. 6, June.

Table 2.3.8 United Kingdom International Transactions in Technology: Royalties, 1976–86, £million

	1976	1979	1982	1985	1987
+	333	381	502	654	262
−	264	317	414	534	236
=	69	64	88	120	26

Notes:
A plus sign () indicates export or receipt.
A minus sign (−) indicates import or payment.

Source: UK Department of Industry (1989) *Business Monitor MA4, Overseas Transactions, 1987*, Business Statistics Office, and UK Department of Industry (1989) *British Business*, 15 September.

Table 2.3.9 Federal Republic of Germany International Transactions in Technology, 1974–87, DM millionᵃ

	1974	1977	1980	1983	1986	1987
+	697	778	1,011	1,313	1,690	1,670
−	1,059	1,895	2,079	2,481	3,378	3,378
=	−830	−1,117	−1,068	−1,168	−1,688	−1,078

Notes:
A plus sign (+) indicates export or receipt.
A minus sign (−) indicates import or payment.
a) Patents, inventions and processes.

Source: Deutsche Bundesbank (1988) *Monthly Report of the Deutsche Bundesbank*, 40, No. 5, May.

respect of both receipts and payments. In practice the proportions of affiliated flows follow the development of a country's outward and inward foreign direct investment positions and their industrial distribution.

The industrial composition of technological transactions varies between countries, although it is naturally concentrated in the more technology-intensive activities. For the United States in 1988, 20 per cent of all affiliated receipts were in the chemicals industry and 55 per cent in the non-electrical machinery group (including computers). In respect of payments, 15 per cent were in chemicals and 18 per cent in non-electrical machinery. The distribution for non-affiliate transactions is similar.

For the United Kingdom and Germany, total receipts in 1987 in chemicals were 40 per cent and 41 per cent, and in electrical engineering (including computers) 12 per cent and 19 per cent respectively. United Kingdom and German payments for the same industries were 21 per cent and 26 per cent (chemicals) and 44 per cent and 46 per cent (electrical engineering) respectively. The United Kingdom data, when analysed by industry (and by country) include a small but unknown quantity of non-technology related transactions.

A geographical analysis of the technology trade of three leading countries is presented in Table 2.3.10. Some transactions unrelated to industrial technology are included in the trade of the United States and the United Kingdom; nevertheless, a reasonably clear picture emerges. Each country conducts the overwhelming proportion of its trade with other developed countries: this is most true of Germany. The larger portion of United Kingdom receipts from less-developed countries may reflect the importance of the Commonwealth, particularly in Asia. Japan has an absolute deficit in technology trade with all three countries; it is the single most important partner for the United States, and for the United Kingdom and Germany after the United States.

The focus of technology trade is clearly between the United States and Europe and between European countries. This will partly result from the distribution of foreign direct investment and the operations of multinational firms. The future development of Japanese bilateral technology trade balances will undoubtedly be a source of great interest and as yet the bulk of Japanese payments are non-affiliate in nature.

2.3.5   Financial flows

Financial flows are transactions within the capital account of the balance of payments. These consist of transfers in the ownership of assets (including the creation and liquidation of claims). This covers transactions in assets such as equities, long-term and short-term bonds and credit transactions.

In practice the key distinctions for the purpose of analysis are not the type of item in which the transaction takes place but the identity of the transactors

Table 2.3.10 The Geographical Distribution of International Technology Transactions of the United States, United Kingdom and the Federal Republic of Germany, Latest Available Year, Persentage Distribution

	W. Europe	EC(12)	UK	E. Europe	USA	Japan	Asia	Other LDCs	Developed countries	LDCs	Value in national currency(M)
United States (1988)											
Receipts	57.5	51.6	12.6	0.3	–	22.5	6.6[a]	2.8	87.9	12.1	10,735
Payments	65.9	43.0	16.6	...	–	17.6	5.2[a]	0.4	94.3	5.7	2,048
United Kingdom (1987)											
Receipts	31.2	26.0	–	na	33.9	6.7	12.3	6.8	80.8	19.1	1,098
Payments	23.7	17.1	–	na	67.8	3.6	0.4	1.5	98.9	1.9	1,074
Federal Republic of Germany (1987)											
Receipts	45.9	28.3	5.9	4.8[b]	25.3	10.2	3.2	5.1	91.6	8.4	1,670
Payments	38.0	22.0	2.9	0.5[b]	57.6	2.7	0.1	0.7	99.2	0.8	3,378

Notes:
Figures are precentages of total.
... Denotes neglible.
na) Not available.
a) Includes Africa.
b) Centrally planned.

Sources: US Department of Commerce (1989) *Survey of Current Business,* 69, No. 6, June; UK Department of Industry (1989) *British Business,* 15 September; Deutsche Bundesbank (1988) *Monthly Report of the Deutsche Bundesbank,* 40, No. 5, May.

(especially in the case of government or official transactions) and the relationship between the transactors (in the case of foreign investment). The recognized categories are those of (i) foreign direct investment; (ii) portfolio foreign investment; (iii) other capital; and (iv) reserves (official transactions) (see International Monetary Fund (1977)).

Foreign direct investment is deemed to exist when a foreign resident participates effectively in the management of an enterprise. To do this some minimum level of equity-holding will be required, after which any transactions in assets with an affiliated firm are flows of foreign direct investment (see Clegg (1987) Appendix C). Foreign direct investment capital outflows therefore consist of purchases of equity, reinvested earnings on existing foreign direct investment, and increases in the net-creditor position of the parent enterprise with respect to the affiliated firm.

All portfolio foreign investment transactions are necessarily of a long-term nature and cover investment in equities and long-term bonds. Long-term capital is defined as that with an original maturity of more than one year, or no stated maturity (such as corporate equities). Other capital transactions comprise many different kinds of capital, including short-term capital, credit and currency transactions. The more detailed entries encountered in balance-of-payment statistics are simply sub-divisions by type of domestic creditor or debtor, such as banks. Official transactions in reserves are related to the financing or regulating of payments' imbalances or to influence the exchange rate of the national currency. Unlike the three types of capital transaction above, which are described as autonomous, official transactions are not undertaken for their own sake and will not be discussed further here.

The distinctions between capital transactions reflect the fact that the rationale of the financial flows generated differs between types of transactors. In the case of foreign direct investment, the motive is that of a firm to engage in productive activity abroad as a means of international competition. Consequently the determinants of foreign direct investment fall within the theory of the multinational enterprise.

Foreign direct investment flows therefore concern the competitiveness of firms and the relative attractiveness of international locations. Portfolio flows reflect either the growth of wealth or a change in the international attractiveness of holding wealth in different countries and currencies, or both. Because portfolio capital is a form of wealth holding, it tends to channel capital to the developed rather than the developing countries. Other capital flows, which include short-term assets, bank lending and trade credits are widespread between countries. However, bank lending notably constitutes a major source of finance for the capital-scarce (capital-importing) countries.

One caveat in respect of foreign direct investment is that in recent years (especially since the advent of exchange-rate instability) the financial positions of multinational enterprises are increasingly managed in a similar way to that

Table 2.3.11   Net Foreign Direct Investment Flows, 1980–86, US $billion[a]

	1980	1982	1983	1984	1985	1986[b]
Developed market economies						
Japan	-2.1	-4.1	-3.2	-6.0	-5.8	-11.6
Major European sources						
Germany, Federal Republic of	-3.9	-2.0	-1.4	-2.2	-2.9	-3.5
Netherlands	-3.3	-1.6	-2.2	-3.4	-2.7	-2.0
United Kingdom	-1.2	-2.4	-2.7	-7.4	-4.7	-5.7
North America						
Canada	-3.2	-2.4	-3.5	-1.3	-6.0	-0.5
United States	-2.4	16.3	11.5	21.4	-0.3	-6.3
Other	3.7	2.9	3.3	-1.4	-2.2	..
Developing countries						
Capital-surplus[c]	-0.4	9.2	5.6	5.5	2.2	2.0
Capital-importing[d]	9.2	11.4	8.4	7.9	8.8	8.0
of which:						
15 heavily indebted	4.6	6.1	3.4	3.2	4.1	3.0
Unidentified[e]	3.5	-27.5	-15.7	-13.2	13.6	..

Notes:
a) Net inflows are shown as positive numbers, net outflows as negative numbers. Significant differences among national reporting practices require extreme caution in making cross-country comparisons of the value of direct investment flows.
b) Data of developed market economies partly estimated; preliminary estimates for developing countries.
c) Excluding Brunei Darussalam.
d) Sample of 98 countries.
e) Excluding countries and errors and inconsistencies in national balance-of-payments data.

Source: United Nations, Department of International Economic and Social Affairs (1987) derived from IMF, *Balance of Payments Statistics* and other nd official national and other sources.

adopted by short-term wealth holders. Consequently the flows of foreign direct investment have become erratic.

The principal developments in the international flow of foreign direct investment are best highlighted by netting foreign direct investment outflows against inflows. This is summarized on a comparative basis for major countries and country groups in Table 2.3.11. Here the leading sources of net foreign direct investment outflows in the 1980s have been Japan, and in Europe West Germany, The Netherlands and the United Kingdom. The growth of Japanese outward foreign direct investment (and net foreign direct investment) flows is linked to its trade performance: in particular to the need to substitute foreign affiliate production for imports from Japan in the main market countries, principally the

United States and the European Community. Rapid growth has also taken place in Japanese foreign direct investment outflows in the service sector: in particular in financial services, in which activities a direct presence in foreign markets is required to compete effectively.

The net foreign direct investment inflows in the United States are both a reflection of the attraction of the United States' domestic market and the rising competitiveness of non-United States firms. Foreign direct investment inflows into the United States have gone some way to financing the United States balance-of-payments deficit. The net outflows of the United Kingdom reflect the stock of United Kingdom foreign direct investment abroad in which earnings are reinvested together with the relative appeal of foreign production locations to United Kingdom firms.

Within the developing countries, the countries designated 'capital surplus' in fact record net inflows of foreign direct investment, in support of the argument that foreign direct investment necessarily concerns native firms' desire to compete abroad. The capital-surplus (oil-producing) economies have few such firms; consequently a net inflow of foreign direct investment is normal for this group of countries. The capital-importing less-developed countries are in a similar position in respect of their indigenous business sector; however, foreign direct investment inflows also provide a transmission of much-needed capital to these countries.

Net portfolio capital flows are presented in Table 2.3.12, from which it can be seen that (up to the mid-1980s) the United States was the major recipient of this form of wealth-holding, while Japan was a leading source-country. The effect of such flows is a private form of balance-of-payment disequilibrium financing that takes place in response to differentials in the rates of return on assets between countries. The capital-surplus less-developed countries became net recipients of portfolio capital flows after 1982 as a consequence of the fall in the world price of oil. The capital-importing less-developed countries have difficulty attracting net inflows of portfolio capital.

Financial flows involving the less-developed countries under the private capital account alone are not the best indicator of changes in the financial position of these countries. Although not strictly an analysis of financial flows, it is more meaningful to employ the concept of the net transfer of resources, defined as the net capital or resource flow minus the net payment of interest and dividends. The net capital flow is calculated to include the use of official reserves, which must then be replenished. Table 2.3.13 presents such an analysis, which makes it clear that the interest repayments on debt are easily able to outweigh not only less-developed countries' ability to pay but the current net-capital inflows. For this reason, less-developed countries have increasingly turned to attracting inward foreign direct investment capital flows as a means of alleviating the international debt crisis (Lecraw (1991)).

Table 2.3.12 Net Portfolio Foreign Investment Flows, 1980–86, US $billion[a]

	1980	1982	1983	1984	1985	1986[b]
Developed market economies						
Europe	5.6	−15.7	−0.6	−0.4	−2.9	..
Japan	9.4	1.0	−3.0	−24.2	−41.4	−68.8
United States	10.5	9.5	1.8	25.6	67.5	88.4
Other	5.5	9.4	4.2	5.2	10.0	..
Developing countries						
Capital-surplus[c]	−24.0	−14.2	5.5	14.5	8.3	..
Capital-importing[d]	1.3	7.1	3.1	2.0	2.3	..
of which:						
15 heavily indebted[e]	1.7	4.4	0.4	−	−0.7	..
Unidentified[f]	−8.2	2.7	−11.0	−23.5	−43.8	..

Notes:

a) Positive number indicate net sales of securities abroad (new foreign issues minus retirements, plus net sales to foreigners of existing securities held in domestic portfolios); negative numbers are net purchases of securities. Data are from balance-of-payments statistics which conventionally exclude placement of official foreign exchange assets but include as inflows liabilities constituting foreign authorities reserves.

b) Available information is insufficient to make estimates for country groups.

c) Excluding Brunei Darussalam.

d) Sample of 98 countries.

e) Argentina, Bolivia, Brazil, Chile, Colombia, Côte d'Ivoire, Ecuador, Mexico, Morocco, Nigeria, Peru, Philippines, Uruguay, Venezuela and Yugoslavia.

f) Excluding countries and errors and inconsistencies in national balance-of-payments data.

Source: United Nations Department of International Economic and Social Affairs (1987) derived from IMF, *Balance of Payments Statisics* and official national and other sources.

2.3.6 Intra-industry trade

Intra-industry trade is defined as the simultaneous import and export of products (or services) belonging to the same industry (Greenaway and Milner (1986)). It is strongly associated with trade in manufactured products and also with trade between developed countries. Much of the interest in intra-industry trade is theoretical in origin: it poses, or appears to pose, a contradiction to the orthodox neoclassical trade theory (which predicts inter-industry trade).

This notwithstanding, the study of intra-industry trade holds significant relevance to policy. The existence of intra-industry trade in manufactures' trade is thought to have facilitated multilateral tariff reductions between developed

Table 2.3.13 Net Transfer of Resources to the Capital-importing Developing Countries, 1979–85, US $billion[a]

	1979	1980	1981	1982	1983	1984	1985[b]
Net transfer mediated through all credits[c]							
Net capital flow	47.9	54.2	62.5	50.8	39.7	32.0	13
Net interest paid	−17.2	−23.6	−34.8	−50.0	−48.3	−53.9	−54
Net transfer	30.7	30.6	27.7	0.8	−8.6	−22.0	−41
Net transfer mediated through direct investment							
Net flow of investment	10.1	9.8	14.2	12.0	8.9	8.5	9
Net direct investment income	−11.4	−13.7	−13.5	−13.1	−11.6	−11.3	−13
Net transfer	−1.3	−4.0	0.7	−1.1	−2.7	−2.8	−4
Net transfer mediated through official grants	12.0	12.7	13.1	10.7	11.0	12.3	14
Total net transfer	41.4	39.3	41.5	10.4	−0.3	−12.5	−31
Memorandum items							
Net transfer to Latin America and Caribbean[d]	15.6	11.9	11.4	−16.7	−25.9	−23.2	−30
Net transfer to sub-Saharan Africa[e]	6.4	6.0	9.5	10.1	7.9	0.8	1

Notes:
a) Net flow of foreign resources available for imports of goods and services (i.e., after payment of foreign capital outstanding). All flows are inflows minus outflows of residents and non-residents. Sample of 93 developing countries.
b) Estimate, rounded to nearest billion dollars.
c) Includes all official bilateral and multilateral credits, including use of IMF credit, and all private credits, short-term as well as long-term.
d) Thirty-one developing countries or territories, accounting for about 92 per cent of the trade of the region.
e) Thirty-seven countries, accounting for about 92 per cent of the trade of the full group.

Source: United Nations, Department of International Economic and Social Affairs (1986) derived from IMF, *Balance of Payments Statistics*, national data and estimates of the World Bank, regional commissions of the United Nations and other sources.

Table 2.3.14   Intra-industry Trade Indices for OECD Countries, 1959–67

SITC Section Code	Intra-industry trade ratios				Increase in total trade 1959–67 (%)
	1959	*1964*	*1967*	*1974*	
(0) Food and live animals	22	25	30	—	72
(1) Beverages and tobacco	40	42	40	—	68
(2) Crude materials	26	28	30	—	49
(3) Mineral fuels	30	29	30	—	80
(4) Oils and fats	41	39	37	—	23
(5) Chemicals	56	60	66	63	122
(6) Manufactures	43	49	49	58	325
(7) Machinery	43	53	59	62	202
(8) Misc. manufacturing	45	53	52	58	149
(9) Commodities, n.e.s.	34	45	55	—	180

Source: Grimwade (1989)

countries (see Chapter 2.4) while at the same time enabling structural and economic adjustment to proceed between countries without the absolute contraction (or elimination) of whole industrial sectors. This implies intra-industry specialization.

The investigation of intra-industry trade is beset with measurement problems (Greenaway and Milner (1986) Chapter 5, Grimwade (1989) Chapter 3). The concept of intra-industry trade is probably best conveyed by the Grubel and Lloyd (1975) index, although numerous alternative and improved measures have appeared. This index measures intra-industry trade as the proportion of a country's total trade (exports plus imports) in a product (industry) for which a balance between exports and imports exists. It is conventionally written as:

$$Bj = \frac{(Xj + Mj) - |Xj - Mj|}{(Xj + Mj)}$$

where Bj is intra-industry trade, and
   Xj and Mj are exports and imports of product j

The straight brackets in the formula indicate that the absolute value is taken. The index is frequently multiplied by 100 to convert it to a percentage, while its properties are that intra-industry trade would be total if Bj equalled 100 and nil if Bj equalled zero. An average measure of intra-industry trade for a country can be obtained by applying industrial trade weights.

The values obtained for intra-industry trade clearly depend on the level of industrial aggregation used: good discussions are found on this in the references noted above. Table 2.3.14 shows some estimates of intra-industry trade for nine

Table 2.3.15   Intra-industry Trade Indices in the Manufactures's Trade of OECD
Countries, 1964–74

Country	1964	1967	1974	Change 1964–74
France	74	77	81	+7
Netherlands	73	72	72	–1
United Kingdom	68	71	77	+9
Belgium-Luxembourg	68	71	79	+11
Italy	58	58	61	+3
West Germany	52	55	58	+6
United States	46	49	54	+8
Canada	40	41	48	+8
Japan	46	49	54	+8
Australia	26	26	29	+3
All countries	53.7	56.5	60.4	+6.7

Source: Grimwade (1989)

broad categories of industry, from which it is seen that there has been a tendency
for measured intra-industry trade to rise over time, particularly in chemicals and
manufacturing. A similar tendency for estimates of intra-industry trade to rise
over time is found at the country level (Table 2.3.15) where the countries recording the largest increases are Belgium-Luxembourg and the United Kingdom.

   These perceived developments in intra-industry trade should ideally be interpreted in the light of other processes occurring in international trade, such as the
increased trade in intermediate products and the rise of intra-firm trade. When
approached at the level of the industry (as dictated by official statistics) it is
difficult to assess the true significance of intra-industry trade.

2.4

The Institutional Framework of Trade

2.4.1 Introduction

Contrary to the exposition found in elementary theory, international trade invariably takes place within the context of international frameworks. The most prominent of these is the General Agreement on Tariffs and Trade which presides over the bulk of world trade and over the periodic multilateral trade negotiations aimed at propelling the world towards free trade. Also included are the regional movements towards trade liberalization and trade preferences for less-developed countries.

At a different level a substantial proportion of world trade occurs under the control of multinational firms, between affiliated enterprises, while the movement towards countertrade side-steps the theme of multilateralism inherent in institutions committed to the liberalization of trade. These special aspects of the governance of trade are addressed in Chapter 2.6.

2.4.2 Multilateral trade negotiations

The General Agreement on Tariffs and Trade emerged in 1947 as the international organization with responsibility for providing a framework for trade relations. There were originally just over 20 signatories to the General Agreement on Tariffs and Trade a figure which has now risen to 96 with some 30 countries under special arrangements following General Agreement on Tariffs and Trade rules in principle and who are afforded treatment as full members in trade concessions.

Therefore the General Agreement on Tariffs and Trade covers the trade between all developed market economies and most less-developed economies; the principal exceptions to date are most of the centrally planned socialist economies. For an outline of the essential framework of the General Agreement on

Tariffs and Trade see van Meerhaeghe (1985); other general introductions are to be found in Caves and Jones (1985) Chapter 13, Gill and Law (1988) Chapter 7, Grimwade (1989) Chapter 1, Jones (1983) Chapter 2, MacBean (1988), and Sodersten (1980) Chapter 17 among others, while the classic analysis of the General Agreement on Tariffs and Trade is that by Curzon (1965).

The aims of the General Agreement on Tariffs and Trade can be summarized as to provide:

(i) a structure for the orderly conduct of international trade;
(ii) a system of rules and codes of conduct which reduce the risk of unilateral action, and thereby that of a trade war;
(iii) a framework for the progressive reduction of barriers to trade (see Greenaway (1983) Chapter 5).

The General Agreement on tariffs and Trade therefore enshrines the principle of free trade as epitomized by comparative advantage, although in practice it is felt to reveal a bias towards catering for the interest of producers rather than consumers (Baldwin (1988)).

The Articles of Agreement of the General Agreement on Tariffs and Trade (Table 2.4.1) are the essence of its method. The first two articles compose the basic obligations of the signatory countries. Articles III to XXIII effectively constitute a code for fair trade, the difficulties of which are discussed in Chapter 2.5. Procedures for application and for the amendment of articles are covered in articles XXIV to XXXV, while articles XXXVI to XXXVIII are directed towards the trade issues of developing countries.

There have been eight rounds of multilateral trade negotiations under the auspices of the General Agreement on Tariffs and Trade; the latest is the Uruguay Round, held from 1986 to 1990. Typically a Round consists of three years of conceptual discussions followed by two years of hard bargaining. The Tokyo Round (1973–9) included for the first time negotiations on non-tariff barriers, while the Uruguay Round has introduced trade in services (see United Nations Department of Economic and Social Affairs (1988) Chapter 3; (1986) Chapter 5; (1989) Chapter 1; and World Bank (1987) Chapter 9).

The most fundamental principle of the General Agreement on Tariffs and Trade is that of non-discrimination between countries supplying the same good (note, however, the exceptions in Section 2.4.3). This is effected by the most-favoured-nation treatment clause included in the bilateral trade agreements concluded between the General Agreement on Tariffs and Trade participants. Bilateral bargaining between developed countries involves the procedure of reciprocal concessions, or first difference reciprocity, on the reduction of trade barriers facing the exports of greatest importance to each of the parties (see World Bank (1987) Chapter 8). This principle has come under increased pressure as certain countries seek equal access in key sectors, thereby adopting a sector-by-sector approach.

Table 2.4.1 The GATT Articles of Agreement

I	Objectives
II	General most-favoured-nation treatment
III	Schedules of concessions
IV	National treatment and internal taxation and regulation
V	Freedom of transit
VI	Anti-dumping and contervailing duties
VII	Valuation for customs' purposes
VIII	Fees and formalities connected with importation and exportation
IX	Marks of origin
X	Publication and administration of trade regulations
XI	General elimination of quantitative restrictions
XII	Restrictions to safeguard the balance of payments
XII	Non-discriminatory administration of quantitative restrictions
XIV	Exceptions to the rule of non-discrimination
XV	Exchange arrangements
XVI	Subsidies
XVII	State trading enterprises
XVIII	Governmental assistance to economic development
XIX	Emergency action on imports of particular products
XX	General exceptions
XXI	Security exceptions
XXII	Consultation
XXIII	Nullification or impairment
XXIV	Customs unions and free trade areas
XXV	The organization for trade cooperation
XXVI	Acceptance, entry into force and registration
XXVII	Withholding or withdrawal of concessions
XXVIII	Modification of schedules
XXIX	Tariff negotiations
XXX	Amendments
XXXI	Withdrawal
XXXII	Contracting parties
XXXIII	Accession
XXXIV	Annexes
XXXV	Non-application of the agreement between particular contracting parties
XXXVI	Trade and development: principles and objectives
XXXVII	Undertaking relating to commodities of special export interest to LDCs
XXXVIII	Outline of joint action on trade and development

The most-favoured-nation clause ensures that the bilateral trade concessions on products are equally available to all members of the General Agreement on Tariffs and Trade (including those participating under special arrangements). Countries completely outside the General Agreement on Tariffs and Trade therefore face appreciably higher tariffs; for example, without most-favoured-nation treatment, the average tariff on exports from the Soviet Union stands some 16 per cent higher.

In the Kennedy Round (1964–7) the negotiations introduced the process of linear or across-the-board tariff reductions on all classes of manufactured products, rather than slavishly bargaining reductions on one item for another. This innovation recognized that the developed countries trade most intensively with each other in the same classes of products, generating intra-industry trade. As a consequence, linear reductions benefit all parties while still observing the principle of reciprocity (Meyer, (1978)). Where trade barriers continue to be employed by countries, the General Agreement on Tariffs and Trade encourages the use of tariffs rather than non-tariff barriers on the grounds that tariffs are more transparent: their economic effects are easier to identify (World Bank (1987) Chapters 8 and 9).

The reductions in trade barriers since the end of the Second World War have been impressive though confined to trade in manufactures. Agriculture has been exempted from the General Agreement on Tariffs and Trade and consequently is still characterized by high trade barriers, including national income support, subsidized inputs, exports subsidies and input levies. A second exemption from the General Agreement on Tariffs and Trade is the movement towards economic integration and free-trade areas (see MacBean, 1988). While it is true that the common external tariff of a customs union should be no higher than the average of its members' individual tariffs before integration, this cannot be guaranteed to apply to the incidence of effective protection (see Section 2.5.2) while integration itself, involving the elimination of all internal tariffs, clearly has the potential to discriminate against cheaper suppliers in non-member countries. The economic analysis of customs unions and free-trade areas suggests that despite possible adverse effects, the world as a whole could benefit from the creation of such islands of free trade (see Hine (1985) Chapter 2).

A further exception is that less developed countries are exempted from the reciprocity requirements in General Agreement on Tariffs and Trade negotiations. This appears to be a good principle, but can be criticized for its tendency to disengage less-developed countries from having to pursue liberalization policies themselves within the world system, and for the favour it confers on less-developed countries' own protectionist lobbies, which include both native firms and the affiliates of foreign multinationals.

Apart from these original exemptions from the General Agreement on Tariffs and Trade (under Article XX) more recent movements away from free trade are evident in the discriminatory treatment of low-cost exports from the less-developed and newly industrializing countries, and from Japan, in particular the growth of managed trade (see Section 2.5.3). These and other shortcomings of the General Agreement on Tariffs and Trade have spawned a substantial literature on the need for reform, especially in respect of the limitations in the agreement's coverage and its evident incapacity in the minds of many to deal with the 'new protectionism'. These issues are discussed in Baldwin (1987), General Agreement on Tariffs and Trade Study Group (1986), United Nations Department of Economic and Social Affairs (1988) and World Bank (1987) Chapter 9.

2.4.3   Preferential trading agreements[1]

Trade preferences, by which is meant more favourable terms than afforded those with most-favoured-nation status, exist in two broad respects: first between countries engaged in economic integration or creating a free-trade area, and secondly those in favour of the less-developed countries.

The premier example of economic integration is the European Economic Community founded by the Treaty of Rome in 1957. The European Community has eliminated tariffs on all internal trade and sets a common external tariff (the Common Customs Tariff) on imports from non-member countries, with the exception of those from associated countries and regions such as the European Free Trade Association (Williams (1988)). The current membership of the European Community (12) is Belgium, Denmark, France, the Federal Republic of Germany, Greece, the Republic of Ireland, Italy, Luxembourg, The Netherlands, Portugal, Spain and the United Kingdom. For a discussion of the economic rationale of the European Community see Hine (1985) Chapters 5 and 6. The issues of economic integration and trade barriers are discussed further in respect of the European Community in Chapter 2.5.

The European Free Trade Association enjoys virtual free trade in industrial goods with the European Community, as well as between its own members (Curzon Price (1982)). A free-trade area, unlike a customs union such as the European Community, does not set a common external tariff on non-member trade. The membership of the European Free Trade Association comprises Austria, Finland, Iceland, Norway, Sweden and Switzerland (Williams (1988)), and the degree of integration of the European Free Trade Association in economic matters with the European Community is likely to continue to progress, with the possible movement towards the formation of a common economic zone. The European Community has association agreements with a number of countries of the South and East Mediterranean (Williams (1988)), although only that with the European Free Trade Association provides reverse preferences for European Community members.

The most recent movement towards free trade on a regional basis within the developed world is the Canada-United States Free Trade Agreement, signed in

1988, after a history of bilateral trade disputes. The provisions include the elimination of almost all tariffs on bilateral trade by 1998, clear rules on customs valuation, national treatment for producers of both countries, the abolition of higher indirect taxes on imports and other non-tariff barriers such as technical standards. The agreement also removes tariffs and quotas on those agricultural goods not subject to national support schemes, and relaxes certain instances of government favouritism towards national producers in purchasing (procurement). Furthermore, the right of establishment is granted except in a number of service sectors (Lipsey and York (1988), Rugman (1988a), (1988b)). The agreement also creates a binational panel to adjudicate on trade disputes that may arise between the two countries regarding unfair trade.

By number the majority of instances of regional integration and free-trade areas occur between less-developed countries. For a detailed listing of less-developed country arrangements see van Meerhaeghe (1985) Introduction.

The Latin American Integration Association was created in 1980 on the demise of the Latin American Free Trade Association (itself created in 1960), the latter having achieved only limited integration. Its members are Argentina, Bolivia, Brazil, Ecuador, Mexico, Chile, Colombia, Paraguay, Peru, Uruguay and Venezuela (Finch (1982)). The Central American Common Market comprises Costa Rica, Guatemala, El Salvador and Nicaragua, while Honduras continues to participate though it officially withdrew in 1968. This region has attained free trade in most industries and sets a common external tariff.

The Andean Group was formed in 1969 by Bolivia, Colombia, Ecuador and Peru; they were later joined by Venezuela, while Chile withdrew from membership. This group are all members of the Latin American Integration Association. It has also experienced difficulty other than in achieving the virtual abolition of internal tariffs on manufactures (El Agraa and Hojman (1982)).

The Association of South-East Asian Nations was formed in 1967 to promote regional cooperation as a response to political instability in South-East Asia. Because the economies of its five original members, Indonesia, Malaysia, the Philippines, Singapore and Thailand (Brunei joined in 1984) have very similar industrial structures, they do not form a trading bloc in terms of the internal intensity of trade; however, collectively the Association of South-East Asian Nations forms a powerful negotiating body with third countries (see El Agraa (1982b), Brooke (1988)).

Other regional organizations include the Caribbean Community and Common Market founded in 1973 (see Hall (1982)), and the West African Economic Community (Communaute Economique de l'Afrique de l'Ouest), an institution preserved from colonial times. Lastly the Economic Community of West African States was founded in 1975 (see Brooke (1988a), (1988b), (1988c) for a detailed account of regional organizations of Africa and the Middle East, and Robson (1982)).

Outside the framework of General Agreement on Tariffs and Trade, the major grouping of non-signatories is the Council for Mutual Economic Assistance. This was founded in 1949 by Bulgaria, Czechoslovakia, the German Democratic Republic, Hungary, Poland, Romania and the Union of Soviet Socialist Republics. In 1962 it admitted non-European members: Cuba, Mongolia and Vietnam. As centrally planned socialist economies, each with domestic state monopolies antithetical to free trade, the aim was to attain a planned socialist division of labour on the basis of bilateral, rather than multilateral, trade within the bloc (Marer and Montias (1982)). The constraints imposed by this system in practice has led to a reorientation of these countries towards exports to the developed market economies, utilizing countertrade arrangements in particular (see Chapter 2.6).

There are two schemes of trade preferences given to imports from the developing countries. The Generalized System of Preferences is the name given to the preferential trade arrangements under the auspices of the General Agreement on Tariffs and Trade, applying to less-developed country imports to the developed economies and signed initially in 1971 by the European Community. The scheme offers developing countries lower tariffs in developed markets than are available under most-favoured-nation treatment. The United Nations Conference on Trade and Development, created in 1964 as a parallel body to the General Agreement on Tariffs and Trade to further the trade interests of less-developed countries, pressed for the introduction of the Generalised Scheme of Preferences. The arrangement is that, in principle, preferential access is extended to some 120 developing countries (known as the Group of 77).

The generalized scheme-of-preferences agreements of most less-developed countries cover manufactures, semi-manufactures and a few agricultural commodities. The most significant exclusions are for products that characterize the exports of the more highly developed less-developed countries (see Chapter 2.5, Section 2.5.3). While tariff concessions under the generalized scheme of preferences are favourable in nominal terms, restrictions are often encountered. This arises because of the provision of duty-free access up to a specified quota of imports, after which most-favoured-nation tariff rates apply. This device is known as a tariff quota: a hybrid of the two forms of protection. Furthermore, trade concessions under the generalized scheme of preferences are not 'bound', meaning that, unlike most-favoured-nation treatment, they can be withdrawn with little notice. It is estimated that in practice less than 20 per cent of less-developed-country exports to the developed countries enter under generalized scheme-of-preferences preferential terms (Williamson (1983) Chapter 13, World Bank (1987) Chapter 9).

The second scheme of preferences for less-developed countries is a regional agreement by the European Community called the Lomé Convention, itself a successor to the Yaounde Convention provided to African countries in 1963 (Commission of the European Communities (1987b), (1987c), Hine (1985) Chapter 6, Leonard (1988) Part II, Chapter 22). The Lomé Convention was agreed initially in 1975 and is renewed every five years. It confers preferential access to the European Community market on a group of 66 African, Caribbean and Pacific countries, themselves often former colonies of European Community countries. While the generalized scheme of preferences offers concessions only on tariffs, the Lomé Convention provides some relaxation of non-tariff barriers and trade regulations, together with exemptions from certain multilateral trade agreements, such as the Multi-Fibre Arrangement (see Section 2.5.3). However, the products covered by the Convention are typically tropical in nature rather than manufactures' trade (which is more important for development) and the arrangements as a whole are thought to divert trade from lower-cost producers in Latin America, the Middle East and Asia (Williamson (1983) Chapter 13).

2.4.4 International commodity trade

International commodity markets

The nature of international trade in commodities or primary products is often quite different from that of manufactures. Primary commodities are defined as goods in or near the first stage of transformation (Gordon Ashworth (1984) Chapter 1). The term therefore covers much agricultural output, base metals and oil. As a group the distinctive feature of commodities is that their short-run demand and supply schedules tend to be inelastic, so that small shifts in supply or demand lead to relatively large changes in their spot-market prices (see Ady (1980) for a classification of commodities by elasticities, and General Agreement on Tariffs and Trade (1987) for commodity price indices sources). This behaviour is most pronounced for commodities that are least associated with the production of luxury goods (see United Nations (1989) Chapter 1 and Williamson (1983) Chapter 13 for overviews of commodities; also United Nations Industrial Development Organization (1987) Chapter 1).

While manufactures are essentially differentiated products, primary products are virtually homogeneous within their type, with few or no close substitutes. For this reason centralized markets have evolved to establish prices in locations such as London, New York and Chicago. Much international trade in these goods is arranged on the basis of contracts concluded in such commodity markets or contracts concluded elsewhere but nevertheless strongly influenced by the central market price.

Not only are the consequences of demand and supply shifts more marked for prices, but the likelihood of such shifts is higher for commodities than for other goods. In the case of agricultural commodities, supply may shift because of climatic changes; in non-agricultural primaries, such as base metals, shifts in demand occur because of the magnified effect of changes in the rate of growth of

Table 2.4.2 The Dependence of Developing Countries on Commodity Exports in 1982–83

Major commodities	Weight (Percentage)	Number of countries accounting for 0.50 per cent or more of total developing country exports	Number of countries for which the commodity accounts for 20 per cent or more of their total exports
Coffee	19.4	28	15
Cocoa	5.1	18	3
Tea	2.6	15	2
Total, beverages	27.1	61	20
Sugar	8.7	18	6
Oilseeds and oil	6.8	26	3
Cotton	4.7	27	6
Wheat	0.7	7	–
Rice	1.5	9	1
Rubber	5.5	10	–
Copper	7.4	11	3
Aluminium	3.6	16	1
Tin	3.6	8	1
Total, other than beverages	42.5	132	21

Source: United Nations, Department of International Economic and Social Affairs (1988)

demand for final products for which they are inputs (Economist Intelligence Unit, (1990a)).

Many less-developed countries specialize in the production of primary goods (Table 2.4.2). The result is that the export earnings of these countries are highly variable (MacBean and Nguyen (1987) Chapter 1). Certain primary commodities enjoy relatively stable conditions of world supply (though not necessarily of demand) such as minerals and metals; in contrast food and agricultural raw materials suffer more from supply-induced world-price instability. The problem is not simply one of price (and therefore earnings) variability but also that if producers collectively expand their capacity, or a significant new producer enters the market, then long-run prices and earnings will fall. Calls for reforms in commodity trade are articulated by groups of producers such as the Cairns group of 13 principal agricultural exporters; however, the problem is a fundamental one. Added to this are the difficulties faced by developing countries with high international debt burdens.

International commodity agreements and the stabilization of export earnings

Because of the special problems of international commodity markets, two forms of international arrangements have arisen: (i) international commodity agreements between producers and consumers, and (ii) compensatory financing schemes to neutralize the effects of unstable export earnings. Of these, only international commodity agreements act on the world price of commodities to counteract the effects of adverse shifts in world demand.

The most persistent cause of variability in a country's export earnings is likely to be domestic supply shifts (the world volume of exports is in general more stable, as supply changes across countries tend to be self-cancelling). This source of instability can be tackled at a national level through stock policies via national marketing boards and loan facilities to encourage producers to build up private stocks (see Gordon Ashworth (1984) Chapter 4).

Instability in world prices may be addressed by international commodity agreements, employing export controls and buffer stocks. Five international commodity agreements have operated during the postwar period: the Wheat Trade Convention, the International Sugar Agreement, the International Coffee Agreement, the International Cocoa Agreement and the International Rubber Agreement (see van Meerhaeghe (1985) Chapter 4, and World Bank (1983)). Export controls have been employed in the sugar and coffee agreements while buffer stocks have been used in natural rubber and cocoa. The tin agreement was the only one to use both export controls and buffer stocks, a fact that led to inadequate stock-building through over-reliance on export controls. Of these agreements, only that for rubber was operating by the end of 1989, an achievement assisted by the fortuitous price-stabilizing effect of synthetic rubber production (Economist Intelligence Unit (1990b)).

International commodity agreements are notoriously difficult to negotiate because producers and consumers perceive their own interests to be in opposition. The provisions incorporated in international commodity agreements are therefore commonly compromised in crucial respects: in the choice of instruments of price stabilization, the level and range of price support, the extent of finance for buffer stocks and the allocation of export quotas. The poor performance of single-commodity international-commodity agreements prompted the proposal of the Integrated Programme for Commodities by the United Nations Commission for Trade and Development, for which a common fund for commodity price stabilization was initiated in 1979 and intended to finance buffer stocks for non-perishable commodities. The clear advantages of such a programme are that the integrated coverage of a range of commodities (with supply changes unlikely to be correlated) spreads the risk to the scheme as a whole, while adequately financed buffer-stock arrangements obviate the need to impose production limits. Despite this the programme has yet to be implemented to anything approaching its full extent.

The value of international commodity agreements is a controversial one: with the exception of fuels, about 58 per cent of primary exports originate from the developed countries. Furthermore, international commodity agreements that employ export quotas are thought to lock developing countries into a fixed pattern of production, so inhibiting diversification into other industries and into higher value-added products (van Meerhaeghe (1985) Chapter 4). Export quotas also interfere with the scope for low-cost exporters to win market share away from higher-cost producers.

The objective of compensatory financing schemes is to even-out fluctuations in export earnings to minimize the disruption to less-developed countries' development programmes. The Compensatory Financing Facility of the International Monetary Fund operates only if the shortfall in earnings from commodities results in an overall balance-of-payments deficit. By contrast the Stabilization of Export Earnings Fund, set up under the first and second Lomé Conventions of the European Community, are commodity-specific (see Section 2.4.3). This scheme guarantees a minimum revenue (through the provision of grants) to African, Caribbean and Pacific countries. The main products covered are cocoa, coffee, cotton, leather, skins, wood, tea and sisal, with the addition of funds for metals under the second convention, notably copper, cobalt and aluminium. In all, 48 primary commodities are included. This arrangement is particularly advantageous to low-income or highly indebted less-developed countries unable to afford a national stock policy.

The stabilization both of world trade in primary commodities and of the fortunes of developing country exporters remains problematic; for a further discussion of the development of the schemes noted above, see United Nations Department of International Economic and Social Affairs (1988) Chapter 3.

Note

1. Most of the organizations appearing here under preferential trading arrangements are discussed more fully in Chapter 3.3.

2.5

Barriers to World Trade

2.5.1 Introduction: the motives for protection and causes of barriers to trade

There are several reasons why the world can never be expected to achieve a state of completely free trade. Inevitably there are natural barriers such as distance and the earth's topography that interfere with the costless exchange of products between countries; despite advances in transport systems and communications these impediments will always exist.

Natural barriers, however, lie largely outside the debate between policy-makers and between academics although they do underscore the need for the right of establishment, especially for industries whose final products are least tradable. The most significant barriers to trade are those imposed by governments and in a few cases by groups of producers. Government-imposed barriers have been the subject of trade negotiations and the general move towards economic liberalization discussed in Chapter 2.4.

The barriers to trade with which this chapter is concerned are all types of protection. This implies there is a degree of competition between industry in the home economy and the rest of the world. Accordingly, a tariff on imports is said to protect the import-competing domestic industry. In general, protection composes much of the trade (or commercial) policy of a country. There are, however, other government-imposed barriers to trade that are not primarily intended to prevent foreign competition, though they may have this effect and indeed may be abused on occasion to limit imports. These obstacles include regulations on matters of public concern, such as prudential regulation in banking and insurance, and technical safety standards and health regulations: matters of sovereignty rather than protectionism.

The instruments of protection include tariffs and non-tariff barriers such as quotas and exchange-rate policy (the latter is discussed in Chapter 1.7). In terms of theory it is recognized that where there is a case for protection, economic efficiency is best served by subsidies on domestic production. Tariffs in turn are preferable to non-tariff barriers (Chacholiades, (1981) Chapter 9); however, it is often more appealing to a government to erect a tariff that discriminates against' foreign residents than to raise domestic taxes to pay for the subsidy. In fact, subsidies that afford protection to exporters are much disapproved of under the General Agreement on Tariffs and Trade (see Article XI): it is often a matter of perspective whether these constitute a distortion (an inefficiency in the economic allocation of resources or the pattern of consumption) in world trade or a welfare-enhancing response to existing barriers (Eaton (1986), Grossman, (1986)). To appreciate why this might be, we need a grasp of the various motives for protection.

Harry Johnson once classified the argument for tariffs as economic, non-economic and non-arguments. Economic arguments relate to raising the economic welfare of a country, either through correcting an inefficient allocation of domestic resources or through exploiting the market power of a country in international trade. Such arguments look at welfare only from the viewpoint of the tariff-imposing country. In the light of the discussion above, the justification for the imposition of tariffs as remedies for domestic distortions are weaker than often supposed; however, they are permitted in specified circumstances under the General Agreement on Tariffs and Trade (see 2.5.2 below). Such domestic inefficiencies often arise because imports have become more competitive, so changing the required economic structure of the economy – in other words, when the potential comparative advantage has shifted. The reallocation of resources between activities is not costless and so a tariff is often sanctioned to alleviate these adjustment costs. The world of international trade is continually changing, with new countries entering and offering more competitive products, so this sort of motive for tariffs should be widespread.

The economic arguments for protection to correct an inefficient industrial structure that does not result from the dynamic nature of the world economy are more suspect. Such problems as a monopolized domestic industry (whereby output is restricted) are best dealt with by anti-monopoly legislation. A further static argument for tariffs, to correct a socially injurious level of consumption of a product, is clearly rather ill-advised unless there is no domestic producer to replace the imports excluded. This is why economists argue that a distortion is best corrected at its source (Corden 1974)), such as using a domestic tax or subsidy rather than by misappropriating trade policy. Nevertheless, these arguments for protection are encountered (Black (1959)). As will be seen in the sections below, the form that protection takes often speaks volumes about the true motives underlying trade policy.

A further economic argument for protection is the exploitation of monopoly power in international markets. Trade theory demonstrates that it is optimal (for the welfare of a country in such a position) for a country (or group of countries, or producers) able to influence world prices to eschew free trade (Caves and

Jones (1985) Chapter 11, Chacholiades (1981) Chapter 8, Williamson (1983) Chapter 5). This is achieved by raising the price of exports relative to imports (the terms of trade) through restricting imports in the case of monopsony (market) power in importing) or restricting exports (market power in exporting). The implications are that large countries able to influence world prices will be most tempted to employ protection. An extension of this must be that countries that act in concert over trade policy (such as the European Community) will be increasingly in this position.

This argument for protection is known as the optimal tariff argument; it makes the assumption that exporting countries do not retaliate with their own tariffs (see, for example, Caves and Jones (1985) Chapter 11, Sodersten (1980) Chapter 13). However, where tariffs have been in place for some time, or novel methods of protection are used (which may not be familiar) protectionism may be able to persist successfully without precipitating a trade war.

Non-economic motives for protection are so-called merely because they lie outside conventional economic analysis. However, in a broad sense they do reflect the preferences of countries for a particular allocation of resources. Examples include the desire for a level of self-sufficiency in industries of strategic (military) importance, a level of domestic production in industries associated with the national character (Chacholiades (1981) Chapter 9) or political motives. The general effect of trade barriers that reduce the value of imports (at world prices) is to cause the overvaluation of the domestic currency (see also Section 2.5.4).

Some commentators have suggested that the success of the General Agreement on Tariffs and Trade in reducing tariff levels may have led to their substitution by non-tariff barriers (Bhagwati (1988)). These latter are seen as more insidious than tariffs, and their increased use in recent years has given rise to the term 'new protectionism' – new in the sense of both the instrument and in contrast with the old protectionism that characterized the 1930s. However, unlike the old protectionism, the new variety has a tendency to discriminate not by product but by country.

The contemporary threats to free trade are the persistent use of non-tariff barriers to alleviate the unpopular pressures for sectoral adjustment in the developed countries. A case in point is agriculture, as noted earlier largely exempted from the General Agreement on Tariffs and Trade and industries in which the newly industrializing countries have developed comparative advantages, such as textiles. Equally the use of exchange controls and import tariffs by less-developed countries as palliatives for balance-of-payments deficits and to protect domestic industries is a common occurrence.

In fact the use of trade protection would seem to owe most to domestic political lobbies (especially producers') rather than to the maximization of a country's welfare as a whole: the higher prices paid by consumers who have been denied cheaper imports is often a considerable loss (see Section 2.5.4. below, and World

Bank (1987) Chapter 8). If trade protection does not then maximize a country's welfare, the fact that it is adopted says much about the power of domestic-interest groups. It would seem that the non-arguments for protection may be among the most influential.

2.5.2 Tariffs

A tariff is a tax or duty levied on a commodity when it crosses national boundaries. There are two variants: the import duty and the export duty. The former is by far the most widespread and familiar. Export duties are sometimes imposed by countries producing primary products when a curtailment of supply is able to raise world prices and so export earnings (Chacholiades (1981) Chapter 8).

In common with all taxes a tariff can assume any of three different forms: (i) the *ad valorem* duty, expressed as a percentage of the value of the commodity traded; (ii) the specific duty, levied as a fixed amount per unit of the commodity traded; and (iii) the compound duty, a hybrid of the *ad valorem* and specific duties. European countries employ import tariffs predominantly of the *ad valorem* type, whereas the United States uses both *ad valorem* and specific duties with equal frequency.

Ad valorem tariffs are related to the value of the commodity (the term literally means 'to the value'). The value selected is normally the price of the import inclusive of cost, insurance and freight, rather than the free-on-board price that excludes the last two cost items. For tariffs of all kinds their published rate is known as the nominal rate.

The motives for adopting tariffs on imports, as opposed to any other form of protection, are a mixture of historical and political factors and administrative economy. Tariffs have long been employed as a means of raising revenue, and the developed countries used to derive a substantial proportion of government revenue from tariffs earlier in their industrialization. With the growth of national income, this motive has become insignificant, but tariff revenue remains a valuable source of finance for developing countries. (The role of tariffs in commercial policy is outlined in Moore (1985) Chapter 4.)

Import tariffs have been the preferred form of protection for developing countries' domestic industries. For a small country (unable to influence world prices) tariffs, unlike, for example, quantitative restrictions, have a predictable upward effect on the domestic price of an imported commodity. This price signal has been employed not only to reallocate resources between industries domestically, but also to encourage inward foreign direct investment by multinational firms.

Tariffs, and all barriers to trade, have a recognized effect on the location of production between countries. This role is best documented and analysed in the literature on the location decisions of multinational enterprises (Caves (1982)

Chapter 3, Clegg (1987) Chapter 2, Hood and Young (1979) Chapter 2). The effect of the tariff is to raise the price of the importable good and thereby the returns to the import-competing sector in the domestic economy. Although tariffs reduce the amount of final goods imported by the country, they may nevertheless increase the import of intermediate goods for that industry.

Such policies are aimed at import-substitution to alleviate balance-of-payments problems and to conserve foreign exchange, and at promoting a favourable pattern and rate of industrial development. A variant of this is the infant-industry argument that a respite from competitive imports will eventually enable efficient domestic product (Corden (1974) Chapter 9). The caveats noted in Section 2.5.1 about the efficacy of trade protection to correct domestic distortions have proved to be by no means purely academic. The instrumental use of tariffs to stimulate inflows of capital and technology are recognized to have led to inefficient inward foreign direct investment. Consequently there has been a reorientation on the part of many less-developed countries towards an open-trade policy and to the adoption of longer-term incentives to local enterprise (Buckley and Clegg (1990a), Graham (1990), Greenaway and Milner (1987)).

The influence of tariffs on location is normally to cause production to move to the country in which the market is sited. However, value-added tariffs can have the opposite effect, causing a stage of production to move to a foreign location where a specific factor of production is available. This is best exemplified by the provisions adopted first by the United States in 1966, under tariff schedules 806.30 and 807.00, which taxed only the foreign value-added component of United States' imports. This is accepted to have provided an impetus to United States firms, including many multinationals, to export intermediate or semi-finished products to low-labour-cost countries (especially in South-East Asia) for processing, assembly and subsequent re-import.

By far the majority of tariffs are levied on the total value-added of imported goods. The effect of such tariffs on domestic consumption depends simply on this nominal rate; however, this is not true of the effect on the degree of protection to domestic industry when intermediate products are imported. Here the concept of effective protection must be employed, according to which the protective effect of a tariff applies only to the value added by the domestic industry (Corden 1971). This approach shows that effective protection rises with the nominal tariff on the imported final good but is inversely related to the nominal tariff on the intermediate import (Corden (1971), (1974), Chacholiades (1981) Chapter 8, Greenaway (1983) Chapter 4). The effective rate of protection to the domestic industry will lie below the nominal rate if the nominal tariff on the final product is lower than that on the intermediate good, and vice versa. If the nominal tariff on the intermediate product, when weighted by the latter's share in total value added, lies above the nominal tariff on the final product, then the final product industry is actually left disadvantaged with respect to foreign competition.

The commonly available nominal tariff rates therefore easily misrepresent the true degree of protection. As developed countries often levy higher tariffs on manufactures than on the raw materials used to make them (tariff escalation), this raises the effective protection to their manufacturing sectors (World Bank (1987) Chapter 8). Effective protection and alternative measures of protective structure are discussed in Greenaway and Milner (1987) and Kirkpatrick (1987).

Since 1947 nominal tariffs on manufactures have fallen from an average of 40 per cent to between 6 and 8 per cent for most developed countries prior to the Tokyo Round (World Bank (1987) Chapter 8). A summary of the average rates of nominal tariffs before and after the Tokyo Round levied by the leading developed countries is presented in Table 2.5.1. Japanese tariff reductions have in fact exceeded those in the Table. Despite the preferences afforded to certain less-developed countries, it is clear that the nominal tariffs they face on their exports are on average, and when trade-weighted, rarely lower than those of the developed countries. The reductions in the non-discriminatory tariffs of the old protectionism have been compelling nevertheless. However, the rise in discriminatory tariffs, along with non-tariff barriers, has been more disturbing.

The 'new protectionism' has followed two routes: the imposition of tariffs and quotas under the special provisions of the General Agreement on Tariffs and Trade, and the adoption of non-tariff barriers which bypass the General Agreement on Tariffs and Trade's rule of law. Non-tariff barriers are looked at in the following section (2.5.3).

The rise of new protectionism has brought with it the term 'administered protection', used to denote the application of penalties against imports that are justified by a quasi-judicial process, in which domestic petitioners seek legal remedies against allegedly subsidized foreign products. These penalties are applied under national trade-remedy laws by governments and amount to a form of protection. Agencies created by statute investigate and determine injury, and sanction the imposition of countervailing duties, anti-dumping and other trade-related actions (Rugman (1988)). The rise of administered protection in the United States is documented by Rugman and Anderson (1987).

The General Agreement on Tariffs and Trade authorizes the use of anti-dumping and countervailing duties under Articles VI (relating to unfairly traded goods). Dumping is an unfair practice, defined as the sale of an export in a market at below the normal price or below the price of a comparable product produced and sold in the exporting country, or sold in a third market. Dumping is employed to dispose of temporary surpluses or used strategically to attain a monopoly position. In such instances the General Agreement on Tariffs and Trade permits the importing country to impose a neutralizing or preventative duty of not greater than the price difference between the exporting and importing markets.

Government subsidies on the production or export of any good which operate either directly or indirectly to increase exports (or reduce competitive imports)

Table 2.5.1 Tariff Averages before and after the Implementation of the Tokyo Round

Country or country group	Tariffs on total imports of finished and semifinished manufactures			Tariffs on imports from developing countries of finished and semifinished manufactures		
	Pre-Tokyo	Post-Tokyo	Percentage change	Pre-Tokyo	Post-Tokyo	Percentage change
European Community						
Weighted	8.3	6.0	28	8.9	6.7	25
Simple	9.4	6.6	30	8.5	5.8	32
Japan						
Weighted	10.0	5.4	46	10.0	6.8	32
Simple	10.8	6.4	41	11.0	6.7	39
United States						
Weighted	7.0	4.9	30	11.4	8.7	24
Simple	11.6	6.6	43	12.0	6.7	44

Source: World Bank (1987)

Table 2.5.2   Frequency of Use of Tariffs and Quotas under GATT Article XIX

Period	Tariff measures	Quantitative restrictions	Total	Ratio of quantitative restrictions to total
1949–58	13	3	16	19
1959–68	20	16	36	44
1969–78	15	28	43	65
1979–86	17	25	42	60

Source: World Bank (1987)

may be subject to a countervailing duty. Under Article VI countervailing duties are authorized only where the imports threaten or cause material injury to a domestic industry. Subsidies are non-tariff barriers, notoriously difficult to assess. The Tokyo Round produced a code on the interpretation and application of General Agreement on Tariffs and Trade provisions on subsidies (Article XVI); however, the distinction between frontier (export-related) and non-frontier subsidies is problematic (Snape (1982)). Subsidies, other than export subsidies, are not prohibited although General Agreement on Tariffs and Trade signatories agree to avoid any that may harm the industries of a General Agreement on Tariffs and Trade trading partner. Because Article VI permits discriminatory action it has encouraged importing countries to allege unfair trading practices on a frequent basis.

Safeguard action in the case of fairly traded products is permitted under Article XIX of the General Agreement on Tariffs and Trade. A tariff or quota can be imposed where serious injury is threatened or caused to the domestic industry; however, this must apply in a non-discriminatory fashion to all exporters of the product. Table 2.5.2 shows that quantitative restrictions have been favoured by importers under Article XIX. For an analysis of the key articles of the General Agreement on Tariffs and Trade see van Meerhaeghe (1985) Chapter 3.

The available information on the use of countervailing actions and anti-dumping cases is presented in Tables 2.5.3 and 2.5.4, from which it can be seen that the European Community alleges anti-dumping far more frequently than the United States, who employs them with approximately equal frequency. The target countries in the United States' countervailing actions have increasingly been less-developed countries, while the developing countries (including newly industrializing countries) probably make up about half of the antidumping cases. The underlying weakness of General Agreement on Tariffs and Trade to address the new protectionism is that it remains the responsibility of national bodies in the importing country to deem unfair trade practices.

Table 2.5.3   The Frequency of US Countervailing Actions, 1970–85

			Final outcome of action			
		Number of				*Average*
Year	*Exporter*	*initiations*	*Affirmative*	*Negative*	*Pending*	*CVD rate*
1970–74	Industrial countries	9	8	1	–	..
	Developing countries	2	2	–	–	..
1975–79	Industrial countries	59	20	39	–	..
	Developing countries	45	18	27	–	..
1980–85	Industrial countries	63	30 (19)	25	8	10.5
	Developing countries	108	69 (26)	30	9	11.5

Note: Numbers in parentheses represent cases condidered affirmative although they were withdrawn from CVD actions and settled through alternative arrangements between the exporting and importing countries.

Source: World Bank (1987)

Table 2.5.4   Countervailing Duties and Anti-dumping Actions Initiated between 1980 and 1985[a]

	US	*Australia*	*Canada*	*EC*
Countervailing duties	252[a]	18	12	7
Anti-dumping actions	280[b]	393	219	254

Notes:
a) US Trade Act, Section 701.
b) US Trade Act, Section 703.

Source: Bhagwati (1988)

2.5.3   Non-tariff barriers

The new protectionism has been characterized by the growth of non-tariff barriers, especially by those arrangements which lie outside the provisions of the General Agreement on Tariffs and Trade. A non-tariff barrier is a government-imposed measure which has the effect of protecting domestic industry from competing imports or assisting the expansion of exports, or both.

Non-tariff barriers such as quotas have a direct effect on trade, and the principle of effective protection applies to imports that are subjected to quotas through their tariff-equivalent effect (Greenaway (1983) Chapter 7). A quota is a quantitative restriction on trade imposed either by governments or by associations of exporters. Quotas imposed with consultation between the trading partners may be bilateral, or multilateral, otherwise they are termed unilateral import quotas. Voluntary export restraints are an example of export quotas arrived at through consultation or negotiation. It is under the auspices of such arrangements that international trade is said to be 'managed' or controlled (Caves and Jones (1985) Chapter 13). One estimate is that in 1980 up to 48 per cent of world trade was managed trade (Grimwade (1989) Chapter 7).

The true protective effect of quotas and all non-tariff barriers is especially difficult to assess because, unlike tariffs, they fix the quantity traded or exclude trade completely, so preventing any estimate of the trade that might have occurred in their absence. The reasons why quotas rather than tariffs appeal to protectionists is precisely because they allow only a known quantity of trade, whereas a tariff is unlikely to achieve this. Tariffs on imports from highly export-oriented countries (with an inelastic supply of exports) would merely be absorbed by the exporters without much influencing the quantity imported (Chacholiades (1981) Chapter 10). The loss of tariff revenue in using a quota (assuming no licence revenue) is a matter of indifference for developed countries.

Import quotas are provided for in the need for safeguard action under the General Agreement on Tariffs and Trade. Export quotas, however, play a significant role in the management of trade. These quotas are discriminatory because they apply to specified exporters; however, they are normally bilateral or multilateral, with the tariff-equivalent revenue usually accruing to the exporter. This rent can be considerable (World Bank (1987) Chapter 8); in the case of one voluntary export restraint on clothing, it amounted to US $725 million, at 1984 prices, between 1981 and 1983, accruing to Hong Kong producers. Such arrangements are thought to encourage collusion between exporters to charge a monopolistic price, although such gains will be small compared to the trade lost. In the case of an international cartel the desire for collusion precedes the fixing of export quotas to exploit collective monopoly power: the best-known example is the Organization of Petroleum Exporting Countries formed in 1960.

The movement towards bilateral and multilateral export quotas began in the 1950s, with restraints placed on Japanese exports of cotton textiles. The Current Arrangement Regarding International Trade in Textiles, known as the Multi-Fibre Arrangement and signed in 1986, has evolved to cover just under 30 less-developed countries and Eastern European exporting countries and 16 developed importing countries; it prescribes trade in textiles and garments of cotton, wool and man-made fibres (Choi, Chung and Marian (1985), Blum (1988)). The Multi-Fibre Arrangement, as with its antecedents, professes to be a temporary measure aimed at the liberalization of trade while alleviating market disruption and adjustment costs in the developed countries. (For a discussion of structural change and trade patterns, see Baldwin (1989) and Sampson (1989).) Some also point to the fact that countries such as Hong Kong have nevertheless been able to develop on the strength of textile exports (World Bank (1987)

Chapter 8), and that less-developed countries benefit from guaranteed access to markets and from the avoidance of *ad hoc* trade disputes.

The Multi-Fibre Arrangement is perhaps the best-known example of a multilateral variable export restraint (Hindley (1980)). Bilateral voluntary export restraints have arisen in such industries as steel, cars, footwear, motorcycles, machine tools and consumer electronics, most of which are exports of industrializing countries. Negotiated export quotas encourage the diversion of imports from countries bound by quota limits (World Bank 1987) Chapter 8) and provide a locational incentive for multinationals and native less-developed-country firms to switch production to other less-developed countries (Bhagwati (1988)).

Variable export restraints are voluntary in name. Their effect is to remove trade from the provisions of the General Agreement on Tariffs and Trade and therefore from the scope of Article XIX which prescribes compensation to exporters for loss of exports. Bhagwati (1988) has suggested that importing countries are able to coerce exporters to enter such agreements by alleging unfair trade practices, thereby strategically abusing the General Agreement on Tariffs and Trade. The result is the substitution of a long-term discriminatory quota arrangement for tariffs. Yet as long-term protection to industry, quotas may be less effective than tariffs: perhaps their choice has more to do with placating powerful domestic-producer interest groups while avoiding tariffs, which are identified with protectionism to a greater extent than negotiated restraints on trade.

While the growth of voluntary export restraints has largely excluded trade in certain products from the General Agreement on Tariffs and Trade, agricultural trade has been exempt since the General Agreement on Tariffs and Trade's inception because of pressure from many developed countries employing subsidies and income support. Subsidies, both non-frontier and frontier-related, can constitute effective non-tariff barriers. Indirect frontier subsidies are found in the form of government provision of favourable export-credit finance, and guarantees and insurance of private trade credit. It is a matter of controversy whether these are a distortion themselves or an efficiency-enhancing response to the weak capital markets in many less-developed countries (Eaton (1986)). The United Kingdom and United States, for example, currently provide such services through the Bank of England Export Credit Guarantee Department and the United States Export-Import Bank respectively (see Chapter 2.6, Section 2.6.2).

Quantitative restrictions other than those noted above which are effective non-tariff barriers include prohibitions, non automatic licensing, state monopolies, import surveillance (including automatic licensing), price-control measures and government procurement favouring national producers. A final group of non-tariff barriers are not directly targeted on imports, although they may exert a powerful effect; these include technical requirements on goods, health

Table 2.5.5 Industrial Country Imports Subject to 'Hard-core' Non-tariff Barriers, 1981 and 1986

	Source of imports			
	Industrial countries		*Developing countries*	
Importer	*1981*	*1986*	*1981*	*1986*
EC	10	13	22	23
Japan	29	29	22	22
United States	9	15	14	17
All industrial countries	13	16	19	21

Note: 'Hard-core' NTBs represent a subgroup of all possible NTBs. They are the ones most likely to have significant restrictive effects. Hard-core NTBs include import prohibitions, quantitative restrictions, voluntary export restraints, variable levies, MFA restrictions, and nonautomatic licensing. Examples of other NTBs which are excluded include technical barriers (including health and safety restrictions and standards), minimum pricing regulations, and the use of price investigations (for example, for countervailing and anti-dumping purposes) and price surveillance. Percentage of imports subject to NTBs measures the sum of the value of a country's import group affected by NTBs, divided by the total value of its imports of that group. Data on imports affected in 1986 are based on 1981 trade weights. Variations between 1981 and 1986 can therefore occur only if NTBs affect a different set of products or trading partners.

Source: World Bank (1987)

and safety requirements and standards, customs' valuation methods, currency controls and transfer restrictions, and special employment requirements. These non-tariff barriers are especially widespread in service sector trade, itself included for the first time in the Uruguay Round of General Agreement on Tariffs and Trade negotiations. Because many services are non-tradable, freedom to compete in foreign markets requires the right of establishment (Kakabadse (1987)). In 1981 the World Bank data suggested that 13 per cent of developed countries' visible imports were subject to hard-core non-tariff barriers, rising to a figure of 16 per cent by 1986, while those facing less developed countries rose from 19 to 21 per cent (Table 2.5.5). Table 2.5.6 highlights the pervasiveness of quantitative restrictions in trade, which are seen to be exploited with the greatest intensity by the developing countries.

The programme to complete the internal market of the European Community under the Single European Act has gone furthest in addressing national sovereignty-related non-tariff barriers; these are among the last barriers to truly unfettered trade, in which persons, goods, services and capital can move freely (see Butt Philip (1989)) because there are no internal tariffs on trade within the European Community (Hine (1985)). The current internal barriers to trade

Table 2.5.6   The Extent of Quantitative Restrictions in International Trade in the 1980s

	Number of restrictions per country			Proportion of commodities affected by restrictions		
	Developed market economies	Developing countries	All countries	Developed market economies	Developing countries	All countries
All commodities[a]	170	355	290	0.19	0.38	0.32
Agricultural commodities	47	100	77	0.29	0.61	0.47
Manufactures	115	243	213	0.15	0.32	0.28

Note: a) Including minerals and precious stones.

Source: United Nations, Department of International Economic and Social Affairs (1988) derived from data compiled by GATT.

are seen as (i) differences in technical regulations between countries; (ii) intra-European-Community border stoppages for the purpose of adjusting indirect tax payments such as VAT and excise duties; (iii) restrictions on competition through national government and public preference for national suppliers; and (iv) restrictions on the freedom to trade and to establish local in-service activities, notably in financial and transport services. (On the reduction of internal barriers see Emerson and others (1988) Chapter 3, Hine (1985) Chapter 5, Leonard (1988) Part III, 6, Pelkmans and Winters (1988) Chapter 2.)

The Cecchini Report (see Cecchini and others, (1988)) deals exhaustively with the issue of European Community internal barriers and estimates that the total potential static and dynamic economic gains from a unified market are around European Currency Units 200 billion (approximately 134 billion or United States $243 billion) in 1988 prices, representing about 5 per cent of the Community's gross domestic product. Furthermore, as a result of the expected greater observance of comparative advantage within the European Community, its trade with non-European Community countries is predicted to rise by 1 per cent of gross domestic product. The formation of a single European Community economy is, *ipso facto*, a movement towards liberalization and deregulation, which will also facilitate the direct operations of non-European Community firms in the market.

2.5.4   Exchange control

Exchange controls are widely used by countries with balance-of-payments deficits or low reserves of foreign exchange such as the developing countries, although many developed countries also place restrictions of some sort on the conversion of domestic into foreign currency. Exchange control is a monetary device to switch expenditure from foreign- to home-produced output or assets. Official permission has to be obtained for the purchase of foreign exchange (usually over a certain minimum), normally from the central bank or government. Scarce foreign exchange is rationed, often according to the nature of the transaction (exchange for foreign investment is most often highly restricted), and to whether the transactor is a corporation or a private individual.

Exchange control requires an elaborate mechanism of bureaucracy to administer it effectively. When the purchase of foreign exchange is restricted, transactors might resort to transfers between non-resident and resident accounts denominated in the home currency, which then have to be officially supervised (see also Section 2.6.3 on the unblocking of funds via countertrade).

The United Kingdom abolished all exchange controls in 1979 (which resulted in an increase in outward-portfolio investment). Under the Delors plan for European monetary convergence, France, Italy and Belgium must have removed their remaining exchange and capital controls by July 1990, Spain and Ireland by 1992 and Portugal by 1994. The remaining controls prevent, for example, French and Italian individuals but not corporations from holding foreign bank accounts, while Italian individuals are not permitted to hold other certain short-term assets abroad. The Organization for Economic Cooperation and Development adopted a code of liberalization of capital movements in 1968, amending it in 1985, under which members agree to eliminate restrictions on the international movement of capital, although no timescale was specified for implementation. (See also Kindleberger (1987, Chapter 3 on capital controls.)

2.5.5   Other government restrictions

As trade in intermediate and semi-finished products has grown, governments have increasingly enquired into where the value incorporated in final products is added. One application of this is the rules of origin used to determine whether an import from a country, for example a less-developed country that is granted tariff preferences, should qualify for the preference. The value-added rule specifies that at least a certain percentage of a product's ex-factory price must be value-added in a particular country. The European Community makes greater use of an alternative called the process rule (see Hine (1985) Chapter 6). The aim is to reduce trade deflection whereby goods substantially made in a non-preferred country are granted preferences by passing through a preferred country.

Rules of origin are also applied to trade within the European Community to determine whether products subject to national voluntary export restraints are to be counted as imports from a non-member country. This has been subject of disputes between European community member countries, for example between the United Kingdom and France in respect of cars. Within the European

Community a consensus seems to have emerged that in general a good should be considered as European-Community-made if at least 60 per cent of its value is added in a European Community member state.

These rules over local content are familiar in developing countries' negotiations with multinationals over the degree of income to be generated locally. All types of country have become increasingly sensitive to the way foreign-controlled production affects the balance of payments. Developing countries in particular have introduced local content requirements as performance criteria. However, in the case of both less-developed countries and developed countries, local content stipulations constitute barriers to trade where on economic grounds of comparative advantage a lower proportion of local value-added is efficient. If local content agreements are being used to alleviate a domestic distortion in the host country, such as unemployment, the question again arises whether a domestic remedy should be introduced rather than involve trade policy.

2.6

Types of World Trade

2.6.1 Introduction

The majority of international trade is conducted on a multilateral basis. This enables countries to run bilateral trade deficits and surpluses simultaneously with different trading partners, yet still achieve an overall balance with the rest of the world as a whole, through claims being transferred between countries using a convertible currency. The advantages of this system are that international trade is fully expanded to exploit the gains from specialization through comparative advantage while consumers enjoy lower prices and a more extensive choice of products.

Countertrade is to be contrasted with multilateral trade in that every import transaction must generate an export of some comparable value. The adoption of countertrade is often a matter of policy at the country level, in which case the intention is that bilateral trade balances between each trading partner. Countertrade has been the basis for trade of countries in the council for Mutual Economic Assistance trading bloc with the developed market economies. For countertrade to take place a coincidence of wants is required between two countries, which greatly reduces the volume of trade able to occur, and therefore the gains from trade as compared with a multilateral system. However, countertrade is not always a matter of government policy; it may characterize international transactions in other circumstances, admittedly when a coincidence of wants is more likely to be present. The matter of finance is at the centre of the choice between multilateral trade and countertrade.

Although it is not usually thought of as a separate type of trade from multilateral trade in principle, international intra-firm trade is sufficiently distinctive in its implications. International intra-firm trade is the export of goods and services between branches, divisions or subsidiaries of the same enterprise. Normally the directly owned foreign operations of parent enterprises are incorporated foreign affiliates rather than branches which have no separate legal identity. A foreign affiliate is deemed to exist when the parent has an effective voice in its management (International Monetary fund (1977)). There is no universally agreed official shareholding level at which this is imputed, but most countries set a lower threshold of between 10 and 20 per cent of the affiliates' equity. In practice, most foreign affiliates that behave in an integrated way with respect to other members of the multinational enterprise record substantially higher degrees of foreign-parent ownership. Therefore the trade between affiliates of the same multinational enterprise and between parent and affiliates is more correctly described as intra-group trade, though the normal usage will be retained here.

The distinctive feature of intra-firm trade is that unlike trade between parties unrelated (or insignificantly related) by ownership, which is usually associated with multilateral trade, trade flows can be governed by administrative fiat (the internal command system of the firm). At one extreme this tendency may be pronounced while at the other a multinational may conduct what intra-firm trade it does along lines similar to that of independent firms. However, the very existence of intra-firm trade points to some exercise of ownership-based control.

2.6.2   Multilateral trade

Multilateral trade between independent exporting and importing parties using convertible currencies is the model implicitly assumed in most accounts of the mechanics of international trade. The theory of comparative costs explains the proximate cause of international specialization and trade, and the gains from trade (see, for example, Caves and Jones (1985) Chapters 5–7). The many firms that engage in international trade, their agents and intermediaries, all derive their profits from sharing in the gains from trade.

The theories of the causes of international differences in the structure of comparative advantage between different activities was covered in Part 1. Comparative advantage is therefore the manifestation of more fundamental determinants of countries' trade patterns, over which governments try to exert influence using national policies and trade policies (see Chapter 2.5). Multilateral trade is identified with the use of national currencies which are convertible into one another. Convertibility may be restricted in certain ways as noted in Section 2.5.4; however this does not interfere with the principle of multilateral trade.

The textbook account of how international trade works frequently gives the impression that final products (for final consumption) characterizes international exchange. In fact, the increased incidence in intermediate product trade, whether in goods or services, is perfectly intelligible within the scheme of multilateral trade. Neither is it of any consequence in this respect that much trade is conducted under long-term rather than one-off contracts or spot-market transactions, as this mostly reflects the nature of the product or the industrial market structure.

Perhaps more significant is the growth of trade within multinationals, examined in Section 2.6.4.

Specialist institutions have evolved to lower the costs of engaging in international trade: in effect to assist exporters and importers in overcoming, or reducing, the barriers to trade. The practical aspects of this are well covered in Part 2 of Brooke and Buckley (1988) and Brooke (1986) Chapter 4. The important point about multilateral trade is that it is in principle decentralized and conducted by firms pursuing profitable opportunities caused by differences in international comparative advantage. At its simplest, international trade might consist of an exporter and importer with the services of two bankers and a shipper (Burton (1984) Chapter 7). However, it may well consist of a far more complex set of agents and relationships (see Buckley and Brooke, 1988).

There are two sets of processes involved in international trade: the finance process by which the exporter is paid, and the trade process (involving the movement of outputs). The sources of international trade risk to the exporter include that of default by the importer, late payment or non-payment, damage to the goods, and exchange risk where the goods are invoiced in foreign currency. Only exchange risk is necessarily peculiar to foreign trade rather than domestic trade; however, the extent of the other risks are augmented by international impediments such as legal, cultural, linguistic and political differences.

Because the physical transfer of outputs tends to be protracted as compared with domestic trade the financial aspects assume greater significance, with special arrangements having evolved regarding credit, either taken out by the exporter to obtain liquidity or by the importer to expedite payment to the exporter. It is clear therefore that banks and other financial institutions enable such impediments to trade to be overcome at lower cost compared with the traders assuming the risks themselves.

Within the financial process the credit terms negotiated will depend on the parties' relative bargaining strengths, the degree of trust on either side, the frequency and regularity of trade between the parties (and therefore the scope for future sanctions against each other), the perceived risk of exporting to the market country, the nature of the product (a capital good which retains a high value over time permits longer credit) and the availability and cost of credit terms to the exporter or importer (Burton (1984) Chapter 7). Depending on the nature of the trade, the parties and the countries involved, further specialist intermediaries may be involved, such as export houses who assume the burden of exporting (Bass and Geddes (1988)).

Government provision of export credit and insurance is available to exporters, for example, for United Kingdom exporters from the Export Credit Guarantee Department of the Bank of England and for United States exporters from the Export-Import Bank in the United States. The theoretical argument for such arrangements is that they overcome inefficiencies in importers' domestic credit markets, and so realize mutually advantageous trade that otherwise might not occur. It can also be argued that such arrangements are subsidies to exporters. In practice they are looked upon as a competitive instrument to expand exports. In the United Kingdom around 40 per cent of exports are insured in this way (Burton (1984), Chapter 7).

The exchange risk borne by either party in international trade is a further source of barrier. This risk may be borne by the exporter, when goods are invoiced in the foreign currency, or by the importer when invoiced in the exporter's home currency, although an acceptable third country's currency may be used to share the risk. It is normal for trade to be invoiced in the exporter's currency; for example, for United Kingdom trade in the mid-1970s, 75.9 per cent of exports were invoiced in sterling while 72.1 per cent of imports were invoiced in the exporter's currency (Carse and Wood (1979)). The use of forward exchange markets to obtain forward cover against adverse movements in exchange rates is one means of reducing risk, but at a cost (see Bass and Geddes (1988)).

International trade therefore has evolved cost-minimizing intermediaries to expand the degree to which gains from trade can be appropriated. At the government or regional level, arrangements may exist to stabilize the fluctuations of currencies and to further the degree of trade, although such exchange-rate policies may be compromised by other national economic objectives (see Chapter 2.7).

2.6.3   Countertrade

While multilateral trade is very much the orthodox account of how trade is and should be conducted, countertrade has only recently come under close scrutiny. Countertrade is defined as a contractual arrangement under which the export of a good is linked to the import of other goods (Casson and Chukujama (1990); see also Paliwoda (1981)). Estimates of the importance of countertrade in the world trading system vary widely, not least because of the covert nature of many countertrade deals. Paliwoda (1988) places countertrade at around one-third of world trade by value and one-half of all East–West trade.

A number of schemes exist for classifying the varieties of countertrade arrangements which are possible (Borner (1986) Chapter 6, Lecraw (1988), Paliwoda (1988)). Recourse to countertrade is recognized to rise in the world economy during depression (as in the case of barter in the 1930s) and during world recession (Casson and Chukujama (1991), Paliwoda (1988)). To this extent it is not a new form of international trade, although its importance has undoubtedly increased since the mid-1970s.

Lecraw (1988) distinguishes seven generic types of countertrade:

(i) barter: the exchange of goods and services with the absence of money, except to balance any discrepancy between export and import values;

(ii) counterpurchase (or parallel trade): involves two linked contracts, the exporter under one contract (normally from the developed country) agrees to purchase a selection of goods from a basket of commodities produced by the importer (normally a developing country). Counterpurchase involves a two-way flow of money payments netting out to zero where the values of exports and imports are equal. Deferred payment for exports is possible and would constitute an interest-free loan;

(iii) buy-back: distinctive in that an input is exchanged for an output, such that an exporter of capital equipment, technology or training services from a developed country accepts part of the output produced as full or partial payment;

(iv) production sharing: similar to buy-back in concept, except that the supplier of the input receives a proportion of the output rather than a predetermined quantity. Used most frequently for natural resource and energy projects;

(v) industrial offsets (or compensation): requirements are placed on the exporter by the importer or importing country to produce part of the product, source parts or assemble the product within the importing country. The responsibility of finding buyers for the output rests with the importing country, although part of this may be designated to the original exporter. The use of offset is most frequent in the defence industry;

(vi) switches: the requirement by a country possessing a trade surplus with a partner country that an exporter from a third country should accept goods and services from the partner in payment for its exports to the first country;

(vii) unblocking of funds: where a country with exchange controls blocks the remittance of funds accumulated in local currency. In this case these funds may be used either by the firm concerned to buy local products, or transferred to another firm for the same purpose. The local products may then be exported.

Barter typically involves primary products or standardized manufactures' trade between a centrally planned socialist economy and a developing country, while counterpurchase is the dominant form of countertrade between developed and developing countries (Casson and Chukujama (1991)).

The risks associated with countertrade are higher than for multilateral trade, as are the negotiation costs, while only about one in 10 countertrade arrangements are finalized and executed (Lecraw (1988)). In particular, moral hazard is often acute, with only high risks being insured: not least because at least one of the countries involved is likely to be afforded high-country-risk status by banks and insurers.

Countertrade is identified with countries exerting stringent limits on foreign equity ownership, although some countries may require some level of foreign capital participation (Lecraw (1988)). The free-market type of ventures analogous to those in countertrade, such as foreign direct investment, joint ventures, licensing and technical service agreements are often prohibited or discouraged by those countries favouring countertrade. A theoretical comparison of the economic efficiency of countertrade with that of multilateral trade (and freedom in foreign equity participation) suggests the latter is almost invariably superior (Casson and Chukujama (1991)). However, countertrade is often seen as the only feasible method of conducting trade in the absence of political and economic reform within the centrally planned socialist economies and developing economies. Also, because the world economic system is not perfect, beset as it is with imperfections in capital markets, incomplete and asymmetric information, incomplete forward and contingent markets for risk-bearing, transport costs, and imperfect final product markets (barriers to entry, including the existence of government-imposed imperfections), countertrade improves the allocation of resources and output generated. Furthermore, the use of countertrade may lead to reductions in certain of these imperfections through information flows and beneficial experience effects, such as increasing trust between parties.

The economic conditions disposing countries to adopt countertrade, in particular counterpurchase, are the degree of commodity concentration of exports, country indebtedness and official policy stance promoting countertrade, while those favouring buy-back are restrictions on foreign equity ownership, a reputation for low-quality goods and low indigenous technological capacity (Casson and Chukujama (1991)). The firm-level factors promoting countertrade are complex, but firms that are flexible with respect to the form of international business may be best able to benefit from engaging in countertrade. (See also United Nations Food and Agriculture Organization (1986).)

Countries most engaged in countertrade can be placed in four groups: (i) the countries of Eastern Europe; (ii) low and middle income countries, especially those with balance-of-payments deficits following the oil crises of the 1970s, and countertrade as promoted by China; (iii) oil-exporting countries with balance of-payments problems needing to finance imports without visibly exceeding the Organization of Petroleum Exporting Countries' export quotas; and (iv) high-income countries employing industrial offsets, especially in defence-related industries (Lecraw (1988)).

As with multilateral trade, countertrade has its own associated institutional framework. Exporters can pursue negotiations and contractual obligations through in-house countertrade units, such as an export department or countertrade subsidiary. External countertrade intermediaries exist to perform the same functions and give advice, while banks are able to finance countertrade transactions when goods are not exchanged simultaneously; these last operations have been problematic for banks more familiar with orthodox trade finance (Lecraw (1988)).

2.6.4 International intra-firm trade

It is not in respect of the mechanics of the trade process that intra-firm trade differs from multilateral trade between independent exporters and importers. While the institutional arrangements adopted may in some way reflect the existence of a long-term relationship between the parties, the observance of export and import regulations and the need for appropriate financial arrangements will still be present.

The distinctive feature of intra-firm trade, especially in an international context, is the scope that exists for the firm to set prices that may not align with those that would exist between independent importers and exporters. This is recognized as a source of inaccuracy in international trade statistics, as are countertrade practices (see General Agreement on Tariffs and Trade (1987)). The setting of prices between divisions of the same firm (or firms within the same multinational group) is known as transfer pricing. As a rule there is no reason to expect that transfer prices will be the same as those set between independent traders for comparable products; it is possible that transfer prices may better reflect and promote the efficient use of resources, because there may not be the same problems of inter-firm bargaining and pricing in imperfect markets. It is also possible that no comparable product exists, because, especially in intermediate-product trade, inputs may be highly specialized (Rugman and Eden (1985b), Eden (1985)).

The growth of intra-firm trade has been reviewed in Casson and Associates, (1986). A number of studies have suggested that within the world's largest firms the proportion of intra-firm trade in visibles is substantial: an average of 50 per cent for those in high research-intensity industries, 37 per cent in medium research-intensity industries and 6 per cent in the least research intensive industries (Dunning and Pearce (1981)). Most assessments of the degree of intra-firm trade are restricted to visibles trade; they measure only exports from the parent to affiliates and do not include affiliate exports to the parent and to other affiliates. This fact may or may not seriously misrepresent the intra-firm trade propensity of multinationals, but it will lead to underestimates of the importance of intra-firm trade in world trade as a whole.

For developed country multinationals, intra-firm exports from the parent to affiliates are typically finished or nearly finished products. In the opposite direction they are usually intermediate products closer to the raw-material stage, or products with value added by low-wage labour. The importance of multinationals in the movement towards the increased international division of labour is therefore clearly evident (Casson and Associates (1986), MacCharles (1987)).

While contributing to increased multilateral trade, multinationals therefore have a degree of discretion over the prices charged, quite unlike independent traders. This discretion extends to intra-firm service trade, such as payments for licences and management services that are less well documented but arguably open to even further discretion than trade in visibles. With intra-firm trade comes scope for the strategic pricing of trade, termed transfer-price manipulation. The objectives of the multinational are thought to be the maximization of profit to the firm as a whole, or global profit maximization and the reduction of risk attaching to this profit. Because the multinational has linked operations in different countries it can seize the opportunity to vary prices on intra-firm trade to achieve worldwide goals (Rugman and Eden (1985a)). The external incentives to engage in transfer price manipulation include differences in corporate tax rates between countries, tariffs on imports, exchange risks, and risks arising from the perception of locally recorded profits as excessive, either by governments, or rivals (encouraging entry) or internally by the local workforce pursuing wage increases, or a joint-venture partner wishing to secure a higher share of the returns (Caves (1982) Chapter 8).

Transfer price manipulation is subject to internal administrative and external limitations (Grimwade (1989) Chapter 4); however, when the motives for transfer price manipulation are systematic by country (such as tariffs and foreign-exchange risks) the impact on exchange rates could be significant, especially for developing countries.

2.7

Exchange Rates

2.7.1 Introduction

The price of foreign currency in terms of domestic currency is known as the rate of exchange and is determined by supply and demand. From the discussion of multilateral trade in Chapter 2.6 it is evident that, broadly speaking, the demand for a country's currency represents the foreign demand for its output and assets (both real and financial), while the supply of its currency results from the country's residents' demand for foreign output and assets. A component of the demand for currency is the official intervention conducted by central banks aimed at influencing the exchange rate itself.

At the international level, as at the national level, currency is demanded as a means of payment and as a store of wealth. Those countries with output and assets favoured by international markets will tend to experience rising exchange rates in the absence of official intervention to the contrary and vice versa. The control of the exchange rate is therefore an expenditure-switching device although, in contrast to tariffs or export subsidies, it acts in an across-the-board manner on all traded items.

Developments that have taken place in the international monetary system have rendered anachronistic the expression of exchange rates with respect to the dollar alone. It is important to assess the performance of a currency against those of the main trading partners. The effective exchange rate fulfils this function, being a trade-weighted index of exchange rates with respect to a basket of currencies. Also taking the form of an index is the real exchange rate, which constitutes a measure of the competitiveness of domestic output relative to foreign outputs. It is calculated using a suitable price index for domestic output divided by a comparable index of foreign prices converted into domestic currency using the effective exchange rate. When the domestic inflation rate is higher than the world inflation rate, the domestic currency must depreciate in value. The real exchange rate is constant when this depreciation exactly offsets the inflation differential.

So an appreciation in the real exchange rate signifies a fall in the competitiveness of domestic relative to foreign outputs. Convention varies in the expression of this measure, however, with some inverting the numerator and denominator (World Bank (1987) Chapter 6). A further variant of the real exchange rate employs a price index for non-traded outputs divided by a price index for tradables. For a country unable to influence world prices, a depreciating real exchange rate of this type measures changes in the relative price signals to switch production into tradables (from non-tradables) and consumption out of tradables and into non-tradables. Accordingly it is a useful concept when assessing the likely balance-of-payments effects of exchange-rate changes. Goods (or services) that are subject to quantitative restrictions become non-traded, because domestic price is set by domestic (rather than world) supply and demand. The two variants of the real exchange rate do not necessarily move together (World Bank (1987) Chapter 6). The real exchange rate measures only price competitiveness, rather than non-price competitiveness, which is particularly important in certain industries.

To appreciate why the present exchange-rate system has evolved to require the complexity of measures noted above, the following sections overview the problems of the international monetary system and the shortcomings of alternative exchange-rate regimes.

2.7.2   Fixed exchange rates

The Bretton Woods Conference in 1944 introduced the World Bank, the International Monetary Fund and the International Trade Organization (whose charter remained unratified and whose function was assumed by the General Agreement on Tariffs and Trade). The International Monetary Fund was charged with world monetary arrangements, and the establishment of a superior means of international adjustment to the gold standard. The gold standard relied on the adequacy of price flexibility to correct imbalances in the balance of payments; in view of the inflexibility of prices the consequence was unemployment in deficit countries (Aliber (1983) Chapter 3).

The Bretton Woods System, as it came to be known, established a regime of fixed exchange rates (in the form of adjustable pegged rates). Under this, national central banks were required to intervene in the foreign-exchange market, buying or selling the national currency against official foreign-exchange reserves to maintain the national currency within the permitted deviations (plus or minus 1 per cent) from an agreed value against the United States dollar. This agreed value was known as the par value or parity. The pegging of currencies' par values against the dollar provided a high degree of exchange-rate stability; the confidence this generated encouraged the expansion of multilateral trade.

It was not intended that the dollar, or any national currency, should bear the burden of providing liquidity as the world economy grew. This was to be provided by gold and national-currency subscriptions to the International Monetary Fund. In practice the borrowing facility this created was under-utilized; the role of the dollar rose not least because it was in plentiful supply following Marshall Aid to Europe, and the continued United States balance-of-payments deficit which was contributed to by United States foreign direct investment outflows to Europe and military expenditure abroad (especially in Vietnam). By the 1960s the United States dollar was the leading component of central banks' reserves. After 1959 the stock of dollars held by foreign residents (and therefore United States liabilities) exceeded United States gold reserves (United States assets). By the end of the 1960s there was much anxiety over the convertibility of the dollar into gold.

The International Monetary Fund introduced a new currency to provide liquidity, called the Special Drawing Right, of which the first issue was in 1970. Originally its value was fixed in terms of gold but today it is expressed as a weighted basket of currencies. The Special Drawing Right's main use is for official transactions although its use for private transactions is intended to grow. The use of the dollar as a reserve asset has also declined, while the price of gold has been able to rise since its official price was abolished in 1976, thereby allowing the value of gold exchange reserves to rise.

The Bretton Woods exchange-rate system presided over the growth of world trade from the end of the Second World War to late 1971. In August 1971 the convertibility of the dollar into gold was suspended and most major countries began floating their currencies (see Section 2.7.3). The meeting at the Smith-sonian Institute in December 1971 gave rise to the Smithsonian Agreement, an attempt to re-establish a pegged exchange-rate system through realigning the value of the dollar against world currencies, and allowing a wider (2.25 per cent) margin about parities. Nevertheless, currencies later returned to floating, the pound doing so in June 1972.

The pegged exchange-rate system is recognized to have a number of advan-tages: (i) the stability of exchange rates allows firms to expand international trade and therefore encourages multilateral trade; (ii) it does not confer any undue advantages on firms with multinational operations over independent exporters and importers: a pegged exchange rate reduces the incentives for opportunism, whereby with floating exchange rates multinationals can, for example, use their short-term funds to speculate by instructing foreign affiliates to lead or lag payments or receipts between member firms in the group (Caves (1982) Chapter 6); and (iii) a pegged exchange rate tends to align inflation rates between countries.

The failings of the Bretton Woods System were not necessarily intrinsic to a system of pegged exchange rates. The central problems were the inadequacy of world liquidity and the fact that the burden of adjustment fell on countries with balance-of-payments deficits (those with net-currency outflows). This problem was foreseen by Keynes, who had proposed an alternative system at Bretton Woods whereby creditor nations (who had run balance-of-payments surpluses) were to be charged interest on accounts in credit at the International Monetary Fund along with debtor nations (with balance-of-payments deficits) on overdrafts. The burden on deficit countries to pursue deflationary policies would therefore be mitigated by surplus countries given an incentive to reflate.

The maintenance of the pegged exchange-rate parities, therefore, depended in the long term upon deficit countries pursuing deflationary domestic macroeconomic policies, and in the short term on drawing on official reserves to support the domestic currency's exchange rate. A devaluation was authorized only when a long-term fundamental balance-of-payments disequilibrium was demonstrable to the International Monetary Fund; devaluation itself constituted a substantial shock to the economy concerned. The effect of speculation is known to exacerbate these problems; as Tew (1988) has pointed out, an adjustable peg system is the speculator's paradise because the direction of any possible parity change can be guessed with almost complete certainty.

2.7.3   Floating exchange rates

A floating exchange-rate system is in a sense a default regime when compared with pegged exchange rates. There are two possible variants: a freely floating exchange-rate system and a managed floating system. The former, where the exchange rate is determined entirely by market forces, has rarely occurred for any appreciable length of time (though see Aliber (1983) Chapter 2). The latter involves national central banks exercising their discretion over whether to intervene to reduce upward or downward pressure on the current exchange rate. While a freely floating system requires central banks to hold no exchange reserves, a managed floating regime is not so economical, as short-term fluctuations in exchange rates will have to be evened out through official intervention.

The advantages of a floating exchange-rate regime largely occur at the official level, while the disadvantages impinge most on exporters and importers. Ideally a floating exchange rate should reflect the real relative demand for goods, services and assets between countries, while relieving central banks of having to give slavish support to unrealistic exchange rates. A floating rate tends to equilibrate total currency outflows with inflows (purchase of foreign output and assets with the sale of domestic output and assets, respectively), as (for a net currency outflow) exports and home assets become cheaper in terms of foreign currency while imports and foreign assets become more expensive in terms of domestic currency, and vice versa for an inflow.

However, to conserve official exchange reserves, a government may seek to control the exchange rate indirectly by controlling domestic interest rates on assets denominated in the home currency. To support the exchange rate this would involve raising interest rates to make home assets more attractive to foreign residents, who will buy the home currency to purchase the assets. This can distort domestic expenditure patterns and, if it persists, reduce the level of domestic investment. For the mechanisms by which automatic balance-of-payments adjustment and the equilibration of the exchange rate are thought to occur (via the income-adjustment process for Keynesians and the monetary stock adjustment process for monetarists) see Crockett (1977) Chapter 3, Krueger (1983) Chapter 3, Tew (1988) Chapter 4.

2.7.4   Forward currency markets and exchange-rate volatility

Increased use of forward currency markets is thought to have been a further result of the exchange-rate instability prevalent since the early 1970s. Nevertheless, studies by Grassman (1973a), (1973b) and by Carse and Wood (1979) showed that only a minority of Swedish and British trade was covered forward (for Sweden 6.0 per cent and 6.8 per cent of imports and exports respectively, and for the United Kingdom 13.5 per cent and 1.9 per cent of imports and exports respectively).

Where an importer has agreed to be invoiced in the importer's domestic currency (the foreign currency) the exporter is liable to receive an uncertain amount on conversion into the exporter's domestic currency at the date payment is made, if the spot market is relied on. This risk can be eliminated for a known cost: that of making a forward contract to sell foreign currency for domestic currency. In those instances where the precise date for future payment is not known, an option contract can be made to sell foreign currency for domestic currency within an agreed period of any length desired in the future. (For a practical example see Bass and Geddes (1988).)

It appears that the greater part of the variability in exchange rates is determined by capital flows rather than by differences in the relative rates of inflation and productivity growth; consequently, changes in exchange rates may often appear to owe relatively little to underlying economic factors. For example, the nominal effective exchange rate of the United States dollar appreciated by around 55 per cent between 1980 and 1985, while the real exchange rate changed by a similar magnitude. Such large changes suggest at least some degree of currency misalignment (United Nations Department of International Economic and Social Affairs (1988) Chapter 3). However, it is imperative to distinguish between short-term and portfolio capital flows and direct foreign-investment flows, the last of which would certainly be expected to contribute to the economic adjustment of the countries concerned (see Dunning (1985)).

The effects of exchange-rate volatility on international trade are reviewed in United Nations Department of International Economic and Social Affairs (1986)

Chapter 4, Annex 4. The results of a number of studies suggest that changes in real exchange rates alter the level of uncertainty in international trade and so adversely affect trade flows, either in terms of volume or volume growth. Exchange-rate theory shows there can be a tendency for exchange rates to alter proportionately more in the short than in the long run; so variability will often be greater, the shorter the period considered (see Krueger (1983) Chapter 4). In these circumstances a system of managed floating is probably the best choice, while cooperation as under the European Monetary System will further assist the process of international trade.

2.7.5   The European Monetary System

The use of floating exchange rates introduces uncertainty into international transactions; exporting firms find it difficult to predict what the future prices of their exports are likely to be, which interferes with the establishment of foreign customers. To some extent the use of forward exchange markets (see the previous section) assists; however, these do not solve the problem of developing foreign markets over the medium and long term. This is an especially significant problem for countries that trade intensively with each other, and particularly for those pursuing economic integration, such as those within the European community. Because of this, after the disappearance of pegged exchange rates under the Bretton Woods System, members of the European community have made attempts to limit intra-European Community exchange-rate volatility.

The European community has also had a view towards the long-term goal of monetary union (or economic and monetary union) since the Hague Summit of 1969. To attain this it is a necessary condition that there should be a progressive stabilization of European Community members' exchange rates. It is not actually necessary to have a single currency to achieve monetary union: as long as exchange rates are fixed then goods, services and assets will effectively be priced in one currency.

The first step was in April 1972 with the 'snake in the tunnel': the tunnel being the permitted bands for fluctuation under the short-lived International Monetary Fund Smithsonian Agreement, the snake being the commitment by European community members to further maintain their cross-exchange-rate fluctuations with respect to each other within 2.5 per cent bands. Certain non-European Community members also followed the arrangement; however, by 1978 the only remaining members were the Federal Republic of Germany, Benelux, Denmark and associate member Norway. The snake was superseded by the exchange-rate mechanism of the European Monetary System (EMS).

The European Monetary System, launched in 1979, provided for:

(i)   the European Currency Unit (ECU) with a value given by the weighted average of a basket of European Community currencies. This now includes all the currencies of the European Community (since September 1989 when the Spanish peseta and the Portuguese escudo joined). The weights of each currency within the basket are intended to reflect each country's 'economic weight' in the system. They are reviewed every five years and whenever the European Currency Unit is enlarged to include further currencies;

(ii) an exchange rate mechanism (ERM) based on a system of fixed parities with, in the case of seven out of the nine Exchange Rate Mechanism members, margins of plus or minus 2.25 per cent of the European Currency Unit;

(iii) short term credit facilities;

(iv) the European Monetary Cooperation Fund (EMCF) as the official holder of non-European Community reserve currencies, also seen as an embryo European central bank.

Each currency has a central (or par) rate, which is a target rate against the European Currency Unit and therefore against each of the other currencies in the mechanism. When a currency joins the Exchange Rate Mechanism, or when there is a realignment, each currency is assigned a central rate in relation to the European Currency Unit. This is then used to establish the central rates against all the other participating currencies. Changes to any central rate must be agreed by all members and cannot be made unilaterally.

The margins of fluctuation for each currency with respect to its own parity in the Exchange Rate Mechanism differ between two groups of countries: the 'narrow' band of 2.25 per cent applies to all countries except for the United Kingdom and Spain, who are allowed the 'wide' band of approximately 6 per cent with respect to the European Currency Unit and the other participating currencies. However, these bands are nominal; for arithmetical symmetry the actual ones used are fractionally different. A bilateral parity grid can therefore be derived for each currency with respect to each other's currency in the Exchange Rate Mechanism. Sterling became a member of the Exchange Rate Mechanism on 8 October 1990, entering with the provision of wide bands. On joining, sterling's central rates were, to give two examples, £1 = 2.95000 deutschmark and £1 = 9.89389 French franc.

A currency is likely to reach an effective upper or lower limiting margin before the theoretical maximum deviation in cross-exchange rates is reached. The hypothetical maximum deviation would be the sum of any two currencies' maximum deviations with respect to the European Currency Unit, but in practice the effective limits are determined by the need for each currency to remain within its bands against all other Exchange Rate Mechanism currencies simultaneously. So, for example, sterling may not be more than 6 per cent above the weakest currency or 6 per cent below the strongest. Consequently its effective limits with respect to other currencies will be constrained to within 6 per cent.

One of the advantages of the Exchange Rate Mechanism over the Bretton Woods System is that it spreads the burden of maintaining exchange rates within permitted ranges. If one currency reaches its limits against another, the central banks of both countries (the strong and the weak currency) have equal obligations to buy and sell at the limited rates. This effectively prevents movement outside the margins. Furthermore, any movement of a currency beyond 75 per cent of its nominal maximum permitted divergence against the European Currency Unit (called the divergence threshold) requires official intervention.

Under the Exchange Rate Mechanism the deutschmark is widely regarded as the de facto 'numeraire' or benchmark currency, in much the same way as the dollar was the *de facto* numeraire in the Bretton Woods System (although gold was intended to be the rightful 'numeraire'). Therefore economic reports on other currencies' performance are commonly made with respect to the deutschmark. However, a problem for the European Monetary System, as for the 'snake' before it, is that when the exchange value of the dollar is expected to fall, international wealth holders buy the strongest European Community currency, the deutschmark, so straining the official foreign-exchange reserves of other European Community countries to maintain their currency's value with respect to the European Currency Unit. To address this problem the European Monetary System provides for each central bank to have access not only to its own foreign-exchange reserves but also to four credit facilities, of which the most important is the Very Short Term Facility (VSTF). Under this last arrangement each central bank makes its own currency available without limit to any other central bank on short-term credit.

The last major realignment of parities was in January 1987, while in January 1990 Italy moved from the wide to the narrow band. If a currency is at its ceiling or floor with respect to the European Currency Unit for a protracted period any realignment is likely to cover not just this currency but also others, so spreading the adjustment costs. This stands in marked contrast to the practice under the Bretton Woods System.

Realignments have become increasingly rare within the European Monetary System, but where they do occur they have mainly been necessitated by the effect of inflation differentials between currencies. To date these differentials have become reduced as Exchange Rate Mechanism economies have converged over time. Even so, the management of the European Monetary System where member countries have divergent inflation rates is still a matter of some controversy (see Corden (1985) Chapter 10, and United Nations Department of International Economic and Social Affairs (1985) Chapter 4).

2.7.6 Multiple exchange rates

The foregoing discussion of exchange rates assumes that all foreign-exchange transactions are executed at a single official or market-determined rate of exchange. In practice governments, and their exchange-control authorities, may fix different permitted rates of exchange for different classes of transactions as a method of direct control on expenditure.

Multiple exchange rates as a means of exchange control are identified with centrally planned socialist economies and with developing countries. Typically complete control over all dealings in foreign exchange is maintained, with a requirement that all exporters sell their foreign-exchange earnings to a central board from which importers are required to buy their foreign currency. Such schemes often impose an unfavourable rate of exchange for imports of luxury goods and for the tourist trade, with a favourable rate of exchange for basic items and business service transactions (Sodersten (1980) Chapter 25). In terms of trade policy such a system of multiple exchange rates is equivalent to a scheme of import tariffs and subsidies on different classes of goods.

Perhaps the best-known but rather different example of multiple exchange rates is the 'green' currency system used by the European Community for the setting of prices in agricultural trade. The common agricultural policy restricts agricultural imports from non-European Community countries and sets minimum prices (or intervention prices) for agricultural produce. These prices are fixed annually by the Community in terms of European Currency Units. Because of the variability of market exchange rates (see Sections 2.7.3 to 2.7.5) agricultural prices would become unstable in member countries, so administered rates specifically for agricultural trade (green exchange rates) are used which do not follow the foreign exchange markets.

When green rates do diverge from market rates a problem is caused because, unlike multiple exchange rates used for exchange control, producers do not actually trade at the green rates. Border levies and restitutions (monetary compensatory amounts) are applied to goods traded between member countries to equate the price received by exporters in different countries (Hine (1985) Chapter 5). There are some 40 green rates employed by the European Community. Such a system eventually causes national support prices to diverge considerably between countries as the gap between green and market exchange rates widens: there is no automatic adjustment mechanism for green exchange rates. The European Monetary System, however, has operated to reduce the degree of divergence between market and green rates.

References

Ady, P. (1980): 'Developed Countries' Attitudes to the Integrated Programme of Commodities and the Common Fund', Chapter 5 in Sengupta, A (ed.): *Commodities, Finance and Trade: Issues in North South Negotiations*. London: Frances Pinter.

Aliber, R.Z. (1983): *The International Money Game* (4th edn). London: Macmillan.

Baldwin, R.E (1987): 'GATT Reform: Selected Issues', Chapter 15 in Kierzkowski, H. (ed.): *Protection and Competition in International Trade*. Oxford: Blackwell.

Baldwin, R.E. (1988): *Trade Policy in a Changing World Economy*. Hemel Hempstead: Harvester-Wheatsheaf.

Baldwin, R.E. (1989): 'Structural Change and Patterns of International Trade', Chapter 2 in Black, J. and Macbean, A.I. (eds): *Causes of Changes in the Structure of International Trade 1960–85*. London: Macmillan.

Baldwin, R.E. and Richardson, J.D. (1986): *International Trade and Finance: Readings* (3rd edn). Boston: Little, Brown and Company.

Bass, R.M.V. and Geddes, M. (1988): 'Credit and Finance', Chapter 2.6 in Brooke, M.Z. and Buckley, P.J.: *Handbook of International Trade*. London: Macmillan.

Bhagwati, J. (1988): *Protectionism*. Cambridge, Mass.: MIT Press.

Black, J. (1959): 'Arguments for Tariffs', *Oxford Economic Papers*, 11, pp. 191–208.

Black, J. and Hindley, B. (1980): *Current Issues in Commercial Policy and Diplomacy*. London: Macmillan.

Black, J. and MacBean, A.I. (1989): *Causes of Changes in the Structure of International Trade. 1960–85*. London: Macmillan.

Black, J. and Winters, L.A. (1983): *Policy and Performance in International Trade*. London: Macmillan.

Blum, C. (1988): 'The Multi-Fibre Arrangement', Chapter 6.6 in Brooke, M.Z. and Buckley, P.J.: *Handbook of International Trade*. London: Macmillan.

Borner, S. (1986): *Internationalization of Industry: An Assessment in the Light of a Small Open Economy – Switzerland*. Berlin: Springer-Verlag.

Brooke, M.Z. (1988a): 'Regional Organizations; Central and South America', Chapter 7.3 in Brooke, M.Z. and Buckley, P.J.: *Handbook of International Trade*. London: Macmillan.

Brooke, M.Z. (1988b): 'Regional Organizations: Africa and the Middle East ', Chapter 7.5 in Brooke, M.Z. and Buckley, P.J.: *Handbook of International Trade*. London: Macmillan.

Brooke, M.Z. (1988c): 'Regional Organizations: the Far East', Chapter 7.6 in Brooke, M.Z. and Buckley, P.J.: *Handbook of International Trade*. London: Macmillan.

Brooke, M.Z. and Buckley, P.J. (1988): *Handbook of International Trade*. London: Macmillan.

Buckley, P.J. and Clegg, J. (eds) (1990a): *Multinational Enterprises in Less Developed Countries*. London: Macmillan.

Buckley, P.J. and Clegg, J. (1990b): 'Introduction and Statement of the Issues', Chapter 1 'in Buckley, P.J. and Clegg, J. (eds): *Multinational Enterprises in Less Developed Countries*. London: Macmillan.

Burton, F.N. (1984): *Contemporary Trade*. Deddington: Philip Allan.

Butt Philip, A. (1989): 'European Border Controls: Who Needs Them?', *Royal Institute for International Affairs. Discussion Paper*, no. 19. London: RIIA.

Carse, S. and Wood, G.E. (1979): 'Currency Invoicing and Forward Covering: Risk-Reducing Techniques in British Foreign Trade', Chapter 7 in Martin, J.P. and Smith, A. (eds): *Trade and Payments Adjustments Under Flexible Exchange Rates*. London: Macmillan.

Casson, M.C. and Associates (1986): *Multinationals and World Trade: Vertical Integration and the Division of Labour in World Industries*. London: Allen & Unwin.

Casson, M.C. and Chukujama, F. (1990): 'Countertrade: Theory and Evidence', Chapter 7 in Buckley, P.J. and Clegg, J. (eds).: *Multinational Enterprises in Less Developed Countries*. London: Macmillan.

Caves, R.E. (1982): *Multinational Enterprise and Economic Analysis*. Cambridge: Cambridge University Press.

Caves, R.E. and Jones, R.W. (1985): *World Trade and Payments*. Boston: Little, Brown and Company.

Cecchini, P. with Catinat, M. and Jacquemin, J. (1988): *The European Challenge: 1992, the Benefits of a Single Market*. Aldershot: Wildwood House.

Chacholiades, M. (1981): *Principles of International Economics*. New York: McGraw-Hill.

Choi, Y.-P., Chung, H.S. and Marian, N. (1985): *The Multi-Fibre Arrangement in Theory and Practice*. London: Frances Pinter.

Clegg, J. (1987): *Multinational Enterprise and World Competition: A Comparative Study of the USA, Japan, the UK, Sweden and West Germany*. London: Macmillan.

Commission of the European Communities (1987a): *The External Trade of the European Community*, European File, 1/87, January. Luxembourg: Office for Official Publications of the European Communities.

Commission of the European Communities (1987b): *The European Community and the Third World*, European File, 15/87, October. Luxembourg: Office for Official Publications of the European Communities.

Commission of the European Communities (1987c): *Generalized Preferences for the Third World*, European File, 16/87, October. Luxembourg: Office for Official Publications of the European Communities.

Commission of the European Communities (1988): *Europe Without Frontiers – Completing the Internal Market* (2nd edn), 3/88. Luxembourg: Office for Official Publications of the European Communities.

Corden, W.M. (1971): *The Theory of Protection*. Oxford: Clarendon Press.

Corden, W.M. (1974): *Trade Policy and Economic Welfare*. Oxford: Clarendon Press.

Corden, W.M. (1985): *Inflation, Exchange Rates and the World Economy: Lectures on International Monetary Economics* (3rd edn). Oxford: Clarendon Press.

Crockett, A. (1977): *International Money*. Sunbury-on-Thames: Nelson.

Curzon, G. (1965): *Multilateral Commercial Diplomacy*. London: Michael Joseph.

Curzon Price, V. (1982): 'The European Free Trade Association', Chapter 5 in El Agraa, A.M. (ed.): *International Economic Integration*. London: Macmillan.

Davies, H. (1988): 'Marketing Knowledge Abroad', Chapter 3.1 in Brooke, M.Z. and Buckley, P.J.: *Handbook of International Trade*. London: Macmillan.

Drew, J. (1979): *Doing Business in the European Community*. London: Butterworths.

Dunning, J.H. (1985): 'Introduction', in Dunning, J.H. (ed.): *Multinational Enterprises, Economic Structure and International Competitiveness*. Chichester: Wiley.

Dunning, J.H. and Pearce, R.D. (1981): *The World's Largest Industrial Companies*. London: Gower Press.

Eaton, J. (1986): 'Credit Policy and International Competition', Chapter 6 in Krugman, P.R. (ed.): *Strategic Trade Policy and the New International Economics*. Cambridge, Mass.: MIT Press.

Economist Intelligence Unit (1990a): *World Commodity Outlook 1990 – Industrial Raw Materials*. London: EIU.

Economist Intelligence Unit (1990b): *World Commodity Outlook 1990 – Food, Feedstuffs and Beverages*. London: EIU.

Eden, L. (1985): 'The Microeconomics of Transfer Pricing', Chapter 2 in Rugman, A.M. and Eden, L. (eds): *Multinationals and Transfer Pricing*. Beckenham: Croom Helm.

El Agraa, A.M. (ed.) (1982a): *International Economic Integration*. London: Macmillan.

El Agraa, A.M. (1982b): 'ASEAN and Overall Conclusions', Chapter 13 in El Agraa, A.M. (ed.): *International Economic Integration*. London: Macmillan.

El Agraa, A.M. and Hojman, D.E. (1982): 'The Andean Pact', Chapter 11 in El Agraa, A.M. (ed.): *International Economic Integration*. London: Macmillan.

Emerson, M. and others (1988): *The Economics of 1992*. Oxford: Oxford University Press.

Enderwick, P. (ed.) (1988): *Multinational Service Firms*. London: Routledge.

Finch, M.H.J. (1982): 'The Latin American Free Trade Association', Chapter 10 in El Agraa, A.M. (ed.): *International Economic Integration*. London: Macmillan.

GATT Study Group (1986): 'The Way Forward', Chapter 14 in Baldwin, R.E. and Richardson, J.D. (eds): *International Trade and Finance* (3rd edn). Boston: Little, Brown and Company.

Geiger, T. (1988): *The Future of the International System: The United States and the World Political Economy*. London: Unwin Hyman.

Gemmell, N. (ed.) (1987): *Surveys in Development Economics*. Oxford: Blackwell.

General Agreement on Tariffs and Trade (1980): *International Trade 1979/80*. Geneva: GATT.

General Agreement on Tariffs and Trade (1987): *International Trade 1986/87*. Geneva: GATT.

General Agreement on Tariffs and Trade (annual): *International Trade*, Geneva: GATT.

Gill, S. and Law, D. (1988): *The Global Political Economy: Perspectives, Problems and Policies*. Hemel Hempstead: Harvester-Wheatsheaf.

Gordon Ashworth, F. (1984): *International Commodity Control*. Beckenham: Croom Helm.

Graham, E.M. (1990): 'Strategic Trade Policy and the Multinational Enterprise in Developing Countries', Chapter 4 in Buckley, P.J. and Clegg, J. (eds): *Multinational Enterprises in Less Developed Countries*. London: Macmillan.

Grassman, S. (1973a): *Exchange Reserves and the Financial Structure of Foreign Trade*. Farnborough: Saxon House.

Grassman, S. (1973b): 'A Fundamental Symmetry in International Payments Patterns', *Journal of International Economics*, 3.

Greenaway, D. (1983): *International Trade Policy: From Tariffs to the New Protectionism*. London: Macmillan.

Greenaway, D. and Milner, C. (1986): *The Economics of Intra-Industry Trade*. Oxford: Blackwell.

Greenaway, D. and Milner, C. (1987): 'Trade Theory and the Less Developed Countries', Chapter 1 in Gemmel, N. (ed.): *Surveys in Development Economics*. Oxford: Blackwell.

Grimwade, N. (1989): *International Trade: New Patterns of Trade, Protection and Investment*. London: Routledge.

Grossman, G.M. (1986): 'Strategic Export Promotion: A Critique', Chapter 3 in Krugman, P.R. (ed.): *Strategic Trade Policy and the New International Economics*. Cambridge, Mass.: MIT Press.

Grubel, H.G. and Lloyd, P.J. (1975): *Intra-Industry Trade: The Theory and Measurement of International Trade in Differentiated Products*. London: Macmillan.

Helpman, E. and Krugman, P.R. (1986): *Market Structure and Foreign Trade*. Cambridge, Mass.: MIT Press.

Hindley, B. (1980): 'Voluntary Export Restraints and Article XIX of the General Agreement on Tariffs and Trade', Chapter 4 in Black, J. and Hindley, B. (eds): *Current Issues in Commercial Policy and Diplomacy*. London: Macmillan.

Hine, R.C. (1985): *The Political Economy of European Trade: An Introduction to the Trade Policies of the EEC*. Brighton: Wheatsheaf.

Hoogvelt, A. with Puxty, A.G. (1987): *Multinational Enterprise: An Encyclopedic Dictionary of Concepts and Terms*. London: Macmillan.

International Monetary Fund (1977): *Balance of Payments Manual (4th edn)*. Washington, D.C.: IMF.

International Monetary Fund (annual): *Balance of Payments Statistics*. Washington, D.C.: IMF.

International Monetary Fund (annual): *Direction of Trade Statistics*. Washington, D.C.: IMF.

International Monetary Fund (annual): *Government Finance Statistics Yearbook*. Washington, D.C.: IMF.

Johns, R.A. (1985): *International Trade Theories and the Evolving International Economy*. London: Frances Pinter.

Jones, C.A. (1983): *The North-South Dialogue: A Brief History*. London: Frances Pinter.

Kakabadse, M.A. (1987): *International Trade in Services: Prospects for Liberalization in the 1990s*. The Atlantic Institute for International Affairs, Atlantic Paper No. 64. London: Croom Helm.

Kierzkowski, H. (1987): *Protection and Competition in International Trades*. Oxford: Blackwell.

Kindleberger, C.P. (1987): *International Capital Movements*. Cambridge: Cambridge University Press.

Kirkpatrick, C. (1987): 'Trade Policy and Industrialization in LDSs', Chapter 2 in Gemmel, N. (ed.): *Surveys in Development Economics*. Oxford: Blackwell.

Krueger, A.O. (1983): *Exchange Rate Determination*. Cambridge: Cambridge University Press.

Krugman, P.R. (ed.) (1986): *Strategic Trade Policy and the New International Economics*. Cambridge, Mass.: MIT Press.

Leamer, E.E. (1984): *Sources of International Comparative Advantage*. Cambridge, Mass.: MIT Press.

Lecraw, D.J. (1988): 'Countertrade: A Form of Cooperative International Business Arrangement', Chapter 24 in Contractor, F.J. and Lorange, P. (eds): *Cooperative Strategies in International Business*. Lexington, Mass.: Lexington Books – D.C. Heath.

Lecraw, D.J. (1991): 'Factors Influencing Foreign Direct Investment by Transnational Corporations in Host Developing Countries: A Preliminary Report', Chapter 8 in Buckley, P.J. and Clegg, J. (eds): *Multinational Enterprises in Less Developed Countries*. London: Macmillan.

Lee, C.H. and Naya, S. (eds) (1988): *Trade and Investment in Services in the Asia-Pacific Region*. Centre for International Studies, Inha University, Korea.

Leonard, D. (1988): *Pocket Guide to the European Community*. Oxford and London: Blackwell and The Economist Publications Ltd.

Linder, S.B. (1961): *An Essay on Trade and Transformation*. New York: Wiley.

Lipsey, R.G. and York, R.C. (1988): *Evaluating the Free Trade Deal: A Guided Tour Through the Canada-US Agreement*, Policy Study No. 6. Toronto: C.D. Howe Institute.

MacBean, A.I. and Nguyen, D.T. (1987): *Commodity Policies: Problems and Prospects.* London: Croom Helm.

MacBean, A.I. (1988): 'The United Nations and Associated Bodies', Chapter 7.2 in Brooke, M.Z. and Buckley, P.J.: *Handbook of International Trade.* London: Macmillan

MacCharles, D.C. (1987): *Trade Among Multinationals: Intra-Industry Trade and National Competitiveness.* Beckenham: Croom Helm.

Marer, P. and Montias, J.M. (1982): 'The Council for Mutual Economic Assistance', Chapter 6 in El Agraa, A.M. (ed.): *International Economic Intergration.* London: Macmillan.

Martin, J.P. and Smith, A. (eds) (1979): *Trade and Payments Adjustment Under Flexible Exchange Rates.* London: Macmillan.

Meyer, F.V. (1978): *International Trade Policy.* London: Croom Helm.

Mirus, R. and Yeung, B. (1986): 'Economic Incentives for Countertrade', *Journal of International Business Studies*, 17, No. 3, pp. 27–39.

Mirza, H. (1988): 'The New International Economic Order', Chapter 1.6 in Brooke, M.Z. and Buckley, P.J.: *Handbook of International Trade.* London: Macmillan.

Moore, L. (1985): *The Growth and Structure of International Trade Since the Second World War.* Brighton: Wheatsheaf.

Negandhi, A.R. (ed.) (1986): *China's Trade with Industrialized Countries: Socio-Economic and Political Perspectives. Research in International Business and International Relations.* Greenwich, Conn.: JAI Press.

Organization for Economic Cooperation and Development (1984): *East-West Trade – Recent Development in Countertrade.* Paris: OECD.

Paliwoda, S.J. (1981): 'East-West Countertrade Arrangements: Barter, Compensation, Buyback and counterpurchase or "Parallel" Trade', *UMIST Occasional Paper*, No. 8105, March.

Paliwoda, S.J. (1988): 'The Socialist Countries of Europe', Chapter 5.7 in Brooke, M.Z. and Buckley, P.J.: *Handbook of International Trade.* London: Macmillan.

Pelkmans, J. and Winters, L.A. (1988): *Europe's Domestic Market*, Chatham House Papers, No. 43. Royal Institute of International Affairs, London: Routlege.

Robson, P. (1982): 'The West African Economic Community', Chapter 8 in El Agraa, A.M. (ed.): *International Economic Integration.* London: Macmillan.

Rugman, A.M. (1988a): 'The Free Trade Agreement and the Global Economy', *Business Quarterly*, Summer.

Rugman, A.M. (1988b): 'A Canadian Perspective on US Administered Protection and the Free Trade Agreement', *Maine Law Review*, 40 , pp. 305–24.

Rugman, A.M. and Anderson, A. (1987): *Administered Protection in America.* London: Croom Helm.

Rugman, A.M. and Eden, L. (eds) (1985a): *Multinationals and Transfer Pricing'.* Beckenham: Croom Helm.

Rugman, A.M. and Eden, L. (1985b): 'Introduction', Chapter 1 in Rugman, A.M. and Eden, L. (eds): *Multinational and Transfer Pricing'.* Beckenham: Croom Helm.

Rugman, A.M. and Verbeke, A. (1987/8): 'Trade Policy in the Asia-Pacific Region: a US-Japan Comparison', *Journal of Business Administration*, 17, Nos. 1 and 2, pp. 89–107.

Sampson, G.P. (1989): 'Structural Change: Accommodating Imports from Developing Countries', Chapter 7 in Black, J. and MacBean, A.I. (eds): *Causes of Changes in the Structure of International Trade 1960–85.* London: Macmillan.

Sengupta, A. (ed.) (1980): *Commodities, Finance and Trade: Issues in North-South Negotiations.* London: Frances Pinter.

Snape, R.H. (1982): 'The Importance of Frontier Barriers', Chapter 15 in Kierzkowski, H. (ed.): *Protection and Competition in International Trade.* Oxford: Blackwell.

Sodersten, B. (1980): *International Economics* (2nd edn). London: Macmillan.

Spero, J.E. (1981): *The Politics of International Economic Relations* (2nd edn). London: Allen and Unwin.

Tew, B. (1988): *The Evolution of the International Monetary System 1945–88* (4th edn). London: Hutchinson.

Tucker, K. and Sundberg, M. (1988): *International Trade in Services.* London: Routledge.

United Nations (annual): *Yearbook of International Trade Statistics.* New York: UN.

United Nations Conference on Trade and Development (1984): *Yearbook of International Commodity Statistics.* New York: UN.

United Nations Conference on Trade and Development (1987): *Handbook of International Trade and Development Statistics*, 1987 Supplement. Geneva: UNCTAD.

United Nations Department of International Economic and Social Affairs (annual): *World Economic Survey.* New York: United Nations.

United Nations, Food and Agriculture Organization (1986): *Commodity Review and Outlook*, FAO Economic and Social Development Series, No. 40. Rome: FAO.

United Nations Industrial Development Organization (annual): *Handbook of Industrial Statistics.* New York: UNIDO.

Utton, M.A. and Morgan, A.D. (1983): *Concentration and Foreign Trade*, National Institute for Economic and Social Research Occasional Papers, 35. Cambridge; Cambridge University Press.

Van Meerhaeghe, M.A.G. (1985): *International Economic Institutions.* Dordrecht: Martinus Nijhoff.

Vernon, R. (1970): *The Technology Factor in International Trade.* Columbia University Press.

Whichard, O.G. (1984): 'US International Trade and Investment in Services: Data Needs and Availability', *Bureau of Economic Analysis Staff Paper*, No. 41, US Department of Commerce, September.

Williams, V. (1988): 'The European Community', Chapter 7 in Brooke, M.Z. and Buckley, P.J.: *Handbook of International Trade.* London: Macmillan.

Williamson, J. (1983): *The Open Economy and the World Economy.* New York: Basic Books.

Witt, S.F. (1988): 'Tourism', Chapter 6.3 in Brooke, M.Z. and Buckley, P.J.: *Handbook of International Trade.* London: Macmillan.

World Bank (1983): 'The Outlook for Primary Commodities', *World Bank Staff Commodity Working Paper*, No. 9, January. Washington, D.C.: World Bank.

World Bank (1987): *World Development Report, 1987.* Oxford: Oxford University Press.

World Bank (1989): *World Development Report, 1989.* Oxford: Oxford University Press.

World Bank (annual): *World Development Report.* Oxford: Blackwell.

Part 3

Institutions of World Trade

Introduction

A feature of the international business environment is the rapid growth of organizations to stimulate, control and influence world trade and the economic performance. Most of this part is about international organizations, mainly founded since the Second World War. Even national institutions are changing their roles. Central banks may still see their main function to be safeguarding national economic health, but they are increasingly influenced by evidence that national economic health is inseparable from international. The time may well be near when a series of regular meetings of finance ministers is listed as a significant international regulatory institution in its own right.

Currently most of the literature concerns a specific body. In particular the World Bank, the International Monetary Fund, the General Agreement on Tariffs and Trade and the European Community have generated an extensive literature, much of it of general application. Among significant and recurring themes are:

(1) tensions between national aspirations and the principles of the international institutions, often laboriously developed;
(2) tensions between the richer and the poorer countries within an institution. (This particularly applies to regional organizations, but also to United Nations' affiliates like the General Agreement on Tariffs and Trade and the United Nations Conference on Trade and Development);
(3) tensions over the assumptions on which judgements are being made (for instance within the International Monetary Fund and the World Bank over the criteria for judging national economic policies);
(4) controversies over priorities;
(5) controversies over the time-scale of reforms.

We start with the multilateral institutions, in which eligibility for membership is not restricted to a region.

Contents

3.1

Multilateral Institutions

Most of the institutions in this chapter are affiliates of the United Nations and, on principle, any country is eligible for membership. Chapter 3.3 ends with two organizations with a more restricted membership which is, nevertheless, not regional in character.

The main significance of the International Monetary Fund, the World Bank and the other bodies examined here for experts on international business is that together they form a framework for the regulation of trade and investment. This regulation stems from a series of attempts to ensure that companies do not ignore national interests and economic policies and to restrain governments from imposing unnecessary restrictions on international business. The framework is made up of the following elements which form the first three sections of this chapter:

(1) international finance, balance of payments and exchange rates;
(2) trade – its liberalization and control;
(3) investment.

Some of the institutions that form an international framework are considered in this chapter. Bilateral, national and regional institutions are outlined in Chapters 3.2 and 3.3.

3.1.1 International finance, balance of payments and exchange rates

Two affiliates of the United Nations – the International Monetary Fund and the World Bank – both created after the Second World War, were designed to promote order in the financial affairs of the world and to reduce the disparities between rich and poor. Both were given special structures to encourage the richer nations to contribute heavily to their funds. Unlike some United Nations agencies, voting power in both of them is by size of subscription. Most of the communist countries did not join either institution; this is now changing, but the altered conditions are not affecting the free market bias in both institutions. On the contrary, privatization – and techniques for reducing the public sector – are being increasingly canvassed.

The International Monetary Fund (IMF)

The Fund was established to promote international liquidity, to assist countries which needed to overcome balance-of-payments difficulties without unduly restricting trade and to assist in maintaining stable exchange rates. The third objective was made largely – but not quite – obsolete when floating rates came to be accepted in the 1970s. The issue remained on the agenda and is being reactivated.

The Fund operates through a series of tranches that are available to member countries in proportion to their subscriptions. The conditions attached to assistance become more onerous as the requirements of a country increase. The Fund provides advice on the restructuring of a nation's finances in return for a loan to help overcome a serious crisis. This service is available to the 152 present members and several non-members are likely to join.

The International Monetary Fund has generated a considerable literature, both explanatory and critical. It publishes its own quarterly review, a series of staff studies and an annual World Economic Outlook.[1] Like other financial and development institutions, the Fund has encountered rapid changes since the early 1970s; these make the problems faced in the first 30 years of its existence appear comparatively straightforward. In particular, floating exchanges, energy crises and debt problems have brought a new dimension to the Fund's activities. The following are among the issues currently under consideration.

Interest rates
Countries with stable economies and established financial institutions are expected to benefit from allowing market forces more influence over interest rates. Where this is considered impractical, it is important that controls are sufficiently flexible to take some account of market forces, especially when they produce inflation. In South East Asia, the relaxation of controls has been successful; in some countries the controls have had to be reimposed to restore order to the financial sector.

Credit allocation
Where controls are required, these should be limited as far as possible; but some form of allocation, in line with closely identified priorities, is preferred to subsidizing interest rates.

Financial institutions

Any reduction in controls has to be accompanied by the development of legal and accounting systems and supervisory institutions to ensure reasonable security for investors. There is room for improving banking systems by management training, adopting new procedures and increasing competition. The supply of funds for investment can be expected to increase with the growth of pension funds and insurance policies.

The emergence of money markets has enabled developing countries to restructure their financial systems, and others are likely to benefit from this. The money market provides finance on sound terms for companies. The Fund is concerned that the 'long established informal financial sector' that exists in developing countries should be used to help mobilize funds and not suppressed.

The International Monetary Fund has been criticized on two main grounds:[2]

(1) That it makes too little effort to stabilize currencies. This has been a recurring complaint since fluctuating currencies became common in 1973, particularly among developing countries which favour fixed exchanges.

(2) That it causes undue problems to client governments by the conditions imposed for assistance: undue supervision and exaggerated deflation.

It appears that the Fund is spurred to action in times of crisis but, when the richer nations are less worried, complacency dominates. Thus the latest (1989) annual meeting of the Fund's members was criticized as being dominated by those recording strong economic growth, and unhelpful to those experiencing declines. 'There are still too many losers among the membership of the International Monetary Fund' (*Sunday Times*, 24 September 1989). A similar sentiment was expressed in the following words: 'The inability to find a satisfactory mechanism for dealing with the consequences for developing country indebtedness of the policy mistakes of the 1970s has been the chief failure of the 1980s' (*Financial Times*, 23 September 1989).

The World Bank

The World Bank is a comprehensive name for three closely related institutions – the International Bank for Reconstruction and Development (IBRD) and its two affiliates: the International Development Association (IDA) and the International Finance Corporation (IFC). The IBRD is the main provider of loans for major risk projects (such as power, transport and irrigation) in developing countries. Frequently it works in association with regional development banks – although these are currently having problems – and other aid organizations. The Bank also provides consultancy services and endeavours to ensure that its aid contributes towards raising the standard of living in the poorest countries and among the poorest citizens. A favourable but still commercial rate of interest has to be charged and this has caused problems to some clients. So has the consultancy work which attempts to ensure that the money is used to the best advantage, but is criticized for imposing free market methods and stringent controls on emerging economies.

To meet the problems caused by the insistence on economic interest rates and stringent repayment terms, the Bank set up the International Development Association (IDA) which grants loans for long periods, with many years interest and repayment free, to the 36 poorest countries. The service is the same in other respects and the Association operates with the same staff. The third institution – the International Finance Corporation (IFC) – exists to support the private sector in developing countries. Funds are provided to enterprises that appear viable but too risky for other lenders, and fresh funds are generated by selling existing holdings when feasible.

The World Bank has been criticized on the grounds that it is a bureaucratic system more responsive to the needs of its staff and the donor countries than to those of its client countries. One critical study examines four models:[3]

(1) *Needs* – where credits are extended to those countries that need them most.
(2) *Deserts* – where credits are extended to those countries that deserve them.
(3) *Benevolence* – where credits are extended in accordance with officially stated goals.
(4) *Politico-economic* – the World Bank is a bureaucracy furthering the interests of its employees.

According to this study, the *politico-economic* model predicts actual performance more accurately than the others.

3.1.2   Trade – its liberalization and control

There are two United Nations' affiliates that were established to influence the world trade system. The General Agreement on Tariffs and Trade was designed to break down barriers and promote free trade; the United Nations Conference on Trade and Development was brought into existence to influence the directions of trade, to enable poorer countries to enter world markets more easily.

The General Agreement on Tariffs and Trade[4]

The final act of the General Agreement on Tariffs and Trade was signed in 1947 by the governments of 23 countries. Membership has now expanded to 96 countries. The Charter evolved out of inconclusive negotiations to establish an International Trade Organization and the deliberations were part of a post-war international cooperation which led to the establishment of most of the institutions examined in this chapter. A legal framework was created for the mutual reduction of tariffs and a code developed for regulating public policies that affect trade. The General Agreement on Tariffs and Trade system is based on the belief that a liberal international trading system confers political and economic advantages to nations of all sizes.

The code is based on three premises. The first requires governments which seek to protect their domestic industries to do so by relying on tariffs. Protection of itself is not prohibited; but protectionist measures should be tariff-based, transparent and imposed at the border. Tariffs are compatible with the market system while other non-tariff, discriminatory measures prevent markets from allocating scarce resources to their most productive use. The second premise is the most-favoured-nation principle. Any advantage given to one General Agreement on Tariffs and Trade member has to be extended automatically and unconditionally to every other. This in effect means that all General Agreement on Tariffs and Trade members should be treated equally by their partners. The third premise is an obligation to participate in negotiations for the gradual reduction of trade barriers.

There have been seven rounds of negotiations and an eighth was launched in September 1986 in Uruguay. The Uruguay Round, as it has come to be known, was scheduled to end in 1990. It is the most extensive and complex yet. There are 15 negotiating groups, two of which consider issues never before examined in the General Agreement on Tariffs and Trade: services and intellectual property rights.

Objectives of the Uruguay Round

The Uruguay Round has been launched at a time when most observers believe that the multilateral trading system is being seriously eroded. Member countries follow policies incompatible with both the spirit and the letter of the General Agreement on Tariffs and Trade. For example, the so-called 'grey area' measures such as voluntary export restraints[5] are not explicitly mentioned in the Charter. Yet they contravene the principles of the Charter because they target particular exporters. The General Agreement on Tariffs and Trade up to now has had no remit to address restrictive or discriminatory policies in services and intellectual property rights.

The major objectives of the Round are to *strengthen and broaden* the system. This will count as achieved if:

(1) governments are prevented from resorting to non-tariff protectionist measures;
(2) developing countries are persuaded to participate more actively in the negotiations and assume the same obligations as other member countries;
(3) The General Agreement's rules are extended to cover fresh topics such as services;

(4) The General Agreement's rules are made more binding so that trade disputes can be resolved swiftly without countries having to take unilateral measures in retaliation for another country's perceived restrictive policies.

The Uruguay Round negotiating groups

In charge of the negotiations overall there is a Trade Negotiations Committee. Reporting to this Committee is a Group of Negotiations on Goods and a Group of Negotiations on Services. The latter is separate from the former because developing countries would not agree to participate in the negotiations on services as contracting parties. Hence a compromise was reached for a Ministerial Declaration with a separate section for services that expressed the intentions of ministers representing participating countries rather than contracting parties. The Group of Negotiations on Services had an ambiguous legal status.

With the Group of Negotiation on Goods there are 14 sub-groups, each of which examines a particular issue and can be classified as follows:

(1) General trade liberalization issues:
    (a) tariffs,
    (b) non-tariff barriers.
(2) Sector-specific trade liberation issues:
    (c) natural resource products,
    (d) textiles, clothing,
    (e) agriculture,
    (f) tropical products.
(3) Improvement of the legal framework:
    (g) General Agreement on Tariffs and Trade articles,
    (h) Most-favoured-nation agreements and arrangements,
    (i) safeguards,
    (j) subsidies and countervailing measures,
    (k) trade-related aspects of intellectual property rights,
    (l) trade-related investment measures.
(4) Improvement of the General Agreement on Tariffs and Trade as an institution:
    (m) dispute settlement,
    (n) functioning of the system.

The following section provides a selective review of the most complex and controversial issues under negotiation.

Subjects for negotiations

(1) Non-tariff measures

The term non-tariff barriers includes quantitative import restrictions, voluntary export restraints, price controls, fiscal measures and other monitoring and administrative measures.

(a) Quantitative import restrictions limit the volume of imports. They include quotas (which may be global, country-specific or seasonal), prohibitions (total, partial or with exceptions), discretionary import authorizations and conditional import authorizations (subject to the importer undertaking particular commitments).

(b) Voluntary export restraints, which are often involuntary, are agreements that limit exports without the importer having to take any explicit border or other administrative measures.

(c) Price controls are collusive arrangements between governments. They include variable levies, minimum prices and voluntary export price restraints.

(d) Fiscal measures are tariff-type charges intended to raise the price of imported products. They include tariff quotas, whereby a higher tariff rate is levied when importers exceed a specified quantity, and seasonal tariffs that are mainly applied to agricultural products.

(e) Monitoring other administrative measures are regulations intended to control imports regarded as sensitive. They include price and volume investigation and surveillance as well as anti-dumping and countervailing duties. Such measures raise uncertainty about market access and make exports riskier.

Non-tariff barriers have been proliferating for several reasons. As a result of previous Rounds, tariffs have been either reduced or fixed and cannot be increased. Consequently, governments have found other means of protecting their industries. They have shown a preference for non-tariff barriers because they are less visible, can be very selective so that they hurt a particular exporter, and do not require authorization by parliaments. In those cases where the exporter agrees to abide by a set price or quantity control of a particular market, the incidence is even more extensive.

The reduction of non-tariff barriers is not an easy task. The General Agreement's practice of reducing these barriers is to define *reciprocal* concessions of equivalent magnitude. But it is difficult to define the equivalence of the many, diverse barriers that exist. Because liberalization under the General Agreement proceeds on the basis of exchanging equivalent concessions, a curious situation arises whereby those countries with more such barriers are in a stronger bargaining position than those with less. Liberalization has so far been prevented because there has been no agreement about whether non-tariff barriers are illegal under the General Agreement's rules. If they are illegal, they must be eliminated without any reciprocal concessions from other countries. Finally, certain countries regard their barriers as part of their overall national economic policies and, therefore, not subject to negotiation.

One of the problems of tackling non-tariff barriers has always been that of identifying and, in particular, of quantifying them. A recent article[6] expounds a measuring technique proposed by the Australian government: the effective rate of assistance (ERA). This had been proposed many years earlier, but its use in helping to achieve some of the aims of the Uruguay Round is now a serious possibility. The proposal is that the net assistance of tariff and non-tariff barriers to industrial inputs and outputs is used as a yardstick for determining how far a country is moving towards free trade.

(2)   Textiles and clothing

Much of the world's trade in textiles is controlled by the Multi-Fibre Arrangement. Each Arrangement is one of a series of bilateral quota-agreements which specify the volume of textiles that developing countries are allowed to export to developed countries. The Arrangements are reviewed periodically, and the one currently in force is the sixth. It was initiated in 1986 and was due to expire in 1991.

Every time a Multi-Fibre Arrangement is negotiated its scope is also expanded. The first (1961–2) was intended to be temporary and covered only cotton products. Subsequent Arrangements have been extended to cover all textiles and clothing including cotton, wool, synthetic, vegetable and silk fibres.

Membership of the Arrangement has also expanded because one of its major effects has been a diversion of trade to non-traditional exporters of textiles. As the exports of traditional textile-producing countries were restrained, companies in those countries moved their operations to other countries not subject to controls. Producers in the protected markets of industrial countries were also encouraged to increase their output.

The Multi-Fibre Arrangement is in direct conflict with the principles of the General Agreement on Tariffs and Trade. It relies on quantitative restrictions which are not applied on a most-favoured-nation basis. Each exporter is allocated a particular quota by each importing country. Industrial countries have argued that an important precondition to the gradual withdrawal of these quotas is the acceptance of reciprocal obligations by developing countries. Developing countries have in turn responded by rejecting the idea of bargaining away restrictions which they consider illegal under the General Agreement; they have also demanded more favourable treatment for low-income countries. There was little scope for an agreement eliminating the Multi-Fibre Arrangement during the Uruguay Round, although powerful voices in the industrial countries also condemned it.[7]

(3)   Agriculture

Most issues raised by the General Agreement on Tariffs and Trade involve a North-South divide; in agriculture, on the other hand, the most vehement opponents are among the industrial countries. For example, the United States and Australia are in the liberal camp that wants an end to trade barriers and government support of inefficient farmers. Ardent opponents to such suggestions are the European Community and Japan. Government intervention in agricultural markets has resulted in huge surpluses in some countries and severe shortages in others. Developed countries have surpluses financed by exorbitant consumer prices and direct government transfers. A case in point is the European Community's Common Agricultural Policy. It has been absorbing two thirds of the Community's expenditure and producing periodic budget crises. The surpluses of developed countries are often dumped on international markets, depressing world prices. A major effect of these low prices is to discourage agricultural production in poor countries, some of which have turned from being net exporters to net importers.

Trade in agricultural products is, in principle, subject to the same rules as other commodities; but there are several important exceptions. First, the general prohibition of import and export quantitative restrictions (quotas) may be waived whenever such restrictions prevent or relieve food shortages and whenever they are necessary to the enforcement of certain domestic policies. Second, agriculture is exempted from the general prohibitions on export subsidies. Price and income support programmes are not prohibited. However, countervailing measures may be applied when such subsidies are shown to cause injury to the producers of the importing country. The subjects of the Uruguay Round negotiations, highlighted by the Punta del Este Declaration, were the improvement of market access through the reduction of tariff and non-tariff trade barriers, the improvement of market competition through the reduction of direct and indirect government subsidies, and the minimization of the adverse effects of sanitary measures and other quality regulations. The United States has recently proposed that agriculture reform should begin by a gradual phasing out of government subsidies. The European Community has rejected that idea. It prefers the establishment of an international arrangement whose purpose would be the allocation of quotas to principal producers so that supplies and prices are managed.

(4) Safeguards
Member countries of the General Agreement on Tariffs and Trade are allowed to impose temporary barriers in order to prevent a sudden influx of imports that might seriously damage domestic industries. Such safeguards are allowed by Article XIX which also provides for compensation of foreign exporters where governments may retaliate if compensation is not forthcoming. This article has never been used as the founders of the General Agreement intended. Trade restrictions have been imposed irrespective of whether the domestic industry has suffered any injury from imports. Because Article XIX does not explicitly stipulate that safeguard action should be non-discriminatory, protectionist measures

have been targeted against particular products and suppliers. This form of selectivity is contradictory to the provisions of Article I which specifies that trade intervention must be non-discriminatory.

Reform of Article XIX hinges on developments regarding Voluntary Export Restraints which are by definition selective. The European Community has been defending what it perceives as its right to resort to selective measures. The strongest opponents of selectivity are developing countries which have been adversely affected by the Multi-Fibre Arrangement. However, even if the issue of selectivity is resolved, member countries would still have to determine which measures to bring within the scope of Article XIX. There is no assurance that all grey area measures would be subject to the General Agreement's disciplines.

(5) Anti-dumping and countervailing measures
These measures regulate the fairness of competition from imports. An anti-dumping duty is levied when imports are sold at a price which is lower in the importing than in the exporting market. The purpose of the duty is to make up the difference in price between the two markets. Countervailing duties are imposed on imports whose price or production costs are subsidized. The use of anti-dumping and countervailing duties is allowed by the General Agreement on Tariffs and Trade. The procedure by which they should be applied is specified by two General Agreement on Tariffs and Trade codes. There are protocols attached to the Charter to which not all the signatories have acceded. The major problem in assessing the dumping margin (the price differential) is in determining the price that prevails in the domestic market of a firm that dumps its products. For several reasons this can often be a difficult task. There may be several prices quoted to different domestic buyers of the dumped product. The product in question may be sold in different forms in different markets. It may be necessary, therefore, to reconstruct a normal price for the product that adequately reflects its true costs. Again this is not easy; the investigators would have to estimate the proportion of the firm's overall investment and operating expenditures that have to be allocated to that particular product.

Inadequacies of the anti-dumping code and of the discretion shown by investigators in determining normal prices have recently been highlighted by international criticism of some practices. The European Community has imposed anti-dumping duties on Japanese photocopiers, dot-matrix printers and electronic scales, all of which are assembled in plants within the Community. It has regarded these assembly plants as screwdriver operations, designed to circumvent duties on assembled products shipped directly from Japan. The Community has also expressed its intention to impose anti-dumping duties on Japanese photocopiers assembled in California. These two incidents show there are no precise international rules in determining the cost and nationality of a product. From a narrow, legalistic perspective many governments would claim that, as long as they are not on the receiving end, anti-dumping practices are working reasonably well. Often, however, these practices have little economic rationale and are increasingly misused by governments whose purpose is the protection of domestic industries rather than the fairness of competition.

(6) Trade-related investment measures
The General Agreement on Tariffs and Trade deals with *products*. It has no rules for the treatment of *companies* as such. Every country has laws regulating the operations of companies in its territory, some of which concern investment, especially investment by foreign companies. Trade-related investment measures are currently outside the purview of the General Agreement. National policies on foreign and domestic investment provide either incentives or disincentives. Tax concessions, subsidized loans and other fiscal exemptions are examples of incentives. Examples of disincentives are local content requirements, trade restrictions, limits on equity control, restrictions on profit repatriation, foreign exchange controls and other performance requirements. There is as yet little understanding of the economic effect of such policies. Nor is it well known how prevalent they are and how they are applied. Because many of these measures are administered at the discretion of the relevant ministry, they are probably not applied equally to all investors. Hence, one of the major problems in bringing the trade-related investment measures under the General Agreement's rules is to specify what they are and determine what effect they have.

The most difficult problem is to define, in a reasonably precise manner, those measures that should be eliminated. Some trade-related investment measures have a legitimate economic function in the sense that they improve national economic welfare. No definition has been proposed so far which can distinguish between legitimate measures and those which distort. It is unlikely, therefore, that the General Agreement on Tariff and Trade will achieve anything beyond the reduction of a few of the measures. Even that prospect is by no means certain, since many countries, especially developing countries, object to anything they perceive as impinging on their sovereign right to determine their national economic policies.

(7) Trade-related aspects of intellectual property rights
The General Agreement on Tariffs and Trade expressly draws exceptions to its rules for patents, copyrights, rules on trade marks and other intellectual property rights. Developing countries as a group want the present system to continue. Industrial countries, in particular the United States, want the Agreement to be strengthened to cover trade-related aspects of intellectual property rights. They believe that violations of their intellectual property rights, especially in developing countries, unfairly deprive their producers of sales revenue. Hence, the major issue is whether developing countries should respect intellectual property legislation in developed countries. Developing countries, however, view such legislation as another form of non-tariff barrier. They also view it as a

barrier preventing the flow of much-needed knowledge and technology from the haves to the have-nots. Such fundamental differences of perspective imply there is little scope for an agreement on trade-related aspects of intellectual property rights. Even if such differences did not exist, an agreement would still be difficult. Most countries have extensive and substantially diverse legal systems for the protection of intellectual property rights. It would not be easy to overhaul and reconcile such systems.

(8) Services

Along with trade-related investment measures and trade-related aspects of intellectual property rights, services are a new issue on the agenda. Disagreement over the inclusion of services in the Uruguay Round ran so deeply that ministers at the Punta del Este meeting instructed their governments to negotiate only as interested countries, not as the General Agreement's contracting parties. Once more the division was between developing and industrialized countries. Developing countries saw one more attempt by industrial countries to infringe their national economic prerogatives. They also perceived themselves as losing to the more efficient Western service multinationals. Industrial countries could see only restrictions on the operations of their companies abroad.

A major, largely political, difficulty in achieving liberalization of trade in services is that some services can only be provided personally by their purveyors. Hence, the provision of some services requires the physical movement of either the provider or the client and may also require that the provider establishes a commercial presence in the market in which it operates. Physical movement and the establishment of a commercial presence are regarded by developing countries to be investment issues and, therefore, outside the scope of General Agreement on Tariffs and Trade. Another problem is that many services are regulated in varying ways and degrees in different countries. Free entry of services from less-regulated markets may thus be incompatible with the objectives of national regulations. In some countries some services are nationalized or are legal monopolies. These can include banking, transportation, broadcasting, medical, other health services and education. Trade is by definition impossible unless such countries modify their domestic economic policies. Other problems include the absence of an acceptable definition of traded services and the lack of comprehensive and detailed data on the production and trade of services.

The United Nations Conference on Trade and Development (UNCTAD)

Established in 1964, the United Nations Conference on Trade and Development was set up partly as a result of Third World dissatisfaction with the General

Agreement on Tariffs and Trade. The dissatisfaction was about a number of issues that included the following:

(1) The voting system. With its one member, one vote, the United Nations Conference on Trade and Development gave a majority vote to the developing countries.

(2) The bias in the regulations. The regulations of the General Agreement on Tariffs and Trade were held to favour the industrial countries because most of the negotiations were over manufactured goods of little immediate interest to a majority of developing countries. Items of special interest to them, like textiles, are taken out of the system and hedged around with special rules (see note 7).

Raw materials, a principal export of developing countries, are either duty free or charged at low rates. This is helpful in the short term, but those low rates on raw materials combined with higher rates on manufactured goods (especially those of a comparatively simple nature) do not encourage the process of industrialization. At the same time, high duties and other restrictions on agricultural produce block the main source of income for most developing countries.

(3) Lack of bargaining power. A perception among the developing countries that they lack bargaining power in the General Agreement.

The impetus behind the United Nations Conference on Trade and Development was not just dissatisfaction with the General Agreement. The cost of entry to world markets was among the issues leading to its formation as well as the value of commodities. Apart from oil, the price of minerals has steadily deteriorated on world markets. In the event, the deliberations of the Conference have proved to be as slow and tortuous as those of the General Agreement, but some measures are in place. The Generalized System of Preferences had provided developing countries with special tariff concessions on a number of exports, while the Integrated Programme for Commodities has attempted to sustain commodity prices. Neither of those schemes has proved notably successful and the search for stronger bargaining positions continues. The Conference has, however, succeeded in bringing the New International Economic Order on to the world agenda; this is discussed in Chapter 3.4.

Other organizations involved in the regulation of trade

A number of other affiliates of the United Nations have been designed to influence trade in some way or another – some as a stimulus, like the various aid organizations; others are also regulatory and specialized on subjects like labour, agriculture or aviation.[8] Most of these influence more than trade and are considered in the next section. The World Intellectual Property Organization (WIPO) is specifically concerned with fees for technology transfer and for copyrights.

3.1.3   Investment

Attempts to liberalize trade have been accompanied by efforts to control international investment. Chosen vehicles have been codes of conduct adopted by several United Nations affiliates, the Organisation for Economic Cooperation and Development, and several regional organizations. The latter (considered in Chapter 3.3) sometimes adopt codes that are mandatory, enforced by national legislation; the world organizations adopt voluntary codes, but these have proved more effective than some of their critics expected. The main reason why governments have supported international action has been described as a love-hate relationship[9] in which governments grant concessions to encourage foreign investment and impose restraints to ensure that investing companies do not violate national economic policies.

The strengths and bargaining power of international companies cause political problems, which are exacerbated by the need for the benefits they bring. As a sweetener to companies, most codes guarantee the security of investment and safeguards against discriminatory treatment. However the main thrust of the codes is to restrain companies not governments. In general these codes:

seek to ensure that companies are more open with their information – revealing the state of play in each subsidiary in an understandable and consistent manner;

seek to ensure that companies treat their subsidiaries as integral parts of the whole, while at the same time dealing with them at arm's length;

seek to ensure that companies do not interfere in the political or economic policies of host countries.

The most elaborate of the codes was drafted by the United Nations Centre for Transnational Corporations.

The United Nations Centre for Transnationals

The United Nations Centre for Transnationals was established to collect information on the activities of international companies and to advise member countries on their dealings with them. The Centre has produced a series of reports on subjects as diverse as the pharmaceutical industry and management contracts, and much else. It has also been involved in drafting a code of conduct, much of which has now been accepted by the General Assembly. A summary of the main clauses is given below.

(1) The code is designed to assist in the control of international ('transnational' is the United Nations' jargon) firms and to ensure that their activities contribute positively to international development.

(2) Companies must respect the sovereignty, laws and policies of the countries

in which they operate, and the right of those countries to regulate their activities. Respect for socio-cultural values and traditions is demanded, as is active opposition to policies of apartheid.

This section proscribes political interference and corrupt practices, while a series of clauses concerns ownership and control. The subsidiary is to be structured in a way that will allow it to play a full part in local development and economic plans; personnel and training policies are to give priority to the benefit of local nationals. Exports from the subsidiary are to be promoted. Financial policies must conform with the laws of the country and not conflict with its economic policies; in particular, the repatriation of capital, the transfer of profits and other cash transactions are to be timed to minimize the damage to the balance of payments. The subsidiary is also expected to avoid practices that may harm the local capital markets, to consult with the government when engaged in share issues or long-term borrowing, and to cooperate in efforts to establish local equity participation.

Transfer prices should be based on an arm's length principle. Restrictive practices, the transfer of technology, consumer protection and the physical environment are all considered in detail. Companies are called upon to disclose full information about their operations for the company as a whole, for the country concerned and (as far as possible) by regions and products, under the headings:

(a) balance sheet;
(b) income statement;
(c) allocation of net profits;
(d) sources and uses of funds;
(e) new long-term investments;
(f) research and development expenditures;
(g) the structure of the enterprise (parent and subsidiary);
(h) ownership distribution;
(i) operations;
(j) employment;
(k) accounting practices;
(l) transfer pricing.

The provision of information is subject to safeguards where confidentiality is important; otherwise, representatives of labour are to be kept fully informed of developments and plans likely to affect the future of the employees.

(3) The third part of the code concerns relationships between companies and governments. There are clauses on the role of foreign companies and the rights of countries to prohibit their entry into certain sectors; their treatment by governments, including their acceptance on an equal footing with domestic companies; the safeguarding of the confidentiality of the information that they

do supply; and their rights in the face of nationalization, and in disputes over compensation and jurisdiction.

(4) Bilateral and multilateral agreements between states on issues arising out of the code are provided for. Governments agree not to use companies to further their policies in other countries but, on the contrary, to try to prevent companies interfering in the internal affairs of host nations.

(5) The code is to be publicized by member countries and administered by the United Nations Commission on Transnationals. The final clauses provide for reconsideration and revision.[10]

The Organisation for Economic Cooperation and Development (OECD)

The Organisation for Economic Cooperation and Development has 26 members, including all the most industrialized nations, and also provides services to their client countries. Its role is primarily consultative with expert staff-servicing committees in most areas of primary production, manufacturing and service industries. The Organisation has also produced its code of conduct for multi-nationals. This was the first comprehensive code promulgated and was agreed by the affiliated governments, employers' organizations and trade unions. Without any legal authority – adherence to decisions of the Organisation is voluntary and the code specifically states that its provisions are voluntary – this code has already produced a number of results,[11] confounding critics who claim that the lengthy process of producing such documents is a cosmetic and pointless exercise.

The World Health Organization

The World Health Organization developed its own code largely as a result of the controversy over formula milk.[12] The manufacturers involved – Nestlé, Bristol-Myers, Abbott Laboratories, American Home Products, Borden, Cow & Gate and Glaxo among them – were accused of damaging the health of infants in the poorer countries by the measures used to sell formula milk. The problem for the companies was that they would have been even more severely criticized if they had refused to allow sales of the product. Formula milk is vital to a baby's survival where breast-feeding is impossible, not an uncommon situation in rich countries and even more likely to occur in countries where the mothers are inadequately fed; it is also safer than unprocessed milk from cows or goats. The companies' position was made more difficult by the fact that a considerable sales effort was needed in an impoverished and tradition-bound society to create a mass market. Without this the price would have been too high, and the manufacturers would then have been accused of over-charging.

As it happened, this accusation was made in any case, but the main charge was that the selling methods gave the customers the impression that good mothers must make every effort to provide their babies with this product, but did not give them sufficient instruction in its use nor emphasize the importance of breast-feeding when possible. On the tins were details about the strength of the mixture required, for instance, but these were hard to follow and impossible if the mother was illiterate. It was also improbable that the water would be sterilized, especially if a long walk to a scarce well was necessary, and formula product did not provide the babies with the immunity carried by the mother's milk. The salesmanship included broadcasting, free samples at clinics and the dressing of sales ladies in nurses' uniforms.

The controversy began in the early 1970s when publicity was given to research results which produced evidence that harm was being done to infants by the formula milk. There were also counter-arguments, including claims that the product had made a large contribution to improved health, that abuses could easily be cured and that the fuss was greatly exaggerated in any case; a mother's instincts usually told her when a product was harming her baby before it was too late. The World Health Organization began to consider the issue in 1972, but in 1974 the publication of a leaflet in Switzerland called *Nestlé Kills Babies* and the subsequent libel action brought the matter to the attention of public opinion in many parts of the world. Boycotts against the manufacturers were undertaken in North America and a variety of organizations entered the argument. In January 1981, the World Health Organization adopted a code of conduct for the promotion of formula milk. But this was not the end of the story. Eight years later in 1989, the controversy continues with allegation and counter-allegation in spite of efforts by Nestlé to remove the causes for complaint.

Other organizations

The Multilateral Investment Guarantee Agency (MIGA) is a new organization that came into existence in 1989 to support private investment in the developing countries. Set up under the auspices of the World Bank, the Agency will issue guarantees as well as providing coinsurance and reinsurance against non-commercial risks (like war and riots), expropriation and restrictions on foreign exchange transfers. Membership is open to all members of the World Bank and the Agency will provide additional services in the form of information, advice and technical assistance.

The International Labour Organization (ILO) has influenced investment considerably by its work on both working conditions and on training. The Organization has also produced a code.[12] This is divided into six sections, of which the first declares that the code covers all types of company (whether in private, mixed or public ownership) and is aimed at supporting the positive contributions to national well-being and reducing the harmful ones. Companies are expected, in the following sections, to respect the sovereignty of the states in which they operate and especially to support freedom of association, collective bargaining and non-discrimination in labour and social policies; they are urged to go beyond the local norms in these policies and to provide relevant training at all levels together with high standards of safety and health. There are provisions for enforcing agreed best practices in industrial relations, and governments are required not to offer incentives in the form of anti-labour measures. The code ends with procedures for regular consultation and the settling of disputes.

3.1.4   Conclusion

This chapter has examined the growing international framework within which international business has to operate. A mutual process of adaptation appears to be occurring as institutions feel their way towards a new international order; at the same time companies are learning to conform to the requirements, and indeed to rise to the opportunities that the gradual increase in security has provided for international operations. The threefold division of the chapter points to the main issues under review – international finance, international trade and international investment. Each is growing its distinctive institutions.

Notes and References

1. The annual publication is *World Economic Outlook: A Survey by the Staff of the International Monetary Fund* is published annually in April by the International Monetary Fund (Washington, DC). The 1989 issue focused on (1) the current situation and short-term prospects for both industrial and developing countries; (2) medium-term prospects and policy issues for industrial countries and for the indebted developing countries. Revised projections are published in October. The quarterly publication is *Finance and Development*. Among recent staff papers are:
   Keller, P.M and Weerasinghe, N.E. (May 1988): *Multilateral Debt Rescheduling: Recent Experience*. IMF.
   Otani, I. and Villaneuva, D. (June 1989): *Theoretical Aspects of Growth in Developing Countries: External Debt Dynamics and the Role of Human Capital*. IMF.
2. See, for example, Abdallah, I.S. (1989): 'The inadequacy and loss of initiative of the International Monetary Fund', *Development Dialogue*, 2.
3. See Frey, B.S. (1984): *International Political Economics*. Blackwell.
4. Note that the General Agreement on Tariffs and Trade is discussed in a different context in Chapter 2.4. The following is a selection of the literature on the subject:
   GATT and the Uruguay Round in general:
   Alo, M. and Aronson, J. (1985): *Trade Talks: America Better Listen*. Council on Foreign Relations.
   Camps, M. and Diebold, W. (1985): *The New Multilateralism*. Council on Foreign Relations.
   Viravan, A. et al. (1986): *Trade Route to Sustained Economic Growth*. Macmillan.

Golt, S. (1988): *The GATT Negotiations 1986–90*. British–North American Committee.

Non-tariff barriers:

Nogues, J. et al. (1986): 'The Extent of Non-Tariff Barriers to Imports of Industrial Countries'. *The World Bank Economic Review*. 1 (1), pp. 181–99.

Textiles:

Keesing, D. and Wolf, M. (1980): *Textile Quotas against Developing Countries*. GPRC.

Koekkoek, K. and Mennes, L. (1986). 'Liberalising the MFA', *Journal of World Trade Law*, 20.2, pp. 142–67.

Agriculture:

Noones, J. (1985): 'Agriculture and Developing Countries in GATT', *The World Economy*, 8.2, pp. 119–33.

Franklin, M. (1985): *Rich Man's Farming: Crisis in Agriculture*, Royal Institute of Internal Affairs.

Safeguards:

Leddy, J.: *A New Safeguard Code*. Washington, Council.

Anti-dumping and Countervailing Measures (1981):

Beseler, J. and Williams, A. (1986): *Antidumping and Antisubsidy Law*. Sweet and Maxwell.

Finger, M. and Nozues N. (1987): 'International Control of Subsidies and Countervailing Duties', *The World Bank Economic Review*, 1.4, pp. 707–25.

Norall, C. (1986): 'New Trends in Antidumping Practice in Brussels', *The World Economy*, 9.1, pp. 97–111.

Trade-Related Investment Measures:

Guisinger, S. (1985): *Investment Incentives and Performance Requirements*. Praeger.

Trade Related Aspects of Intellectual Property Rights:

Stalson, H. (1987): *Intellectual Property Rights and US Competitiveness in Trade*. Washington, National Planning Association. 1987.

Services:

Nicolaides, P. (1988): *Liberalising Trade in Services*. Discussion Paper No. 3, Royal Institute of International Affairs.

Nicolaides, P. (1989): 'The Problem of Regulation in Traded Services', *Aussenwiktschaft*.

5. *Voluntary Export Restraints* whereby an exporter agrees to limit its sale of some goods in a particular market (prudent marketing is an important tool of the new protectionism). The restraints are frequently used as a response to an increase in the share of exports in the circumstances that Article XIX of GATT was designed to control – emergency protection when an industry is faced with a sudden surge of imports. The ostensibly voluntary nature of Voluntary Export Restraints removes them from the scope of Article XIX and therefore from the control of the GATT.

'There is a widespread view – partly connected with this invasion of the GATT – that Voluntary Export Restraints are dangerous and undesirable instruments' (Black and Hindley). Lists might include textiles, footwear, leather products, electronic goods, automobiles, ball-bearings, cutlery and zip fasteners. GATT estimate that about five to ten per cent of world trade is affected. See Black, J. and Hindley, B. (eds) (1980): *Current Issues in Commercial Policy and Diplomacy*. St Martin.

6. See Banks, G. (June 1989): 'A role for ERAs in the GATT forum?' *The World Economy*, 12.2, pp. 219–36.

7. This view was powerfully expressed in two studies published in 1984. See: Wolf M. and others: *Costs of Protecting Jobs in Textiles and Clothing*. Trade Policy Research Centre. Silberston, Z.A. (1984): *The Multi-Fibre Arrangement and the UK Economy*. Her Majesty's Stationery Office.

   For a comment see: 'The MFA is too costly a joke', *The Economist*, 22 December 1984. For a review of the working of the Arrangement by the Director General of Comitextil, see: Blum, C. (1988): 'The Multi-Fibre Arrangement', Chapter 6.6 in Brooke, M.Z. and Buckley, P.J., *Handbook of International Trade*. Macmillan. For a detailed study see: Macgovern, E. (1982): *International Trade Regulations: GATT, the United States and the EEC*. Globefield.

8. Affiliates of the United Nations not mentioned on these pages but with some relevance to international business include: International Atomic Energy Agency, International Civil Aviation Organization, International Fund for Agricultural Development, International Maritime Organization, International Telecommunications Union, United Nations Development Programme, United Nations Disaster Relief Office, United Nations Environment Programme, UNESCO (United Nations Educational, Scientific and Cultural Organization), United Nations Fund for Population Activities, United Nations High Commissioner for Refugees, United Nations Industrial Development Organization, United Nations Institute for Training and Research, Universal Postal Union, World Food Council and World Food Programme. Brief details of these organizations can be found in standard reference works such as the *Statesman's Yearbook*, Macmillan.

9. See Brooke, M.Z. and Remmers, H.L. (1978): *The Strategy of Multinational Enterprise* (2nd edn) pp. 184. Pitman.

10. The following sources of information provide summaries and analyses of the codes: Centre for Transnational Corporations, *The CTC Reporter*, No. 12, United Nations, 1982; *Commission on Transnational Corporations*, supplement no. 8, United Nations Economic and Social Council, 1982. *Towards International Standardisation of Corporate Accounting and Reporting*, United Nations, 1982; *Measures Strengthening the Negotiating Capacity of Governments in their Relations with Transnational Corporations*, United Nations Centre on Transnationals, New York, 1983. This has been updated by papers dated 31 January 1986 (No. E/C 10/1986/11) and 10 February 1986 (No. E/C 10/1986/4); *National Legislation and Regulations Relating to Transnational Corporations*, United Nations Centre on Transnational Corporations, New York, 1983. A review of the subject can be found in Mousouris S.G. (1988): 'Code of conduct facing multinational corporations', Chapter 28, of Walter, I. (ed.): *Handbook of International Business*. Wiley. See also Kline, J.M. (1985): *International Codes and Multinational Business*. Greenwood.

11. The OECD code is published by each of the member governments. The British edition is: *International Investment: Guidelines for Multinational Enterprises*, HMSO command 6525, 1976. For a detailed discussion of the significance of the code, see: Blanpain, R. (1977): *The Badger Case and the OECD Guidelines for Multinational Enterprise*. Kluwer. There is a summary in the *Journal of the Royal Society of Arts*, May 1978, pp. 326–34.

12. See *The International Code of Marketing of Breast Milk Substitutes*, FAO, 1981. See also Muskle, E.S. and others (Spring 1986): 'The Nestlé infant formula audit commission', *Journal of Business Strategy*, 6.4, pp. 19–32.
13. *The Tripartite Declaration Concerning Multinational Enterprises and Social Policies*. ILO, 1981.

3.2

Multilateral Treaties and National Institutions

The international and regional organizations, outlined in Chapters 3.1 and 3.3, are accompanied by a network of national institutions and multilateral treaties designed both to promote and to constrain international business. The treaties are usually drafted in the context of international agreements like General Agreement on Tariffs and Trade or the International Monetary Fund, but many are negotiated by countries which prefer to deal direct between governments rather than through international organizations.

3.2.1 Bilateral and multilateral treaties

The treaties are of two principal kinds: those concerned with taxation and those that are about trade relations. The parties are not necessarily national governments: one may be an institution like the European Community.

Taxation treaties

Double taxation and other tax agreements between countries cover much of the world, although in different forms. Some years ago, the United Nations produced guidelines for tax treaties between industrial and developing countries.[1] Among the clauses were the following:

(1) Foreign investment generates profits which, if not reinvested in the host country, need to be transferred elsewhere; it also entails payments which have to be remitted abroad. Such financial transfers may exert great pressure on the balance-of-payments position of developing countries.

(2) It is also recognized that foreign investment, properly integrated, can make a positive contribution to the economic and social well-being of developing countries.

(3) The international investment climate largely determines the growth of investment flows from developed to developing countries. The elimination of international double taxation has helped as it provides a mechanism for mutual agreement in the settlement of differences.

(4) Few tax treaties have been concluded between developed and developing countries, but many of the latter alleviate the effective tax burden on foreign investors by unilaterally offering them major tax incentives which may include income tax exemptions.

(5) Bilateral tax treaties can solve many of the double taxation problems by reconciling the differences that arise between the concepts of various types of income and their geographical source, establishing a common method of determining how certain items of income shall be classified and taxed. In many cases, capital-exploring countries have granted relief under bilateral treaties in forms that they are not prepared to extend indiscriminately by statute.

(6) For equal countries, a bilateral treaty would not be hampered by considerations that losses and gains will be of equal magnitude to both countries. A loss of revenue that may be of little importance to a developed country may constitute a heavy sacrifice to a developing one. For many developing countries, the scarcity of foreign exchange resulting from the outflow of tax-exempt locally produced income may be of even greater importance than the loss of revenue.

(7) Developing countries have been reluctant to enter into tax treaties, unless they can assume that the treaties will ensure that the risk of tax revenue and foreign exchange losses will be offset by other provisions.

Among the issues discussed in the literature are: *Double tax treaties* that affect numerous countries including most of the industrialized.[2] Sometimes these treaties enter into considerable detail and differentiate between occupations. *Tax avoidance and evasion*[3] takes the researcher into a range of topics varying from straightforward fraud to the many grey areas of transfer pricing and charging for services.

Trade relations treaties

The improvement of trade has been the subject of innumerable treaties negotiated over the last 40 years. Sometimes these are between two countries, sometimes between groups of countries. A sample of such treaties is discussed here.

The Lomé Convention is an arrangement whereby European Community countries admit goods from the poorer of their previous colonies duty free. The Convention has safeguards designed to ensure that other countries do not use its privileges by trading via a Lome country; it also has restrictions on some politically sensitive products. An article that takes a generally favourable view of the working of the Convention makes the following points.[4]

(1) The Lomé Convention is the most generous of the European Community's hierarchy of preferences for developing countries; the trade cooperation

provisions have the objective of promoting trade between the African, Caribbean and Pacific States (ACP) and the Community, and between themselves.

(2) Products originating in Lomé Convention states should be imported into the Community free of customs duties and charges having equivalent effect, and the Community shall not apply to imports of products originating in those states any quantitative restrictions or measures having a similar effect.

(3) Partners to the Convention retain tariff autonomy, so the origin of traded goods has to be determined to prevent third countries deflecting exports to the Community via Lomé Convention countries with a lower tariff on these goods than the Community. Such trade deflection would undermine the Community Common External Tariff, and therefore the margin of tariff preference received by the states. Consequently the Community and the states are keen to uphold the rules of the Convention.

(4) Because of their social and economic structures, many Lomé Convention states may wish to increase their exports of labour-intensive manufactured goods and attract foreign investment into export-oriented manufacturing sectors. The Community may resist such an increase in imports while at the same time seeking to increase exports to the states.

(5) Under the terms of the Convention, the only way the Community can influence the volume of trade-manufactured goods with the Lomé Convention countries is through the safeguard clause and through the definition of originating products.

(6) The possibility of having to resort to the safeguard clause has been used to restrict the growth of export capacity of cotton textiles by Lomé Convention states which export significant volumes (at least 1 per cent of Community volumes) of ultra-sensitive and sensitive goods.

(7) The safeguard clause should only be used in extreme circumstances since the political costs of implementing outweigh any short-term economic benefits to producers in the European Community.

A more critical article questions some of the consequences of the Convention, and asks especially whether it is increasing or reducing the dependence of the member countries on their former colonial masters.[5] The following are the main suggestions:

(1) Lomé aid is compatible neither with infinite development and independence, nor with further under-development and countinuing dependence. Lomé aid has contributed to the development of the member states, but has resulted in no obvious reduction in their dependence.

(2) Unless the recipient countries are alert, European Community economic assistance could facilitate a continuing dependent development.

(3) Lomé confers upon the member countries powers of project determination and intervention in the deliberation of the Fund unmatched by those of previous Conventions, or by any other bilateral or multilateral donors.

(4) The bulk of Community aid now goes to production, but none has been

channelled to regional cooperation ventures between the Lomé Convention members and other non-African, Caribbean and Pacific countries.

(5) The Community needs to guard against projecting the Lomé aid arrangement as an alternative to the measures enumerated in the Action Programme for the establishment of a new international economic order – especially since the aid promised has frequently been reduced.

Trade between the European Free Trade Area (EFTA) and the European Community entered a new era – it has been claimed – in April 1984 with the first of a series of meetings designed to promote closer cooperation between the two institutions. The following main points were made in the articles in which the claim was made.[6]

(1) Ever since the conclusion of free-trade arrangements, the European Free Trade Area has been asking for a simplification of the rules of origin in order to become recognized as one tariff zone or customs area. The bilateral nature of the free-trade arrangements permits products consisting of components from all Community countries to be freely traded in all European Free Trade Areas countries, whereas products manufactured in one member country should theoretically not include foreign components above a certain permitted percentage in order to be freely traded within the European Community. The Luxembourg Declaration highlighted this imbalance.

(2) Community exports to the European Free Trade Area are over 22 per cent of its total exports to the outside world, and imports from the area more than 14 per cent of its total imports from outside. The Association and the Community together account for almost 40 per cent of world trade. Inflation rates in the European Free Trade Area are lower than those in the Community and unemployment less than one third of that of the European Community.

(3) The Association and the Community have joint programmes for uniform standards in the high-technology areas, especially telecommunications. In the fiscal year 1986–7, the European Free Trade Area will contribute 600,000 Swiss francs to this work; for information technology alone, 15 to 16 new European standards will emerge.

(4) The Single Administrative Document (SAD) is a sign of cooperation between the European Free Trade Area and the European Community, since it will replace 60 to 70 different forms for exporting industrial products. The European Free Trade Area countries insist that the introduction of the Single Administrative Document throughout Western Europe should be accompanied by a further simplification of the origin rules in trade between the European Free Trade Area and the European Community through the long-term certificate system whereby an exporter only has to apply for an authorization once a year.

(5) The Community has used anti-dumping procedures against the European Free Trade Area firms which, according to the Association's experts, are not in conformity with the Free Trade Agreements.

(6) Public procurement is a difficult area for relations between the European Free Trade Area and the European Community. Even within the Community, only a limited proportion of procurement contracts are genuinely open to bids from firms in other countries. Small nations, like the Association members, depend to a large extent on free competition, and would gain from more liberalized procedures for public procurement.

(7) Since the Luxembourg meeting in 1984, relations between the European Free Trade Area and the European Community have developed in a more systematic way than in the previous 24 years, yet a lot of work is done informally. This could be an advantage as more room is left for pragmatic, unbureaucratic solutions.

Trade with China

In spite of recent setbacks, trade with China has been developed through a series of agreements in which the European Community has taken an initiative. An account of some of the issues develops the following themes.[7]

(1) The value of Chinese trade quadrupled between 1975 and 1985, and China has attracted much foreign investment, a large proportion of which is from Community Member States.

(2) The Chinese stress the political dimension of the relationship with the European Community. After initially criticizing the Community as a puppet of the United States, the Chinese now perceive it as a potential diplomatic ally with a common interest in developing the international system away from the sole control of the superpowers.

(3) The Community is more interested in the economics of the relationship, especially in terms of trade and investment, the latter being almost exclusively from the Community to China.

(4) The 1978 European Community–China Trade Agreement was basically a five-year non-preferential agreement. Despite a commitment to promote and intensify trade the agreement lacked real substance. It was replaced in 1985 by a more extensive agreement. This included a section on economic cooperation, to be encouraged across a wide range of activities including industry, agriculture, energy and transport. Also offered were joint production and ventures, technology transfer, financial cooperation, visits, seminars and a general exchange of information.

(5) The Chinese believe that one of the two goals of China's basic national policy is to promote a sustained, steady growth of China's economy by the execution of the policy of reform and an opening to the outside world.

(6) Although China has not turned into the lucrative export market of over a billion consumers for which many had hoped, it remains an important new partner for the Community.

United States and Canada: a bilateral trade treaty

The long gestation period of this controversial treaty between two rich nations has been reviewed in the following terms.[8]

(1) Canadians believe that the multilateral trading system alone is inadequate to ensure a more productive and internationally competitive economy, and look to further trade liberalization through commercial integration with the United States.

(2) Some business circles support a common market approach, involving the removal of all barriers to the flow of goods, money and people between the two countries. Others have called for a free-trade arrangement which would eliminate existing tariff and non-tariff barriers. The Standing Committee on Foreign Affairs of the Canadian Senate preferred an industrial free-trade area, while the Canadian government favoured limited, sectoral free-trade agreements, with the option of a broader arrangement.

(3) Once the final tariff reductions agreed in the General Agreement on Tariffs and Trade Multilateral Trade Negotiations came into operation in 1987, negotiations for the free-trade area would cover a ten-year transition period, couched in North American terms.

(4) The free trade area would:

(a) exclude agricultural, mineral, fishery and energy products;
(b) eliminate all tariffs and protectionist non-tariff barriers over a ten-year period, with the United States moving at a faster pace than Canada;
(c) provide safeguards in the form of an escape clause;
(d) enable both countries to set up adjustment assistance programmes;
(e) contain an understanding on the use of permissible subsidies;
(f) relax the enforcement of competition laws by both countries with respect to specialization agreements and mergers;
(g) create a joint monitoring agency and an appeal mechanism.

(5) Several arguments were used in favour of the free-trade area. Free access to the United States market would ensure the survival of Canada's secondary manufacturing sector. Canada is the only industrialized country, apart from Australia, without access to an internal market or regional bloc of 100 million people or more. The outflow of Canadian investment to the United States would be reduced since it would no longer be necessary to surmount its walls.

(6) Roughly 65 per cent of trade between Canada and the United States is already duty free. Two-thirds of Canada's dutiable exports to the States face tariffs of five per cent or less. After the agreed tariff cuts in 1987, the average United States tariff on manufactured goods would be around four per cent, compared to nine per cent in Canada. This means that 80 per cent of Canadian

exports would enter the United States free of duty, while 15 per cent would be subject to tariffs of five per cent or less, and the remainder would face duties of over five per cent.

3.2.2 National institutions

Much of the official stimulation and control of international trade and investment is carried out by national institutions. These can be government or regulatory bodies; they can act unilaterally, through discussions with opposite numbers in other countries, or in collaboration with multilateral, bilateral or regional organizations. They form a critical part of the pattern outlined in these chapters.

National policies reflect both the short-term needs of a country which may be faced with balance-of-payment problems, inflationary pressures, rising unemployment, or any of a number of other temporary calls for action. The policies may also reflect longer-term strategies such as import substitution or export promotion. The latter is strongly advocated by bodies like the World Bank, but the choice is not regarded as an either/or option by most countries. Protectionist measures survive in the most industrialized. One analysis of government strategies has been proposed by Rugman.[9] He put forward a matrix of country policies against company advantages. The country specific advantages are resource based or technology based. The advantage in each sector can be either natural, where a country is rich in resources that are saleable on world markets, or traditional, as in the case of the industrial countries and technology. The advantage can also be brought into existence or enhanced by government action; such a policy can be difficult to implement.

Governments aim to influence corporate policies by micro as well as macro measures. The latter include investment incentives – which have become increasingly competitive and were considered in the previous chapter – and by investment restrictions. Table 3.2.1 shows the incidence of investment restrictions on specific industry sectors in a number of countries.

Central banks

Central banks are frequently used to implement industrial policies. A number of issues have been discussed in identifying their roles in international economic policies, including the following.

(1) The reason for the existence of central banks and their part, for instance, in controlling the foreign lending of the commercial banks.[10]

(2) The operation of specific financial systems and how they react to pressure.[11]

(3) Other options for performing the role of a central bank. The argument of Collyns[12] is that the circumstances of smaller developing countries often make

Table 3.2.1   Investment Restrictions

	Brazil	France	Germany	Italy	Japan	Sweden	Switz-erland	United States
Agriculture	–	×	–	–	×	–	–	–
Arms	–	×	–	–	–	–	–	–
Banking	–	×	×	×	–	×	×	×
Drink	×	×	–	–	×	–	×	–
Energy	–	–	–	–	–	–	×	–
Financial	–	×	–	–	–	×	–	–
Fishing	×	×	–	×	–	×	–	–
Gambling	–	×	–	–	–	–	–	–
Insurance	–	×	–	×	–	×	×	–
Leather	–	–	–	–	×	–	–	–
Legal	–	×	–	–	–	–	–	–
Mining	–	–	–	–	×	–	–	×
Press	–	–	–	×	–	–	–	–
Property	–	–	–	–	–	×	×	–
Publishing	–	×	–	–	–	–	–	–
Radio, TV	×	–	×	–	×	×	×	–
Salt	–	–	–	–	×	–	–	–
Telecom	×	×	×	×	×	×	×	–
Tobacco	–	×	–	–	×	–	–	–
Transport	×	×	×	×	×	×	×	×
Utilities	–	–	–	×	–	×	–	–

Note: × means that foreign investment is restricted in the industry sector by the country.

central banks impractical or irrelevant. Such economies, often based on foreign-owned commercial banks that finance commerce and exports, may be dominated by a limited range of exports and terms of trade that are beyond domestic influence. Monetary policy, too, is different in such economies. Domestic output is determined more by supply conditions and the country's terms of trade than by levels of domestic demand. Another problem is a shortage of capable manpower available for staffing a central bank; this is especially felt when an unstable government saps the independence of the bank.

The existence of other options has been demonstrated by the establishment of transitional authorities in Fiji (1973), Solomon Islands (1976), Seychelles (1976), Belize (1978) and the Maldives (1981). These arrangements are described as stages in development from a currency board into a fully fledged central bank. Transitional monetary authorities can economize human resources and concentrate on basic talks such as issuing currency, providing banking services to the public and private sectors and managing foreign exchange reserves.

Another option is for a group of countries to form a monetary union. This is expected to improve the allocation of resources as exchange risks are reduced and internal barriers to the flow of funds are lowered. There is also a reduced need for foreign exchange reserves as balance-of-payments risks are pooled and transactions within a region can be conducted in a regional currency. The West African Monetary Union is an example.

(4) The profitability, or otherwise, of central bank intervention in the money markets.[13]

3.2.3 Conclusion

A review of international competitiveness[14] designed to demonstrate the dangers of over-competitiveness, also shows the range of options being proposed for countries. A main division is between those which believe in industrial strategies for nations and those which emphasize the operation of market forces – although most believe that both have their place. This chapter has outlined the measures taken by governments to influence international trade in addition to their participation in international and regional treaty organizations. In the case of members of the European Community, bilateral treaties come under the auspices of the regional organizations. Governments are influenced by varying opinions and pressures towards either regulation or liberalization. The latter naturally seems more advantageous to those with existing advantages; regulation, or at least some form of strategy implementation, is perceived to help in either playing for time during a period of economic readjustment or in a process of industrialization.

Notes and References

1. See: *Manual for the Negotiation of Bilateral Tax Treaties between Developed and Developing Countries*. United Nations Department of International Economic and Social Affairs, 1979. See also: Newman, J.: *United Kingdom Double Tax Agreements*, 1979. This subject is also discussed in Chapter 3.4: The New International Economic Order. See also: Bedrossian, A. and others: 'Tax trades as a source of Government revenue – a reestimation', *Scottish Journal of Political Economy*, June 1985.
2. Many accountancy companies (such as Arthur Andersen) publish details of bilateral double-taxation agreements. For a specialist view, see *International Conference on the Double Taxation of Copyright Royalties Remitted from One Country to Another*. UNESCO, 1979.
3. See for example *Colloquy on International Tax Avoidance and Evasion*. Strasbourg, 1980.
4. See McQueen, M.: 'Lomé and the protective effect of rules of origin', *Journal of World Trade Law*, March-April 1982.

5. See Rajana, C. 'The Lomé Convention', *Journal of African Studies*, June 1982.
6. See Hurni, B.: 'Efta-EC relations, aftermath of the Luxembourg Declaration', *Journal of World Trade Law*, September to October 1986.
7. Redmonds, J. and Lan, Z.: 'The European Community and China: New Horizons', *Journal of Common Market Studies*, December 1986.
8. See Sarna, A.: 'The impact of a Canada-US Free Trade Area', *Journal of Common Market Studies*, June 1985. See also Rugman, A.M.: 'Canada's agenda for bilateral trade negotiations', *Business Quarterly*, Spring 1986.
9. See Rugman, A.M.: 'Multinational enterprises and strategies for international competitiveness', paper presented to the Annual Meeting of the Academy of Management, International Management Division, Chicago, August 1986. See also Scott, B.R. and Lodge, G.C. (eds) (1985): *Competitiveness in the World Economy*. Harvard Business School.
10. See Goodhart, C.: 'Why do banks need a central bank?', *Oxford Economic Papers*, March 1987.
11. See for instance Rowley, A.: 'Critical MAS before explosion', *Far Eastern Economic Review*, December 1985 (on Singapore); Sricharatchanga P.: 'Regulation by decree', *Far Eastern Economic Review*, November 1985 (on Thailand); Bradley, M. and Jansen, D.: 'Federal Reserve operating procedure in the eighties: a dynamic analysis', *Journal of Money, Credit and Banking*, February 1985; Longworth, D.: 'Canadian intervention in the foreign exchange market', *Review of Economics and Statistics* (on Canada); Lee, M.: 'Chinese Exchequers', *Far Eastern Economic Review*, May 1985 (on China).
12. See Collyns, C.: 'Alternatives to central banks in small developing countries', *Finance and Development*, December 1982; Timberlake, R.: 'The central banking role of clearing-house associations', *Journal of Money, Credit and Banking*, February 1984.
13. See Beenstock, M. and Dadashi, S.: 'The profitability of forward currency speculation by central banks', *European Economic Review*, April 1986.
14. See Rugman, A.M.: 'National Strategies for International Competitiveness', *Multinational Business*, no. 3, 1985. Among the citations on strategies are: Stopford, J.: 'The international environment and the required adjustments to assure international competitiveness of European industry', paper presented at Brussels Workshop, June 1984; Scott, B.R. and Lodge, G.P. (eds) (1985): *US Competitiveness in the World Economy*. Harvard Business School; Nielson, R.P.: 'Industrial policy: the case for national strategies for world markets', *Long Range Planning*, 17.5, 1984, pp. 50–9. An example of emphasis on market forces is: Hindley, B.: 'Empty economics in the case for industrial policy', *The World Economy*, September 1984, pp. 277–94. A collection of papers arising from a Competitiveness Initiative of the Economic and Social Science Research Council was published in the *Journal of Marketing*, 4.2, Winter 1988.

3.3

Regional Organizations

A typical treaty of today is the regional alliance designed to serve mainly, sometimes solely, economic purposes; such alliances contrast with those of the past which were negotiated primarily to serve military and political purposes, with economic motives in the background. As it happens, one of the institutions mentioned in this chapter – the Association of South East Asian Nations – did start as a military alliance; the insurgencies that brought it into existence have gradually faded away (the last remains are thought to have been put to rest as this chapter was being written in late 1989), and the Association has grown into a regional economic body.

The success of the European Community, albeit sometimes more appreciated by non-Europeans than Europeans, has stimulated the emergence and growth of other regional organizations. There are about 65 organizations which bring together three or more countries with formal links, including the economic. These are distinguished from multilateral treaties because they establish a separate organization with its own staff. The types of regional organization that are of interest to international business scholars are the economic communities (aiming for a high level of integration), the free-trade areas (aiming for free trade between members but not a common external tariff) and the regional banks.

Five examples to illustrate the principle characteristics of these organizations are employed in this chapter: the European Community, the Andean Group, the Caribbean Community and Common Market, the Association of South East Asian Nations and Development Banks.

3.3.1   The European Community

The European Community has generated a considerable literature, including at least one Journal mainly devoted to its interests.[1] A number of issues are discussed in the literature, mostly concerned with:

(1) the management of the Community itself (its constitution, decision-making and financing);
(2) relations between the Community institutions and regulations and those of the member states: the emergence of a single market;
(3) relations between the Community and the rest of the world;
(4) finance: the European Monetary System, the European Currency Unit, the European Development Bank and the finance sector. This subject is treated separately because of its scope and comprehensiveness;
(5) The Common Agricultural Policy.

(1)   The management of the Community

A special feature of the European Community is its ability to legislate – to propose laws which, once adopted, become binding on the member states. This is not a sacrifice of sovereignty *in law*, since Community regulations still have to be passed by national parliaments; but it is *in fact* because these parliaments are almost certain to accept them. To refuse to ratify a significant piece of legislation would be to leave the Community. Up to now no country, except Greenland, has left. A balance of advantage in staying in has always overcome nationalist scruples about loss of sovereignty, however forcibly expressed.

The decision-making process[2] was framed to make it unlikely that any member would wish to leave and, in the light of experience, this process is gradually being modified. The modifications include a redefinition of the roles of the four main institutions – the Commission, the Council of Ministers, the European Parliament and the Court of Justice. The Commission is the full-time executive of the Community, appointed by the member states; it proposes new legislation after consultation with interested parties throughout Europe. The proposals are then put to the Council of Ministers who decide whether to proceed. For most of the Community's existence, the Council has had to decide unanimously; but a big step forward in modifying the procedures came in 1987 when the Single European Act brought in majority voting on most issues. The Council of Ministers, made up of the foreign ministers of the member states, considers proposed legislation in the light of national interests and, once agreed, passes it to the European Parliament. This was established as an advisory, not a legislative, body but a gradual change has been towards increasing its power; it now has authority over the budget and the pace of change has been increased by the Single European Act. Now that Parliament is elected by universal suffrage, along the same lines as national parliaments, it is claiming greater authority still. A power struggle between the European Parliament and the Council of Ministers, already evident, is likely to intensify. The Council currently remains the initiator and ultimate decision-taker, but members of the European Parliament are discovering their powers and will find ways to enhance them; at the time of writing, however, the role of parliament remains advisory.

Procedural modifications have been designed to speed up decisions aimed at completing the internal market (the 1992 initiative) and to foster communication on the European Monetary System, economic and social cohesion, research, technology, transport and the environment. The processes remain lengthy – there is no time limit to legislation – and subject to much lobbying at national and Community level. Publicity has been designed to build up a spirit of common citizenship among the people of the Community countries; this publicity has also contributed to promoting demands for turning Parliament into an institution more like that to which the citizens are accustomed in their own countries. Efforts to persuade people to 'think European' have been producing this side effect, which is not always welcome to member governments and which is raising the profile of the Parliament.

Social and industrial policies are emerging designed to provide more uniform conditions of work for citizens and of legislation for companies. The European company has been stalled for many years; proposals for greater worker participation (the Vredeling Proposal) have also been delayed, but the European Economic Interest Grouping has been brought into existence. This is designed to enable businesses to enter into agreements across frontiers without the formalities of joint ventures which may only be suitable for large companies, and without fear of intervention as a result of the competition policy. Based on an existing French law, this arrangement is the first Community-wide formula to ease business integration.[3]

(2) Relations between the Community institutions and regulations and those of the member states[4]

An important task of the Community is to create an *internal market*. The first task of abolishing internal duties and establishing a common tariff for goods imported to member countries was established long ago (in 1968). The creation of a common market and the abolition of non-tariff barriers have proved more difficult. The range of issues being tackled is wide and includes the following:

The methods of levying Value Added Tax and excise duties, and the rates at which they are levied. The way these taxes are being applied in some member states has the effect of turning them into customs duties in all but name. The goods are stopped at frontiers and extra tax is charged. The difficulties of overcoming this are reflected in the special attention paid to this issue. As a result of a decision in 1987, any harmonization of taxes and duties needs a unanimous decision of the Council of Ministers which, even then, could allow exceptions.

Food law has been gradually harmonized in regulations concerned with public health, consumer protection, fair trading and official inspection.

Manufacturing standards have been laboriously harmonized over the years and many more are included in the 1992 initiative. A new approach, adopted in the

1980s, concentrates on performance issues such as safety, rather than the details of technical structure, thus allowing regulations to be agreed more readily.

Frontier formalities, the checks and inspections at frontiers, remain controversial.

Business law is being more closely integrated. A general distinction is now being made between *harmonization* – whereby all member countries must have a common law – and *mutual recognition* which means that any member country will accept products, practices or qualifications which are recognized in any other member.

Competition policy has, on the whole, been a success story for the Community. This is an issue on which there has been a common interest arising from two motives. One is the need for a competition policy that takes account of the market power of international companies. While these companies may dominate in a national market, they may be relatively small by international standards; this means that national competition policies may be ineffective, and a continent-wide law is required. The other need for a competition policy is that it helps to make the market a reality. Measures designed to break down customs and other barriers could easily be used by companies to build up considerable power. For the market to become free and efficient requires controls over agreements between companies as well as their market share. For this reason, the legislation has not only been used against large takeovers, but even more frequently against restrictive agreements on, for instance, agencies. However, most franchising agreements are exempt from the provisions of competition law. The exemption was introduced following a court ruling in the mid-1980s declaring that a specific agreement infringed the competition laws. The companies involved in this ruling were subsequently given special individual clearances by the Commission. Technical licensing agreements have also been exempted.[5]

(3)   Relations between the Community and the rest of the world[6]

Agreements between the Community and other countries take a number of forms. There are *Association Agreements* with Cyprus, Malta and Turkey. These may be expected eventually to lead to membership. There are *Trade Agreements* with members of the European Free Trade Association, most members of the Council for Mutual Economic Assistance and a number of countries in South East Asia and Latin America. There are also *Cooperation Agreements* with other regional organizations like the Association of South East Asian Nations, the Andean Pact, the Central American Common Market, Maghreb, Mashraq and some individual countries including Israel.

Many of these, especially the trade agreements, have already been mentioned under the heading of multilateral treaties (Chapter 3.2). Special mention should be made of the Lomé Convention with 66 African, Caribbean and Pacific (ACP) countries, former European colonies. For the member countries, a European Development Fund has been established. Most of the aid provided through this fund (about 80 per cent) is spent in outright grants, the rest for loans at low rates of interest. Contracts awarded in connection with the fund are competed for on equal terms by companies throughout the Community and include major construction projects and rural development schemes (55 per cent), supply contracts (30 per cent) and service and consultancy projects (15 per cent).

Dumping and protectionism

A perennial issue on the agenda of the European Commission is that of dumping. This is a complex issue: examples are hard to identify and cases difficult to prove. One article on the subject – entitled: 'EC: dumping from non-market economies'[7] – discussed a specific instance: the import of ball-bearings from the non-market economies of Eastern Europe. In this case, the problem of proof was exacerbated by the lack of a market price in the exporting countries. To overcome this, Japanese prices were taken as a yardstick. This, in turn, raised another difficulty. The imports from Eastern Europe were of an inferior quality to those from Japan and so could be regarded as applying to a different market. In view of the fact that the imports had not increased, it was decided that no injury had occurred and the dumping case was dropped. Although so specific, this case neatly illustrates two of the problems that arise in dumping cases.

The reverse of the dumping issue is that of protectionism. Glowing phrases like 'opportunity Europe' are matched in other parts of the world by harsher statements about 'fortress Europe'. Trade wars are threatened by the strong (such as the United States) while weaker economies, especially those in the Pacific Rim, are changing their directions of trade to avoid what they see as a threat of protectionism in Europe.

(4) Finance: the European Monetary System (the European Currency Unit), the European Development Bank and the finance sector[8]

Subjects related to finance have been segregated in a separate section because of their width and range. They include institutions, a currency and the harmonization of the banking sector.

The European Monetary System (EMS)

The aim of the System is to establish 'closer monetary cooperation leading to a zone of monetary stability in Europe'. This covers the two closely related objectives of exchange-rate stabilization and a bringing together of the economic and monetary policies of the member states. Among the components of the system is the *European Currency Unit* (ECU). This is made up of a basket of currencies reflecting the balance between the economies of member countries at any given time. It was established with four objectives:

(a) to fix the central rates in the exchange mechanism;
(b) as a point of reference for calculations within the mechanism;
(c) for denominating creditor and debtor balances resulting from any intervention in Community currencies;
(d) as a reserve instrument and means of settlement between central banks in
the Community.

With the increase of settlements in ECUs and the beginnings of bonds
denominated in ECUs, the currency is gaining credibility and looks set to form
the basis of a European currency, although the current emphasis is on mutual
recognition of one another's monetary units.

Another component of the system is the Exchange Rate Mechanism (ERM).
Participating countries are given a bilateral central rate against each of the other
currencies and fluctuations are permitted within a limited range (plus or minus
2.25 per cent at present, higher for Spain and the United Kingdom). Central
banks are under an obligation not to permit fluctuations outside the limits.
There is also a 'divergence indicator' which indicates approaching danger; action
at this stage is presumed but not compulsory. To support the Exchange Rate
Mechanism there are some credit mechanisms which provide short- and medium-
term credits to countries near their limits. Realignments of the exchange rates
are a further defence which was, in fact, used seven times in the four years
beginning March 1979 alone.

The finance sector
The right of free establishment for banks and their freedom to provide services
was established in the mid-1970s. This did not enable national banks to spread
freely across borders because of national regulations which applied to local as
well as foreign banks. In some countries, for instance, a market demand has to
be established before the setting up of a new bank. The aim of the Commission,
in this and other sectors, is to ensure that a bank is regulated by the laws of its
own country; if it complies with them and qualifies as a European Bank, it can
open branches in any Community country. The second banking directive, giving
effect to this aim, was finally approved in November 1989. These moves should
be seen in the context of pressures in member countries towards a liberalization
of the banking sector combined with greater protection for consumers. At the
same time the European Commission has made it clear that the competition laws
will apply to the banks and prevent, for instance, interest-rate fixing agreements.[9]

(5) The Common Agricultural Policy[10]

For long stereotyped as an example of slow, tortuous decision-making, the
complexities of an agricultural policy have often been underestimated. In fact,
most individual countries find it difficult to maintain a balanced agriculture –
both surplus and famine are common in different parts of the world. Regulatory
systems, both manipulating support prices and reducing surpluses and source,

have produced some results and in 1989 the agriculture budget was considered to be under control: progress from the days when it was regarded as an open-ended commitment.

3.3.2   The Andean Group

The most advanced regional organization in Latin America in terms of its regulatory and coordinating systems is the Andean Group. The record of regional organizations in the area has demonstrated many of the difficulties that such organizations encounter. Military and political difficulties with and between countries have held up developments, as have inequalities of wealth. One organization – the Latin American Free Trade (LAFTA) – broke up because the poorer member countries considered they were being treated unfairly and that the richer countries were gaining more of the benefits. A successor organization – the Latin American Integration Association (LAIA) – has a more loose-knit constitution which allows for greater flexibility. It has different regimes for the richer, middle-range and poorer members. All members of the Andean Group also belong to the Integration Association; most are in the middle-income regime.

The Andean Group now consists of Bolivia, Colombia, Ecuador, Peru and Venezuela; these countries share economies that depend on primary industries – agriculture and extraction. Tariffs have been virtually abolished for manufactured goods between the countries which plan to develop a full common market. By the Cartagena Agreement of 1984, member countries committed themselves to tackle problems of foreign debt. Progress was initially slow between countries which needed to build a communications infrastructure between themselves, and a main thrust has been towards mutual projects in priority sectors designed to promote industrialization. In these two aims – infrastructure and selected common projects – the Andean Group is typical of regional organizations in developing countries. Control of foreign companies is also on the agenda. In the Group's early days, the controls were fairly comprehensive; member countries were interested in presenting a common front to reduce exploitation, as they saw it. More recently the controls have been modified and incentives to foreign investment have been reconsidered although 100 per cent ownership of local companies is still not permitted.[11]

3.3.3   The Caribbean Community and Common Market[12]

This institution developed out of an earlier, less ambitious, project and has had setbacks caused by crises in its member countries, notably Jamaica and Guyana. It covers a wide range of economies, with Trinidad and Tobago the wealthiest, and this has caused tensions. As in Latin America, the poorer countries have claimed they are at a disadvantage. The main objectives are economic integration, a common external tariff and development planning. Joint projects began in 1976 with the founding of the Caribbean Food Corporation; more recently there have been several projects in the extractive industries, along with attempts to lessen dependence on external investment. A neighbouring group – the Organization of Eastern Caribbean States – has virtually developed into a single country.

3.3.4 The Association of South East Asian Nations (ASEAN)

This Association was founded in the 1960s with a range of objectives. Originally political and military concerns were uppermost, since some member countries were suffering from insurgency. As the military threat receded, economic considerations came to the fore and the Association began to develop in the late 1970s. Since then, the economies of most of the member states have expanded rapidly and some have recorded sensational growth rates; but there has been little integration of those economies, and trade between them is limited as a proportion of their total trade. Nevertheless the Association has managed to negotiate agreements with other groupings on favourable terms.

A number of common projects have been started, mainly in chemicals and engineering but also in finance. This latter came on the horizon at the end of the 1970s with the third Association of South East Asian Nations banking conference in Jakarta.[13] This set up an Asean Finance Corporation (AFC) to participate in and initiate new industrial investment by providing equity capital and low-cost funds, and to underwrite equity and debt issues for new enterprises. The Corporation also guarantees convertible or straight debenture issues for Association of South East Asian Nations' ventures, as well as Association of South East Asian Nations' credits going outside the Association but for the benefit of enterprises based in member countries. This latter measure was designed to foster joint ventures with foreign companies, and provide a link to encourage investment from outside the area, especially from Japan. The Corporation was left with the political problem of ensuring cooperation in its schemes from the member countries. One debate that has yet to be resolved is how far the Association of South East Asian Nations expects to go towards closer integration; another is the probable development of a wider free-trade area covering other Pacific Rim countries.[14]

3.3.5 Development banks

A number of problems have been identified and examined as a result of the slow progress made by the development banks. An article on the *African Development*

Bank[15] explained a problem that has also been encountered by others but has affected them less – the role of politics. It is alleged that over-politicization has led to a shortage of capital and the use of consensus as a means of resolving even technical issues. The per caput lending during the first ten years of the Bank's existence was only $0.45 a head, a small fraction of that achieved by other development banks. At the same time a shake-up was reported in the *Asian Development Bank*. This was a result of a cut back of one-fifth in the staff designed to make the Bank more efficient. A few years later, in 1984, the Bank changed course by entering into equity investments to stimulate money markets and industrial projects in member countries.

3.3.6   Conclusion

A number of common threads have been noted by commentators on regional organizations.

Slow decision-making. Most insist on unanimity – the European Community has only modified this rule – and this becomes more difficult as an institution develops. Common interests become less common when the finer details are under discussion.[16]

Conflict between poorer and richer members. At least one organization broke up on this issue. It is common for poorer member countries to perceive that the wealthier are gaining more advantage from the treaty; naturally the richer deny this, frequently claiming that they put more resources into mutual projects.

Nationalism and regionalism. One problem is that of promoting regionalism among countries that have an immediate concern of promoting nationalism. This difficulty has been found, for example, in the Economic Community of West African States (ECOWAS) some of whose members – like Ghana and Nigeria – have needed to establish a national allegiance against divisive tribal outlooks. As a result, it is not easy to foster a wider regional loyalty at the same time.

The initiation of common projects. One means by which wider loyalties are being built up, and citizens of member countries persuaded of the practical advantages of membership of regional organizations, is through cooperative projects. In the regional organizations of developing countries, especially, emphasis is placed on projects to create a climate of cooperative action in which other institutions can emerge. These exist in many sectors, but particularly agriculture, chemicals and finance. The Common Agricultural Policy of the European Community is also a community project, but in a context that is regulatory rather than innovative. In the European Community, greater emphasis is placed on common projects undertaken by organizations or individuals – commercial or educational, for instance – rather than official actions as such.

Notes and References

1. *The Journal of Common Market Studies.*
2. This account of the decision-making process of the European Community will be all too familiar to European scholars; it is included here for the benefit of our wider readership. Booklets outlining the structure and allocation of powers of community are available free from the Directorate-General of information which has offices in many countries outside Europe as well as within.
3. See also Chapter 4.5. The law enabling the existence of a European Economic Interest Grouping (EEIG) was created in 1985 and became operative in 1989. It provides a legal framework for joint ventures on a number of activities such as production, sales, data processing, research and much else; it is also flexible about who can take part, including private companies, public institutions and professionals. The terms of the law can be found in the *Official Journal* of the European Communities, no. L 199, 31 July 1985, p. 1.
4. Among articles on this subject, see: Pinder, J.: 'European Community and nation state: a case for neo-federalism', *International Affairs*, Winter 1985–6; Johnson, G.: 'Perspectives on the European Economic Outlook', *Barclay's Review*, August 1984; Hager, W.: 'Protectionism and security: how to preserve free trade in Europe', *International Affairs*, Summer 1982.

   On the implications of the Single European Act, see: Fitzmaurice, J.: 'An analysis of the European Community's cooperation procedures', *Journal of Common Market Studies*, 26, 1987–8, pp. 389–400; McAleese, D. and Matthews, A.: 'The Single European Act and Ireland: implications for a small member state', *Journal of Common Market Studies*, 26.1, September 1987, pp. 39–60. See also Cecchini, P. and others: (1988), *1992: European Challenge.* Gower.
5. The Commission produces an annual *Report on Competition Policy* (Luxembourg: Office for Publications of the European Community). For a report suggesting that competition policy is indeed one of the successes of the European Community, but that there is still much to be done, see: Smellie, R.: 'Competition policy of the European Community: a conference report', *Government and Opposition*, Summer 1983.
6. Among articles on this subject are: Zlebura, G. et al.: 'Internationalization of capital and the role of the European Community', *Journal of Common Market Studies*, September–December 1982; Mayer, W.: 'Theoretical considerations on negotiated tariff adjustments', *Oxford Economic Papers*, March 1981; Marsh, P.: 'EEC foreign policy and the political management of East-West economic relations', *Millenium*, Spring 1980; Weiss, F.: 'A political economy of EC trade policy against the less developed countries', *European Economic Review*, February to March 1987; Pearce, J.: 'Europrotectionism: the challenge and the cost', *World today*, December 1985; Hull, R.: 'European-ASEAN relations: a model for international partnership?' *Asian Affairs*, February 1984; Ball, R.: 'The Common Market's failure', *Altantic Community Quarterly*, Spring 1984; Kondonassis, A.: 'Some major trade and development programmes of the European Economic Community with the LDCs: towards a common development policy?' *Journal of Economic Issues*, June 1984; Lunn, J.: 'Determinants of US direct investment in the ECC: further evidence', *European*

Economic Review, January 1980. See also Croxford, G.J. and others: 'The reform of the European Development Fund: a preliminary assessment', *Journal of Common Market Studies*, 26, 1987–8, pp. 25–38.

7. *Journal of World Trade Law*, September–October 1986.
8. Among articles on this subject see: Tugendhat, C.: 'Opening up Europe's financial sector to intra-community competition', *Banker*, January 1985. See also Ormstrom Muller, J.: 'Economic effects of Monetary Compensation Amounts', *National Westminster Bank Quarterly Review*, November 1983.
9. A letter on this subject from the Commissioner responsible for competition to the European Banking Federation was quoted in the *Financial Times* on 17 November 1989.
10. See Gardner, B.: 'The common agricultural policy: the political obstacle to reform', *Political Quarterly*, April–June 1987.
11. For an account of the earlier efforts of the Andean Group to steer foreign investment into industries and locations determined by the group see: Grosse, R.: 'Foreign Investment Regulation in the Andean Pact: the first ten years', *Inter-American Economic Affairs*, Spring 1980. See also Grosse, R.: 'The Andean foreign investment code's impact on multinational enterprises', *Journal of International Business Studies*, Winter 1983, pp. 121–33. A more general article on the pact is Ferris, E.G.: 'Andean pact and the Amazon treaty: reflections of changing Latin American relations', *Journal of Interamerican Studies*, May 1981.
12. Discussions on various aspects of CARICOM can be found in Williams, M.: 'An analysis of regional trade and payments arrangements in CARICOM, 1971–83', *Social and Economic Studies*, December 1985; Bennett, K.: 'An evaluation of the contribution of CARICOM to intra-regional Caribbean trade', *Social and Economic Studies*, March 1982; Bennett, K.: 'Mobilising foreign exchange reserves for economic growth in CARICOM', *Social and Economic Studies*, December 1981. A further development in CARICOM was The Georgetown Declaration of 4 July 1986 (see *Caricom Perspective*, July–December 1986, supplement). The declaration laid special emphasis on joint ventures, but also other objectives including trade policy.
13. See Sacerdotl, G.: 'Breakthrough by ASEAN's Bankers', *Far Eastern Economic Review*, February 1980. See also Awarichara, S.: 'Asean closes economic ranks', *Far Eastern Economic Review*, October 1980.
14. These policy issues are discussed in a number of articles, including Rieger, H.: 'Asean: a free trade area or a customs union?', *Far Eastern Economic Review*, May 1986; Colbert E.: 'Regional cooperation and the tilt to the West', *Proceedings of the Academy of Political Science*, 1986. This article also looks at other organizations in the area such as the South East Asia Treaty Organization (SEATO). Soesastro, H.: 'ASEAN and the Political Economy of Pacific Cooperation', *Asian Survey*, December 1983; Imagawa, E.: 'Initiating a Pacific Basin plan', *Japan Quarterly*, April–June 1985; Atarashi, K.: 'Japan's economic cooperation policy towards the ASEAN countries', *International Affairs*, Winter 1984–5; Limqueco, P.: 'Contradictions of development in ASEAN', *Journal of Contemporary Asia*, no. 3, 1983.
15. See 'Some unresolved problems in the African Development Bank,' *World Development*, November–December 1981. The articles on the Asian Development Bank referred to later in the paragraph are Clad, J.: 'Building for the past', *Far Eastern Economic Review*, April 1987; Ensor, P.: 'The ADB's adventure', *Far Eastern Econ-*

omic Review, February 1984. The contrast between those two titles is symptomatic of a change in the Bank itself. Other articles on development banks include the following:

Asian Development Bank

Clad, J.: 'Unhappy returns', *Far Eastern Economic Review*, November 1986; Rowley, A.: 'Ideology before need', *Far Eastern Economic Review*, February 1985; Ocompo-Kelfors, S.: 'ADB counts the cost', *Far Eastern Economic Review*, February 1984; Bowring, P.: 'Quiet revolution', *Far Eastern Economic Review*, May 1983; Bowring, P.: 'ADB prepares its cost', *Far Eastern Economic Review*, February 1981; Wihtol, R.: 'Asian Development Bank: development financing or capitalist export promotion?', *Journal of Contemporary Asia*, no. 3, 1979.

African Development Bank

'African Development Bank, special anniversary report: 20 years of growth', *Africa*, September 1984; Mung'omba, W.: 'ADB spells out its priorities', *Africa*, March 1983; Fordwor, K.: 'Some unresolved problems of the African Development Bank', *World Development*, November–December 1981; Ngwube, D.: 'ADB banks on agriculture', *Africa*, January 1981.

Development banks: general

Krassner, S.: 'Power structures and regional development banks', *International Organization*, Spring 1981; Schoultz, L.: 'Politics, economics and US participation in multilateral development banks', *International Organization*, Summer 1982.

16. The present author's favourite example is in the Treaty of Rome itself where (in the English version published by Her Majesty's Stationery Office in 1967) in a 231-page document designed to revolutionize Europe, two pages are devoted to the subject of bananas. While major issues took up less space relative to their significance, the importing of one product occupied nearly one per cent of the words of the Treaty because of an argument over which countries should be encouraged (or even allowed) to supply it. A similar role is accorded to wattle in the British Treaty of Accession.

3.4

The New International Economic Order into the 1990s

3.4.1 Introduction

Over four decades after the onset of independence much of the developing world is still confronted by a vast gulf in living standards between itself and the industrialized countries. Table 3.4.1 and Graph 3.4.1 illustrate the scale of the difference. In 1988, though the developing countries comprised three quarters of the world's population and three fifths of its territory, they nevertheless accounted for only a tiny proportion of the total world Gross National Product. The average per caput Gross National Product of the developing economies (ranging from wealthy Kuwait to impoverished Bangladesh) amounted to a mere five per cent of the per caput Gross National Product of industrialized countries. This situation persists despite considerable effort on the part of developing countries. For example, Graphs 3.4.2 and 3.4.3 show that developing countries have grown considerably faster than industrialized countries in terms of both Gross National Product and trade over the last few decades, but (apart from the pressures of population growth with the downward impact on per caput incomes) it is clear that the magnitude of the task needed to achieve 'development' in a short time-scale necessitates much more rapid rates of growth than hitherto achieved by developing countries as a whole (the Newly Industrializing Countries of East Asia being the main exceptions).

However, though developing countries occupy a relatively large position in the international trade framework (nearly 30 per cent of total trade in Table 3.4.1), and, indeed, the Newly Industrializing Countries have relied on trade expansion as one component of their industrialization strategy (Graph 3.4.3), it can be argued (see Section 3.4.2) that their economic options are severely constrained by the world economic system. In this context, the New International Economic Order is 'an economic and political concept, variously interpreted, which encapsulates the developing countries' demands for a greater access to the world's economic, financial and technological resources. These demands are born

Table 3.4.1   Industrial and Developing Countries: Comparative Data, 1988[1]

	Industrial countries	Developing countries
Area[2] (million Km[2])	32.0	80.4
Population[3] (millions)	818	3,960
Total GNP (US$ billion)	13,928	3,200
Total GNP Per Capita (US$)	17,000	800
Total Exports (US$ billion)	1,970	730
Total Imports (US$ billion)	2,040	760

Notes:
(1) Excluding East European countries.
(2) World area (including Eastern Europe) = 135.9 mn km2.
(3) World population (including Eastern Europe) = 5,200 million people.

Source: Dresdner Bank Statistical Survey, September 1989.

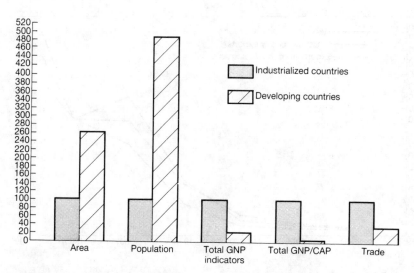

Graph 3.4.1   A Comparison of Industrialized and Developing Countries, 1988 (Selected Indicators: Industrialized Countries = 100)

Source: Dresdner Bank Statistical Survey, September 1989.

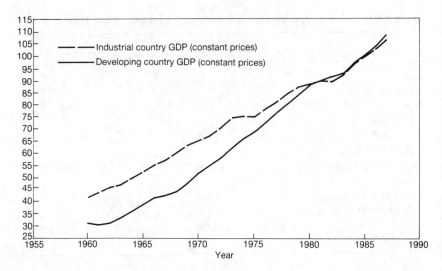

Graph 3.4.2   Industrial and Developing Country GDP Growth, 1960–1988 (Indexes: 1985 = 100)

Source: IMF *International Financial Statistics Yearbook*, 1989, Washington.

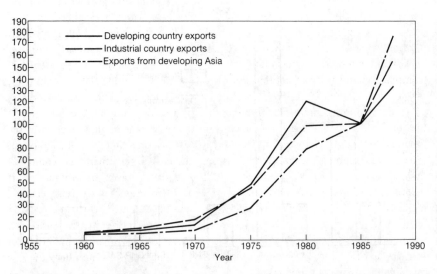

Graph 3.4.3   Industrial and Developing Country Export Growth, 1960–1988 (Indexes: 1985 = 100)

Source: IMF *International Financial Statistics Yearbook*, 1989, Washington.

of disappointments following political independence, the recognition that the pace and pattern of development is constrained by economic and technological dependence on industrialized countries, and the fear that the chasm between developed and developing nation-states will surely increase unless the existing international structures and relationships are transformed.' (Mirza (1988)). The progress of the New International Economic Order is examined in Section 3.4.3 following an examination of the principal issues underlying the developing country demands in the next section.

3.4.2 The principal issues, demands and proposals

The issues and proposals discussed below are based on the United Nations sponsored concept that all states should have a fair access to the world's resources. Another idea underlying the New International Economic Order is that the economic expansion of the developing countries can be to the benefit of the industrialized countries. Both of these ideas will be referred to later.

Commodities

Until recently the vast bulk of the trade between industrialized countries (the North) and developing countries (the South) consisted of the former specializing in, and exporting, manufactured goods, while the latter specialized in, and exported, agricultural goods and raw materials ('commodities'). This specialized production and exchange is usually referred to as the *old international division of labour* and is resented by developing countries because it is felt that the demand, composition and price of commodities is determined by industrialized countries, while they have little influence on manufactured goods. The reasons for this state of affairs are manifold and include: (i) the demand for commodities is frequently derived demand and depends on the requirements of a given industry (mainly located in industrialized countries) at any one time; (ii) technological progress is more rapid in manufacturing industries and therefore commodity-dependent developing countries are 'locked into' slower growth rates; (iii) manufactured goods are more 'marketable' and, for example, whereas technologically induced productivity increases can be retained through product differentiation of manufactured products, this is not normally the case with commodities – in fact price falls; and (iv) multinational companies, mainly from the industrial North, control commodities at one stage or another, be this production, distribution or sales.

The above arguments can be extended or qualified, but they amply indicate the South's great concern over commodity trade. Graphs 3.4.4 and 3.4.5 support these concerns to some extent. As Graph 3.4.4 shows, the price of commodities (a weighted index of 33 commodities excluding petroleum) rose very slowly

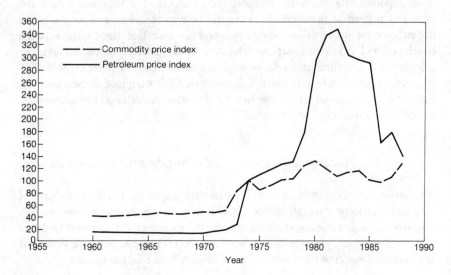

Graph 3.4.4 Commodity and Petroleum Prices: Changes, 1960–1988 (Indexes: 1974 = 100)

Source: IMF *International Financial Statistics Yearbook*, 1989, Washington.

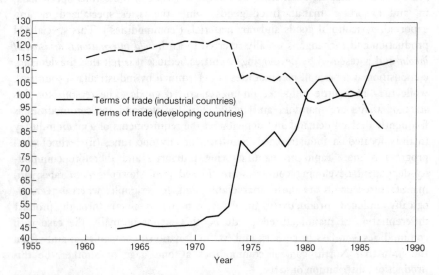

Graph 3.4.5   Changes in the Terms of Trade, 1960–1988 (Indexes: 1985 = 100)

Source: IMF *International Financial Statistics Yearbook*, 1989, Washington.

during most of the 1960s and, following a sharp set of increases in the 1970s, seems to have resumed this trend, although there seems to be a greater price instability. A similar picture can be painted for petroleum, but even more so. The sharp increase in petroleum prices in the 1970s – and the equally sharp fall in the 1980s – is indicative of an international power struggle and, indeed, an example of how a group of countries, the Organization of Petroleum Exporting Countries, attempted to establish a (partial) new international economic order. A number of other developing countries also managed to establish cartel-based price increases in other commodities during the 1970s, but this was certainly aided by fears of energy and raw materials shortages gripping many firms in the industrialized countries at the time. The rise in commodity (including petroleum) prices was short-lived because of the commercial (i.e. firms found alternative sources or developed less resource-intensive methods of production) and political (i.e. the international diplomacy of the industrialized countries and linked international institutions such as the International Monetary Fund and the Organization for Economic Cooperation and Development) consequences. The dramatic fall in petroleum and other commodity prices in the 1980s is nevertheless a good example of the problems associated with such specializations in the international division of labour. If the price of commodities was deflated against the increases in the price of manufactured goods, the effect would be even more dramatic and would clearly affect the terms of trade between countries (as would other factors). Graph 3.4.5 shows the movement of the terms of trade over the last three decades and, as the developing countries protest, apart from the 1970s, these have generally been moving against them.

Given the price and price instability problems associated with commodities, developing countries argue strongly for an 'integrated programme for commodities' which will stabilize the commodity market, extend developing-country control over activities such as the processing, distribution and marketing of commodities, and compensate for any shortfalls in export earnings resulting from a sudden fall in prices. This is a major theme in the New International Economic Order negotiations. Furtado and others (1989) show the huge losses suffered by sub-Saharan countries in Africa following the decline in commodity prices and the dollar (the chief currency in which the goods are priced) in the 1980s.

Manufacturing

In order to reduce their dependence on commodities and ensure higher living standards, developing countries have diversified into manufacturing industries. The most successful examples are the Newly Industrializing Countries of Asia and Latin America which are now a major part of the *new international division of labour* which entails a new type of trade specialization between industrialized and developing countries: chiefly a respective specialization and trade in high- versus low-technology manufactures (though the concept and reality is much more complex). Nevertheless a number of major problems remain, especially for the non-Newly Industrializing Countries.

One major issue is that industrialized countries still produce and control most technology. Thus 'low technology' industries such as textiles, clothing and electronics have been transferred, but more advanced industries remain in the industrialized countries, although India, South Korea, Taiwan, Brazil and other Newly Industrializing Countries have managed to generate some very advanced technologies. One reason why technology transfer is limited is that technical knowledge, skills, patents and other types of information are the main basis upon which Northern (especially multinational) companies have established their privileges and profits. Technology transfer is thus not deemed to be good business practice, although in some cases it may be a firm's best option.

Secondly, partly as a result of Newly Industrializing Countries successes, developing countries have increasingly faced difficulties in exporting to industrialized countries because of tariffs, non-tariff barriers and other forms of protection (see Castro (1989) for a more detailed analysis). Thirdly, more recently, a number of concessions won in previous New International Economic Order negotiations have been removed or reduced by a number of industrialized countries. For example, the United States is curtailing the coverage of the General System of Preferences privileges (see Table 3.4.4 for a discussion of this) which have previously allowed developing-country firms easier access into its markets (Kirkman (1989)). Finally, there is a considerable push by industrialized countries to force 'liberalization' and 'reciprocity' on developing countries (this was a major theme in the Uruguay Round of the General Agreement on Tariffs and Trade in 1990) whose domestic industries could well suffer from the onslaught of more advanced and competitive companies from the industrialized countries.

In response, a series of proposals have emanated from the South concerning manufacturing and trade. These include: (i) the reduction of trade restrictions and the elimination of tied trade; (ii) a code on technology transfer, a reform of the patent system and the prevention of the reverse flow of technology (i.e. the migration of skilled personnel from developing to industrialized countries); (iii) a code of conduct to reduce restrictive practices and encourage Multinational Corporations to transfer technology, skills and resources more readily to developing countries; and (iv) an increase in financial flows to the South, including aid and foreign direct investment.

Financial Flows

Though most investment in developing countries has been financed by domestic savings, external finance, has been required by non-oil-developing countries. This has been forthcoming from a number of countries, chiefly the industrialized

Table 3.4.2   Aid and Foreign Direct Investment Flows to Developing Countries, 1987
(billions of US$)

	Aid	FDI
Africa	11.1	0.8
East Asia	2.2	2.5
Other Asia	7.2	1.3
Middle East	6.3	0.8
Latin America	3.6	4.1
Total	30.4	9.5

Source: World Bank, World Development Report, 1989, Oxford University Press.

Table 3.4.3   Long-term Lending to Developing Countries, 1987 (billions of US$)

	Total debt outstanding	Net flows	Net transfers
Africa	109	10	6
East Asia	102	−9	−16
Other Asia	142	11	5
Middle East	260	3	12
Latin America	384	5	−19
Total	996	16	−38

Notes:
Net flows are new inflows of lending minus principal repayments.
Net transfers are net flows minus interest repayments.

Source: World Bank, World Development Report, 1989, Oxford University Press.

countries, but also Organization of Petroleum Exporting Countries and the socialist countries. As Tables 3.4.2 and 3.4.3 show, most external finance is in the form of aid, bank loans and foreign direct investment. Bank loans have been considerable in recent years, but as Table 3.4.3 indicates, these have now become a net drain on resources as banks have reduced their lending to developing countries and interest rates have increased. In 1987 there was a net *outflow* of United States $38 billion from developing countries to foreign lenders, chiefly banks. Foreign direct investment remains small and slanted toward the richer developing country, and a number of proposals are aimed at trying to increase the inflow of private investment and ensure a wider distribution between countries.

In 1968 industrialized countries promised to give one per cent of their Gross National Products in aid and since then a target of 0.7 per cent has been established. Only five countries, Denmark, France, The Netherlands, Norway (over 1 per cent) and Sweden have exceeded the 0.7 per cent target and these are all relatively small countries, apart from France. Other major donors, including the United States of America and the United Kingdom, have barely exceeded 0.25 per cent. Because of the scale of the United States of America and Japanese economies, they are the two largest aid givers. Japanese aid has been expanding rapidly in recent years and may exceed that of the United States of America some time in the 1990s. As a result of the 1968 promise, developing countries consistently urge that industrialized countries raise their aid to the intended level. There are also calls to ensure more aid goes through multilateral channels such as the World Bank so that source countries have less control and cannot therefore tie the aid to purchasing goods from the donor country, for example.

Other issues

A number of New International Economic Order proposals relate to issues which are only indirectly concerned with the present international economic order. One set of proposals relates to the fate of land-locked and small-island economies which are often under-developed because of their geography. Another issue concerns the massive resources of the sea and sea bed which have been declared 'the common heritage of mankind' by the United Nations. Negotiations on the extraction and distribution of the sea's resources have been conducted in the United Nation's Conference on the Law of the Sea (UNCLOS) and a draft treaty was agreed in 1982. However, the United States refused to sign the treaty and many other industrialized countries have yet to ratify it. The law of the sea therefore remains a hot issue in the New International Economic Order dialogue.

   The above section has only summarized the more important debates in the New International Economic Order; further information can be gained from the sources mentioned at the end of this chapter. Some of the issues emerging for the 1990s are also discussed in Section 3.4.5.

3.4.3   The main actors and the evolution of the New International Economic Order

A vast array of entities are involved in the continuing dialogue for a New International Economic Order and some of the more important ones are discussed below. A history of the New International Economic Order is presented in Table 3.4.4 which is worth examining before reading the remained of this section.

Table 3.4.4 A Brief Chronology of the New International Economic Order

1955	Twenty-nine newly independent countries take part in a conference in Bandung (Indonesia). They call for stable prices and demand commodities.
1961	At the first conference of the Non-Aligned Movement (founded in 1956), held in Belgrade, twenty-five developing countries call for a new international order to redress international terms of trade and allow them greater access to the world's resources.
1962	As more developing countries become independent and join the United Nations, their power grows in the General Assembly. Consequently, seventy-seven developing countries play a key role in the passage of a UN resolution for a conference on trade and development (UNCTAD). Despite the opposition of industrialised countries UNCTAD I convenes in 1964.
1963	Group of 77 (G77) comes into existence through a formal association of the above developing countries.
1964	UNCTAD I. The first United Nations Conference on Trade and Development is held in Geneva. G77's chief success is to ensure that UNCTAD becomes a permanent and special organ of the United Nations. It is to meet every four years and, because voting is on the basis of one country one vote, it is to play a crucial role in pressing the developing countries' call for a new international economic order (NIEO). Developing countries also call for preferential treatment in trade relations, but nothing definite is agreed. There is some discussion of an IMF facility to finance shortfalls in
	commodity earnings; and industrialized countries offer to give up to 1% of their GNP in aid.
1968	UNCTAD II convenes in New Delhi. The General System of Preferences (GSP) is established. GSP is essentially an undertaking by industrialised countries to treat the trade of selected developing countries preferentially, for example through a reduction in tariffs on selected industries and products. During the 1970s GSP becomes relatively important in developing countries' export success, but later protectionism reduces the value of GSP. An aid target of 1% of GNP is again agreed on, but no date for the achievement of this target is set. There is no general accord on commodity trade, but an international sugar agreement later results. However, the, the European Community refuses to sign, thereby negating the agreement's value.
1972	UNCTAD III convenes in Santiago. Little emerges from this conference and it is considered a failure. G77 proposes a comprehensive series of measures on trade, production, multinational companies, the IMF voting system, and the allocation of new SDRs. Internal dissension in G77 and a negative response from industrializing countries ensures that no substantive agreements are reached. The developing countries ask for more SDRs (Special Drawing Rights, essentially the IMF's 'money') to finance development, but during 1970−74 only 4% of new SDRs are allocated to developing countries.
1973	OPEC (the Organisation of Petroleum Exporting Countries)

(Cont.)

Table 3.4.4 (*Cont.*)

forces a manifold increase in oil prices. The era of cheap energy ceases overnight and industrialized countries, already suffering from a slowdown in growth rates and international financial difficulties, are thrown into disarray.

1974 The position of developing countries is further strengthened by the sixth special session of the United Nations General Assembly. The assembly adopts a charter on the Economic Rights and Duties of States. A new international economic order is on the cards and the term NIEO comes into common usage. There is of course considerable opposition from the industrialized countries, but henceforth they find that they have to negotiate the whole range of international economic issues together, rather than individually.

1975 The North–South Conference on International Economic Cooperation (CIEC) convenes in Paris at the request of industrialized countries. Only nineteen developing countries (seven from OPEC) are invited and industrialized countries attempt to isolate OPEC by discussing only the energy issue. OPEC insists on discussing all commodities and the conference collapses.

1976 UNCTAD IV takes place in Nairobi with G77 riding on the crest of a power-wave, but industrialized countries manage to diffuse most of G77's far-reaching proposals. The main result is the adoption of an Integrated Programme for Commodities, aiming at the stabilization of prices at a 'just' level and the achievement of greater developing country control over commodity distribution and marketing. International

Commodity Agreements (ICAs) were later negotiated in cocoa, coffee, rubber, jute, tin, and sugar, but prices did not stabilize because a common fund to finance shortfalls in revenues was not in operation. At the end of UNCTAD VI (July 1983) the capital of this 'common fund' stood only at 37% of the required amount.

1977 CIEC reconvenes in Paris, when industrialized countries agree to discuss all commodities, finance, and trade within the framework of the NIEO. There are no results and developing countries still cynically believe that the main purpose of CIEC is to discuss the price of oil.

1979 UNCTAD V takes place in Manila after more oil price rises and amid a protectionist trend in industrialized countries. G77 proposes changes in the conditionality of IMF loans, but these are rejected. It is agreed that codes of conduct for transnational companies (multinationals) and technology transfer will be formulated and that UNCTAD will monitor protectionist trends.

1981 A North–South summit takes place in Cancun, Mexico. This conference is arranged after the publication of the first Brandt Commission report, (*North–South: A Programme for Survival*) by Chancellor Bruno Kreisky (Austria), President Lopez Portillo (Mexico), and Prime Minister Pierre Trudeau (Canada) and addresses itself to the entire gamut of NIEO issues, but especially the 'emergency programme' identified by Brandt. This programme refers to a large-scale transfer of resources to the poor countries, an international energy strategy, a global food programme and reforms in the international economic system. Although the emergency programme is also designed to help industrialized countries in the midst of a world recession, the summit is a failure, chiefly because of the negative attitudes of the United States President, Ronald Reagan.

1983 UNCTAD VI convenes in Belgrade amid a serious and intensified crisis in the world economy. Experts are generally agreed that because of the complex interdependence between countries and key economic problems, any solution will have to be fundamental and far reaching. A key element of the crisis is the *international debt crisis* and related problems such as the decline in commodity prices, soaring interest rates and growing protectionism. The last is partly the consequence of the successes of the NICs and the development of the *new international division of labour*. Developing countries underline the link between market restrictions, foreign exchange earnings and debt and argue that the debt problem is symptomatic of world recession. UNCTAD VI proposes three interlinked solutions: a reduction in protectionism, an increased flow of resources to developing countries and a softening of IMF 'conditionality'. The results of the conference are meagre indeed because the views of G77, G7, etc. regarding the appropriate solution diverge considerably.

1987 UNCTAD VII – see text.

There are a few positive results, including a new commitment by industrialized countries towards achieving aid targets (0.7% of GNP) by 1985 and new provisions to assist especially needy land-locked and island developing countries.

1985 Publication of *Global Challenge. From Crisis to Cooperation: Breaking the North-South Stalemate* by the Socialist International after a meeting chaired by Michael Manley. The analysis of the report is an updated and extended version of that in the two Brandt Commission reports, and again a number of steps are outlined to ensure global recovery. The report falls on deaf ears since most OECD countries are still controlled by right-wing governments pursuing deflationary 'monetarist' policies.

1987 The Havana Declaration. G77 declares the 1980s 'the last decade of development' and argues that the world economic crisis is having a grave effect on many developing country economies. The collapse of commodity prices, the debt crisis, stagnation in aid, a flow of resources from developing economies to industrialized ones, protectionist measures, and the worsening structural problems of least developed countries are seen as the most dramatic manifestations of the debt crisis and are placed on the agenda for discussion at UNCTAD VII.

Institutions

Most negotiations regarding the New International Economic Order occur in United Nations-related organizations, the most significant of which is the United Nations Conference on Trade and Development (see Table 3.4.4). Other major United Nations organizations within which the New International Economic Order is discussed and negotiated include the United Nations Industrial Development Organization, the United Nations Conference on the Law of the Sea, the United Nations Development Programme, and the United Nations Educational, Scientific and Cultural Organization. The Bretton Wood organizations, the International Monetary Fund, World Bank and GATT with their key role in the international economy are also crucially involved. A new United Nations organization producing valuable material for the New International Economic Order debate is the World Institute for Development Economics Research which is based in Helsinki and is an offshoot of the United Nations University (UNU).

UNCTAD: The United Nations Conference on Trade and Development was initially proposed in 1962 and first convened in 1964. Unlike many other United Nations organizations, The United Nations Conference on Trade and Development is technically not a separate entity from the United Nations itself. It has a permanent secretariat within the United Nations secretariat and is a special body of the United Nations General Assembly. Since it was specifically designed to foster and coordinate activity on behalf of developing countries, its role in the New International Economic Order dialogue remains paramount and is reviewed both in Table 3.4.4 and Section 3.4.4.

The Bretton Woods Institutions: The development and roles of the main Bretton Woods Institutions, the International Monetary Fund, the General Agreement on Tariffs and Trade and the World Bank, have already been described, but mention must be made here of some of their impact on developing countries and the New International Economic Order. It is worth noting at this stage that the principal shareholders of the Bretton Woods Institutions are the industrialized countries and therefore the policies of these institutions frequently, though not necessarily, reflect the interests of the industrialized world.

The International Monetary Fund, originally designed to promote trade expansion through international monetary cooperation and foreign exchange stability, has increasingly played a major role in these straitened times, particularly in response to the international debt crisis. Hard-pressed developing countries have increasingly turned to the International Monetary Fund for loans, but have seldom found the conditions imposed reasonable. Indeed, International Monetary Fund 'conditionality' can be seen as one element of the industrialized countries reasserting their power in the international order, following some erosion of their influence during the 1970s. In consequence, the latest New International Economic Order proposals ask the industrialized countries to increase the International Monetary Fund's financial resources and relax conditionality.

The World Bank's role as a conveyor of aid to developing countries has always been considered beneficial, although its promotion of the private sector market-based activities has sometimes been resented. In recent years the World Bank has increasingly aimed to increase its aid to the least developed countries in line with New International Economic Order proposals. In recent years the United Nations Development Programme has challenged the free-market assumptions of the World Bank and has played an increasingly influential role in the New International Economic Order debate. In its first annual *Human Development Report* published in 1990, a direct response to the World Bank's *World Development Report*, the United Nations Development Programme declared that 'the link between growth and human progress is not automatic' and backed this up with a 'Human Development Index'. The United Nations Development Programme is likely to continue to play a major role in the New International Economic Order debate in the 1990s.

The General Agreement of Tariffs and Trade was originally intended as a temporary substitute for International Trade Organization. The International Trade Organization would have handled problems arising in commodities trade, but did not come into existence because the United States Congress rejected its charter. Since then the General Agreement on Tariffs and Trade has continued in existence and, although mainly a rich countries' club, its rules have been of some benefit to developing countries. The most-favoured-nation clause, for example, means that a tariff reduction offered to any country must also be offered to all other members of the General Agreement on Tariffs and Trade. In recent years, with growing complexity in international trade, the rise of protectionism, bilateral trade deals and the expansion of international trade in services, there is an increasing acknowledgement of the need for a fully-fledged International Trade Organization. In the 1990 Uruguay Round of General Agreement on Tariffs and Trade negotiations, the Economic Community proposed the establishment of a Multilateral Trade Organization (MTO) which would administer the General Agreement on Tariffs and Trade, the General Agreement on Tariffs and Trade codes and an agreement on trade in services. The negotiations have not yet been concluded, but difficulties have arisen to the extent that the Organization for Economic Cooperation and Development has been proposed as a new forum for trade negotiations. The Economic Community is not in favour of this, but if the Organization for Economic Cooperation and Development became the main forum for multilateral trade negotiations, the interests of developing countries would undoubtedly suffer because of their further marginalization.

Other Bodies: Many other bodies are also involved in the New International Economic Order debate, both pro- and anti- New International Economic Order proposals. The Trilateral Commission, for example, has strong links with the Organization for Economic Cooperation and Development, but is constituted as a 'private' think tank, albeit with powerful members from business, politics and other elites in North America, Europe and Japan. Founded by David Rockefeller, Zbigniew Brzezinski and other 'eminent citizens' in the wake of the crises of the 1970s, the Trilateral Commission is essentially an interest group for international big business. In this respect it is critical both of New International Economic Order demands and the protectionist tendencies of many industralized countries. The Brandt Commission, on the other hand, is pro- New International Economic Order. The 'Independent Commission on International Development Issues', chaired by German ex-Chancellor Willy Brandt, was founded in 1977 at the suggestion of Robert McNamara, President of the World Bank. The Commission's report and proposals were published in a comprehensive document, *North-South: A programme for Survival*, which called for a rapid solution for underdevelopment and the world economic crisis. It was argued that the development of the South (through a massive transfer of resources from the North) was not only just, but would also benefit the North by establishing rapidly growing markets in developing countries. Despite a consequent international conference at Cancun, Mexico, in 1981 and the publication of a further report, *Common Crisis*, the recommendations of the Commission were not heeded. Nevertheless, many aspects of the report's proposals found their way into United Nations Conference on Trade and Development VI and are also visible in some recent suggestions to resolve the international debt crisis.

Countries

The Group of 77: The Group of 77 represents the developing countries in all major New International Economic Order negotiations. As the name implies, the original membership consisted of 77 countries, but now stands at over 120. The Group of 77 came together out of mutual interest and was instrumental in establishing the United Nations Conference on Trade and Development in 1962. The principal issues of concern to the Group of 77 have already been discussed, but it is worth noting that, not unexpectedly given the large number of countries involved, there are intra-group differences of opinion and approach. The least radical group consists of the East Asian Newly Industrializing Economies, such as Singapore and South Korea, clearly because they have done well within the existing international order. The Organization of Petroleum Exporting countries have also differed in terms of priorities and methods, especially when the price of oil was high. Nevertheless, despite the differences and rivalries, the Group of 77 has continued to negotiate on a coherent basis. This is because: (i) the fundamental interests of these countries still coincide; (ii) regular meetings are held to thrash out differences; and (iii) a number of countries, notably Yugoslavia, India and Egypt, carry sufficient moral weight to effect a compromise when differences arise.

Group B Countries: In the United Nations Conference on Trade and Development countries are divided into four groups. Groups A and C are developing countries, Group B are industrialized countries (the 'West') and Group D are the *socialist* countries. The response of the Group B countries to proposals for a New International Economic Order has essentially been one of containment. Many proposals are readily conceded on the grounds of justice, but others are opposed, wherever necessary, especially when the existing economic regime is challenged. One particular worry is that the Group of 77 tries to impose non-market or legally binding regulations too readily and seeks deadlines which are too strict. Thus Group B countries argue strenuously for a voluntary, market-based agreement on the transfer of technologies (the Group of 77 wants amendments to the patent system), and a market solution for the price-instability of commodities. Some of Group B's fears are genuine and indicate a profound belief in the efficiency of the free market, but the Group's vested interests in the existing order are immense and obviously contribute to their position on the New International Economic Order. However, Group B is not a monolithic bloc and considerable differences exist among members. At present, the United States is the most stridently anti- New International Economic Order, but other countries, notably Scandinavia, are sympathetic to the proposals presented by the Group of 77.

Group D Countries: In the past the socialist countries have generally supported the general principles of the New International Economic Order and usually voted with the Group of 77 at the United Nations Conference on Trade and Development. At present, however, given the immense changes in Eastern Europe, it is not clear what position will be taken in the 1990s. It is worth bearing in mind, however, that these countries may be regarded, to some extent, as competitors for aid and other financial resources from the Organization for Economic Cooperation and Development countries.

3.4.4   United Nations Conference on Trade and Development VII

The United Nations Conference on Trade and Development VII began almost exactly where the United Nations Conference on Trade and Development VI ended. Few of the promises made at earlier meetings had been fulfilled and the world economic crisis and all its grave manifestations were still at the top of the agenda (see the Havana Declaration, Table 3.4.4). The topics for discussion were thus familiar and included proposals for: (i) the expansion of financial flows to developing countries in the wake of the international debt crisis; (ii) the early establishment of the Common Fund for Commodities and related measures; and (iii) the reduction on restrictions to international trade.

In general, the United Nations Conference on Trade and Development VII was a disappointment, since it resulted in few concrete measures to solve the world economic crisis or alleviate the problems of the least developed countries.

Much of the failure can be explained by the opposition of many industrialized countries, especially the United States. In terms of the debt crisis there was a broad agreement that 'an equitable, durable and mutually agreed solution will only be reached by an approach based on development, within the framework of an integrated, cooperative, growth-orientated strategy that takes into account the particular circumstances of each country' (Final Act of the United Nations Conference on Trade and Development VII, 10 August 1987). Though this was a step forward, there were no specific measures agreed to resolve the problem; nor has a viable, coherent approach emerged since. Similarly, though the industrialized countries agreed to meet the target of 0.7 per cent of their Gross National Product to go as aid to developing countries (of which 0.15 per cent is to go to the least developed countries), no specific date was set. Japan offered to increase its aid substantially and, though aid remains a small proportion of its Gross National Product and is orientated towards East Asia, this has meant that in the 1990s Japan could well become the world's largest aid donor, ahead of the United States of America. Finally, there was considerable agreement regarding the need to expand international trade and investment, and especially the need to halt and reverse protectionism. Yet again this remains merely lip-service from the point of view of many developing countries. The General Agreement on Tariffs and Trade's Uruguay Round is extremely important in this respect and the future of international trade and investment in the 1990s will be determined by the outcome.

3.4.5 Conclusion

To any objective observer, the history of the debate for a new international economic order is chequered by a long haul of failure dotted with the occasional success. Successes include commitments by industrialized countries towards the General System of Privileges, aid, International Commodity Agreements, codes of conduct for multinational companies and technology, and a law of the sea. Yet commitment and action are different things and heady promises have seldom been kept. Many of the major problems of the 1980s remain unresolved and, indeed, living standards in many developing countries are below those achieved in the 1970s. In large measure this is the consequence of a hard-line political climate in the industrialized countries during the 1980s, especially a belligerent United States of America which was willing to impose its will by tactics ranging from International Monetary Fund conditionality to military action.

A search for solutions (to the international debt crisis, trade surpluses, protectionism etc.) is on at the beginning of the 1990s, but new issues are emerging which will determine the shape of the international order at the century's end. These issues include: (i) Japan's accommodation within the international order and its attitude towards developing countries; (ii) the consequences of West

European integration and the North American Free Trade Area (for example, there may be trade diversion from developing countries); (iii) the final outcome in Eastern Europe and the impact of this on international trade, investment and financial flows; (iv) the results of the debate on the environment and how the North aids the South in, for example, reducing atmospheric pollution and saving rain forests; and (v) how the Organization for Economic Cooperation and Development countries use their dominant position in the world community, following the collapse of the Eastern Bloc and declining resistance from developing countries.

It is not clear at this stage whether the emerging international economic order will be a reconstructed, relatively liberal international trade and investment regime akin to that prevailing in the 1950s and 1960s or, if the quest for a Multilateral Trade Organization fails, a world of regional groups (North America, West Europe and Japan being the likely nuclei). Either way, the position of the developing countries remains precarious and the Group of 77's search for a new international economic order must continue.

References

Until the middle of the 1980s, the New International Economic Order was a relatively coherent topic and many publications were produced with this particular theme in mind. Since then the debate has become diversified and diffused into related issues and material of relevance is being produced in various fora, in the context of many issues and topics. These references can only hint at the immense wealth of publications available on the topic. Up-to-date information is best obtained from the various institutions mentioned in this chapter, especially the United Nations Conference on Trade and Development, but also the United Nations Development Programme, the World Bank, the United Nations Educational Scientific and Cultural Organization, the World Institute for Development Economics Research and others.

The Brandt Commission (1980): *North-South: A Programme for Survival*. London: Pan Books.

The Brandt Commission (1983): *Common Crisis*. London: Pan Books.

Castro, Juan A. de (1989): *Protectionist Pressures in the 1990s and the Coherence of North-South Trade Policies*. United Nations Conference on Trade and Development Discussion Paper No. 27, Geneva.

Commission of the Churches Participation in Development (1979): *For a New International Economic Order*. World Council of Churches, Geneva.

Cooper, R.N. et al. (1977): 'Towards a Renovated International System', *Trilateral Commission Task Force Reports: 9–14*. New York: New York University Press.

Furtado, Celso, Jayawardena, Lal and Yoshitomi, Masuru (1989): *The World Economic and Financial Crisis*. World Institute for Development Economics Research, Helsinki.

The IFDA Dossier, Nyon, Switzerland. Published by the International Foundation for Development Alternatives (IFDA) this journal contains valuable articles and discussion from a grass-roots viewpoint.

Mirza, Hafiz (1986): *Multinationals and the Growth of the Singapore Economy*. Beckenham: Croom Helm.

Mirza, Hafiz (1988): 'The New International Economic Order' in Brooke, Michael Z. and Buckley, Peter J.: *The Handbook of International Trade*. London: Macmillan.

Overseas Development Institute (1983): Briefing Paper Series: *UNCTAD VI: Background and Issues*. London.

Overseas Development Institute (1989): Briefing Paper Series: *The Developing Countries and 1992*. London.

OECD (1983): *The Generalized System of Preferences*. Paris.

OECD (1983): *World Economic Interdependence and the Enduring North-South Relationship*. Paris.

Pavlic, Breda and Hamelink, Cees J. (1985): *The New International Economic Order: Links Between Economics and Communications*. UNESCO, Paris.

Sklar, H. (1980): *Trilateralism*. New York: South End Press.

The Socialist International (1985): *Global Challenge. From Crisis to Cooperation: Breaking the North-South Stalemate*. London: Pan Books.

South Magazine, London. A general monthly magazine with a wide coverage of 'business' issues related to developing countries.

UNCTD (1987): *Revitalizing Development, Growth and International Trade: Assessment and Policy Options*. Geneva.

The UNCTAD BULLETIN, Geneva. Published nearly every month: a good way to stay abreast of the New International Economic Order dialogue.

UNDP (1990): *Human Development Report 1990*. Oxford: Oxford University Press.

WIDER Study Group Series (1989): *World Economic Summits: The Role of Representative Groups in the Governance of the World Economy*. WIDER, Helsinki.

WIDER World Economy Group Report (1989): *World Imbalances*. WIDER, Helsinki.

Part 4

National Characteristics

Introduction

Part 4 examines the relationship between nation states and multinational enterprises. Chapters 4.1 and 4.2 examine the effects of foreign direct investment on host and source countries and Chapter 4.3 analyses the special problems arising for less-developed countries. Chapter 4.4 examines the elusive concept of culture in international business. Chapters 4.5 and 4.6 analyse variations in national commercial legal systems and in accounting systems.

Contents

4.1

The Effects of Foreign Direct Investment on the Host Country

This section examines the impact of foreign direct investment on host countries. The effects of foreign direct investment are felt in many areas, among the most important of which are (1) employment effects, (2) balance-of-payments and trade impact, (3) the effect on industrial structure, (4) transfer of technology issues, (5) location effects, (6) planning and multinational enterprises, (7) demonstration effects and other social consequences and (8) the impact on national sovereignty. Each of these will be dealt with in turn. The section ends with a conclusion that evaluates the effects of foreign direct investment with respect to alternative means of transferring resources internationally.

It is necessary to begin with a warning against excessive generalization. The effects of foreign direct investment will differ according to the type of investment and the socioeconomic conditions in host and source countries. There are three main types of foreign direct investment related to the predominant motive for investment: (1) market-orientated foreign direct investment, (2) cost-orientated investment and (3) raw-material orientated vertical foreign direct investment. These types will have a very different impact on conditions in host countries. The characteristics of individual source and host countries, too, will affect the analysis. Particularly important here is the level of development of the host country (Lecraw (1983)). A series of case studies covering developed and developing countries is examined in Dunning (1985).

4.1.1 Employment effects in the host country

Employment effects in the host country are similarly affected by our views on what would have happened in the absence of the inward investment. The net-employment effects depend on the extent to which employment in the multinational entrants has displaced local projects. Displacement of local projects is least likely in highly specialized products and high-technology areas. It is more likely where only standard technology, management and marketing skills are required. Even so, a decrease in local employment will occur only if it is assumed that the foreign investment is less labour-intensive than the (theoretical) project it has displaced. This capital-intensity problem is particularly acute in less-developed host countries where, it is argued, inward investment is inappropriate because it is more capital-intensive than local conditions dictate. In general, studies of this issue have found inward foreign investment to be more capital-and skill-intensive than local competitors, though this is not a universal finding.

The skill intensity of inward investment creates both beneficial and detrimental effects on the host. The more skill-intensive is the output of multinationals in the host country, the more local value-added accrues. However, foreign investment is alleged to create and foster labour elites in les-developed countries, leading to social tension and divisiveness. However, foreign investment has been found to be more responsive to regional incentives than local investment and multinationals have done much to reduce regional inequities in host countries (such as the large investment of foreign multinationals in regionally high unemployment areas of the United Kingdom such as Wales and Scotland).

Inward investment will have employment-creating effects outside its immediate impact via the income firms' purchase of inputs, services, construction demand and sub-contracting. The multiplier effects of the firms' expenditure will stimulate activity and employment. However, there is a danger that most of the benefits of such a secondary impact will flow abroad and a current preoccupation of governments is to increase the local content of purchases by incoming investors. The low level of contact with the local economy can lead to a dual economy whose existence is analysed in Chapter 4.3 below.

A source of concern for host countries is the degree to which inward investment deprives local entrepreneurs of the opportunity to flourish. First, it is argued that the opportunities open to them are pre-empted by the entry of multinationals. Secondly, it is suggested they can be outclassed by foreign investors and driven out of business. Thirdly, they may prefer to work in a safe job in a multinational in the host country rather than take a risk in order to create jobs for others. Thus the argument is that the host country becomes less dynamic following the entry of foreign investors. This effect depends on the support to domestic entrepreneurs, the supply of venture capital and the strength of the indigenous business culture.

Contrary to existing prejudices, employment in foreign multinationals in advanced countries has been found to be at least as stable, if not more so, than employment in local firms (see Chapter 4.2). In less-developed countries, however, there is a great deal of concern that multinationals, particularly in off-shore-production-type facilities, are becoming more footloose and are relocating production in response to changes in labour costs or government policies, particularly tax incentives. This footloose behaviour is only possible where the fixed-capital requirements of the investor are low; otherwise relocation is expensive.

In summary, the employment impact on the host country depends on the nature of the production in question, conditions in the host country and local alternatives to inward investment as a means of funding economic activities.

4.1.2   Balance-of-payments and trade effects for the host country

The balance-of-payments effect on the host country consists of a once-for-all positive effect on the capital inflow, followed by an ongoing impact made up of outflows to service the resource inflow and a set of indirect effects. The outflows will be (a) dividends and interest in respect of the capital imported, (b) royalties in respect of technological imports, (c) fees for management and other skills and (d) payments for imported inputs and services. The indirect effects concern the impact on exports and on import substitution as well as the effect on host-country economic aggregates such as income and demand.

It is possible to simulate the balance-of-payments impact of inward foreign direct investment but this depends on the choice of assumptions on the costs of resources imported and the direction and strength of indirect effects. One important indirect effect in many cases is the access of the host country to the marketing and distribution network of the multinational firm. This enables many less-developed host countries to increase exports and overcome the marketing-entry barriers that are a constraint on their exporting efforts. The consequent danger is that the host country becomes dependent on the exports of the firm to earn foreign exchange. As foreign exchange is a key factor constraining the growth of many less-developed countries, the balance-of-payments impact of multinationals is a source of concern and often of conflict. Exchange-control regulations are frequently used in less-developed countries to prevent outflows; this can severely restrict the strategies of foreign investors. Host countries are frequently concerned that multinationals are manipulating internal prices of goods and services transferred across national boundaries (transfer prices) to the firm's gain and the host-country's loss. See Rugman (1985).

4.1.3   The effects of foreign investment on industrial structure in the host country

The major concerns of industrialized host countries are (1) the anti-trust or anti-monopoly aspects of inward investment, and (2) the protection of key areas of the economy from foreign control.

It is clear that foreign direct investment is related to imperfect competition and the possession of competitive advantages. Company size and foreign direct investment are also closely linked. However, the major area of concern is that direct investors indulge in monopolistic practices such as price fixing, prevention of entry into industry, product differentiation and excessive promotional expenditures. There is clearly a conflict between the efficiency-enhancing attributes of foreign direct investment (based on innovation, scale economics, efficient management, marketing and organization) versus the anti-competitive elements. Policies in industrialized countries have tried to penalize the misuse of monopoly power while not discouraging size in itself. There are many cases where the entry of foreign investment has broken up an entrenched domestic monopoly and thus had a favourable effect on domestic industrial structure.

The protection of key areas of industry from entry by foreign investors has rarely had a purely industrial structure justification. More usually restrictions on inward investment have been based on strategic, political planning or technological grounds. However, it has been argued that the centrality of certain industries should preclude foreign ownership. Further, there have been occasional arguments that distortions are introduced by foreign ownership. At a typical level of 10–15 per cent of domestic industry being foreign-owned in industrial countries, this argument is difficult to sustain.

In less-developed countries, the argument that the domestic economy is distorted by inward investment has more force. It is argued that foreign investment is instrumental in creating a dualistic economic structure where the (largely foreign-controlled) modern sector exists as an enclave in a largely unaffected traditional domestic economy. Because of the high purchase of inputs from abroad and sales of exports from the enclave, linkage effects in purchases from the host economy are minimal. Thus the host country benefits little from spillovers either by purchases or stimulus to local entrepreneurs. The domestic sector is unimproved by the investment and remains backward. This lack of interaction results from the unequal access to resources which the two sectors enjoy. Dualism is strong enough to cut industry differences and remains an endemic condition in many economies. Policies designed to improve the domestic sector so that it can take advantage of potential links to the foreign modern sector are difficult to implement; the dynamic of the modern sector cannot often be tapped by taxation, because this deters further investment and may frighten off the multinationals. Consequently, retained value, the share of product that remains in the host country, is low, and the benefits of inward investment for the economy as a whole are limited (Lall (1985)). A critical perspective on multinationals in development is given in Lall and Streeten (1977).

4.1.4 The international transfer of technology and skills

Multinational firms are a most important vehicle for the transfer of technology between nations and particularly from advanced to poorer nations. One of the main means of effecting this transfer is foreign direct investment. It is not, however, the only means. Foreign direct investment represents a packaged transfer of capital, technology, management and other skills, which takes place internally within the multinational firms. This internalized transfer can be contrasted with market transactions. Each element of the package can be transferred separately by market means. Thus capital can be loaned, technology sold through licensing agreements of various forms, management and other skills transferred through management contracts and other skills can be bought for a fee. This unbundled set of resources can then be put together in the host country under domestic control. These market relationships represent the major alternatives to foreign direct investment as means of the international transfer of resources. In order to accommodate the desires of host countries, particularly less-developed countries, for a lessening of foreign control, a number of new forms of international resource transfer have come to prominence. (Buckley, Chapter 3 in Buckley and Casson (1985)). These include joint ventures, turnkey agreements, management contracts, international sub-contracting and contractual joint ventures.

The problems with such arrangements are simply either that it may be impossible to unbundle the resources (technology, for instance, may be unavailable outside the direct foreign investment route because the multinational feels this is the best way to appropriate all the returns), or that the host country may pay more in terms of fees to acquire the resources than it would do via direct investment. This will be particularly true where coordination is difficult to effect. Moreover, putting the resources together effectively requires skilled management and administrative personnel – a crucial scarce resource in less-developed countries.

It is not only in less-developed countries that the technological implications of direct foreign investment give cause for concern. Many industrialized countries are concerned that foreign multinationals will take over their technology-intensive firms and independent technological development will prove impossible. Moreover, many European firms are concerned that United States firms will restrict the use of technology in their European affiliates for fear of it being lost to Eastern Europe and the Soviet Union. The control of technology (particularly the national control) thus brings direct foreign investment into the political domain. National policies on technology generation are frequently obscure and contradictory and direct foreign investment is only one means of technology generation and transfer. Nevertheless, the growing importance of technological competition between firms and nations means that attention to the technological consequences of direct foreign investment among policy makers is increasing in host countries. See, for example, Mirza's (1986) case-study of Singapore.

4.1.5   The location policies of multinationals in host countries

Foreign direct investors tend to be more responsive to regional incentives in the host country and to favour relatively underdeveloped areas, for a number of reasons. (1) Foreign investors often need to get permission to invest from host governments; conditions may be attached that may be related to regional policies. (2) Foreign investors need to be seen as good citizens; locating in a needy region is a good way of winning goodwill. (3) Multinationals are generally more responsive to factor-price signals (including subsidies). (4) In the regions, there is often a captive labour market and the foreign investor can become the centrepiece of the local community – examples of this are German investors in the Irish Republic. (5) Foreign entrants have no prior commitments to particular regions and institutions. They are more footloose than domestic firms. (6) Foreign investment takes place in the more footloose industries with fewer strict location constraints.

Consequently, the host country can effect its locational policies by attracting foreign investors. This fact, and the other benefits of inward investment, have led to excessive competition between potential host countries to attract inward investment.

4.1.6   Government planning and direct foreign investment

It is a valid generalization that the degree of government intervention in the economy is a crucial parameter in the relationship between governments and direct investors. Governments of both source and host countries are concerned that multinational firms can circumvent planning. Physical controls, production quotas and output restrictions or incentives can be upset by the import and export activities of multinationals. Monetary planning can be circumvented by multinationals' access to funds elsewhere; fiscal policy can be upset by tax avoidance and the use of transfer pricing.

There is little evidence that foreign firms are less responsive to government controls and exhortations than local firms in general. In fact, with one or two well-publicized exceptions, foreign firms tend to be regarded as more responsive because they need in particular the host-government's goodwill. While there is little doubt that multinationals have the greater potential to avoid or reduce the impact upon them, there is little evidence that multinationals behave any differently from local firms in seeking to ameliorate the consequences of government policies.

Where multinationals are perhaps unique is in their bargaining power before they enter a particular country. Here concessions are often sought and secured. Their bargaining strength is reduced after entry, when a commitment has been made to a particular country. Then, like domestic firms, multinationals are to a considerable degree captive and subject to constraint by the host government (Lecraw (1984)).

One crucial aspect in this relationship is taxation. Tax revenues for the host country represent a major share of the contribution made by foreign direct investment. Tax revenues from foreign investors can be used to accelerate development and growth and provide welfare and other services. However, in their rush to attract inward investment, many host countries use taxation as an incentive to entice multinationals. Consequently, the more footloose firms are able to play off one country against another to obtain the lowest level of taxation. This, however, is an exceptional situation; most multinationals do not have a wide choice of potential locations for investment and are targeted on one country from the outset. In many cases, therefore, the tax taken from multinationals is an important contribution of direct investment.

4.1.7   Social and political effects of foreign direct investment

Many of the criticisms of foreign direct investment from the host country's point of view are not economic but concerned with the social and political effects of inward investment. The concern is that the acceptance of foreign control of part of the host economy not only leads to economic dependence but also to political subjugation, restricting the range of feasible political choices for fear of economic reprisals. This leads to worries in less-developed countries of neocolonialism where control of the economy rests in the investing countries through the agency of multinational firms, acting as the tools of source country policies. Similar fears also apply even to the advanced, industrialized economies of Europe, which absorb foreign investment from the United States of America.

The traditional liberal model of the economy sees firms as autonomous and governments as external actors. Marxist and dependence models take multinationals and their protector governments as joint tools of exploitation, creaming off profits from poor to rich countries (Gilpin (1975), Hymer (1971)). There is also an underlying model that acceptance of foreign direct investment also means choosing a capitalist road and the choice of a Western rather than the Soviet camp in the geopolitical game. (See, for example, Kidron (1965), Vaitsos (1974)).

New institutional modes are an attempt to break down this pattern. The use of joint ventures, sub-contracting turnkey ventures, countertrade agreements and management contracts are institutions that allow some of the benefits of foreign investment to be combined with some measure of host-country control. Resource transfer can thus be effected without the overt strings of foreign ownership. The success of these intermediate modes is in many cases unsure but may represent a beginning in breaking-down the impasse imposed by political conflict.

The social effects of foreign investment are also adduced to be most harmful in less-developed countries. It is argued that foreign investment damages local culture and, by introducing demonstration effects, biases local development towards a Western (United States) pattern, damaging indigenous creativity. A bias toward inappropriate products and spending is induced, which has damaging social, political and economic consequences, not least of which is dependence on imported products. Foreign investment creates a Westernized modern elite that is divorced from the needs of the bulk of the population, inducing social tension and creating a divided society.

All these tensions are evident in less-developed countries and can be observed even in the most advanced. Perhaps in these models too much emphasis is given to the role of multinationals and too little to the general consequence of industrialization and the impact of mass communications. The issue of whether these tensions are an inevitable concomitant of economic growth is too wide an issue on which to comment here.

4.1.8   National sovereignty and bargaining power

The widest area of concern on the effects of foreign direct investment relates to the issue of national sovereignty. Many host countries fear their national autonomy will be restricted if they accept foreign investment and that it will be more difficult to follow independent policies. Naturally, governments make the value judgement that national sovereignty is worthwhile although they may be prepared to trade it off against economic benefits such as integration with a common market in the case of the European Community. At root, the concern with foreign direct investment is that sectors of the economy are controlled by foreigners. The application of laws extra-territorially through the multinational firm can restrict domestic policy-makers. This question arises with regard to the imposition of sanctions against certain countries. It seems likely that the potential drain on national sovereignty involved in foreign direct investment is far less than the actual impact, but such political worries are bound to remain in the minds of host-country decision-makers.

In terms of the relative bargaining power of multinationals and host-country governments, several key factors are at work. The multinational's bargaining power is dependent on its size and resources, the alternative investment opportunities open to it, the degree of penetration it has achieved and the absence of local constraints. The host-country's bargaining strength depends on the quality, skills, experience and honesty of its officials, the resources it has to offer and the extent of their uniqueness, the existence of substitutes for the resources it is attempting to acquire, the size of its market and the degree to which it can get support from other nation-states.

The bargaining process can swing back and forth according to economic conditions and the type of investment under consideration. For instance, a footloose assembly-type operation may have many alternative locations and the multinational may be able to drive a hard bargain in terms of extra incentives, but a specific project requiring a scarce key input (raw material) or requiring access to a large market may give the initiative to the host country.

4.1.9   Conclusion

This section has examined the effects of foreign direct investment on host countries by reference to the choices. Foreign direct investment is not the only means of international resource transfer but it is possibly the most important. Apart from government transfers, the other choices are trade in final goods (export and imports) and market transactions in resources (such as licensing and management contracts). Many host governments prefer these arrangements because they feel they offer a means of reducing foreign control over their economies. However, foreign direct investment allows managers of multinationals to direct foreign operations more closely and often represents the most profitable means of doing business abroad and meeting the competition. There is clearly a role for bargaining and compromise. Multinational firms and governments are seeking new institutional arrangements to circumvent conflict. However, foreign direct investment is likely to remain of major importance in the world economy for the foreseeable future.

References

Buckley, Peter J. (1985): 'New Forms of International Industrial Collaboration', Chapter 3 of Buckley, Peter J. and Casson, Mark: *The Economic Theory of the Multinational Enterprise*. London: Macmillan.

Buckley, Peter J. and Artisien, Patrick F.R. (1985): *Multinationals and Employment*, IRM Multinational Report, No. 5, July–September 1985. Geneva. Published in German as Buckley, Peter J. and Artisien, Patrick F.R. (1986): *Die Multinationalen Unternehmen und der Arbeitsmarkt*. Frankfurt: Campus Verlag GmbH.

Dunning, John H. (ed.) (1985): *Multinational Enterprises, Economic Structure and International Competitiveness*. Chichester and New York: John Wiley & Sons.

Gilpin, Robert (1975): *US Power and the Multinational Corporation: The Political Economy of Foreign Direct Investment*. London: Macmillan.

Hymer, Stephen H. (1971): 'The Multinational Corporation and the Law of Uneven Development' in Bhagwati, J.N. (ed.): *Economics and World Order*. New York: World Law Fund.

International Labour Office (1981): *Employment Effects of Multinational Enterprises in Industrialized Countries.* Geneva: ILO.

Kidron, Michael (1965): *Foreign Investment in India.* Oxford: Oxford University Press.

Lall, Sanjaya (1985): 'A Study of Multinational and Local Firm Linkages in India' in Lall, S. (ed.): *Multinational's Technology and Exports.* London: Macmillan.

Lall, Sanjaya and Streeten, Paul (1977): *Foreign Investment, Transnationals and Developing Countries.* London: Macmillan.

Lecraw, Donald J. (1983): 'Performance of Transnational Corporation in Less Developed Countries', *Journal of International Business Studies*, Vol. 12, No. 1, Spring/Summer.

Lecraw, Donald G. (1984): 'Bargaining Power, Ownership and Profitability of Transnational Corporations in Developing Countries', *Journal of International Business Studies*, Vol. XV, No. 1, Spring/Summer.

Mirza, Hafiz (1986): *Multinationals and the Growth of the Singapore Economy.* London: Croom Helm.

Rugman, Alan M. and Eden, Lorraine (eds) (1985): *Multinationals and Transfer Pricing.* London: Croom Helm.

United Nations Commission on Transnational Corporations (1983): *Transnational Corporations in World Development: Third Survey.* New York: United Nations Centre on Transnational Corporations.

Vaistos, Constantine V. (1974): *Intercountry Income Distribution and Transnational Enterprises.* Oxford: Clarendon Press.

4.2

The Effects of Foreign Direct Investment on the Source Country

This chapter follows Chapter 4.1 in examining the effect of foreign direct investment on: (1) employment, (2) balance of payments and trade, (3) industrial structure, (4) technology transfer and (5) other issues, in the context of the source country. Relationships between multinational firms and their home countries are an important component of the international political economy.

4.2.1 Employment effects in the source country

The employment effects of multinationals must be put in the context of the role of such firms in the world economy. The United Nations Centre on Transnational Corporations examined 369 of the world's largest industrial multinationals and found that in 1980, these firms employed over 25 million people worldwide. (United Nations Centre on Transnational Corporations (1983)). This represents about one quarter of the total employment in the manufacturing sectors of developed market economies. The International Labour Office (ILO) estimate that a further 10 million people are employed in multinational service industries worldwide. (International Labour Office (1981)) In an era of rising unemployment, concern for the location of employment and trends in job losses and gains are a major preoccupation of governments. The power of multinationals to shift activity and employment between countries makes them objects of suspicion, particularly given the immensity of the resources under their control.

The key issue for the source country is: could the employment of multinationals created abroad through foreign direct investment be located in the home country? Could jobs be saved at home by preventing or controlling foreign direct investment? Does investment abroad substitute for jobs at home? A study of the United Kingdom shows that between 1977 and 1981, 67 United Kingdom-based multinationals created 230,000 jobs abroad while shedding over 300,000 jobs at home (Stopford and Dunning (1983)). The context of these questions is vital.

A central issue in the debate on employment impact concerns the alternative position, i.e. what might have happened if the foreign direct investment had not taken place. Essentially, this implies assumptions on whether or not the final market could have been penetrated from the firm's home base rather than the preferred location. Where the final market is the host-country market, this will depend on the degree of protection of that market, the nature of the product, the importance of a 'presence' in the market to achieving sales there, the relative costs of exporting from the source country versus production in the market and the nature of competition.

Where the final market is a third country one (neither source or host country), the issue is one of relative location costs and whether costs in the home country can be sufficiently reduced to make exporting competitive within the chosen location. Where the final market is the home country itself, the case that foreign production is substituting for home employment is stronger but not conclusive. Many multinationals argue that by locating some stages of production outside the home country, usually in cheap-labour locations, they are preserving jobs at home; the jobs that remain at home would be lost without the cost-reducing foreign investment. This type of offshore production has been a rapidly growing response of European and American companies to Japanese competition. The argument of the Western multinationals here is that if they did not invest abroad, the whole of the production would be lost to Far Eastern competition.

Location abroad through foreign direct investment does not necessarily lead to a decrease in home employment. (1) In the case of market-oriented investment, the consequent increase in employment arising from exports from the home country may more than balance the loss of employment in the production of final goods. This is dependent on an increase in foreign market penetration following the investment. (2) Foreign investment may have dynamic effects whereby the long-run competitive position of the firm is improved, thereby preserving and possibly increasing employment at home. (3) Some foreign investments cannot substitute for jobs at home – for instance, those to secure essential inputs unavailable at home for geological, climatic or other reasons (oil, bananas, cotton). (4) Some foreign markets are closed to exports and can only be penetrated by direct investment. This may arise because of protectionism (by policies such as tariffs and quotas) or other government regulations, the nature of the products in question, transport costs (cement) or services that cannot be transported (like banking and retailing).

The conclusion is that it is difficult to generalize on the domestic employment impact of foreign direct investment. The several studies that have been carried out are inconclusive and often flawed (see Buckley and Artisien (1985), (1987) for details). The assumptions of the models used to analyse employment impact are usually static, but global competition is dynamic. Perhaps the best set of assumptions is that foreign direct investment substitutes for exports in the short run, thus imposing employment losses on the source country, but in the long run it substitutes for investment by competing firms (host country or other multinationals) and thus preserves domestic employment.

A study of British manufacturing investment overseas by Shepherd, Silberston and Strange (1985) examined 23 firms in seven (broadly defined) manufacturing industries. The study concentrated on the decision to set up manufacturing abroad. A number of key factors were felt to be important: the way the firm perceived its production advantages, its ability to bear risk, the attraction of foreign markets and various locational considerations. The nature of the industry, the nature of the firms' products and the competitive environment were important influences on the foreign-investment decision. Market size and market growth were, not surprisingly, the key attractions of foreign markets in general. The decision to invest in the market was determined by (in order of importance): proximity to the market, formal and informal trading restrictions and transport costs. In most cases firms felt they did have a choice of foreign-market servicing methods: 50 per cent felt they could have exported and 60 per cent could have licensed in the absence of foreign direct investment. In general firms with well-established standardized products incorporating relatively low value-added and comparatively simple technology were the ones that carried out the bulk of foreign investment in manufacturing.

A related issue concerns the nature of jobs created or lost in the source countries. Studies of this issue suggest that those added or maintained in the source country are of a higher skill level than those lost. Indeed, it has been suggested that foreign direct investment is an important mechanism for restructuring the home economy towards higher value-added activities – a mechanism currently being used in Japan to achieve just this objective.

4.2.2 Balance-of-payments and trade effects on the source country

The impact of foreign direct investment on the balance of payments is complex, involving both direct and indirect effects. Foreign direct investment involves a capital transfer, but it also involves the transfer of a package of complementary resources that may involve technology, management skills, labour and other resources as well as capital.

The balance of payments is affected by (1) the outflow of capital when the investment is made, although this is often largely financed from host-country sources; (2) there is then a return flow of income in the form of dividends, remitted earnings, other income payments, possible payments for technology (royalties, fees) and other resources; (3) there will be an effect on the exports of the source country; initially, there may be an export of equipment, followed by a flow of materials, parts, components and technology from the parent; the foreign subsidiary may serve as a sales outlet for the parent's products; there may be a stimulus to source-country exports from the parent firm's contacts and suppliers through increased awareness of the source country; alternatively, the foreign investment may substitute for exports of final products; (4) the foreign affiliate may export back to the source country, thus increasing source-country imports; (5) other balance-of-payments effects may arise through travel, transportation, services and interest on loans, although these are likely to be minor; (6) finally, if foreign assets are sold, there will be repatriation of capital to the source country.

These effects are likely to differ according to individual cases. Of most interest are the balance of flows in respect of capital and the ongoing effect of the foreign investment on source-country exports. As with employment effects, the balance-of-payments effects of foreign direct investment depend on the relevant alternative, in particular the degree to which exporting to the final market is a viable alternative. In the case of the United Kingdom, the Reddaway Reports, though now dated (1967), (1968), found that new foreign investment made a total net annual gain to the British balance of payment of £4 for each £100 invested. This was made on the basis of an assumption that if the investment had not taken place, rival foreign firms would have invested.

4.2.3 The effect on industrial structure in the source country

Traditionally, source countries have been relatively unconcerned about the effect of outward investment on their industrial structure, believing that rational decision-making within multinational firms would mean they would be left with the higher-order activities, while low value-added activities would be located abroad. However, with the concern for de-industrialization currently in evidence in advanced countries, this has changed. The nature of competition in world markets has become increasingly global; this increased interdependence has caused renewed attention to be paid to the activities of multinational firms. Retrenchment and disinvestment have focused attention on job losses in key industrial sectors so that outward investment is no longer viewed neutrally.

The lack of an industrial policy within the European Community has shown the competing nature of policies in member states and trade functions between Japan, the United States of America and the European Community have focused attention on industrial structure. Job losses in traditional industries are endemic and often regionally concentrated, so focusing political pressure on regional industrial structures. So far, this has not led to controls on outward investment but many opposition parties (such as the British Labour Party) see exchange controls as a means of restricting outward direct investment. It is by no means clear that prevention of foreign investment will increase domestic investment (particularly in declining industries) as the two are imperfect substitutes. Nevertheless, restrictions on foreign investment may become politically favoured, as may restructuring of domestic industry by protectionism and state subsidy.

4.2.4   The international transfer of technology and skills

There have been calls for restrictions on the outflow of technology from advanced countries, notably from the United States of America. Such calls often come from labour lobbies. The restrictions are felt to be a means of protecting domestic industry and labour from foreign competition. Such bodies argue that the combination of high technology with cheaper foreign labour will destroy the competitive strength of the technology-exporting country. The counter argument (put by the multinationals themselves) is that it is mainly older, obsolescent technology that is exported; its export allows its life to be extended, to the advantage of the firm and the source country. This product-cycle model has had much to recommend it but is now less applicable, given the more rapidly changing technological environment and global management skills (Vernon (1979)). A final note is that technology is difficult to control, as it resides ultimately in the minds of individuals; attempts to restrict its diffusion are doomed to failure. If direct foreign investment is the preferred means of the international transfer of proprietary technology, this is likely to be because it maximizes the returns for the firm transferring it.

4.2.5   Other effects on the source country

From the source country's point of view government foreign investments often represent hostages to fortune, giving foreigners an opportunity to blackmail the source country by seizing (or threatening to seize) assets and personnel. The source-country government, as guarantor of the well-being of its citizens and underwriter of its nationals' assets, may well be drawn into conflicts it would wish to avoid by the existence of foreign affiliates.

4.2.6   Home government policies

National policies towards the freedom of outward direct investment are highly correlated with commitment to free market and private enterprise. Largely, the United Kingdom has adopted a policy of *laissez-faire* (Stopford and Turner (1985)); the United States of America has generally allowed outward investment but frequently waivers on the edge of protectionism or regulation, reacting defensively to becoming a net importer of direct investment. Japan and France have had a much greater degree of government involvement (Savary (1985)).

Ideally, a policy on outward investment should be part of an integrated industrial policy. It is seen as such in the case of Japan where labour-intensive, lower value-added activities are allowed and even encouraged to go offshore, largely to East Asian countries. Government finance is available in Japan for uncompetitive industries and resource-procuring investments to set up abroad. The context of policies on outward investment is that of the restructuring of the world economy (Taylor and Thrift (1986)). Intra-industry specialization and the relocation of activities are producing international industry structures that allow component and activity specialization within the 'same coordinating firm, or network of firms (Casson (1986), Ballance (1987)). Within this restructuring, the policies of individual source-country governments are only one factor – often a factor that host-country policy directly militates against.

Consequently, policies are now of necessity multinational, or at least binational. In the face of this new international division of labour, single-country policies (such as exchange control) are becoming increasingly ineffectual. Lack of coordination among trading blocs (the European Community) and other groupings (the Organisation for Economic Cooperation and Development) merely emphasize the impasse.

There is no clear definition of winners and losers in the outward-investment game. Consequently, policies, with the exception of Japan, which is in a unique position with a high yen and highly internationally competitive sectors, are at best in place by historical accident, at worst through lack of attention and default. In formulating such policies, far greater attention is needed to the dynamics of international competition (Porter (ed.) (1986)).

References

Ballance, Robert H. (1987): *International Industry and Business: Structural Change. Industrial Policy and Industry Strategies.* London: George Allen & Unwin.

Buckley, Peter J. and Artisien, Patrick F.R. (1985): 'Multinationals and Employment', *IRM Multinational Reports*, July–September. Published in German as *Die Multinationalen Unternehmenund der Arbeitsmarkt.* Frankfurt, Campus Verlag.

Buckley, Peter J. and Artisien, Patrick F.R. (1987): *North-South Direct Investment in the European Communities: the Employment Impact of Direct Investment by British, French and German Multinationals in Greece, Portugal and Spain.* London: Macmillan.

Casson, Mark and Associates (1986): *Multinationals and World Trade.* London: George Allen & Unwin.

International Labour Office (1981): *Employment Effects of Multinational Enterprises in Industrialized Countries.* Geneva: ILO.

Porter, Michael E. (ed.) (1986): *Competition in Global Industries.* Boston: Harvard Business School Press.

Reddaway, W.B. and others (1967, 1968): *Effects of UK Direct Investment Overseas: Interim and Final Reports*. Cambridge University Press.

Savary, Julien (1985): *French Multinationals*. London: Frances Pinter.

Shepherd, David, Silberston, Aubrey and Strange, Roger (1985): *British Manufacturing Investment Overseas*. London: Methuen.

Stopford, John M. and Dunning, John H. (1983): *Multinationals: Company Performance and Trends*. London: Macmillan.

Taylor, Michael and Thrift, Nigel (eds) (1986): *Multinationals and the Restructuring of the World Economy*. Beckenham: Croom Helm.

United Nations Centre on Transnational Corporations (1983): *Transnational Corporation in World Development: Third Survey*. New York: United Nations Centre on Transnational Corporations.

Vernon, Raymond (1979): 'The Product Cycle Hypothesis in a New International Environment', *Oxford Bulletin of Economics and Statistics*, No. 41, pp. 255–67.

4.3

Multinational Enterprises and Less-developed Countries

During the past 30 years or so the ebb and flow of debate on the role of Multinational Enterprises in less-developed countries has encompassed a wide range of specific issues. Rather than attempting to catalogue these issues, or to provide a full discussion or resolution of any of them, our purpose here is to suggest that improved understanding of specific topics, and thus of the broad relationship between multinational enterprises and less-developed countries, can be facilitated by the delineation of three types of issue. These issues concern (1) efficiency, (2) distribution, and (3) sovereignty and self-reliance. In this chapter we elucidate and illustrate these three general issue types and then discuss two noted areas of controversy – appropriate technology and export-processing zones – in the light of this framework.

4.3.1 Efficiency

Here we are concerned with the issue of whether, purely at the economic level, there exist complementarities between multinational enterprises and less-developed countries such that they may operate in conjunction to increase world economic welfare. Thus we ask: does the operation of multinational enterprises in less-developed countries raise world economic welfare to a level that could not have been achieved in any other way? A naive revealed-preference answer to this might suggest that some such beneficial complementarity must exist because multinational enterprises willingly set up subsidiaries in less-developed countries. Therefore, these subsidiaries must be contributing to the overall profitability of the multinational enterprise groups of which they are part; they must also be making a useful contribution to the growth and/or development of the countries in which they operate, since they are at least tolerated by them.

Our knowledge of multinational enterprises tells us this is far too naive a view to take. The general overseas expansion of multinationals is based upon imperfections including the oligopolistic market structure in which they seek to maximize returns from their advantages and also the imperfections in factor markets that limit the ability of host countries to seek the unpackaging of the multinational enterprise. The viability of the multinational enterprise operations in less-developed countries is also often predicated upon imperfections: notably protection against imports and the dualistic structure of the host economy. So we can argue that the mere existence of multinational enterprises in less-developed countries does not demonstrate their viability as necessary agents of real development. The issue needs to be discussed in more detail and potential aspects of efficient complementarity between multinational enterprises and less-developed countries carefully delineated. Though the fact that multinational enterprises do operate in less-developed countries suggests the existence of some form of complementarity, it may be an artificial and inefficient one, created by imperfections.

It is intuitively plausible that a potentially productive complementarity may frequently be discernible between the ownership-specific advantages of multinational enterprises and the location-specific advantages of the less developed countries. Thus the suggestion is that the multinational enterprises possess certain productive assets (e.g. technology, management expertise, marketing skills and global market networks) to which less-developed countries do not have access and which are necessary for them to realize their potential. Similarly the multinational enterprises may find circumstances in which the full realization of the potential returns from their advantages may require operations in less-developed countries to obtain access to location advantages (e.g. low-cost labour, raw materials and a large or fast-growing protected market).

It has been suggested, notably by Kojima (1978), that the extent to which the potential complementarity outlined above is realized effectively may be strongly dependent on the type of host-country industrialization strategy within which the multinational enterprises operate.

Though there is empirical evidence suggesting that in an import-substitution strategy, foreign firms may have saved less-developed countries foreign exchange, it has also been indicated that persistence with a policy of encouraging this type of investment will be misguided from the less-developed countries' viewpoint and will also lower the efficiency of the world-trade mechanism. Thus, while some early import-substituting multinational enterprise investment was effective in aiding less-developed countries' production in areas where the country might have a latent comparative advantage, it is frequently argued that the process has been taken too far, with foreign investment encouraged in advanced industries whose activity in no way relates to the comparative advantages of less-developed countries. Such capital-intensive investments, based on advanced technology, are inherently inefficient in less-developed countries; they can only compete with imports by high levels of tariff protection sustained permanently, and not temporarily, as would be justified by the infant-industry argument.

This type of investment is characterized by Kojima (1978, p. 15) as anti-trade-oriented, since the local production replaces trade that would, and should, have occurred under the dictates of comparative advantage. Where such investment occurs in a less-developed country it may be a partial cause of several undesirable characteristics. Thus it may both depend upon and help create income inequality and is likely to do little to overcome unemployment problems; indeed, it could make these worse by destroying labour-intensive local output. Kojima argues that this type of trade-destroying investment is exemplified by the operations in less-developed countries of many American multinational enterprises.

More suitable than import substitution, in Kojima's analysis, is export-oriented investment in less-developed countries, in which particularly relevant strengths of the multinational enterprise (e.g. design and marketing skills and an established global marketing network) are complementary to the producing strengths of the host countries (e.g. cheap labour and raw-material resources). Such multinational enterprise involvement, it is suggested, does allow the less-developed country to realize its potential comparative advantage, will be competitive in export markets, and will thus be trade-creating. Kojima believes the pursuit of this type of complementarity to have motivated Japan's manufacturing investments in its poorer Asian neighbours.

Though empirical studies (for a survey, see Casson and Pearce, 1987, pp. 113-4) do not tend to support that part of Kojima's exposition that finds Japanese and United States multinational enterprises exemplifying the outward- and inward-looking strategies, his line of argument does illustrate the efficiency perspective in the multinational enterprise less-developed country relationship.

4.3.2   Distribution

Here we are concerned with how the gains (or losses) that accrue from multinational enterprise operations in less-developed countries are divided between the partners. Thus it would not be enough to find that multinational enterprises in less-developed countries lead to a growth in world economic welfare that could not otherwise have been achieved. There is, in fact, a fear that the position of the multinational enterprise as the owner of crucial productive advantages, and with a great deal of flexibility as an entity with a world-wide organization, may be able to coopt for itself a greater share of the benefits of its less developed-country operations than is strictly equitable. Clearly the idea of what is a just distribution of the surplus created by multinational enterprise operations in less-developed countries is a slippery one, involving accurate pricing of factors of production such as technology and management. This becomes even more contentious when the profitability of a multinational enterprise project in a less-developed country is due less to the efficient use of various productive factors optimally combined than to market distortions and imperfections created, or sustained, by host-government policy. Under such conditions the distribution of surplus would inevitably be strongly influenced by bilateral bargaining between the multinational enterprise and less-developed-country government.

However, if we admit that the concept of a fully just distribution is a difficult one to deal with, it does not alter the fact that many economists will argue strongly that a real issue exists here. Even if it is not precisely obvious what a fair distribution would be, it is clear that under current circumstances the actual outcome is a long way from any such fair outcome, with the multinational enterprises benefiting at the expense of less-developed countries.

Two lines of argument would be advanced to support this view:

(i) that imperfections in the markets for the factors of production in which multinational enterprises are strong allow them to earn monopoly rents on these factors.

(ii) that when distribution is mainly dependent on bilateral bargaining between multinational enterprises and less-developed-country governments, the multinational enterprise is in the stronger position. We now proceed to elaborate this point.

Several writers (notably Streeten (1974) pp. 265–71, Vaitsos, (1974) pp. 311–5) have suggested that, however technically efficient a multinational enterprise project in a less-developed country may be, a host country will only be sure of achieving benefits from it after a successful outcome to negotiations between its government and the foreign firm. Such negotiations are likely to be a crucial factor in determining the distribution of the surplus created by the project.

At the time of setting up a project the host government and the investor will negotiate over a set of conditions, such as tax concessions, tariff protection for final products and tariff concessions on important inputs, labour training, export targets and levels of local value-added. If we sum these up as a package of 'concessions', then it is perfectly possible that at the point of entering into negotiations there will be a gap between the minimum level of concessions that the firm is willing to accept and the maximum level of concessions the government is prepared to offer. Any level of concessions within this gap will be acceptable to either party. Nevertheless at the bargaining the firm will try to force the level of concessions as near as possible to the maximum the government is prepared to offer, while the government will try to push the level as near as possible to the minimum acceptable to the firm.

The outcome of this bilateral negotiation will depend on many factors including level of knowledge and bargaining experience and skill. In terms of knowledge the foreign firm will, in all likelihood, be in the stronger position. The multinational enterprise will probably know more about the host economy and the government's plans for the economy than the government can find out about the activity of the whole multinational enterprise network and its future plans.

Indeed, while the government may enter the negotiations with its future plans clearly laid down, and with little scope for manoeuvre during the bargaining, the multinational enterprise's great flexibility may mean it has several future options open to it according to the negotiations' outcome. This is a great source of power.

The outcome is that in many cases where a less-developed country (correctly) accepts a project on efficiency grounds, it may well have paid more for it in terms of concessions than it would have needed were it better informed and generally in a stronger position *vis-à-vis* the multinational enterprise.

The delineation of the bargaining range above assumes that the multinational enterprise has sufficiently distinctive ownership advantages, and the less-developed country sufficiently distinctive location-advantages, for them to have distinguished each other as preferred partners. The existence of similar multi-national enterprises and similar less-developed country hosts, to those involved in the bargaining, may narrow the range of the bilateral negotiations, but these alternatives are assumed not to be large enough in quantity, nor similar enough in quality, to collapse the acceptable terms of agreement to a unique, market-determined solution. Recently, researchers have begun to attempt empirical investigation of the determinants of bargaining success in multinational enterprise/host government negotiations. For a summary of several of these pioneering studies, see Casson and Pearce (1987) pp. 122–3.

The transfer prices at which goods and services are moved across borders, but within multinational enterprises, are often alleged to provide these firms with scope for distorting the distribution of the benefits of their operations against certain host countries. For further discussion of the effects of transfer prices, and some attempts to evaluate their use, see, for example, Vaitsos (1974) and Rugman and Eden (1985).

4.3.3　Sovereignty and self-reliance

However favourably a multinational enterprise may be regarded by a particular less-developed country, with respect to efficiency and distribution criteria, its foreignness *per se* will probably be, to some degree, evaluated negatively. Thus all countries, to varying extents, place a value on independence. Sovereignty and self-reliance issues then relate to the ways in which the multinational enterprise's operations might compromise (or possibly enhance) the economic independence of the host countries in the short- or longer-term periods.

We consider the economic sovereignty issues to be short-term ones, relating to ways in which multinational enterprises' behaviour may undermine the effectiveness of certain areas of host-country policy. The general flexibility and power of multinational enterprises, especially as manifested in intra-group transfers, are perceived as having the potential to constrain less-developed-country governments' autonomy in areas such as fiscal policy, monetary policy and trade policy. Again, host-government ability to organize or control the structure of industry may be restricted by multinational enterprise activity.

The issues we categorize here as relative to self-reliance concern the ways in which the operations of multinational enterprises in less-developed countries, over sustained periods of time, may either undermine the viability of independent indigenous enterprise or assist in the realization of its potential. One facet of this (Casson and Pearce (1987) pp. 107–8, Lall (1979)) concerns the effects of multinational enterprises on host-country industrial structure, i.e. levels of concentration and prevalent modes of competition. One line of speculation might suggest that multinational enterprise entry could benefit competition by increasing the number of firms, and, perhaps, stimulating renewed competition (and improved efficiency) by disrupting an established oligopolistic equilibrium among indigenous firms and inducing them to embrace new practices and technology. By contrast it is also possible that multinational enterprises may reduce competition, by fairly or unfairly (e.g. using subsidized predatory-pricing) outcompeting local firms and securing monopoly positions for themselves. Increased concentration may also result if local firms feel stimulated to merge as a means of deriving a basis for effectively competing with multinational enterprise entrants.

The speculations put forward above, on the potential effects of multinational enterprises on less-developed countries' industrial structure, tend to assume that multinational affiliates and local firms are substitutes, in the sense of competing for the same market. This, however, is not the only possible relationship between multinational enterprise subsidiaries and less-developed country firms; in some cases, these firms may be complements. Such complementarity may reflect matching technical specializations of the firms or factors relating to optimal use of capacity. Jansson (1982) provides a useful analytical framework for the analysis of such linkages between foreign and indigenous enterprises in less-developed countries. Thus a sub-contracting of relationships may be developed that might benefit local firms, either by providing them with an additional outlet for their existing productive capability or by contributing to a general upgrading of this capability, if the multinational enterprise supplies technology (especially process know-how) to enable them to fulfil their role adequately (Casson and Pearce (1987) pp. 108–10).

4.3.4 Multinational enterprises and appropriate technology for development

Most attempts to delineate the plausible components of an effective complementarity between multinational enterprises and less-developed countries would be likely to include technology as part of the package of inputs provided by the multinational enterprise. However, doubt is frequently expressed as to whether the technology used by multinational enterprises does actually contribute to the type of efficiency distinguished earlier. The starting point for scepticism about the technology used by multinational enterprises in less-developed countries is that the bulk of the companies' technology is created for use in the developed countries. This suggests the techniques innovated in developed countries will be oriented to a production environment of high labour costs and a market comprising a large group of discerning high-income consumers. This technology is then perceived as likely to be too capital-intensive, too skill-intensive and too oriented towards high product quality to achieve the desired type of efficient complementarity with less-developed countries.

This a priori argument that the multinational enterprise's technology may be inappropriate for use in less-developed countries may be mitigated by acknowledging that the crucial characteristics of multinational enterprises – their geographically dispersed operations, their depth of technical knowledge, know-how and creativity – may facilitate adjustment to more effective operations in less-developed countries either through selection or adaptation.

In the case of selection, the multinational enterprise can match the technology needed to produce particular component parts or final goods, or to perform distinctive stages of a production process (see the discussion of export-processing zones below), within a host less-developed country's productive environment. Clearly this type of selection is likely to be most prevalent in export-oriented operations, where cost-competitive production is desired. Where a multinational enterprise is motivated by this type of global-optimizing specialization of production, it is unlikely to add adjustment of its existing technology to selection in implementing such less-developed-country facilities. This is partly because one major motivation for adjustment (small market size) will be irrelevant, and because the multinational enterprise does not want to compromise the quality of export-oriented output by further de-skilling of the production process. It may be considered that, in principle at least, selection is motivated by the pursuit of the type of efficiency introduced earlier.

Probably of more concern are the multinational-enterprise-producing subsidiaries focused on the servicing of local less-developed markets. The operations often arise when a potentially profitable less-developed-country market cannot be effectively supplied through trade, because of natural barriers such as transport costs or artificial barriers such as tariffs. Selection of suitable technology is rarely feasible here; local market conditions tend to delineate the product to be manufactured and the technology for doing so is already defined. The option then is to adapt that extant technology to the less-developed-countries' production environment. Evidence suggests that, where economic incentives make it worth their while to do so, the established knowledge and creative capability of multinational enterprises make them the most effective agents for the conversion of existing technology to new situations. However the fact that the multinational enterprise subsidiary is frequently in possession of a protected monopoly position in the less-developed country often removes much of the incentive to indulge in adjustment. The operation of familiar capital-intensive processes may place less pressure on subsidiary management than the implementation of experimental (though potentially more profitable) labour-intensive processes. Evidence suggests that where multinational enterprise subsidiaries do adjust the production processes of local-market-oriented subsidiaries in less-developed countries, the main motivation is to respond to the smaller scale of output needed, rather than different factor costs. Casson and Pearce (1987) pp. 96–105 survey the evidence on these issues.

The discussion of multinational enterprise technology in less-developed countries also embodies elements of the self-reliance issue. Thus a frequently articulated fear has been that allowing multinational enterprises a significant role in leading industrial sectors of a less-developed country may make that country's industrial development technologically dependent on the direction taken by these firms' innovative activity. This creative activity by the multinational enterprise is seen as likely to be only minimally influenced by the needs of less-developed countries. Dependence on multinational enterprises is seen as precluding the substantial development of a technology fully capable of realizing the industrial potential of the less-developed country.

It may be that this fear of dependency is most plausible in the case of rationalized export-oriented production where the motivation for technological development is new products for developed-country markets; the selection of less-developed countries as production sites is predominantly a convenient by-product. This type of activity may also be perceived as subverting the less-developed countries' sovereignty, since adequate planning for this part of the industrial sector is likely to be outside the scope of indigenous decision-makers, depending as it does on the implementation of external scientific progress. The picture is perhaps less bleak for local-market-oriented subsidiaries. Though we have suggested these subsidiaries are unlikely to commit substantial resources to one-off major adaptations of existing technology, they may gradually take some initiative in evolving a distinctive technology for local circumstances. This may increasingly incorporate sub-contracting to local suppliers, whose technological capability may be enhanced in the process.

The type of technology utilized also has distribution implications. Where production is oriented towards the use of capital- and skill-intensive techniques, using sophisticated equipment to produce high-income products, a relatively small share of the benefits are likely to accrue to the local population or government. For example, the implied reliance on imported machinery and/or component parts may restrict local value-added and also enhance scope for transfer-pricing by the multinational enterprise. Such potential for distortion in the distribution of benefits is likely to be greatest when the multinational enterprise's activity is predicated upon marketing imperfections or patterns of demand that emerge from a highly skewed income distribution (that may itself partly reflect the employment pattern of this type of subsidiary). Where the operations are based upon a more efficient complementarity between the multi-national enterprise and less-developed country, the scope for the technology utilized to provide the potential for distortion of the benefits is likely to be lessened.

4.3.5 Multinational enterprises and less-developed country export-processing zones

One of the most controversial forms taken by multinational enterprise invest-ment in less-developed countries in recent years has been that described as export-platform investment. This occurs in industries that overall are quite technologically advanced, but in which distinct labour-intensive stages of pro-duction can be distinguished. The firms then locate this particularly labour-intensive stage of production in less-developed countries with other stages in the vertically-integrated-production sequence located in developed countries, which usually provide the market for the output. The motivation for this is to perform these labour-intensive stages of production as competitively as possible by using the large supplies of low-cost labour available in many less-developed countries. The predominant form that the process then takes is to import the product into the less-developed country at a partial stage of completion, have the labour-intensive process performed on it there and re-exported back to the developed country either as a finished good or for further processing. In many industries, such as electronics, the motivation for the setting up of such plants, by United States multinational enterprises in particular, has been defensive. Thus the sectors of the industry that have been most strongly inclined to utilize this type of operation appear to have been those most vulnerable to price-competitive imports, and thus most in need of new sources of low-cost inputs.

The essential characteristics needed for a product to be amenable to this type of operation are (a) that it has a labour-intensive stage whose value-added accounts for a reasonably large part of the final value of the product, and (b) that the good has a sufficiently high value-to-transport-cost ratio, to avoid transport costs cancelling out the production cost savings. If the goods can also be econ-omically transported by air, the flexibility gained may save on inventory costs.

The growth in the use of this type of specialized production facility was stimulated by institutional factors in both the multinational enterprises' parent countries and in the less-developed countries. The most influential factor on the parent-country side has been tariff provisions that allow goods involved in such a process to be assessed for duty, on re-entry to the parent country, only on the value-added overseas and not on the full-value of the goods as imported (e.g. United States tariff schedules 806.30 and 807.00).

On the host-country side, many less-developed countries have made positive efforts to encourage the growth of such processing stages within their economies. The most prevalent form of encouragement has been the setting up of export-processing zones. These are specially designated industrial areas or estates which (a) allow all imports (including capital goods) and exports free of tariff or other trade restrictions, (b) incorporate all the infrastructure, factories, port or airport facilities necessary, and (c) offer special packages of financial inducements including tax holidays, low-tax rates and the hire of factory space at concessional rents.

In evaluating the use of export-processing zones by multinational enterprises we may consider that, assuming both the companies and less-developed countries have accurately evaluated their own inputs and those of the other party, a potentially mutually beneficial, efficient complementarity will be established. However, when we address the distribution and self-reliance aspects of this type of operation, more problematic speculations arise. It may seem likely that the type of inputs (predominantly unskilled labour) that underlie the less-developed country's contribution to export-processing zones are available in quite a range of countries. Because of this, competition between countries to obtain multinational enterprise partners for export-processing zones may have led to the offering of excessively generous incentive packages. The result may be that when the multinational enterprise selects a particular location for an export-processing-zone facility, the supporting packages of incentives it receives will be greater than that needed to have induced it to undertake such an operation. Thus the distribution of benefits of the efficient complementarity are biased towards the multinational enterprise.

Another often-discussed problem with export-processing zones, which carries distribution connotations, is the suggestion that the calculation of the costs of such a facility do not adequately incorporate those that may be borne by some members of the local workforce in the form of a deterioration in health. Eyesight problems and nervous stress are often put forward as external costs involved in certain export-processing-zone operations. It may be further argued that the way multinational enterprises operate in export-processing zones is not oriented to providing the types of spillovers or learning effects likely to enhance the long-term industrial self-reliance of less-developed countries. Though the technology used is assumed to be more suited to less-developed countries than much used by multinational enterprises, it is likely to be highly process-specific; little beneficial spillover into local industry is to be expected. In the main, the managerial skills used are likely to be most concerned with the day-to-day supervision of a disciplined labour force and routine accounting. Because the firm's activity is only one stage in a wider production process, whose organization is essentially centralized, little expertise in independent decision-making is likely to be developed. In a similar way, the fact that the firm's transactions are predominantly limited to those with other units of the same multinational enterprise group, rules out the development of marketing expertise. One skill that might be usefully learnt by local personnel in export-processing zones is that relating to the techniques of quality control.

4.3.6 Conclusion

We have not tried to provide a simple overall opinion of the value of multinational enterprises to the development of less-developed countries, nor even to seek a resolution of particular topics that have emerged as sources of friction between them. Our aim has been to outline a framework that defines particular distinctive aspects of the relationship between multinational enterprises and less-developed countries and to suggest that understanding the different categories of issues implied by this framework may help to clarify the crucial facets of any particular area or controversy.

References

Casson, M.C. and Pearce. R.D. (1987): 'Multinational Enterprises in Less Developed Countries', in Gemmell, N. (ed.): *Surveys in Development Economics*. Oxford: Blackwell, pp. 90–132.

Jansson, H. (1982): *Interfirm Linkages in a Developing Economy. The Case of Swedish Firms in India*. Acta Universitatis Upsaliensis, Studia Deconomiae Negotiorem 14, Uppsala.

Kojima, K. (1987): *Direct Foreign Investment: A Japanese Model of Multinational Business Operations*. London: Croom Helm.

Lall, S. (1979): 'Multinationals and market structure in an open developing economy: the case of Malaysia', *Weltwirtschaftliches Archiv*, 115, pp. 325–48.

Rugman, A.M. and Eden, L. (eds) (1985): *Multinationals and Transfer Pricing*. London: Croom Helm.

Streeten, P. (1974): 'The theory of development policy' in Dunning, J.H. (ed.): *Economic Analysis and the Multinational Enterprise*. London: Allen & Unwin, pp. 252–79.

Vaitsos, C.V. (1974): 'Income distribution and welfare considerations' in Dunning J.H. (ed.): *Economic Analysis and the Multinational Enterprise*. London: Allen & Unwin, pp. 300–41.

4.4

Culture and International Business

When Captain Cook asked the Chiefs of Tahiti why the men ate apart from women, they looked at him in wonder and disbelief at such a foolish question. They thought and thought, and finally one offered the only explanation they had: 'Because it is right'.

(Farb (1978) p. 351)

4.4.1 The significance of culture

Culture is the human condition and can be defined as an evolving system of concepts, values and symbols inherent in a society – a learned system of behaviour which organizes experience, determines an individual's position within social structures and guides actions in a multitude of situations, known or unknown. (See Harris (1974) for a good discussion of the hoary theoretical difficulties associated with the concept.) The usefulness of culture and other anthropological tools for analysing business systems (and related topics) is widely acknowledged (for further discussion see Triandis and Lambert (1987), Deal and Kennedy (1982), Morey and Luthans (1985) and Smircich and Calas (1987)).

This chapter will examine some of the broad issues of relevance regarding 'culture and international business', but it will be impossible to discuss any topic in depth. The interested reader is directed to the abundance of good literature available, some of which is listed in the references. The issues will be discussed in terms of national culture, business/industrial culture and corporate/organizational culture; and to aid the analysis, the case of a British company operating in Japan will be used for illustrative purposes. The chapter will conclude with a short treatment of cultural change and an outline of current academic directions.

4.4.2   National culture and international business

Though culture is a quintessential feature of all societies, there is clearly a wide variety of inter-related cultural systems spread across the globe. Thus the cultures of Sweden and Norway can be regarded as being similar. They have a direct relationship and shared values with other North European countries, while their cultural links with China are tenuous. However, humanity is much more closely knit than it thinks. For example (1) Norway and Egypt both ultimately share an underlying morality (Christianity-Islam) derived from a Middle Eastern complex of religions; (2) China has been the source of inventions and ideas today used the world over; and (3) the modern nation-state, though the focus of some shared values, is clearly a grid placed over a more intricate patchwork of allegiances (and especially so where the social fabric is defined by tribes, clans or other non-national identities).

At one level, the existence of commonalities is reassuring for international business since this permits the design and marketing of global products. Unfortunately marketability and competitiveness are often defined at the margin or by extremes, so even the most global of products will need to be adapted to specific conditions. Thus cultural differences (defined nationally for ease of analysis) need to be taken into account whether trading overseas or producing in a foreign country. In general this requires little more than being aware of local tastes and habits (the colour white is unlucky in some countries; a nod does not always signify assent). For example, Yau (1988) describes marketing strategies based on certain Chinese values; Kreutzer (1988) suggests a detailed segmentation of West Asian markets on the basis of class, cultures and sub-cultures; and Riddle (1986) argues that cultural issues are more intense in the services sector. A simple example of the need to produce for local conditions is the recent belated appearance of Arabic language software for computer systems (Arab-British Commerce (1988)). A British firm selling in the Japanese market would be faced with intense linguistic difficulties and problems meeting the stringent requirements of Japanese customers, not least regarding quality standards (Buckley, Mirza and Sparkes (1987), (1989)).

There are also implications for the training of managers dealing with other countries, particularly expatriates who may need to settle in a specific country for a matter of years. Mendenhall and Oddou (1986) and Earley (1987) analyse the different types of intercultural training available and argue that it is frequently insufficient (at least for American managers abroad). Similarly, training and issues of corporate strategy arise when sensitivity to local attitudes means that indigenous managers and production workers are employed to run an overseas plant. Where indigenous managers are not employed Grimaldi (1986) argues that international management will be more capable of establishing good relationships with local workers if national (especially popular) culture is interpreted rather than simply observed. He uses the example of the Carnival as the most potent manifestation of values and motives in Latin America. One of the largest studies on culture and work patterns is that of Hofstede (1980) which ranked cultures along four dimensions: power distance, individualism, uncertainty avoidance and masculinity. Similarities and differences between cultures were identified and the analysis is clearly of interest to international business strategy. Hofstede's work has been much criticized methodologically ('culture is correlated with culture' – Roberts and Boyancigiller (1984)), but it cannot be ignored. The Japanese public has shown a preference for goods produced in Japan, while local employees tend to prefer foreign companies with a long-term commitment to the country (because of life-time employment): the British company needs to take matters such as these into account.

4.4.3   Business/industrial culture and international business

The business culture refers to the general behaviour and values of the corporate sector and the environment within which commercial transactions occur; the related industrial culture describes the general values of the production system, including industrial relations – and attitudes towards quality, reliability and technological change. Many analyses tend to view business/industrial culture as a microcosm of national culture, reflecting general concepts and values faithfully. In fact the relationship is rather complex, particularly because the business/industrial culture depends on a country's level of development (and mode of production), as well as conscious efforts to promote certain relationships, such as the transplantation of foreign production and management systems by late developing countries. Furthermore the national culture is to some extent determined by the production system: the small nuclear family in most developed countries can be directly ascribed to the modern factory system and associated consequences such as urbanization; such a demographic transition is now happening in many newly industrializing countries.

The interaction between historical, socio-cultural and business/industrial factors is complex and the results difficult to predetermine. Simplistic ascriptions of specific business attitudes or techniques to national culture are best avoided (Buckley and Mirza (1985)). Western international business is frequently posited as fundamentally similar, in contradistinction to Japanese or developing country multinationals, but a closer examination does not bear this out. There are frequently huge differences between views about trade, international business and related matters. The internationalization by companies from western countries frequently reflects the indigenous business culture: Mackarzina and Staehle (1986) give examples of multinationals from many European countries – their international strategies and management practices are by no means homogenous. One might even suggest similarities in business cultures and multinational activity between early (Britain, the United States and The Netherlands) and late (Germany, Japan, Sweden, Korea) developers, but such a view would have to be heavily qualified.

What of our unsuspecting British company in Japan? The first important aspect of Japanese business culture it would probably notice would be the significance of relationships. Business is not essentially a contractual one between unrelated entities, but is conducted between friends. Much time is devoted to building up friendship and commitment. The company will find this eventually pays dividends – but requires a lot of resources and a long-term view: possibly an attitude less common in British business culture. On a similar note, Japanese business is arguably more expansion-minded and likely to take risks. This mode of behaviour clearly has implications for the competitiveness of the British company globally and its subsidiary in Japan. Rosch and Segler (1987) discuss 'communication with the Japanese' further. A second point for the company to note is that Japanese business culture tends to view foreigners with suspicion (a form of xenophobia), regard women as unsuited to managerial positions (Adler (1987), Carney and O'Kelley (1987)), and place a premium on age. These are broad generalizations, but in terms of building a serious relationship, the British company should not (unfortunately) choose a young woman as chief executive! An entirely Japanese management team may be most suitable. Finally, how would such a team function and could this behaviour be easily integrated into the organization? There are key differences. For example, DeFrank and others (1985) discuss the underlying cultural variables affecting management practices and find that Japanese managers are more adept at consensus decision-making and establishing good relationships with blue collar workers, albeit at the expense of considerable personal stress. Given the apparently large difference in management practices between Western and Japanese executives, many companies have tended to give considerable autonomy to Japanese affiliates (Buckley, Mirza and Sparkes (1991)).

4.4.4   Corporate/organizational culture and international business

Organizational culture (including that of corporations) can be viewed as being analogous to national culture. A system of concepts, codes of action and values determine how an organization and its components behave and pursue their goals. These goals and values need not be coherent, but it is usually assumed that where they are, an organization functions more effectively. Deal and Kennedy (1982) argue that a successful business corporation requires a strong culture which consists of specific components: core values (Sear's quality at a good price), heroes or role models, rites and rituals (Beyer and Trice (1987) show how rites define different types of organization) and a network for inculcating corporate values into the workforce.

Smircich and Calas (1987) would probably wince at the Deal and Kennedy analysis since they argue that the anthropology-derived concept of organizational culture was originally a literature of opposition, but 'to the extent that culture has been incorporated into the positivist, technical interest as part of the traditional organizational literature, the organizational culture may be dominant, but dead' (p. 229). Their wide-ranging article is invaluable in analysing the role of culture in the organizational literature (see Table 4.4.1). One issue of relevance to this chapter is the question whether organizational/corporate culture (from a functionalist, technical perspective) is internal (created by management and historical development) or external (based on the general mores of society). Clearly there is no dividing line and much of the functionalist literature must perforce assume a heavy internal weighting in order to explain the huge differences between organizations in a single national culture.

From the international business perspective, there are two major themes of relevance: (1) are organizational cultures internationally transferable and (2) in terms of comparative international management, are differences in organizational cultures related to effectiveness? The latter theme, to some extent, underlies the former in as much as differences in effectiveness would spur attempts at adoption of successful corporate cultures. Though many authors suggest otherwise, the relationship between organizational (or national) culture and effectiveness remains ambiguous (see Reynolds (1986) and Buckley and Mirza (1985) among others).

The question of transferability has two elements: (1) how readily can organizational cultures from one country be transferred to another (e.g. should the overseas subsidiary of a multinational company operate in exactly the same way as the parent firm?) and (2) how readily can organizational cultures from a given company/country be transferred to a company in another country? (Is Matsushita's putatively successful organizational culture transferable to General Electric?) The two elements are not unrelated and both depend on the extent to which organizational culture is *national* culture-bound and whether the components to be transferred (such as attitudes to quality control) can be identified and made palatable to the recipient. With regard to the first element, many companies are aware of the difficulties in international operations arising from differences between the organization's values and the culture of the host company; and there is a tendency to operate in accordance with local custom. However, this notion should not be pushed too far since cultures are essentially different in degree; and even at the extremes, as with a technologically advanced company in a developing country or a Spanish company in China, there is some literature to suggest there is a degree of universality in work goals and management/worker values across cultures, the adaptations of our British company in Japan notwithstanding (see Sekaran (1981) and Ronen (1979)). The recent

Table 4.4.1 Three Frameworks for Analysing the Organizational Culture Literature

Themes	Paradigmatic Perspective	Theory of Knowledge Perspective
	Culture from a Functionalist Perspective	*The Technical Interest*
Cultures as Variables Comparative Management – culture as external variable, synonymous with country. Corporate culture – culture as internal variable, influencing systemic balance and performance.	Organizational culture as a management tool. Managers can control culture through controlling communication practices, and thus influence organizational performance. Some research seeks to define a relationship between objectified cultural events (for example, storytelling, rituals, language) and objective circumstances (productivity, turnover).	Research guided by an interest in manipulation and control of the natural and social environment. Based on a physical science model, features empirical testing of hypotheses and generalizable claims. Success of theory depends on ability to operate on the environment producing predicted effects. Technical knowledge is traditionally what has been called science.
	Culture from an Interpretive Perspective	*The Practical Interest*
Culture as Root Metaphor Organizational cognition – organizations as structures of knowledge; shared frames of reference or rules.	Organizations viewed as cultures; focus shifts to the processes of organizing as the enactment of cultural development. Culture is the process through which social action and interaction become constructed and reconstructed into an organizational reality. The symbolic constitutes what is taken for granted as organizational life. Culture and communication are vehicles through which reality is constituted in organizational contexts. Interpretive focus places communication at the center of organizational culture.	Research motivated by the desire to understand meaning in a specific situation so that a decision can be made and action taken. A specific decision, not a generalizable rule, is the goal of knowledge seeking. Literary and historical analysis are models of the practical search of knowledge. Methodology involves the interpretation of the meanings manifest in human interaction. The ultimate claim to validity is consensus of the interested parties on the meaning of the situation.

	The Emancipatory Interest
Organizational symbolism – organizations as shared meanings; patterns of symbolic discourse. Unconscious processes and organization – organizations as reflections and manifestations of unconscious processes.	An interest in increasing the level of human autonomy and responsibility in the world. Builds on Freudian and Marxist perspectives in that it stresses the recovery of rationality and responsibility from the blockages of ideology and false consciousness. Methodology of self-reflection in that questions assumptions in which the current situation is grounded. It addresses the appropriateness of shared meanings. The validity criterion is the contribution of such knowledge to the potential for autonomous, responsible human action.

Quoted from: Smircich and Calas (1987), p. 234.

internationalization of Japanese companies is a good testing ground for the question of whether organizational cultures can be transferred. Trevor (1988) in an analysis of Toshiba's operations in Britain shows that at least some elements of the company's organizational attitudes and management style can be transferred overseas (and are frequently sufficiently universal values/techniques which can be adapted by British companies); and Hayashi (1987) illustrates the fact that Japanese companies are adapting their management systems to the values of their workers in the United States and elsewhere. Pascale and Athos (1981) suggest that Japanese management can be successfully applied by companies in other countries. There is some truth in this, although it is fair to point out that Matsushita (on which their analysis is based) is not generally regarded as having a typically Japanese corporate culture.

4.4.5   Cultural change and international business

The significance of cultural change to international business is threefold. First, changes in the national culture affect business and international business both directly (through evolving attitudes and tastes) and indirectly (through the effect on business/industrial culture). Meyerson and Martin (1987) show that the impact of such change on organizations in general can be multifarious and examine three paradigms seeking to examine the impact. Secondly, organizational/ corporate cultures are often prone to rapid change, particularly as a consequence of environmental factors such as (international) competition, technological development and political intervention. There is a huge literature on political risk (multinationals are, for example, less likely to invest in riskier countries), a topic that can be subsumed under 'cultural change'. Feldman (1986) examines the effect of the deregulation of AT & T (a political action with dramatic indirect international consequences) on the culture of Bell Telephone. Bartlett and Yoshihara (1988) suggest that Japanese multinationals are less efficient in organizational adaptation than those from North America and Europe: if correct, this clearly has implications for international competition.

Finally, note should also be made of the impact of international business on cultures. While many national cultures are quite robust, some can be gravely affected by the economic impact of foreign companies or their importation of values and attitudes. This can occur through the sheer scale of local production on small communities, employment practices (such as the exploitation of cheap female labour), the inculcation of organizational values and the establishment of elite or inappropriate consumption patterns. This issue is of concern in many countries (le défi americain, for example), but is of particular relevance to developing countries. United Nations Centre on Transnational Corporations (1988) gives examples of this impact on local cultures; Mattelart (1979) discusses the wider issues.

4.4.6 Conclusion

The relationship between the multifaceted concepts of culture and international business is highly complex and this survey barely covers a fraction of the issues. Morey and Luthans (1985) show that the general concept of culture is being constantly refined for more effective use, while Smircich and Calas (1987) question the uses to which the culture is put. At the international level more research needs to be done and Triandis and Albert (1987) identify some gaps in the literature. They suggest research particularly on: (1) communications problems faced by managers abroad, (2) effective culture orientation programmes for managers going overseas, (3) minority-majority interactions in national cultures and organizations, (4) comparative work on the dimensions of cultural differences, (5) studies of culturally heterogenous work-teams and (6) the organizational forms of commercial and non-commercial (the World Bank, the International Monetary Fund) multicultural organizations. This listing is by no means exhaustive and the field is wide open. A word of caution is in order however; unless the ambiguous concepts intrinsic to culture and international business are theoretically refined, adequately operationalized and tested with sound methodologies, the results may be worse than useless. They could be dangerous.

Note

1. Primordial cultures exist among other animals; and sociobiologists are prone to use these (not to mention sheer instinct) to explain the behaviour of business*men*, e.g. their penchant for fast foreign cars and cigars. However, such an approach is beset with theoretical and methodological flaws and is best avoided.

References

Adler, Nancy J. (1985): *International Dimensions of Organizational Behaviour*. Kent State University Press.

Adler, Nancy J. (1987): 'Pacific Basin Managers: A Gaijin, Not a Woman', *Human Resources Management*, Vol. 26, No. 2.

Adler, Nancy J. and Jelinek, Mariann (1986): 'Is "Organization Culture" Culture Bound?', *Human Resources Management*, Vol. 25, No. 1.

Al-Mubarak, Mohammed I. (1988): 'Empirical Analysis of the Effects of Environmental Interdependence and Uncertainty on Purchasing Activities: A Cross Cultural Study, *Industrial Marketing and Purchasing*, Vol. 3, No. 1.

Amsa, P. (1986): 'Organizational Culture and Work Group Behaviour: An Empirical Study', *Journal of Management Studies*, Vol. 23, No. 3.

Arab British Commerce (1988): 'Ready-made solutions for the small user', January–February.

Bartlett, Christopher A. and Yoshihara, Hideki (1988): 'New Challenges for Japanese Multinationals: Is Organization Adaptation their Achilles Heal?', *Human Resources Management*, Vol. 27, No. 1.

Berger, P. and Luckmann, T. (1966): *The Social Construction of Reality*. New York: Doubleday.

Beyer, Janice M. and Trice, Harrison M. (1987): 'How an Organization's Rites Reveal Its Culture', *Organizational Dynamics*, Vol. 15, No. 4.

Bolt, James F. (1988): 'Global Competitors: Some Criteria for Success', *Business Horizons*, Vol. 31, No. 1.

Brislin, R.W., Lonner, W.J. and Thorndike, R.M. (1973): *Cross-cultural Research Methods*. New York: Wiley.

Buckley, Peter J. and Mirza, Hafiz (1985): 'The Wit and Wisdom of Japanese Management: An Iconoclastic Analysis', *Management International Review*, Vol. 25, No. 3.

Buckley, Peter J. and Mirza, Hafiz and Sparkes, John R. (1987): 'Direct Foreign Investment in Japan as a means of Market Entry', *Journal of Marketing Management*, Vol. 2, No. 3.

Buckley, Peter J., Mirza, Hafiz and Sparkes, John R. (1991): *Success in Japan: How European Companies Compete in The Japanese Market*. Oxford: Basil Blackwell.

Carney, Larry S. and O'Kelley, Charlotte G. (1987): 'Barriers and Constraints to the Recruitment of Female Managers in the Japanese Labour Force', *Human Resources Management*, Vol. 26, No. 2.

Casimir, F.L. (ed.) (1978): *Intercultural and International Communication*. Washington: University Press of America.

Danandjaja, Andreas A. (1987): 'Managerial Values in Indonesia', *Asia Pacific Journal of Management*, special issue II: Culture and Management Styles in Southeast Asia. See special issues I and II for other articles on this topic.

Davies, Julia, Easterby-Smith, Mark, Mann, Sarah and Tanton, Morgan, (1988): *The Challenge of Western Management Development: International Alternatives*. Routledge.

Davidson, Marilyn J. and Cooper, Cary L. (1987): 'Female Managers in Britain – A Comparative Perspective', *Human Resources Management*, Vol. 26, No. 2.

Deal, Terrence and Kennedy, Allen (1982): *Corporate Cultures: The Rites and Rituals of Corporate Life*. Addison Wesley.

DeFrank, Richard S., Matteson, Michael T., Scweiger, David M. and Ivancevich, John M. (1985): 'The Impact of Culture on the Management Practices of American and Japanese CEOs', *Organizational Dynamics*, Vol. 13, No. 4.

Earley, Christopher P. (1987): 'Intercultural Training for Managers': A Comparison of Documentary and Interpersonal Methods', *Academy of International Management Journal*, Vol. 30, No. 4.

England, George W., Negandhi, A. and Wilpert, B. (eds) (1979): *Organizational Functioning in a Cross-Cultural Perspective*. Kent State University Press.

Farb, Peter. (1978): *Humankind: A History of the Development of Man*. London: Jonathan Cape.

Farh, Jing-Lih, Podsakoff, Philip M. and Cheng, Bor-Shiuan (1987): 'Culture-Free Leadership Effectiveness versus Moderators of Leadership Behaviour: An Extension and Test of Kerr and Jermier's "Substitutes for Leadership"', *Journal of International Business Studies*, Vol. XVIII, No. 3.

Farris, George F., Senner, Eldon E. and Butterfield, Anthony (1973): 'Trust, Culture and Organizational Behaviour, *Industrial Relations*, Vol. 12, No. 2.

Feldman, Steven P. (1986): 'Management in Context: An Essay on the Relevance of Culture to the Understanding of Organizational Change', *Journal of Management Studies*, Vol. 23, No. 6.

Fernandez, J.O. (1975): *Black Managers in White Corporations*. New York: Wiley.

Fortune (1988): 'More Yanks Work for Foreigners', 1 August New York.

Grimaldi, Antonio (1986): 'Interpreting Popular Culture: The Missing Link Between Local Labour and International Management', *Columbia Journal of World Business*, Vol. XXI, No. 4.

Hall, E.T. (1976): *Beyond Culture*. New York: Doubleday.

Hanke, Jean J. and Saxberg, Borje O. (1985): 'Isolates and Deviants in the United States and Japan: Productive Nonconformists or Costly Troublemakers?', *Comparative Social Research*, Vol. 8, No. 3.

Haaland, John E. (1988): 'People and Organizations of the Future (Body, Mind, Spirit, Culture)', *Human Resource Planning*, Vol. 10, No. 4.

Harris, Nigel (1974): *Beliefs in Society*. Penguin, Harmondsworth.

Hayashi, Kichiro (1987): 'The Internationalization of Japanese-Style Management', *Nioppon Steel News*, August.

Hofstede, Geert (1980): *Culture's Consequences: International Differences in Work-Related Values*. Beverly Hills: Sage.

Inzerilli, Giorgio (1983): 'Culture and Organizational Control', *Journal of Business Research*, Vol. 11, No. 3.

Jablin, Frederic M., Putnam, Linda L. Roberts, Karlene H. and Porter, Lyman W. (1987): *Handbook of Organizational Communication: An Interdisciplinary Perspective*, Beverly Hills: Sage.

Jaeger, Alfred M. (1986): 'Organization Development and National Culture: Where's the Fit?', *Academy of Management Review*, Vol. 11, No. 1.

Jones, Gareth R. (1983): 'Transaction Costs, Property Rights and Organizational Culture: An Exchange Perspective', *Administrative Science Quarterly*, Vol. 28, No. 3.

Joynt, Pat and Warner, Malcolm (eds) (1985): *Managing in Different Cultures*. Oslo: Universitetsforlaget.

Kelley, Lane and Worthley, Reginald (1981): 'The Role of Culture in Comparative Management: A Cross-Cultural Perspective', *Academy of Management Journal*, Vol. 24, No. 1.

Kets De Vries, Manfred, F.R. and Miller, Danny (1986): 'Personality, Culture and Organization', *Academy of Management Review*, Vol. 11, No. 2.

Kreutzer, Ralf T. (1988): 'Key Factors for the Development of Marketing Strategies for West Asia', *Singapore Marketing Review*, Vol. III, No. 1.

Landis, D. and Brislin, R.W. (1983): *Handbook of Intercultural Training*, Vol. 2. New York: Pergamon.

Laurent, A. (1983): 'The Cultural Diversity of Western Conceptions of Management', *International Studies of Management and Organization*, Vol. XIII, No. 1.

Macharzina, K. and Staehle, W.H. (1986): *European Approaches to International Management*. Berlin: Walter de Gruyter.

Mattelart, Armand (1979): *Multinational Corporations and the Control of Culture*. Brighton: Harvester Press.

Mendenhall, Mark and Oddou, Gary (1986): 'Acculturation Profiles of Expatriate Managers: Implications for Cross-Cultural Training Programmes', *Columbia Journal of World Business*, Vol. XXI, No. 4.

Meyerson, Debra and Martin, Joanne 1987: 'Cultural Change: An Integration of Three Different Views', *Journal of Management Studies*, Vol. 24, No. 6.

Morey, Nancy C. and Luthans, Fred (1985): 'Refining the Displacement of Culture and the Use of Scenes and Themes in Organizational Research', *Academy of Management Review*, Vol. 10, No. 2.

Muhlbacher, Hans, Vyslozil, Wilfried and Ritter, Angelika (1987): 'Successful Implementation of New Market strategies', *Journal of Marketing Management*, Vol. 3, No. 2.

Nonaka, Ikujiro (1988): 'Creating Organizational Order Out of Chaos: Self-Renewal in Japanese Firms', *California Management Review*, Vol. XXX, No. 3.

Pascale, R. and Athos, A. (1981): *The Art of Japanese Management*. New York: Warner.

Peters, T. and Waterman, B. (1982): *In Search of Excellence*. New York: Harper and Row.

Renwick, G.W. (1981): *The Management of Intercultural Relations in International Business*. Chicago: Intercultural Press.

Reynolds, Paul D. (1986): 'Organizational Culture as Related to Industry, Position and Performance: A Preliminary Report', *Journal of Management Studies*, Vol. 23, No. 3.

Riddle, Dorothy L. (1986): *Service-Led Growth: The Role of the Service Sector in World Development*. New York: Praeger.

Roberts, Karlene H. and Boyacigiller, Nakiye A. (1984): 'Cross-National Organizational Research: The Grasp of Blind Men', in Staw and Cummings 1984, op. cit..

Ronen, S. (1979): 'A Cross National Study of Employees' Work Goals', *International Review of Applied Psychology*, Vol. 28, No. 1.

Rosch, M. and Segler, K.G. (1987): 'Communications with Japanese', *Management International Review*, Vol. 27, No. 4.

Sekaran, Uma (1981): 'Are US Organizational Concepts and Measures Transferable to Another Culture? An Empirical Investigation', *Academy of Management Journal*, Vol. 24, No. 2.

Schein, Edgar A. (1983): 'The Role of the Founder in Creating Organizational Culture', *Organizational Dynamics*, Vol. 12, No. 1.

Smircich, Linda and Calas, Marta B. (1987): 'Organizational Culture: A Critical Perspective', in Jablin et al., op. cit..

Staw, Barry M. and Cummings, L.L. (eds) (1984): *Research in Organization Behaviour: An Annual Series of Analytical Essays and Critical Reviews*, Vol. 6. Greenwich: JAI Press.

Terpstra, Vern (1978): *The Cultural Environment of International Business*. Cincinnati: South-Western Publishers.

Trevor, Malcolm (1988): *Toshiba's New British Company: Competitiveness through Innovation in Industry*. London: Policy Studies Institute.

Triandis, Harry C. and Albert, Rosita D. (1987): 'Cross-Cultural Perspectives', in Jablin and others, op. cit..

Triandis, Harry C. and Lambert, W.W. (eds) (1980): *Handbook of Cross-cultural Psychology*. Boston: Allyn and Bacon.

UNCTC (1988): *Transnational Corporations in World Development: Trends and Prospects*. New York: UN, Chapter XIV is most relevant.

Wilkins, Alan L. and Ouchi, William G. (1983): 'Efficient Cultures: Exploring the Link between Culture and Organizational Performance', *Administrative Science Quarterly*, Vol. 28, No. 3.

Yau, Oliver (1988): 'Chinese Culture Values: Their Dimensions and Marketing Implications, *European Journal of Marketing*, Vol. 22, No. 5.

4.5

Commercial Legal Systems

4.5.1 Introduction

Looking into commercial legal systems means looking into the entire legislative infrastructure which affects, in one way or another, entrepreneurial undertakings of any kind. Commercial legal systems comprise the civil and commercial code of given countries, their trade laws, company laws, labour laws, banking and credit laws, laws governing the handling of foreign exchange matters, laws on the protection of industrial property rights, tax laws, social security laws, competition laws, and many others.

In this chapter, the following subjects out of the variety just cited will be looked at more closely: the different forms of private (direct) investment, developments in the field of foreign exchange legislation, the protection of industrial property rights as well as legislation on taxation and social security.

The legislation just mentioned mainly refers to laws which are based on the national legislation of the different countries. There are also a great number of bilateral and multilateral agreements and conventions which may also influence the commercial legal system as practised in a given country.

International organizations are preoccupied with different aspects which influence commercial legal systems; to the extent found to be useful for this specific purpose, they are referred to under the individual heading.

A great wealth of literature has been published in recent years on the underlying subjects whereby more and more attention is devoted to the situation in and the relationship with developing countries (see the References at the end of this chapter).

4.5.2   The different legal forms of private (direct) investment and issues related thereto

1.   In general

Private (direct) investment is currently being rediscovered by many countries as a means for the promotion of economic and technological development and as a way of fighting unemployment, to name just two examples out of a great variety of functions. In connection with the debt crisis to which many countries are exposed, the advantages of private (direct) investment capital versus loan capital[1] is recognized, too, as a highly desirable stabilizing factor in their economies.

The expansion of international economic cooperation resulted in the development of increasingly sophisticated forms of investment, in addition to the classical forms of equity capital investment such as:[2]

(1)   the holding of the capital of wholly-owned subsidiary companies abroad (either in the legal form of a stock corporation or a limited liability company);

(2)   the holding of substantial shareholdings in foreign companies;

(3)   portfolio shareholdings abroad;

(4)   the participation in foreign partnerships; and

(5)   investment through a foreign branch,

namely through forms of investment[3] with reduced or non-equity participation, the main types of such new forms being joint ventures, turnkey projects, licensing agreements, management and technical assistance contracts, franchising and international sub-contracting.

In addition to these new forms of investment, there are two means of undertaking foreign investment which are currently meeting the particular interest of the international business community, namely (a) the Economic Interest Groupings, and (b) Debt-Equity Conversion Schemes.

The Economic Interest Groupings are a form of international enterprise currently promoted by the Commission of the European Communities (EC) with the purpose of achieving the market integration planned for 1992. The underlying regulation of the Commission of the European Communities came into effect on 1 July 1989. This form of international enterprise closely follows the French legal form of the Groupement d'Interet Economique;[4] the most prominent example for that type of cooperation is the AIRBUS production.[5]

As to Debt-Equity Conversion Schemes, there are different opportunities employing such schemes. Broadly speaking a scheme works as follows: a potential investor acquires a hard-currency loan at a reduced rate in the secondary market (for hard currency) which he then converts into local currency to be employed in the acquisition of equity capital or the conversion of loan capital into equity capital of a local company. Countries seen to be particularly appropriate candidates for this procedure include highly indebted developing countries such as Argentina, Bolivia, Brazil, Chile, Colombia, Ecuador, Mexico, the Philippines and Venezuela.

2. International organizations active in this field

Many international organizations are preoccupied with issues in the area of international direct investment: the Organization for Economic Cooperation and Development as well as related organizations, namely the Business and Industry Advisory Committee to the OECD (BIAC) and the Trade Union Advisory Committee to the OECD (YUAC); the United Nations (in particular) the United Nations Centre on Transnational Corporations, New York (UNCTC); the United Nations Industrial Development Organization, Vienna (UNIDO); the World Bank with its different arms, particularly the International Finance Corporation (IFC) and the Multilateral Investment Guarantee Agency (MIGA) and the International Centre for the Settlement of Investment Disputes (ICSIC) (all Washington), and the International Chamber of Commerce, Paris, to name but a few.

3. Conventions in the field of investment protection

Private direct investment may be protected by various forms of protection schemes: multilateral investment protection agreements (the most prominent being MIGA), bilateral investment protection agreements (some 300 such agreements exist between different countries),[6] unilateral investment protection schemes as offered by home country governments, or by private agencies and insurance companies.

Although the primary task of such agreements is the determination of refunds and damages in case of expropriation (including repatriation of capital, profits, salaries), bilateral investment protection measures have prevented expropriation in many cases.

4.5.3 Legislation in the field of the protection of intellectual property rights[7]

1. In general

Intellectual property is generally understood to include two main topics: *industrial property*, chiefly in inventions, trademarks, industrial design, and appellations of origins, and *copyright*, chiefly in literary, musical, artistic, photographic and cinematographic works. Legislation in this field is concerned with the protection of these rights, the exclusive right of exploitation, and the repression of unfair competition. Legislation on these matters differs from country to country on several important points.

Laws relating to intellectual property rights are generally concerned only with acts accomplished or committed in the country itself. As a consequence, any certificate issued to protect such a right is effective only in the country in which a government agency has granted that certificate. There are eight exceptions to this rule, the most important being:

(1) *in the field of patents*: the European patent, granted by the European Patent Office in Munich which has effect in 13 European countries;[8]

(2) *in the field of trademarks*: the international trademarks' registrations made under the Madrid Agreement (see multilateral agreements, below), which has effect in 27 countries;

(3) *in the field of industrial designs*: the international deposits made under the Hague Agreement (see multilateral agreements, below), which has effect in 21 countries.

In order to obtain guaranteed protection in foreign countries for their own citizens, 11 countries established the International Union for the Protection of Industrial Property in 1883 by signing the Paris Convention for the Protection of Industrial Property. In the meantime, the number of member countries has increased to 98 (as at 30 June 1988).

Following the *leitmotif* that:

Protection of industrial property is not, of course, an end in itself: it is a means to encourage industrialization, investment and honest trade. All this is designed to contribute to more safety and comfort, less poverty, and more beauty in the lives of men,

12 special conventions[9] have been concluded so far under the aegis of the Paris Union.

The main purpose of these conventions is thus to be seen in the strengthening of cooperation among sovereign nations in the field of industrial property by way of ensuring that the protection is adequate, easy to obtain and, once obtained, effectively respected.

2.   International organizations active in this field

The leading international organization in the field of the promotion of the protection of intellectual property rights is the World Intellectual Property Organization (WIPO) in Geneva,[10] one of the 16 specialized agencies of the United Nations system of organizations. The World Intellectual Property Organization has 119 members.

In recent years, the World Intellectual Property Organization has devoted much attention to helping developing countries build up their own system of protecting intellectual property rights through the provision of advice, training and the furnishing of documents and equipment. One of the means of achieving this objective was the elaboration of *WIPO Model Laws for Developing Countries* on Inventions; on Marks, Trade Names, and Acts of Unfair Competition; on Industrial Designs; on Appellation of Origin and Indication of Source; on Copyright; and on the Protection of Performers, Producers of Phonograms and Broadcasting Organizations.

3. Multilateral conventions in the field of the protection of intellectual property rights

The following conventions are currently in existence that aim to protect intellectual property rights internationally:

A) International protection of industrial property
TREATIES PROVIDING FOR SUBSTANTIVE PROTECTION
Paris Convention, of 20 March 1883, for the Protection of Industrial Property.
Madrid Agreement, of 14 April 1891, for the Repression of False or Deceptive Indications of Source on Goods.
Nairobi Treaty, of 26 September 1981, on the Protection of the Olympic Symbol.

TREATIES FACILITATING PROTECTION IN SEVERAL COUNTRIES
In the field of patents
Patent Cooperation Treaty, of 19 June 1970.
Budapest Treaty, of 28 April 1977, on the International Recognition of the Deposit of Microorganisms for the Purposes of Patent Procedure.
In the field of trademarks
Madrid Agreement, of 14 April 1891, concerning the International Registration of Marks.
Trademark Registration Treaty, of 12 June 1973.
In the field of appellations of origin
Lisbon Agreement, of 31 October 1958, for the Protection of Appellations of Origin and their International Registration.
In the field of industrial designs
Hague Agreement, of 6 November 1925, concerning the International Deposit of Industrial Designs.

TREATIES ESTABLISHING INTERNATIONAL CLASSIFICATION
Strasbourg Agreement, of 24 March 1971, concerning the International Patent Classification.

Nice Agreement, of 15 June 1957, concerning the International Classification of Goods and Services for the Purposes of the Registration of Marks.

Locarno Agreement, of 8 October 1968, establishing an International Classification for Industrial Designs.

Vienna Agreement, of 12 June 1973, establishing an International Classification of the Figurative Elements of Marks.

International Convention, of 2 December 1961, for the Protection of New Varieties of Plants.

B)   International Protection of Literary and Artistic Property (Copyright)
TREATY PROVIDING FOR THE PROTECTION OF COPYRIGHT

Berne Convention, of 9 September 1886, for the Protection of Literary and Artistic Works.

TREATIES PROVIDING FOR THE PROTECTION OF NEIGHBORING RIGHTS

Rome Convention, of 26 October 1961, for the Protection of Performers, Producers of Phonograms and Broadcasting Organizations.

Geneva Convention, of 29 October 1971, for the Protection of Producers of Phonograms Against Unauthorized Duplication of their Phonograms.

Geneva Convention, of 21 May 1974, Relating to the Distribution of Programme-Carrying Signals Transmitted by Satellite.

CONVENTIONS NOT YET IN FORCE

Vienna Agreement on the protection of typefaces and their international deposit.

Geneva Treaty on the international recording of scientific discoveries.

Madrid Multilateral Convention on double taxation of copyright royalties.

4.5.4   Legislation in the field of social security[11]

1.   In general

The range of legislation in the field of social security varies widely from country to country. Many components influence the social security system of a given country, such as the political system, cultural traditions and the degree of economic and social development. Social security systems play a protective role in case of crises by relieving individual cases of distress as well as helping to avoid major upheavals in the community as a whole.

The following areas are generally refered to as social security:[12] old age, invalidity and survivors; sickness and maternity; employment accident and occupational diseases; unemployment; family allowances; complementary pensions; provident funds; mutual benefit societies; social assistance and welfare; and rehabilitation. One of the most important indicators determining the range and quality of the social security system of a given country is its economic situation, primarily in the long run and, to a lesser extent, in the short term.

For countries with a high GNP per caput it is much easier to finance a comprehensive social security system, in comparison with countries that have to rely mainly on subsistence farming. In the short run, the current economic situation of a country (its degree of unemployment or its rate of inflation) may influence its government's policy with regard to social security legislation.

Recent trends and issues can be summarized as follows: The uncertain economic climate has brought about a slowdown in the progress of social security in some countries, and great efforts have had to be undertaken to maintain the effectiveness of progress through adaptation and flexibility. High unemployment as it is experienced by many market economy countries has its effects not only on the financing of the payment of unemployment benefits, but also in terms of missing contributions to other areas of social security.

2. International organizations active in this field

The most important international organization in the field of social security is the International Social Security Association (ISSA), founded in Geneva in 1927 to protect, promote and develop social security throughout the world. The International Social Security Association has 252 affiliate members and 59 associate members in 129 countries. The International Social Security Association pursues its aims through three main programmes of activity: technical activities, regional activities and research and documentation activities. The International Social Security Association also publishes various services on social security on a worldwide basis.

3. Conventions in this field

Where persons who are covered by the social security system of their country leave that country, the issue arises as to what happens to their acquired rights, and to what extent are they covered by the social security system in their new country of residence.

International situations with respect to social security represent a highly specialized area. In order to remove or mitigate negative effects for the persons concerned, a number of countries entered into bilateral agreements on social security governing the rights and duties of the different parties involved, For European Community citizens moving from one member state to another, the underlying European Community provisions (which, in fact, have the character of a multilateral agreement) make sure that persons are covered by social security, usually according to the system of their country of residence.

4.5.5　Legislation in the field of taxation

1.　In general

The tax systems employed by individual countries are, at least in theory, a function of the degree of the economic and social development, the political system, traditions and other factors. However, the permanent need for tax reforms in many countries reveals that the optimal system has not yet been found. Although a model tax system which would take into account the necessities of countries with differing degrees of economic development has not yet been established, well-established principles were recently elaborated which bring about some clarity.

An analysis of a fiscal system which is internationally comparable requires a classification of the different types of taxes on the basis of generally accepted principles. Indeed, much work has been done by different international organizations to establish such principles; for example the Organization for Economic Cooperation and Development in its classification of taxes, the International Monetary Fund's tax classification system, the United Nations' System of National Accounts, and the European Communities' European System of Integrated Economic Accounts.[13]

The major elements of the classification principles as established by these organizations looks as follow (simplified classification):

    A.　The taxes on income
        a.　Corporate income taxes
        b.　Individual income taxes
    B.　Social security contributions
        (see section on social security, above)
    C.　Taxes on payroll
        a.　Payroll taxes
        b.　Similar taxes levied on workforce
    D.　Taxes on property
        a.　Real estate/land taxes
        b.　Capital/wealth taxes
        c.　Inheritance/estate/gift taxes
        d.　Capital transfer taxes
    E.　Taxes on goods and services
        a.　Turnover/sales taxes
        b.　Excise taxes/duties
        c.　Production taxes
        d.　Import taxes
        e.　Export taxes

F. Custom duties
  a. Import duties
  b. Export duties
G. Stamp duties
H. Other taxes

There are no clear-cut tendencies in the development of tax systems that can be observed on a worldwide basis. Within the Organization for Economic Cooperation and Development member countries, the trend towards a greater reliance on direct taxes as it was observed until three to four years ago seems, however, to have been broken off; indirect taxes provide an increasing share in the total revenue of many states.

The member states of the European Community are expected to follow the guidelines to bring about a harmonization of the tax systems, whereby excise duties and the turnover tax (VAT) are given priority. The next area for harmonization attempts will be the taxes on income (corporate income tax/ individual income), also to integrate corporate and individual income taxes in one way or another. In developing countries, an increasing interest in the European style of value-added tax is currently observed.

2.   International agreements in the field of taxation

International cooperation, especially in the form of investment, can result in double taxation which may either be avoided by unilateral measures of the home countries, or by bilateral or multilateral agreements, the so-called tax treaties. Bilateral measures for the avoidance of double taxation are based on tax treaties concluded between two states. Tax treaties basically define the different types of taxes that are covered, the different types of income (and capital, where applicable) that are affected, the way in which the right to levy a tax is allocated and the tax revenue thus shared, as well as what methods there are to avoid double taxation, and what kinds of procedures are to be followed in case of cross-border information requirements and disagreement.

Bilateral tax treaties usually follow the pattern as prescribed in the model conventions. The Organization for Economic Cooperation and Development developed two model tax conventions, in 1963 and 1977, together with an extensive commentary which has, in itself, achieved the status of an authoritative international legal reference. In 1980, the United Nations presented a model tax treaty specifically devoted to the tax relationship between developing and industrialized countries. The 1977 Organization for Economic Cooperation and Development model tax convention relies more on the concept of residence taxation, whereas the United Nations model puts more emphasis on the concept of source taxation.

Multilateral measures for the avoidance of double taxation are based on a tax treaty as it was concluded by the governments of at least three nations. The following multilateral tax treaties are currently in force: that concluded by the countries of CMEA (Comecon), one of the member countries of the Cartagena Agreement, by the Nordic countries of Europe (Denmark, Finland, Iceland, Norway and Sweden) and that of the West African Economic Community (Burkina Faso, Ivory Coast, Mali, Mauretania, Niger and Senegal).

Notes

1. The absence of interest payments falling regularly due, without taking into consideration the actual economic result delivered by the capital invested in the host country.
2. See Jehle (1988).
3. OECD (1987) 'International Investment and Multinational Enterprises – Recent Trends in International Direct Investment'. Paris, p. 24.
4. Based on Decree 67–821 of 23 September 1967.
5. See Mattausch (1984).
6. See Peters (1988).
7. Direct and indirect quotations always refer to publications released by the World Intellectual Property Organization.
8. Austria, Belgium, France, the Federal Republic of Germany, Greece, Italy, Liechtenstein, Luxembourg, The Netherlands, Spain, Sweden, Switzerland, United Kingdom.
9. Nine are called 'Agreements', three are called 'Treaties'.
10. World Intellectual Property Organization, 34, chemin des Colombettes, CH 1211 Geneva 20, Switzerland.
11. Direct and indirect quotations always refer to publications released by the International Social Security Association.
12. This classification follows that of the International Social Security Association.
13. For a direct comparison of the Organization of Economic Cooperation and Development classification of taxes with other international classifications, see Organization of Economic Cooperation and Development, Revenue Statistics of Organization of Economic Cooperation and Development Member Countries 1965–1984. Paris, 1985, 50–51.

References

Abizadeh, S., and Wyckoff, J.B. (1982): 'Tax System Components and Economic Development – An International Perspective', *Bulletin for International Fiscal Documentation*, p. 483.

Alworth, J.S. (1986): 'International Aspects of Capital Income Taxation: A Survey of Recent Developments and Possible Reforms', Conference Paper, International Institute of Public Finance.

Anderson, E. (1983): 'Corporate Tax Laws as Instruments of Economic Policy: Some Finnish Experiments', *Bulletin for International Fiscal Documentation*, p. 35.

Avery Jones, J.J. (1986): 'Interpretation of Tax Treaties', *Bulletin for International Fiscal Documentation*, p. 75.

Basile, A. and Germidis, D. (1984): 'Investing in Free Export Processing Zones', OECD – Development Centre Studies, Paris.

Baum, W.C., and Tolbert, S.M. (1985): *Investing in Developing Countries – Lessons of World Bank Experience*. Oxford: Oxford University Press.

BIAC (1987): BIAC Brochure on the *OECD Declaration on International Investment and Multinational Enterprise*, BIAC Committee on International Investment and Multinational Enterprise, Paris.

Bird, R.M. (1983): 'Income Tax Reform in Developing Countries: The Administrative Dimension', *Bulletin for International Fiscal Documentation*, p. 3.

Buckley, P.J. (1979): 'Foreign Investment Success for Smaller Firms', *Multinational Business*, No. 3.

Buckley, P.J. (1983): *New Forms of International Industrial Cooperation: A Survey of the Literature with Special Reference to North-South Technology Transfer*. Aussenwirtschaft, p. 195.

Buckley, P.J. (1985): 'New Forms of International Industrial Cooperation', in *The Economic Theory of the Multinational Enterprise*, Buckley and Casson (1985) Chapter 3. London: Macmillan.

Buckley, P.J., and Pearce, R.D. (1979): 'Overseas Production and Exporting by the World's Largest Enterprises – A Study in Sourcing Policy', *Journal of International Business Studies*, No. 1.

Bundesstelle für Aussenhandelsinformation (1983): 'The Federal Republic of Germany as a Business Partner', Köln.

Caley, M. (1986): 'Changes in Revenue Structures – Recent Trends in Company Taxation', Conference Paper, *International Institute of Public Finance*.

Cnossen, S. (1986): 'Tax Harmonisation in the European Community', *Bulletin for International Fiscal Documentation*, p. 545.

Cnossen, S. (1986): 'The Role of Excises in OECD Member Countries', Conference Paper, *International Institute of Public Finance*.

Commission of the European Communities 1983: 'Tax and Financial Measures in Favour of Investment', COM (83), 218 final.

Deutsche Bundesbank (1986): 'Internationale Organisationen und Abkommen im Bereich von Währung und Wirtschaft', *Sonderdruck der Deutschen Bundesbank*, Nr. 3. Frankfurt.

Dräger-Stiftung (1985): 'Zielsetzung Partnerschaft – Die weltwirtschaftliche Bedeutung von Auslandsinvestitionen und Technologietransfer', Band 9, Lübeck/Bonn.

Esser, J. and Meessen, K.M. (Hrsg.) (1983): 'Kapitalinvestitionen im Ausland – Chancen und Risiken/Capital Investment Abroad – Chances and Risks', Verlag Industrie-Förderung.

Fuest, W. and Kroker, R. (1985): 'Unternehmensbesteuerung im internationalen Vergleich', *IW-trends*, p. 16.

Guisinger, S. (1987): 'Attracting and Controlling Foreign Investment', *Economic Impact*, p. 18. United States Information Agency, Washington.

Guisinger, S. (1987): 'Investment related to trade', *The Uruguay Round – A Handbook on the Multilateral Trade Negotiations*, Finger and Olechowski (eds). Washington: A World Bank Publication.

International Chamber of Commerce (1987): 'Promotion of Private Foreign Direct Investment in Developing Countries'. Paris.

International Social Security Association (1987): 'Developments in social security and ISSA activities 1984–1986'. Geneva.

Jehle, E. (1988): 'How to Bring Down Frontiers in International Business – The Impact of Intelligent Fiscal Policies', Paper presented at a Conference of the Academy of International Business, UK Chapter, 15–16 April 1988. London.

Kayser, G., Kitterer, B.H.J., Naujoks, W., Schwarting, U. and Ullrich, K.V. (1981): 'Investieren im Ausland – Was deutche Unternehmen draussen erwartet', *Deutscher Industrie-und Handelstag*. Bonn.

Krayer, D. (1978): 'Das Europäische Patentübereinkommen', *Internationale Wirtschaftsbriefe*, No. 15, 10 August.

Laney, L.O. (1987): 'The Evolving Market for Third World Debt, Economic Impact', p. 49. United States Information Agency, Washington.

Loewenheim, U. (1982): 'Europäisches Patent-und Markenrecht', *Internationale Wirtschaftsbriefe*. No. 24, 27 December.

Maktouf, L. and Surrey, S.S. (1983): 'Tax Expenditure Analysis and Tax and Budgetary Reform in Less Developed Countries', *Law and Policy in International Business*, p. 739.

Massone, P. (1981): 'Developments in Latin America: Adjustment of Profits for Inflation', *Bulletin for International Fiscal Documentation*, p. 3.

Mattausch, H. (1984): 'Die Besteuerung des französischen Groupement d'Intérêt Economique und seines deutschen Mitglieds', IWB No. 15, 10 August.

Michaelopoulos, C. (1986): 'A Look at Private Direct Investment, Finance and Development', *Singapore Economic Bulletin*, p. 13.

Nieuwkerk, M.V. and Sparling, R.P. 1985: 'De internationale investeringspositie van Nederland', *Monetaire Monografieën De Nederlandsche Bank NV*. Deventer: Kluwer.

NMB Bank – Frans van Loon (1987): 'Asset Trading and Debt Conversion', NMB Bank Brochure. Amsterdam.

OECD (1983): 'Investing in Developing Countries'. Paris.

OECD (1983): 'International Investment and Multinational Enterprises – Investment Incentives and Disincentives and the International Investment Process'. Paris.

OECD (1983): 'World Economic Interdependence and the Evolving North-South Relationship'. Paris.

OECD (1984): 'Tax Expenditures – A Review of The Issues and Country Practices'. Paris.

OECD (1985): 'Statistiques de recettes publiques des pays membres de l'OCDE/Revenue Statistics of OECD Member Countries 1965–1984'. Paris.

OECD (1986): 'Personal Income Tax Systems under Changing Economic Conditions; The Ratio of Personal Tax Receipts to GDP'. Paris.

OECD (1986): 'Venture Capital – Context, Development and Policies'. Paris.

OECD (1987): 'Development Co-operation – Efforts and Policies of the Members of the Development Assistance Committee'. Paris.

OECD (1987): 'Financing and External Debt of Developing Countries – 1986 Survey'. Paris.

OECD (1987): 'External Debt Statistics – The Debt and Other External Liabilities of Developing, CMEA and Certain Other Countries and Territories'. Paris.

OECD (1987): 'International Investment and Multinational Enterprises – Recent Trends in International Direct Investment'. Paris.

OECD (1988): 'Direct Investment in Developing Countries – Report on a Meeting of Management Experts under the OECD Labour/Management Programme'. OECD External Relations Division, Paris.

Oman, C. (1984): 'New Forms of International Investment in Developing Countries'. OECD Development Centre Studies, Paris.

Peters, P. 1988: Investment Treaties: An Updating: Contribution to the discussion on legal aspects of a NIEO'. Paper prepared for The Netherlands branch of ILA.

Max Planck Institute for Comparative Public Law and International Law (continous) Public International Law – A Current Bibliography of Articles. Heidelberg: Springer Verlag.

Plasschaert, S.R.F. (1985): 'The Suitability of Schedular, Global and Dualistic Patterns of Income Taxation, with Particular Refence to LDCs'. Conference Paper, International Institute of Public Finance.

Ritter, W. (1979): 'Steuerbeziehungen mit der Dritten Welt', *Deutsche Steuer-Zeitung*, p. 419.

Roberti, P. and Bernardi, L. (1985): 'Comparing Social Security Systems: Pitfalls and Insights', Conference Paper, *International Institute of Public Finance*.

Shome, P. (ed.) (1986): *Fiscal Issues in South-East Asia*. Oxford University Press.

Tanzi, V. (1982): 'Tax Policy in Middle-Income Countries: Some Lessons of Experience', *Bulletin for Internatioal Fiscal Documentation*, p. 411.

Uhling, C. (1986): 'The Role of Entrepreneurial Cooperation', Intereconomics, p. 283.

United Nations Centre on Transnational Corporations (1980): 'Users Guide to the Information System on Transnational Corporations – A Technical Paper', New York.

United Nations Centre on Transnational Corporations (1980): 'Supplement to National Legislation and Regulations Relating to Transnational Corporations', New York.

United Nations Centre on Transnational Corporations (1983): 'Measures Strengthening the Negotiating Capacity of Governments in Their Relations With Transnational Corporations – Joint Ventures among Firms in Latin America', New York.

United Nations Centre on Transnational Corporations (1983): 'Transnational Corporations in World Development – Third Survey', New York.

United Nations Centre on Transnational Corporations (1983): 'National Legislation and Regulations Relating to Transnational Corporations – A Technical Paper'. New York.

United Nations Centre on Transnational Corporations (1985): 'Environmental Aspects of the Activities of Transnational Corporations: A Survey', New York.

United Nations Centre on Transnational Corporations (1985): 'Trends and Issues in Foreign Direct Investment and Relating Flows', New York.

United Nations Centre on Transnational Corporations (1986): 'National Legislation and Regulations Relating to Transnational Corporations', Volume V. New York.

Wallace, C.D. (1988): *Foreign Direct Investment and the Multinational Enterprise: A Bibliography*. Dordrecht: Martinus Nijhoff Publishers.

Wellons P., Germidis D. and Glavanis B. (1986): 'Banks and Specialized Financial Intermediaries in Development', OECD Development Centre, Paris.

WIPO: 'World Intellectual Property Organization (1988): General Information', Geneva.

World Bank (1988): 'World Development Report 1988 – Opportunities and Risks in Managing the World Economy, Public Finance in Development, World Development Indicators'. Washington.

4.6

Accounting Systems

4.6.1 Introduction

Business organizations need accounting systems to record their business transactions and must summarize these transactions to report on their performance to their owners and creditors. Reports of the organization's assets and earnings are also necessary as a basis for ensuring that they contribute as taxpayers to the communities in which they operate. However, the particular arrangements for fulfilling these roles differ considerably from one country to another, depending upon the legal codes operating in particular countries, the methods of financing business in each country, the different taxation arrangements employed, the strength of the accounting profession in each country and their different cultural characteristics.

Such differences make it difficult for investors and businessmen to use accounting data to assess or compare the performance of firms in different countries. The growth of multinational business and the development of more international capital markets have brought to the fore these problems of accounting comparability. Businessmen and investors thinking of trading with or purchasing shares in a foreign company have to base their decisions on information contained in the company's published financial report, prepared according to local accounting norms which may be quite different from those that apply in the investor's own country.

Accounting systems perform a variety of functions. They serve to maintain a day-to-day record of an organization's trading relationships with others – its purchases of materials and services from suppliers and its sales to customers, and any indebtedness arising from these transactions. Accounting systems also provide periodic information about the financial position of the enterprise (through balance sheets) and its trading results (through profit-and-loss statements) for the benefit of the enterprise's owners and creditors. These performance reports in turn may well be used by owners and others as a basis for deciding whether to invest in the enterprise. Reports of trading results can also assist in the calculation of the organization's tax liability. Finally, trading results can serve as performance indicators to be used in industrial or national planning.

Underlying all accounting systems are fundamental accounting principles such as the recording of assets and liabilities at their *historical cost*; drawing up financial statements on the premise that the business is a *going concern*; *consistency* in applying accounting principles from period to period; recording costs as they are *accrued*; *realizing* revenues only when they are earned; *matching* revenues and the costs of these sales; *prudence* in measuring business income; and disclosing items only if they are *material*. Pursuit of these principles should lead to accounting reports which give a *true and fair view* of the business's financial position and operating results. However, although accounting principles and reporting practices should provide a means of international communication, in practice the interpretation of measurement principles and reporting practices reflect the different economic and political climates of separate nations.

The extent of differences in the interpretation of accounting principles and in financial reporting practices is indicated in a world-wide survey undertaken by Price Waterhouse International which compared accounting practices in over 60 countries, highlighting, through detailed tables, the differences between nations (Price Waterhouse International (1979)). A survey of accounting practices among member countries undertaken by the Organization for Economic Cooperation and Development (1980) revealed similar differences in the application of accounting principles between countries and wide variations in accounting disclosure policies.

Many authors have sought to explain these differences in terms of the historical development of accounting in different social and political climates which have caused accounting systems to evolve in different ways. Parker, for example, stresses this explanation, though he sees virtues in this diversity in providing comparative data for the development of accounting systems (Parker (1979)). Zimmerman also takes this historical view, though he foresees developments in international-communications technology serving to reduce future disparity (Zimmerman in Holzer (1984)). As awareness of disparities has grown, so also has academic and business interest in the subject, to the point where a recent survey of international accounting literature by Samuels and Piper included some 34 pages of bibliography on the subject, most published over the past decade (Samuels and Piper (1985)).

4.6.2 Causes of international differences in accounting practices

In attempting to make sense of observed differences in the application of accounting principles and financial reporting practices between countries, various writers have sought to analyse the causes of these differences. One of the more persuasive analyses by Nobes (Nobes and Parker (1981), Nobes (1984)) suggests four main factors which have an effect: differences in legal systems; the predominant types of business organizations and their ownership; differences in taxation rules; and the strength of the accountancy profession in various countries. The following observations borrow heavily from this analysis, as each of these influences is explored in turn.

1. Nature of the legal/commercial system

As Chapter 4.5 makes clear, legal systems differ markedly across the world. Many European countries like France and West Germany have formal legal systems where the law attempts to cover all eventualities and must be obeyed to the letter. Company law in such countries tends to prescribe precise, detailed rules for asset valuation, income measurement and the format of accounting reports, so that company accounting becomes a branch of company law. Japan has a similar formal, legal and commercial code. By contrast, countries like the United Kingdom and the United States of America rely much more upon common-law systems, supplementing a limited amount of statute law by case law developed through the courts. This emphasis on the spirit rather than the strict letter of the law creates a more flexible approach to company law, leaving companies greater discretion about how to calculate and disclose accounting results.

Systems of government economic planning can also lead to detailed specification of the nature and form of company accounts in particular countries. For example, in France the Plan Comptable General provides standardized formats, prescribed depreciation rates and asset-valuation rules which are compulsory for companies, in the interests of providing industry performance data for use by government in planning. The French Economics Ministry in its role of controller of the economy provides a chart of accounts, definition of terms, model financial statements and rules for measurement and valuation for each industry. The standard accounts have to be completed by companies each year for national statistics purposes; published financial statements use the model formats and tax returns are based on the model measures. By contrast, in countries like the United Kingdom and the United States of America, which do not have such detailed government intervention, there is less uniformity in accounting formats and rules.

At the foremost extreme of formality one can point to accounting systems in socialist countries such as the Soviet Union. Here, accounting for the self-supporting Khozraschet enterprises places a heavy emphasis upon the fulfilment of plans as the basic objective of the enterprise, as Berry points out (Berry in Holzer (1984)). Each enterprise is headed by a director, and employs a chief economist, responsible for planning and setting production norms and a chief book-keeper, concerned with financial reporting. Enterprises prepare detailed official reports to their superior industry-planning authorities including balance sheets, production expenses, output-plan fulfilment and labour-plan fulfilment which are collated by the Central Statistical Administration for the benefit of the State Planning Authority – Gosplan. The state bank Gosbank is also able to exercise external control over enterprises because of its importance in providing working capital, while the state investment bank Stroybank exerts influence through its financing of enterprises' capital outlays.

2. Types of business organization and ownership

Most countries have adopted joint-stock companies as their main form of business organization, recognizing the need for public reporting of business results as an acceptable price to pay for the advantages of being able to raise capital by issuing shares and offering limited liability. However, the prevalence of joint stock companies and patterns of share ownership can significantly affect the form of the business results report.

In countries like the United Kingdom and the United States of America where the bulk of private-sector economic activity is undertaken by a few hundred large joint-stock companies, each of which is owned by many thousands of shareholders, we would expect detailed reports of company performance to be made to owners and pressure for disclosure. We would also expect to find independent professional accountants auditing these reports of business performance to reassure owners that company managers have reported a true and fair view of the company's affairs.

Though large joint-stock companies are also the predominant form of business organization in West Germany, most company shares are held or controlled by a few large banks. Here business performance reports tend to be more creditor-oriented than owner-oriented and need to be less detailed since banks can often nominate directors and thus directly obtain information. By contrast, where most companies are small, privately-owned, family businesses, as in France and Japan, there is less demand for detailed published accounting reports or for audited accounts. At the extreme limit, where most businesses are sole proprietorships, there is little or no need for accounting reports other than for tax assessment purposes. This is often the situation in developing countries where most people are self-employed peasant farmers or small traders.

Countries like the United Kingdom and the United States of America that have large numbers of big limited companies also have active stock exchanges where such company shares are traded. Trading in shares again creates pressure for disclosure from shareholders; as a requirement of having their shares quoted on an exchange, companies must often comply with strict disclosure requirements. By contrast in countries like France and Italy where fewer companies have their shares traded on stock exchanges like the French Commission des Operations de Bourse and the Italian Commissione Nazionale per le Societa a la

Boorsa, there has been less pressure for disclosure until recently. As Oldham (1975) points out, there is a strong preference in most of Europe (except the United Kingdom) for fixed-interest rather than risk bearing shares, encouraging a relatively passive shareholder stance.

3. Taxation rules

Rules of taxation assessment of companies can have a significant effect on accounting practice. Many countries like France, West Germany, Italy and Japan require that expenses claimed for tax purposes must usually be the same as those charged in the financial accounts. This reflects the predominance of taxation as the main reason for preparing accounts in many of the countries. By contrast, in countries like the United Kingdom whose commercial rules of accounting were developed prior to many tax rules, the taxation authorities have to adjust the commercial accounts for their purpose.

The alternative systems can give rise to widely varying accounting results, making profit comparisons between countries difficult. For example, in Germany where the commercial accounts (Handelsbilanz) should be the same as the tax accounts (Steuerbilanz) the tax regulations lay down depreciation rates to be used for particular assets; if these allowances are to be claimed for tax purposes, they must be charged in the financial accounts. By contrast in the United Kingdom the amount of depreciation charged in published financial accounts is determined by commercial judgement of the appropriate rate at which to write off assets; the amount of depreciation charged for tax purposes may be quite different, being determined by capital allowances within the tax rules. Similar problems arise with bad debt provisions. These are determined by tax laws in many European countries, but in the United Kingdom may be determined on a basis of commercial prudence in the company accounts yet on a different basis in the taxation computation.

4. Strength of the accounting profession

The size and competence of a country's accounting profession is likely to be strongly influenced by many of the factors mentioned above. For example, the lack of a substantial body of private shareholders in most large continental European companies means the need for auditors is much smaller than in the United Kingdom and the United States of America, so the accounting profession is generally smaller in Europe. The establishment of formal planning and accounting systems, as in France, reduces the scope for interpretation in preparing accounts, affecting both the number and the quality of the accounting profession there. In Japan independent professional accountants were virtually unknown until after the Second World War and only with the growth of joint stock companies – the Kabushiki Kaishas – has the requirement for an independent audit of larger listed-companies' accounts fostered the growth of a trained accounting profession (Choi and Hiramatsu (1987)).

In turn, the lack of a large and influential profession can make it more difficult to introduce advanced accounting methods and auditing requirements. In some European countries and in Japan there may be insufficient professionally qualified persons competent to undertake audit work, so that the statutory requirement for a rigorous audit to be undertaken has to be restricted to larger quoted companies.

In concluding his review of the causes of differences in accounting practices between countries, Nobes (1984) stresses the importance of the mix of users of accounting information in determining the dominant source of rules for accounting practice. He points out that in many continental European countries the importance of governments as controllers of the economy and collectors of taxes has led to the dominance of company laws, commercial codes and tax regulations. By contrast in Anglo-Saxon countries the accounting profession has tended to exercise control over accounting practice, developing accepted accounting-measurement practices which have more recently taken the form of detailed accounting standards.

In turn, the accounting systems in force in developing countries tend to reflect their colonial antecedents, as Enthoven points out. (Enthoven in Nobes and Parker (1981).) However, developing countries have certain accounting problems in common, regardless of which general accounting tradition they have inherited. These are often related to the excessively detailed accounting regulations and requirements imposed upon enterprises by government, poor verification of the quality of accounting information and the inadequate number and skills of the accounting profession in most developing countries.

4.6.3   Some examples of differences in measurement and disclosure practices

Only through detailed studies of accounting practices in various countries of the type reported by Nobes and Parker (1981) and Holzer (1984) can the reader gain a full appreciation of differences between countries. Our present review is much less ambitious, touching upon a few examples to leave the reader with some impressions of differences.

Accountants generally tend to measure business assets in terms of their original cost. However, the historic cost formula is rarely applied rigidly; some assets may be adjusted from historic cost to current market value or may be adjusted for general price level changes. At one extreme West Germany employs historical cost in a rigid, unsupplemented manner. At, the other extreme in The Netherlands some companies present their main accounts in replacement cost terms, preferring the subjectivity of estimating replacement costs to the distortion from fairness which arises from historical cost-accounting during inflationary periods. The United Kingdom lies between these two extremes, preparing accounts on an historical cost basis but experimenting with supplementary replacement cost accounts.

Furthermore, accountants generally make depreciation charges against fixed assets to spread the historical cost of fixed assets over a number of accounting periods over which they are expected to be of service. Yet the amount of depreciation charged can vary greatly. In the United Kingdom and most Anglo-Saxon countries where depreciation is not affected by tax requirements charges are based upon commercial judgements about the lives of fixed assets. By contrast, in continental European countries like France and West Germany where financial accounts conform closely to tax regulations, and where tax rules allow accelerated depreciation over a shorter period than the asset's expected life, larger depreciation charges will be made in the accounts than is commercially warranted, understating profits.

Again, accountants tend to make provisions which act as charges against profits in anticipation of certain expected expenses such as bad debts. However, the extent of their prudence in creating provisions varies greatly from country to country. For example, in the United Kingdom and most other Anglo-Saxon countries the amount provided for bad debts is based upon a commercial judgement. By contrast in continental European countries where a provision for bad debts is not allowed for tax purposes, none may appear in the accounts, with the risk that income is overstated.

As industrial and commercial operations have come to be carried out by groups of companies rather than individual companies, holding companies have developed and the need has grown for consolidated accounts to reflect the combined results of the group. However, financial statement consolidation practices can vary widely between countries. In the United States and United Kingdom all subsidiary companies' results would be consolidated in preparing group accounts, including overseas subsidiaries. By contrast, in West Germany, though consolidation was made obligatory for public companies in 1965, foreign subsidiaries need not be consolidated, so that German group accounts can understate group assets and income where the group has overseas subsidiary companies. In France, consolidation of accounts was rare until recent times, though the European Community Seventh Company Law Directive is likely to change this situation. In 1987 the Organization for Economic Cooperation and Development issued a report on consolidation policies in its countries that details many of these differences (Organisation for Economic Cooperation and Development, (1987)).

Choi, Hino and Min (1983) highlight the effect of different financial accounting and commercial practices in making a comparison of accounting ratios virtually meaningless in most cases. They take the particular example of United

States and Japanese companies, pointing out how the debtors-to-sales ratio or average-collection-period ratio differs considerably between United States and Japanese firms. The larger Japanese collection periods may simply reflect Japanese commercial traditions of lifetime employment, with repayment extensions being granted to buyers during business downturns to ensure the buyer's continued future patronage. Again, lower profitability ratios and profit margin ratios for Japanese companies may reflect their preference for sales growth as the primary objective and a drive to increase market share as a means of assuring profits in the long run.

4.6.4   Harmonization

In recent years there has been a strong movement towards international harmonization of accounting both on an international basis or within smaller regional groupings of countries like the European Community. There are a number of reasons for this movement. First, the rapid growth of international trade over recent decades has created increasing interdependence between countries, heightening awareness of differences in accounting approaches between them. Secondly, the growth of multinational enterprises with their global investment and financing strategies has created a need for greater comparability of accounting measures between countries. Thirdly, the development of international capital markets, with more sophisticated investors who operate on a worldwide basis, has created a need for more standardized information about company performance. Finally, the parallel growth of large professional accounting practices which operate on a worldwide basis, such as Price Waterhouse International and Arthur Andersen, has added a further spur to standardization, as their international teams of accountants seek to reconcile differences in accounts on behalf of clients.

Many authors highlight the growing economic social and political power of multinational companies as being at the heart of the harmonization process, stressing the need for information to analyse the activities of multinationals as the driving force for internal accounting standard-setting (Gray, Shaw and McSweeny (1981)). Many commentators have pressed for greater disclosure by multinational companies to assist in monitoring their activities (Emmanuel and Gray (1983)).

Harmonization seeks to increase the compatability of accounting practices in different countries by setting limits to the extent to which they are permitted to vary. The process of reducing differences does not imply complete standardization of accounts. Differences in the fundamental purpose of accounts in various countries are probably too great to make complete standardization possible. Indeed, some writers have expressed concern that the imposition of universal accounting standards will merely produce accounting statements which are superficially standard but which mask underlying differences in purpose and philosophy (Berry and Parker (1987)). Furthermore, harmonization is generally directed only at large, multinational, quoted companies, rather than local, small, closely-held companies.

On a global basis the efforts of the International Accounting Standards Committee (IASC) have contributed to standardization. This body was formed in 1973 with the aim of improving the comparability of measurement and reporting by all enterprises. The International Accounting Standards Committee has joint representation of professional accounting bodies from nine founder-member countries and has subsequently widened representation by admitting many other associate members to the group. The objectives of the International Accounting Standards Committee set out in its constitution involve maintaining an International Accounting Standards Committee to formulate and publish standards to be observed in the presentation of audited financial statements and to promote their worldwide acceptance and observance. Choi and Mueller (1978) summarize the essential features of the International Accounting Standards Committee in a review of international accounting standards and organizations.

The commitment of the European Community (EC) countries to the principle of ultimate economic unity has enabled the EC to go much further in achieving common enforceable standards than has been achieved on a worldwide basis. European harmonization efforts have taken the form of new company laws brought into effect as a result of European Community directives. Nobes (1980) and Oldham (1975) both comment extensively on the nature of these directives and their effects. Most notable among these are the Fourth, Seventh and Eighth Directives, outlined below.

The Fourth Company Law Directive, issued in 1978, had to be passed into law by member states within two years, with a further 18 months for national legislation to come into force. Most countries in Europe have now implemented the Directive: the provisions of the Fourth Directive were incorporated in United Kingdom legislation by the 1981 Companies Act. The Directive stipulated the form and content of the annual accounts of limited-liability companies, required the audit of such accounts and extended disclosure requirements. The Directive also set out rules to be employed in the valuation of assets, emphasizing the historical cost basis of valuation and the conventions of going concern, prudence and consistency in asset valuation. Specifically the Directive sets detailed rules concerning measurement of depreciation and valuation of inventories. Finally the Directive permitted member states to allow small companies to publish less detailed balance sheets and to avoid an audit.

The Seventh Company Law Directive, issued in 1983, was incorporated into national legislation by 1988 and implemented by 1990. The directive is concerned with the preparation of consolidated accounts by groups of limited-liability companies. It requires groups of companies to prepare consolidated balance sheets and profit-and-loss accounts and requires the audit and publication of consolidated accounts. The Eighth Company Law Directive was issued in 1984 with incorporation into national legislation by 1988 and implementation by 1990. It stipulates minimum educational and experience requirements for auditors engaged in statutory audits within the European Community and insists on the auditor being independent of the audited company. Both directives have taken somewhat longer to implement than originally envisaged.

Oldham (1987) traces the effects of the directives on the accounting practices of member states. He notes how they have served to increase the content of published accounts and accompanying notes, overcoming traditional secrecy and improving the information value of company reports. He also notes how they have placed greater priority on the provision of a true and fair view of a company's or group's assets, liabilities and profits, de-emphasizing the distorting effect of rigid accounting rules employed for tax or national planning purposes.

4.6.5   Conclusion

Despite these harmonization efforts, significant differences in accounting methods between European countries remain. Furthermore, on a broader world stage, differences are more marked and entrenched. Consequently in the present climate the only advice one can offer international users of accounting data is 'caveat emptor' – let the buyer beware! For although useful guideline articles for businessmen can offer some outline idea of the nature of accounting systems in a particular country (see, for example, French, Ozawa and Sato (1987)), in the absence of a detailed knowledge of these differences, grave misjudgements can be made about company performance. For as Choi and others (1983) point out, differences in measures of financial return may be influenced as much by differences in accounting measurement conventions as the underlying performance being measured.

References

Berry, I.R. and Parker, D.: 'The Divergence of Accounting Practices', *Management Accounting*, December 1987 pp. 26–7.

Berry, M. (1984): 'Accounting in Socialist Countries', in Holzer H.P. (ed.): *International Accounting*: New York: Harper and Row.

Choi, F.D.S., Hino H. and Min, S.K.: 'Analysing Foreign Financial Statements: The Use and Misuse of International Ratio Analysis', *Journal of International Business Studies*, 1983. Reproduced in Choi, F.D.S. and Mueller, G.G.: *Frontiers of International Accounting: An Anthology*. UMI Research Press, 1985.

Choi, F.D.S. and Hiramatsu, K. (eds) (1987): *Accounting and Financial Reporting in Japan: Current Issues and Future Prospects in a World Economy*. London Van Nostrand Reinhold.

Choi, F.D.S. and Mueller, G.G. (1978): *An Introduction to Multinational Accounting*. New York: Prentice Hall.

Emmanuel, C.R. and Gray, S.J. (1983): 'Segmental Disclosure by Multibusiness Multinational Companies: A Proposal, Accounting and Business Research 1978'. Reproduced: in Gray, S.J. (ed.): *International Accounting and Transnational Decisions*. Sevenoaks, Kent: Butterworth.

Enthoven A. (1981): 'Accounting in Developing Countries', in Nobes, C.W. and Parker, R.H. (eds): *Comparative International Accounting*. Oxford: Philip Allan. 2nd edn. 1985.

French, M., Ozawa, M. and Sato, J.: 'Learning the Art of Japanese Business', *Accountancy Age*, April 1987, pp. 36–40.

Gray, S.J., Shaw, J.C. and McSweeney, L.B. (1983): 'Accounting Standards and Multinational Corporations', *Journal of International Business Studies*, 1981. Reproduced in Gray, S.J. (ed.): *International Accounting and Transnational Decisions*: Sevenoaks, Kent: Butterworth.

Holzer, H.P. (ed.) (1984): *International Accounting*. New York: Harper and Row.

Nobes, C.W.: 'Harmonization of Accounting Within the European Communities: The Fourth Directive on Company Law', *International Journal of Accounting: Education and Research*, Spring 1980. Reproduced in Gray, S.J. (ed.) (1983): *International Accounting and Transnational Decisions*. Sevenoaks, Kent: Butterworth.

Nobes, C.W. (1984): *International Classification of Financial Reporting*, Beckenham: Croom Helm.

Nobes, C.W. and Parker, R.H. (1981): *Comparative International Accounting*. Oxford: Philip Allan. 2nd edn. 1985.

Oldham, K.M. (1975): *Accounting Systems and Practice in Europe*. Aldershot, Hants: Gower. 3rd edn 1987.

Organisation for Economic Cooperation and Development (OECD): *International Investment and Multinational Enterprises: Accounting Practices in OECD Member Countries*. OECD, Paris 1980.

Organisation for Economic Cooperation and Development (OECD): *Consolidation Policies in OECD Countries, Report by Working Group on Accounting Standards*, No. 2, OECD, Paris 1987.

Parker, R.H. (1979): 'Explaining National Differences in Consolidated Accounts', in Lee, T.A. and Parker, R.H. *The Evolution of Corporate Financial Reporting*. Walton-on-Thames, Surrey: Thomas Nelson.

Price Waterhouse International: *International Survey of Accounting Principles and Reporting Practices*. Fitzgerald, R.D., Stickler, A.D. and Watts, T.R. (eds). Price Waterhouse International, 1979.

Samuels, J.M. and Piper, A.G. (1985): *International Accounting: A Survey*. Beckenham, Croom Helm.

Zimmerman, V.K. (1984): 'Introducing the International Dimension of Accounting, in Holyer, H.P. (ed.) *International Accounting*. London: Harper and Row.

Part 5

International Investment

Introduction

International investment is a crucial element in international business. This part examines types of international investment (Chapter 5.1) covering long-term versus short-term investment and disinvestment. The increasing diversity of forms of international investment is noted. Chapter 5.2 examines the growth of such investment, paying attention to service and manufacturing multinationals and the internationalization of smaller firms. The direction of international investment is described in Chapter 5.3. The industrial structure of international investment is reviewed in Chapter 5.4 while Chapter 5.5 examines the barriers to international investment.

Contents

5.1

Types of International Investment

International investment can be divided into long-term and short-term investment, usually by the (arbitrary) term date of one year. Long-term international investment can itself be divided into portfolio and direct varieties. An increasing diversity of international investment in many dimensions can be identified. Finally, attention must be paid to the phenomenon of international disinvestment.

5.1.1 Long-term versus short-term international investment

The International Monetary Fund (IMF) defines long-term capital as transactions in securities with an original term maturity of over one year or no stated maturity. In many cases, original maturity has no bearing on the length of time for which an investment will be held, so some countries (including the United Kingdom) do not distinguish between short-term and long-term capital in their balance of payments accounts.

The foreign exchange market

Every transaction across the international exchanges involves a transfer of foreign exchange. Because the timing of such transactions is not instantaneous, they will involve the transfer of assets (trade credit, promissory notes) for a limited period of time. These offsetting transactions result in the build-up of short-term capital movements to fund transactions. A risk-averse trader may also enter into forward purchases of foreign exchange in order to alleviate the risk of changes in currency parities (a premium will be paid for this service). These and other means of financing transactions result in short-term capital movements. Often, the trader's motive will be to reduce the amount and time of exposure to foreign-exchange risk.

As well as import and export financing, it will also often be necessary to retain working capital in a foreign currency. This necessitates recourse to the foreign-exchange market. Speculators and arbitrators will also use the market, but for purposes of gain on their own account rather than to facilitate a trade or investment transaction. National Central Banks will also intervene in the market in order to support the value of their own currency or to carry out national policy or agreed concerted international actions.

Short-term international finance

Short-term international deposits range from call money and overnight funds to investment with an arbitrary one-year maturity. Borrowers, mainly government and multinational companies, raise significant amounts of capital international money and capital markets. Recent years have seen numerous new financial instruments and international financial centres developed to meet these needs. (See Eiteman and Stonehill (1986) for a review.)

The Eurocurrency markets have grown into the most important sources for short-term credits and deposits. They have also evolved into a medium-term market for syndicated loans to finance large outlays. The first such market, the Eurodollar market, grew in the dollar-scarce years after the Second World War: centred on London, it began by the recirculation of United States dollars held by Eastern European governments, unwilling to deposit the dollars in the United States. The existence of high-yielding, safe, liquid investments led to a growth in demand and the creation of new international markets in financial instruments. A Eurodollar is simply a United States dollar time-deposit in a bank outside the United States. Other convertible currency markets followed, leading to Eurobanks: financial intermediaries simultaneously bidding for time-deposits and making loans in a currency other than its home-country currency.

A major outgrowth of the Eurocurrency markets is Eurodollar credit (or Eurocredit) – bank loans to firms, government institutions or banks denominated in Eurocurrency and extended by banks in countries other than the country of the currency in which the loan is denominated. The length of Eurodollar loans varies but six months is routine. The creation of a separate Asian dollar market followed, based on the availability of dollars in the Asia-Pacific region which the owners had no wish to declare to governments. This is mainly an inter-bank market.

Several international finance centres perform the functions of an offshore

Table 5.1.1   Borrowing on the International Financial Market[a] (Billions of Dollars)

	1984	*1985*	*1986*
Bonds	111.5	167.7	226.4
Syndicated loans	57.0	42.0	47.8
Note-issuance facilities	17.4	36.3	21.4
Other back-up facilities	11.4	10.5	5.6
Total	197.3	256.5	301.2
Eurocommercial-paper programmes	"	11.2	56.7
Other non-underwritten facilities	"	10.6	8.5
Equities	"	2.7	11.7
Grand total	197.3	281.0	378.1

Note: a) Excluding merger-related stand-bys and renegotiations.

Reproduced from: UNCTC (1988) p. 107.

Source: Organization for Economic Cooperation and Development, *Financial Market Trends*, No. 37, May 1987, p. 5.

market. Offshore financial markets provide financial services for non-residents, usually dealing in foreign currency-based securities.

Medium- and long-term international finance

The growth of the international bank has paralleled the Eurocurrency market. International bonds are Eurobonds or foreign bonds. A Eurobond is underwritten by an international syndicate of banks and other securities firms; it is sold exclusively in countries other than the country in whose currency it is denominated. A foreign bond is underwritten by a syndicate composed of members from a single country, sold principally within that country and denominated in that country's currency, although the user is from a different country.

Eurobonds are issued by large firms, governments, government enterprises and international institutions. They have the advantages of law-regulatory interference, less stringent disclosure terms than many national regulatory authorities allow and favourable tax status. There has been a recent rapid growth in Euroyen bonds; competition in this market produces constant innovations, which, although allowing users greater variety, cause headaches to regulatory bodies and statistical authorities.

International trading for equities is becoming the norm. Lending through development banks is also a major factor in providing capital in less-developed countries. Table 5.1.1 shows the rapid recent growth of the international financial market, total borrowings on which had reached over $378 billion in 1986.

5.1.2   Types of international investment: direct versus portfolio investment

Direct investment can be distinguished from portfolio investment by the following five factors (Buckley and Roberts (1982)).

(1) The fundamental aspect of direct investment as opposed to portfolio investment is that investor purchases the power to exert control over the management of the enterprise or facility. This power of control will vary with the distribution of the equity in the company in question. For instance, an investor holding 30 per cent of the voting equity in a company, where no other investor holds more than 10 per cent, is more likely to be able to exercise control, in spite of his minority holding, than he would if he held 49 per cent, with the other 51 per cent in one person's or company's hands. National definitions of what constitutes control differ. Operating definitions of foreign direct investment used by national authorities vary greatly; for instance the United States of America used a 10 per cent foreign ownership threshold while Japan and West Germany use 25 per cent. A comprehensive review of extant data on foreign investment and international production is given in Dunning and Cantwell (1987).

(2) Direct investment usually involves the movement of factors of production other than capital, whereas portfolio investment is a pure capital movement. These factors may be technology, management and other forms of corporate knowledge.

(3) There is a fundamental difference in the ultimate target of the two types of international investment. Portfolio capital will tend to move to sectors in the host country that have an advantage over their counterparts in the source country, in order to earn a higher rate of financial return. Exactly the opposite is likely to occur with direct investment, for it will often flow to industries in the host country where the source country has the advantage but where this advantage can be transferred to the foreign country to the investor's ultimate gain. Thus direct investment is closely linked to the use of internal markets within multinational firms (Buckley and Casson (1976), (1985)).

(4) The vast majority of portfolio investment is carried out by individuals and financial institutions, not industrial or service companies. Portfolio investment takes place through the capital market whereas direct investment involves the creation or purchase of assets directly by companies. This may be for reasons other than immediate financial gain such as the safeguarding of a source of raw material or the threat to an export trade leading to defensive investment.

(5) Direct investment may not produce a flow of capital across the international exchanges. Portfolio investment involves the international flow of capital through the issue of new securities (bonds and stocks) or the purchase and sale of existing stocks and bonds through security exchanges or through a variety of short-term credit instruments. Direct investment, however, may occur by equity

being exchanged for knowledge of patents or technology, or in exchange for machinery. Alternatively, foreign direct investors may raise all the capital in the host country. The directly investing company may reinvest profits already earned abroad (for instance, from an existing subsidiary) rather than repatriating them. This results in an increase in foreign direct investment, like the other two cases, with no actual international flow of funding. Again, national treatments of reinvestment differ. (See Dunning and Cantwell (1987).)

Forms of foreign direct investment

Foreign direct investment can be examined from three viewpoints: by mode of entry and operation, by activities performed and by motives.

Mode of entry and operation
There are two key choices in mode of entry and operation in foreign direct investment: the ownership decision (wholly-owned or joint-venture) and the buy-or-build decision (greenfield entry versus takeover). These choices are discussed in Section 6.4 below.

Activities Performed
The scope and size of a foreign direct investment are dependent upon the range of activities performed by the foreign unit. It is a fallacy to believe that a foreign direct investment need be large or involve a sizable amount of capital – one person working from a basement, with an inventory and a car makes a perfectly adequate sales subsidiary in many cases. What is crucial is control of the operation, not its size.

We can imagine a spectrum of activities running from a sales-only subsidiary, through simple packaging operations to assembly to full production, to a full range of activities including research and development being performed abroad.

Motives
Foreign direct investments differ by motive. The most important motives are: (1) market-oriented (including defensive investment, to protect market share built-up in other ways and tariff-jumping investment), (2) cost-oriented, either for cheap labour (of which offshore production is a variant) or for raw-material vertical integration either backwards or forward; and finally (3) technology-oriented, either to acquire or to use technology.

Special types of foreign investment

Expatriate investment occurs when an entrepreneur (or company) migrates and starts the firm in the new homeland, financed by capital from his old homeland

(Buckley and Roberts (1982)). Management control is not exercised from the source country and such investments rapidly become indigenous to the host country. They involve a once-for-all outflow of capital but no compensating returns of dividend or other income.

Syndicate investment comes about when a group of individuals pool their capital and invest overseas. This may be considered direct or portfolio, depending on whether control is involved.

New forms of international investment are considered in Chapter 1.3 above. The term international cooperation is a better term, as investment in the conventional sense of new asset-creation may not actually be involved (Buckley and Casson (1985) Chapter 3, Oman (1980)). These new forms of cooperation can be analysed in terms of their equity or non-equity nature, their time and space limitations if any, the scope of transfer of resources and rights and the mode of transfer (internal or external). Such new forms include joint ventures, minority holdings, fade-out agreements, licensing, management contracts, turnkey ventures and even contractual joint ventures and international sub-contracting (see Chapter 1.3).

5.1.3   The increasing diversity of international investment

International investment in all its forms has become a much more diverse phenomenon in recent years. Short-term capital flows have multiplied as new financial instruments have burgeoned. Longer-term sources of lending have multiplied as the debt crisis has been prolonged. The types, scope and sources of foreign direct investment have also increased.

Foreign direct investment

This increasing diversity is manifested particularly in foreign direct investment. The dominance of the traditional Anglo-Saxon foreign direct investors (United States of America and United Kingdom) has been challenged by Japan and Continental European investors. The number of significant origin-countries has increased markedly. A selection of studies on these significant outward investors include those based on Sweden (Swedenborg (1979), Hornell and Vahlne (1986)), France (Savary (1984)), Italy (Onida and Viesti (eds) (1988)), Canada (Rugman and McIlveen (1985)), Spain (Nueno and others (1981)) and Belgium (Van den Bulke (1986)). Franko (1976) covers the outward investment of the countries of continental Europe. Rugman (1986) compares the performance of European and North American multinationals. The literature on Japanese foreign direct investment is covered in Section 1.4.7.

Attention has also recently been drawn to foreign direct investment from less-developed countries ('Multinationals of the South') (See *inter alia* Kumar and Mcleod (1981), Lecraw (1977), Wells (1983), Lall (1983), Khan (1986), and Agarwal (1985)) and to multinationals from Socialist Countries ('Red Multinationals') (Hamilton (ed.) (1986)). The phenomenon of multinationals from smaller countries has existed for some time with small but high-income countries such as The Netherlands, Switzerland and Norway being the source of powerful, well-established multinationals (Agmon and Kindleberger (1977)).

This increasing range of origin countries and firms is matched by an increasing range of industries and forms of foreign direct investment. The service industries have attracted particular attention to the decade of the 1980s, particularly the increasing internationalization of banks. However, other service industries such as travel and tourism, advertising agencies, insurance companies, accountancy practices, hotels, restaurants, transportation companies, publishers, law practices, retailers, securities and financial firms and construction companies also operate on an increasingly international scale. This phenomenon is so marked that the most recent United Nations Centre on Transnational Corporations (UNCTC) survey devotes a large section to the service industries (United Nations Centre on Transnational Corporations (1988)).

The forms of doing business abroad are also increasing in range. The new forms of international involvement (or investment (Oman (1980))) are growing in importance as substitutes for, and often complements to, foreign direct investment. As part of a spectrum with pure exporting at one end and foreign direct investment at the other, we can identify foreign agencies, foreign distributors, foreign licensing, franchising, management contracts, foreign minority holdings, fade-out agreements, turnkey ventures, contractual joint ventures, international sub-contracting joint ventures, foreign sales subsidiaries and foreign assembly as intermediate points. The picture is more complex than this and these modes of international cooperation can be analysed in many more dimensions (Buckley (1985)). In fact, they raise many interesting conceptual issues (Buckley and Casson (1988)).

In addition, small multinationals have long been recognized to be important in the totality of foreign direct investment (Buckley, Newbould and Thurwell (1988), White and Campos (1986)). See Section 5.2.3.

A phenomenon more recently recognized is that of state-owned multinationals, not only from Socialist countries but also from the capitalist West (Anastassopoulos and others (1987)). These issues – the increasing variety of origin country, of industry and of form – are taken up in Chapters 5.3, 5.4 and 5.5 below.

5.1.4   International divestment

Foreign divestment, or disinvestment, has attracted increasing interest in recent years, particularly as the international recession has reduced economic activity. However, the literature on foreign divestment has lacked clarity in terms, definitions and a consistent theoretical basis. This section attempts to restructure this literature, based on initial work by Casson (1987).

Several important distinctions must be made in analysing divestment. First, it is important to distinguish between divestment of ownership and divestment of control. This is analogous to the discussion in Section 5.1.2 above. A fall in ownership from 100 per cent to 51 per cent will not lose control but one from 51 per cent to 49 per cent may. It is often changes of control, not ownership, that attract attention. Secondly, a distinction must be made between voluntary and involuntary divestment. Expropriation is considered in Section 5.5 below. Thirdly, a particular class of divestment is the management buy-out. Wright and Coyne (1985) define a management buy-out as: 'the case where some representatives of the management of the company ... have negotiated to purchase the company from its current owners ... and organized the finance to support the purchase'. The transfer of ownership should be completed with the former owners having no substantial further ownership interest in the newly formed company.

Voluntary divestment may be equilibrium adjustment, error correction or precipitated by a change in the time preference of investors (Casson (1987)). Equilibrium adjustment is a rational response of a firm to changed circumstances, either external (technological change) or internal (changed management-personnel or policy). Error correction involves divesting in a facility which was invested in mistakenly. Finally, the emergence of a bias towards the short-term in investor preferences may result in investors preferring companies with high short-run returns versus those with high long-run streams of income. It may in many, perhaps most, cases be difficult to disentangle these types of divestment but they provide a useful analytical toolkit.

Much attention in practice has centred on United States divestment in Europe, either at case-study level (e.g. Young and Hood (1977), Grunberg (1981), Casson (1987)) or in a particular host-country or region (Van den Bulke and others (1979) on Belgium, Young, Hood and Hamill (1985) on Scotland, Gaffikin and Nickson (1984) on the British West Midlands). Studies that compare employment losses from multinationals with domestic firms have found little difference in employment losses between these groups (McAleese and Counahan (1979) for the Irish Republic, Van den Bulke and Halsberge (1983) for Belgium (although Van den Bulke's earlier study found that foreign multinationals had more coherent rationalization policies)).

Casson (1987) makes the point that divestment and investment decisions must be considered together as part of the company's overall strategy. They may be part of a restructuring, relocation or retooling strategy in the face of changed industry circumstances, changed location conditions or changed technology. To examine divestment only as rationalization in the face of decreased final demand is to see only part of a more complex picture.

References

Agarwal, J.P. (1985): 'Intra LDCs Foreign Direct Investment: A Comparative Analysis of Third World Multinationals', *The Developing Economies*, Vol. XXIII No. 3, September, pp. 236–53.

Agmon, Tamir and Kindleberger, C.P. (1977): *Multinationals from small countries.* Cambridge, Mass: MIT Press.

Anastassopoulos, Jean-Pierre, Blanc, Georges and Dussage, Pierre (1987): *State Owned Multinationals.* Chichester: John Wiley.

Buckley, Peter J. (1985): 'New Forms of International Industrial Cooperation' in Buckley and Casson (1985) *op cit.*

Buckley, Peter J. and Casson, Mark (1976): *The Future of the Multinational Enterprise.* London: Macmillan.

Buckley, Peter J. and Casson, Mark (1985): *The Economic Theory of the Multinational Enterprise.* London: Macmillan.

Buckley, Peter J. and Casson, Mark (1988): 'A Theory of Cooperation in International Business', in Contractor, F.J. and Lorange, P. (eds): *Cooperative Strategies in International Business.* Lexington, Mass: Lexington Books.

Buckley, Peter J. Newbould, Gerland D. and Thurwell, Jane (1988): *Foreign Direct Investment by Smaller UK Firms* (2nd edn). London: Macmillan.

Buckley, Peter J. and Roberts, Brian (1982): *European Direct Investment in the USA Before World War I.* London: Macmillan.

Casson, Mark, (1987): 'Foreign Divestment and Rationalization in the Motor Industry', in *The Firm and the Product*, Chapter 8. Oxford: Basil Blackwell.

Dunning John H. and Cantwell, John (1987): *IRM Directory of Statistics in International Investment and Production.* London: Macmillan.

Eiteman, David K. and Stonehill, Arthur I. (1986): *Multinational Business Finance.* Reading, Mass: Addison-Wesley.

Franko, Lawrence G. (1976): *The European Multinationals.* London: Harper & Row.

Gaffikin, F. and Nickson, A. (1984): *Jobs Crisis and the Multinationals: Deindustrialization in the West Midlands.* Nottingham: Russell Press.

Grunberg, L. (1981): *Failed Multinational Ventures: The Political Economy of International Divestments.* Lexington, Mass: Lexington Books.

Hamilton, Geoffrey (ed.) (1986): *Red Multinationals or Red Herrings?* London: Frances Pinter.

Hornell, Erik and Vahlne, Jan-Erik (1986): *Multinationals: The Swedish Case.* Beckenham, Kent: Croom Helm.

International Monetary Fund (1979): *Balance of Payments Manual* (4th edn). Washington D.C.: IMF.

Khan, Kushi M. (1986): *Multinationals of the South*. London: Frances Pinter.

Kumar, Krishna and Mcleod, Maxwell G. (eds) (1981): *Multinationals From Developing Countries*. Lexington, Mass: D.C. Heath.

Lall, Sanjaya (1983): *The New Multinationals: The Spread of Third World Enterprises*. Chichester: John Wiley.

Lecraw, Donald J. (1977): 'Direct Investment by Firms from Less Developed Countries', *Oxford Economic Papers*, Vol. 29, No. 3, pp. 442–57.

McAleese, Dermot and Counahan, M. (1979): ' "Stickers" or "Snatchers"? Employment in Multinational Cooperations During the Recession', *Oxford Bulletin of Economics and Statistics*, Vol. 41, No. 4, pp. 345–58.

Nuneo, Pedro, Martinez, Nieves and Sarle, Jose (1981): *Las Inversiones Espanolas en el Extranjero*. Barcelona: Ediciones Universidad de Navarra.

Oman, Charles (1980): *The New Forms of Investment in Developing Countries*. Paris: OECD Development Centre.

Onida, Fabrizio and Viesti, Gianfranco (1988): *The Italian Multinationals*. Beckenham: Croom Helm.

Rugman, Alan M. (1986): 'European Multinationals: An International Comparison of Size and Performance' in Macharzina K. and Staehle, W.H. (eds): *European Approach to International Management*. Berlin: Walter de Gruyter.

Rugman, Alan M. and McIlveen, John (1985): *Megafirms: Strategies for Canada's Multinationals*. Toronto: Methuen.

Savary, Julien (1984): *French Multinationals*. London: Frances Pinter.

Swedenborg, Brigitta (1979): *Multinational Operations of Swedish Firms*. Stockholm: Almquist & Wicksell.

United Nations Centre on Transnational Corporations (1988): *Transnational Corporations in World Development*. New York: UNCTC.

Van den Bulke, Daniel (1986): 'The Role and Structure of Belgian Multinationals' in Macharzina, K. and Staehle, W.H.: *European Approaches to International Management*. Berlin: Walter de Gruyter.

Van den Bulke, Daniel, Boddewyn, J.J. Marten, B. and Klemmer, P. (eds) (1979): *Investment and Divestment Policies of Multinational Corporations in Europe*. Farnborough, Hants: Saxon House.

Van den Bulke, Daniel and Halsberge, E. (1983): 'Divestment and Loss of Employment: A Comparison between Foreign and Belgian Enterprise'. EIASM Workshop: Oslo.

Wells, Louis (1983): *Third World Multinationals: The Rise of Foreign Investment from Development Countries*. Cambridge, Mass: MIT Press.

White, Eduardo and Campos, Jaime (1986): *Alternative Technology Sources for Developing Countries: The Role of Small and Medium Sized Enterprises for Industrialized Countries*. Buenos Aires: CEDERI.

Wright, Mike and Coyne, John (1985): *Management Buyouts*. Beckenham: Croom Helm.

Young, Stephen and Hood, Neil (1977): *Chrysler UK: A Corporation in Transition*. New York: Praeger.

Young, Stephen, Hood, Neil and Hamill, James (1985): *Decision Making in Foreign-Owned Multinational Subsidiaries in the United Kingdom*. Geneva: International Labour Office.

5.2

The Growth of International Investment

This chapter concentrates on the growth of foreign direct investment and the multinational enterprise. Chapter 5.3 covers the major home and host countries of foreign direct investment and Chapter 5.4 covers the industrial structure of that investment. Here we examine overall trends: predictions of the growth of the multinational enterprise, the growth of manufacturing multinationals, the growth of service multinationals and the internationalization of smaller firms.

It is important to distinguish between the growth of foreign direct investment and the growth of multinational enterprises. Foreign direct investment underestimates the extent to which multinational companies control foreign assets. Less than full ownership is necessary to control assets and the purchase of foreign assets can be financed through borrowing or raising equity in host-country capital markets. Consequently, figures for foreign direct investment need to be supplemented by data on the growth of multinational enterprises.

Foreign direct investment has grown faster than world trade since 1960. In the periods 1961 to 1973, 1974 to 1980 and 1981 to 1986 world output and world trade grew at annual averages of 5.5 per cent and 8.1 per cent in the first period, 3.6 per cent and 4.4 per cent in the second and 2.7 per cent and 2.7 per cent in the third (United Nations Centre on Transnational Corporations (1988)). Foreign direct investment in the comparable periods 1960 to 1975, 1975 to 1980 and 1980 to 1985 grew at 22.6 per cent, 19.1 per cent and 5.9 per cent annual averages (Dunning and Cantwell (1987)).

5.2.1 Predictions of the growth of the multinational enterprise

Many predictions have been made concerning the growth of multinational enterprises. Most rely on straight-line projection or on naive scenarios. In 1968,

Polk predicted that by the end of this century, the largest 200 or 300 multinationals would account for one half of the world's output (Polk (1968)). The figures above show that foreign direct investment has outpaced world output and world trade. However, multinational firms cannot be said to be replacing world trade, although they can be said to be exercising control over it.

Examinations of the growth of the multinational enterprise, measured in terms of rate of growth of worldwide sales, have found significant non-linearities in its relationship with firm size. Using a specification

$$g = f(s, s^2) \qquad \text{(Equation 5.1)}$$
$$\text{or } g = f(\phi, \phi^2), \text{ where } \phi = \text{logs} \qquad \text{(Equation 5.2)}$$

where g is rate of growth of the firm's sales
and s is firm size at the beginning of the period,

growth has been found to be negatively related to size but positively related to size squared. This u-shaped relationship suggests that in the periods tested (from the late 1950s to the late 1970s), growth may show as firms approach a critical size, but after this point, for the very largest firms, there may be stimuli to further growth (Rowthorn (1971), Buckley, Dunning and Pearce (1984)).

The relationship between a firm's size and its profitability, specified on the same basis, is not as strong or as stable as that between size and growth. Difficulties of specifying profitability accurately and differences in accounting traditions nationally make it difficult to arrive at hard and fast conclusions of the independent influences of size on profitability (Buckley, Dunning and Pearce (1984), Stopford and Dunning (1983)). However, at the firm level, internalization of know-how and research and development establishes the connection between multinationality, growth and profitability (Buckley and Casson (1976), (1985)). This suggests that an approach disaggregated to the level of individual firms and groups of firms by industry and nationality is likely to prove more fruitful for the testing of hypotheses.

5.2.2   The growth of manufacturing multinationals

Table 5.2.1 shows that despite the recent rapid growth of service multinationals, global foreign direct investment is still dominated by manufacturing or, more accurately, non-service firms. These firms account for over 50 per cent of the major countries' outward foreign direct investment, with the exception of Japan which is heavily influenced by the investments of its general trading companies (*sogo shosha*).

A comprehensive study of the world's largest industrial enterprises and their growth between 1962 and 1983 has been carried out by Dunning and Pearce (1985). The rate of the growth of employment of these firms grew by a mere 2

Table 5.2.1 Service and Industrial Transnational Corporations, Selected Home Countries

Item	United States[a] Excluding banks			United States[a] Including banks			Federal Republic of Germany[b]		Japan[c]		United Kingdom[d]
	1977	1982	1984	1977	1982	1984	1976	1985	1977	1984	1981
Number of TNCs											
Total	3,078	2,008	1,995	3,189	2,141	"	2,589	3,963	1,223	1,488	"
Services	1,093	690	673	1,204	823	"	1,097	1,863	409	541	"
Number of Affiliates											
Total	23,219	17,123	16,751	24,666	18,339	"	9,059	14,964	3,589	4,937	"
Controlled by service parents	5,870	4,058	3,943	6,838	5,119	"	"	"	1,538	1,916	"
In services	12,711	9,457	9,085	13,595	10,339	"	5,258	9,429	1,586	2,671	"
Stock of FDI as per cent of total FDI											
Controlled by service TNCs	18	14	"	21	19	"	29	32	"	"	24
In services	37	33	31	41	38	37	42	48	38	52[e]	34

Notes:
a) Excluding non-business entities. The Netherlands Antilles are not excluded from FDI stock. The substantial decline in the total number of United States TNCs and their affiliates is a result of changed reporting procedures. The cut-off point below which full data for affiliates do not have to be reported was increased from $500,000 in 1977 to $3 million in 1982 and to $10 million in 1984.
b) Excluding individuals.
c) Excluding banks and insurance companies.
d) Excluding oil, banking and insurance.
e) 1985.

Reproduced from UNCTC, 1988, p. 399.

Source: UNCTC, based on official sources.

Table 5.2.2   Alternative Measures for the Share in the Total Outward FDI of the
United States, 1982

	Assets	*Sales*	*FDI stock*	*Employment (thousands)*	*Value-added*[a] (billions of dollars)
	(billions of dollars)				
1 All foreign affiliates	1,349	1,027	207	6,816	185
2 Service affiliates	922	458	77	1,786	58
2 as per cent of 1	69	45	37	26	31
3 Banking	574	87	10	159	7[b]
3 as per cent of 1	43	9	5	2	4
4 Services other than banking	349	370	67	1,627	51
4 as per cent of 1	26	36	32	24	27

Notes:
a) Net income, employee compensation and foreign income taxes.
b) Net income and employee compensation only.
Reproduced from UNCTC, 1988, p. 372.

Source: United States, Department of Commerce. US Direct Investment Abroad: 1982, Benchmark
Survey Date (Washington, D.C., Superintendent of Documents, 1985).

per cent in the decade 1972 to 1982, in contrast to a 46 per cent increase in 1962
to 1972. Employment fell marginally between 1977 and 1982. Over 28 per cent
of total sales was accounted for by the sales of foreign affiliates. The degree of
internationalization varied greatly: the proportion of foreign production in total
sales varied from 84 per cent in United-States-owned manufacturing multinationals to 11 per cent for Japan, though Japanese foreign production was
increasing rapidly in 1982 and has continued to do so. United States of America
firms had the largest average firm size among the world's giants but this size
superiority has fallen markedly and persistently since 1962.

5.2.3   The growth of service multinationals

Foreign direct investment in services accounts for about 40 per cent of the
world's stock of foreign direct investment and 50 per cent of annual flows
(United Nations Centre on Transnational Corporations (1988)). Table 5.2.2
shows for the United States (the only country for which detailed data are available) that these assets-measure of foreign investment in services boosts its share
to 69 per cent (compared to 37 per cent when foreign direct investment stocks
are used) and a sales measure to 45 per cent. The employment share of foreign-

based services is only 26 per cent and using value-added gives services a share of 31 per cent.

Figures for the stock of foreign direct investment in services are shown in Table 5.2.3 for the countries where this is available in decending order of share of services – from Spain 65 per cent (1984) through Japan 57 per cent (1986), United States of America 43 per cent (1986), United Kingdom 35 per cent (1984) to The Netherlands 22 per cent (1984). The generally rapid growth of the share of services in flow figures is shown in Table 5.2.4; it includes rates of 20 per cent growth (Japan) and 19 per cent (United States of America) and for outward direct foreign investment and inward rates of growth of 22 per cent for the United Kingdom (which includes the effects of the deregulation of London financial markets (Big Bang)) and 20 per cent for Australia. There is evidence of rapidly gaining interdependence in world service markets. (See also Enderwick (1988)).

5.2.4 The internationalization of smaller firms

The increasing internationalization of small- and medium-sized enterprises has made a major impact on the growth of international investment.

In the case of United Kingdom foreign investors, an estimated 1,500 enterprises had 9,100 foreign affiliates. Two-thirds of these foreign investors (1,000 firms) with net assets of less than £2 million accounted for under 1 per cent of the total net book value of United Kingdom foreign direct investment at the end of 1981 (*British Business*, 2 March 1984). This is in sharp contrast to the 34 enterprises with net assets of over £200 million and 1,550 overseas affiliates that account for 55 per cent of the total stock of British foreign investment.

When foreign investment into the United Kingdom is examined, it is found that about 3,000 foreign companies had United Kingdom affiliates, three quarters (2,150) of these had United Kingdom affiliates with a book value of less than £2 million, accounting in total for about 2 per cent of inward direct foreign investment in the United Kingdom (excluding oil, banking and insurance). In contrast, 21 foreign companies had assets valued at over £150 million in the United Kingdom, and account for one third of the total (*British Business*, 2 March 1984). Inward investment was less concentrated than outward: the 100 largest inward investors account for 60 per cent of total direct investment; the 100 largest outward investors account for 80 per cent – again excluding oil, banking and insurance.

A similar pattern is found in other countries. Foreign investment into France, for instance, is highly concentrated. The top five foreign investors in 1978 accounted for 16 per cent of all such investment, the top 10 for 25 per cent, the top 88 for 56.5 per cent and the top 172 for 68.4 per cent (Savary (1984) p. 34). French outward investment is highly concentrated. The 28 largest industrial

Table 5.2.3 Outward Stock of Foreign Direct Investment in Services, Selected Developed Home Countries by Descending Order of Share in Services, Various Years (value and percentage)

Country and currency	Year	Value		Share of services in total FDI percentage)
		Total FDI	FDI in services	
Spain	1975	24.9	12.3	49
(billions of pesatas)	1980	95.5	46.2	48
	1984	283.7	184.3	65
Japan	1965	0.9	0.2	25
(billions of dollars)	1970	3.6	1.4	38
	1975	15.9	5.8	36
	1977	22.2	7.9	35
	1980	36.5	14.0	38
	1985	83.6	43.4	52
	1986	106.0	60.4	57
Austria	1979	6.8	3.7	54
(billions of schillings)	1982	11.3	5.9	53
Federal Republic of Germany[a]	1966	10.6	1.1	10
(billions of Deutsche mark)	1976	49.1	20.0	41
	1980	84.5	36.2	43
	1984	145.4	68.0	47
	1985	147.8	70.3	48
Australia	1978	1.4	0.7	47
(billions of Australian dollars)	1983	3.4	1.6	47
Finland[b]	1975	1.2	0.2	14
(billions of Finnish marks)	1980	2.8	1.0	35
	1985	10.6	4.6	44
	1986	14.1	6.1	44
United States[c]	1950	11.8	3.8	32
(billions of dollars)	1957	25.4	7.8	31
	1966	51.8	16.3	32
	1977	147.2	60.4	41
	1985	250.7	108.3	43
	1986	276.1	119.1	43
France[d]	1980	51.0	20.7	41
(billions of francs)	1985	149.0	63.4	43
Sweden				
(billions of dollars)	1982	6.3	2.5	40

Table 5.2.3   (*Cont.*)

Country and currency	Year	Value Total FDI	Value FDI in services	Share of services in total FDI percentage)
United Kingdom	1971	9.3[e]	2.2[e]	24
(billions of pounds)	1981	45.5	16.2	36
	1984	75.7	26.4	35
Italy	1974	2,285.0	1,011.0	44
(billions of lira)	1976	2,941.0	958.0	33
	1980	6,484.0	1,987.0	31
	1984	20,498.0[f]	6,657.0[f]	33
Canada	1973	7.8	2.4	31
(billions of Canadian dollars)	1980	25.8	6.8	26
	1984	41.7	12.0	29
Switzerland[g]				
(billions of Swiss francs)	1986	55.5	15.4	28
Netherlands[g]	1973	43.6	5.3	12
(billions of guilders)	1983	119.9	27.2	23
	1984	143.7	31.7	22

Notes:
The definition of the services sector used here is a broad one: it includes construction and public utilities, wherever possible. The data in this chapter are not necessarily consistent with those reported earlier in this Survey because, wherever possible, they have been adjusted to include all services in the category 'services'. The principal reason for any discrepancy is that when it comes to industry/country data used in the earlier chapters, the reporting of industry distribution is less detailed than in the case of overall data. In addition, some countries compile detailed data only periodically, in FDI benchmark-survey years (for example, every five years in the United States). In non-benchmark years, data are less disaggregated, making it difficult to single out some services categories.

a) Data for 1966 are not fully comparable with those for later years.

b) Calculations of the stock based on cumulative outflows since 1967. Services include 'other industries'.

c) Services data include services related to the petroleum industry which consist of trading and transportation Services in this industry and oil and gas field services. Investment in finance, insurance and real estate in the Netherlands Antilles are excluded for 1977, 1985 and 1986.

d) Calculations of the stock based on cumulative outflows during the periods 1975–1980 and 1975–1985. Services include items that cannot be classified.

e) Excludes banking and insurance in countries other than the United States. These data are, therefore, not fully comparable with later years.

f) A proportion of the investment recorded by the Bank of Italy under banking and finance has been reallocated to manufacturing. This is probably mostly investment channelled via holding companies in Luxembourg and Liechtenstein to the industrial sector of other countries.

g) Based on the industry affiliation of the parent corporation.

Reproduced from: UNCTC, 1988, pp. 373–4.

Source: UNCTC, based on various official and other sources.

Table 5.2.4 Foreign Direct Investment Flows in Services of Major Home and Host Countries, by Descending order of Share in Services, 1975–1980 and 1981–1985 (billions of national currencies and percentage)

Country	Average annual flows		Share of services[a]		Change between 1975–1980 and 1981–1985 (percentage points)
	1975–1980	1981–1985	1975–1980	1981–1985	
Outward FDI					
Japan[b]					
Total	4.0	9.4	41.8	62.2	+ 20
Developed market economies	1.8	5.1	59.3	66.4	+ 7
Developing countries	2.2	4.3	27.1	57.3	+ 30
Germany, Federal Republic of[c]	8.9[d]	12.7	49.1[d]	58.4	+ 9
Australia	0.2	1.0	53.6	57.0	+ 3
United States[e]					
Total	15.6	9.1	34.3	53.2	+ 19
Developed market economies	11.7	6.2	29.4	52.9	+ 24
Developing countries	3.9	2.9	48.6	53.7	+ 5
Finland	0.3	1.5	48.7	47	– 2
France					
Total	7.4	19.6	44.1	43.5	– 1
Developed market economies	5.6	15.2	47.6	46.6	– 1
Developing countries	1.8	4.4	33.3	33.1	–
United Kingdom[f]					
Total	2.3	5.0	43.6	38.2	– 5
Developed market economies	1.9	4.0	40.4	33.1	– 7
Developing countries	0.5	1.1	56.4	57.0	+ 1
Canada					
Total	1.7	3.8	20.2	30.9	+ 11
Developed market economies	1.4	3.4	25.3	31.7	+ 6
Developing countries	0.3	0.4	-1.0	24.6	+ 26

Netherlands[g]					
Total	6.8[h]	8.3[i]	39.8[h]	29.6[i]	− 10
Developed market economies	"	7.3[i]	7.3[i]	"	"
Developing countries	"	1.0[i]	"	41.9[i]	"
Inward FDI					
Australia	1.0	2.1	60.9	80.5	+ 20
Finland	0.2	0.2	65.9	79.8	+ 14
Germany, Federal Republic of[c]	3.8[d]	5.0	68.9[d]	72.8	+ 4
Canada	0.4	−1.1	58.8	69.9	− 11
France	5.5	9.7	61.6	64.5	+ 3
United Kingdom[f]	1.4	1.7	36.8	59.1	+ 22
United States	7.6	17.6	43.7	48.6	+ 5
Netherlands	2.0[h]	1.4	50.4[h]	46.6	− 4
Japan[b]	0.3	0.7	27.8	31.0	+ 3

Notes:

a) Since geographically segmented data are often based on a more restricted definition of services, the figures are not fully comparable with total figures and those reported elsewhere. For Canada and the United Kingdom (inflows, 1975–1980), agriculture, forestry and fishing are included in services, and for the United Kingdom, services inflows also include mining for 1975–1980; the amounts involved are, however, relatively insignificant. Unallocated FDI has been excluded from calculations.

b) Billions of dollars.

c) Dots are calculated as changes in FDI stocks.

d) 1977–1980.

e) Excluding the Netherlands Antilles.

f) Until 1983, oil companies are excluded.

g) Based on the sector of the Netherlands investor.

h) 1980.

i) 1982–1985.

Reproduced from UNCTC, 1988, pp. 375–6.

Source: UNCTC, based on national data.

investors accounted for 67.8 per cent of the turnover of foreign production subsidiaries, the 66 largest for 83.9 per cent and the 123 largest for 92.5 per cent (Savary (1984) p. 22).

A possible exception to the modest scale of foreign investment by smaller firms is Japan. Ozawa estimates that about half the total number of Japanese foreign investments are made by enterprises with under 100 million yen capital stock or 300 or fewer employees (United Nations Conference on Trade and Development (1984)). Until the first half of the 1970s, Japan's smaller foreign investors concentrated on developing countries close to Japan and as much as 87.6 per cent of their ventures were located in the neighbouring Asian countries. More recently their focus has shifted to developed countries: North America (primarily the United States of America) accounted for as much as 39.5 per cent of Japanese small firms' foreign investments in 1982. Asia's share has declined but in the early 1980s it was attracting about half of the new manufacturing investments made by smaller firms. Most such investors only have one foreign location (United Nations Conference on Trade and Development (1984)).

There is some evidence that the number of small and medium firms becoming foreign investors is growing; according to a recent study in the German Federal Republic, companies with less than 500 employees accounted for 56 per cent of the firms with investment plans in the developing countries (White (1983)). In a study of small-firm foreign investors in Latin America, White and Feldman found that the number of firms with less than 500 employees in their home countries was quite significant. They show that the number of European firms of this size accounted for 28.3 per cent of subsidiaries and joint ventures in Brazil, 18.5 per cent in Mexico, 13.9 per cent in Peru and 14.0 per cent in Venezuela. However, in terms of amounts invested, small firms accounted for 1 per cent to 2 per cent of the total investment of the respective country of origin. It is notable that their technology transfer via licensing was also significant (White (1983) pp. 272–3). Indeed, it has recently been hypothesized that smaller firms are likely to become important users of new forms of international cooperation such as licensing, joint ventures, turnkey operations and production sharing (Oman (1984)). While such operations economize on capital outlay, they tend to be management-intensive; this may choke off the ability of small firms to enter into the more complex forms of such arrangements (Buckley (1985)). Licensing and joint ventures remain viable options, although our study shows that the tolerance of small firms to joint-venture arrangements can be low and such arrangements can adversely affect success.

References

Buckley, Peter J. (1985): 'New Forms of International Industrial Cooperation' in Buckley, Peter J. and Casson, Mark (1985): *The Economic Theory of the Multinational Enterprise*. London: Macmillan.

Buckley, Peter J. and Casson, Mark (1976): *The Future of the Multinational Enterprise.* London: Macmillan.

Buckley, Peter J. and Casson, Mark (1985): *The Economic Theory of the Multinational Enterprise.* London: Macmillan.

Buckley, Peter J., Dunning, John H. and Pearce, Robert D. (1984): 'An Analysis of the Growth and Profitability of the World's Largest Firms 1967 to 1977', *Kyklos,* Vol. 37, No. 1, pp. 3–26.

Duninng, John H. and Cantwell, John (1987): *IRM Directory of Statistics of International Investment.* London: Macmillan.

Dunning, John H. and Pearce, Robert D. (1985): *The World's Largest Industrial Enterprises 1962–1983.* Aldershot: Gower Press.

Enderwick, Peter (ed.) (1988): *Multinational Service Firms.* London: Routledge.

Oman, Charles (1984): *New Forms of International Investment in Developing Countries.* Paris: OECD.

Polk, Judd (1968): 'The New World Economy', *Columbia Journal of World Business,* Vol. 3, pp. 7–16.

Rowthorne, R. (1971): *International Big Business.* Cambridge: Cambridge University Press.

Savary, Julien (1984): *French Multinationals.* London: Francis Pinter.

Stopford J.M. and Dunning, J.H. (1983): *Multinationals: Company Performance and Global Trends.* London: Macmillan.

UNCTAD (1984): *International Transfer of Technology to Developing Countries by Small and Medium Sized Enterprises.* Geneva: UNCTAD Secretariat TD/B/C6/119.

UNCTC (1988): *Transnational Corporations in World Development: Trends and Prospects.* New York: UNCTC.

White, Eduardo (1983): 'The Role of Third World Multinationals and Small and Medium Sized Companies in the Industrialization Strategies of Developing Countries', in *Industrial Development Strategies and Policies for Developing Countries.* Vienna: UNIDO.

5.3

Direction of International Investment

This chapter is divided into three major sections. The first refers to the direction of outward foreign direct investment – the sources of international capital and the home country of the investor. The second examines the host or recipient countries, the importers of foreign capital. The final section examines the net flows of foreign direct investment.

5.3.1 Source countries

Multinationals are highly concentrated by country of ownership. The largest three source countries have controlled more than 60 per cent of world foreign investment from the beginning of the century, although the identity of the three countries has changed. (Table 5.3.1 shows the concentration rates to be 92.8 per cent in 1900, 90.1 per cent in 1914 and 87.5 per cent in 1930. Table 5.3.2 gives 75.7 per cent in 1960, 65.1 per cent in 1975, 62.6 per cent in 1980 and 61.5 per cent in 1985.)

However, recent changes in world economic power have seen the rapid rise in Japanese, Dutch and Swiss foreign investment, the re-emergence of Germany after its second expropriation this century and the beginnings of foreign direct investment from nations that had previously only been host countries, including a small number of significant Third World foreign investors.

It is conceivable that the concept of nationality of ownership is in need of more careful redefinition. Casson showed that when financial markets are globally integrated, a firm may produce in one set of countries, be funded by debenture holders in another, and have its risk borne by equity holders in yet a third (Casson (1985)). Its management culture may derive from yet another set. The implicit assumption in the literature is that these sets (except production) can be identified with one, or unusually, two countries of ownership and casual empiricism suggests that we have not yet reached the truly international

Table 5.3.1 Stock of Foreign Investment held Abroad by Percentage Distribution, 1900, 1914, 1930.

Country	Per cent		
	1900	*1914*	*1930*
US	2	6.3	35.3
UK	50.8	50.5	43.8
France	21.8	22.3	8.4
Germany	20.2	17.3	2.6
Switzerland	neg.	neg.	neg.
Canada	neg.	0.5	3.1
Japan	neg.	neg.	neg.
Netherlands	4.6	3.1	5.5
Sweden	neg.	0.3	1.3
Others	neg.	neg.	neg.
Total amount (billions of $US)	23.8	38.6	41.6

Notes:
The percentages are calculated from figures for total foreign investments, i.e. including portfolio investments overseas.
All figures are derived from *actual*, not licensed, amounts.
Source: Woodruff, W: *The Impact of Western Man*. St Martins Press, 1967.

corporation as envisaged by Kindleberger (1969) p. 182. Most of the largest multinationals can still be identified unequivocally with one or two nations of ownership. This may not continue to be the case if markets permit separation of the above functions.

Econometric studies of nationality of ownership effects in foreign direct investment show them to be highly significant, frequently more significant than industrial differences in explaining growth, profitability and policy decisions. A plausible hypothesis here is that multinationality is greater for firms based in traditionally open economies which form part of a wider social and ethnic grouping than for firms based in traditionally closed economies which are socially and politically isolated (Buckley and Casson (1976)). Post-imperial countries, the UK, The Netherlands, Belgium and France exhibit a high propensity to invest abroad, partly as a result of the reduction in psychic distance from common post-governance structures.

When annual-flow figures for foreign direct investment are measured, as in Table 5.3.3, the recent change in major source countries becomes very marked. In 1975, the United States accounted for over 51 per cent of the total; in 1983

Table 5.3.2 Outward Stocks of Foreign Direct Investment, by Major Home Country and Region, 1960–1985 (billions of $US)

Countries/regions	1960			1975			1980			1985		
		percentage of			percentage of			percentage of			percentage of	
	Value	total	GDP	Value	total	GDP	Value	total	GDP	Value	total	GDP
Developed market economies	67.0	99.0	6.7	275.4	97.7	6.7	535.7	97.2	6.7	693.3	97.2	8.0
United States	31.9	47.1	6.2	124.2	44.0	8.1	220.3	40.0	8.2	250.7	35.1	6.4
United Kingdom	12.4	18.3	17.4	37.0	13.1	15.8	81.4	14.8	15.2	104.7	14.7	23.3
Japan	0.5	0.7	1.1	15.9	5.7	3.2	36.5	6.6	3.4	83.6	11.7	6.3
Germany, Federal Republic of	0.8	1.2	1.1	18.4	6.5	4.4	43.1	7.8	5.3	60.0	8.4	9.6
Switzerland	2.3	3.4	26.9	22.4	8.0	41.3	38.5	7.0	37.9	45.3	6.4	48.9
Netherlands	7.0	10.3	60.6	19.9	7.1	22.9	41.9	7.6	24.7	43.8	6.1	35.1
Canada	2.5	3.7	6.3	10.4	3.7	6.3	21.6	3.9	8.2	36.5	5.1	10.5
France	4.1	6.1	7.0	10.6	3.8	3.1	20.8	3.8	3.2	21.6	3.0	4.2
Italy	1.1	1.6	2.9	3.3	1.2	1.7	7.0	1.3	1.8	12.4	1.7	3.4
Sweden	0.4	0.6	2.9	4.7	1.7	6.4	7.2	1.3	5.8	9.0	1.3	9.0
Other[a]	4.0	5.9	3.1	8.5	3.0	1.7	17.4	3.2	1.9	25.6	3.6	3.3
Developing countries	0.7	1.0	"	6.6	2.3	"	15.3	2.8	"	19.2	2.7	"
Centrally planned economies of Europe	"	"	"	"	"	"	"	"	"	1.0[b]	0.1	"
Total	67.7	100.0	"	282.0	100.0	"	551.0	100.0	"	713.5	100.0	"

Notes:
a) Australia, Austria, Belgium, Denmark, Finland, Greece, Ireland, New Zealand, Norway, Portugal, South Africa, Spain.
b) 1983 rough estimate.

Reproduced from UNCTC, 1988, p. 24.

Source: United Nations Centre on Transnational Corporations, based on J. Dunning and J. Cantwell, IRM Directory of Statistics of International Investment and Production (New York, New York University Press, 1987); and official national and international data.

Table 5.3.3 Distribution of Foreign Direct Investment Outflows, by Major Home Country 1975–1985

Country groups by region	1975	1980	1981	1982	1983	1984	1985	Annual averages 1975–1980	Annual averages 1981–1985
Developed market economies	98.9	98.1	99.4	96.6	97.3	98.6	98.0	98.8	98.0
Western Europe	36.6	47.2	53.6	59.0	60.5	59.2	50.4	44.4	55.6
France	4.7	5.4	8.3	8.6	4.7	4.9	3.7	4.5	5.5
Germany Federal Republic of	7.2	7.3	7.6	8.6	8.8	10.0	8.2	7.7	8.6
Italy	1.1	1.2	2.6	3.1	5.8	4.6	3.0	1.0	3.8
Netherlands	8.3	10.4	8.7	10.1	10.1	11.6	5.3	9.4	8.8
Switzerland	"	"	"	"	1.4	2.6	6.0	"	"
United Kingdom	10.9	19.8	22.6	22.0	22.5	18.8	18.7	17.4	20.8
Japan	6.5	4.2	9.1	13.8	9.9	13.8	10.7	5.5	11.0
United States	51.4	38.0	22.9	19.0	9.9	13.2	25.4	42.4	19.0
Developing Countries	1.1	1.9	0.6	3.4	2.7	1.4	2.0	1.2	1.8
World[a]	100	100	100	100	100	100	100	100	100
billions of dollars	27.6	57.6	54.1	32.7	36.5	43.1	59.9	40.3	45.3

Note: a) Excluding the centrally planned economies.

Reproduces from UNCTC, 1988, p. 77.

Source: United Nations Centre on Transnational Corporations, based on International Monetary Fund, balance of payments tape; and other official national and international sources.

this had declined to under 10 per cent before recovering to top 25 per cent in 1985. Indeed, taking annual averages for 1981 to 1985, the United Kingdom was the largest outward investor.

Further, it can be hypothesized that certain national cultures are more viable than others as bases for managing internal markets. Such culturally inspired managerial styles may reduce the costs of organizing internal markets and provide an impetus to multinationality. Foreign direct investment enables the internal transfer of efficient managerial culture unavailable to host-country firms (Buckley, (1983)). The identification of 'hierarchy' as the alternative to 'market' as modes of organization (Williamson (1975)) may have obscured the role of national cultures in evolving internationally viable competitive systems within firms. Evidence is presented in Tables 5.3.4 and 5.3.5.

Table 5.3.4, based on direct investment-flow figures, shows an average propensity to invest abroad, calculated by the proportion of foreign direct investment to Gross National Product in the same year. Table 5.3.5 takes the ratio of outward direct investment stocks to corporate assets. On both measures, the United Kingdom emerges as having the highest propensity to invest abroad. The contrast, in 1983, between the United Kingdom with 31 per cent of foreign direct investment to total corporate assets with Japan's 1.4 per cent is very marked.

Table 5.3.6 examines the ratio of foreign to domestic employment among the world's largest firms. The figures range from Swiss firms 350 per cent and Dutch firms 280 per cent down to French firms 25 per cent and Japanese firms 25 per cent, although the latter is almost certainly an overestimate.

Despite this heavy concentration of foreign direct investment, recent years have seen a diversification in source countries. Multinationals from smaller countries, from less-developed countries and from socialist countries have attracted attention (see Section 5.1.3 above).

The impact of multinationals

The independent impact of multinationals on growth and performance has been a source of controversy. Adding a term in M (degree of multinationality: sales of foreign affiliates excluding goods imported from the parent for resale divided by total worldwide group sales) to the equation that includes size, nationality and industry as well as testing for significance via an F test has given mixed results in the explanation of profitability and growth (Buckley and others (1978), (1984)). Part of the reason for the difficulty lies in the problem of accurately measuring the degree of multinationality but the direction of causation is also unclear. Multinationality may be suggested to increase profitability as firms seek the highest possible returns from their worldwide foreign investments. However, profitability may be depressed if foreign indirect investment is undertaken to

Table 5.3.4   Selected Countries: the Average Propensity to Invest Abroad[a]

Country	Average propensity to invest overseas: Rank in				
	1965	1971	1977	1965	1977
United Kingdom	8.6	12.1	18.2[b]	1	1
Netherlands	7.8	11.9	14.5	2	2
Sweden	4.7	5.0	7.9[b]	4	3
USA	7.3	4.5	6.7	3	4
W. Germany	2.3	4.9	5.1	7	5
Norway	0.3	2.6	4.7[c]	15	6
Belgium	2.3	6.2	4.2	7	7
Canada	2.3	2.8	4.0	7	8
France	3.5	2.6	3.7[b]	5	9
Japan	0.9	1.5	3.6[b]	12	10
Venezuela	0.0	N.A.	3.3	18/21	11
Italy	3.0	4.1	3.2	6	12
Finland	0.4	4.4	2.9	14	13
Australia	1.1	3.3	2.3[b]	11	14
Brazil	0.0	0.02	2.3[b]	18/21	14
Austria	1.8	2.2	2.0[b]	10	16
Colombia	0.0	0.5	1.7[c]	18/21	17
Spain	0.3	0.6	1.3	15	18
S. Africa	0.7	2.6	1.0[c]	13	19
Philippines	0.2	0.7	0.9	17	20
S. Korea	0.0	1.2	0.7	18/21	21

Notes:

a) The average propensity to invest abroad = $\dfrac{\text{Flow of FDI}}{\text{GNP in same year}} \times 1{,}000$

b) 1976 figure

c) 1975 figure

All figures are calculated from actual, not licensed, capital movements.

Source: Calculated using figures derived from the IMF publications: *International Financial Statistics* and *The Balance of Payments* Yearbook (various issues).

diversify a firm's income, for a given return, to reduce variability. Consequently, further testing of the impact of this variable is dependent on clear assumptions on the strategy of the firms. Shapiro (1983) suggests that advantages attributed to multinationality are in fact specifically related to particular nationalities (in the case of Canada, to United States ownership) rather than being general. Tests are necessary to discriminate between these effects more carefully.

Table 5.3.5 Selected Home Countries: Ratio of Outward Foreign Direct Investment Stocks to Total Corporate Assets (percentage)

| | United States | | | | |
Year	All corporations	Non-financial corporations	Japan	Federal Republic of Germany	United Kingdom[a]
1945	1.8	"	"	"	"
1950	2.1	4.2	"	"	"
1955	2.4	5.6[b]	"	"	16.0
1960	2.9	"	"	"	18.0
1965	3.1	6.8	"	1.4	18.3[c]
1970	3.2	6.8	0.4[d]	2.3[e]	22.7
1975	3.1	6.4	0.9	3.4	21.8
1980	3.0	5.3	0.9	4.8	22.6
1981	2.9	5.6	1.2	5.6	27.1
1982	2.6	5.4	1.4	5.9	29.0
1983	2.2	4.8	1.4	6.3	31.0
1984	2.1	4.7	1.7	7.2	"
1985	2.1	4.7	1.5	"	"

Notes:
a) 1975.
b) 1966.
c) 1971.
d) 1969.

Reproduced from UNCTC, 1988, p. 27.

Source: United Nations Centre on Transnational Corporations, based on official national sources.

5.3.2   Host countries

Although only a few countries in the world are significant outward foreign direct investors, most receive some inward investment. The bulk of the flows are between advanced market economies but much of the interest centres on the low proportion of foreign direct investment that goes to less-developed countries and in particular to the least-developed countries.

The stock of foreign direct investment for individual regions is shown in Table 5.3.7. The proportion of the stock of such investment has remained at about 75 per cent in advanced market economies and 25 per cent in less developed countries over the decade 1975 to 1985. The flow figures, shown in Table 5.3.8, are remarkably stable, ranging from a low of 19.3 per cent (1980) to a high of 29.3 per cent (1975) over this period.

The importance of foreign direct investment to less-developed countries indi-

Table 5.3.6   Estimates of Direct Employment by Multinational Companies in the Home and Host Country Operations, by Country of Origin of Enterprise

Country of origin of enterprise	Year	Total	of which At home	of which Abroad	Ratio Foreign employment: Domestic Employment %
Austria	1983	400	300	100	33.3
Belgium	1975	345	163	182	111.7
Canada	1984	1,764	1,058	706	66.7
France	1981	3,930	3,139	791	25.2
Germany, Federal Republic of	1983	9,632	7,224	2,408	33.3
Italy	1981	1,000	750	250	33.3
Japan	1985/86	4,630ᵃ	3,704ᵃ	926	25.0
Netherlands	1980	1,454	383	1,071	279.6
Sweden	1984	950	665	285	42.9
Switzerland	1986	744	165	579	350.9
United Kingdom	1981	5,250	3,165	2,085	65.9
United States	1984	24,560	18,171	6,389	35.2

Note: a) Considered an underestimate value.

Source: UNCTC, 1988, p. 213 and author's estimates.

Source: International Labour Office, based on a variety of sources and compilations prepared by the Starnberg Institute.

vidually and collectively is shown in Tables 5.3.9 to 5.3.11. Table 5.3.9 shows that for less-developed countries as a whole, debt was 44.7 per cent of Gross Domestic Products in 1985 (up from 14 per cent in 1975), while foreign direct investment represented only 8.7 per cent of Gross Domestic Products. In developing countries as a whole, foreign direct investment represented only 3.1 per cent of gross fixed-capital formation and 17.2 per cent of long-term capital inflow in the periods 1980–4 and 1980–5 respectively (Table 5.3.10).

However, the impact of this investment is disproportionate as Table 5.3.11 shows. For instance, foreign-owned companies represent over 54 per cent of employment in manufacturing in Singapore, 70 per cent of manufacturing production assets in Zimbabwe, 63 per cent of manufacturing production in Singapore and 44 per cent in Malaysia and nearly 90 per cent of manufactured exports in Singapore and 70 per cent in Costa Rica.

An explanation of why so little foreign direct investment goes to less-developed countries must rely on location effects. Location effects enter the theory of the multinational firm in two main ways. First, as location endowments (Dunning (1981)) of host countries, stimulating in the traditional Ricardian

Table 5.3.7 Inward Stocks of Foreign Direct Investment, by Major Host Region, 1975–1985
(billions of $US)

Countries/regions	1975 Value	1975 percentage of total	1975 GDP	1983 Value	1983 percentage of total	1983 GDP	1985 Value	1985 percentage of total	1985 GDP
Developed market economies	185.3	75.1	4.5	401.0	75.6	5.1	478.2	75.0	5.5
Western Europe	100.6	40.8	5.8	159.6	30.1	5.6	184.3	28.9	6.6
United States	27.7	11.2	1.8	137.1	25.9	4.2	184.6	29.0	4.7
Other[a]	57.0	23.1	7.0	104.3	19.7	6.0	109.2	17.1	5.7
Japan	1.5	0.6	0.3	0.5	0.9	0.4	6.1	1.0	0.5
Developed countries and territories	61.5	24.9	6.4	138.4	24.4	7.4	159.0	25.0	8.5
Africa[b]	16.5	6.7	15.7	19.6	3.7	9.4	22.3	3.5	10.8
Asia[c]	13.0	5.3	3.2	40.1	5.8	4.9	49.6	7.8	5.7
Latin America and the Caribbean[d]	29.7	12.0	8.9	73.2	13.8	11.9	80.5	12.6	13.6
Other[e]	2.3	0.9	2.1	5.4	1.0	2.4	6.6	1.0	3.4
Total[f]	246.8	100.0	4.9	539.4	100.0	5.5	637.2	100.0	6.1

Notes:

a) Australia, Canada, Japan, New Zealand, South Africa.

b) Botswana, Cameroon, Central African Republic, Congo, Cote d'Ivoire, Egypt, Gabon, Ghana, Kenya, Libyan Arab Jamahirrya, Malawi, Mauritius, Morocoo, Nigeria, Senegal, Seychelles, Sierra Leone, Togo, United Republic of Tanzania, Zaire, Zambia, Zimbabwe.

c) Bangladesh, China, Hong Kong, India, Indonesia, Malaysia, Pakistan, Philippines, Republic of Korea, Singapore, Sri Lanka, Taiwan Province, Thailand.

d) Argentina, Barbados, Brazil, Chile, Colombia, Dominican Republic, Ecuador, Guyana, Jamaica, Mexico, Panama, Paraguay, Peru, Trinidad and Tobago, Uruguay, Venezuela.

e) Fiji, Papua New Guinea, Saudi Arabia, Turkey, Yugoslavia.

f) Excluding the centrally planned economies of Europe, for which no precise data are available.

Reproduced from UNCTC, 1988, p. 25.

Table 5.3.8 Distribution of Foreign Direct Market Inflows by Major Region, 1975–1985 (percentage)

Country groups by region	1975	1980	1981	1982	1983	1984	1985	Annual averages 1975–1980	1981–1985
Developed market economies	70.6	80.5	73.6	69.8	76.8	78.5	76.7	76.6	75.2
United States	12.1	32.4	44.7	31.1	27.0	51.7	38.9	24.6	39.2
Western Europe	47.0	41.0	47.4	32.9	37.0	19.8	33.7	43.3	30.4
Japan	0.9	0.6	0.4	0.9	0.9	"	1.2	0.3	0.6
Other	10.2	6.7	1.2	4.5	11.6	6.7	2.8	8.4	4.5
Developing countries	29.3	19.3	26.4	30.2	23.2	21.3	23.3	23.4	24.8
Africa	2.3	0.4	3.2	3.8	3.6	3.1	3.4	2.5	3.3
Latin America and the Caribbean	15.3	11.9	13.6	14.4	7.7	7.0	9.1	12.5	10.5
Western Asia	3.3	0.6	"	0.7	0.7	1.2	1.0	1.9	0.8
Other Asia and Oceania	7.4	6.1	9.3	10.8	10.7	9.6	9.1	6.2	9.9
Southern Europe	0.9	0.2	0.4	0.2	0.2	0.4	0.4	0.3	0.4
World[a]	100	100	100	100	100	100	100	100	100
billions of dollars	21.5	52.2	56.8	44.5	44.1	49.0	49.3	32.1	48.7

Note: a) Excluding the centrally planned economies of Europe.
Reproduced from UNCTC, 1988, p. 76.

Source: United Nations Centre on Transnational Corporations, based on International Monetary Fund, balance-of-payments tape; and other official national and international sources.

Table 5.3.9 Developing Regions and Selected Countries: Indicators of the Relative Importance of Foreign Direct Investment and Debt Stocks, 1975 and 1985 (percentage)

Region/country	1975			1985			
	FDI	Debt	Debt as percentage of exports	FDI	Debt	Debt as percentage of exports	Bank debt to total debt
	As percentage of GDP			As percentage of GDP			
Developing countries[a]	6.3	14.0	109.6	8.7	44.7	182.3	55.4
Africa	15.0	18.9	72.4	12.6	63.2	174.8	36.3
Algeria	"	29.8	84.9	"	122.9	122.0	51.2
Cote d'Ivoire	12.6	25.9	66.7	19.1	128.4	203.0	46.3
Egypt	0.5	36.1	177.0	20.3	110.3	320.0	31.4
Morocco	2.3	19.5	69.2	6.0	119.0	335.7	37.6
Nigeria	20.9	3.2	12.1	5.4	26.3	152.0	48.6
Asia[b]	4.7	16.4	102.7	5.9	30.4	137.7	49.1
Indonesia	3.2	14.7	148.6	6.4	43.3	105.1	43.2
Korea, Republic of	2.8	30.6	103.3	1.9	58.1	148.2	70.2
Malaysia	24.7	19.7	40.9	28.6	59.8	105.1	66.3
Philippines	3.1	17.7	84.8	6.1	80.7	324.7	54.8
Thailand	3.4	9.2	45.0	5.9	50.5	187.4	53.4

Latin America and the Caribbean	8.9	19.3	150.1	13.6	62.2	310.7	69.9
Argentina	5.9	16.9	183.3	12.9	73.6	466.3	69.1
Brazil	5.6	19.1	237.0	13.9	56.0	358.9	73.1
Chile	5.7	59.7	244.4	14.0	134.4	447.9	67.5
Colombia	7.4	20.9	122.7	11.8	38.1	247.2	49.6
Ecuador	11.6	16.5	63.6	8.3	69.3	263.6	67.1
Mexico	5.5	17.7	243.8	8.9	54.9	324.3	78.2
Peru	11.0	32.9	300.0	15.4	90.2	400.0	49.7
Uruguay	"	18.6	116.7	"	111.9	376.9	46.9
Venezuela	13.7	5.4	14.9	15.0	75.6	221.9	82.1
Europe	2.1	14.1	79.5	3.2	33.6	88.2	48.1
Turkey	1.6	9.3	100.0	0.8	58.4	217.6	43.9
Yugoslavia	0.5	18.8	72.5	0.3	43.5	128.7	54.4

Notes:
a) The countries included in each regional average are essentially the same as those of Table 5.3.7.
b) Excluding the Middle East.

Reproduced from UNCTC, 1988, p. 129.

Source: United Nations Centre on Transnational Corporations, based on official national and international sources and on J. Dunning and J. Cantwell, *IRM Directory of Statistics of International Investment and Production.* New York: New York University Press, 1987.

Table 5.3.10 Developing Regions: Foreign Direct Investment Inflows as a Proportion of Domestic Capital Formation, Total Foreign Capital Inflows and Debt Service, 1975–1979 and 1980–1985 (percentage)

	Gross fixed capital formation		Total long-term capital inflow[a]		Interests payments on foreign debt	Total debt servicing
	1975–1979	1980–1984	1975–1979	1980–1985	1980–1985	1980–1985
Developing countries	3.0	3.1	14.5	17.2	30.1	18.1
Africa	3.8	3.9	13.0	19.4	29.2	14.0
South and South East Asia	1.4	2.0	17.2	19.3	38.1	20.8
Latin America and the Caribbean	3.7	3.8	18.0	18.8	15.7	10.2
Western Asia	1.6	0.5	2.0	1.3	"	"
Southern Europe	12.6	10.4	4.2	8.2	2.5	1.2

Note: a) Only countries for which data were available are included in the regional totals.

Reproduced from UNCTC, 1985, p. 139.

Source: United Nations Centre on Transnational Corporations, based on official national and international sources.

Table 5.3.11 Indicators of the Importance of Foreign Affiliates in Manufacturing Production and Exports of Developing Countries/Territories (percentage)

Region/country/territory	Employment	Production	Exports
Africa			
Sierra Leone	13.0 (1981)	"	"
Zaire	30.4 (1974)	"	"
Zimbabwe	"	70.0 (1982)[a]	"
Asia and Oceania			
Fiji	29.0 (1977)	31.8 (1980)[b]	"
Hong Kong	9.8 (1984)	13.9 (1981)	16.5 (1984)[c]
India	13.0 (1977)	7.0 (1979)	"
Korea, Rpublic of	9.5 (1978)	19.3 (1978)	24.6 (1978)
Malaysia	19.7 (1975)	44.0 (1978)	34.6 (1980)
Philippiness	8.6 (1976)	"	51.5 (1983)
Singapore	54.6 (1982)	62.9 (1982)	89.7 (1983)
Taiwan Province	16.7 (1981)	"	25.6 (1981)
Latin America			
Argentina	18.9 (1981)	29.4 (1983)	26.6 (1983)
Brazil	23.0 (1977)	32.0 (1977)	32.3 (1980)
Chile	"	28.0 (1979)	21.7 (1979)
Colombia	"	29.0 (1983)	16.9 (1980)
Costa Rica	"	"	70.1 (1980)
Mexico	21.0 (1970)	27.0 (1972)	42.4 (1977)
Peru	13.5 (1975)	25.2 (1974)	8.0 (1978)
Trinidad and Tobago	44.0 (1977)[d]	"	"
Uruguay	"	11.5 (1978)	12.6 (1978)
Venezuela	"	35.9 (1975)	"

Notes:
a) Assets.
b) Sales.
c) As percentage of profits.
d) Includes petroleum. Employment in foreign affiliates in oil is 70 per cent.

Reproduced from UNCTC, 1988, p. 159.

Source: United Nations Centre on Transnational Corporations, based partly on J. Dunning and J. Cantwell, *IRM Directory of Statistics of International Investment and Production*. New York: New York University Press, 1987; and other international papers.

fashion trade flows and giving rise to factor flows. Secondly, location factors provide the motives for the different types of foreign direct investment. The key motives are:

market induced direct investment,
raw material induced direct investment, and
labour induced investment, a subset of which is
offshore production.

When we examine further the less-developed countries that do receive inward investment, they represent quite a distinct sub-set of all developing countries. Either they have large protected markets (Brazil, Argentina, India) or they have significant raw-material resources that are geographically concentrated (oil, copper) or they are newly industrializing – they attract inward investment to a cheaper-labour country with a well-developed infrastructure and to an enclave industrial environment (Singapore, South Korea). In each of these cases the impact on the host country will be very different (see Chapter 4.1 above). Examples of the analysis of inward investment in each case are Kidron (1965) on India, Moran (1974) on Chile and Mirza (1986) on Singapore. A survey of multinational enterprises in less-developed countries is Casson and Pearce (1987). See also Chapter 4.3 above.

5.3.3 Net flows of foreign direct investment

Inflows and outflows of foreign direct investment are not unconnected. Examination of net flows can be illuminating. It is possible to classify countries into net importers or net exporters of capital. The switch from net exporter to net importer of foreign direct investment can be dramatic and even traumatic as the United States of America found in the mid-to-late 1980s. It has been suggested that an investment development cycle may be useful in analysing the dynamics of the investment and income (Dunning (1981), (1986)). This cycle has been analysed using the elements of Dunning's eclectic theory which traces shifts in location advantages, internalization decisions and ownership advantages (Dunning (1988)).

References

Buckley, Peter J. (1983): 'New Theories of International Business', in Casson, Mark (ed.): *The Growth of International Business*. London: George Allen & Unwin.
Buckley, Peter J. and Casson, Mark (1976): *The Future of the Multinational Enterprise*. London: Macmillan.
Buckley, Peter J. and Casson, Mark (1985): *The Economic Theory of the Multinational Enterprise: Selected Papers*. London: Macmillan.

Buckley, Peter J., Dunning, John H. and Pearce R.D. (1978): 'The Influence of Firm Size, Industry, Nationality and Degree of Multinationality on the Growth and Profitability of the World's Largest Firms 1962–72', *Weltwirtschaftliches Archiv*, Band 114, Heft 2, June, pp. 243–57.

Buckley, Peter J., Dunning, John H. and Pearce R.D. (1984): 'An Analysis of the Growth and Profitability of the World's Largest Firms 1967–1977', *Kyklos*, Vol. 37, No. 1, pp. 3–26.

Casson, Mark (1985): 'The Theory of Foreign Direct Investment' in Buckley and Casson (1985) *op cit.*

Casson, Mark and Pearce, Robert D. (1987): 'Multinational Enterprises in LDCs', in Gemmell, Norman (ed.): *Surveys in Development Economics*. Oxford: Basil Blackwell.

Dunning, John H. (1981): *International Production and the Multinational Enterprise*. London: George Allen & Unwin.

Dunning, John H. (1986): 'The Investment Development Cycle and Third World Multinationals' in Khan, Kushi M. (ed.): *Multinationals of the South*. London: Frances Pinter.

Dunning, John H. (1988): 'The eclectic paradigm of international production: A restatement and some possible extensions', *Journal of International Business Studies*, Vol. 19, No. 1, Spring, pp. 1–32.

Dunning, John H. and Cantwell, John (1987): *The IRM Directory of Statistics of International Investment and Production*. London: Macmillan.

Kidron, Michael (1965): *Foreign Investments in India*. Oxford: Oxford University Press.

Kindleberger, C.P. (1969): *American Business Abroad*. New Haven: Yale University Press.

Mirza, Hafiz (1986): *Multinationals and the Growth of the Singapore Economy*. Beckenham: Croom Helm.

Moran, Theodore (1974): *Multinational Corporations and the Politics of Dependence: Copper in Chile*. Princeton: Princeton University Press.

Shapiro, D.M. (1983): 'The Comparative Profitability of Canadian and Foreign Owned Firms', *Managerial and Decision Economics*, Vol. 4, No. 2, pp. 97–106.

United Nations Centre on Transnational Corporations (1988): *Transnational Corporations in World Development: Trends and Prospects*. New York: UNCTC.

Williamson, Oliver E. (1975): *Markets and Hierarchies: Analysis and Anti-Trust Implications*. New York, Free Press.

Woodruff, W. (1967): *The Impact of Western Man*. New York: St Martin's Press.

5.4

The Industrial Structure of Foreign Direct Investment

This chapter reviews theoretical explanations of industry structure (5.4.1) and then goes on to review the broad industry structure of foreign direct investment (5.4.2), international competition (5.4.3), individual industries and the internationalization of service industries (5.4.5).

5.4.1 Theoretical explanations of industry structure

Foreign direct investment and multinational firms are concentrated by industrial sector. The theory of the multinational enterprise based on the internalization of markets vertically, in research-intensive industries and in skill-intensive activities (Buckley and Casson (1985) Chapters 2 and 8) suggests that the types of industries outlined in Table 5.4.1 will be dominated by multinational firms.

In a study of the foreign penetration of United Kingdom industry, the following characteristics were associated with foreign penetration at industry level:

high wage rates;
high salary levels;
ratio of staff: operatives;
ratio of royalty payments to net output;
industry concentration; and
advertising expenditure as a percentage of net output.

The first five were significant in a rank correlation analysis at 1 per cent level, the sixth at the 5 per cent level (Buckley and Casson (1976)). Such a nexus of characteristics is consistent with an industry group dependent on the internalization of specialized knowledge, embodied largely in skilled individuals and technology-intensive machinery, which protects its position by erecting barriers to entry based on product differentiation and quality competition.

Further significant differences between domestic and foreign firms emerge in

Table 5.4.1   Industries Dominated by Multinational Firms

Industry	*Examples*
PRIMARY	
Perishable agricultural products requiring careful monitoring of product quality	Bananas Tobacco
Raw materials whose deposits are geographically concentrated	Oil Copper
MANUFACTURING	
High-technology, research-intensive industries with intermediate flows of specialized knowledge and skills	Computers Pharmaceuticals
Capital-intensive industries requiring the services of sophisticated plant and machinery	Earth-moving equipment Heavy electrical machinery
SERVICES	
Skill, knowledge and communication-intensive services	Banking Distribution
Location dependence services	Oil services Insurance

Source: Buckley and Casson, 1985, p. 198; Buckley, 1987, p. 20.

the management of industrial relations and labour utilization in a study of foreign investors in the United Kingdom (Buckley and Enderwick (1985)). The industrial relations practices of foreign multinationals in the United Kingdom differ in type and degree from local firms. Foreign firms take some workplace relations out of joint negotiations and indulge in single-employer bargaining. They also rely more heavily on formalized agreements and plant- or company-based agreements. A more effective use of labour is a major source of a foreign multinational's productivity advantage; this arises from a simplified union representation and increased worker flexibility. However, this increased utilization of labour is achieved at a price. This price is usually higher wage rates but also more conflict over labour utilization issues; a higher incidence of unconstitutional disputes results. The policies of foreign firms in dealing with these difficulties attempt to increase the cost to employees of taking industrial action.

There is a wages differential in British industry between foreign and domestic firms, even after account has been taken of plant size. Indeed, the largest differentials occur in the small and the very large plant sizes (Buckley and Enderwick (1985)). This positive differential arises because of productivity levels, plant bargaining and policies designed to buy out restrictions on labour utilization and to discourage unionism. In testing an exit-voice model of strike activity in United Kingdom industry (Enderwick and Buckley (1983)), strike activity was found to depend on both structural and cost factors. Multinationals attempt to discourage strike action by a high-wage policy but transnational production enables national unions to exploit their leverage in disrupting integrated activities.

Studies of the growth, profitability and policy decisions of multinational firms have consistently shown important industry differences (Buckley, Dunning and Pearce (1984)). Representing industry differences by dummy variables and assuming that industry effects (and, later, nationality effects) are additive, Equation 5.1 (See Section 5.2.1 above) becomes:

$$G = a + bs^2 + cs^2 + \sum_{i=1}^{n} d_i I_i + \sum_{j=1}^{m} t_j N_j + e \qquad \text{(Equation 5.3)}$$

where b, c are regression coefficients,
    a is the intercept
    I_i takes a value 1 for industry i and O otherwise,
    N_j takes a value 1 for nationality j and O otherwise,
    di and f j are differences from arbitrarily chosen d_{m+1} and f_{m+1} respectively,
    e is the error term.

Industry effects are then tested by omitting all industry terms from Equation 5.3 and testing the ratio of incremental variance explained by inclusion of these terms in the full equation to the remaining incremental variance in the full equation by means of an F-test. In general, industry differences on growth and profitability and policy are significant. To develop this hypothesis, industry differences have been replaced by groupings based on research intensity, with limited success, possibly because research and development is measured at industry, not firm level and so this measure misses intra-industry differences in research and development intensity (Buckley and Pearce (1984)).

5.4.2 The broad industry structure of foreign direct investment

The broad division of foreign direct investment into extractive, manufacturing, services and other – including agriculture, real estate, communications, retail and public utilities – is shown in Table 5.4.2. The Table shows foreign investment in services to be important and growing rapidly. In 1985, foreign direct investment in services was larger than in manufacturing for the Federal Republic of Germany, Japan and the UK. For The Netherlands it was equal to manufacturing investment.

The fact that manufacturing still exceeds service investment for the United States of America is largely due to the continuing growth of United States offshore production, notably in-band manufacturing firms on the Mexican border (United Nations Centre on Transnational Corporations (1988)). Electronics firms continue to develop in the newly industrializing countries of South East Asia. The flow of manufacturing foreign direct investment to less-developed countries is subject to two opposing forces: the continuing lower costs of labour in less-developed countries versus organizational and technological pressures to produce near, or within, major markets (just-in-time production systems, low inventory pressures and increasing protectionism).

The breakdown of small multinational firms by sector is shown in Table 5.4.3. Smaller Japanese foreign investors are concentrated in manufacturing; smaller United States multinational firms are more oriented to manufacturing than other sectors; and of smaller Canadian firms with foreign investments, manufacturers form a minority.

Foreign investment by smaller firms covers a wide range of industries. White (1983) p. 274 characterizes the operations as highly specialized, covering one or two product lines, with short production runs, often serving the contractual markets given by other industries. Typical industries include metal-working, capital-goods production, textiles and clothing, food, furniture, ceramic products and non-metallic products. These industries are well represented in the sample of United Kingdom outward investors in Buckley, Newbould and Thurwell (1988).

Smaller Japanese foreign investors cover a variety of labour-intensive light manufacturing such as light-metal articles, furniture, bags, footwear, apparel, toys and plastic products. The 1980s saw many more smaller firm foreign investors in electrical machinery, non-electrical machinery and transport equipment as smaller suppliers and sub-contractors follow large enterprises abroad (United Nations Conference on Trade and Development (1984)).

These findings provide empirical support for the conjectures that balanced growth in small-firm industries is conducive to success.

5.4.3 International competition

While most attention in the spread of multinational firms has been concentrated on foreign production financed by international direct investment, in analysing international competition it is vital to include the other two modes of market servicing: licensing and exporting. In the division of world markets it is essential to include the total foreign sales of nations; that is:

Table 5.4.2 Selected Developed Market Economies: Sectoral Distribution of Outward Stock of Foreign Direct Investment, 1975 and 1985 (percentage)

Countries	Extractive		Manufacturing		Services[a]		Other[b]	
	1975	1985	1975	1985	1975	1985	1975	1985
Canada[c]								
Total	21.1	22.9	50.5	46.2	28.4	30.9	"	"
Developing Countries	21.2	46.4	18.2	20.4	60.6	33.2	"	"
Developed market economies	21.1	18.6	60.3	50.9	18.6	30.4	"	"
Germany, Federal Republic of[d]								
Total	4.1	3.8	48.3	43.0	41.9	48.3	5.7	4.9
Developing Countries	12.6	9.9	64.1	57.7	23.4	32.4	"	"
Developed market economies	2.1	3.0	47.7	43.0	50.2	54.1	"	"
Japan[e]								
Total	28.1	15.5	32.4	29.2	36.2	51.8	3.4	3.5
Developing Countries	31.9	21.9	43.8	32.7	19.1	41.5	5.1	3.9
Developed market economies	23.6	9.2	19.1	25.7	56.0	62.0	1.3	3.1
Netherlands[f]								
Total	46.5	55.4	38.6	22.2	14.7	22.1	0.3	0.3
Developing Countries	34.1	41.9	38.7	23.3	25.9	34.8	1.2	"
Developed market economies	48.9	57.9	38.5	22.0	12.5	19.8	0.1	0.3

United Kingdom[g]								
Total	11.1	33.3	59.5	31.8	29.4	34.8	"	
Developing Countries	18.2	31.9	48.2	24.7	33.6	43.4	"	
Developed market economies	8.9	33.6	63.0	33.4	28.1	32.9	"	
United States								
Total	26.4	23.1	45.0	37.9	24.3	33.7	4.3	5.2
Developing Countries	20.0	27.6	44.9	31.7	24.5	34.5	10.5	6.4
Developed market economies	26.4	19.9	48.4	41.1	22.2	34.4	3.0	4.5

Notes:

a) Breakdown by region and sector is available for a narrower definition of services for the United States and the Federal Republic of Germany than is used elsewhere in the survey. However, the trend is the same for both definitions. For Canada, the Federal Republic of Germany and the United Kingdom, agriculture, forestry and fishing are included in services.

b) Other. For United States, agriculture, forestry and fishing, construction, mining (1985), transportation, communication and public utilities (1985), retail trade; for the Federal Republic of Germany, loans from dependent holding companies to other foreign associated enterprises; for The Netherlands and Japan, agriculture, forestry and fisheries; for Japan, establishment of branches and purchases of real estate.

c) Canadian data are for 1975 and 1983.

d) Data for the Federal Republic of Germany are for 1976 and 1985.

e) Japanese stock data based on cumulative flows rather than on the historical book values as is the case in other countries.

f) Data for The Netherlands are for 1975 and 1984, the extractive sector is on the historical book values as is the case in other countries. Is defined as mining, oil and chemicals.

g) Data for the United Kingdom are for 1974 and 1984. For 1974, oil companies, banks and isurance companies are excluded.

Reproduced from UNCTC, 1988, p. 86.

Source: United Nations Centre on Transnational Corporations, based on official national sources.

Table 5.4.3 Number of Small Multinational Corporations, Classified by Country of Origin, Size and Sector

Country of Origin	Size	Manufacturing	Other sectors	Total	Percentage of all MNCs
Canada	Sales up to $18.4 million	80	515	595	58.4
Japan (1984)	Up to 300[a] employees	238	103	341	23.0
United Kingdom (1981)	20 to 499 employees	"	"	1,177	78.0
United States of America (1982)	Up to $100 milion assets	508	406	914	43.3
France	20 to 499 employees	"	"	1,600[b]	80.0

Notes:
a) Less than 100 employees for services corporations.
b) Includes non-equity technology transfer.
Source: UNCTC, 1988, p. 37.

Total foreign sales = Exports + sales from foreign licenses
+ sales from foreign affiliates.

In practice it is difficult to estimate each of these forms, particularly foreign licensing, but the concentration of attention and policy on one form of foreign market servicing alone can lead to incorrect, often counterproductive results. Tariff charges, for instance, to protect a home market may lead to foreign multinationals jumping the tariff wall in defensive investment moves. Attempts to improve exporting from a particular source country will be frustrated unless other forms of foreign-market servicing are taken into account. A comprehensive attempt to estimate the total foreign sales in the United Kingdom is undertaken in Buckley and Prescott (1988). A comparative analysis of world competition is undertaken by Clegg (1987) in which the patterns of direct foreign investment of the United States of America, Japan, the United Kingdom, Sweden and the Federal Republic of Germany are compared.

The main institutional agent of international competition is the multinational corporation. The United Nations Centre on Transnational Corporations has compiled data on 600 multinational manufacturers (including agricultural production) with sales of over $1 billion in 1985. The industrial breakdown of

Table 5.4.4   Large Multinational Corporations by Primary Line of Business, 1985

Primary line of business	Total sales Number	Total sales (Billions of US dollars)	Percentage
Mining	19	47.9	1.6
Petroleum and gas	52	762.6	24.6
Food, beverages, tobacco	77	324.0	10.4
Paper, printing	51	116.9	3.8
Chemicals	95	419.9	13.5
Basic metals	56	204.4	6.6
Machinery and equipment	175	759.5	24.5
Motor vehicles	39	392.1	12.6
Others	36	76.6	2.5
Total	600	3,103.9	100.0

Source: UNCTC, 1988, p. 34.

these firms is shown in Table 5.4.4. The group is dominated in terms of sales by machinery and equipment, petroleum and gas, chemicals and motor vehicles. All these broad industries and their major sub-divisions are global oligopolies in which small numbers of large firms compete on a world scale.

The existence of such global industries has led to an over-enthusiastic exposure of global strategies, treating the world as a single market. But how widely applicable is the globalization model? In its pure form, with implications of a global product, standardized marketing techniques and centralized control, the answer is probably that not many sectors, industries or product divisions conform to a homogeneous worldwide strategy. Perhaps the model is an idealized view of the market-servicing policies at the opposite end of the spectrum of size and international experience from first-time investors? It is also not without its normative elements. National markets in many areas remain firmly idiosyncratic. The focus on successful multinationals leads us to ignore the many failed attempts to impose a foreign (or international or global) product on an unwilling national market. Moreover, the existence of market niches leaves global marketers vulnerable to competitors from non-standardized products.

A more cautious version of the globalization model is now widespread. Porter's recent work (1986) suggests there is no single global strategy (Young (1987)). Rather, any strategy is constrained by the value chain (vertical integration), configuration (location costs of interrelated activities internalized within the firm) and coordination issues. This leads to a typology of global strategies. A related categorization by White and Poynter (1984) distinguishes the types of integration among networks of foreign affiliates (miniature replica, marketing satellites, rationalized manufacture, product specialist and strategic independent) that have much in common with Casson's typology of industries (1986). It is clear, however, that it is essential to analyse competition and industrial structure at the international level in most industries (Ballance (1987)).

5.4.4 Individual industries

Industry studies remain firmly rooted in a single nation or, at best, in a European or North American context. Despite the growth of international competition, much writing on industrial economics, market analysis and business policy remains firmly in a national context. Exceptions to this trend are current writings on European competition as exemplified by Macharzina and Staehle (1986) with individual chapters on cars, steel, petrochemicals, aerospace clothing and microelectronics; and writers on global competition such as those in Porter (1986) which includes chapters on shipbuilding and civil aircraft. Where individual industries are studied on a global scale, it tends to be a sub-set of industries that are favoured, notably automobiles (Maxcy (1981)), pharmaceuticals (James (1977)), electronics (Scibberas (1977)), extraction (Thoburn (1981)) and oil (from Penrose (1968) onwards e.g. Rees and Odell (1987)). Far more attention needs to be paid to the dynamics of global competition at industry level. Such studies should include the interaction with international trade. The building blocs for such an integration are available as the studies by Casson and Associates (1986) show. The Casson studies of vertical integration in world industries include the motor industry, bearings, synthetic fibres (where the pioneering study by Hufbauer provides an early exemplar), tin, copper, bananas and shipping.

5.4.5 The internationalization of service industries

The internationalization of service industries has recently attracted a great deal of attention, not least because of the detail in which it is mapped by the United Nations Centre on Transnational Corporation (1988). The internationalization of banking, securities and financial services, insurance, trade-related services (wholesale and retail), business services (accounting, advertising, market research and legal services), construction, publishing, transportation and leisure-related services (hotels, airlines, fast food and restaurant chains) has grown to a point where it accounts for about 40 per cent of the world's stock of foreign direct investment and 50 per cent of annual flows.

The form of internationalization in the service industries is not necessarily via foreign direct investment. In hotels and restaurants the franchise is an important

Table 5.4.5 International Franchising by United States Firms, by Location of Number of Establishments, 1985

		Developed market economies		Developing
Type of franchised business [a]	Total	Total	Canada	countries [b]
Restaurants	6,122	4,767	1,542	1,355
Auto and truck rental services	5,758	3,972	714	1,786
Business aids and services	3,905	3,663	1,279	242
Non-food retailing	3,510	3,285	1,599	225
Automotive products and services	2,203	1,924	1,045	279
Retailing (food other than convenience stores)	2,140	1,813	959	327
Construction, home improvement, maintenance and cleaning services	1,693	1,603	695	90
Hotels, motels and campgrounds	515	387	276	128
Recreation, entertainment and travel	177	160	66	17
Laundry and dry-cleaning services	132	123	112	9
Educational products and services, rental services (equipment), convenience stores, and miscellaneous	4,033	3,681	767	352
TOTAL	30,188	25,378	9,054	4,810

Notes:
a) Excluding automobile and truck dealers, gasoline service stations and soft-drink bottlers.
b) Including New Zealand with a total of 402 outlets.
Reproduced from UNCTC, 1988, p. 421.

Source: United States, Department of Commerce, *Franchising in the Economy 1985–1987.* Washington, D.C., Government Printing Office, 1987.

form of international expansion. In this form of contractual relationship, the franchisor (source firm) provides the business system, trademark or brand, quality-control system and mode of operation, and the franchisee – often but not always a smaller firm – operates the business under the franchisor's (global) brand name. It can be seen from Table 5.4.5 that although restaurants and hotels are the most salient form of franchising operation, this mode covers a vast range of services and is particularly important in car rental, business services, food and non-food retailing and automotive products as well as in construction and maintenance. (See Enderwick (1988) for a review and Seymour (1987) on construction.) By contrast, much of the expansion in banking and financial services has been via the traditional direct investment route; non-equity ventures are a rarity. Indeed, foreign direct investment in banking has grown more rapidly than that in other sectors in recent years (United Nations Centre on Transnational Corporations (1988). See also Rajan (1987)). A further important trend is the internationalization of general trading companies, including the Japanese sogo-shosha, the Korean general trading company and the long-established colonial traders, together with many recent imitators.

References

Ballance, Robert H. (1987): *International Industry and Business.* London: George Allen & Unwin.

Buckley, Peter J. (1987): *The Theory of the Multinational Enterprise* (The Uppsala Lectures in Business, 1986). Stockholm: Almquist & Wicksell.

Buckley, Peter J. and Casson, Mark (1976): *The Future of the Multinational Enterprise.* London: Macmillan.

Buckley, Peter J. and Casson, Mark (1985): *The Economic Theory of the Multinational Enterprise.* London: Macmillan.

Buckley, Peter J. and Enderwick, Peter (1985): *The Industrial Relations Practices of Foreign-Owned Firms in British Manufacturing Industry.* London: Macmillan.

Buckley, Peter J., Newbould, Gerald D. and Thurwell, Jane (1988): *Foreign Direct Investment by Smaller UK Firms.* London: Macmillan.

Buckley, Peter J. and Pearce, Robert D. (1984): 'Exports in the Strategy of Multinational Enterprises', *Journal of Business Research*, Vol. 12, No. 2, June, pp. 209–26.

Buckley, Peter J. and Prescott, Kate (1988): 'The Structure of British Industry's Sales in Foreign Markets', *Managerial and Decision Economics*, Vol. 10, No. 3, pp. 189–208.

Casson, Mark and Associates (1986): *Multinationals and World Trade.* London: George Allen & Unwin.

Clegg, Jeremy (1987): Multinational Enterprise and World Competition. London: Macmillan.

Enderwick, Peter (ed.) (1988): *Multinational Service Firms.* London: Routledge.

Enderwick, Peter and Buckley, Peter J. (1983): 'The Determinants of Strike Activity in Foreign Owned Plants: Evidence from British Manufacturing Industry 1971–3', *Managerial and Decision Economics*, Vol. 4, No. 2, pp. 83–8.

Hufbauer, G.C. (1966): *Synthetic Materials and the Theory of International Trade.* London: Gerald Duckworth.

James, Barrie G. (1977): *The Future of the Multinational Pharmaceutical Industry to 1990.* London: Associated Business Programmes.

Macharzina, K. and Staehle, W.H. (eds) (1986): *European Approaches to International Management.* Berlin: Walter de Gruyter.

Penrose, Edith T. (1968): *The Large International Firm in Developing Countries: The International Petroleum Industry.* London: George Allen & Unwin.

Porter, Michael E. (1986): *Competition in Global Industries.* Boston: Harvard Business School Press.

Rajan, Amin (1987): *Employment in Multinational Banking: Recent Trends and Future Prospects.* Geneva: ILO.

Rees, Judith and Odell, Peter (1987): *The International Oil Industry: An Interdisciplinary Perspective*. London: Macmillan.

Sciberras, Edmond (1977): *Multinational Electronics Companies and National Economic Policies*. Greenwich, Conn: JAI Press.

Seymour, Howard (1987): *The Multinational Construction Industry*. London: Croom Helm.

Thoburn, John (1981): *Multinationals, Mining and Development: A Study of the Tin Industry*. Aldershot: Gower.

UNCTC (1988): *Transnational Corporations in World Development: Trends and Prospects*. New York: UNCTC.

UNCTAD (1984): *International Transfer of Technology to Developing Countries by Small and Medium Sized Enterprises*. Geneva: UNCTAD Secretariat TD/B/119.

White, Eduardo (1983): 'The Role of Third World Multinationals and Small and Medium sized Companies in the Industrialization Strategies of Developing Countries', in *Industrial Development Strategies and Policies for Developing Countries*. Vienna: UNIDO.

White, R.G. and Poynter, T.A. (1984): 'Strategies for Foreign Owned Subsidiaries in Canada', *Business Quarterly*.

Young, Stephen (1987): 'Business Strategy and the Internationalization of Business: Recent Approaches', *Managerial and Decision Economics*, Vol. 8, No. 1, pp. 31–40.

5.5

Barriers to International Investment

This chapter examines the major barriers to inward and outward foreign investment. Government intervention on inward investment is considered in Section 5.5.1 and it includes disclosure requirements, taxation, limitations on entry and ownership and performance requirements that may include employment or export provisions or requirements to transfer technology. Expropriation is considered in Section 5.5.2. Barriers arising from low income and low growth are examined in Section 5.5.3. The general trend towards deregulation is considered in Section 5.5.4. Section 5.5.5 examines the political risk of foreign investment and ways of managing it. Section 5.5.6 analyses source-country barriers to outward investment and Section 5.5.7 covers supranational problems.

5.5.1 Government intervention in host countries

It is essential to begin by referring to the motives behind the foreign investment decision. The form of government intervention is related to the type of investment. Three major motives can be discerned:

(1) market-oriented foreign direct investment;
(2) raw-material-based investment;
(3) cost-reducing investment.

The first type, market-oriented investment, is naturally oriented towards countries with large home markets, often in response to rapid market growth or the threat or reality of tariff imposition (Buckley and Pearce (1979), (1981), (1984)). Much of this type of investment takes place in the advanced industrialized countries or in large, rapidly growing and less-developed countries (Brazil, Mexico, Argentina); some takes place in the newly industrializing countries (Malaysia, Korea). Foreign investment in service industries, a rapidly growing phenomenon on the world scene, falls into this category, as services

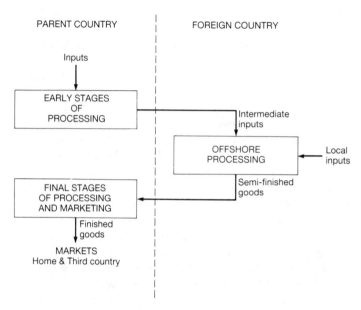

Figure 5.5.1   A Typical Offshore Production Process

have to be performed *in situ*. As the advanced countries become more service-oriented, so we can expect foreign investment in such areas to dominate all other types.

The second type, raw-material or extractive investment, has traditionally been the source of much contention between host and source countries. Historical factors, which have led to extraction technology reposing in advanced countries and raw materials in colonized and less-developed countries, have increased tension. Recent host-country attempts to gain control by nationalization, expropriation and indigenization have led to massive restructuring of operations and the search for new forms of institutional arrangements (Oman (1980), Buckley (1985).

The final type of motive is cost reduction (raw-material control can be considered a sub-set of this motive but it raises many other issues). Two major types can be distinguished: labour-cost-reducing investment and tax-haven investment.

In many industries, labour is an element of cost that can be reduced by relocation. The search for cheap labour has led to multinationals reorganizing their operations so that the labour-intensive stages can be relocated. When the output of these stages is reintroduced into the production flow of the firm located in the advanced country, the process is referred to as offshore production. A typical offshore process is shown in Figure 5.5.1. A further form of cost reduction is that achieved by tax reduction, the extreme form of which is location of some activities in tax havens.

At an extreme level of generality, it may be said that the first type of direct foreign investment has caused little controversy in the host country, largely because it is import-substituting and ostensibly increases investment and employment there. However, it has caused some concern in source countries because of the fear that foreign production is substituted for exports leading to job losses at home. This has prompted enquiries such as the Hufbauer and Adler Report, the Tariff Commission Report, a Report by the Subcommittee on Multinationals (and many others) in the United States of America and the Reddaway Reports in the United Kingdom (Hufbauer and Adler (1968), Tariff Commission Report (1979), Organization of Economic Cooperation and Development (1976), Reddaway and others (1967), (1968)).

The second type of investment has caused most controversy. Data from the Harvard Business School's Multinational Enterprise Study shows that manufacturing and service firms are relatively immune from expropriation in the Third World. Only 30 plants of United States manufacturing companies were expropriated between 1960 and 1974. This was just 1.2 per cent of United-States-owned manufacturing plants in the Third World. Two governments, Allende in Chile and Sukarno in Indonesia, were responsible for 80 per cent of the seizures (Faundez and Picciotto (1978), p. 15, Bradley (1977)). Burton and Inoue (1984), reporting other estimates, put this figure at 1.6 per cent.

The more recent study (Burton and Inoue (1984)) provides limited support for the hypotheses that agriculture and finance are prone to asset expropriation in the early stages of economic development and manufacturing in the late stages. It also lends support (though this is not explicitly tested) to the view that the higher the service element in operations, the lower the threat of expropriation. The overall threat of asset expropriation is relatively small (Burton and Inoue, p. 414).

Labour-cost-reducing investment has been condemned in advanced countries but welcomed with massive incentives and tax-free zones by Third World countries desperate to increase output, employment and exports. Runaway industry and the export of jobs have been condemned in the United States and other capital-exporting countries. Multinationals, however, have gained from lower-cost activities and offshore plants have increased enormously in operating efficiency and the range of functions performed. Access to advanced countries' markets is a major contribution of this type of investment for host-Third-World countries who are denied this access in many instances; the use of the distribution networks and contacts of the investing companies is a major contribution to their exports.

In view of these objections on the part of host countries to the acceptance of foreign direct investment and the political problems generated, multinationals have been pushed into developing alternative means of market servicing such as joint-ventures licensing, franchising and other new forms. Major government-imposed constraints on inward investment include disclosure requirements, taxation-provision limitations on entry and ownership, performance requirements and requirements to transfer technology to the host country.

Disclosure requirements

Multinationals often complain that host-country regulations require the disclosure of a larger amount of confidential operations than is required of local companies. This can be commercially damaging.

Taxation

It has frequently been claimed that multinationals pay a higher overall rate of tax than uninational firms because they are caught between overlapping fiscal jurisdictions. It is also the case that multinationals can benefit by slipping between the cracks of taxation authorities. Of particular recent concern has been the adoption of the unitary taxation scheme by several United States states.

Limitations on entry and ownership

Almost every country in the world has a list of proscribed industries in which foreign control is not permitted. These include industries of strategic importance, communications industries, publishing, television, news media and other variously defined essential industries. Other arguments adduced for control include the infant-industry argument: that a time of protection is needed for a nascent domestic industry (and that an efficient capital market would fund it after a waiting period) and arguments derived from market-failure considerations, balance-of-payments arguments and protection of domestic technology.

A variant of prohibition is the insistence on local control of some or all industries. This has led to a growth of joint ventures (Beamish (1988)) and other new forms of international involvement (Oman (1980), Buckley (1985)) that are institutional attempts by host governments to reap the benefits of foreign expertise without foreign control; from the multinational's point of view they are the means of accessing a market that is otherwise closed.

Performance requirements

International investment is restricted by the insistence of host governments on performance standards for foreign entrants. These may take the form of employment requirements or employment requirements for nationals, particularly in management and other skilled positions. Exporting quotas may also be laid down.

Technology transfer requirements

Further disincentives to international investment may arise from the host-country's insistence that the most modern technology must be imported. In view of the importance of protecting proprietary rights (and extracting a full return from technological advances), this may prove a severe imposition on potential investors.

5.5.2   Expropriation

The most extreme form of government intervention is expropriation. Table 5.5.2 shows expropriation acts by year and Table 5.5.3 their time pattern.

5.5.3   Barriers arising from low incomes and low growth

Foreign direct investment is motivated by access to markets and productive resources. Where markets are small, fragmented and slow-growing, domestic resources are usually relatively unproductive. This is the essential problem for the least-developed countries in attracting inward investment. Table 5.5.4 shows the United Nations Centre on Transnational Corporations' summary of adverse factors inhibiting foreign investment in a selection of low-income countries: these include small size, negative growth and location (e.g. land-locked countries). The index has some correlation with the lack of inward investment. To improve the correlation, adverse political factors (including political instability) should be added (see Section 5.5.5 below).

The proportion of foreign direct investment that goes to the least-developed countries is insignificant. The United Nations Centre on Transnational Corporations calculate, on the basis of 1984 data for 40 low-income developing countries, foreign direct investment amounted to under one per cent of gross domestic investment in all but seven countries (United Nations Centre on Transnational Corporations (1988), p. 196). This does not, however, prevent multinational firms from having dominant roles in particular sectors within these countries – often much of this investment dates from the pre-colonial period.

One policy measure that has been widely utilized to attract inward direct investment into low-income countries is the establishment of export-processing zones. Major problems in the success of such zones include the provision of adequate infrastructure (particularly power supplies and transport facilities). Most such zones tend to employ a preponderance of female labour, often with severe negative social consequences in the host country.

Table 5.5.2 Expropriation Acts, by Year

Year	Number of acts	Percentage of total	Number of countries expropriating
1960	6	1.0	5
1961	8	1.4	5
1962	8	1.4	5
1963	11	1.9	7
1964	22	3.8	10
1965	14	2.4	11
1966	5	0.9	3
1967	25	4.4	8
1968	13	2.3	8
1969	24	4.2	14
1970	48	8.4	18
1971	51	8.9	20
1972	56	9.8	30
1973	30	5.2	20
1974	68	11.8	29
1975	83	14.5	28
1976	40	7.0	14
1977	15	2.6	13
1978	15	2.6	8
1979	17	2.9	13
1980	5	0.9	5
1981	4	0.7	2
1982	1	0.2	1
1983	3	0.5	3
1984	1	0.2	1
1985	1	0.2	1
Total	574[a]	100.0[b]	

Notes:
a) The data is missing for four acts.
b) Error due to rounding.
Reproduced from UNCTC, 1985, p. 315.
Source: Data for 1969 to 1979 are from Kobrin, 1984, p. 333 (unpublished). For the data for 1980–5, see Michael Minor, *The Expropriation of Foreign Direct Investment in Developing Countries: Trends from 1980–1985* (unpublished).

Table 5.5.3   Time Pattern of Expropriations, 1960–1965

Period	Number of acts	Percentage of total	Average number of acts/year
1960–1964	55	9.6	11.0
1965–1969	81	14.1	16.2
1970–1975	336	58.5	56.0
1976–1979	87	15.2	21.8
1980–1985	15	2.6	2.5
1960–1985	574	100.0	22.1

Reproduced from UNCTC, 1988, p. 315.

5.5.4   Deregulation

The deregulation of business has been a major trend in the late 1970s and the 1980s in the advanced capitalist economies. Attempts to remove the burden of government from the private sector have led to the removal of many constraints: but the necessary increase in other regulatory bodies – witness the deregulation of the London financial markets. A parallel policy trend has been the privatization of nationalized or state-owned industries. The scope for the private sector has increased; as a result, barriers to the increasing interpenetration of economies by multinational firms have declined.

5.5.5   Political risk and foreign direct investment

Recent changes in the world economy have thrust the assessment of political risk to the forefront of foreign investment decisions. The liberalization of Eastern Europe and the changes in the Soviet Union have created a great deal of investment interest in these hitherto relatively unexplored areas for multinationals. However, the uncertainty posed by rapid political change is a barrier to undertaking the necessary investment. The assessment of political risk is ultimately the responsibility of the investing firm that must decide the weight given to this factor in the overall decision. A variety of market assessment indicators that attempt to quantify political risk are commercially available. However, these indicators must alter rapidly in times of political change; they may have great difficulty in anticipating such events as the fall of the Shah in Iran and the quiet revolutions in Eastern Europe of the late 1980s and early 1990s. A comprehensive summary of definitions of political risk is given by Kobrin

Table 5.5.4   Selected Low-income Countries: Adverse Factors Inhibiting Foreign Investment

	Small size[a]	Negative growth[b]	Location[c]	Total number of adverse factors
Afghanistan		d	×	1
Bangladesh				0
Benin	×			1
Bhutan	×		×	2
Burkina Faso	×		×	2
Burma				0
Burundi	×		×	2
Central African Republic	×	×	×	3
Chad	×	×	×	3
Comoros	×	×	×	3
Djibouti	×	×		1
Equatoria Guinea	×	d		1
Ethiopia				0
Gambia	×			1
Guinea	×			1
Guinea-Bissau	×	×		2
Ghana		×		1
Haiti	×			1
Kenya				0
Lao People's Dem. Rep.	×	d	×	2
Madagascar		×		1
Malawi	×		×	2
Maldives	×		×	2
Mali	×		×	2
Mozambique		d		0
Nepal			×	1
Niger	×	×	×	3
Rwanda	×		×	2
Sao Tome and Principe	×		×	2
Senegal		×		1
Sierra Leone	×			1
Somalia		×		1
Sri Lanka				0
Sudan		d		0
Togo	×			1
Uganda		×	×	2
United Republic of Tanzania		d		0
Vietnam		×		1
Zaire		×		1
Zambia		×	×	2

Notes:

a) Small size is defined here as a gross national product below $US 2 billion in 1985.

b) Annual growth of per capital GNP less than or equal to 0 per cent between 1965 and 1985.

c) Land-locked countries or countries consisting of a small archipelago.

d) Classification open to dubt owing to poor quality or lack of data.

Reproduced from UNCTC (1988) p. 201.

Source: United Nations Centre on Transnational Corporations, based on Table XII.I and other international sources.

(1979). A simple method for building political risk into investment decisions is given by Brooke (1988). For examples of forecasting political risk and its management, see Ting (1988), Ghadar, Kobrin and Moran (1983). Political risk may stimulate outward investment from an unstable country as well as attract inward investment to a stable one. For a test of the impact of political risk on outward investment, see Tallman (1988).

A recent large-scale assessment of the global environment for foreign direct investment (United Nations Centre on Transnational Corporations (1988)) broadly comes to the conclusion that inward investment is now more politically secure. The acceptability of multinationals is now higher than at any time since the 1950s because of the desire of host countries for investment, employment, technology and skills and because of the increasing flexibility of the multinationals towards ownership policies, operations and strategies. National policies are now much more welcoming to inward investment. Previous implicit acceptance of multinationals has now become an explicit welcome. This does not mean that political risks have disappeared, nor that the political element in an explanation of the behaviour of multinational enterprises should be ignored (Boddewyn (1988)). Even in the United States, political tensions can be aroused by the fear of foreign control, particularly if it is concentrated by region, sector, or country of ownership (Graham and Krugman (1989)).

5.5.6 Source-country barriers to foreign direct investment

Barriers to foreign direct investment in the source country have generally been declining and are continuing to decline. Exchange controls as a policy weapon are now limited in advanced, industrialized countries and remain general only in centrally planned economies and the more highly regulated Third World countries.

However, other things being equal, governments prefer domestic investment to foreign investment. Although there is a realization that domestic investment is not a perfect substitute for foreign investment, attempts are made via the taxation system, the political system and even the legal system to bias the investor's preferences towards home rather than abroad.

5.5.7 Supranational barriers to international investment

Instruments at supranational level concerned with foreign direct investment are aimed both at facilitating international investment and at its regulation. Examples of facilitation are bilateral agreements on the promotion and protection of investment, which normally include provisions on standards of treatment (fair and equitable), national treatment and most-favoured-nation status, provision for compensation and due process of law in cases of nationalization and expropriation, rules on the transfer of profits and capital repatriation and procedures for the settlement of disputes.

Regional agreements may include general principles of conduct and protection measures as well as facilitation measures. Many of these regional agreements cover less-developed countries (e.g. the Andean Pact) or are primarily concerned with issues of development (Lomé Conventions).

Certain key facilitation issues are also covered in international instruments such as the Convention on the Settlement of Investment Disputes (World Bank), Codes of Liberalization of Capital Movements (Organization of Economic Cooperation and Development), Convention Establishing the Multilateral Investment Guarantee Agency (Organization of Economic Cooperation and Development, adopted but not yet in force). Other international instruments are regulatory and are in response to certain regional problems (Revised Code of Conduct for Companies from the European Community with Subsidiaries, Branches, or Representatives in South Africa) or particular product issues (International Code of Marketing of Breast-milk substitutes: The World Health Organization). More general agreements cover Transborder Data Flows, Transfrontier Movements of Hazardous Wastes, and Multilaterally Agreed Equitable Principles for the Control of Restrictive Business Practices (United Nations Conference on Trade and Development).

The more general and grandiose Codes of Conduct have caused concern in the international business community. These include the Organisation of Economic Cooperation and Development's Declaration on International Investment and Multinational Enterprises (1976), adopted in 1976, the draft United Nations Code of Conduct on the Transfer of Technology (under negotiation) and the draft United Nations Code of Conduct on Transnational Corporations. A listing of the main international instruments relating to multinational enterprise is given in the publication *Transnational Corporations in World Development: Trends and Prospects* (1988) pp. 338–9.

The United Nations code of conduct has been under discussion since the draft code was submitted in 1982. During this time the climate of opinion has shifted dramatically from one sympathetic to the creation of a watchdog at international level to a more concerted approach to liberalizing flows of international investment rather than regulation. Similarly, the United Nations Conference on Trade and Development Code of Conduct on the Transfer of Technology runs the risk of curtailing international investment by failing to allow multinational firms to capitalize returns on transfers of technology. The switch of concern away from the costs and towards the benefits of international investment must have an impact on the eventual form of these important codes (Buckley (1989)). The switch in emphasis on regulation is most evident in less developed countries

(Buckley and Clegg (1990)) and in the newly liberalized countries of Eastern Europe, who do not appear to want to let their desire for inward investment be shackled by restrictive international agreements. Moreover, they hope to become significant international investors in their own right, admittedly from a low base (McMillan (1987)).

However, there are legitimate areas where international regulation is desirable, if not essential. These include supranational regulation of transfer prices in internal markets, environmental protection, the sociocultural impact of multinationals, consumer protection, the settlement of international disputes and the resolution of conflicts of jurisdiction and investment insurance. The success of these ventures will be judged by the efficiency of the specific action while minimizing the barrier to investment implicit in any legislation.

References

Beamish, Paul (1988): *Multinational Joint Ventures in Developing Countries*. London: Routledge.

Bergsten, C. Fred, Horst, Thomas and Moran, Theodore H. (1978): *American Multinationals and American Interests*. Washington, D.C.: Brookings Institution.

Boddewyn, Jean J. (1988): 'Political Aspects of MNE Theory', *Journal of International Business*, Vol. 19, No. 3, Fall, pp. 341–64.

Bradley, D. (1977): 'Managing Against Expropriation', *Harvard Business Review*, July/August.

Brooke, Michael Z. (1988): 'Country Characteristics: An Overview' in Brooke, Michael Z. and Buckley, Peter J. (eds): *Handbook of International Trade*. London: Macmillan.

Buckley, Peter J. (1985): 'New Forms of International Industrial Cooperation' in Buckley, Peter J. and Casson, Mark: *The Economic Theory of the Multinational Enterprise*. London: Macmillan.

Buckley, Peter J. (1989): 'The Implications of the Economic Theory of the Multinational Enterprise for Control at International Level' in Buckley, Peter J.: *The Multinational Enterprise: Theory and Applications*. London: Macmillan.

Buckley, Peter J. and Clegg, Jeremy (1990): *Multinational Enterprises in Less Developed Countries*. London: Macmillan.

Buckley Peter J. and Pearce, R.D. (1979): 'Overseas Production and Exporting by the World's Largest Enterprises', *Journal of International Business Studies*, Vol. 10, No. 1, Spring, pp. 9–20.

Buckley, Peter J. and Pearce, R.D. (1981): 'Market Servicing by Multinational Manufacturing Firms: Exporting versus Foreign Production', *Managerial and Decision Economics*, Vol. 2, No. 4, December, pp. 229–46.

Buckley, Peter J. and Pearce, R.D. (1984): 'Exports in the Strategy of Multinational Firms', *Journal of Business Research*, Vol. 12, No. 2, June, pp. 209–26.

Burton, Fred and Inoue, H. (1984): 'Expropriation of Foreign Owned Firms in Developing Countries', *Journal of World Trade Law*, Vol. 18, No. 5, September October.

Faundez, Julie and Picciotto, Sol (1978): *The Nationalization of Multinationals in Peripheral Economies.* London: Macmillan.

Ghadar, Fariborz, Kobrin, Stephen J. and Moran, Theodore H. (eds) (1983): *Managing International Political Risk: Strategies and Techniques.* Washington, D.C.: Ghadar and Associates.

Graham, Edward M. and Krugman, Paul R. (1989): *Foreign Direct Investment in the United States.* Washington, D.C.: Institute for International Economics.

Hufbauer, G.C. and Adler, F.M. (1968): *Overseas Manufacturing Investment and the Balance of Payments.* Washington, D.C.: US Treasury Department.

Kobrin, Stephen J. (1979): 'Political Risk: A Review and Reconsideration', *Journal of International Business Studies*, Vol. X, No. 1, Spring/Summer, pp. 67–80.

McMillan, Karl H. (1987): *Multinationals From the Second World.* London: Macmillan.

OECD (1976): *Declaration on International Investment and Multinational Enterprises.* Paris: OECD.

Oman, Charles (1980): *The New Forms of Investment in Developing Countries.* Paris: OECD Development Centre.

Poynter, Thomas A. (1985): *Multinational Enterprises and Government Intervention.* Beckenham: Croom Helm.

Reddaway, W.B. et al. (1967 and 1968): *Effects of UK Direct Investment Overseas: Interim and Final Reports.* Cambridge: Cambridge University Press.

Tallman, Stephen B. (1988): 'Home Country Political Risk and Foreign Direct Investment in the United States', *Journal of International Business Studies*, Vol. 19, No. 2, Summer, pp. 219–34.

The Tariff Commission Report (1979): *Implications of Multinational Firms for World Trade and Investment and US Trade and Labor.* Washington D.C.: US Congress, Senate Committee on Finance.

Ting, Wenlee (1988): *Multinational Risk Assessment and Management.* Westport, Conn: Greenwood Press.

UNCTC (1988): *Transnational Corporations in World Development: Trends and Prospects.* New York: UNCTC.

Part 6

Management

Introduction

Part 6 reviews the body of knowledge on management decision-making. The underlying theories that influence decision-making have been examined in Part 1 and the environment in Part 2. The chapters in Part 6 look at the issues from the other side, as it were: the side of the influencers rather than the influences. They review studies carried out on international strategies and methods of operation along with related subjects like planning, finance, marketing, control and staffing and the multidimensions of accounting.

Contents

6.1

Strategic Decisions

The distinction between successful exporters like Boeing, successful importers like Sears Roebuck and successful multinational investors like IBM is a bogus one.

(Stopford and Turner (1986) p. 24)

This quotation neatly encapsulates the comprehensiveness of international corporate strategies, the guidelines of the corporate thrust abroad. A sense of direction, objectives and a driving force together with reactions, responses and adaptations make up the bundle of influences known as strategies. The trend of recent writing has been to expand the meaning of the word, avoiding too narrow a definition. Included have been:

the application of general strategies to international operations;
the development of specifically international strategies;
the adaptation of the company to foreign operations;
the adaptation of departments and other sub-units to foreign operations.

The word 'strategies' has been used by various authors to cover all those definitions or any combination and there has been considerable confusion over its meaning. Sometimes strategy appears to be identified with organization – not just a prime factor (as with the 'strategy and structure' school considered in Chapter 6.10); at others it is confused with planning. Some books have the word 'strategy' in the title and planning in the sub-title as if the two were identical; but usually strategy is understood as a first stage, the fixing of objectives and of the most probable routes for attaining those objectives.

Sometimes a publication implicitly adopts a number of different meanings. In the first four chapters of Wortzel and Wortzel (1985), for instance, the phrase 'international strategies' means:

how companies respond to international competitors (Chapters 1 and 2);
how companies decide where to locate their facilities (Chapter 3); and

whether companies decide to determine their major policies centrally or locally (Chapter 4).

None of those uses conveys the sense of direction crucial to the strategist, although Chapter 3 does discuss the uses and constraints on what the author calls 'global scanning'. Many of the concepts listed in the following paragraphs are derived from Ansoff's work which has been added to by others but not superseded.[1]

6.1.1   International strategy formation: major issues

The issues considered in this section are: the development of *objectives; general strategies* that will take a company abroad under suitable circumstances; and influences on the *choices* made between the objectives, specifically *international strategies*. Other relevant concepts are considered in Section 6.1.2.

Objectives

Objectives are crucial to the process of strategy formation. They provide the stimulus, indeed the reason, for the strategies as well as the criteria (in the form of targets) for evaluation. But the setting of objectives is not a tidy, one-off activity. It is normally a continuous process of change and adaptation, punctuated by occasional bursts of reappraisal in which objectives are not necessarily formulated: they may just emerge. Those companies that do formulate their objectives usually do so for the business as a whole; specific aims for the overseas business are sometimes found, especially where there is an international division.

Objectives are discussed under other headings like 'corporate mission' or 'company philosophy'. Both phrases summarize an often implicit approach – how a company sees itself and its strengths.

General strategies

The principal strategic options are listed below. These represent the most likely answers to fundamental questions about the direction or purpose of a company. A choice of any of the options may lead to the decision to go international under appropriate conditions.

(1)   Organic expansion, increasing sales of the same products.   This will lead to international operations when the costs of servicing the foreign markets are less than those at home or when the domestic market is saturated.

(2) Horizontal diversification, expansion into other products in the same sector. This is a common method, often found to be the most successful. A typical example is an electrical company that moves into television and radio manufacture after establishing a market in household goods, or an insurance company adding motor business to life policies. These moves do not necessarily result in foreign operations; sometimes horizontal expansion is chosen in preference to international but, even then, a merger with a firm that is already international will take a company abroad.

(3) Vertical diversification, when a company moves into the business of its customers or suppliers. In accordance with internalization theory, this expansion route will be undertaken when the costs of the internal market are below those of the external. There are hidden costs in either case that are often difficult to identify; these include problems caused by internal company politics when suppliers are purchased. Whatever the problems, vertical expansion frequently leads to international operations.

(4) Concentric marketing, when a company expands into unrelated businesses using similar marketing skills. This is most relevant to larger, cash-rich concerns, like tobacco companies aiming to reduce dependence on a market with little or no growth potential into one that also involves fast-moving consumer products like packaged foods or cosmetics.

(5) Concentric technology, when a company moves into other businesses that use similar technical skills.

(6) Conglomerate strategies, when companies buy other companies, unrelated to their core business, usually to obtain a viable portfolio that provides both growth and income. One research into United States conglomerates[2] showed that the growth abroad bore little relation to the product-mix at home. The main determinants were: transaction costs, the firm's previous experience in the host country and the spread of risks. This article suggests that when multinationals were first systematically studied (in the 1950s), few foreign subsidiaries were in unrelated businesses, but that by 1975 this had grown to 75 per cent for United States multinationals.

(7) Niche strategies, when a company has found a position in its domestic market – usually used of a smaller company that avoids direct competition with larger firms in a market controlled by an oligopoly. When it is perceived that the same niche is available in other countries, this becomes an international strategy.

Another classification is proposed by Robock and Simmonds[3] with a distinction between entering a few foreign markets and entering many; this is followed by the manner in which the entry strategy is matched to the competition – whether aggressively or defensively, for instance. This takes less account of the varied options available to a company, but does have the advantage of bringing the effects of competition into the process of strategy formation.

The choice

Any of these strategies can be used in combination with others; the niche strategy is likely to be so used. The choice of strategy will be related to a number of considerations, including:

(1) Experience. A process of organization-learning directs attention towards strategies that have been successful in the past and away from those that have not. Reviews of the evidence are likely to be biased by such experience and strong support is needed before embarking on an alternative strategy.

(2) Personality and organization. Biases are introduced by personal preferences and by existing units of the organization which lobby for resources.

(3) Targets. The setting of targets (like x per cent compound growth annually in return on investment) will lead to a search for new strategies when the existing business is seen to be incapable of achieving the targets. The targets, which will also form criteria for appraising the various options, can include return on investment, value added, cash flow or growth.

International strategies

Four issues are considered under this heading: the choice of an international strategy in its own right, the options available, the motives for operating internationally and the processes.

(1) An international strategy. Looking abroad to fulfil objectives can be seen as an alternative to the options already listed. This is a specifically international strategy employed when the company sees its main advantage to lie in developing the core business outside the home country, when the home market is saturated or when some of the varied businesses are by nature international.

(2) The options. A general decision to operate abroad is then broken down into a choice between the various options available to implement the decision. These are usually classified as export, knowledge agreements or investment. Each of these three main strategies covers a list of sub-options, discussed in separate chapters. In the past, scholars were inclined to treat them separately, as if in watertight compartments. They were either interested in export or in

investment: usually in investment. The strategic approach which regards export, investment, and licensing, as a means of servicing markets, rather than as independent phenomena, has now gained acceptance.

In practice, the choices are restricted by legislation (either encouraging or preventing local investment, for instance), by taxation which favours one method of operating against another, and by other special features of a particular market including its size and attractiveness.

(3) Motives for operating internationally. These have been discussed already in terms of the advantages to be gained from entering foreign markets and of reducing dependence on domestic markets. In practice, around 40 per cent of first moves abroad are estimated to be unplanned responses to export opportunities. Most investment comes later as a means of defending a market.

The service industries are seen to develop abroad differently but, in recent times, have done so very rapidly. Channon lists three motives for banks to move abroad: to maintain a position in the money markets, to match competitors and to meet the needs of existing customers.[4] That last motive seems the most common among the service industries and some manufacturers, but taking a successful business idea abroad has also been noted – especially in sectors like retailing.

(4) The processes of international growth. The thrust abroad can be seen in terms of a process, which may or may not be actively pursued. One commonly accepted view of the process is known as *incrementalism*.[5] This states that a company does not usually move in one step from a purely domestic concern to a fully fledged multinational; on the contrary, the process is a gradual one passing through a number of stages – perhaps selling in different regions of its own country before starting to operate outside. Once abroad, export precedes investment, and a learning curve enables a company gradually to build up a substantial international operation. This theory ties up with research findings that most foreign investment is defensive, supporting a market that already exists against competitive or governmental pressures. Incrementalism has also been supported by a body of research carried out, mainly through case studies, in a number of countries; the theory is also widely believed to be true by practitioners and consultants. It has been contrasted[6] with 'strategic choice' where a company anticipates the results of the process. Incremental theory relates to two developments, either of which can outdistance the other. One is the learning process, in which the company builds its own bank of experience, knowledge and contacts that enables it to move forward with confidence. The other is the physical process in which the moves are made step by step rather than in leaps.[7]

The theory of incrementalism has also been challenged, and clearly does not apply to all circumstances – large firms or those in stable and predictable markets, for instance – and there is an ambiguity inherent in the data. Clearly, too, incrementalism is less plausible in the service industries. This may be a reason why sectors like retailing were late on the international scene. There are other sectors, like extraction and mining, where incrementalism is hardly a relevant concept; there are also some entrepreneurs who manage to break out of every mould. But, allowing for all the exceptions, there does seem to be a typical process of gradual development rather than a springing on to the international scene in one planned swoop.

A related theory holds that policies, forced upon a company for defensive reasons, become available for market entry or other more aggressive uses. This applies to direct investment, stimulated by the need to defend one market but then available for entering others. A corporate infrastructure is brought into existence that includes the know-how, staff, facilities and other resources needed. Once the infrastructure is in place, vested interests are built up to support further expansion abroad.

Yet another relevant concept is that of a *threshold*. This interprets what happens when a company passes a stage in the development of its international operations at which the management system requires renewal; the existing system can no longer support the business that develops once the threshold has been crossed. One writer mentions 'threshold fear' as a factor inhibiting export,[8] but there is more than one threshold in the development of international strategies. Among those identified are:

(1) that between the time when a firm is mainly domestic and when export becomes a significant part of the business (say when export exceeds 20 per cent of sales);
(2) that between the time when a company develops international business through export and licensing and when it begins to own foreign investment (say when the investment reaches about 5 per cent of net assets);
(3) that between the time when a company has some foreign investments and when it becomes dependent on them (say when the investment reaches 20–30 per cent of net corporate assets).

The percentage figures are arbitrary, but give some idea of when the threshold is passed. This is illustrated in Figure 6.1.[9]

Departmental strategies

Individual departments, often but not necessarily marketing, are likely to develop international strategies before the company as a whole. For instance, the first thrust abroad may come from the purchasing department looking for fresh sources of supply, or it may come from finance looking for lower interest rates or tax havens. The activities of each department are considered later but, in general, a company can use the international contacts and experience gained from these activities for the benefit of the whole. There is little evidence,

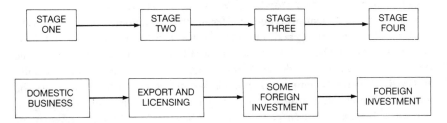

Figure 6.1. The Thresholds a Company Crosses as its International Strategies Develop

The arrows represent the thresholds described in the text.

Note: There is no inevitable progression between stages. Some can be missed, or the company can move backwards.

however, that this is what actually happens. Supply is a subordinate function and finance usually follows rather than anticipates the calls of marketing. The literature on multinationals is full of potential advantages that have not been actualized.

6.1.2 Other relevant concepts

Corporate culture and other socio-psychological methods of classification

One influence on the formation of strategies is the corporate culture within which the strategies are generated. If this is outward-looking, pressures towards operating abroad are likely to be accepted. Concentration on the core business is another aspect of company culture that leads abroad when the home market is saturated. This is not an aspect of international strategy that has been much discussed but it may well account for the different ways in which companies respond to similar stimuli.

The use of socio-psychological methods of classification: one attempt to use socio-psychological techniques in analysing corporate strategies was first promoted by Perlmutter in a much-quoted article.[10] This classified companies into ethnocentric − one-country-centred − polycentric − several-country-centred − and geocentric − world-centred. More recent updates have added a fourth category: regioncentric[11] (see Chakravarthy and Perlmutter (1985)). This approach has been followed by other authorities (see, for instance, Rutenberg (1982)) but is liable to the criticism that such a means of generalizing about corporate bodies can only be valid in a most general sense, if at all. The application of psychological characteristics to organizations raises a number of questions about how such characteristics can be ascertained. Even a phrase like 'corporate strategy' is suspect: does it refer to strategies adopted by a company as a whole, by its governing body, by its chief executive or by its public relations officer or whoever else? This problem is usually met by investigating what the company has done and declared intentions which appear to be generally accepted. To define a company orientation is much more doubtful; there may be many conflicting 'orientations' within it and the 'myths and folklore' to which Perimutter refers are often contradictory. Phrases like 'corporate mission' or 'company culture' suggest a more modest attempt to analyse the kind of influences at work in a particular concern.

Corporate mission

'Mission' is another concept used to express the underlying stimulus to corporate strategy.[12] The word is seen as the set of ideas that provide answers to questions like: in which activities does this firm see its particular advantages against the competition? Once the relationship between mission and strategy is established, further questions present themselves. These include the approach to markets, whether this is country-by-country or by looking at the world as a whole, and the degree of standardization or differentiation that matches the mission.

Levels of international involvement

The idea has been put forward that strategies can be analysed in terms of levels of involvement.[13] Five are proposed:

(1) companies that have neither discussed nor investigated the possibility of operating abroad;
(2) companies that have discussed and investigated the possibility, but taken no action;
(3) companies that have exported but are not currently doing so;
(4) companies that are exporters but not investors;
(5) companies that are both exporters and investors.

Clearly, that particular classification is biased towards the earlier stages of foreign business. A more refined taxonomy which distinguishes between licensing arrangements and investment, as well as the nature of the global spread, could provide a means of measuring and perhaps predicting strategies.

6.1.3 Trends

Opinion has moved away from attempts to explain international strategies from the point of view of motives within the company and to concentrate rather on the lure of world markets. In the next chapter an opposite trend is identified in studies of export. In the development of general international strategies, phrases like the 'global market place', unknown a few years ago, have become commonplace and are used to refer to a general response of a company to the world environment (see note 12). In spite of criticisms that it exaggerates a modest trend, the phrase is increasingly used. It is also used in a number of senses, including the view that increasingly products are not just aimed at one national market – that indeed many countries are too small to provide an adequate return on the growing costs of new product development – and that many factors are growing more international. Companies that deploy their resources internationally are likely, in the end, to defeat domestic competitors. Some writers see competition as the main factor in determining international strategies.[14] The phrase 'global positioning' takes this line of thought further by bringing together in a system active framework the influences on policy development, location and operations.

Control
A recent article points out a bias in the literature towards 'degree of control' in determining market entry strategies.[15] In this literature, control means the ability to determine a company's activities in a market – does a wholly owned subsidiary permit greater 'control' than a licensing arrangement? – rather than the technical implementation of a company's control system. This ability is regarded as the 'single most important determinant of both risk and reward'. In reviewing the literature, the article argues that in fact there is a trade-off between control and transaction costs; models suitable for analysing the trade-off are proposed. It may well be that this article is recording a swing away from the emphasis on control towards more concern with costs.

Strategy versus performance

At a time when survival has been higher on the agenda of many companies than growth, it is natural that short-term considerations should be more strongly opposed to long-term strategies. 'Short-termism', as it has come to be called, has been used to contrast the international thrusts of companies from different countries. Both British and American companies are often accused of over-emphasizing short-term considerations, as opposed to the Japanese who are said to take a longer-term approach. These assertions merit more thorough examination than they have been given in the past; they are not necessarily axiomatic.

International strategies for non-dominant companies

An important sub-theme is the niche strategy, the place of the 'non-dominant firm' developed by Mascarenhas (1986). This article summarizes a number of strategies whose logic is to attack less competitive markets quickly, to capture maximum geographic advantage from new products, to segment markets in order to avoid direct confrontation with leaders, to open up new markets by redesigning or customizing the corporate approach focusing on secondary rather than primary markets, to improve procurement internationally and to analyse the limits to a competitor's international marketing. Avoiding direct conflict with major international companies is a theme about which much more is likely to be heard with increasing concentration on the small firm.

International strategies for professional organizations

An unusual article by Nigel Mansfield[16] discussed the international strategies of a professional group: British consulting engineers. This showed that the value of overseas work by the consultants rose from about £1 billion worth in 1970 to over £50 billion in 1985. The main reasons given were: an optimum means for expansion and a maximum use of experience gained at home.

Notes

1. See Ansoff, H.I. (1965): *Corporate Strategy*. McGraw-Hill.
2. See Caves (1987).
3. See Robock and Simmonds (1983) pp. 284–5.
4. Channon (1977) p. 125.
5. Newbould and others (1987).
6. See Robock and Simmonds (1983) p. 273.
7. See Johanson and Vahine (1977).
8. See Dichtl and others (1983).
9. See Brooke and Remmers (1978) p. 5.
10. Perimutter, H.V. (1969): 'The tortuous evolution of the multinational Corporation', *Columbia Journal of World Business*, January–February, pp. 9–18.
11. See Chakravarthy and Perimutter (1985). For an example of other authorities who have followed Perimutter, see Rutenberg (1982).
12. Robock and Simmonds (1983), Chapter 13.
13. By Barrett and Wilkinson in Turnbull and Paliwoda (1986).
14. See Wortzel and Wortzel (1985) Chapter 1. The phrase 'global positioning' is quoted from Stopford and Turner (1985).
15. Anderson and Gatignon (1986).
16. Mansfield, N.R. (1986): Some international issues from the early 1980s facing British consulting engineers', *Proceedings of the Institution of Civil Enqineers, Part I*. October, No. 80, pp. 1211–31.
    Mansfield has since published further papers on the subject.
    For examples, see:
    Mansfield, N.R., Wheeler, C. and Young, S. (1987): 'The use of information for exporting construction services'. Report for Scottish Development Agency, April.
    Mansfield, N.R. (1987): 'International issues for British consultants', Proceedings of the Institution of Civil Engineers, Part 1, Vol. 82, December, pp. 1217–28.

Young, S., Wheeler, C. and Mansfield, N.R. (1987): 'A summary of some information and assistance sources and access routes for firms conducting international construction business'. Information paper, University of Strathclyde, December.

References

Allul, R.J. (1989): 'Formulating global strategy', *Planning Review*, Vol. 7, No. 2, March–April, pp. 22–8.

Anderson, E. and Gatignon, H. (1986): 'Modes of foreign entry: a transaction cost analysis and propositions', *Journal of International Business Studies*, Vol. 17, No. 3, Fall, pp. 1–26.

Brooke, M.A. and Remmers, H.L. (1978): *The Strategy of Multinational Enterprise* (2nd edn). Pitman.

Caves, R.E. (1987): *American Industry: Structure, Conduct and Performance* (6th edn). Prentice-Hall.

Chakravarthy, B.S. and Perlmutter, H.V. (1985): 'Strategic planning for a global business', *Columbia Journal of World Business*, Vol. 20, No. 2, Summer, pp. 3–10.

Channon, D.F. (1986): *Bank Strategic Management and Marketing*. Wiley.

Channon, D.F. (1977): *British Banking Strategy and the International Strategy*. Macmillan.

Channon, D.F. (1979): *Multinational Strategic Planning*. Macmillan.

Davidson, W.H. (1982): *Global Strategic Management*. Wiley.

Dichtl, E. et al. (1983): 'The foreign orientation of management as a central construct in export-centred decision-making process', *Research for Marketing*, Vol. 10, No. 1, pp. 7–14.

Doz, Y. (1986): *Strategic Management in Multinational Companies*. Pergamon.

Dymsza, W.A. (1984): 'Global strategic planning: a model and recent developments', *Journal of International Business Studies*, Vol. 15, No. 2, Fall, pp. 169–83.

Ghertman, M. and Allen, M. (1984): *An Introduction to the Multinationals* (Eng. edn). London: Macmillan.

Ghoshal, S. and Bartlett, C.A. (1987): 'Managing across borders: the new strategic requirements', *Sloan Management Review*, Vol. 28, No. 4, Summer, pp. 7–17.

Goodnow, J.D. (1985): 'Developments in international mode of entry analysis', *International Marketing Review*, Vol. 2, No. 3, Autumn, pp. 17–30. (This paper reviews theory and suggests some software for analysis.)

Greenly, G.E. (1989): *Strategic Management*. Prentice Hall.

Hedlund, G. and Kverneland, A. (1984): 'Investing in Japan – The Experience of Swedish Firms', Stockholm: Institute of International Business.

Hedlund, G. and Kverneland, A. (1985): 'Are Strategies for Foreign Markets Changing? The Case of Swedish Investment in Japan', *International Studies of Management and Organization*, Summer.

Hedlund, G. and Kverneland, A. (1986): 'Why is there so little foreign direct investment in Japan?', *Advances in International Marketing*, Vol. 1. Greenwich, Connecticut: JAI Press.

Hedlund, G. and Zander, I. (1986): 'Swedish MNC's Strategies for Europe. Preliminary Report for the Penelope Project', Research Paper Vol. 86, No. 14. Stockholm: Institute of International Business.

Hoogvelt, A. and Puxty, A.G. (1987): *Multinational Enterprise: an Encyclopaedic Dictionary of Concepts and Terms*. Macmillan.

Johanson, J. and Vahine, J.-E. (1977): 'The internationalization process of the firm – a model of knowledge development and increasing foreign market commitments', *Journal of International Business Studies*, Vol. 8, No. 1, Spring/Summer, pp. 23–32.

Kogut, B. (1985): 'Designing global strategies: profiting from operational flexibility', *Sloan Management Review*, Vol. 27, No. 1, Fall, pp. 27–38.

Leontiades, J. (1985): *Multinational Corporate Strategy: Planning for World Markets*. Heath.

Lorange, P. et al. (1986): *Strategic Control*. West Publishing.

Mansfield, N.R. (1986): 'Some international issues from the early eighties facing British consulting engineers', *Proceedings of the Institute of Civil Engineers*, No. 80, October, pp. 1221–31. (Strategic issues for a professional institute.)

Mascarenhas, B. (1986): 'International strategies of non-dominant firms', *Journal of International Business Studies*, Vol. 17, No. 1 Spring, pp. 1–25.

Mayer, R. (1984): *International Business: Issues and Concepts*. Wiley.

Neghandi, A.R. (1985): 'Management strategies and policies of American, German and Japanese multinational companies', *Management Japan*, Vol. 18, No. 1, Spring, pp. 12–20.

Newbould, G.D. et al. (1987): *Going International: The Experience of Smaller Companies Overseas* (2nd edn). Associated Business Press.

Ohmae, K. (1989): 'The global logic of strategic alliance', *Harvard Business Review*, March–April, pp. 143–56.

Porter, M.E. (ed.) (1986): *Competition in Global Industries*. Harvard.

Robock, S.H. and Simmonds, K. (1983): *International Business and Multinational Enterprise* (3rd edn). Irwin.

Root, F.R. (1982): *Foreign Market Entry Strategies*. American Management Association.

Rugman, A.G. (1985): 'Multinationals and Global competitive strategy', Vol. 15, No. 2, pp. 8–18.

Rutenberg, D.P. (1982): *Multinational Management*. Little, Brown.

Schrage, M. (1989): 'A Japanese giant rethinks globalization', *Harvard Business Review*, July-August, pp. 70–85.

Stopford, J.M. and Turner, L. (1986): *Britain and the Multinationals*. Wiley.

Taylor, M. and Thrift, N. (1986): *Multinationals and the Restructuring of the World Economy*. Croom Helm.

Turnbull, P. and Paliwoda, S.J. (1986): *Research in International Marketing*. Croom Helm.

Vernon, R. and Aharoni, Y. (eds) (1981): *State-owned Enterprises in the Western Economies*. Croom Helm.

Vernon, R. (1984): 'Japan's multinational in the 1980s', *Diamond Weekly* (in Japanese), 14 January.

Wortzel, H.V. and Wortzel, L.H. (1985): *Strategic Management of Multinationals: The Essentials*. Wiley.

6.2

Export

Export is used in this chapter of the direct sale of goods or services between independent companies in different countries. Trade between two units of the same company is considered under investment. By this definition, export, once occupying almost the whole of international trade, now accounts for less than half the value of goods and services crossing frontiers. Even so, it is a common, increasingly common, activity although confined to a minority of firms. In the United States, for instance, 250 out of 350,000 manufacturing firms account for 80 per cent of exports, while a large majority never sell abroad at all.[1]

Research into export over the last ten years has focused on the difference between the exporter and the non-exporter, when circumstances appear the same. This has been traced back into the condition of the company, its resources and its products, before export is undertaken and forward through various stages of development. Another change is in the approach to the subject. Export has traditionally been treated as an independent subject with little connection with other aspects of trade, like foreign investment on which most research was concentrated. More recent publications treat export in its own right, as an integral part of the thrust abroad. Concentration on the strategic aspects of international trade has placed export in a different perspective. In the process, the phrase 'export marketing' has been largely replaced by 'international marketing', and the subject correspondingly widened.

A new wave of research into the role of export in international strategies is reflected in the contents of this chapter , which include: factors supporting or inhibiting export; export strategies; and the environment of the exporter.

6.2.1 Export: origin, development and performance

Recent academic work has been concerned with subjects like pre-export, performance and the obstacles to export. These are covered in this section under the headings: 'pre-export' and 'factors supporting or inhibiting export'.

Pre-export

Research has been concentrated on a number of groups of companies: those that began to export and then abandoned the attempt, those that never began and why they did not, those with successful export records. The thrust of studies on pre-export is towards assessing the factors that condition subsequent performance. A virtuous circle has been identified in which pre-export activity leads to a commitment to export; this, in its turn, leads to active export behaviour. If successes follow, the commitment is reinforced and the circle is completed. In contrast, inactive pre-export behaviour leads to a tentative commitment, followed by a passive approach. If, as so often, this leads to poor results, the commitment is further reduced. This completes the vicious circle – possibly broken by a withdrawal from exports that are then claimed to be unprofitable. The following issues have been found to distinguish active from inactive pre-export behaviour.

(1)   Attitude of decision-makers
A major trend of recent studies has been to emphasize the significance of management attitudes in determining whether or not a company responds to commercial influences in favour of export. The attitudes identified are not just in the form of 'We support exporting', but include values (understanding of and sympathy for citizens of other countries) and breadth of vision and willingness to innovate. The penetration of foreign markets is more likely to be undertaken by companies accustomed to adopting new ideas. In this it resembles other forms of innovation. An attitude favourable to export may well be supported by contacts, experiences and even personal tastes that favour the idea of operating abroad. The ability among senior executives to speak foreign languages may be an additional factor.

(2)   Track record of decision-makers
A company needs a record of general management ability and good performance to embark upon exports. The idea that it is possible to turn one's back on failure at home by selling abroad is not usually recommended. On the contrary, a company takes abroad its strengths, in order to build on them.

(3)   Ability to sell in different regions of the home country
It has been demonstrated, in more than one sample[2] that many successful exporters have first penetrated regional markets within their own country. This has given them insight into handling markets where there are subtle local differences, as well as into packaging and distribution, before tackling such issues on the more complex international scale. Product adaptation is another skill that may be learnt through regional sales.

(4) Developing useful contacts

Much export depends on contacts; developing and cultivating businesses which can play a part in, or advise on, the move abroad is another part of pre-export.

(5) The saleable product or service

The product advantage remains crucial, although it is often assumed in modern studies of export. One reason for its comparative neglect is that an increasing range of products have found their way into international trade. The folklore is increasingly filled with stories of unlikely goods or services being sold abroad, and there seems to be little future in attempting to identify 'saleable products'. The criterion is success at home, especially in finding an appropriate niche, a willingness to adapt to foreign needs and to accept that the niche may be different abroad. One study has also illustrated the importance of productivity and product development in export.[3]

(6) The triggering mechanisms

The phrase 'triggering mechanism' has been used of a number of factors that stimulate a will to export. Probably the most common is the arrival of a chance order or an enquiry from abroad. It has long been recognized that this may be a trap: it may trigger off exports before a company is ready. The subsequent failure and disillusionment has been thoroughly documented. In one sample 60 per cent of respondents agreed they had been persuaded into exporting before they were ready, while as many as 86 per cent of those who failed had begun by experiencing some successes.[4] Other trigger mechanisms from outside the company include:

a perception that the market is saturated;
a perception that there are foreign markets that are less competitive; and
pressures or suggestions from official bodies like chambers of commerce, trade associations or other exporters.

From within a company, the search for export markets may result from a realization that:

profit and growth targets cannot be achieved on the domestic market;
there is excess capacity which can be absorbed by sales abroad; and
the international potential of a product or service has come to be understood.

Any of these factors will produce export if it is seen by the decision-makers as a viable option – another reason for the emphasis on attitudes.

Summary

A substantial body of research has now been built up under titles like 'pre-export' and 'internationalization'. Export is seen as an innovative and experimental activity in a company for which adequate preparation is essential. The preparation takes in resources, abilities and attitudes without which foreign trade may be triggered before a company is able to cope.

Factors supporting or inhibiting export

The search for factors to explain why some companies respond to the export lure and others do not – and why some succeed and others fail under similar circumstances – has led to a concentration on internal advantages and hazards. One study that criticizes this approach emphasizes the importance of an 'ecological view', a firm's response to the environment rather than to its own strengths and weaknesses.[5] Another critique has listed 17 obstacles to exporting. Under factor analysis, these were subsumed under the following headings (the mean values are given in brackets): exogenous economic constraints rated the most significant (3.5), comparative distance (2.6), lack of export commitment (2.6), national export policies (2.6) and the strength of the competition (2.1). This was a single-industry study of an industry in which the force of external economic conditions (like the effects of exchange rates and of foreign import tariffs) may well have been particularly high; but if this is accepted as a reason why this study is out of line with others, the need for further single industry studies is clear. Samples of country, region or size of company may give average results that do not reflect the actual situation of companies in specific sectors.

Another list[6] places special emphasis on: sufficient opportunities at home (73 per cent of sample), complexity of foreign trade (66 per cent) and government constraints (65 per cent). Costs and lack of capital also come high on the list along with foreign competition. Among writers that emphasize the internal factors,[7] a number of advantages are identified, including the expectations of managers (beliefs about the probable outcome of exporting and the growth and security of the markets), levels of commitment (how thoroughly the market planning is undertaken, for instance) and distinctive assets, including technology, expertise and unique products that give a firm special advantages.

Export propensity is a concept that summarizes findings both before and after the phrase was made current in Olsen and Wiedersheim-Paul (1978). In their model, propensity – the difference between a firm which is likely to export and one which is not – consists of a complex pattern of interacting characteristics and stimuli. Initially, corporate characteristics – product, market and potential – combine with export stimuli to influence the decision-makers. They, in their turn, perceive the stimuli, internal and external, in ways that will lead to decisions that vary according to the perceptions. The characteristics of the decision-makers that influence this perception are divided into their 'cognitive style', the way they collect and evaluate information, and their 'degree of international orientation'. This latter, picked up in other writings, refers to attitudes that are likely – or unlikely – to stimulate export. As a result of mediating the characteristics and the stimuli through the perceptions, the decisions can be either actively to seek export sales, to accept them passively or not to export at all. The whole model is an attempt to identify where the *propensity* is or is not likely to be present. Other writers[8] have distinguished subjective managerial characteristics, like personality and value, and objective ones such as availability of qualified staff.

Psychic distance (sometimes called psychological distance) is a concept that has gained currency and is used in some writings listed in this section. The phrase is often used vaguely, but is useful in accounting for difficulties new exporters face in coping with strange cultures. When this concept is given a normative status – 'the successful exporter limits the psychic distance' – its force is more questionable. The small, inexperienced company may find greater opportunities and less competition in just those markets where the psychic distance is greatest.

Critical mass is another important concept, affirming that success in an export market depends on achieving a critical market share. The calculation of the critical share will depend on how the market is defined, but there is evidence that some failures may be due to ignoring the need for gaining an adequate share in a selected segment or niche before tackling other markets.[9]

6.2.2 Export strategies

Once the decision has been made that export is the correct strategy for a company, a number of sub-strategies become available. These can be classified in a number of ways including the type of market, the approach to the market or the route adopted. Robinson (1984) has produced a comprehensive list.[10]

Conventional wisdom has suggested a choice between conflicting criteria. On the one hand the company should limit its export efforts to a small number of markets which can be covered intensively and in which a viable market share can be achieved as soon as possible. As against this is pressure to hedge the risks of each market by entering others in which the national economy, the competition and other influences will have different consequences.

One study has classified export strategies according to both the spread of markets and the attitude to international markets.[11] The latter are divided into 'marketer' (adapts products and segments), 'quasi-marketer' (limited adaptability) and 'seller' which does not adapt. Each of these strategies can be used in the world or in neighbouring markets, but not necessarily to the same effect.

Another method of classification is according to whether the sale is made at home or abroad and whether a third party is involved. This is illustrated in Figure 6.2.1; the numbers in the following list correspond with those in the Figure.

(1)   To a foreign buyer at home
This is the simplest and quickest route abroad where it is feasible. It may be possible in consumer goods where a foreign buyer for a large retail company

	At home	Abroad
Without third parties	(1) To a foreign buyer	(2) To a foreign buyer (3) To a foreign subsidiary
With third parties	(4) To an export house	(5) To a foreign agent/distributor
	(6) Through cooperation on the part of exporting companies	

Figure 6.2.1   A Typology of Export Options

visits a country. There are also occasional opportunities to sell to other foreign purchasing organizations, including government agencies; but competition for large orders is such that this cannot commonly be carried out entirely in the home country. It is generally assumed that sales at home are not greatly different from other domestic sales and are mainly opportunistic in nature; this subject has not been much studied except in the context of buyer–seller relationships. The seller still has to organize delivery but may use the services of a freight forwarder.

(2)   To a foreign buyer abroad
This is the traditional method of export to which old-established exporting countries are deeply wedded. Interviews with directors of many British companies, for instance, elicit responses along the lines of: 'We put all our export effort into travelling salesmen, supported by members of the board who travel widely.' Direct sales have advantages where there is a limited or spasmodic market, especially for capital goods, but nowadays these are counterbalanced by the needs for a local presence which:

provides a more rapid response to opportunities;
provides a closer monitoring of developments;
provides the customer with greater confidence in after-sales service and the provision of spares;
matches the competition; and
assists the company to concentrate on key markets.

(3)   To a foreign branch or subsidiary
Sales to a foreign unit of a company are considered in Chapter 6.4.

(4) Sales to an export house at home

This is suitable for the small company for whom it provides a relatively trouble-free method of expanding sales. It is unlikely to be a viable method for making a sustained impact on foreign markets, however, for it does not take the company through the learning process necessary to develop an export strategy. An understanding of foreign markets and of selling, distributing, currency exchange and the other issues that make up export marketing is not acquired through an intermediary. On the other hand, some research has demonstrated that export management companies in the United States promote exports effectively; much depends on the relationship between the exporter and the export-management company and the contractual structure of this relationship.[12]

Similar advantages and disadvantages apply when direct sales abroad are serviced through an export house at home. In this case there should be more feedback from the foreign market to stimulate product adaptation, but most of the elements of export will not be learnt. The company will not cross the threshold that leads to export until a comprehensive foreign policy is adopted.

(5) To a foreign agent

The most viable option for the long-term exporter without facilities abroad is to operate through a foreign agent. This is also an aspect of export on which many studies have concentrated. Relationships with agents are found to cause difficulties, summarized in the following notes.

(a) *Definition.* The word 'agent' is here used as a generic term for a range of activities. Macmillan and Paulden (1979) identify 28 different kinds of agreement which have varying legal meanings in different countries. These shade into one another and can be seen as a continuum of arrangements with freelance sales representatives at one end and, at the other, companies that fulfil all the business activities – warehousing, after-sales service and credit (del credere) agents at the other. Agent companies are given different names with different implications in each country. In commercial jargon there is a major distinction between, for instance, the agent and the distributor. For present purposes, both are considered as elements along a continuum.

Commercial and company law in various countries incorporates agency agreements in different ways. A significant issue is the degree of protection afforded against the foreign principal. In some countries those agency agreements in which the agent undertakes a full marketing programme are especially protected. If the agreement is terminated, compensation for loss of goodwill has to be paid to the agent; this is calculated on the basis of loss of anticipated profits, usually from two to seven years. This is a classic trap for exporters from countries like Britain and the United States which do not have such a law. Such a regulation will probably be extended throughout the European Community in due course. Another legal issue is that of restraint of competition. A principal often attempts to prevent an agent dealing in competitors' goods and an agent attempts to obtain an exclusive franchise. Under certain conditions such arrangements may fall foul of competition regulations. In the European Community, for instance, most of the cases brought under the competition policy have been about restrictive clauses in agency agreements.

(b) *Collaboration agreements.* Some companies find any form of collaborative agreement difficult to manage. An intimate knowledge of one another's businesses is implied, while corporate policies and cultures have to be brought together more closely than in other commercial relationships, such as buyer to supplier. An agency agreement is likely to be a company's first collaboration across frontiers and may well be the first at home or abroad. This means that the principles and procedures necessary for handling such an agreement are not in place; the first experience may be traumatic. For the larger, more experienced, company there is another kind of problem when the methods of dealing with a collaborator do not fit into an administrative system – collaboration increases occasions of uncertainty that a company usually attempts to reduce. There is uncertainty about the agent's business methods and priorities; this is compounded by a potential conflict of interest over supply, pricing, market segment and other policies. The conflict can occur whether or not the company is experienced but is likely to be more intractable with the larger firm.

(c) *Conflicts of interest.* An agency agreement starts from a common interest – a point often overlooked by academic studies in which interviews are conducted after the problems have begun to appear. The principal has a product or service but neither the resources nor the necessary knowledge to enter the market; the agent is assumed to know the market but to be looking for products. This initial identity of interest – and the euphoria that results from a satisfactory initial meeting – can lead to inadequate agreements with agents who have been selected with insufficient appraisal. The problems that result become apparent later.

One problem is that of time-scale. Quick returns may be required by one partner, either because that is the strategy for a particular product or for entering a foreign market or – more urgently – because of a cash crisis. If the other partner is looking for long-term growth and wants to put all available resources into developing the market instead of making a profit, a conflict can soon break out. Either the principal or the agent can opt for a short- or long-term policy.

There are also numerous opportunities for conflict in the marketing policies. For example the agent may have a different view of a market segment from the principal. This view may well be supported by a knowledge of buying habits in the agent's country; at the same time the principal may consider that the agent's proposals are damaging to a carefully constructed corporate image and cannot be tolerated for that reason. Disputes like this are hard to resolve, since there is no profit-and-loss calculation to which appeal can be made. The difficulty over supply arises because the principal is concerned with numerous markets, each demanding priority; the agent is concerned with its market only.

The conflicts of *interest* are often exacerbated by conflicts of *opinion* and difficulties caused by lack of *resources*. An ironical example of this latter is a problem of success. If a business develops rapidly, it can outgrow its agent's resources. The principal is then faced with the alternative of either changing the agent company – a poor reward for good performance – or injecting funds into it. The importance of conflict resolution is emphasized by a Swedish study[13] of 140 companies involved in export cooperation projects in which only about a quarter were rated a success.

(d) *Methods of conflict reduction.* One method of limiting, or eliminating, a conflict has been mentioned: injecting funds into the agent company. This can be carried out in a number of different ways, including a long-term loan, some equity, or a direct purchase. Many a subsidiary has started its existence as an agent. Another is by improved selection (methods for selecting agents are similar to those for selecting licensees, outlined in the next chapter). Yet another is by maintaining close contact, so that problems can quickly be resolved at a high level in both the principal and agent companies. The exact form that this contact should take is a matter of controversy. There is some evidence that the closer the relationship resembles that between a company and a subsidiary, the better the performance. This is not easy to achieve and the subject merits further investigation. The opposite extreme, which appears to be common, is characterized in one paper as: 'the local agent represents a cheap, quasi-disposable export channel requiring a low level of commitment, a low level of expenditure and very often very little effort in their selection'.[14]

Criteria for appraising an agent's performance will vary according to the type of arrangement. In some cases there is detailed monthly reporting on sales, income, market share and other key indicators; in others there is an annual report. Many arrangements in between those two extremes are known. The formal reports may or may not be accompanied by meetings between senior representatives of the principal and agent companies; there is a strongly held belief that regular meetings are important for good performance; but there is an almost equally strongly held view that the time and expense of regular meetings cannot be justified. The appropriate method of appraisal will follow from the kind of relationship established.

Concentrating on the terms of the agreement is another form of conflict reduction. At interviews, executives are inclined to belittle the importance of the contract, emphasizing the need to build a business relationship. As against this, it has been pointed out that the relationship is more firmly established if the details of the agreement have been closely discussed beforehand. The discussion is a useful discipline. Not every conflict is resolved, and a failure can be met either by breaking the agreement or by buying the agent. Many a subsidiary has come into existence in this way.

(6) Through cooperation on the part of exporting companies
Export promotion schemes frequently contain offers of collaboration for promoting exports. These take a number of forms including a group of non-competing companies jointly attacking a market or a large exporter acting as agent for a

small company (the so-called piggy-back scheme). The extent of such arrangements and their effectiveness has been little explored. Terpstra lists a number of successful schemes in the United States,[15] but the evidence remains limited. Organizational problems that constrain collaboration deals – like conflicts of interest and an unwillingness to share information – particularly appear to affect export cooperation projects.

The selling of systems, an increasing preoccupation of exporting companies, involves cooperation of a different order. A number of the options available for establishing, organizing and controlling a project that includes a systems package are detailed in a Swedish case study of the capital goods industry.[16]

Exporting by small firms

Studies of the export activities of small firms have been carried out in numerous countries, often sponsored by government departments. One example is the work of Garnier in the University of Sherbrooke in studies of the printing and electrical industries sponsored by the Canadian Department of Trade and Commerce.[17] See also Darling and Postnikoff (1985).

6.2.3   The environment of the exporter and other issues

A detailed research study showed the following issues listed in order of importance, as the major export questions for the late 1980s.[18] Changes in the international trade framework (the General Agreement on Tariffs and Trade), methods of dealing with the international debt situation, the development of United States trade policy and trade law, exchange rates, countertrade, protectionism, trade in services, trade imbalances between industrialized countries, trade controls, high-technology trade, employment effects of trade, energy trade, development of trading blocs, foreign direct investment, agricultural trade, newly industrialized country trade and international tax issues.

All-embracing would be a suitable sub-title for this section. The world economic order, the economy of each individual nation, international law, national legal and tax systems and the cultural differences between countries are a few of the elements that complicate the environment of the exporter. These issues, including the political problems of both exporting and importing countries, are considered elsewhere. This section concentrates on protectionism, dumping, documentation and distribution.

Protectionism

Writers on protectionism usually regard it as a bad thing; they quote economic theory to demonstrate the waste involved.[19] Against this is ranged a great deal of opinion from governments, companies, trade unions and other interested organizations. Their view is usually expressed in the form of 'Free Trade is ideal, but this industry needs protection until ...' The words after the 'until' vary from supporting an infant industry to winning time for adjustment in a declining one. The place of protectionism in theory, as well as in the councils of international organizations, is discussed elsewhere in this book; meanwhile, companies have to reckon that it will not suddenly disappear and will affect their selection of markets. Almost every list of factors that discourage export includes this subject.

Protection is normally divided into two parts – the tariff and the non-tariff barriers. The former are seen as relatively simple to cope with: the tariff is a straight addition to the price, and a calculation will determine the conditions under which the market would be viable. Exchange rate movements can have a similar effect to tariff barriers. If a currency is devalued, imports become more expensive. The rate is not entirely under government control in countries where it is floating, but the effect remains.

The non-tariff barriers are more troublesome: in particular, they are hard to predict. Each country has its own particular laws on matters such as health and safety; these are likely to have been stimulated by the pinpointing of problems – perhaps as the result of a scandal, and lobbying by a pressure group. Such laws may not have been aimed at foreign producers, but may have the effect of forcing foreign companies to abandon the market or make substantial adaptations to their products. These accidental barriers can be distinguished from obstacles imposed with the purpose of making life difficult for importers, the adopting of arbitrary standards of acceptability. There is a third category which makes for special problems in the service industries. This is concerned with professional practices and standards that have been hallowed by tradition. They may have statutory force, and legislation may include support for professional status as well as measures to counter malpractices from which a particular country has suffered.

Dumping

A notoriously difficult condition to identify, dumping is the practice of selling products at what is assumed to be below cost price in order to destroy competition. The trend of recent cases has been to use methods like import controls (usually labelled voluntary and negotiable) rather than direct legal action to limit suspected examples of dumping.

Documentation and distribution

Although little discussed in academic literature, there are a number of issues connected with documentation and distribution.

(1) Comparative advantage. Documentation procedures have a cost, and the way they are applied can constitute a non-tariff barrier. The additional costs of transportation, including frontier formalities and other procedures, affect the comparative advantage of a product.

(2) Organization. Documentation and delivery across frontiers are two of the distinctive features of international business which influence the decision to establish a specialist department. Failure to employ adequate skills in this field is a common cause of traumatic experiences which influence changes in the corporate structure.

(3) Management. In the teaching of export, it has been suggested, documentation has been over-emphasized at the expense of strategy. For management, however, documentation and distribution remain important concerns. Neglect at this point can damage both profitability and the relationship with the customer.

Other issues

The financing of exports, product policies, pricing and the buyer–seller relationship are considered in later chapters.

Notes

1. See Darling and Postnikoff (1985).
2. See, for example, Welch and Wiedersheim-Paul (1980a).
3. See Schneeweis (1985).
4. See Bilkey, W.J. and Tesar, G. (1977): 'The export behaviour of smaller sized firms', *Journal of International Business Studies*, Vol. 7, No.1, Spring/Summer, pp. 93–8. See also Czinkota (1982).
5. See Reid (1983). The statements in the following sentences are from Bauerschmidt and others (1985), p. 121.
6. See Kaynack and Kothari (1984).
7. See, for example, Cavusgil and Nevin (1981) and Dichtl and others (1984).
8. See, for instance, Dichtl and others (1984).
9. See Attiyeh and Wenner (1979).
10. See Robinson (1984), p. 40.
11. See Cooper and Kleinschmidt (1985).
12. See Bello and Williamson (1985).
13. See Strandell, A.C. (1985): 'Export cooperation: company experience', a typescript report of the National Industrial Board (SIND) of Sweden, September.
14. See Wheeler, C.N. and Livingstone, N.G. (1986): 'The agent and export strategy: a study of manufacturers and exporters of machinery in the Strathclyde Region', unpublished paper, Marketing Department, University of Strathclyde, March.

15. See Terpstra (1983), pp. 330–3.
16. See Mattson, L.-G. (1980/1): 'Cooperation between firms in international systems selling', Department of Business Administration, University of Uppsala, reprint series.
17. See Garnier, G. (1982): 'Comparative export behaviour of small Canadian firms in the printing and electrical industries', in Czinkota and Tesar (1982). This was based on two reports produced for the Department of Trade and Commerce in 1978.
18. The list is quoted from Czinkota (1986). Participants in the research included legislators, administrators, executives and academics. The whole article should be read.
19. The subject of protectionism recurs frequently in Chapters 3.1 to 3.3 where efforts to curb it through treaty organizations are detailed. Relevant trade theory is discussed in Part 1. Examples of writings on the subject are: 'The costs of protectionism', *EFTA Bulletin*, No. 25, July–September 1984, pp. 4–5. See also 'The appropriate response to trade barriers and unfair trade practices in other countries', *American Economic Review*, No. 74, May 1984, pp. 81–7.

References

Aranda, L. (1986): 'International training programmes for success', *Training Development Journal*, No. 40, April, pp. 71–3.

Attiyeh, R.S. and Wenner, D.L. (1979): 'Critical mass: Key to export profits', *Business Horizons*, December, pp. 28–38.

Bauerschmidt, A. et al. (1985): 'Common factors underlying barriers to export: studies in the US paper industry', *Journal of International Business Studies*, Vol. 16, No. 3, Fall, pp. 111–23.

Bello, D.C. and Williamson, N.C. (1985): 'Contractual arrangements and marketing practices in the indirect export channel', *Journal of International Business Studies*, Vol. 16, No. 2, Summer, pp. 65–82.

Bilkey, W.J. (1985): 'Development of export marketing guidelines', *International Marketing Review*, Vol. 2, No. 1, Spring, pp. 31–40.

Brooke, M.Z. and Buckley, P.J. (1988): *Handbook of International Trade*. London: Macmillan.

Burton, F.N. and Shlegelmilch, B.B. (1987): 'Profile analysis of non-exporters versus exporters grouped by export involvement', *Management International Review*, Vol. 27, No. 1, pp. 38–48.

Cannon, T. (1979): 'International and export marketing', *Managemet Bibliographies and Reviews*, Vol. 5, No. 2.

Cavusgil, S.T. (1984): 'Organization characteristics associated with export activity', *Journal of Management Studies*, Vol. 21, No. 1, January.

Cavusgil, S.T. and Nevin, J.R. (1981): 'Internal determinants of export marketing behaviour: an empirical investigation', *Journal of Marketing Research*, No. 18, February, pp. 114–19.

Citrin, D. (1985): 'Exchange rate changes and exports of selected Japanese industries', *IMF Staff Papers*, Vol. 32, No. 3, September, pp. 409–29.

Clifton, E.V. (1985): 'Real exchange rates, import penetration, and protectionism in industrial countries', *International Monetary Fund Staff Papers*, No. 32, September, pp. 513–36.

Cooper, R.G. and Kleinschmidt, E.J. (1985): 'The impact of export strategy on export sales performance', *Journal of International Business Studies*, Vol. 16, No. 1, Spring, pp. 37–55.

Czinkota, M.R. (1986): 'International trade and business in the late 1980s: an integrated US perspective', *Journal of International Business Studies*, Vol. 17, No. 1, Spring, pp. 127–34.

Czinkota, M.R. and Tesar, G. (eds) (1982): *Export Management*. Praeger.

Darling, J.R. and Postnikoff, J.F. (1985): 'Strategic information for small business', *Journal of Small Business Management*, Vol. 23, No. 4, October, pp. 28–37.

Davies, G. and Freebury, C. (1987): 'The Management of Documentation by British Exporters', *International Journal of Physical Distribution and Logistics Management*, Vol. 17, No. 6.

Dichtl, E. and others (1984): 'Export-decision of small and medium-sized firms: a review', *Management International Review*, Vol. 24, No. 2, pp. 49–60.

Dichtl, E. and others (1983): 'The foreign orientation of management as a central construct in export-centred decision-making process', *Research for marketing*, Vol. 10, No. 1, pp. 7–14.

Glover, K.A. (1983): *Developing foreign export as a market entry strategy*. HBS Case Services, Harvard Business School.

Green, J.T. and Allaway, A.W. (1985): 'Identification of export opportunities', *Journal of Marketing*, No. 49, Winter, pp. 83–8.

Joynt, P. and Welch, L. (1985): 'A strategy for small business internationalization', *International Marketing Review*, Autumn, pp. 64–73.

Kaynack, E. (1985): 'The role of product planning for export marketing', *Service Industries Journal*, No. 52, July, pp. 200–14.

Kaynack, E. and Kothari, V. (1984): 'Export behaviour of small and medium-sized manufacturers: some policy guidelines for international markets', *Management International Review*, Vol. 24, No. 2, pp. 61–9.

Macmillan, C. and Paulden, S. (1979): *Export Agents* (new edn). Aldershot: Gower.

Olsen, H.C. and Wiedersheim-Paul, F. (1978): 'Factors affecting the pre-export behaviour of non-exporting firms', in Ghertman, M. and Leontiades, J. (eds): *European Research in International Business*, pp. 283–305. North Holland.

Piercy, N. (1981): 'Company internationalization: active and reactive exporting', *European Journal of Marketing*, Vol. 15, No. 3.

Reid, S.D. (1983): 'Firm internationalization costs and strategic choice', *International Marketing Review*, Winter, pp. 44–56.

Robinson, R.D. (1984): *Internationalization of Business*. Dryden Press.

Sarathy, R. (1985): 'High technology exports from newly industrializing countries: the Brazilian commuter aircraft industry', Vol. 27, No. 2, Winter, pp. 60–84.

Schlegelmilch, B.B.: 'Can export performance be explained by attitudinal differences?' *Managerial and Decision Economics*, No. 7, pp. 249–54.

Schlegelmilch, B.B.: 'Controlling country and industry specific influences on export behaviour', *European Journal of Marketing*, Vol. 20, No. 2, pp. 54–71.

Schlegelmilch, B.B. (1985): 'Internal determinants of export behaviour of British and

German firms', *Proceedings of the European Marketing Academy Conference*, April, Schelefeld.

Schneeweis, T. (1985): 'A note on international trade and market structure', *Journal of International Business Studies*, Vol. 16, No. 2, Summer, pp. 139–52.

'Strategies for exporting', (1986): *Research and Development*, No. 28, July, pp. 23–4.

Terpstra, V. (1983): *International Marketing* (5th edn). Dryden Press.

Turnbull, P. and Paliwoda, S.J. (1986): *Research in International Marketing*. Croom Helm.

Walters, P.G. (1985): 'A study of planning for export operations', *International Marketing Review*, Vol. 2, No. 3, Autumn, pp. 74–81.

Welch, L.S. and Wiedersheim-Paul, F. (1980a): 'Domestic expansion: internationalization at home', *South Carolina Essays in International Business*, No. 2, December.

Welch, L.S. and Wiedersheim-Pual, F. (1980b): 'Initial exports – a marketing failure', *Journal of Management Studies*, Vol. 17, No. 3, October.

Yaprak, A. (1985): 'An empirical study of the differences between small exporting and non-exporting US firms', *International Marketing Review*, Vol. 2, No. 2, Summer, pp. 72–83.

Yavas, V. and Glauser, M.J. (1985): 'Successful exporting to the Arabian Gulf region: a survey of Bahrain consumers', *Journal of Marketing Management*, Vol. 1, No. 2, Winter, pp. 195–200.

Yorke, D.A. (1984): 'Market profit centres: fiction or an emerging reality?' *Management Accounting*, February, pp. 21–3.

6.3

Knowledge Agreements

The title is used to cover licensing, franchising and the numerous other forms of contractual arrangement between independent companies in which know-how is sold. The role of these agreements in world trade (where they still play a minority party) and the circumstances under which they are likely to be used are discussed in Part 1; their use is seen to depend on the relative costs and benefits of the external market or that internal to the company. This chapter will examine the installation and operation of the agreements, beginning with a list of some of the forms they take. The definitions below are generally accepted by academics, but the names are often interchanged by practitioners, who use words like licensing, franchising, management contracts or joint ventures for the same exercise.

Licensing is the sale of technical knowledge in the form of patents, specifications, blueprints and other documents, together with the back-up services necessary to ensure that the resultant products are manufactured, sold and maintained efficiently.

Franchising is the sale of a package of commercial know-how including trade-marks, signs, emblems and other features which together make a viable business possible. The use of a franchised package by an independent company is usually conditional upon the observance of rules about the training of staff, customer service, quality control and other requirements.

Contract manufacture is used of arrangements in which one company manufactures another's products for a fee. In this case the contract manufacturer's plant is performing a single function; the principal carries out all the other functions from design to marketing.

Technical cooperation (aid, assistance) agreements include a license but also the management methods required for the successful development of the business.

Apart from the more acceptable name (particularly for newly industrializing and formerly socialist countries) these agreements are indistinguishable from management contracts.

Management contracts are the sale of a total management package by a contractor to a client. In a basic contract, the contractor provides all the business functions and manages the contract venture as a subsidiary while ensuring that it becomes a viable business in its own right when the contract period ends. Sometimes the contractor holds a small proportion of equity in the venture.

The management contract is more comprehensive than the other types of knowledge agreement; it differs in other ways too. One difference is that the one-to-one relationship between principal and client is normally replaced by a three-sided arrangement that includes a contract-venture enterprise. The client and the venture may be identical, but frequently a separate entity is established by the principle and the client. This is similar to the joint venture considered under 'investment' (Chapter 6.4). The three-sided arrangement both causes problems and cures them. It complicates the system of communications and thus the potential for misunderstanding. On the other hand, it simplifies the division of authority and ensures a certain objectivity by the partners in dealing with a third party – the contract venture they have jointly established.

Construction contracts differ from other arrangements on this list: they operate in one industry sector and the contract is limited to a specific project on whose requirements the time scale and remuneration are based. The trend towards package deals, observed in many sectors, is particularly advanced in construction where a favoured system is for a main contractor to offer a range of services. In addition to design and construction these include financing, procurement and the management of local and other sub-contractors. The total package is often called a turnkey project.

Turnkey projects is a phrase sometimes used of the total package and sometimes of the last stage – the operation of the complete project until the owners can operate it as a going concern. At this stage the range of skills required broadens to include the operation as well as the construction of projects which vary considerably and include hydro-electric schemes, steelworks, petrochemical plants and hospitals. If the turnkey is prolonged it becomes indistinguishable from a management contract.

(*Note* that in the construction industry the phrase 'management contract' is normally used in a different sense from that in this chapter. It is employed of a main contractor who undertakes to manage sub-contractors. Nevertheless the construction industry also uses management contracts as defined here.)

A consortium is the coming together of a number of companies on the basis of sharing in a project rather than as sub-contractors. The sharing may be as equal partner or it may be on the basis of a percentage of the equity carrying a proportional share of the voting power. Originally established in the construction industry to share the risks and expertise demanded by large-scale projects, the consortium idea spread to banks which financed large undertakings. It has now spread to other industry sectors including many in new technologies, like deep-sea mining. A specialized type of high-tech consortium is an inter-governmental agreement, usually to develop military hardware but also including civil aircraft.

With the increasing cost and time horizon of high-tech project, international consortia are likely to become increasingly common. Most of them are linked to other forms of agreement like licensing (usually cross-licensing) and management contracts.

Transfer of technology and expertise

Academic studies, apart from those listed in Part 1, have concentrated on the transfer of technical and managerial expertise; but strategic considerations, like a relatively low-cost and low-risk method of market entry are of increasing significance. The transfer of technology was considered in Chapter 1.3 and will be looked at again under the management of research and development in Chapter 6.9.

6.3.1   Knowledge agreements: strategic factors

Knowledge agreements between them provide a number of options for entering and servicing markets. The strategic considerations differ and one may be used where another has failed. Relative to both export and investment, these agreements are considered low-cost and low-risk; companies often regard them as low-profit as well. The truth of these statements depends on how costs, risks and profits affect a company at a given time. As with many similar business decisions, an apparently low-cost option may turn out to be otherwise if a different basis is taken for the calculation. Licensing agreements, for instance, can become loss makers rather than revenue earners if not supported by adequate research. Nevertheless, on principle, knowledge agreements are suitable means of entering markets that would otherwise be considered too risky. Probable advantages, along with likely problems and other considerations, are examined in the following list.

Licensing

(1)   Advantages

    A means of operating in a market where import restrictions or transport costs make other methods impossible.

A means of acquiring additional revenue from the results of research and development.

A means of limiting the need for capital and exposure to risk where local manufacture is required.

There are special advantages when rapid coverage in numerous markets is required to forestall competition.

(2) Disadvantages

The licensor has little control over the marketing policies of the licensee. The impact on the market and the volume of production are usually under local control.

The income may well be less because the influence of competition and of government restrictions, sometimes both, ensures that royalties are kept low – and may be reduced when an agreement comes up for renewal.

There is the further possibility of an opportunity cost where the licensee is not exploiting a market fully but can prevent imports of a principal's product from elsewhere.

Major problems occur when the licensee proves inadequate.

One of the most commonly mentioned objections to licensing (and to other forms of knowledge agreement) is the possibility of promoting a competitor. The licensee acquires the technology and then uses it to enter the principal's markets elsewhere. The agreement will be designed to prevent this, but enforcement is not easy and, in any case, once the patent has expired the licensee is free to exploit it. Further, without infringing the terms of the licence, the licensee may be able to develop the know-how transmitted and use it to compete.

There are two answers to this problem. One is that its existence emphasizes the importance of establishing a satisfactory relationship. If the business develops in a way that is satisfactory to both parties, the problem of competition should not arise. It is when the licensor ignores the arrangement, and only makes contact when royalties are due, that the licensee company is most likely to go its own way. Research into international business in many different contexts – such as agents, management contract ventures and associate companies – has demonstrated the importance of a business relationship nurtured by frequent communication. The other issue is also a common feature of international business studies – the principle of transferred problems, which states that a problem does not necessarily disappear when a supposed solution is found; it frequently reappears under another guise. In this case, and investment saved on one item is spent on another – research at home to keep ahead with new developments in the world market place.

(3) Conflict

A significant conflict of interest between the two parties to an agreement occurs when the licensee wants to export to areas serviced by other units or agents of the principal. In this case there is often a direct conflict with other units of the company, while a prohibition on exports may fall foul of local regulations.

Franchising

The advantages are similar to licensing. In this case a proven body of commercial skills can be sold worldwide with a minimum investment, although many franchisors invest heavily in support schemes – like training and publicity – from which their franchisees benefit. For the principal, the problems of franchising are minimal. An unsuccessful franchisee can be replaced more readily than a licensee, and there are fewer implications for other of the principal's activities, except the maintenance of world standards: a reputation acquired in one country can spread to another. For this reason, great emphasis is usually placed on training programmes for the staff of franchisee companies; they need to operate to standards sets by the principal.

Two difficulties are raised more frequently than others. One is that global standardization often has to be modified in practice, and in unexpected ways. The other difficulty is that of quality control. Many companies that go in for franchising agreements also cater for international travellers – like hotels and car rental firms – and a bad experience in one country can damage the market in others. Hence strict quality control is a preoccupation of franchisors.

Management contracts

Arrangements whereby a complete management package is bought under contract stand between basic licensing ventures, on the one hand, and 100 per cent ownership at the other. Some management contracts resemble licensing or franchising agreements; others include some equity on the part of the contractor. Many of the advantages arise from this ability to develop out of and to overcome the problems of other types of arrangement.

Advantages for the contractor

Producing revenue from management expertise.

Providing the benefits of direct investment where this has become impossible or too risky.

Rescuing a licensing or franchising arrangement where the client has proved incapable of developing the business.

Providing support for other international ventures, projects and consortia.

Management contracts may also be important for selling other products or services of the contractor.

Another advantage for the contractor company is that a contract can be helpful to its reputation. In the case of direct sales or licensing, if the customer or client is not capable of using the equipment properly, a contractor's prestige can be damaged. It may be necessary to inject management skills at least in the early stages of a project.

Advantages for the client (and in some cases the client's country)

A means of acquiring expertise without the strings attached to foreign equity participation.

A quick route to a viable business.

An acceptable means of using foreign skills.

Management contracts are an advantage when it comes to negotiating loans with development banks. The foreign contractor gives an assurance of viability.

Disadvantages

The contractor is wary of providing a competitor, as with licensing. Otherwise there is less risk than in investing or exporting, but this is countered by fewer returns and the uncertainty that accompanies a contract when it is short-term.

The client is afraid of becoming over-dependent on the contractor. Some developing countries prefer consultancy arrangements. Some clients, and some governments, suspect any package arrangement on the grounds that it may be a vehicle for overcharging.

A distinction has been made between explicit and implicit management contracts. A study of contracts in Algeria,[1] a socialist country that used this mode of business widely, showed that *all* were implicit – that is, to support other objectives, mainly technology transfer. The explicit contract in which only management expertise is transferred is uncommon in any country, although the distinction is a fine one especially in service industries. In manufacturing, a so-called technology contract – such as a technical cooperation agreement – may be primarily about management. At least a specific technology is likely to have its distinctive management requirements and its appropriate management style without which the technology will not work.

Technical cooperation agreements

These come between licensing and management contracts. They are particularly relevant in socialist nations where no other arrangement may be possible, and in other countries where the word 'management' is suspect either for ideological reasons or because of local susceptibilities. Technical cooperation is a package that carries technical, commercial and managerial knowledge. It possesses both the advantages and disadvantages of a management contract which it closely resembles. The special advantage for the contractor is the ability to generate business in difficult markets.

Contract manufacturing

Advantages

There are a number of advantages in contract manufacture. They include the following.

Overload on existing facilities can be met without committing capital in new fixed assets.

Manufacture can be undertaken in areas of low labour cost for shipment back to industrial countries. There are, in fact, many applications of this, some of them not usually considered 'manufacture', like the sending of company records to Jamaica from the United States for keying on to disk.

Contract manufacturing can bring the advantages of licensing with, in addition, the ability of the principal to control the marketing programme.

Disadvantages

As with licensing, there is the possibility of promoting a competitor. There is also the possibility that the contractor finds the commitment greater than expected. Support services may have to be injected if the client proves inadequate.

Turnkey contracts

An offer to operate a new plant or other project for a period before handing over to the new owner is both useful for marketing and a safeguard for the reputation of the contractor. Both these benefits are also characteristic of other knowledge agreements.

Conclusion

Knowledge agreement is a generic title for a variety of activities demanding widely divergent skills. Most of the agreements – licensing, management contracts, franchising and technical cooperation, for instance – offer increased market share with a minimum of capital at risk. To the client they offer a ready-made business for which the learning curve with its attendant costs is much less than for the normal process of developing a business. For governments, particularly in developing countries, the agreements help to promote trade and bring in foreign expertise; they do so without the strings attached to foreign investment or the costs to the balance of payments incurred by exports.

As against these advantages, the disadvantages seem insubstantial. The fear of establishing a competitor has on occasions proved justified, but can be put down to weakness on the part of the contractor. Investment is believed to produce greater returns in the long run, but this is hard to prove. Clients and some governments see foreign control as still a problem, but this is at least negotiable.

So why do knowledge agreements remain a second-best option, covering a small part of the total movement of funds across frontiers? The answer may be due to organizational reasons as much as to economic ones. The well-known *principle of undivided control* states that, all other things being equal, an organization will seek to reduce the areas of uncertainty by eliminating collaborators where possible – and all knowledge agreements are collaborative by definition.[2] Another organizational issue is that of status within the company. Foreign investment is a top-level decision, to be handled by the most senior managers often including the chief executive. Export is handled at a lower level, although responsibility for export may be in the hands of a senior executive. Knowledge agreements, on the other hand, are often within the discretion of lower levels. They are not accorded top executive consideration, and so are not promoted or maintained as effectively as direct investment. It is notable that franchising, often the exception to this general rule, is also the fastest growing type of agreement.

Problems between the partners are discussed later in this chapter; meanwhile, the difficulties of generating income may well be considered both a consequence and a cause of the low status of knowledge agreements. Sometimes the services provided are not even charged for, on the grounds that the principal benefits in other ways, including sales to the client.

6.3.2 Knowledge agreements as a means of generating income[3]

Assessing the benefits to the contractor of a knowledge agreement is a complex calculation. On the one hand there is more to consider than direct fee income, on the other the costs are various and often elusive. In the following notes, monitoring is considered under a separate heading – although a cost, it is also a form of guarantee without which the income may disappear.

Fees and other benefits

The direct fees can be on a percentage, a per product or a time basis. In negotiating a contract, the principal will be seeking to reduce the influence on the income of the client's activities; while the client company will wish to ensure the opposite – that it is paying out of results achieved.

The percentage basis can be subdivided again into a fraction of sales or of profits. The principal is likely to prefer sales because the influence of the client is reduced. The client company, for its part, prefers profits; a commission based on sales is potentially more expensive, even to the extent of reducing the profits to zero. This conflict of interest is naturally the subject of considerable negotiation and sometimes of serious dissatisfaction. While such arrangements are common, the percentages obtainable have been reduced by competition. As a result principals are increasingly seeking other forms of remuneration, of which one is per product.

A fee based on production is especially relevant to licensing, technical assistance and contract manufacture. In a licensing agreement, the royalty may be paid on each product manufactured under the licence. This does not differ greatly from a percentage of sales; it can avoid disputes where the licence is for a component rather than an assembled product. In this case a percentage on sales may be difficult to calculate.

A fee based on time, like £x a year for the use of the licence, is the form of payment most favoured by principals. This fee base removes the influence of the client on the results, and its use is notably more common in forms of business where the latter has the least bargaining power. These include most kinds of franchising as well as management contracts in sectors like tropical agriculture. From the client's point of view, this is unsatisfactory because it does not stimulate activity on the part of the principal. A mixture of methods is sometimes negotiated to benefit both parties.

A major additional benefit for the principal arises where other income is derived apart from fees. The client may be a customer, and the supply of goods or services may be more important than the supply of technical or commercial information. There can also be other forms of spin-off that are profitable to the contractor. A marginal research project can become viable if licences generate additional income.

There are other opportunity benefits in licensing. If, for instance, a market would be lost without local manufacture, the greater earning power elsewhere of any capital that would have been committed for an investment instead of a licensing agreement is likely to be included in the calculation.

Costs

The costs to the principal vary according to the inputs. For a basic licensing agreement the marginal costs may be negligible – only the servicing of a particular client. Only a limited number of licensing agreements are basic in this sense; as soon as extra management or technical support is required the costs increase. Some of these may be recoverable under the contract, but others may not. A frequent cause of complaint by principals is that licensing and franchising agreements turn out to be open-ended. The costs in back-up from head office can be much higher than expected. In the case of management contracts, also, an arrangement which seemed undemanding when it was negotiated gradually absorbs more time on the part of head-office management. This is particularly the case when the client is a government or quasi-official enterprise. Any substantial problem then becomes a top-management concern, whoever negotiated the original agreement. The will be direct costs to head office as well as opportunity cost. Table 6.3.1 is an analysis of costs designed for appraising

Table 6.3.1 Knowledge Agreements: an Analysis of Costs

Accounting costs (A)	*Opportunity costs (O)*
Direct (A1): the salaries and benefits of staff allocated to the project (pro rata for those part-time); the technical costs involved in transferring the knowledge and setting up the project; the cost of materials required in setting up the project; legal, marketing, research and administrative costs directly related to the project; training of client's staff.	Loss of exports (O1): the margins lost on exports that could have been made to the market. Alternative use of managerial time (O2): the limits imposed on other project by the use of managerial time. Alternative use of financial resources (O3): the danger that money is spent on non-lucrative resources. This also applies to the costs of other corporate resources.
Indirect (A2): Support from head office in legal and management time; the capital costs incurred in research and development to sustain the project.	Dangers of establishing a competitor (O4): the possibility that once versed in the business, the client will end the agreement and become a competitor.

Total costs = A [A1 + A2] + O [O1 + O2 + O3 + O4]

Source: based on Brooke, 1985, Table 4.3.4, p. 170.

the performance of management contracts; with some adaptation, it applies to other knowledge agreements.

The training of a client's staff often causes controversy. In a franchise, this is usually a contracted cost for both parties; it may not be so well-defined in other agreements. In a licensing arrangement, a principal may decide that its corporate reputation demands an improvement in the technical performance of the client's staff; while the client may argue that the principal must bear the costs of extra training not provided in the agreement.

Monitoring

The systematic monitoring of the results of the agreement – in the licensee, the franchisee, the contract venture or whatever – is both a guarantee and a cost to the principal. It can also be a cost-effective method of training when the client company learns to control its own business more effectively by observing the monitoring system of the principal. Studies of management contracts discovered numerous examples of this, including a close watch on the leakage of funds – for example through delinquent accounts or rising stocks. Monitoring also provides the system within which the relationship between principal and client is formalized.

6.3.3 Conditions for success

The first condition for success, as with exporting, is adequate preparation within the company. In the case of knowledge agreements, all involve collaboration with an independent foreign company – so a satisfactory relationship is essential. Most research into such relationships has concentrated on export preparation and foreign agents; some of it also includes licensing and most of the work on agents is relevant to licensees. Those elements in success that are most important for knowledge agreements are:

a saleable package;
an ability to keep the knowledge ingredient (whether technical, commercial or managerial) up-to-date;
an adequate system for monitoring the foreign business;
adequate methods for selecting and appraising collaborators;
a satisfactory agreement negotiated in the light of both the common and conflicting interests of the partners – which have been discussed openly during the negotiations.

6.3.4 The environment of knowledge agreements

Licensing and the other types of agreement detailed in this chapter are even more sensitive to the business and political environment than export and deals with agents.

Legal arrangements, for instance, vary greatly from country to country. They take four forms: (1) the protection of intellectual property; (2) regulation of agreements; (3) the assertion of competition policies; and (4) other controls on the transfer of knowledge and the protection of local business.

The duration of a patent is from zero in countries that have no legislation on the subject to a maximum of 20 years. Even countries that do offer protection, do not do so in some products. Italy, which normally offers protection for the maximum of 20 years from the date of application, does not give patent protection to pharmaceutical products. There are similar regulations on trade marks, although the maximum of 20 years is less common. Copyright is the third element of legislation on intellectual property; it is supported by international agreement (the Berne Convention) and is usually for a longer period. Most countries also have regulations stipulating conditions that can or cannot be written into agreements. In the case of management contracts, some developing countries require government consent. In general, regulations concerning intellectual property are currently under negotiation in various organizations including the General Agreement on Tariffs and Trade and the European Community; the latter is also currently discussing the patenting of pharmaceuticals.

The Anti-Trust laws in the United States are an example of competition legislation which has a long history and has been used to attack licensing and other agreements. Among clauses that can fall foul of the legislation are those that insist on a licensee granting back to the principal any improvements made to the product, or that apportion rights between licensees, or in which the licensor fixes conditions of sale or prices. There are many others, the principle being to prohibit clauses that restrict competition in any way. Many of these arrangements are also prohibited by the competition laws of the European Community; but there are reservations to encourage mutual agreements between enterprises in different states so long as there is no serious restraint of trade.

Notes

1. Reported in Burton, F.N. and Hammoutene, A. (1987): 'The management contract as a mode of international industrial competition: myth or reality?' presented to an Academy of International Business, United Kingdom annual meeting, Lancaster, April. The 'explicit' contract is called the basic contract in Brooke (1985), a detailed study of the subject.
2. In international business studies the principle can be traced back to Stopford, J.M. and Wells, L.T. (1972): *Managing the Multinationals*, Basic Books and Longman. Chapter 8 is entitled: 'The drive for unambiguous control'. In organization-studies the principle can be traced back at least to Cyert, R.M. and March, J.G. (1963): *A Behavioural Theory of the Firm*, Prentice Hall. One of the 'major relational concepts' identified in this book is 'uncertainty avoidance' (pp. 118–20).
3. For a discussion of methods of remuneration for management contracts see Brooke (1985), Chapter 4.3. Chapter 4.2 considers the question of monitoring.

References

Brooke, M.Z. (1985): *Selling Management Services Contracts in International Business.* Holt, Rinehart and Winston.

Brooke, M.Z. and Buckley, P.J. (1988): *Handbook of International Trade* (new edn). Macmillan.

Buckley, P.J. and Davies, H. (1981): 'Foreign licensing in overseas operation', *Research in International Business and Finance*, pp. 75–89. JAI Press.

Casson, M. (1979): *Alternatives to the Multinational Company.* Macmillan.

Contractor, F.J. (1985): 'A generalized theorem for joint-venture and licensing negotiations', *Journal of International Business Studies*, Vol. 16, No. 2, Summer, pp. 23–50.

Contractor, F.J. (1985): *Licensing in International Strategy*. Quorum Books, Greenwood Press.

Etele, A. (1985): 'Licensing and the pricing of technology', *Management Decision* Vol. 23, No. 3, pp. 53–61.

McDonald, D.W. and Leakey, A.S. (1985): 'Licensing has a role in technology strategic planning', *Research Management*, No. 28, January to February, pp. 35–40.

Walter, I. and Murray, T. (1982): *Handbook of International Business*. Wiley.

6.4

Investment and the Multinational

Foreign investment is a much studied aspect of foreign business and its implications occupy many chapters in this book. It is a complex phenomenon which can be approached from many angles – economic, socio-psychological, political and legal among them. Underlying theories, including those of motivation, have already been examined. This chapter looks at the management issues.

Theories designed to explain the phenomenon of international investment and its motives are detailed in Chapter 1.4. The options are outlined in Figure 6.4.1 which starts from the division into direct and portfolio investment. Like most such distinctions, the division is not watertight and is, as a rule, defined differently for academic purposes than by businesses or for accounting or tax purposes. There are grey areas but the distinction used here is between a direct investment which brings with it some exercise of management, and portfolio investment where only ownership (shareholder) rights are pursued. This definition means that a company may own only one per cent of the equity of another[1] but, if there is also an agreement that management functions (like control) are exercised, it becomes a direct investment. This is an extreme example, and usually such an arrangement would be classed as a management contract; but the percentage at which a holding is regarded as an investment is arbitrary and makes no difference to the exercise of management. At 51 per cent there is a legal change, an agreement is no longer required and, in some countries, the accounts must be consolidated (in others this is carried out at a higher percentage); but, if the foreign company is treated as a subsidiary and integrated into the corporate system for control purposes, there may be no managerial difference between one per cent and 100 per cent. The fact that there are usually some differences arises from the nature of the agreement, and the extent to which the partner exercises rights beyond those of a shareholder.

Figure 6.4.1 sets out the options in diagrammatic form. One of the differences in joint ventures stems from the nature of the other shareholders: each of the ownership options is divided into two, whether the other owners are one or more

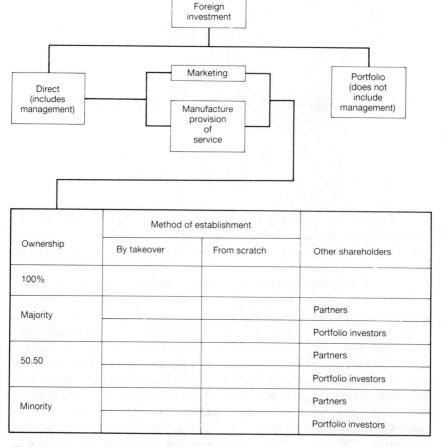

Figure 6.4.1　The Options for Foreign Investment

partners or whether they are portfolio investors. The other distinction shown in the figure is between the two methods of forming the subsidiary: either by takeover or from scratch. These distinctions are discussed later in this chapter. Meanwhile the first issue is the decision process which establishes and sustains the foreign investment.

6.4.1　Foreign investment: the decision process

A process can be identified between the explanations and motives, which underlie theories of the multinational, and the perceptions of managers through which

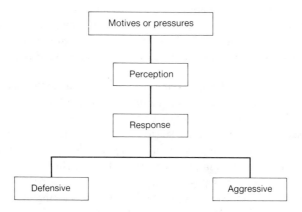

Figure 6.4.2 The Process that Results in Foreign Investment

the motives are translated into decisions. The problems that bring foreign investment on to the managerial agenda are of two main kinds: the need to defend a market and the need to enter fresh markets. The process is sketched out in Figure 6.4.2.

It is usually agreed that the main problem that stimulates foreign investment is the need to defend a market. One survey showed that nearly 80 per cent of a sample of companies gave 'defence' as a reason for new foreign investment – and these were established multinationals.[2] The process of establishing a marketing subsidiary will differ from that aimed at a full subsidiary for manufacture or the provision of a service.

A marketing subsidiary

A subsidiary for marketing a company's products is likely to be established when:

(1) existing arrangements have proved inadequate – sales outstripping an existing agent, for example;
(2) competitors are establishing a local presence and winning customers by doing so;
(3) warehousing, after-sales services or the stocking of spares is required;
(4) a local presence is required to provide greater credibility.

Any combination of the four is possible, and the pressure to invest locally becomes strongest when at least two are seen to operate together. The argument from competition is usually the most powerful.

The main resistance to a marketing subsidiary comes from two considerations.

(1) the cost is greater than any anticipated benefit;
(2) the requirements of customer relations are not met by a marketing subsidiary when, for instance, the level of management required for dealings
with the customer cannot be made available in a marketing subsidiary.

The second argument strongly reinforces the first but both may need closer
scrutiny than is sometimes accorded. A subsidiary will not be brought into existence unless it can satisfy a company's normal criteria for return on investment
but the consequences of loss of market have to be considered. Once established,
a subsidiary can be instructed on its discretion levels and about the occasions
when senior management from head office must be brought in.

For small companies, it is possible to give a subsidiary a regional remit, thus
offsetting the costs against the opportunities for developing the market in a
group of countries. For a larger company, this can also have an advantage. For
example, a company that has grown by acquisition may find itself possessed of a
network of arrangements, many conflicting and some incompatible. The marketing subsidiary with a regional remit is well placed to rationalize such a network
sensitively, without undue loss of market share.

A subsidiary for manufacture or the provision of a service

A number of conditions have been identified which are likely to bring a subsidiary into existence. These include:

Defensive conditions

The conditions are labelled 'defensive' because if they are ignored, an existing
market share may be much reduced or lost altogether. Direct export or licensing
is no longer adequate for servicing the market. The list has been culled from the
authors' own research and from other sources listed in the references. It is
impossible to put a numerical weighting by each item because of the different
bases of different studies, but the first three are those most frequently mentioned.

(1) A market threatened by competition. This common perception is
supported by evidence of groupings of multinationals in specific centres.
When one invests, others will follow suit to protect their market share.
(2) A market threatened by government constraints – new or increasing tariff
or non-tariff barriers, import restrictions or quotas. Import substitution
legislation is included under this heading, as are other demands or
measures for local facilities.
(3) A market threatened by increasing costs of imports caused by greater
differentials in pay and other production factors, increased facilities for
local production or unfavourable movements in the exchange rate.

(4) A market threatened by costs and delays in the physical distribution system.
(5) Problems with agents or licensees. There can arise even when the venture is a success, if the business outgrows the agent's resources.
(6) Problems with after-sales and other technical and support services.
(7) The need to protect patents by local manufacture.
(8) The need to ensure supplies of materials and components, and at an acceptable standard of quality.
(9) the need to protect shareholders at home from the effects of the economic cycle by investing in more than one economy.

Market entry reasons
A number of instances arise when defence is not the reason. These may be aggressive – where investment is considered as the most suitable means of market entry – or neutral when a company has to invest where its business is or when it is attracted to invest by some external influence like a government incentive.

(1) When investment is the most suitable or only method of entry. This is frequently the case with service industries. Retailers can go abroad by franchising but often choose investment.
(2) When investment abroad enables a company to extend its provision to existing customers. This is also true of service industries like banks and for manufacturers of components. There may be a defensive element in this case – if a customer threatens to change to a supplier of services or components which is already operating internationally.
(3) When underemployed resources at home can be used more profitably abroad, or when global planning makes more effective use of resources.
(4) When costs can be reduced by the foreign investment.
(5) When foreign investment provides access to fresh sources of technical knowledge or other expertise. This is sometimes cited as a reason for maintaining a subsidiary which is not meeting normal criteria for return on investment.
(6) The need to expand abroad to meet corporate targets – including growth, market share or return on investment – which cannot be met by domestic expansion.
(7) As a response to external influences like government incentives or approaches by third parties.
(8) As a response to pressures within the company from groups or individuals advocating foreign investment as a result of insights or ambitions.

Any of these conditions or reasons can set in train a process of investigation or pilot schemes which can lead to the build-up of facilities abroad.

The thresholds

One threshold was identified in an earlier chapter on export; in the case of investment there are two thresholds at which difficulties are known to occur. In a first investment, the anticipated costs and problems are likely to mean a postponement after the need for an investment is established and a case has been made out. There then comes a second threshold when the foreign investment becomes a significant part of the business. This threshold has been widely identified, along with the strains and stresses brought about by the need to adapt the management system to the changed circumstances.

The Harvard studies, for instance, defined a multinational as a company with 25 per cent of its investment in at least six foreign countries.[3] While 25 per cent is an arbitrary figure, it represents a significant proportion. By the time that figure is reached, the foreign operations can no longer be treated as a side-line. The actual proportion at which the threshold becomes apparent to the company is likely to vary according to size, industry sector, country of origin, style and attitudes of management and a number of other factors. While no company would reorganize and set up an international management system for 1 per cent of the business, few companies could fail to do this for 30 per cent – and somewhere in between, a threshold is being recognized.

Some writers identify other thresholds as the company becomes more geographically diverse; words like 'geocentric' and 'global' are used to express different approaches to the view that there is at least one further threshold which a company can cross – although such words are apt to be employed in a nebulous sense.

Note on the use of analogies

The word *threshold* is used here to signify the crossing of a space beyond which conditions change radically. This could be described as a spatial analogy and allows the extra thought that there is still complete freedom of movement. A company can cross a threshold, decide that the new business methods are unprofitable and move back by disinvesting; or it can move to a totally fresh position. Some of the writers cited prefer the word *evolution*. This is an analogy from nature. Apart from the question of the appropriateness of using a word that implies a lengthy process of natural selection, the analogy from nature implies less freedom of action than is the case. Some inevitability is assumed. There is also an assumption that a new stage has been achieved which is somehow higher than the one before, and that a move back would be a retreat. But this is not necessarily the case in a business, which is seeking the most profitable solution to a problem, not the next peak in an evolutionary process. All analogies have their limitations, but the word 'threshold' appears more neutral than 'evolution'. Even so, it hardly conveys the dynamic forces that are causing upheavals in the system – upheavals that will be considered further in Chapter 6.10.

6.4.2 Ownership

The title conjures up a major issue for the international investor – whether to aim at 100 per cent ownership or some form of shared participation. Most companies nowadays recognize there is a range of options; they will select the one that appears to suit the circumstances of a particular market best. There are still some companies that only accept an investment of 100 per cent, while many more take 100 per cent where possible; on the other hand, there are companies that prefer a joint venture. It used to be said that nationality was a determining factor, but that is becoming harder to sustain.

The approach to ownership is a subject that has seen more radical change than any other. Twenty years ago, little had been written on joint ventures, reflecting the fact that most companies hardly even considered them an option. Today joint ventures are much discussed, but the 'drive to unambiguous control'[4] is still strong among companies even while new joint ventures are being reported almost daily; they are now compulsory in most developing countries. Accounts of joint ventures often consider their relative success or failure rather than how they fit into a general pattern of international investment. This will be outlined here, but first a note on the meaning of the phrase. 'Joint venture' is frequently used of any participation in the shareholding of a company, but this covers a number of arrangements which have very different implications. The shares may be held by two or more companies, each of which is a direct investor – in other words they all have some involvement in the management of the venture; or the shares may be held by most of the participants as portfolio investment. Figure 6.4.3 shows the principle.

Policy differences

Research has shown there are differences of policy between companies that have 100 per cent ownership and those that do not,[5] the following among them:

Capital structure. The capital of a joint venture is usually structured like that of a local company. The leverage (gearing) of a wholly-owned subsidiary is higher, sometimes much higher. The company is anxious to commit as little permanent capital, equity, as possible and to make high local borrowings. The high gearing is irrelevant if there is only one owner, since it only has a marginal effect on the owner's capital standing.

Dividends. On dividends too, the joint venture behaves like a local company and pays out a similar proportion of its earnings. The wholly-owned subsidiary pays out according to the capital requirements of the company as a whole – varying from a zero dividend, if developments in the subsidiary are planned, to 100 per cent of the profit if funds are needed elsewhere in the group.

Other shareholders	Proportion of shareholding		
	Majority	50–50	Minority
One or more companies *			
Any number of portfolio investors †			

Figure 6.4.3   Methods of Participation in a Joint Venture

Notes:
* The companies that share the direct investment may be from any country; a typical joint venture is where the foreign company has a local partner, but many arrangements are more complex.
† These would normally be in the host country. One of the purposes of selling shares in a local subsidiary (as opposed to the parent company) is to comply with the law in countries where local participation is compulsory and – even where it is not – to involve the local money market.

The examples of capital structure and dividends demonstrate that there are differences; companies do feel constrained by the existence of local shareholders. Many other constraints have been listed by various writers including the operation of the corporate control system, pricing policies and the allocation of markets. Whether these restrictions are a necessary consequence of a joint venture or not may well be doubted. Some firms operate their control system with subsidiaries in which they have a minority holding; many others regard this as impossible.

Among writers on the subject, Robock and Simmonds recognize that 100 per cent ownership leaves a company with more flexibility, but assert that 'many firms find that divestment of some equity can provide more than offsetting benefits through protection against controls'.[6] A more positive approach is represented by the finding that a local partner can assist in making a greater impact, and in producing a viable market share more rapidly.

Writing in the early 1970s, Stopford and Wells found there was general opposition to joint ventures among American businessmen but, in spite of the opposition, a great many took part in them. This ambivalent attitude was shown by the fact that only 33 of their sample of 187 companies had no joint ventures abroad; while all foreign subsidiaries were joint ventures for a similar number. The authors related propensity to joint venture with strategy. Companies that employed strategies demanding tight control were opposed to joint ventures. The strategies included use of marketing techniques to differentiate products, rationalization of production facilities, control of raw materials and development of new products ahead of the competition.[7] Companies in the sample that preferred joint ventures did so largely on the grounds of seeking access to local resources. Quick entry to new markets and access to raw materials were frequently mentioned resources. Also mentioned, mainly by smaller companies, was the need for local partners to increase the skills available to the company in raising funds, in managing and in marketing.

Other writers have put together lists of costs and benefits associated with joint ventures. Such lists usually include the words: 'in many countries they are compulsory'. Some items on the lists are given in Table 6.4.1.

It will be noted that although the disadvantages take up more space in the table, this does not make them more powerful. No attempt has been made to weight the issues for the following reasons:

(1) As authors differ considerably in their emphases, it would be meaningless to say that x authors have identified a particular advantage or disadvantage.

(2) The situation is changing all the time. As we write fresh, and often more complex, joint ventures are being announced frequently in the business press. It seems reasonable to assume that there is a process of organization-learning at work that is already making many of the disadvantages seem less substantial. There can be little doubt that this process will continue.

Conclusion

A number of points arise from a review of writings on joint ventures which include the following.

(1) Despite changes in the business environment, the drive for undivided control is still strong.

(2) The disadvantages of joint ventures are mitigated when the other partners are portfolio investors rather than active participants.

(3) Many of the disadvantages appear more obvious to those who have not undertaken joint ventures. Experience can make the problems less significant.

(4) The advantages are especially clear for companies wishing to make an impact on difficult markets – the risks are reduced and entry is made easier.

(5) Disadvantages can be mitigated by close attention to detail in devising agreements and in establishing a satisfactory business relationship including frequent high-level meetings.

(6) For companies dependent on closely integrated, international strategies, there will always be advantages in minimizing any conflict of interest with

Table 6.4.1   The Advantages and Disadvantages of Joint Ventures

	Advantages	*Disadvantages*
Political/legal	Compulsory in some countries, favoured by governments in most; especially beneficial when governments are customers.	Danger of falling foul of competition legislation (especially quoted by United States' firms uncertain of implications of Anti-Trust Laws). Problem includes sharing of information.
Financial policies	Limited commitment of risk capital.	Constraints on international policies.
Control policies		Problems caused by dilution of control.
Marketing policies	Can reduce costs and time of market entry; can tap.	Constraints on international policies; advantages can also be achieved by takeover; constraints on allocation of markets with company.
Production and research and development policies		Constraints on international standardization and rationalization.
Staffing policies	Attraction of local experts.	Restrictions on international management development schemes. Partner may not possess.
Planning policies	Access to wider resources.	Constraints on global planning procedures and deployment of resources. Danger of rigidity: partner may impede rapid change to meet changes in global markets.

Note: The issues listed in this table are assembled from the sources referenced in note 6. No attempts have been made to weight them because emphases differ greatly.

partners. For companies with less need of integration and greater reliance on local resources, joint ventures will be an advantage.

References

Publications on joint ventures

Beamish, P.W. (1985): 'The characteristics of joint ventures in developed and developing countries', *Columbia Journal of World Business*, Vol. 20, No. 3, pp. 13–19.

Beamish, P.W. and Banks, J.C. (1987): 'Equity joint ventures and the theory of the multinational enterprise', *Journal of International Business Studies*, Summer, pp. 1–16.

Buckley, P.J. and Casson, M. (1988): 'A theory of cooperation in international business', In Contractor, F. and Lorange, P. (eds): *Cooperative Strategies in International Business* pp. 31–53. Lexington.

Cartwright, S. and Cooper, C.L. (1989): 'Predicting success in joint ventures organizations in information technology', *Journal of General Management*. Vol. 15, No. 1, Autumn, pp. 39–46.

Frayne, C.A. and Geringer, J.M. (1987): 'Self-management: A key to improving international joint venture performance', *Proceedings*, Conference on International Personnel and Human Resource Management, Singapore.

Geringer, J.M. (1986): 'Criteria for selecting partners for joint ventures in industrialized market economies'. Unpublished doctoral dissertation, University of Washington.

Gomes-Casseres, B. (1987): 'Joint venture instability: Is it a problem?', *Columbia Journal of World Business*, Summer, pp. 97–107.

Gullander, S. (1976): 'Joint ventures and corporate strategy', *Columbia Journal of World Business*, Spring, pp. 104–14.

Harrigan, K.R. (1987): 'Strategic alliances: their new role in global competition', *Columbia Journal of World Business*, Summer, pp. 67–9.

Hayward, K. (1986): *International Collaboration in Civil Aerospace*. Frances Pinter.

Killing, J.P. (1982): 'How to make a global joint venture work', *Harvard Business Review*, Vol. 60, No. 3, May–June, pp. 120–7.

Killing, J.P. (1983): *Strategies for Joint Venture Success*. Praeger.

Kogut, B. (1988): Joint ventures: theoretical and empirical perspectives. *Strategic Management Journal*, Vol. 9, No. 4, pp. 319–32.

6.4.3 Establishing and managing a foreign subsidiary

Once decisions about the location and ownership of a new facility have been taken, the means of establishment and the system of management are decided. The means of establishment will be closely linked to the ownership decision, but either a wholly-owned subsidiary or a joint venture can be set up from scratch or by taking over an existing company. In the case of a joint venture there is a third course of action – that no new company is established: the partner becomes the joint venture.

Table 6.4.2 Methods of Establishing a Foreign Subsidiary

	By greenfield venture	*By takeover*
Political/legal	Government grants may be available.	Local hostility may lead to constraints; risks of action under competition laws.
Costs	Controllable – accurate estimates for buildings and equipment *should* be available; production costs may be less for new plant.	More difficult to control or assess; takeover may be more or less costly.
Market share	Market entry and market share may be costly and take time.	Facilitates market entry and building of market share; other problems of start up are also made easier. The firm taken over has an existing order book.
Choice of location	Open.	Restricted.
Management	Need to recruit; no need to spend time in assimilating existing staff.	Already available as is local knowledge.
General	Avoids resentment and perhaps backlash to foreign takeover.	Disturbs the competitive structure of the industry. Less severe problems of integration often occur.

The little evidence available suggests that takeovers and starting from scratch (often known as greenfield ventures) are nearly equal,[8] but the balance of advantage may be shifting towards the greenfield. Table 6.4.2 lists the current position. This table shows there is a close balance between costs and benefits. The choice is likely to be connected with industry sector and nationality. High-tech firms are inclined to favour the greenfield method where they do not inherit an existing corporate culture. Political conditions that favour this method seem to be increasing – hostility towards takeovers and the imposing of conditions when they take place. On the other hand expanding companies are often short of skilled managers and are looking to bring them into the organization by takeover. The search for high-quality management teams is a part of the search for a subsidiary, and its result may affect other decisions like location and even nationality. The search also extends to technical expertise. In some sectors, like advertising, the greenfield method is rare because of the costs of building up a viable market share. Takeovers have the advantage of an existing order book.

Other decisions

Once the method of establishment is settled, a legal framework is required. This is normally a subsidiary that provides limited liability and may have tax advantages. The alternative is a branch, a considerably less common arrangement; attempts are currently being made to make branches easier to establish within the European Community to facilitate a free choice of location throughout the Community. There then follows a series of other decisions, covered in later sections, including organization, control and the management of each department.

6.4.4   Portfolio investment

Less discussed than direct investment, portfolio plays as large a role in the international flow of funds and is almost certainly expanding more rapidly.[9] Indeed, the internationalization of the money markets is an outstanding feature of recent years. Similar motives come into play as with direct investment, especially that of spreading income across a variety of economies. The smaller, newer stock exchanges (like those of the Philippines and South Korea) are growing particularly rapidly. Another feature is the growth of international currencies and bonds. A large part of portfolio investment arises from diversification policies of fund managers who are sought after by companies anxious to sell their shares in international markets. The eagerness to sell equity as widely as possible contrasts with the dislike of joint ventures. The wider the spread of equity, the greater the managers' power over against shareholders. For other forms of portfolio investment beside equity a large variety of instruments are appearing to match demand. Commodities and futures are playing an increasing part in the flow of funds as well as equities and loans.

6.4.5   Disinvestment

The obverse side of investment is disinvestment which has been increasingly studied over the last 15 years.[10] Any sale of equity abroad is a disinvestment which can, therefore, be total or partial. It can, again, be either voluntary or compulsory. Contrary to some beliefs, most disinvestment is not as a result of nationalization or expropriation. In one survey only four per cent of the instances investigated turned out to be from either of these causes; 33 per cent were through liquidations, and the majority of 63 per cent as a result of a sale of assets.[11] Any of these courses may be a sign of withdrawal or advance. Not all forms of disinvestment are disasters.

Rationalization

This is a principal cause of voluntary disinvestment, and a continuous process. Many foreign investments are opportunistic, undertaken because an agent is for sale, a well-managed company is available for takeover, a threat to a market has become urgent or any of numerous similar reasons. Under such circumstances disinvestment is part of corporate growth, not a retreat. New technologies, actions by competitors or changes in a market may also stimulate a disinvestment through which a company rationalizes while growing.

Other voluntary sales of assets

Any closure of facilities in which equity is reduced in a subsidiary is disinvestment. Apart from rationalization, the reasons may include: lack of viability in a particular market; there are seen to be commercial advantages in selling equity in the subsidiary to a local partner or to local shareholders; funds raised from a sale can be more profitably employed in another unit of the company.

Compulsory disinvestment

This usually takes the form of nationalization or indigenization. The compulsory purchase, or confiscation, of foreign assets by governments is less common than it used to be, which is not to say that it may not increase. The current trend in many parts of the world is towards the state sale of assets rather than the reverse. On the other hand, indigenization, the compulsory sale of foreign assets to local citizens, is likely to increase as the stock of savings in a particular country grows. Local entrepreneurs will bring pressure to bear on governments in developing countries to make more openings for themselves.

6.4.6   Investment in industry sector and geographical area

One of the trends in the literature on multinationals is towards specific industry sectors or geographical areas. The United Nations Centre on Transnational Corporations' publications have concentrated on these topics, in addition to the relations between companies and governments, but a number of monographs also exist. The following list of studies begins with primary production.

Primary industries – agriculture, extraction and mining

Many of the studies of developing-country investment (see below) concentrate on agriculture and mining. Among specialist studies in mining is: *Transnational Corporations and Contractual Relations in the World Uranium Industry: A Technical Paper* (1983): United Nations Centre on Transnational Corporations. An apparently narrow scope masks a study that raises a wide range of international investment issues. Uranium is a specialist fuel with a limited number of buyers mainly in the atomic energy industries. The suppliers are numerous companies, both in mining and other forms of energy supply (principally oil). National security and commercial insecurity have combined to keep newcomers out of the industry, while world over-production has ensured that prices have been even more volatile than those of other commodities. The early high prices, and high expectations, led to exploration for fresh sources and the promise of prosperity to many countries. The subsequent slump has meant problems, especially for a country like the Niger whose development plans were built around uranium.

Secondary industries – manufacture

Most of the classic studies of multinationals confined themselves to manufacturing. Three industries account for the bulk of specialized sectors – automotive, electrical and pharmaceuticals – although there are company histories, especially in firms dominated by well-known entrepreneurs, in most established industries. A study of the global textile industry (Toyne, B and others (1984): *The Global Textile Industry*, Allen & Unwin) contains little on international investment.

Automotive

A historical review of this industry is to be found in Maxcy, G. (1981): *The Multinational Motor Industry*, Croom Helm. This book also considers company–government relations in a sector where the main companies are large employers in several countries and in which rationalization is frequently undertaken. According to Maxcy, most foreign investment has come about as a result of tariff barriers or for defence against other changes as in relative wage costs or exchange rates. See also: *Transnational Corporations in the International Auto Industry* (1983), United Nations Centre on Transnationals.

Electricals and electronics

Almost unnoticed, the electrical industries have taken over as typical employers from more traditional sectors. This stands as a sub-theme to the major moves from agriculture to manufacture to services which have characterized the industrial nations and are now spreading to the Third World. In Britain, for instance, electronics showed the highest growth among the few manufacturing sectors that grew at all in the early 1980s.[12] The world growth figures were outstanding.

Transnational Corporations in the International Semiconductor Industry (1986), United Nations Centre on Transnational Corporations, reviews foreign investment in an industry whose size has multiplied by about five in the United States and Europe over ten years, and by considerably more in Japan. The study shows the structure of an industry which, in spite of a few giants, retains many large multinational manufactures. It also shows a trend towards concentration, and especially to vertical integration, as well as the growth of operations in developing countries (mainly in the Far East). The rapid growth of these latter – three of the Korean electronics companies are now themselves multinationals – is likely to increase competition dramatically, however much the market grows.

Pharmaceuticals
This is another sector on which the United Nations Centre on Transnational Corporations has produced a report – *Transnational Corporations and the Pharmaceutical Industry* (1979). This report suggests that a two-tier structure is emerging. One tier consists of a limited number of 'specialist innovative' companies dominating the new products market; the other is a larger number of 'broad-line generic' suppliers. The costs of research and the requirements of clinical testing in each country lie behind this trend. The specialist innovative multinationals are expected to continue to diversify into other products to hedge against the risks of the long-term research required for new drugs. They will also manufacture generics. Government control of purchasing is also likely to increase in order to contain the drugs' bills incurred by national health authorities.

Tertiary industries – services

The service sector is a diverse group which includes finance, insurance and advertising as well as transport and tourism. As the proportion of manufacturing to service industries has declined, generalizations are still being made which are irrelevant to the service sector, but the balance is changing. General literature on the multinational service industries increased greatly in the 1980s. One issue that came to light is the influence on foreign investment of non-tariff barriers. Financial and insurance services, for instance, are the subject of regulations protecting local and professional interests in most countries. International forums are currently discussing such practices. Another characteristic is that service companies – including the financial, but also advertising, market research and many others – are under pressure to develop international networks to provide a global service for their customers.

References

The following are some recent publications on the service industries internationally:

Boddewyn, J.J. and others (1986): 'Service multinationals: conceptualization, measurement and theory', *Journal of International Business Studies*, Vol. 17, No. 3, Fall, pp. 41–57.

Dixon, D.F. and Smith, M.F., (1983): 'Theoretical foundations for services marketing strategy', in Berry, L.L. and others: *Emerging Perspectives on Marketing Services*. American Marketing Association.

Enderwick, P. (ed.) (1988): *Multinational Service Industries*. Beckenham: Croom helm.

Gray, P.H. (1983): 'A negotiating strategy for trade in services', *Journal of World Trade Law*, No. 17, September–October.

Herman, B. and Hoist, B. van (undated): *International Trade in Services: Some Theoretical and Practical Problems*. Netherlands Economic Institute.

Advertising

Like other services, international advertising is provided by a mixture of multinational firms and international consortia of national firms. The largest multinationals are almost all American or Japanese. In addition to the need to provide for international customers, growth has been explained by the rapid growth of advertising almost everywhere. Market entry, for the investor, is usually by takeover. A greenfield project proves too expensive since it takes a long time (eight to ten years) to build up a viable market share. Publications on international advertising include the following:

Peebles, D.M. and Ryans, J.K. (1984): *Management of International Advertising*. Allyn & Bacon

Transnational Corporations in Advertising (1979). United Nations Centre on Transnationals.

Weinstein, A.K. (1977): 'Foreign investment by service firms: the case of international advertising agencies', *Journal of International Business Studies* No. 8, Spring–Summer, pp. 83–91.

Banking

In addition to their need to follow customers abroad, the banks have become foreign investors to match their competitors and to ensure for themselves a place in the international money markets. The foreign subsidiary is frequently a joint venture, even a minority holding; this is partly to circumvent non-tariff barriers, local restrictions on banking activity, and partly to restrict capital committed to allow a wider international spread. In the case of United States' Banks, among others, foreign investment has enabled them to free themselves from constraints at home. Their subsidiaries in London, for instance, were able to provide services forbidden by United States banking laws. Publications on international banking include the following:

Grubel, H.G. (1985): *Multinational Banking*, Research notes and discussion papers No. 56. Institute of South East Asian Studies.

Pecchioli, R.M. (1983): *The Internationalization of Banking: The Policy Issues*. Organisation for Economic Cooperation and Development.

Transnational Banks (1981). United Nations Centre on Transnationals.

Geographical areas

Under this heading are included investment from and to specific areas. Among the publications are the following:

Investment from industrialized countries

Dunning, J.H. (1986): *Japanese Participation in British Industry*. Croom Helm.

Hornell, E. and Vahlne, J.-E. (1986): *Multinationals: the Swedish Case*. Croom Helm.

Italia Multinazionale: L'internazionalizzione dell' industria italiana (1986). Vol. I, 24 Ore, Edizioni del Sole.

Rugman, A.M. (1986): 'The role of multinational enterprises in US-Canadian economic relations', *Columbia Journal of World Business*, Vol. 21, No. 2, Summer.

Rugman, A.M. (1984): 'The strategic management of Canada's multinationals: who needs high tech?', *Business Quarterly*, Fall.

Savary, J. (1984): *French Multinationals*. St Martin's Press.

Stopford, J.M. and Turner, L. (1986): *Britain and the Multinationals*. Wiley.

Investment from developing countries

Investment to Developing Countries: Activities of Transnational Corporations in South Africa and Namibia and the Responsibilities of Home Countries with Respect to their Operations in this Area (1986). United Nations Centre on Transnational Corporations.

Mirza, H. (1986): *Multinationals and the Growth of the Singapore Economy*. Croom Helm.

Transnational Corporations in South Africa and Namibia: United Nations Public Hearings (1986). Volume II, Verbatim Reports. United Nations Centre on Transnational Corporations.

Transnational Corporations in World Development (1983): United Nations Centre on Transnational Corporations.

Wells, L.T. (1983): *Third World Multinationals: The Rise of Foreign Investments from Developing Countries*. MIT Press.

Notes

1. In this chapter, the word 'investment' is used in the conventional sense, implying some ownership. This is not to ignore the logic of the view that all foreign activities imply some investment (a point made in the last chapter).

2. See Brooke (1986) p. 100. Maxcy (1981) p. 270, (see Section 6.4.6 below) asserts that, in his sample, defence is the only reason for foreign investment. There is a suspicion, to put it no higher, that other reasons are becoming more important and are likely to show up more in studies in the future.

3. See Stopford and Wells (1974), p. 5.

4. See Chapter 6.3, note 2.

5. An early example of such research was presented in Brooke. M.Z. and Remmers, H.L. (1970): *The Strategy of Multinational Enterprise* (1st edn). Longman. See especially pp. 260–71 and p. 313.

6. Robock and Simmonds (1983) pp. 257–8. The following discussion, together with Table 6.4.1, draws on Stopford and Wells (1974) pp. 99–124; Vernon and Wells (1976) pp. 22–7; Walter and Murray (1982) pp. 31. 19–20; Terpstra (1983) pp. 349–54; Robinson (1984) pp. 152–78; as well as the author's own research: see Brooke

and Remmers (1978) pp. 200–23; Brooke (1984) pp. 193–4 and 278–81, and Brooke (1985) pp. 72–82. A method for a cost-benefit analysis is to be found in Robinson (1984) pp. 170–4.

7. Stopford and Wells (1974) pp. 100 and 106; the following sentences refer to Chapter 9 called 'The quest for additional resources'.

8. Nearly equal in numbers, that is. See, for example, a report in the *Financial Times* entitled 'Survey: Finance and Investment' (6 May 1980). This report stated that 54 per cent of new foreign direct investment in the United States at the time was by greenfield ventures.

9. 'Almost certainly', because accurate figures are not available. One estimate (from figures published in the *Statistical Abstract of the United States 1984*, US Bureau of the Census 1984, p. 818) says that United States income from unincorporated affiliates was 76.7 per cent of that from direct investment, but the figure changes to 62.3 per cent if retained earnings are taken into account. For one aspect of portfolio investment – foreign pension funds in the United States – see Ehrlich (1983).

10. See, for example Boddewyn, J.J. (1983); Grunberg, L. (1981); Hood and Young (1982); Marois, B. (1979); Van den Bulcke, D. (1979); and Wilson, B. (1980). Note that some authorities use 'disinvestment' and some 'divestment', the latter when there is a compulsory element. The word divestment is avoided here.

11. See Torneden, R. 1975: *Foreign Disinvestment by US Multinationals*, Praeger. A pioneer study of disinvestment is reported in Sachdev, J.C. 1976: 'Disinvestment – corporate strategy or admission of failure', *Multinational business*, No. 4, pp. 12–19. Van den Bulcke has published a series of studies of disinvestment: see Van den Bulcke and others (1979). See also: 'Disinvestment by American multinational companies: the case of Belgium', *Bulletin de l'IRES*, 1979, No. 55, UCL, Louvain la Neure; 'Disinvestment and loss of employment: a comparison between foreign and Belgian enterprises', EIASM, Workshop on European Unemployment and Productivity, Oslo, 1982.

12. With 1980 as a base year of 100, in 1985:
    computers and office machinery stood at 270.9;
    telecommunications equipment at 123.7;
    processing plastics (125.0) and basic industrial chemicals (118.6) were the only other major manufacturing sectors that had not fallen below 100.

General References

See also publications on joint ventures in Section 6.4.2 and on sectors and industrial areas in Section 6.4.6.

Boddewyn, J.J. (1983): 'Foreign divestment theory: is it the reverse of FDI theory?' *Weltwirtschaftlikes Archiv*, Vol. 119, No. 2.

Brooke, M.Z. (1984): *Centralization and Autonomy*. Holt, Rinehart and Winston.

Brooke, M.Z. (1985): *Selling Management Services Contracts in International Business*. Holt, Rinehart and Winston.

Brooke, M.Z. and Remmers, H.L. (1978): *The Strategy of Multinational Enterprise* (2nd edn). Pitman.

Clarke, I.M. (1985): *The Spatial Organization of Multinational Corporations.* Croom Helm.

Ehrlich, E.E. (1983): 'Foreign pension fund investments in the United States', *Federal Reserve Bank of New York Quarterly Review* No. 8, Spring, pp. 1–12.

Grunberg, L. (1981): *Failed Multinational Ventures.* Lexington Books.

Hood, N. and Young, S. (1982): *Multinationals in Retreat: the Scottish Experience.* Edinburgh University Press.

Juhl, P. (1985): 'Economically rational design of developing countries' expropriation towards foreign investment', *Management International Review,* Vol. 25, No. 2, pp. 44–52.

Marois, B. (1979): 'L'art de desinvestir', *Revue francaise de gestion,* May–June.

Robinson, R.D. (1984): *Internationalization of Business.* Dryden Press.

Robock, S.H. and Simmonds, K. (1983): *International Business and Multinational Enterprise.* Irwin

Terpstra, V. (1983): *International Marketing* (3rd edn). Dryden Press.

Van den Bulcke, D. and others. (1979): *Investment and Divestment Policies of Multinational Corporations in Europe.* Saxon House.

Vernon, R. and Wells, L.T. (1976): *Manager in the International Economy* (3rd edn). Prentice-Hall.

Walter, I. and Murray, T. (1982): *Handbook of International Business.* Wiley.

Wilson, B. (undated): *Disinvestment of Foreign Subsidiaries.* UMI Research Press.

6.5

International Control and Planning

'Control' and 'planning' are words that can be used to describe a broad area of thought or a bundle of techniques. This chapter is devoted to the international application of techniques, but the writers quoted do not necessarily make the distinction which is clarified in the following paragraphs.

Control is used of the exercise of authority between superior and subordinate units in an organization. This use finds a place in Chapter 6.10 under centralization and decentralization. In this chapter, however, *control* is used of techniques: the reporting system and other means by which commercial information is passed from one unit to another. Items of information are selected to provide a guide to the success or failure of the subsidiary. Control, in this sense, is equivalent to monitoring. It is usually administered by a finance department and is also considered under finance and accounting (Chapters 6.6 and 6.12).

The distinction between the exercise of authority and the techniques of monitoring is not watertight and one focus of interest is the relationship between the two. Do they go together? Is an elaborate monitoring system a sign of centralization or — on the contrary — does it make decentralization possible? These questions are much discussed.

Planning is similarly used in more than one sense. The strategic options that form the basis of corporate planning were considered in Chapter 6.1, while the information on which the plans can be developed is considered elsewhere. This chapter looks at the process along with the techniques. Although they usually occur in different bodies of literature — planning is to be found under business policy and control (as used in this chapter) under finance and accounting — the two subjects come together in practice since the planning provides criteria by which the control information can be tested, while the reports form a major input to the planners. Figure 6.5.1 outlines the interrelationships, sometimes implicit rather than overt, which influence studies of these subjects.

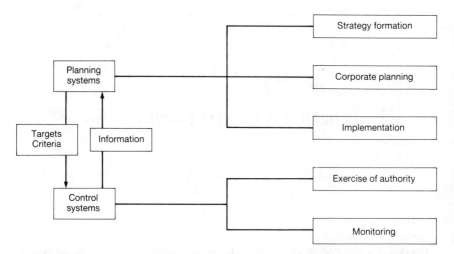

Figure 6.5.1   A Model for the Study of Interrelationships in the Control and Planning Systems

6.5.1   Control

Studies of control systems are concerned with the following issues in addition to the interrelationships already discussed.

(1) *Contrasts in understanding* the purpose of the system. Managers at different levels, both at home and abroad, have been found to interpret control systems differently. Head-office executives are likely to concentrate on the need for management information which alerts them to opportunities and problems worldwide. Control may be seen as a means of assessing bonuses, an insurance policy against disaster, a tool to discipline subsidiary managers, a means of management education (drawing attention to specific priorities) or as a method of appraisal on the results of which both the continued existence of subsidiary and the careers of its managers can depend. For a general discussion of ambiguities in control systems, see Daft and MacIntosh (1984).

(2) *Distortions caused by extraneous factors.* The value of information is limited by factors that are difficult to incorporate or allow for in reporting systems. These factors include internal distortions caused by transfer pricing and external influences like exchange rates, terms of trade and local regulations.

Exchange fluctuations are among the influences on which attention has been concentrated; but the attention is based on a number of different points of departure. An article by Lessard and Lorange (1977), for instance, identifies the means by which exchange-rate considerations can be kept out of comparisons of performance with budget. Eliminating such a bias is more difficult when evaluating a subsidiary by corporate standards.

An investigation into the effects of currency exchange in a sample of 70 United States' multinationals was reported by Gernon (1983). The investigation showed that, after a change in rules for external reporting by the Financial Accounting Standards' Board, 60 per cent of the companies were also using that standard for internal purposes. A consequence of this, it was pointed out, was that evaluations (and the salary adjustments that went with them) became dependent on currency fluctuations over which managers had no control. The article reports that 'the translation issue presented more unresolved problems when attempting to conduct an effective evaluation of foreign operations than did any other issue'.

It is also suggested that top-level managers do not know how to interpret performance figures presented in local currencies. This suggests that, whatever the detailed monitoring carried out by a controller's department, the higher tier of management is looking at results biased by exchange fluctuations. This issue is picked up in a study of British companies (Demirag (1988)), but the author also shows that a higher proportion of his sample used local currencies than in the American studies. In both countries it was agreed by a majority that, whatever the practices, exchange movements should be eliminated.

(3) *The degree of participation* in the development and operation of a system. It has been suggested that there are cultural differences on this issue. One research, for instance, suggested that Japanese controllers prefer less participation than American (Daley and others, 1985). Another suggested a similar difference between Mexican and American (Whitt (1979)).

(4) *The relationship between control and planning.* This relationship itself divides into two – the use of control information as a main input into planning and the effect on the control system of the length of the planning horizon.

(5) *The range of tools employed.* Doz and Prahalad (1984) argue that too narrow a range of control techniques produces unsatisfactory results.

(6) *The strength of the controls.* There are a number of measures used in the literature of the strength of controls; these include:

the amount of information required and how detailed it needs to be; an example from Japanese firms is provided by Pascale and Athos (1981);
the frequency of reporting and its scheduling; and
the penalties, real or assumed, for not reporting on schedule.

(7) *The role of internal auditors.* It is widely believed among practitioners that travelling auditors are the most cost-effective means of control. Studies frequently appear to overlook such perceptions. An apparently loose control system can, in fact, be effective as a result of frequent internal audits.

6.5.2 Planning

Formal corporate planning has expanded in the last 30 years with the growth and diffusion of new concepts and techniques. Studies have frequently brought strategy and planning together – the phrase 'strategic planning' was in vogue during the 1970s – but the study of planning is usually concerned with the methods through which both strategies and operations are devised. Internationally there are two issues: that part of a company's planning which concerns its international operations and the process of disseminating corporate planning techniques internationally within a company. Most research has concentrated on the former which can itself be divided into three parts:

strategic (long-term – what do I want to do?);
tactical (medium-term – how do I organize my resources to make that happen?);
operational (short-term – how do I make day-to-day arrangements in organizing my resources?).

All three have to be modified by *contingency planning* – things never work out as intended.

Corporate planning – strategic

International Strategic Planning is the subject of a seminal article[1] which develops a model showing the options that companies use. This article places corporate planning in its context as a framework for decision-making. The model is based on an assessment of the strengths and weaknesses of a company together with those of its subsidiaries and competitors. A second line concerns opportunities, risks and strategic issues by geography and by product. This is followed by a third line of objectives by geography and product as well as strategies for entry and expansion. As so often with models of this type, any illogicalities in the order are met by drawing arrows pointing in many directions; however irritating, these do bring out the complexity of strategic planning. The model also covers the skills needed to evaluate the political, economic, social, legal, technical and commercial environments.[2]

An interesting issue is the degree of structure in the planning system. The author assumes that the more detailed the system, the less flexible, and that companies adopt less structured systems when they need greater flexibility; but this is not necessarily the case – a less detailed system can also be rigid, if it does not contain provision for change. Lists are provided of factors and criteria useful in evaluating the competition; the author surprisingly suggests that these lists have to used in a qualitative rather than a quantitative analysis. As well as the shortage of information in some countries, the lack of quantitative data is partly due to the difficulty of defining a competitor; if this is a unit of a company, it may be difficult to make a reliable calculation. The article ends with an evaluation of some methods of opportunity and risk analysis, notably that of the Boston Consulting Group. Of its use by one firm, he says that this method 'is more sophisticated than may appear on the surface'.

Diffusion of planning

A specifically international issue is the degree to which corporate planning activities are diffused worldwide. A group of investigators based at Columbia University[3] has brought together evidence of a fairly rapid spread. They suggest that foreign subsidiaries often take up head-office (American) practices with even more enthusiasm than the parent company itself. The word 'enthusiasm' may mask a considerable pressure to adopt practices believed to have been responsible for the parent company's international growth. One of these articles (Capon and others 1984) demonstrates a similar ambiguity about the role of planning to that found for control. Questions were asked about planning as a device for conflict resolution, for dealing with uncertainty and risk, for allocating corporate resources and for sequencing future activities among other related uses. There was little unanimity and only a high level of agreement in answers to questions about resources and future activities. Planning was seen narrowly as a bundle of techniques to aid the decision-maker and not broadly as a process for steering the company.

Notes

1. Dymsza (1984).
2. Other models can be found in Davidson (1982) Chapter 8.
3. See Capon and others, 1980 and 1984.

References

Control

Choi, F.D.S. and Mueller, G.G. (1984): *International Accounting*. Prentice hall.

Daft, R.L. and Macintosh, N.B. (1984): 'The nature and use of formal control systems for management control and strategy implementation', *Journal of Management*, No. 10, pp. 43–66.

Daley, L. and others (1985): 'Attitudes towards financial control systems in the United States and Japan', *Journal of International Business Studies*, No. 16, pp. 91–110.

Demirag, I.S. (1988): 'Assessing foreign subsidiary performance: the currency choice for UK MNCs', *Journal of International Business Studies*, Summer, pp. 257–75.

Doz, Y. and Prahalad, C.K. (1984): 'Patterns of strategic control within multinational corporations', *Journal of International Business Studies*, Fall, pp. 55–72.

Eiteman, D.K. and Stonehill, A.I. (1986): *Multinational Business Finance* (4th edn). Addison-Wesley.

Flamholtz, E. (1983): 'Accounting, budgeting and control systems in their organizational context: theoretical and empirical perspectives', *Accounting, Organizations and Society*, No. 8, pp. 153–69.

Gernon, H. (1983): 'The effect of translation on multinational corporations' internal performance evaluation', *Journal of International Business Studies*, Spring/Summer, pp. 103–12. (The author refers to a Financial Accounting Standards Board document of 1975.)

Lessard, D.R. and Lorange, P. 1977: 'Currency changes and management control: resolving the centralization/decentralization dilemma', *Accounting Review*, July, pp. 628–37.

Pascale, R.T. and Athos, A.G. (1981): *The Art of Japanese Management*. Simon and Schuster.

Whitt, J.D. (1979): 'Motivating lower level management of Mexican affiliates', *Management Accounting*, June, 46–9.

Planning

Capon, N. and others (1980): 'International diffusion of corporate and strategic planning practices', *Columbia Journal of World Business*, Fall, pp. 5–13.

Capon, N. and others (1984): 'A comparison of corporate planning practice in American and Australian manufacturing companies', *Journal of International Business Studies*, Fall, pp. 41–54.

Davidson, W.H. (1982): *Global Strategic Management*. Wiley.

Dymsza, W.A. (1984): 'Global strategic planning: a model and recent developments', *Journal of International Business, Studies*, Vol. 15, No. 2, Fall, pp. 169–83.

6.6

International Money Management

6.6.1 Introduction

Most large firms operate a centralized reporting and management system for long-term investment planning, the raising of long-term finance, and for monitoring the control of working capital by operating divisions. Although firms may be prepared to treat their operating divisions as profit centres, responsible for their own costs and revenues, they are rarely willing to allow divisions to operate as investment centres responsible for raising and deploying their own funds. Central treasury control enables a firm to improve the terms on which it raises long-term capital through large-scale share issues or borrowings; and to minimize the need for raising capital externally by using cash surpluses generated in some divisions to finance the cash requirements of other divisions. Consequently, decisions about the source from which funds are raised and the use to which funds are put are invariably centralized, especially when companies operate in a number of different countries.

Companies involved in exporting, importing or operating on a multinational basis are subject to the risk of losses from exchange-rate changes. They may also make gains, but this is unlikely to be a problem. A British company exporting $1.8 million of products to a customer in the United States when the current exchange rate is £1=$1.80 (or $1=55.55p) would expect to receive £1 million for these products. If, during the period between concluding the sales contract and receiving the dollars the exchange rate were to fall to, say, £1=$1.90 (or $1= 52.63p) the company would find that when it came to convert its dollar-receipts into sterling through the foreign exchange market, its sterling receipts would be £947,400 rather than £1m; this would reduce or even eliminate any profit on the transaction. On the other hand if the exporter were to experience a rise in the dollar exchange rate *vis-à-vis* sterling, the sterling receipts from exports would rise, creating windfall profits.

A British firm importing DM 3m of products from a supplier in Germany when the current exchange rate is £1=DM3 (or DM1=33.3p) would expect to pay £1m for these products. If during the period between concluding the purchase contract and paying the DM to the supplier the exchange rate of the DM were to rise to say, £1=DM 2.9 (or DM1=34.48p) then the firm would find that when it came to convert its sterling payments into deutschmark through the foreign exchange market, its sterling payment would be £1,034,500 rather than £1m, which again could serve to reduce or eliminate profit on the transaction. On the other hand, if the exporter were to experience a fall in the deutschmark against sterling, the sterling cost of German purchases would fall, creating a windfall profit. Multinational firms are subject to exchange-rate losses (or gains) from their exports and imports of raw materials, components and finished products and also from the changing value of their overseas assets, interest and dividend payments and other flows.

When exchange rates vary daily, under a floating exchange-rate regime or a regime of internationally agreed fixed exchange rates which are subject to periodic revision, firms are subject to exchange-rate risks like those above. The pages that follow contain a brief exploration of how firms identify the nature and extent of the risks to which they are subject; whether they pursue an active or passive stance in relation to these risks; and the various internal and external means they can adopt to minimize such risks. The intention is to provide a brief overview of such international money-management problems; readers requiring more detail about these topics can consult one of the basic texts in this area such as Shapiro (1989), Eiteman and Stonehill (1989), Buckley (1986), and McRae and Walker (1980).

6.6.2 Foreign trading-risk exposure

Companies that operate on an international basis are exposed to a number of possible financial risks over and above the normal trading risks encountered by domestic firms. First, they face a degree of political risk such as the expropriation of their overseas assets or reduction in the value of such assets through the price of dividend restriction policies, or restrictions on the repatriation of capital or dividends imposed by host countries. A firm may also face the risk of losses from dramatic exchange-rate changes brought about by market reaction to major political or economic policy changes in a country, as Cosset and Rianderie (1985) demonstrate. Chapter 6.12 offers a fuller discussion of these political risks and the steps which multinational firms can take to counter them.

In addition, international firms may face increased risks of failure to pay by customers. The usual bad debts problem encountered by firms may be exacerbated where firms deal with foreign customers because of the increased difficulties of checking the credit-worthiness of overseas customers, of pursuing debtors through unfamiliar legal systems and of repossessing goods following non-payment where these are outside the country.

The potential additional credit risk on overseas sales makes it imperative for an exporter to agree the terms of a transaction with its importing customer before goods are shipped – including price, insurance, freight, date of shipment, date of payment and payment method. Various payment methods carry different credit risks and speeds of cash collection. At one extreme the exporter could arrange cash with order, which would guarantee him immediate payment, or less stringently could insist on cash on delivery. However, such terms are unattractive to purchasers who bear the whole burden of financing the shipment and are rarely used. At the other extreme the importer could arrange open-account terms with the exporter under which the account will be settled at a predetermined date after the goods have been shipped. Here financing of the deal falls on the exporter; and since the exporter loses control of the goods which pass to the customer he is in a weak legal position if payment is not subsequently forthcoming. Between these extremes a variety of payment methods may be employed, including the use of bills of exchange and documentary letters of credit. To cover the risk of default an exporter may seek credit insurance through such schemes as the United Kingdom Export Credit Guarantee Department, which in return for a premium reimburse the exporter in the event of default by the purchaser. Furthermore, when countries accumulate large overseas debts because of balance-of-payments deficits, they are likely to impose exchange controls and other currency restrictions which may make it difficult for firms to collect and repatriate revenues even from sound customers.

Research has concentrated on the means of predicting when and where such payments problems are likely to arise. Abdullah (1985) proposed an index based on five characteristics which would be expected to provide such a warning. These were: a significant erosion in a country's international liquidity; a faster growth in external debt than export earnings; an increase in the inflation rate; a deterioration in export earnings; and adverse political developments. Abdullah demonstrates how the index can be applied to specific countries.

In recent years much attention has been directed towards the financial risks to firms from exchange-rate changes. The subject of exchange-rate exposure has been intensively studied over the past two decades or so, particularly since the movement to a worldwide floating exchange-rate regime in the early 1970s. Where a company has assets, liabilities or income-streams denominated in currencies other than its own, these assets, liabilities and income-streams are exposed to exchange risk in so far as a currency exchange-rate movement will change (for better or worse) their parent- or home-currency value. Researchers such as Jacque (1981) and Hekman (1983) categorize exchange risks, distinguishing three broad types.

(1) *Transactions exposure* arises from foreign currency transactions, both capital items such as foreign currency dividend and loan payments; and trading items such as foreign currency debtors and creditors arising from selling and purchasing goods or services. The export and import examples cited earlier were typical transactions exposures, where between the contract date and the date

where the debt is settled the firm is exposed for the amount of the debt. Such transactions exposures may result in an actual cash loss (or gain) to the company and any realized losses (or gains) will affect the company's tax position.

(2) *Translation exposures* arise when consolidating foreign subsidiaries' balance sheets and income statements expressed in local currencies into the parent company's group accounts are denominated in the parent's currency. The exchange rates used to translate assets, liabilities, revenues and expenses can change, affecting the parent currency-translated value of these assets. Chapter 6.12 discusses the nature of this problem and the various methods of translation that may be employed, so we need not dwell on these here. Suffice it to say that gains and losses on transactions are usually adjusted through the parent company's reserves so as not to affect the reported profit.

(3) *Economic exposure* is the effect of unexpected exchange-rate changes upon a firm's future cash-flows from operations. Economic exposure is the most important for the long-term health of a group of companies, since it reflects the effects of exchange-rate changes upon company sales volumes, prices and costs.

In measuring, monitoring and controlling exchange-rate exposure the above distinction is important, for some categories of exposure are easier to measure and control than others. The financial impact of transactions exposure is easiest to measure, because it is expressed in terms of the amounts of loans, debtors and creditors outstanding in any foreign currency, multiplied by the percentage exchange-rate change, to show the foreign exchange gain or loss. Even here, though, complications arise, since it can be argued that transaction exposure arises as soon as orders are placed rather than from the date of invoicing of sales or purchases, as Bond (1990) reminds us, so that the total amounts of working capital at risk are larger than mere debtors and creditors. Translation exposure requires the projected balance sheets and income statements of each subsidiary or group of subsidiaries expressed in a particular foreign currency to be assessed, then multiplied by the likely percentage exchange-rate change for that currency, in order to determine the likely foreign exchange gains or loss.

Economic exposure is the most difficult to measure since it is so wide-ranging and long-term. Buckley's (1986) listing of the effects of changing exchange rates communicates the broad ranging nature of economic exposure, where he mentions effects such as: the effects of devaluation upon a firm's export sales volumes, profit margins and cash flows; the effects of devaluation upon import-competing, domestic sales volumes, margins and cash flows; the costs of imported inputs after devaluation; and the levels of fixed and working capital.

Taxation treatment of foreign exchange gains and losses differs between countries and between different types of exposure. In most countries foreign exchange gains on normal trading transactions are regarded as trading income and taxed accordingly while exchange losses are allowable against trading income, though gains or losses on long-term capital transactions may be treated as capital gains or losses. However, since detailed tax regulations and tax rates differ from country to country, a multinational company would seek to arrange for foreign exchange gains to arise in countries with low tax rates and for foreign exchange losses to arise in countries with high tax rates, where they are tax allowable and where the company has taxable income to offset against losses, in order to minimize the firm's global tax bill. Taxation of translation gains and losses may involve more complex considerations, with differences in regulations, tax rates, double taxation agreements, transfer prices and tax havens all complicating matters, as Chapter 6.12 outlines. However, here again firms may seek to plan their tax affairs centrally to minimize their overall tax burden. Consequently it is important that tax and treasury planning are interlinked, to incorporate the effects of tax considerations on financing, capital expenditure and operating decisions.

6.6.3   Strategies for managing exchange-rate risk

A firm has two options on exchange risk management: aggressive and active or defensive and passive. Aggressive policies are usually advocated when it is felt that international markets for foreign exchange and capital are characterized by imperfections caused by government interference in currency and capital markets; these cause short-run exchange rates and interest rates to deviate from market expectations as embodied in forward exchange rates. To the extent that senior managers of a firm feel they are able to forecast future exchange rates and outguess market, they may seek to make as much profit as they can through changes in currency rates. Maximizing foreign exchange gains could mean seeking debt financing denominated in softer currencies that are likely to depreciate and reduce the domestic currency burden of loans; and invoicing sales in what are expected to be harder currencies that are likely to appreciate.

Alternatively firms may adopt defensive policies where senior managers believe that foreign exchange and capital markets are reasonably efficient so that forward exchange rates reflect future market trends, and it is impossible consistently to outguess the market. The defensive firm considers itself to be in the business of making and selling goods or services and adopts a foreign exchange stance designed to minimize losses from changing exchange rates. Minimizing potential losses could mean matching the currency denomination of assets with liabilities to minimize exposure; and attempting either to invoice export sales in its domestic currency or, where this is not possible, automatically covering the outstanding debt through hedging.

The extent to which a firm adopts either position depends upon the risk aversion of its senior managers, since aggressive policies may enable windfall gains to be made from currency changes but also entail a downside risk of losses. Risk-averse managers may prefer to forgo potential currency gains in order to minimize exposure to currency losses. Companies rarely fall neatly into one category or another but rather lie on a continuum of risk aggressiveness between these extremes and may vary their postures on foreign exchange risk over time. Collier, Davis, Coates and Longdon's 1990 report of a survey of 23 large British and United States multinationals shows a wide range of risk attitudes and associated ideas on treasury management. The other factor that determines the degree of 'aggressiveness' of a firm's posture is its ability to forecast exchange rates and in particular consistently to outguess the forward rate.

Long-term exchange rate forecasts are generally qualitative in nature and based upon the relative industrial efficiency of two countries. Medium-term forecasts are often based upon forecast relative inflation rates, following the purchasing power parity principle.[1] Short-term forecasts seek to measure deviations in a currency's exchange rate from its fundamental medium-term value, they are frequently based upon forecast relative interest rates following the interest rate parity principle, as Soenen and Aggarwal's (1987) survey results show. McRae and Walker (1980) review the evidence on forecasting accuracy. They suggest the empirical studies indicate that relative inflation rates serve as a reasonable predictor of medium-term exchange rates but that short-term deviations from these rates do occur which are broadly explicable in terms of interest-rate differences. The overall evidence on the effectiveness of forecasting in improving upon forward exchange rates is somewhat mixed, but to the extent that managers of many multinational companies believe they can outguess the market they adopt moderately aggressive exchange-rate positions.

6.6.4   Information systems

Appropriate information systems for monitoring currency flows within a company are required for both aggressive and defensive systems. Information systems should enable the extent of foreign currency exposure in different currencies to be identified so that managers can take appropriate steps to deal with these exposures. Some currency and cash management can be done at local operating levels as part of the normal processes of freeing cash tied up in working capital. However, overall management of currency exposure requires continuous flows of information from subsidiaries to the group treasury department on their foreign-exchange exposure. Such information should be forward-looking, embracing forecasts of balance sheets and income statements to help identify translation exposure, and cash-flow forecasts to assess transaction exposure. Information on orders received, sales made, orders placed and purchase invoices received in each currency need to be reported regularly and frequently to group treasury to assist in dealing with transaction exposure. From such data the treasury department can forecast foreign-currency receipts and payments and their anticipated date of receipt or payment as a basis for planning how to deal with the exchange-rate risks involved.

In order to concentrate all currency exposure in their central treasury function, some larger multinational companies have turned the treasury department into a separate company through which all trade is invoiced and then re-invoiced. Group companies invoice exports to other group companies through the re-invoicing company in the currency of the exporter, which in turn invoices the importing company in its own currency. In this way all the exchange risk is borne by the re-invoicing company. In the same way, all export sales to outside parties and imports from outside suppliers can be channelled through the re-invoicing centre in order to concentrate the currency risk there. Finally, the re-invoicing centre may take responsibility for group borrowings and act as banker to the group, concentrating responsibility for capital flows there. Baker and Aggarwal (1984) review the ways in which some major United States multinationals have organized their exposure management function; their results suggest a wide variety of approaches.

6.6.5 Methods of managing exchange-rate risk

There is a wide range of methods for managing exchange-rate risks, though these many be subdivided into two broad groups: internal techniques that can be used as part of a multinational firm's financial management procedures to minimize its exposure to exchange risk; and external techniques that rely upon contractual arrangements to insure against exchange losses that may arise from any exposed-currency positions, which have not been eliminated by internal measures. The outline of techniques presented below follows this broad distinction.

A)   Internal techniques for managing exchange-rate risk

A large multinational firm with a wide range of currency flows arising from its production and marketing operations has a range of techniques available for reducing exposed-currency positions or preventing them from arising.

One useful device is to offset the respective indebtedness of subsidiary companies which trade with one another, so that companies merely need to settle their indebtedness for the net amount owing. Taking a simple example of bilateral netting, if a US subsidiary of a British multinational group owes a German subsidiary the deutschmark equivalent of £3 million, while the German subsidiary owes the United States subsidiary the dollar equivalent of £2 million, then the actual cash remittance can be netted out, such that the US subsidiary pays the Germany subsidiary only the net amount of £1m worth of deutschmarks. By reducing the amount of intra-company receipts and payments of £5 million to the residual net amount of £1 million, the two companies save on the costs of converting currencies and transferring them through foreign-currency exchanges. More sophisticated multilateral netting schemes can also be employed which involve several subsidiaries trading with one another. Such netting requires centralized control of payments and sophisticated communication systems to ensure that subsidiaries notify the central treasury department of impending payments and receipts, as the treasury department prepares for periodic settlement dates for indebtedness.

A further means that an international firm may employ to minimize resort to foreign exchanges is currency matching. This entails matching currency inflows from external and inter-group sales with currency outflows from external and inter-group purchases, using receipts in a particular currency to make payments in that currency, thus reducing the need to go through foreign-exchange markets. Natural matching can only occur where there is a two-way cash flow in the same foreign currency, though it is also possible to undertake parallel matching of receipts and payments in two currencies whose exchange rates are expected to move closely in parallel. Again, the practice of currency matching necessitates a high degree of centralized treasury management and detailed notification by subsidiaries of their expected receipts and payments.

Multinational firms can also adjust credit terms between subsidiary companies which trade with one another in order to minimize exchange exposure. By paying obligations in advance of their due date (leading) or delaying payment of obligations beyond their due date (lagging), firms can facilitate currency matching and minimize exposure. Alternatively, firms may employ leading and lagging as part of an aggressive strategy for managing exchange risk to maximize expected exchange gains by taking advantage of expected devaluations and revaluations of currencies. Again, leading and lagging require central information-gathering and decision-making to ensure that the timing of intra-company settlements is optimal from a group point of view. Where leading and lagging are employed, this distorts the liquidity and profitability of subsidiary companies, so in evaluating the performance of managers of subsidiaries it becomes necessary to evaluate performance in pre-interest terms. Furthermore, because of the effects of leading and lagging on exchange rates and balance-of-payments figures, many governments have restricted the scope for such activities by specifying standard credit terms and by means of exchange controls.

Management of its assets and liabilities enables a multinational firm to control its exposure to transaction and translation exposures. Managers may adopt an aggressive approach seeking to increase exposed assets, revenues and cash flows denominated in strong currencies and to increase exposed liabilities, expenses and cash outflows in weak currencies to maximize their chances of windfall currency gains; or they may adopt a defensive posture, matching the currency denomination of assets and liabilities, revenues and expenses, and cash inflows and outflows to minimize foreign exchanges losses or gains.

In some respects, asset and liability management involves little more than good general working capital management practices such as minimizing cash tied up in stocks, collecting money quickly from debts, delaying payment to creditors where possible and remitting funds rapidly to head office. However, where an overseas subsidiary is located in a weak-currency country, there is an even stronger incentive to pursue these practices to reduce net current asset exposure in the weak currency and minimize exchange losses between making local sales, and collecting on the debts. As part of this process, the firm may consider various ways of accelerating the receipt of funds, both within countries and between countries, through such means as electronic fund transfers, direct debiting of customers' accounts and cable or telex remittances which reduce postal and cheque-clearing delays in transmitting cash.

The multinational firm, in managing assets and liabilities, must consider not only its working capital but also its longer-term financing and investment policies. Managements taking an aggressive exchange-exposure stand will seek to increase lending and reduce borrowing in strong currencies and expand borrowing and reduce loans in weak currencies, to maximize the gains to be made from exchange-rate changes. Rhee, Chang and Koveos (1985) stress the importance of borrowing in the weakest currency and lending in the strongest. Where subsidiary companies are located in weak-currency countries both aggressive and defensive headquarters' managers would seek to minimize translation exposure on their subsidiary's assets and investments by increasing borrowings in the same currency. Different interest rates between countries may also influence a firm's decision on which capital markets to use for borrowing since this affects the cost of capital, though since differential interest rates reflect the underlying relative strengths of currencies, interest-rate and exchange-rate considerations are generally interdependent.

Dealing with broader economic exposure involves trying to anticipate the effects of unexpected changes in exchange rates on the firm's future cash flows from operations; as such it involves a broader range of operating and strategic decisions. In the short run this may involve increasing local selling prices of products to counter the adverse effects of exchange-rate movements, to the extent that local competition, national price controls or administrative delays make it possible to implement quickly a fully matching price increase. Alternatively, the multinational firm may attempt to shift its sales mix to hard-currency countries or seek to source its supplies from soft-currency countries. In the longer term, it may necessitate the multinational firm shifting its production facilities from hard-currency to soft-currency countries.

Eiteman and Stonehill (1989) argue that the best means for a multinational to manage its economic exposure is to diversify its sales, location of production facilities and raw materials sources; and to diversify its financing base by raising funds in several currencies and in several capital markets. Such diversification creates opportunities for the firm to react to opportunities presented by disequilibrium in product, foreign exchange or capital markets. For example, where exchange-rate movements alter comparative costs in the firm's plants located in different countries, headquarters' managers may shift sourcing policies, thus increasing output from the cheaper plant and cutting output from the more expensive one. Again, where interest-rate differentials open up between markets that are not fully reflected in exchange rates, the multinational firm can switch its financing sources to lower its overall cost of capital.

B) External techniques for managing exchange-rate risk

Once a firm has adopted whatever internal methods are available to reduce its currency exposure, there is an increasingly varied range of financial instruments it can employ as part of its contractual arrangements to protect itself against currency risk. These instruments can be used by a firm to insure, hedge or cover against the possibility of losses from exposed exchange positions associated with its commercial transactions. A fuller discussion of these instruments can be obtained from international finance texts such as Buckley (1986) and McRae and Walker (1980); from treasury management texts like Heywood (1978) and Lassen (1982); or from more specialist books like those by Brown (1983) and Westwick (1986).

One of the most commonly used instruments for protecting exposed currency positions are forward foreign-exchange contracts with banks. Forward markets are available in most major currencies; by buying or selling currency in the forward market at a guaranteed forward exchange rate, a firm may protect itself against the effects of future changes in exchange rates upon its currency holdings or owings. For example, the earlier British exporter entering into an export contract on 30 September to sell $1.8 million of products would expect to receive $1.8 million from the customer on 31 December if the contract provided for three months' credit. If the spot exchange rate were £1=$1.80 ($1=55.55p) on 30 September the company might anticipate that its dollar receipts would be worth £1 million. However, the sterling amount which the company would actually receive for its $1.8 million on 31 December would depend upon the spot exchange rate at that date, which is unlikely to remain unchanged over the 90-day exposure period. There is a risk that the dollar might depreciate against sterling to, say, £1=$1.90 ($1=52.63p) on 31 December so that the final sterling receipt would be only £947,400. To avoid the possibility of such a loss the British exporter could, at the same time as agreeing the export contract on 30 September, sell the dollar receipts in the forward exchange market at a fixed 90-day forward rate of, say, £1=$1.82 ($1=54.95p) for delivery at the payment date of 31 December. Whatever then happens to the sterling/dollar exchange rate over the next 90 days, the contractual rate is fixed at 1:1.82. Hence on 31 December the company should receive its customer's payment of $1.8 million which can be delivered to the bank handling the forward deal, with the exporter receiving a sterling credit of £989,000 as agreed in the forward contract.

The cost to the exporter of providing forward cover and eliminating the exchange-risk element in the transaction is essentially the amount of the foreign currency debt multiplied by the difference between the spot exchange rate at the contract date of 30 September and the forward exchange rate, which in this case amounts to 1.8 million times (55.55p–54.95p) = £11,000. The size of this cost will depend upon the extent to which the forward rate on the foreign currency is at a discount (or a premium) compared with the spot exchange rate; for example, here the dollar is at a slight market discount compared with its spot rate.

When shipping delays occur or customers fail to adhere to credit terms, settlement dates cannot be predicted exactly. Here exporters or importers may resort to an option date forward contract or forward option which fixes the exchange rate when the forward contract is made but leaves open the exact maturity date for the firm to decide, as long as it falls within the option period. Returning to our earlier example, our exporter might agree a forward option on 30 September to sell $1.8 million forward at a forward rate of £1=$1.82 on a 90–120 day option, so that he can opt to sell the dollars any time between 31 December and 31 January, depending upon when the American customer pays up.

An alternative way of handling unspecified settlement dates is a swap deal involving the simultaneous buying and selling of a currency for different maturities. Returning to our earlier example, the British exporter would begin by covering the $1.8 million export sale with a forward currency sale, using a fixed date of 31 December delivery as the best estimate of when the American customer will pay. If a precise payment date is later agreed which is before the initial futures contract expires, say 30 November, then the initial settlement date of 31 December can be adjusted to the exact date of 30 November by a forward/forward swap. This is a pair of forward currency deals, the first involving a forward purchase of $1.8 million on 31 December to offset the original forward contract to sell $1.8 million on 31 December; the second involving a forward sale of $1.8 million on 30 November to cover the exposure on the original export deal. Where the precise payment date falls after the arbitrary date of 31 December chosen for the initial forward contract, the forward cover can be extended to, say, 31 January, by a spot/forward swap. This involves the exporter in a spot purchase of $1.8 million on 31 December to meet the original forward sale contract; and a new forward sale contract for $1.8 million for delivery on 31 January, to extend the cover on the export sale.

In practice, option date forward contracts are the preferred method of dealing with uncertain settlement dates, especially where a firm's export sales comprise a large number of small transactions with different settlement dates where it would be administratively costly to cover each individual transaction. In such cases it is easier to take out a single large forward option contract to cover the aggregate value of the expected currency receipts. Kwok (1987) suggests there is little difference in effectiveness between hedging individual transactions as opposed to combining them in one integrative hedging scheme.

Forward contracts are a popular means of covering transactions exposures, and contracts can be arranged for most major currencies for periods up to a year ahead. However, forward markets for currencies of small countries tend to be thinner, with smaller traded amounts, so it is more difficult to secure forward cover in such currencies. Nevertheless, as Soenen and Aggarwal found in their survey of 259 United Kingdom, Dutch and Belgian companies, forward-exchange contracts were much the most popular means of foreign exchange hedging.

Another means of protecting exposed currency positions is a financial futures contract: an agreement to sell or buy a standard quantity of a specific currency for delivery at one of four specified dates in the forthcoming year. The price or exchange rate of the currency future will be determined by demand and supply among dealers on the trading floors of organized futures exchanges such as those in London (London International Financial Futures Exchange) and Chicago (Chicago International Monetary Market). A company like the earlier British exporter can hedge against adverse exchange-rate movements of the dollar by taking a position in future contracts that is equal and opposite to its currency exposure, in order to lock in current exchange rates on future currency transactions. Dollars futures are traded in standard units of $100,000 for delivery in March, June, September or December, so the British exporter expecting to receive $1.8 million on 31 December would contact a broker at the end of September when the export contract is signed and ask him to purchase 18 standard contracts to sell dollars in December at the going market price/exchange rate. The broker would perform this service for the exporter in return for a commission and the exporter would be expected to pay a small proportion of the value of the contracts to the clearing house. Thereafter, when the American customer pays his $1.8 million debt, the British exporter can close his selling position in the futures market by making an offsetting deal of 18 standard dollar-purchase contracts.

Though futures markets provide a means of hedging transactions exposures, they do have disadvantages in this regard. First, financial futures markets exist for only a small range of the larger trading currencies like dollars, sterling and deutschmarks, so they cannot be used for certain currencies. Secondly, futures markets have only four delivery dates per year which may be difficult to match with the timing of a trader's export/import currency exposure. Finally, deals are done for standard quantities of currency which may make it difficult to achieve an exact hedge for a particular sum of currency exposed.

Yet another means of protecting exposed-currency positions is a currency option. Currency options provide the right, but not the obligation, to sell or buy a particular currency at a particular exchange rate at any time before a specified date. Option contracts are for standardized amounts, for example $50,000; and are for standard periods expiring in March, June, September and December.

Call-or-buy options confer the right to purchase a standardized amount of foreign currency at a specific exchange rate during a specified time period; while put-or-sell options confer the right to sell a standardized amount of foreign currency at a specific exchange rate. Option writers sell options in return for a premium and they have an obligation to perform if the option is exercised: they will have to sell the foreign currency at the stated exchange rate if a call-or-buy option is exercised or buy the foreign currency at the stated exchange rate if a put-or-sell option is exercised. Once an option has been written, it can be resold by the original buyer through organized option markets in Philadelphia, Chicago or London, for example, where its price will depend upon the market's view of future changes in the spot exchange rate of the underlying currency and the time left before the option expires.

Returning to our earlier example: the British exporter making a sale in September, and expecting to collect $1.8 million from this sale on 31 December, would be concerned about possible currency losses if the dollar exchange rate were to fall below the current spot rate of £1=$1.80 ($1=55.55p). To protect against this potential loss, in September the exporter could buy 36 standard ($50,000) put-or-sell options at an exchange rate of £1=$1.80 ($1=55.55p) which are due to expire in December. Thereafter, if the exchange rate of the dollar falls to say, £1=$1.90 ($=52.63p) then the value of the put options would increase and the exporter could make a net profit on expiry date to the extent that the spot currency price (52.63p) is below the option exercise price (55.55p) by an amount greater than the premium paid for the option. This profit would serve to compensate the exporter for the currency-exchange losses in converting his $1.8 million sales receipts back into sterling at a less favourable exchange rate.

Options may be particularly attractive to firms pursuing an aggressive exchange-rate management policy since they can be used to protect against the downside exchange risk on foreign currency debts or owings, while leaving open the upside potential for currency gains. However, premiums paid for options can be expensive. De Maskey and Baker (1989) acknowledge the high cost of options as a covering technique compared with currency futures but stress their offsetting flexibility. Furthermore, the currency options traded on the major markets are for standard capital amounts and have standardized maturity dates which make it difficult to match them with the exact amount and timing of exposure cover required by a company. However, there is now an active over-the-counter market in tailor-made options written by banks and sold privately to the customer who seeks currency cover.

As an alternative to covering or hedging in forward, futures and options markets, a firm can use short-term currency borrowing as a means of protecting itself against exchange-rate changes. For example, the earlier British exporter could, when arranging the export contract for $1.8 million on 30 September, simultaneously arrange to borrow $1.8 million repayable in three months and immediately convert this $1.8 million into sterling at the spot exchange rate of £1=$1.80 ($1=55.55p). Thereafter on 31 December when the American customer pays the $1.8 million which he owes the British exporter, this is used to repay the dollar loan. This borrowing transaction covers the British exporter against exchange risk since the export proceeds are converted immediately from dollars into sterling. However, the British exporter will have to pay interest at prevailing United States interest rates on the dollar loan for three months (and will receive interest on the converted sterling at prevailing British interest rates).

Where export sales have imprecise settlement dates they can still be covered by short-term borrowing by using foreign currency overdraft loans. For example, our British exporter would arrange a $1.8 million loan on 30 September for a period of up to, say, four months, then immediately convert the proceeds into sterling and remit them; he would repay this dollar loan as soon as his American customer pays up. Where the British exporter expects a continuing stream of small export sales and dollar receipts rather than a single large export order he can arrange a dollar borrowing facility for the aggregate of these sales at a fixed rate of interest. Thereafter, as each export contract is finalized, the exporter borrows dollars equal to the amount of the sale and converts these borrowed dollars into sterling at the spot exchange rate. As customers pay for their goods, the dollars they pay are used to repay some of the dollar borrowings.

The cost of this kind of hedging largely comprises the difference between the foreign currency interest which the British exporter has to pay on his borrowings and the home interest he earns on the repatriated currency. This technique can only be used as an exposure management tool for countries with reasonably developed local borrowing facilities, which do not restrict such borrowing as part of their exchange-control regulations.

As an extension of the currency-borrowing technique, a multinational company can cover itself against exchange-rate exposure by opening a bank account in each of the major currencies in which it trades, and maintaining an overdraft in each currency equal to the amount of its net debtors in that currency. For example, our British exporter would maintain a dollar account and each time he makes a dollar sale he will increase his dollar overdraft; while each time an American customer pays up in dollars, these will be used to pay off part of the overdraft. In this way the foreign currency assets and obligations of the British exporter would be balanced, so neutralizing the effects of any exchange-rate changes upon the company's sterling assets/liabilities. Currency overdrafts are particularly useful where a company has a large number of small export transactions in a variety of foreign currencies.

Foreign-currency bank accounts are also useful where a firm has both exports (and debtors) and imports (and creditors) with the same country, since it can use the account to deposit its receipts and make its payments in the local currency, netting any such receipts and payments so that only any net balance in the account is exposed and needs to be covered in the forward currency market.

A further means a company may employ to minimize its exchange exposure is a currency swap deal with another company: the two firms agree to swap an initial amount of currency at an agreed rate of exchange, exchange interest payments on these exchanged amounts and subsequently re-exchange the initial currency amounts at the maturity date. For example, our British exporter, having made an export deal for $1.8 million on 30 September and expecting to be paid this sum on 31 December, might enter into a swap deal with an American exporter, selling £1 million worth of goods to Britain who will be owed sterling by his customer in three months' time. Here our British exporter would arrange a swap on 30 September of $1.8 million for £1 million at the current spot exchange rate of £1=$1.80 ($1=55.55p). Now the British exporter owes £1 million in sterling and would agree to meet the sterling interest payments on this outstanding sum; while the US exporter will now owe $1.8 million and would meet the dollar interest payments on this sum. Under the terms of the swap agreement on 31 December the British exporter would re-exchange the sterling for dollars at the agreed exchange rate of £1=$1.80 to coincide with the payment of his trade debt by the American customer. Effectively the swap deal enables the British exporter to avoid hedging his export deal by means of dollar borrowing, but instead to hedge his export deal by sterling borrowing.

Swap deals often enable borrowers to gain access to currency markets that would otherwise be closed to them or to arrange loans on more competitive interest terms than would otherwise be the case. For example, our British exporter would no doubt find it easier and cheaper to arrange a sterling loan than a dollar loan, while his US partner would similarly find it easier and cheaper to raise a dollar loan. In this way, swaps can serve to reduce the credit costs of servicing exports and imports. Currency swaps need to be tailor-made to meet the individual needs of particular exporters and importers seeking to borrow particular amounts of particular currencies for particular periods of time. Major banking intermediaries have developed a marriage-broking role in matching partners for currency swaps. Swap deals merely exchange foreign-currency exposures; they do not involve the legal swapping of trade debts, so under swap deals the parties are still responsible for any bad debts if customers do not pay up when their goods become due for payment. Park (1984) examines some of the variants of swap deals that have developed over recent years and their advantages to participants.

Where an exporter agrees payment by his customer in the form of a bill of exchange, the exporter can arrange to discount the bill and receive payment before the settlement date, so protecting himself against exchange-rate exposure during the credit period. For example, if our British exporter drew up on 30 September a $1.8 million bill of exchange, redeemable on 31 December, and then arranged for this to be accepted immediately by the American buyer, then on 30 September the British exporter could discount the bill either with a US bank for, say, $1,710,000 which would be repatriated immediately at the current exchange rate of £1=$1.80 ($1=55.55p), or with a British bank for £950,000. Either way, the exporter is covered against exchange risk in return for the discount on the face value of the bill charged by the bank, in this case £950,000 or $90,000, less any interest earned on the repatriated £950,000 over the three months.

Like discounting, factoring can be used to cover export owings against exchange risk. Here our British exporter selling goods for $1.8 million on 30 September and expecting payment on 31 December would simply sell this $1.8 dollar debt on 30 September to a commercial bank or specialist factoring organization. The bank or factor will pay the exporter much less than the $1.8 face value of the debt, say $1.7 million or £944,300, because the bank or factor must then assume the risk that the customer may default, the exchange-rate risk over the three months and the interest-financing burden over the three months. This makes factoring an expensive method of cover, though it can help to reduce the exporter's sales accounting and credit collection costs.

Forfaiting provides yet another way for a firm to cover its export owings against exchange risk as well as the political and commercial risk of non-payment by an importer. Forfaiting operates in the same way as factoring, though forfaiting is often employed for arranging medium-term export financing for large items of capital equipment which typically are bought by state-owned firms and paid for in instalments spread over several years. Thus a British exporter selling goods for $1.8 million on 30 September and expecting four payments of $450,000 at yearly intervals could sell this $1.8 million dollar debt to a specialist finance firm (called a forfaiture) for an amount much less than the face value of the debt, forfaiting any subsequent rights to the debt. The forfaiter assumes any risk of non-payment of the debt, bears any exchange-rate risks over the period of the debt and provides credit financing for the sale.

Finally, an exporter may secure exchange-rate risk cover through government export credit agencies like the United Kingdom Export Credit Guarantee department or the United States Eximbank. In return for an additional premium, such agencies will cover an exporter not only against the risk of default by customers on credit sales but also against the financial consequences of adverse exchange-rate movements.

While the various external exchange-rate risk management schemes outlined above can all serve to hedge currency exposure, they are all secondary to the main internal techniques that serve to minimize the amount of a firm's exposure. Many of these internal techniques amount to little more than the efficient control of long-term investments and short-term working capital. However, in large multinational firms these practices require a degree of centralized monitoring and control which inevitably restrict the autonomy of operating divisions in the interests of avoiding sub-optimal money management.

6.6.6 Conclusion

Growth in world trade and the development of multinational businesses over recent decades has increased the volume and scope of international payments. At the same time the regime of floating exchange rates which has prevailed since the early 1970s has served to increase the uncertainty involved in international operations. These developments have heightened the interest of multinational enterprises in developing strategies for dealing with foreign-trade exposure, including the management of political, trade-credit and exchange-rate risks. In order to minimize the impact of these risks upon profit, a degree of centralized monitoring and control of money flows is necessary.

Once a multinational firm has adopted whatever internal measures it can to ameliorate the impact of such risks through diversifying its sources of finance, production facilities and markets, and by devices like payments netting, then it may need to resort to the use of various external means of managing risk. Fortunately, the growth of world trade and multinational companies has been paralleled by a growth in the size and complexity of money and capital markets, with banks and other financial institutions in New York, London and Tokyo offering integrated, worldwide, 24-hour borrowing and currency conversion facilities to trading companies. This growth in money and capital markets has fostered the development of increasingly sophisticated financial services such as forward currency markets, financial futures and currency options to serve the needs of international business.

Note

1. For an outline of the basic factors affecting exchange rates the reader may find Copeland (1989) useful.

References

Abdullah, F.A. (1985): 'Development of an Advance Warning Indicator of External Debt Servicing Vulnerability', *Journal of International Business Studies*, Vol. 16, No. 3, Fall, pp. 136–44.

Baker, J.C. and R. Aggarwal (1984): 'Foreign Exchange Risk in Multinational Companies – The Exposure Management Function', *The Business Graduate*, January.

Bond, G. (1990): 'Managing Currency and International Cash', *Management Accounting*, May, pp. 30–1.

Brown, B. (1983): '*The Forward Market in Foreign Exchange*'. Croom Helm.

Buckley, A. (1986): *Multinational Finance*. Philip Allan.

Collier, P., Davis, E.W., Coates, J.B. and Longden, S.G. (1990): 'The Management of

Currency Risk: Case Studies of US and UK Multinationals', *Accounting and Business Research*, Vol. 20, No. 79, pp. 206–10.

Copeland, L.S. (1989): *Exchange Rates and International Finance*. Addison Wesley.

Cosset, J.C. and Rianderie, B.D. (1985): 'Political Risk and Foreign Exchange Rates: An Efficient Market Approach', *Journal of International Business Studies*, Vol. 16, No. 3, Fall.

de Maskey, A. and Baker, J.C. (1989): 'Foreign Currency Options: Their Use by Multinational Corporations and Banks', *Foreign Trade Review*, Vol. 22, No. 3, October–December pp. 243–57.

Eiteman, D.K. and Stonehill, A.I. (1989): *Multinational Business Finance* (5th edn). Addison Wesley.

Hekman, C.R. (1983): 'Measuring Foreign exchange Exposure: A Practical theory and its Application', *Financial Analyst's Journal*, September–October, pp. 59–65. Reproduced in Choi, F.D.S. and Mueller, G. (eds) (1985): *Frontiers of International Accounting: An Anthology*. UMI Research Press.

Heywood, J. (1978): *Foreign Exchange and the Corporate Treasurer*. A. and C. Black.

Jacque, L. (1981): 'Management of Foreign Exchange Risk: A Review Article', *Journal of International Business Studies*, Spring/Summer pp. 81–101. Reproduced in Gray, S.J. (ed.) (1983): *International Accounting and Transnational Decisions*. Butterworth.

Kwok, C.Y. (1987): 'Hedging Foreign Exchange Exposures: Independent versus Integrative Approaches', *Journal of International Business Studies*, Vol. 19, No. 2, Summer, pp. 37–52.

Lassen, R. (1982): *Currency Management*. Woodhead-Faulkner.

McRae, T.W. and Walker, D.P. (1980): *Foreign Exchange Management*. Prentice Hall.

Park, Y.S. (1984): 'Currency Swaps as a Long-Term International Financing Technique', *Journal of International Business Studies*, Vol. 15, No. 4, Winter, pp. 47–54.

Rhee, S.G., Change, R.P. and Koveos, P.E. (1985): 'The Currency of Denomination Decision for Debt Financing', *Journal of International Business Studies*, Vol. 16, No. 3, Fall, pp. 143–50.

Shapiro, A.C. (1989): *Multinational Financial Management* (3rd edn). Allyn & Bacon.

Soenen, L.A. and Aggarwal, R. (1987): 'Corporate Foreign Exchange and Cash Management Practices', *Journal of Cash Management*, March/April.

Westwick, C.A. (1986): *Accounting for Overseas Operations*. Arthur Anderson/Gower.

6.7

International Marketing Management

International marketing is a two-way process by which product and customer are brought together across national frontiers. This comprehensive definition includes many of the subjects covered in earlier chapters; Table 6.7.1 shows where. The present chapter focuses attention first on market research and then on the issues generally understood as elements in the marketing mix.

The concept of international marketing has grown from an extension of local marketing to a global outlook, bringing with it ideas and tools that have transformed national markets.[1] This process still has a long way to go, while the interpretation of current developments is also likely to change. Product policies and buyer behaviour are two aspects that have been closely investigated; one study of international marketing strategies examines:[2]

whether to aim for market share or short-term profits;
the orientation to new opportunities in the environment;
whether to concentrate on adaptation (keeping up with the state of the art) or innovation;
the degree of aggression to be shown in pricing, product-line extension, promotion and dealer-incentive policies; and
the development of a market-oriented organization.

A contemporary subject of debate is the extent to which marketing policies can be standardized around the world. This issue is considered further under 'product' and 'promotion', but the debate is wide-ranging and persistent. The year 1986, for instance, saw an international conference on the subject and a major review of the debate.[3]

General references

Hart, T. and others (1982): 'How global companies win out', *Harvard Business Review*, May–June, pp. 98–108.

Table 6.7.1   International Marketing

Subject	Chapter
Marketing strategy	6.1
Options for servicing markets	6.2
	6.3
	6.4
Marketing strategies	6.7
Market research	6.7
Product policies	6.7
Pricing policies	6.7
Promotion policies	6.7
Countertrade	6.7
External relations	6.7
Buyer behaviour	6.8
Organization of marketing department	6.10

Levitt, T. (1983): 'The globalization of markets', *Harvard Business Review*, May–June, pp. 85–93. This article is summarized by the sentence: 'Companies must learn to operate as if the world were one large market – ignoring superficial regional and national differences.' An opposing point of view can be found in:

Hofstede, G. (1983): 'The cultural relativity of organizational practices and theories', *Journal of International Business Studies*, Vol. 14, No. 2, Fall, pp. 75–89.

6.7.1   Market research

International market research demands a broader approach than a merely domestic one. It is examining business activity in a variety of commercial environments which offer a wide choice of markets.

Terpstra prefers the title 'International Marketing Intelligence' and lists some major differences from domestic research including:

the importance of cultural, political and economic variables that can be ignored at home;

the importance of international economic and political considerations;

the different nature of competition, often itself international; and

the fact that the firm is operating in and between a number of markets.

Differing expectations encountered in various markets could be added to this list.[4] Researchers and clients will be operating in different commercial and cultural environments; they will also be using different approaches. They will ask themselves how standard the methods of research can or should be – a question further stimulated when investigating product standardization. Among the problems of such research, one is that a negative question may be easier to answer than a positive. It is less difficult to find out what is unacceptable than what is acceptable. Another problem is to find statistics that are compatible between countries. There are a number of well-known traps, like the search for a market segment through figures that are often out-of-date and from a different base than those at home. The figures are also averages, which may mean different things – like the scope for selling to an upmarket sector in a country with a low standard of living. The search for the most reliable information which is, at the same time not out-of-date, is a continuing challenge. This is linked to another question – how much research can be carried out in the home country and how much must be done abroad? The answer will depend on the depth required and the sources of intelligence available to the company.

In practice, companies that do not already have a presence in a particular country will usually commission an agency to conduct the research. But this does not answer the questions, it changes the emphasis; and there are a number of options available for commissioning research abroad.

(1) Where there is a subsidiary serving the country or the region, research will normally be its responsibility.
(2) Where there is not, research can either be booked with an international specialist firm or consortium, or with a local company that services the target market.

Market research is one specialist activity of business which is supported by a powerful profession. The issue of professionalism and the safeguarding of standards is important. Apart from national professional bodies, there are cross-frontier organizations like the European Society of Market Research (ESOMAR) whose publications should be consulted.

A special opportunity of international research is that of comparative analysis. The points of similarity and difference can be identified to guide research within a particular market. The use of input-output tables can also show the interdependencies of given sectors in target areas. The interpretation of the results of these two kinds of analyses is a subject for academic study.

Barnard (see note 4) has distinguished between the main purposes for which international research is conducted: markets (size, structure, competition), strategies (the image, buyer motivation, product awareness) and problem solving. The last includes product packaging, price, promotion and other issues considered in the rest of this chapter.

6.7.2   Product policies

A number of product policies have been identified in international studies. The most distinctive and, it seems, the most researched is that of standardization and adaptation; others include segmentation, life cycle, product acceptability (including national and cultural differences) and legal constraints.

Standardization is a distinctive issue that uses the characteristic skills of the marketing function. It involves difficult decisions that often have to be taken on ambiguous evidence. Modern research has derived from a pioneer study by Buzzell.[5] Buzzell wrote that the 'prevailing view' was that marketing strategy was a 'local problem'; the main tenor of the article was to question that view. Fifteen years later, the grounds of the discussion have changed radically and the 'limits of standardization' might be a more suitable title for an article on the subject. The debate has also widened to cover all aspects of the marketing mix, although product policies are generally regarded as the most amenable to standardization. In fact, standardization today is usually presented as one of a series of strategy options, the most cost-effective when it is available. Keegan, for instance, lists five options for foreign markets:[6]

(1) *Production-promotional extension.* This is the standardization option, in which both products and promotions are standardized.

(2) *Product extension – promotional adaptation.* In this option, a standard product is sold by different promotional methods in some of its markets.

(3) *Product adaptation – promotional extension.* This is a case in which the product changes to suit local factors such as tastes, climate and regulations, but a similar promotion is used.[7]

(4) *Dual adaptation* is where both product and promotion is changed as a result of market research reports on the local market.

(5) *Product invention* is where the special needs of a particular market are met by a new product.

There is a certain irony in the fact that increased marketing consciousness has given sensitivity to the market a high priority, at the same time as international standardization has increased. The international success of Japanese consumer electronics has contributed to the change, as has food and drink from the United States. Nevertheless, the third strategy – where the promotion is maintained while the product is adapted – may well be more common than has yet been demonstrated. More changes of approach can be expected.[8]

Adaptation

Whatever the merits of standardization, a number of factors make adaptation essential. These can be divided into optional factors, like cultural differences, where the need to adapt may be a matter of opinion and unavoidable factors such as the climate. Legal constraints have become much more prevalent and persuasive. They include measures for consumer protection and health and safety regulations. A discussion of adaptation in terms of marketing concepts and theories as well as products can be found in Turnbull and Paliwoda (1986). One point they make concerns the relationship between a product's reputation and that of its country of origin. More adaption may be required if the country's image is not a good one.[9] Another publication lists international product strategies as technical innovative, product adaptation, product conformity, availability and security, and low price.

Segmentation

The main issue here is that a product segmentation policy may also have to be adapted. Differing class structures, for instance, will influence market opportunities; other modes of segmentation will also differ.

Product life-cycle

The product life-cycle has been recorded as the basis of a major theory of international investment in Chapters 1.2 and 6.4. The argument there centres around the possibility of extending the life of a product by moving manufacture to an area where the costs of production are less than those in the home country, once the period of innovation has passed. *The extension of the product life cycle* is a phrase covering a use of the concept in a more mundane sense to describe an extension of sales to less sophisticated markets when a product has become obsolete in its country of origin.

6.7.3 Pricing policies

The subject of pricing illustrates the difference between the study of basic theory and that of managerial decision-making. Models of marginal revenues and marginal costs provide insights that may be lacking to some practitioners, but the latter have to steer through a maze of considerations – a mixture of calculation, hunch, trial and error and lobbying on the part of various rival interests within the firm as well as the influence of customers, competitors, regulatory bodies and other elements of the business environment. Terpstra divides the subject into four.[10]

1   Export pricing

As with domestic pricing policies, there is discussion between cost-related and market-related policies. Authors on marketing advocate the latter for numerous cogent reasons, but enquiries within companies reveal that a cost-related policy is frequently adopted because it reduces uncertainties. Calculations designed to assess a price that the market will bear are often considered to require too many ambiguous judgements. On the other hand, a market-related price can help a company decide on the viability of export in the first place. Terpstra presents an example in which the free-on-board price of a product is 37 per cent of the market price in the foreign country.

2 Transfer pricing

One of the most written-about subjects in international business, the pricing of products or services between units of the same company, inevitably recurs under different headings. A significant subject of political controversy, it has implications for company–government relationships as well as for the control system, the tax position and general strategies. For the marketing manager there is a paradox in that the market-related prices he otherwise advocates may prove unrealistic. If a market price exists, there is no problem; but frequently products are transferred within a company for which there is no reference price. Dealings between a parent company and a subsidiary can hardly be regarded as those between sellers and buyers in a free market, whatever the legal theory.

Not surprisingly, research has shown that a majority of companies rely on cost plus for transfer pricing, whatever their normal pricing policies.[11] However, marketing decisions cannot be taken in isolation, and transfer pricing is likely to be regarded as a top-management decision. In particular, the advantages of its use as a mechanism for transferring funds and saving taxes (under certain restricted conditions) have to be set against the costs involved in using a manipulative mechanism, the damage caused to the control system when prices distort performance indicators, along with the consequent damage to staff incentives and cover paths. There are also costs involved in developing bad relations with taxation and other arms of government. These issues are further explored in Chapter 6.8.

3 Foreign market pricing

A major issue of pricing policy in any market has been called the 'message in the price'.[12] This refers to the way in which the price will convey something of the company's intentions for the product and its market segment. Like many an intangible issue, the message is much harder to identify in a foreign market. Upmarket, for instance, can be demonstrated in different ways in different cultures, as can the meaning of a phrase like 'value for money'. In general, pricing policies can be expected to reflect a company's objectives, including the degree of penetration sought in a particular market and, indeed, the status of export.

4 Coordinating pricing in international marketing

This fourth characteristic reflects the general issues of standardization and control. The mandatory fixing of prices in foreign markets may cause legal difficulties; the results may have to be achieved by negotiation and consent, whether the sales are conducted by a subsidiary or through a third party. Many companies prefer to leave pricing discussion to the local operator, but the results can be disastrous if the wrong message is conveyed in the price.

6.7.4 Promotion policies

All the issues considered in this chapter so far are relevant to promotion. There are also specific policies relating to selling, sales promotion, advertising and publicity. The measurement of advertising effectiveness and the motivation of foreign sales forces are two that have been researched.[13] Other research has been into the processes of developing international advertising campaigns.[14] A criticism of global promotion policies was made by an advertising agency; it made the point that, for all but the most upmarket products, even a pan-European approach was dangerous.

6.7.5 Countertrade

Countertrade (barter) is seen as an answer to the problems of trade for a country with balance-of-payments problems and a shortage of hard currency. Although it has a long history, 20 years ago this means of paying for imports was regarded as a rarity mainly used by the socialist countries. Since then it has spread to the Third World and some industrial nations. A number of distinct types of countertrade have emerged, such as the direct transfer of unrelated goods for all or part of the price (barter), an agreement to buy some of the products of equipment sold or licensed to a local company (buyback), or other similar contractual arrangements.

One of these is counter-purchase, currently a growing form of countertrade. In this case two contracts are made, closely related to one another. In the first, the original seller agrees with a buyer to sell a given quantity of goods at a price. In the second contract, the original seller agrees to buy goods from the buyer in part or whole payment for the original sale. A new profession of specialist intermediary has grown up to handle the results of counter-purchase, in cases where the original seller is not in a position to do so. The intermediary firm saves the costs of market research and other expenses of entering the new market represented by the counter-purchasers. It also aims to ensure that future deals are not frustrated by the problem of fulfilling the counter-purchase obligation. On the other hand, it can be seen as a non-tariff barrier as well as a symptom of currency shortage.

Countertrade has been regarded as a sign of an increasing bargaining power as a national market becomes more attractive. A recent study has further pointed out that countertrade can be a normal and rational process of developing trade conditions where the superiority of market-mediated transactions is not well established:[15] in other words, tightly controlled or developing economies where financial instruments – like factoring and futures – are not available. The study hypothesizes a number of circumstances in which the various methods of countertrade could be expected to prove advantageous, including the buyback of natural resources where the costs of other methods of obtaining them are higher, where the quality of the technology is difficult to monitor except through a buyback arrangement, or when direct ownership (internalization) is too costly. None of these explanations are directly related to balance-of-payment difficulties. Hence the author argues that such difficulties are additional in a complex of motivations, and may themselves bring different pressures to bear. Countertrade may be more reliable for the supplier as well as more practical for the buyer. The assumption of this article, as of most writings on the subject, is that countertrade is not likely to be acceptable in the long-term when normal market conditions apply.

6.7.6   External affairs

A recent trend has been to concentrate more attention on the role of business in society; this has led to the development of departments dedicated to public affairs. A pioneer academic study demonstrated how a number of activities had been brought together in a new type of department which coordinated the relationships between a company and elements in its non-commercial environment – government, education and so on.[16] This and other publications on the subject list the department's activities as:

representing the company and advocating its interests to governments and international organizations like the United Nations and the Organization for Economic Cooperation and Development;
representing the company on national and international bodies of employers and on business-orientated pressure groups;
representing the company in relations with other pressure groups (environmental, for example) and other political, cultural or social organizations;
establishing contacts with educational bodies and offering support to research, education and charitable causes;

providing the rest of the company with advice about issues on which a corporate response is required, including social responsibility; briefing managers on current controversies and assisting them in presentations to the public; other activities, including advertising and public relations, designed to enhance the reputation of the company and meet criticisms.

An interesting feature of an external affairs department is that it carries a stage further the trend to integrated umbrella units of organization mandated to produce corporate policies and guidelines of which marketing itself was an earlier example. In the case of external affairs, however, it has been brought into existence by the particular pressures affecting a multinational firm. The department has a domestic activity that could continue to be covered either by its own managers or by public relations. A special department is perceived to be necessary when a company finds itself beset by delicate issues which have both national and international implications.

Notes

1. The conditions under which global marketing makes sense are discussed in McNally and Locke (1986) in the light of two case-studies. See also Baker (1985). For a warning about the dangers of knowledge possessed by head office being blindly applied in the subsidiaries, see Kashani (1989).
2. See Doyle and others (1986).
3. The international conference 'Standardizing entry positioning and distribution strategies' was held under the joint auspices of the marketing Science Institute and the European Institute For Advanced Studies in Management. A summary of the proceedings can be obtained from the Marketing Science Institute, 1000 Massachusetts Avenue, Cambridge, MA 002138, USA. For a review of the subject, see Walters (1986); for an advocate of standardization, see Levitt (1983) and for one against, see Hofstede (1983).
4. See Terpstra (1983), Chapter 7. For a general review of international research, see Barnard (1982a, b). Techniques for foreign market research are examined in Douglas, S.P. and Craig C.S. (1982): 'Marketing research in the International Environment', Chapter 30 of Walter and Murray.
5. See Buzzell, R.D. (1973): 'Can you standardize multinational marketing?' Chapter 32 in Thorelli, H. *International Marketing Strategy*. Harmondsworth: Penguin.
6. See Keegan (1980). The headings in the text are his.
7. For an example, see Rabin, S. (1982): 'International Marketing Mix', in Walter and Murray, pp. 32–5. The author refers to a drugstore product which is sold for headaches in one country and for stomach disorders in another.
8. Examples of recent publications on this subject are Quelch and Hoff (1986) and Greenberg (1986).
9. Turnbull and Paliwoda (1986). The following sentence refers to Turnbull and Walla (1986) p. 268.

10. Terpstra (1985), Chapter 14. The reference in the following paragraph is to p. 505. For another discussion of international pricing policies, see Baker and Ryans (1982). See also Walter and Murray (1982) pp. 32.6–32.7 and 33.7–33.12.
11. For a general discussion of this and other related issues, see Plasschaerts (1979).
12. 'Possibly the most important issue is that of the message in the price' (Brooke, 1986, p. 123). A detailed study of 'product positioning', a related concept, can be found in Johanson and Thorelli (1985).
13. See, for example, Miracle (1984). Professor Miracle has written a number of other articles on advertising internationally: see references.
14. See, for example, Peebles and others (1978).
15. Mims and Young (1986) pp. 28–9. The bibliography at the end of this article (p. 39) should be consulted. The reference in the next sentence is to a booklet entitled *The Euroconsumer, Marketing Myth or Cultural Certainty*, Benton D'Arcy Masius and Bowles. See also Aggarwal (1989).
16. See Boddewyn (1975). A more recent discussion of a public affairs department can be found in Robinson (1984), Chapter 10. Boddewyn uses the phrase 'external affairs', Robinson 'public affairs'; other names are also employed.

References

Aggarwal, R. (1989): 'International business through barter and countertrade', *Long Range Planning*, Vol. 22(3), June, pp. 75–81.

Baker, J.C. and Ryans, J.K. (1982): 'International Pricing Policies and Practices of Industrial Product Manufacturers', *International Marketing: Management and Direction*, Vol. 1, No. 3, pp. 127–33.

Baker, M.J. (1985): 'Globalization versus Differentiation as International Marketing Strategies', *Journal of Marketing Management*, Vol. 1, No. 2, Winter, pp. 145–55.

Barnard, P.D. (1982a): 'Conducting and coordinating multi-country quantitative studies across Europe', *Journal of the Market Research Society*, Vol. 24, No. 1, January.

Barnard, P.D. (1982b): 'Marketing research in non-Western economies', *Journal of the Market Research Society*, Vol. 24, No. 2, April.

Boddewyn, J.J. (1975): *Corporate External Affairs*. Business International.

Bradley, M.F. (1986): 'Key factors affecting international competitiveness', *Journal of Irish Business and Administrative Research*, Vol. 7, No. 2, Winter.

Brooke, M.Z. (1986): *International Management*. Hutchinson.

Cavusgil, S.J. and Nairn, J.P. (1981): 'State of the art in international marketing', in Eris, B.M. and Roering, K.J. (eds): pp. 195–216.

Chisnall, P.M. (1989): *Strategic Industrial Marketing*. Prentice-Hall.

Douglas, S.P. and Craig C. J. (1982): *International Marketing Research*. Prentice-Hall.

Doyle, P. and others (1986): 'Japanese marketing strategies in the UK: a comparative study', *Journal of International Business Studies*, Vol. 17, No. 1, Spring, pp. 27–46.

Greenberg, E.R. (1986): 'Swings in the International Market Place', *Management Review*, Vol. 75, No. 61–2, June.

Hampton, G.M. and van Gent, A.P. (eds) (undated): *Marketing Aspects of International Business*. Kluwer-Nijhoff.

Henzier, H. and Kall, W. (1986): 'Facing up to the globalization challenge', *McKinsey Quarterly*, Winter, pp. 52–68.

Hofstede, G. (1983): 'The cultural relativity of organizational practices and theories', *Journal of International Business Studies*, Vol. 14, No. 2, Fall, pp. 75–89.

Johanson, J.K. and Thorelli, H.B. (1985): 'International Product Positioning', *Journal of International Business Studies*, No. 163, Fall, pp. 57–75.

Kacker, M. (1982): *Marketing and Economic Development*. New Delhi: Deep & Deep Publications.

Kacker, M. (1983): 'Benefits uncertain in European acquisitions of US retailers', *Marketing News*, 4 March. American Marketing Association.

Kacker, M. (1983): 'Role of transnational retailers', proceedings of the Annual Conference, May. *Academy of Marketing Science*, USA.

Kacker, M. (1983): 'Transatlantic investment in retailing', *The Conference Board Research Bulletin*, No. 138.

Kacker, M. (1985): 'Transatlantic trends in retailing', Greenwood.

Kacker, M. (1986): 'Coming to terms with global retailing', *International Marketing Review*, Spring.

Kacker, M. (1986): 'The metamorphosis of European retailing', *The European Journal of Marketing*, Vol. 1, No. 20.

Kashari, K. (1989): 'Beware the pitfalls of global marketing', *Harvard Business Review*, September–October, pp. 91–8.

Kaynak, E. (1982): *Marketing in the Third World*. Praeger.

Kaynak, E. (1985): *Global Perspective in Marketing*. Praeger.

Kaynak, E. (1985): *International Marketing Management*. Praeger.

Kaynak, E. and Savitt, R. (eds) (1984): *Comparative Marketing Systems*. Praeger.

Keegan, W.J. (1980): *Multinational Marketing Management*. Prentice-Hall.

Levitt, T. (1983): 'The Globalization of Markets', *Harvard Business Review*, May–June, pp. 92–102.

McNally, G.J. and Locke, W.W. (1986): 'Global Marketing – a sensible business option?' *Business Marketing*, Vol. 21, No. 4, April, pp. 64–7.

Mims, R. and Young, B. (1986): 'Economic Incentives for Counter-Trade', *Journal of International Business Studies*, Vol. 17, No. 3 Fall, pp. 27–39.

Miracle, G.E. (1984): 'Progress in Research on International Advertising', *Current Issues and Research in Advertising*, pp. 135–66.

Miracle, G.E. (1985): 'Advertising regulation in Japan and the USA: an introductory comparison', *Waseda Business and Economic Studies*, No. 21, pp. 35–69. Tokyo.

Miracle, G.E. and Nevett, T.R. (1987): *Voluntary Regulation of Advertising* (a comparative analysis of the United Kingdom and the United States). Lexington.

Miracle, G.E. and Rijkens, R. (1986): *European Regulation of Advertising: Supranational Regulation of Advertising in the European Economic Community*. North Holland.

Morello, G. (1986): 'The consumer in world trade', in Visser, H. and Schoorl, E. (eds): *Trade in Transit*, pp. 303–13. Martinus Nijhoff.

Peebles, M. and others (1978): 'Coordinating International Advertising', *Journal of Marketing*, Vol. 42, No. 1, pp. 28–34.

Plasschaert, S.R.F. (1979): *Transfer pricing and multinationals; A review of concepts, mechanisms and regulations*. Saxon House.

Quelch, T.A. and Hoff, E.J. (1986): 'Customizing global marketing', *Harvard Business Review*, Vol. 64, No. 3, June, pp. 59–68.

Robinson, R.D. (1984): *Internationalization of Business*, Chapter 2. Dryden Press.

Schlegelmilch, B.B. and others (1986): 'Marketing research in medium fixed UK and US firms', Industrial Marketing Management No. 15, pp. 177–82.

Scott, W.G. (1985): 'Un nuovo strumento del marketing internazionale: il countertrade', [Countertrade: a new tool of international marketing] in *Problemi di Gestione dell' Impresa*, pp. 72–91. Milan: Universita Cattolica.

Terpstra, V. (1983): 'Critical Mass and International Marketing Strategy', *Journal of the Academy of Marketing Science*, Summer, pp. 269–82.

Terpstra, V. (1983): 'Research Agenda for International Marketing', *Journal of International Business Studies*, Spring-Summer.

Terpstra, V. (1983): 'The Role of Economies of Scale in International Marketing', in *Marketing Aspects of International Business*. pp. 59–72. Boston: Kluwer.

Terpstra, V. (1983): *International Marketing* (3rd edn). Australia: Dryden Press.

Terpstra, V. (co-author) (1984): 'Intraregional Foreign Direct Investment in Pacific Asia', *Asia Pacific Journal of Management*, September.

Terpstra, V. (co-author) (1984): 'The American Challenge in International Advertising', *Journal of Advertising*, Fall.

Terpstra, V. (1985): 'International Product Policy', reprinted in Wortzel (ed.): *Strategic Management of Multinational Companies*, pp. 383–91. Wiley.

Terpstra, V. (1985): 'The Changing Environment of International Marketing', *International Marketing Review*, Vol. 2, No. 3, Autumn, pp. 7–16.

Turnbull, P. and Paliwoda, S.J. (1986): *Research in International Marketing*. Croom Helm.

Turnbull, P. and Walla, J.P. (1986): *Strategies for International Industrial Marketing*. Croom Helm.

Walter, I. and Murray, T. (1982): *Handbook of International Business*. Wiley.

Walters, P.G.P. (1986): 'International marketing policy: a discussion of the standardization construct and its relevance for corporate policy', *Journal of International Business Studies*. Vol. 17, No. 2, Summer, pp. 55–69.

Welch, L.S. (1985): 'The international marketing of technology: an interactive perspective', *International Marketing Review*, Vol. 2, No. 1, Spring, pp. 41–3.

6.8

International Logistics Management

Logistics concerns the issue of physical distribution: the movement of goods and components through the manufacturing organization, the marketing channel and on to the ultimate user or consumer. Given this holistic picture it is perhaps easy to understand why this theoretical area is often referred to as 'total distribution management' as it involves the whole organization that exists between suppliers of inputs and purchasers of the final product. In many cases this not only involves intra-company divisions but also extra-company intermediaries (agents, wholesalers, distributors and retailers).

The basic premise on which logistics centres in the maintenance of the best possible service at the least cost (Hussey (1972). This involves logistics managers making trade-offs between what they perceive to be the optimal organization structures for servicing their targeted customers and the resource constraints of the firm. As resource constraints often result in firms pursuing 'second-best' strategies, maximizing the potential from available options is also important.

The logistics-management function is critically dependent on designing organizational structures to facilitate not only the successful movement of goods, but also the interaction with customers: an important part of securing sales and long-term contracts.

6.8.1 International organizational structures

There is a complex array of organizational structures available to firms. International business literature divides these into three generic forms: exporting, licensing and foreign direct investment. Factors that distinguish these three modes of foreign-market servicing relate to internalization and location theories. Exporting is distinguished from licensing and foreign direct investment by the location effect and the majority of value-adding activity taking place in the domestic market; in the other two forms production takes place in overseas markets. Licensing can be differentiated from exporting and foreign direct investment by the internalization effect. Licensing involves a market sale of intermediate goods or corporate assets by the manufacturer, final production being externalized (Buckley and Casson (1976) (1985)). These generic strategies principally relate to the location and internalization of production activities, although they have an important impact on the organizational structure of activities further down the marketing channel. International marketing and channel literature takes the distribution channel as the organizational perspective, placing greater emphasis on the distinction between direct and indirect routes to foreign customers. A multiplicity of channel forms can be identified (Walsh (1978), Cateora and Hess (1979), McMillan and Paulden (1979)). They can be summarised into five basic patterns (Cunningham (1986)):

(1) Agents (exclusive and non-exclusive);
(2) Sales representatives
    (a) operating from the United Kingdom (supplier based)
    (b) based in the customer country;
(3) Sales office;
(4) Sales subsidiaries;
(5) Manufacturing subsidiaries.

The location and internalization of activities again play an important part in distinguishing between the alternative structures. Sales representatives operating from the supplier country can be distinguished from the other forms by the location effect, being the only mode where personnel are sited at a distance from the foreign market. Agents and foreign-market sales representatives (often tied to overseas wholesalers and distributors) are external intermediaries posing problems of motivation and control to the manufacturer (Jensen and Meckling (1976)).

It would not be unreasonable to suggest, therefore, that the choice of organizational structures is dependent on balancing the pros and cons of:

(a) Location of activities – domestic or host market;
(b) Internalization of activities – company controlled or handled by external organizations;
(c) Direct or indirect contact with customers – relationships handled directly by the manufacturer or indirectly through an intermediary.

The choice of organization form is dependent on three groups of factors: the nature of the product, the nature of the market and the nature of the firm. It is beyond the scope of this analysis to present these factors in detail (for examples see Alexander and Berg (1965), Christopher (1972) but certain issues pertinent to international logistics management are worth comment.

Product factors

The geographic distance involved in transporting products to international markets and the accompanying costs have an important bearing on locational and internalization issues. Where products are bulky or heavy, the firm will attempt to minimize the distance between the production unit and the final customer. This often involves manufacturing overseas either through foreign direct investment or a licensing agreement. The generation of economies in transport results in firms shipping large consignments to foreign markets demanding warehousing and bulk-breaking services in the host market. These services are frequently externalized and handled by foreign-market intermediaries.

The level of technology embodied in the product can also be an important influential factor. High-tech products are often assumed to demand company-employed salesmen and service engineers to translate effectively the technological advantages to customers. However, many intermediaries can offer suppliers a well-trained salesforce and service department (Rosson (1984)) with the added advantage of established customer contacts and an understanding of need requirements.

Foreign market factors

Cultural distance is perhaps one of the key factors shaping the organization format suppliers develop for international markets. Particularly at an early stage in their involvement the foreign market is something of an 'unknown quantity' and the foreign manufacturer has little experience on which to draw. Employing the services of intermediaries is often considered to be a way of compensating for market-knowledge deficiencies, encompassing a well-developed market understanding through the enlisting of external services (Hardy and McGrath (1988)).

Other important market factors relate to government legislation and intervention in various international markets. A firm may only be granted access to a particular market on the grounds that it uses local suppliers (in the case of manufacturing investment) or utilizes the services of local intermediaries (in the case of exporting) thus restricting available organizational options.

Alternatively, local laws may limit the amount of control a manufacturer has over the marketing of his product when employing the services of intermediaries. Rosson (1984) highlights vertical trading restrictions in the European Economic Community. He highlights the fact that price-fixing and exclusive agreements are prohibited, which may potentially inhibit high levels of performance. Rosson also addresses the problem of terminating relationships with intermediaries in some international markets where laws make this virtually impossible or only available through the payment of sizeable compensations.

Firm factors

The resources available to the firm determine available options. Establishing operations that permit regular contact with customers is more expensive to implement for international operations than domestic. This arises from the duplication of certain activities, notably stockholding, sales, marketing and servicing in the local market. Cunningham (1986) also argues that firms underestimate the resources needed to build relationships with foreign customers against well-entrenched competition and customer loyalty.

The objectives of the international operation also influence the choice of organizational structure. Firms testing the viability of operating abroad or seeking to maximize returns from mature or declining product groups are more likely to choose the most cost-effective route to the international market, implementing the services of intermediaries. Conversely, firms wishing to extend their customer base and market share are more likely to take a longer-term strategic view. Establishment overseas is considered to promote awareness and afford better understanding of indigenous customers' needs and requirements.

Managerial strengths can also be a determining factor. Firms that traditionally employ intermediaries often opt for this approach when entering new markets. They seek to capitalize on established networks for liaising with intermediaries, adapting communication channels to the new market and extra-company organizations. Alternatively, firms with experience in setting up their own activities in foreign markets can draw on established procedures for assessing markets, establishing operations, recruiting staff and implementing strategies.

Marketing channel structures and the location and internalization or externalization of production are inextricably interlinked (Buckley, Pass and Prescott (1990)). Where production is sited abroad, channel activities (warehousing, sales, marketing and servicing) are probably integrated into the foreign operation. Additionally, proximity to local suppliers of components and raw materials not only suggests a greater likelihood of purchasing management being conducted in the foreign market but also offers firms advantages of global sourcing. However, small overseas production units may lack the bargaining power afforded to large centralized production plants. Where production is externalized in the case of licensing, purchasing and marketing channel activities may be supplied by the licensee. Valla (1986) views this kind of external structure as akin to utilizing the services of an independent agent as regards the supplier/distributor/customer relationship.

This is not to suggest, however, that channels of distribution are built around production activities. The interdependence of the production function and the marketing channel means that factors affecting one automatically impact on the other. For example, where firms are compelled to produce abroad as a result of local legislation or in order to gain access to public procurement, establishment of operations will necessarily involve considerations of channel activities. Building warehouse facilities, creating distribution networks or gaining access to indigenous networks, recruiting sales, marketing and service personnel or employing local intermediaries are all integral to planning foreign ventures. Alternatively where competitive success relies on rapid delivery or just-in-time delivery to retailers, the essential decision to stock goods abroad may have repercussions on the choice of production location.

6.8.2 Cost factors

One of the important functions of logistics management is to minimize the cost of moving raw materials and components into the company and on from final production to the consumer or end-user. This entails the logistics manager pursuing cost-reduction strategies in materials management and the marketing channel. The importance of location and of internalization verses externalization have already been broached. Here these themes are developed to highlight the cost-management aspect of international logistics.

Location theory suggests firms seek to reduce costs by siting various activities in areas where immobile inputs are cheapest. Several forces are assumed to impact on location choice (Buckley and Casson (1976)):

(1) the ability to generate scale economies in certain functions by centralizing activities in large-scale units;
(2) specialized activities, such as research and development, may exert a locational pull on activities favouring establishment where inputs are cheaper or more cost-effectively utilized and centralization where scale economies apply;
(3) the ability to wield monopsony power over suppliers in certain locations, forcing down input prices and locating where supplies are abundant;
(4) government intervention may dissuade manufacturers from establishing operations in least-cost locations;
(5) centralizing high-communication-cost activities that minimize excess costs of communication interference and distortion.

These forces have different implications for the various elements within the logistics function.

Raw material and component input

Scale economies can be generated in raw material and component input by centralizing production. Inputs can be directed towards a single focus; there is no need to ship semi-finished goods and components between production units. This not only reduces transportation costs but also management time in coordinating such effort. Where manufacturing is located abroad, management of input involves balancing the benefits of using domestic suppliers and the additional transportation costs this involves, against searching for new overseas suppliers and building new relationships. Although monopsony power over suppliers is likely to be greatest if the firm centralizes production domestically (Davies (1984)) there are benefits to be earned from reducing transportation costs by manufacturing abroad. If input management is controlled centrally, the distance involved may prevent the organization conducting a comprehensive search of available sources, making identification of the most cost-effective source of supply difficult. Conversely if input management is undertaken in the host market, administration costs for the whole organization will rise because of the duplication of administrative effort. This extra cost may be balanced against the benefits accrued from the proximity to the market this approach affords. Identification of suppliers and monitoring of their activities is enhanced through a local position from which information can be more easily gathered.

Another advantage of using local suppliers stems from the shorter delivery times involved and the amount of stock the manufacturer consequently needs to hold. The benefits are obviously greater for firms operating in markets where demand tends to fluctuate or where inputs are perishable.

Physical distribution

The costs of physical distribution are inextricably interlinked with the location of production and stockholding. Physical distribution costs obviously rise as geographic distance increases. This is compounded in an international context by the need to cross oceans to reach particular overseas markets for many international players. This requires the utilization of different forms of transportation such as shipping and airlines rather than lorries and freight trains. This adds to the administrative costs of the organization, not only because it requires the development of new systems but also because of the increased amount of handling required at airports and docks (Davies (1988)). In servicing far-flung geographic locations transportation costs may be higher than those associated with overseas production, determining the choice of foreign direct investment as the most cost-effective strategy. Vernon's product-cycle approach to internationalization (1966) provides a simple cost-based model of the foreign market servicing strategy of firms, based on production and transportation costs:

$$\text{Invest abroad when } MPC_X + TC > APC_A$$

where: MPC_X = marginal cost of production for export
       TC = transport cost to target market
       APC_A = average cost of production abroad.

The argument is that marginal costs are appropriate because domestic production will continue whether or not the firm decides to export, whereas a foreign production plant has to bear the full average cost of production. The model highlights the importance of transportation costs in the decision to export or invest in manufacturing facilities overseas. Transport costs are not, however, the only additional costs a firm must consider when moving goods across international boundaries. Taxes and tariffs have an important impact on the costs of physical distribution. Horst's (1971) work on the influence of tariff and tax rates across different countries demonstrates that the choice of foreign-market servicing breaks down into special cases according to the operating conditions of the firm and differential tax and tariff levels in home and host countries. In this context, the task for the cost-minimizing organization is to assess the trade-off between higher costs of exporting when tariffs are high and the profit-generating advantages high tariffs produce through differential pricing opportunities.

Marketing channels

There are several alternative channel structures available to firms. Traditional marketing channels are those in which firms utilize the services of inter-mediaries. Administered channels refers to those in which one channel member is able to wield power over others as a result of some element of superiority. For instance, financial strengths, better information systems, reputation, tech-nological leadership or monopoly power can all result in one channel member controlling or at least directing the activities of the channel (Brown (1984)). Vertically integrated channels are those in which operators integrate forwards or backwards, drawing other levels of channel activity into their own control. Horizontal marketing channels involve different operators merging their activities. Multichannel marketing systems involve manufacturers operating through more than one channel. Each channel type has a different cost structure that must be considered when firms are choosing the most economical option available in the light of available resources, future market-growth potential and other financial commitments.

Traditional marketing channels involve the cost of cultivation and preser-vation of channel intermediaries and rising costs of the increased volume of busi-ness. The pattern for administered channels is similar, although transaction costs will rise less rapidly due to cost-minimization directives of the leader achievable through the centralization of strategic planning. Another cost advantage of the administered channel is that it suppresses sub-optimization by individual units within the channel, which tends to reduce profits in the traditional system. Where manufacturers integrate forward by setting up greenfield channel activi-ties the initial fixed cost is high, although variable costs decrease with increased sales due to scale economies and learning curve advantages. Integration through acquisition provides a similar cost structure, although the decline in variable costs may be more rapid because of the established experience of acquired

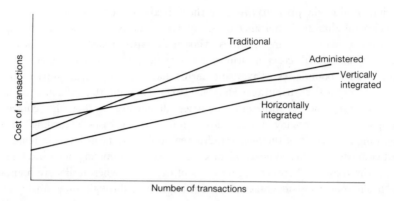

Figure 6.8.1 Transaction Costs of Various Channel Structures

Source: Buckley, Pass and Prescott (1990)

intermediaries. Both forms of integration also include ongoing management costs of inventory and distribution, absent in traditional marketing channels (Diamantopoulos (1987)). Horizontally arranged channels where the costs are divided between more than one party involve both lower initial outlay and variable costs than vertically integrated channels. Obviously costs associated with multi-channel systems depend on which combination of channels is employed. Figure 6.8.1 presents these relative costs diagrammatically.

In the long-term as firms increase the number of transactions, integrated channels become more cost-effective. Increasing the number of transactions may also be more easily achievable through integrated systems as a result of the greater control the manufacturer is able to exert over the system and the greater ease with which information flows through internalized organizational structures. In the long-term, the horizontally integrated channel emerges as potentially the most cost-effective strategy. However, the lack of centralized control and, in the case of domestic-manufacturer integration, the buying-in of local experts with local market knowledge may make this option less desirable.

6.8.3 Dynamics of foreign operations

The process of foreign market expansion is not a static concept. Buckley and Casson (1976) developed a model of the switch from exporting to foreign investment based on Vernon's (1966) product-cycle hypothesis. The model focuses on the fixed and variable costs involved in different market-servicing modes. They propose that as the market grows, variable costs decline and a switch occurs from low fixed-cost to low variable-cost strategies (see Figure 6.8.2).

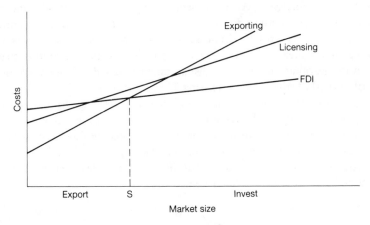

Figure 6.8.2   The Optimal Timing of the Switch to FDI

Source: Buckley and Casson (1985)

If the cost of physical distribution is assumed to make up a sizeable proportion of the variable costs within each market-servicing mode, then it can be
seen at point S; the additional distribution costs involved in exporting outweigh
the costs of foreign direct investment, where closer proximity to the market and
the avoidance of crossing national boundaries prevails. At this point greater
cost-saving advantages will be earned by foreign direct investment rather than
exporting, even though initially, at low transaction volumes and market size,
foreign investment would have proved an expensive exercise. Licensing, which
can often involve distribution of components from licensor to licensee and
policing costs within its operating costs, does not emerge as a preferable alternative in this example.

The Uppsala School (Johanson and Wiedersheim Paul (1975)) proposed a
more behavioural-based model to explain the changing strategies of internationalizing firms over time. They advocated that firms begin exporting to
nearby markets using cost-effective, risk-averse indirect strategies, utilizing the
services of indigenous intermediaries. With increased learning and experience
and as the overseas operation becomes more important to the firm they become
more directly involved with personnel on the ground. Ultimately firms are
thought to establish sales and marketing offices abroad. Other writers, while
changing the profile of the various stages involved, reaffirm that the internationalization process takes a structured sequential form (Wind, Douglas and
Perlmutter (1973), Johanson and Vahlne (1977), Bilkley and Tesar (1977)). Later
writers also extended the concept beyond a simple focus on exporting to include
foreign direct investment in production.

These two stepwise models fail to explain, however, why firms initially enter markets through foreign direct investment or why firms with considerable international experience continue to utilize the services of intermediaries. Turnbull (1986a) suggests this results from strategies being more dependent on the operating environment, industry structure and firm's marketing strategy than on a stagewise learning continuum. His arguments, based on the work of the International Marketing and Purchasing Group are reiterated by Valla (1986). Valla goes on to argue that adoption of additional marketing channels is a more likely approach to increased international involvement than changing the existing organizational arrangement to an alternative form. Incrementally adding benefits to existing operations is viewed as a more satisfactory way of building operations than changing to an alternative form that undermines the experiences, developed systems and contacts already established.

6.8.4 Customer service

Cost factors are balanced against service elements in the logistics management function. In much of the logistics management literature this trade-off is centred around delivery lead-time (service) and the costs of locating abroad versus exporting from the domestic market. Where rapid delivery is a prerequisite of securing sales, the closer the manufacturer is to the market, the shorter are the lead-times on delivery. This enhances customers' faith in the ability of manufacturers to service their needs adequately and may be a key factor in determining the choice of supplier. Exporting firms may, on occasion, fail to supply on time according to their delivery promise. This may be through no fault of their own: dock strikes, poor weather conditions, delayed flights or sea crossings may prevent them. Nevertheless the failure to deliver on time may make the buyer less willing to approach them again. This introduces the notion of the cost of lost sales into the analysis, making overseas production (or perhaps just stockholding) beneficial to the company seeking to maximize sales. The cost of lost sales is shown diagrammatically in Figure 6.8.3 (Berg (1971)).

The location of stockholding and warehousing is dependent on the location of production. Where foreign direct investment and licensing strategies are followed, such activities are necessarily located in the host market. However, where firms export, they may choose to ship goods from domestically held stock, use a foreign external wholesaler or distributor, or establish their own wholesaling activities overseas. The optimum location of inventory is dependent on lead-times required to prevent lost sales and the technology of warehouse design that favours large centralized units. The trade-off, then, is between the cost of lost sales and the economies of scale.

LaLonde and Zinszer (1976) propose three stages to customer service: pre-transaction, transaction and post-transaction. Pre-transaction elements relate to written corporate policies for providing service to customers and develop-

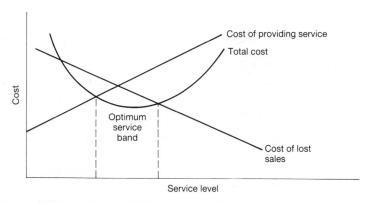

Figure 6.8.3 The Cost of Lost Sales

Source: Berg (1971)

ment of organizational structures to supply such levels of service. Transaction elements refer to performing the physical distribution function, taking orders holding adequate inventory and delivering on time. Post-transaction services are those provided to assist the customer in using the product and gaining satisfaction from their purchase. These three stages comprise a wide array of service elements, the required mix depending on the specific product and market (Christopher (1985)). Common across all elements is the ability of the firm to identify and satisfy customer needs. The International Marketing and Purchasing Research Group advocate the building and maintaining of supplier/customer relationships as the key to satisfying the needs of industrial clients. They propose that successful strategic marketing depends upon both parties taking an active role, being prepared to adapt their behaviour to facilitate the exchange process. Although early research focused on simple two-party interactions, later work recognizes that many supplier/customer relationships involve intermediaries.

Turnbull (1986b) ascribes seven roles of sales subsidiaries within the tripartite interaction between suppliers, intermediaries and customers:

(1) Market intelligence – provision of information and identification of market opportunities;
(2) Market commitment – to encourage customer confidence through a strong market presence and competitive stance;
(3) Relationship management – to establish and maintain close relationships with customers;
(4) Administration – taking and processing orders responding to enquiries and documenting transactions;
(5) Technical problem-solving – providing technical services to customers before and after sales;

(6) Commercial problem-solving – providing technical services to customers before and after sales; and

(7) Social distance – to minimize social, cultural and language barriers.

The critical issue is how firms develop interaction processes to harness the roles of the various parties to the mutual benefit of all players. There is no single solution to this. The most effective organization structure and interactive system is dependent on four factors (Hakansson (1982)):

(a) The elements of interaction – product, information, financial and social exchanges;

(b) Characteristics of the parties – size, structure, strategy, technology, resources, objectives, attitudes and experience;

(c) The environment – market characteristics, macroeconomic factors, culture, geography and social systems;

(d) The atmosphere – power dependence, conflict cooperation and social distance, arising from attitudes and perceptions.

Although no simple prescriptions for success can be offered, the International Marketing and Purchasing research highlights some of the recent steps taken by firms to enhance the establishment and development of relationships with their customers.

Investing more human resources into the operation is seen as a way of increasing commitment (Valla (1986)). Encouraging more personnel to become involved with their counterparts in the customer organization at various functional levels is designed to strengthen the bond between supplier and customer and raise the level of trust and understanding. Alternatively, basing staff from the supplier organization in the target market to assist the agent is another way of displaying commitment. Here the intention is to persuade the agent to work harder on the principal's behalf. Increasing commitment can also take the form of establishing sales offices or manufacturing facilities abroad, demonstrating a more permanent presence and a higher level of credibility to actual and potential customers.

Employing local nationals in sales offices and subsidiaries or as local sales representatives helps firms to overcome language and cultural barriers (Cunningham (1986)). Cunningham goes on to suggest:

A major dilemma arises in devising an organization structure and modus operandi which ensures that language and cultural gaps between supplier and customer are being narrowed (by using foreign nationals in agencies' subsidiaries and customer-country based salesmen) at the same time as providing an increased level of technical interaction with customers. This latter is provided usually by English speaking British engineers who may not be able to bridge the cultural gap adequately.

Strategies for International Industrial Marketing,
Turnbull and Valla (eds), p. 232

In order to overcome this dilemma some firms have opted to combine the two approaches, employing indigenous managers to conduct sales and marketing functions and company specialists to provide technical support. Greater control over operations and combinations of approaches that allow different customer-group requirements to be met emerge as favourable approaches. Flexibility in production and channel organizations also allows firms to react to dynamic environments.

Although many of the above policies for improving customer relationships suggest that internalization of activities and location of personnel abroad are preferable, these strategies are costly. Financial constraints restricting the resources available for overseas investment can result in managers seeking to optimize performance from what may be considered sub-optimum strategies.

6.8.5 Optimizing available strategies

Within external channel systems, building relationships with channel members and developing structures conducive to channel efficiency are important functions of the logistics manager. It is often assumed there is a natural disharmony between channel members who seek to maximize their profits at the expense of others. Developing an efficient system depends on promoting cooperation and minimizing conflict.

Conflict may arise for several reasons. Rosson (1984) identified three factors that inhibit performance in external market channels:

(a) Divided loyalties. Overseas distributors often sell more than one manufacturer's products. Producers therefore compete for their time. They sell most of those products that earn the highest returns and that require less active selling as a result of, for example, market pull generated through extensive advertising, attractive product features or greater reliability requiring less after-sales service.

(b) Seller–buyer atmosphere. Where the distributor is treated as a customer by the manufacturer, the roles assumed by the two parties will typically be those of seller and buyer. The buyer will attempt to bid down prices as far as possible and will assume that once he has title to the products he has control over sales. He will not promote sales by passing on information to consumers such as product-adaptation advantages or promotional efforts, neither will he be inclined to pass information to the seller on customer preferences and changing requirements.

(c) Unclear future intentions. Manufacturers often use distributors as a way of testing market opportunities and learning about the market as part of a longer-term objective of setting up their own facilities at a later date. In the long-run the distributor knows that building up sales for the manufacturer will result in termination of the distributorship.

Pricing levels can also be a source of conflict. Intermediaries may reduce prices in order to move stock, lowering the financial returns for all parties. Other sources of conflict may stem from the manufacturer's product being perceived by the distributor as uncompetitive, and helpful suggestions, based on close market knowledge, being rejected by the manufacturer.

Overcoming conflict may be achieved through cooperation. By working closely with distributors, setting acceptable price levels for both players, giving, receiving and acting on information and providing adequate support (such as sales and service training and promotional literature) the manufacturer can promote loyalty and break down the buyer–seller atmosphere. The major outstanding problem is the likelihood that a manufacturer will establish his own operations in the long-run. Successfully managed relationships may dissuade them from taking this option. However, where this is the long-term aim, the only option facing the firm is to reveal their objectives (Rosson (1984)). The distributor will know where he stands and as a result of the manufacturer's frankness he will be more likely to make the most of the opportunity.

Another way of overcoming conflict is through control. This can be achieved by the manufacturer setting sales quotas requesting regular reports and making frequent visits. Christopher (1972) suggests that control can be achieved through cooperation initiated by the dominant player in the channel. He highlights advertising and promotion, stock monitoring, staff training and risk sharing as important functions the dominant unit can perform to aid channel integration. He also suggests that cooperation enhances communication flows within the channel, benefiting decision-making at all stages. Rewards and sanctions are other possible ways the dominant player can control other channel members. Munro and Beamish (1987) argue, however, that good performance from the intermediary cannot be achieved through increased compensation or threats. Instead, providing additional support has a more positive effect on performance.

Internalized systems are not without their conflicts. Subsidiary and head-office managers may have conflicting attitudes and opinions. Pricing policies, marketing and promotion campaigns and target-market and channel-structure requirements are influenced by the market and local operating conditions and are thus more apparent to subsidiary managers. These should be communicated to the head office in order that conflict be minimized. If firms recognize that local market conditions affect the desirable approach, and only set sales quotas, conflict may be minimized by affording subsidiaries greater autonomy.

Summary

The logistics management function is a complex management role traversing many functional areas within the organization. The complexity of the function is intensified by the myriad of organizational structures and channel approaches the international firm may choose. The greater propensity in international dealings to externalize activities and the dynamics of internationalization also add to the management challenge.

Integrating external operations into the organizational structure, minimizing costs and maintaining service levels requires good relationship management and systems that provide the support and cooperation necessary to integrate the channel. It is also important for the system to be flexible in order that dynamics in modes of market servicing and channel structure can be accommodated in the logistics function. Cost minimization and provision of services are closely related to location and internalization versus externalization decisions, usually the responsibility of the international strategy division. This suggests that logistics managers should work closely with international strategists. This level of strategic importance, not usually conferred to domestic logistics managers, gives international logistics management a strategic rather than an administrative character. Logistics management requires an holistic view of the internal and external organization. Controlling the product flow from inputs through to final user and balancing cost saving and service in the long-term is important to firms' successful internationalization.

References

Alexander, R.S. and Berg, T. (1965): *Dynamic Management in Marketing*, Homewood, Richard D. Irwin Inc.

Berg, Thomas L. (1971): 'Designing the Distribution System' in Stevens, W.D. (ed.): *The Social Responsibility of Marketing*. Chicago, American Marketing Association.

Bilkey, W.J. and Tesar, G. (1977): 'The Export Behaviour of Small Wisconsin Manufacturing Firms', *Journal of International Business Studies*, 8, Spring/Summer.

Brown, Wilson (1984): 'Firm-like Behaviour in Markets: the Administered Channel', *International Journal of Industrial Organisation*, 2.

Buckley, Peter J. and Casson, Mark (1976): *The Future of the Multinational Enterprise*. Macmillan, London.

Buckley, Peter J. and Casson, Mark (1985): *The Economic Theory of the Multinational Enterprise: selected readings*. Macmillan, London.

Buckley, Peter J., Pass, C. and Prescott, Kate (1990): 'Foreign Market Servicing by Multinationals: and Integrated Treatment', *International Marketing Review*, Vol. 7, No. 4, pp. 25–40.

Cateora, Philip R. and Hess, John M. (1979): *International Marketing* (3rd edn). Richard D. Irwin Inc. Homewood.

Christopher, M. (1972): 'The Marketing Channel' in Christopher, M. and Wills, D. (eds): *Marketing Logistics and Distribution Planning*. George Allen and Unwin, London.

Christopher, M. (1985): *The Strategy of Distribution Management*. Gower.

Cunningham, Malcolm T. (1986): 'Industrial Firms in European Markets: the British approach to Europe', in Turnbull, Peter W. and Valla, Jean-Paul (eds): *Strategies for International Industrial Marketing*. Croom Helm, New York.

Davies, Gary (1988): *Managing Export Distribution*, Heinemann, London.

Diamantopoulos, A. (1987): 'Vertical Quasi-integration Revisited: the Role of Power', *Managerial and Decision Economics*, Vol. 8.

Hakansson, H. (ed.) (1982): *International Marketing and Purchasing of Industrial Goods – an Interaction Approach*. John Wiley and Sons, New York.

Hardy, Kenneth G. and McGrath, Allan J. (1988): *Marketing Channel Management: Strategic Management and Tactics*. Scott, Foresham.

Horst, Thomas D. (1971): 'The Theory of the Multinational Firm – Optimal Behaviour under Different Tariff and Tax Rates', *Journal of Political Economy*, 79.

Hussey, David (1972): 'Physical Distribution: the Environmental Context' in Christopher, M. and Wills, D. (eds): *Marketing Logistics and Distribution Planning*. George Allen and Unwin, London.

Jensen, M.C. and Meckling, W.H. (1976): 'The Theory of the Firm: Managerial Behaviour, Agency Costs and Ownership Structures', *Journal of Financial Economics*, Vol. 3.

Johanson, J. and Vahlne J. (1977): 'The Internationalization Process of the Firm – a Model of Knowledge Development and Increasing Foreign Market Commitment', *Journal of Management Studies*, 8, Spring/Summer.

LaLonde, B.J. and Zinszer P.H. (1976): *Customer Service: Meaning and Measurement*. NCPDM, Chicago.

McMillan, C. and Paulden, S. (1979): *Export Agents: a Complete Guide to their Selection and Control*. Gower Press, London.

Munro, H.J. and Beamish, P.W. (1987): 'Distribution Methods and Export Performance' in Rosson, Philip J. and Reid, Stanley D. (eds): *Managing Export Entry and Expansion*. Praeger, New York.

Rosson, Philip J. (1984): 'Success Factors in Manufacturer–Overseas Distributor Relationships in International Marketing' in Kaynak E. (ed.): *International Marketing Management*. Praeger, New York.

Turnbull, P.W. (1986a): 'The Interaction Approach to Marketing Strategy – an Introduction', in Turnbull, P.W. and Valla, Jean-Paul (eds): *Strategies for International Industrial Marketing*. Croom Helm, New York.

Valla, Jean-Paul (1986): 'Industrial Firms in European Markets: the French approach to Europe', in Turnbull Peter W. and Valla, Jean-Paul (eds): *Strategies for International Industrial Marketing*. Croom Helm, New York.

Vernon, R. (1966): 'International Investment and International Trade in the Product Cycle', *Quarterly Journal of Economics*, 80, June.

Walsh (1978): *International Marketing*. McDonald and Evans.

Wind, Y., Douglas, S.P. and Perlmutter, H.V. (1973): 'Guidelines for Developing International Marketing Strategies', *Journal of Marketing*, 37, April.

6.9

The Management of International Research and Development

6.9.1 Scope of the study

Alternative modes of operation

In recent years, it has become obvious that companies need to develop a technology strategy that comprises economic decisions on the acquisition of knowledge from various sources, the storage of knowledge and the means of its retrieval, as well as the internal or external use of the knowledge. Research and development is only one of a multitude of possibilities for knowledge acquisition such as acquisition of firms, buying of patent rights or licences and using contract research. There has been much debate over the years about the best way of organizing research and development. Issues raised have included the value of separating research from development and the optimum size of laboratories: too small is seen as not offering critical mass in key areas; too large is less effective because of, for example, problems of organization structure and communication.

In the past, research and development has been primarily seen as a headquarters' function: an activity performed in the same nation in which the headquarters of a company is located. In recent years, research and development activities have been increasingly located in nations different from the home nation of a company's headquarters.[1] Figure 6.9.1 shows various modes of operating research and development abroad.

This chapter is concerned with those research and development activities that are performed by a company outside of the nation in which its headquarters is located: either in a self-standing research and development facility[2] (wholly-owned subsidiary); or in a research and development facility in conjunction with production or marketing activities (wholly-owned subsidiary). This definition excludes research and development joint ventures with companies abroad or other forms of cooperative agreements;[3] and knowledge acquisition in foreign

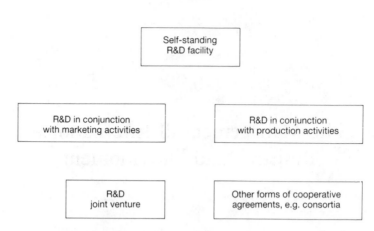

Figure 6.9.1   Modes of Operating R&D Abroad

countries. Both these call for specific legal or institutional arrangements that differ considerably from the cases considered here. One of the major differences concerns the constraints on the quantity or quality of knowledge acquisition or knowledge transfer under these arrangements.

Hakanson and Zander found that many of the overseas laboratories of Swedish firms they studied arose as a by-product of acquisitions.[4] Ronstadt found a similar situation.[5] More recently, Suverkrup looked at the acquisition goals of the United States and German firms and found that 'offensive marketing reasons, technological considerations and regional diversification play the most important role'.[6] A temporal comparison showed that technology reasons have become more important, with emphasis placed on gaining access to new technology and know-how through cooperation with the R&D department of the acquired company and exchanging know-how with the new subsidiary. Differences were also identified between high-technology and low-technology companies in the United States; the former are more interested in using a good research environment, transferring certain research and development results and using the higher research productivity available abroad.

Acquisitions for technological reasons can be planned. An interesting example is that of Thomson, France's largest consumer electronics company, which linked with JVC in a joint venture to assemble video cassette recorders in Europe. Subsequently it acquired the United States consumer electronics divisions of General Electric and RCA, following a series of similar purchases in Europe, and began development and technology for a new generation of video recorders. 'Thomson began producing its own video cassette recorders at a new high tech German plant late last year, and now looks likely to dump JVC altogether and make a grab for both the European and the United States markets.'[7]

The results of research and development may be exploited internationally from the home base through licensing as was done most effectively by Pilkington with its float glass technology.[8] Depending on the nature of the technology, the amount of local adaptation needed and the entry barriers put forth by, for example, the local political system, a company may decide to perform research and development in the home country only and exploit the research and development results internationally.

Another British innovation, the CAT scanner from EMI, was less successful for the company which chose not to license the innovation but to attack the major markets directly. This was partly due to the lack of appropriability and complementary assets under the control of the producer. This lack of strength enabled the potential user to delay the introduction until the user country had caught up. This situation is noted by Rugman and others who state: 'The possession of a firm-specific advantage in product or process technology is often seen to be the most important determinant of the bargaining power of the multinational enterprises.'[9] The fact that the Pilkington process has no competitors after 30 years, whereas the other technology has many, supports this argument well.

The issues of acquiring overseas research and development facilities and of exploiting research and development on a global scale constitute facets of the management of research and development in an international realm. Since the emphasis of this chapter is on the decision parameters involved in operating wholly-owned research and development facilities abroad, these facets will not be explored further.

The management challenge

Many issues must be raised when considering possible structures for companies operating on a global basis. Those relating to business groups are covered elsewhere in this book, but the way in which these have affected research and development must be taken into account. For example, it had been reported that: 'An important part of ICI's structure, and one which emphasizes its commitment to act as a global company, are its 10 broad business groups. Communication and commitment across the company is greatly helped by a management planning policy which moves key people between countries and across product groups. But a final way of promoting fresh ideas and flexibility in the company has been via the research and development structure, a part of the company which spans all the business groups. After a flirtation in the 1970s with centralized research and development operations, the company has spun off most of its business divisions to get a better link between scientific and marketing staff.'[10] They have also established an elaborate network of internal scientific committees as a 'way of ensuring that scientific ideas can flow across business boundaries'[11] – something that is clearly necessary if advantage is to be taken of the knowledge base available worldwide.

The issues of global research and development management are examined more closely by De Meyer and Mizushima under the above heading. They state: 'We have no record of companies which would indicate that it is easier to do research and development on a global scale than in a geographically centralized approach. Globalization of research and development is typically accepted more with resignation than with pleasure. In one of our own cases, internationalization was almost described as an unavoidable nightmare, closer to a marketing gimmick than to an effectively contributing research and development outlet.'[12] Why then do organizations choose to locate research and development facilities overseas? And why should research and development abroad constitute a specific set of problems as compared with other national, however decentralized, research and development organizations of a company? We see four major reasons:

(1) Nations develop different legal frameworks that may support or constrain research and development in specific ways. Companies could try to evade constraints and make use of the supports.

(2) Nations differ with respect to their cultures. Some cultures could be favourable to the specific spectrum of activities that lead to knowledge acquisition; others could be unfavourable. Companies could try to make use of the more favourable environments and to avoid the less favourable ones.

(3) Cultural rivalries within international corporations may lead to the setting up of various research and development facilities in different countries. Such intra-company rivalry may go as far as several research and development facilities working on the same tasks, thus competing against each other and thereby establishing a dual system.

(4) Research and development personnel could be reluctant to seek employment in foreign countries for emotional reasons (the legal or cultural reasons have already been covered). Companies that experience a shortage of research and development personnel in their home base could therefore move their research and development facilities to where they expect to find the desired research and development personnel.

If one of these differences occurs, it constitutes specific problems for research and development management. These problems are different from those that are due to a decentralization of research and development activities within one nation, such as the attempt to move research and development closer to the segments of a heterogeneous market. However, it is difficult to distinguish such reasons from the ones given above in empirical investigations.

6.9.2   Research and development location in foreign countries

The importance of research and development abroad

Given the poor quality of national research and development data, it seems to be of little use to compile and compare time-series data on research and development activities performed in countries different from the home country of a company. Even cross-sectional data are hard to come by and to compare.

A recent survey by the Swiss statistical office reports that 35.2 per cent of the total Swiss industrial research and development expenditure is spent abroad.[13] In the report it is assumed that similar results may be achieved for other small nations that served as a home base for large multinational enterprises, such as The Netherlands. From a questionnaire study conducted among the 780 largest German industrial companies, we found that 17 per cent of their research and development budgets was spent abroad, and 11 per cent of their research and development personnel were employed outside of Germany; however, only 16 per cent of the answering firms were engaged in research and development outside Germany, and in these firms the shares of research and development personnel employed abroad amounted to 31.7 per cent.[14] For the United States and Japanese firms, shares of the research and development budget spent abroad seem to be much smaller. The study just quoted finds a share of 8.2 per cent for the United States, and of 1.9 per cent for Japanese firms. However, both figures are biased due to a highly skewed distribution of firms towards big units. The share of foreign research and development personnel on total research and development personnel for seven German companies was 19 per cent in a study conducted in 1983.[15] In an earlier study, Pausenberger found that German companies spent 11 per cent of their research and development budget abroad and employed 15 per cent of their research and development personnel abroad .[16] Jungnickel quotes lower figures for 1974: 10 per cent of research and development budget and 11 per cent of research and development personnel.[17] In a 1971 study on the top 500 United States firms, Creamer and others show that 10 per cent of the budget is spent abroad.[18] The same result was reached by Mansfield and others for a sample of 55 large United States companies.[19] For Sweden, figures of 14 per cent are reported by de Meyer and Mizushima.[20]

These national figures suggest the following four hypotheses:

(H.1) The data of the most recent study by Brockhoff imply that more capital-intensive research and development activities are performed abroad, and that companies locate more development-oriented work abroad. Against the background of high capital costs in Germany, such a behaviour of German companies is understandable. Although this argument suggests cost-oriented behaviour by managers, questionnaire data do not seem to support this.[21] This might be explained by the often-observed phenomenon that managers' actual behaviour differs from what they say in interviews or questionnaires. But if costs play a much larger role (than assumed until now) in the decision to locate research and development abroad, then development activities especially should be performed abroad. This could mean that such a large amount of development is conducted abroad that a number of development results will be transferred back to the home country of the company. Thus, it turns out that not only may research be a global activity but also development.[22]

(H.2) If a nation serves as a home country to multinational industrial companies, the more of their research and development budgets will be spent abroad the smaller the supply of local scientific personnel and the larger the importance of research and development in the industry considered.

Data collected for individual firms primarily in the chemical industry suggest that German and Swiss firms seek a more rapid expansion of their foreign research and development expenditures as compared with their local research and development expenditure growth.[23] From the above hypothesis we might argue that a scarcity of factor supply is a prime reason for this behaviour. However, German companies invest their research and development money mostly in other European nations (47.5 per cent of the external research and development budgets) and in the United States (41.3 per cent of the external research and development budgets), where they compete not only with the local demand for research and development personnel but also with the demand from other multinationals. This leads to two further assumptions:

(H.3) Research and development is spent abroad if the home nation constrains the research and development activities. German chemical producers claim this is a main reason for moving genetics research to the United States.

(H.4) Research and development is spent abroad when the receiving nation constrains sales if these are not adequately backed up by local research and development activities. This has been claimed with respect to pesticides in India or pharmaceuticals in France. In fact, the development of such constraints has been adopted as strategy for local economic development in those nations that rely heavily on the sales of certain raw materials, such as oil and gas.[24]

An antagonistic behaviour in this respect may be seen in the current attempts of Japanese companies to establish research and development in European countries.[25] In a proactive manner, these companies are now performing all functions of the value-added chain in Europe. However, it remains to be seen what the content and thrust of these newly founded research and development facilities will be.

Clearly, the little information we have reflects a complex issue. In order to gain more clarity about the decision to locate research and development abroad we shall look carefully and deeply at the factors underlying this decision.

Reasons for research and development abroad:

(1)   Cost considerations

The difference of institutional, legal and cultural frameworks between nations influences the factor costs of performing research and development. Labour cost per hour is the most obvious item to be considered. Another important item is location cost where potentially dangerous apparatus or big installations are involved. The perception of danger can vary between nations; the objective possibilities of coping with it can also be different, for instance by avoiding densely populated areas when locating installations. A similar argument refers to the size of installations. As the price of land varies between regions according to the supply and demand relationships, it may be worthwhile to consider this in location decisions.

An interesting example of these kinds of consideration is provided by the Mercedes Benz Corporation. Its attempt to buy a test track and accompanying installations in a thinly populated agrarian part of Germany failed because of opposition from environmental groups. The company started to consider alternatives that went beyond the German border.

Assuming that a certain research and development result can be achieved with a certain number of man weeks, the time worked per year is another cost item to be considered. The regular number of hours worked per week differs between countries; for example, in Germany the actual hours per week worked in industry was 40.3 for 1988, while in Great Britain this figure amounted to 42.3.[26] It is hard to take a lead in the race to be first to market if the number of hours worked per year is markedly lower in one country than in another. Attempts to introduce shift-work in laboratories are constrained by the necessary level of creativity. With the advent of computer-aided design and computer-aided manufacture only a limited amount of development work might be organized in a multiple shift process.

A second factor to consider in this respect is the quality of labour relations that might differ between countries and therefore influences the number of hours worked.

Labour cost per hour is different in different nations. ICI is rapidly building up research and development – especially development – in the United States and Japan and expects a continuing shift of development resources overseas alongside fast-growing markets. But the company retains 'great confidence in both the quality and the relatively low cost of science in Britain. Cost per scientist can be less than half that in some other countries. It helps to account for ICI's smaller investment in research and development than, say, its big German competitors.'[27]

(2)   Market considerations and technology transfer

Sales could be enhanced by overseas research and development apart from the points already discussed with respect to legal or institutional constraints for doing foreign business. Pausenberger and Volkmann discuss various aspects of increasing a business by getting close to the customers to improve communications about their needs or by taking the environmental conditions under which a customer works into consideration in product development.[28] This can be illustrated by referring to the environmental effects of the use of pesticides or to educational differences with respect to the safe operation of production processes.

Mansfield and others show that 'there is a direct and statistically significant relationship between a firm's percentage of sales derived from abroad and its percentage of research and development expenditures carried out overseas'. Furthermore, 'a firm's percentage of sales from foreign subsidiaries has a highly significant positive effect on its percentage of research and development expenditures carried out overseas while its percentage of sales from exports has a significant negative effect'.[29]

Being close to the foreign market with one's own research and development facility is of special importance in those cases where users are a valuable source of innovative ideas and products.[30] By utilizing the user innovations one may broaden the market. The existence of lead users in the foreign market may thus influence the decision to establish overseas research and development facilities.

Research and development presence in foreign markets could also be image-increasing which might have indirect effects on sales. Practitioners say imported goods come from strangers, locally produced goods of foreign manufacturers come from guests, but that goods that are locally produced and backed up by local research and development come from citizens. This illustrates the case in point, at least as long as doing business with a fellow-citizen is valued more highly than doing business with a guest or a stranger.

Legal actions may not only serve as constraints but also open up new markets. These may need research and development back-up. Castrol[32] reports that as early as 1983 they spotted a marketing opportunity for an oil specially designed for engines fitted with a three-way catalytic converter. A two-year research programme led to the first launch of GTX3 in Austria in October 1985. The oil has been introduced gradually throughout Europe, mainly to coincide with the introduction of the legislation in different countries. As would be expected, take-up rates have varied between countries and marketing campaigns have had to be tailored to the specific characteristics of the different nationalities. This case effectively illustrated the need to design marketing strategies to help bring market and technology together.

(3) Organizational considerations
The research and development process itself could be influenced by international research and development facilities, but some of the influences can be detrimental. The integration of research and development results or new ideas into the whole organization may be hindered by a 'not invented here' syndrome that

could gain special importance if the ideas or results have to cross borders. The communication system will not only be affected by distance,[32] but also by language, research traditions and other differences.

(4)   Other influences

The overseas location of research and development can help to increase the spectrum of ideas. The possibilities of job rotation to foreign countries can be a motivating factor for at least some research and development personnel. Given equal competence, research and development tasks can be moved to those locations that are organizationally best-equipped to perform the tasks (where this could relate to ease of team building, labour relations, ease of working on crash projects and others).

Management of international research and development activities faces the task of deriving synergy from these activities. Otherwise the 'sum of the local development activities cannot be added up to a global approach to R&D'.[33] Various organizational options are available to serve this need. Much prominence has been gained by:

a hub model, with centralized decision-making at the home laboratory and a distribution of more or less supporting tasks to the different laboratories;

a network model, with a mission-oriented task distribution among the different laboratories: either constrained to foreign markets; or charged with global technological responsibility for a company in a specific field of technology; or charged with global product responsibility for a company for a specific group of products.

a competitive model, where each laboratory is a profit centre determining its own spectrum of activities.

Various intermediate or mixed assignments of tasks are possible. We do not yet have a clear view on which form of organization is superior under certain conditions. Only plausible possibilities can be suggested.

Some thought has been given to the question whether foreign research and development facilities develop according to a specific life-cycle model, in terms of assuming specific tasks in an observable and typical order. Ronstadt identified four types of global research and development laboratories, which he described as:

(1) transfer technology units designed to help subsidiaries transfer manufacturing technology to the parent as well as providing technical services to local customers;

(2) indigenous technology units established to develop new and improved products for the local markets, not necessarily using technology from the parent organization;

(3) global technology units aimed at developing new products and processes for simultaneous application across many markets; and

(4) corporate technology units aimed at generating new technology of a longer-term and more exploratory nature.[34]

In the companies Ronstadt studied in the United States, he found evidence that start-ups could occur in any of these stages, and that there was no necessary progression or life-cycle. However: 'Once started, there seems to be evidence that the majority of R&D investments follows the evolutionary pattern from technology transfer unit over indigenous technology unit to global technology unit. This model is of course in agreement with the theory about the international product lifecycle.'[35]

Behrmann and Fischer looked at the foreign research and development groups of American transnationals and found more than half had an initial emphasis on technical support, moving from this position to doing applied research and development.[36] They also found that units with a higher emphasis on new product development and exploratory research were more likely to be established directly and not through evolution.

Considerable doubt must be raised, however, that foreign research and development investment follows certain patterns in a time-related manner. De Meyer and Mizushima argue that globalization of competition sheds doubt on the assumption.[37] The diversity of reasons outlined in the preceding paragraphs denies a specific time-related development. It also suggests that reasons beyond the influence of a company may change over time. For instance, the locus of scientific activity could move from one country to another. Forced or voluntary brain drain is a possible reason for this.

(5)   Risk reduction

Knowledge acquisition may be considered as complimentary to uncertainty reduction. Uncertainty is inherent in all actions that relate to future periods. In the efforts to fill perceived or manifest human needs, we may observe different uncertainties. Pearson argues that uncertainty of ends, that is future or present distributions of needs, and uncertainty of means, namely technologies to achieve these needs, can distinguished.[38] It is shown that this is of special relevance to explaining and possibly controlling innovation processes. The same idea proves to be fruitful for understanding the different reasons for performing research and development abroad. From Figure 6.9.2 it is apparent that, if both types of uncertainties are low, knowledge acquisition may be easily performed by a home-base research and development facility – unless other than risk-related reasons can be advanced for performing foreign research and development. If technological uncertainties appear to be low, but market uncertainties are high, foreign research and development will be used primarily to reduce market uncertainties by improving customer relations, contacting lead users, generally speaking by application engineering.

Let us now consider a situation where market uncertainties are low and technological uncertainties are high. In this case a primary task of foreign research and development units will be to contribute to lowering the major

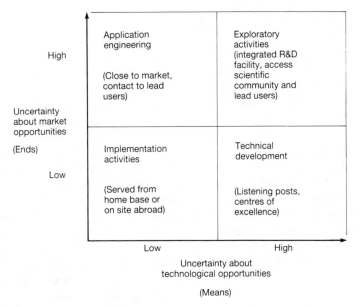

Figure 6.9.2 Uncertainty Map

source of uncertainty. Tying into the network of knowledge production, serving as a listening post,[39] and perhaps contributing to knowledge acquisition by one's own efforts, will therefore be primary tasks. If both types of uncertainty are rather high it seems necessary to operate a research and development facility that integrates all steps from basic research to application engineering in an effort to deal with the uncertainties.

These classifications could occur in any national enterprise as well. They have, however, developed a specific international importance in recent years. As has been shown in the managerial literature as well as in trade statistics, markets are sought through global selling. Local adaptations support this and enable global presence in many cases. At the same time it has become obvious that the production of technological knowledge may shift between locations and, as it is considered as a factor in building competitive strength, attempts are made to protect it from use by foreigners.[40] Thus, as the cost of international technology transfer is raised, it becomes more and more interesting to place research and development facilities in foreign locations.

6.9.3 Conclusion

The research on the location and management of research and development facilities abroad has so far been mostly descriptive in nature. It does not provide any evidence on their effectiveness and efficiency. In a recent study we found that a considerable number of research and development managers feel that their foreign research and development facilities do not meet expectations. We therefore suggest that performance measures should be included in future research.

Research on organization structure and the strategic thrust of overseas research and development has identified a number of typologies, such as the hub or network model and the four types of Ronstadt. However, the uncertainty map suggests that a more dynamic model is necessary and that studies need to take into account both technological and marketing considerations. Different strategic roles of foreign research and development facilities may be captured in the uncertainty map as well as the implications resulting from changes of the factors which influence the decision to operate research and development abroad.

The conclusions, therefore, are that there is no way to manage research and development on a global basis but that flexibility, coordination, commitment and a proactive stance are vital ingredients for success. In this the quality and motivation of people is paramount. The global dimension of research and development adds to the complexity through greater distances and cultural differences. These inevitably affect communication patterns, organization structure and career management, key areas to which particular attention needs to be paid.

Notes

1. The international aspects of the location and management of R&D have been a subject of concern for several years. However, in the early 1970s research and development abroad was seen as providing a valuable and necessary communication link between customers and central R&D facilities and thereby stressing more the development activities of R&D abroad. See Hough, E.A. (1972): 'Communication of Technical Information Between Overseas Markets and Head Office Laboratories', *R&D Management*, Vol. 3, No. 1, October, pp. 1–5.
2. Like, for example, 'Siemens Corporate Research, Inc.' in Princeton, New Jersey, USA. (Zaininger, K.H. (1990): 'Aspects of Global Management of R&D Resources', in Khalil, T.M. and Bayraktar, B.A.: *Management of Technology II*. Proceedings of the Second International Conference on Management of Technology, Industrial Engineering and Management Press, p. 273.)
3. Like the operation between the German chemical company Hoechst and the Massachusetts General Hospital in Boston. (Wortmann, M. (1990): 'Multinationals and the Internationalization of R&D: New Developments in German Companies', *Research Policy*, No. 19, p. 181.)
4. Håkanson, L. and Zander, U. (1986): *Managing International Research and Development*. Mekanforbund.
5. Ronstadt, R. (1977): *Research and Development Abroad by US Multinationals*. New York: Praeger.
6. Suverkrup, Ch. (1990): 'Innovations and US-German Acquisitions', in Khalil, T.M. and Bayraktar, B.A.: *Management of Technology II*. Proceedings of the Second

International Conference on Management of Technology, Industrial Engineering and Management Press, p. 444.

7. *International Management*, February 1990, p. 31.
8. Maidigue, M.A. (1980): 'Entrepreneurs, Champions and Technological Innovation', *Sloan Management Review*, Vol. 21, No. 2, Winter pp. 59–76.
9. (MNEs stands for Multinational Enterprises.) Rugman, A.M. and others 1985: *International Business. Firm and Environment*, p. 300. McGraw Hill.
10. *Financial Times*, 9 August 1989, p. 12.
11. *Financial Times*, 9 August 1989, p. 12.
12. De Meyer, A. and Mizushima, A. (1989): 'Global R&D Management', *R&D Management*, Vol. 19, No. 2, p. 139.
13. Buri, M., Suarez de Miguel, R. and Walder, B. (1989): *Forschung und Entwicklung in der Schweiz 1986*, p. 43 ff. Bundesamt fur Statistik.
14. Brockhoff, K. (1990): *Starken und Schwachen Industrieller Forschung und Entwicklung*, Chapter 10. Umfrageergebnisse aus der Bundesrepublik Deutschland: Poeschel.
15. Wortmann, M. (1990): 'Multinationals and the Internationalization of R&D: New Developments in German Companies', *Research Policy*, No. 19, p. 176.
16. Pausenberger, E. (1982): *Technologiepolitik Internationaler Unternehmen*, zfhf, Vol. 34, No. 12, pp. 1025–54.
17. Jungnickel, R. and others (1977): *Einfluss Multinationaler Unternehmen auf Aussenwirtschaft und Branchenstruktur der Bundesrepublik Deutschland*. Hamburg: HWWA.
18. Creamer, D., Apostolides, A.D. and Wang, S.L. (1976): *Overseas Research and Development by United States Multinationals, 1966–1975*. Conference Board.
19. Mansfield, E., Teece, D. and Romeo, A. (1979): 'Overseas Research and Development by US-based Firms', *Economica*, No. 46, pp. 187–96.
20. De Meyer, A. and Mizushima, A. (1989): 'Global R&D Management', *R&D Management*, Vol. 19, No. 2, p. 136.
21. Empirical research on the reasons for locating R&D abroad has identified 'costs' as only of secondary importance (e.g. see Rondstadt, R. 1977: *Research and Development Abroad by US Multinationals*. Praeger.)
22. This notion may be supported by the recent emergence of centres of excellence. 3M, for example, established 'Regional Technology Centres' in countries like Germany and Japan (Krogh, L.G. 1990: '3M's International Experience', in Khalil, T.M. and Bayraktar, B.A.: *Management of Technology II*. Proceedings of the Second International Conference on Management of Technology, Industrial Engineering and Management Press, pp. xxxiii–xxxix.
23. Brockhoff, K. (1989): *Forschung und Entwicklung, Planung und Kontrolle* (2nd edn), p. 86 ff. Oldenbourg; Buri, M., Suarez de Miguel, R. and Walder, B. 1989: *Forschung und Entwicklung in der Schweiz 1986*, p. 43. Bundesant fur Statistik.
24. Such policies have been adopted by the UK and Norway with respect to operations in the North Sea Continental Shelf. Documents are reprinted in Foders, F. and Wolfrum, R. (1989): *Meereswirtschaft in Europa, Rechtiliche und okonomische Rahmenbedingungen für deutsche Unternehmen*, p. 281 ff. Mohr/Siebeck.
25. Japanese investments in Britain gave rise to a controversial public debate.
26. *Statistische Jahrbuch 1989 für das Ausland*, p. 222.
27. *Financial Times*, 25 January 1989, p. 10.
28. Pausenberger, E. and Volkmann, B.: 'Forschung und Entwicklung in internationalen

Unternehmungen', *RKW-Handbuch Forschung*. Entwicklung, Konstruktion, Loseblattssmmlung, Berlin, Beitrag 8400.
29. Both quotations are from Mansfield, E., Teece, D. and Romeo, A. (1979): 'Overseas Research and Development by US-based Firms', *Economica*, No. 46, pp. 187–96.
30. Von Hippel, E. (1988): *Sources of Innovation*. Oxford University Press. For 'lead user concept' see Urban, G.L. and von Hippel, E. 1988: 'Lead User Analyses for the Development of New Industrial Products', *Management Science*, No. 34, pp. 569–82.
31. *Financial Times*, 9 April 1987, p. 22.
32. Allen, T.J. (1977): *Managing the Flow of Technology*. MIT Press.
33. De Meyer, A. and Mizushima, A. (1989): 'Global R&D Management', *R&D Management*, Vol. 19, No. 2, p. 136.
34. Ronstadt, R. (1977): *Research and Development Abroad by US Multinationals*. Praeger.
35. De Meyer, A. and Mizushima, A. (1989): 'Global R&D Management', *R&D Management*, Vol. 19, No. 2, p. 137.
36. Behrman, J.N. and Fischer, W.A. (1980): *Overseas R&D Activities of Transnational Companies*. MIT Press.
37. De Meyer, A. and Mizushima, A. (1989): 'Global R&D Management', *R&D Management*, Vol. 19, No. 2, April, p. 137.
38. Pearson, A. (1990): 'Innovation Strategy', *Technovation*, No. 10.
39. Nixdorf reports that it has set up such listening posts in various locations in the US (Nixdorf, Annual Report 1982).
40. 'President's Commission on Industrial Competitiveness: Global Competition', *The New Quality*, 1985. Dwyer, P. (1989): 'The Battle Raging over Intellectual Property', *Business Week*, Vol. 22, No. 5, pp. 80–7.

References

Allen, T.J. (1977): *Managing the Flow of Technology*. MIT Press.
Behrman, J.N. and Fischer, W.A. (1980): *Overseas R&D Activities of Transnational Companies*. MIT Press.
Brockhoff, K. (1990): *Starken und Schwachen industrieller Forschung und Entwicklung*. Umfrageergebnisse aus der Bundesrepublik Deutschland, Poeschel.
Brockhoff, K. (1989): *Forschung und Entwicklung, Planning und Kontrolle* (2nd edn), Oldenbourg.
Buri, M., Suarez de Miguel, R. and Walder, B. (1989): *Forschung und Entwicklung in der Schweiz 1986*, Bundesamt fur Statistik, pp. 43 ff.
Creamer, D., Apostolides, A.D. and Wang, S.L. (1976): *Overseas Research and Development by United States Multinationals, 1966–1975*. Conference Board.
Dwyer, P. (1989): 'The Battle Raging over Intellectual Property', *Business Week*, 22 May, pp. 80–7.
Financial Times, 9 April 1987.
Financial Times, 9 August 1989.
Foders, F. and Wolfrum, R. (1989): *Meereswirtschaft in Europa*, Rechtliche und okonomische Rahmenbedingungen für deutsche Unternehmen, Mohr/Siebeck.
Håkanson, L. and Zander, U. (1986): *Managing International Research and Development*. Mekanforbund.

Hough, E.A. (1972): 'Communication of Technical Information between Overseas Markets and Head Office Laboratories', *R&D Management*, Vol. 3, No. 1, October, pp. 1–5.

International Management, February 1990, p. 31.

Jungnickel, R., and others (1977): *Elinfluss multinationaler Unternehmen auf Aussenwirtschaft und Branchenstruktur der Bundesrepublik Deutschland*. Hamburg, HWWA.

Krogh, L.G. (1990): '3M's International Experience,' in Khalil, T.M. and Bayraktar, B.A.: *Management of Technology II*. Proceedings of the Second International Conference on Management of Technology, Industrial Engineering and Management Press, pp. xxxiii–xxxix.

Maidigue, M.A. (1980): 'Entrepreneurs, Champions and Technological Innovation', *Sloan Management Review*, Vol. 21, No. 2, Winter, pp. 59–76.

Mansfield, E., Teece, D. and Romeo, A. 'Overseas Research and Development by US based Firms', *Economica*, No. 46, pp. 187–96.

Nixdorf AG: *Annual Report*, 1982.

Pausenberger, E. (1982): *Technologiepolitik Internationaler Unternehmen*, zfbf, Vol. 34, No. 12, pp. 1205–54.

Pausenberger, E. and Volkmann, B. 'Forschung und Entwicklung in internationalen Unternehmungen', *RKW-Handbuch Forschung*. Berlin: Entwicklung, Konstruktion, Loseblattsammlung.

Pearson, A. (1990): 'Innovation Strategy', *Technovation*, No. 10.

President's Commission on Industrial Competitiveness: Global Competition, (1985): *The New Quality*. Washington, D.C.

Ronstadt, R. (1977): *Research and Development Abroad by US Multinationals*. Praeger.

Rugman, A.M. and others (1985): *International Business, Firm and Environment*. McGraw-Hill.

Statistisches Jahrbuch 1989 für das Ausland.

Suverkrup, Ch. (1990): 'Innovations and US-German Acquisitions', in Khalil, T.M. and Bayraktar, B.A.: *Management of Technology II*. Proceedings of the Second International Conference on Management of Technology, Industrial Engineering and Management Press, p. 444.

Urban, G.L. and von Hippel, E. (1988): 'Lead User Analyses for the Development of New Industrial Products', *Management Science*, No. 34, pp. 569–82.

von Hippel, E. (1988): *Sources of Innovation*. Oxford University Press.

Wortmann, M. (1990): 'Multinationals and the Internationalization of R&D: New Developments in German Companies', *Research Policy*, No. 19, pp. 175–83.

Zaininger, K.H. (1990): 'Aspects of Global Management of R&D Resources', in Khalil, T.M. and Bayraktar, B.A.: *Management of Technology II*. Proceedings of the Second International Conference on Management of Technology, Industrial Engineering and Management Press, pp. 269–79.

This chapter was prepared for this book by Alexander von Boehmer and Prof. Dr Klaus Brockhoff of Forschungsstelle für Technologie und Innovationsmanagement, Christian-Albrechts-Universität zu Kiel, and Alan W. Pearson, Director, R&D Research Unit, Manchester Business School, University of Manchester.

6.10

Organization

Two issues that are related, but in no way dependent on one another, are the subject of this chapter: structure and centralization. Both are much written about but the depth of research is variable. Some writings accept a wide range of variables, but fail to produce a research plan which recognizes the range or the complexity of the data; others ignore the wide range and reproduce simplistic, conventional explanations. Experienced executives are often more sensitive, especially to the issues involved in centralization and decentralization, than many academics; the present author can testify to that, after prolonged discussions with managers who are impressed with the subtleties to be resolved.

6.10.1 Structure

The framework within which the spider's web of international communications operates can be examined from a number of angles. A logical starting point is to consider the objectives.

Objectives

Most of the work on organization has been concerned with the structure and how it is derived. Less consideration has been given to the purposes that structure is called upon to serve. These include:

authority,
communication,
career,
decision-making,
expertise, and
responsibility.

Writers on organization are often preoccupied with communication, but the other elements are equally essential to an effective structure.

Authority means the process by which control is exercised over the units and sub-units of an organization. It also refers to the need for stimulus and discipline in the relationship between the units, and the ability to provide motivation.

Communication means all forms of message-passing both upwards and downwards including mandatory orders, advice, queries, suggestions and requests for information as well as the more formalized procedures of the reporting and monitoring systems.

Career means the provision of an adequate career structure, a subject usually overlooked by theorists but of the greatest importance to participants; an organization that does not provide an adequate career structure can be expected to fall.

Decision-making in terms of where and how decisions are taken has been the focus of much attention and is considered later in this chapter under the heading 'Centralization and decentralization'.

Expertise. The allocation of expertise in different units of an organization is a major issue inside the larger multinationals. The discussion relates to the subject of internal markets and cost-benefit analysis, although more judgemental and personal issues are also involved. The final decision may depend on the availability of key personnel or the dispositions of competitors.

Responsibility is closely related to both authority and expertise: it is the means by which an organization allocates responsibility to its participants.

Structure

The need for an international structure stems from the origins of international operations. When a company begins to do business abroad, there is a need to adapt the organization; some argue that the need should be recognized earlier.[1] The stress at this stage is on the need for representation on the board and specialization at an appropriate level. The embryo international organization may be represented by a person part-time, like the director who is charged with answering to export matters on the board agenda in addition to his other duties, or the clerk who completes the export documentation in addition to his other duties. From these beginnings can develop an export department with its own management structure or even an export division. In American companies, although less often elsewhere, an international division sometimes develops in a company even before there is foreign investment. But it is the emergence of investment that begins the process towards the multinational organization which has been the subject of many specialist studies. The studies are of two kinds: those that start from some theory of organization change and those that generalize from organization options.

Strategy and structure

The best-known theory of change is the one stemming from the work of Chandler.[2] This links the emergence of new structures with changes in strategy. As expounded by Stopford and Wells, the process starts in three stages: (1) is a simple structure for a small organization led by one man; (2) is a functional structure with the organization divided into departments each of which is concerned with foreign operations; and (3) operates through divisions which have some (but a varying) degree of autonomy. Once the third stage is reached, an international division will usually be in place for the management of the foreign business. As this division increases in size, a number of factors will lead to its dissolution. It may be replaced by the product divisions operating worldwide; it may be replaced by geographical divisions responsible for regions, or there may be a combination of product and region.

A number of factors – including, in the short term, the availability of management – influences the choice of structure, but this is ultimately dependent on the strategy chosen for product or geographical diversification. After 1967, some companies began to experiment with a structure that combines both regional and product management within one system: the grid structure. The progress from one stage to another and between the international division and the other global options is seen as 'evolutionary'. As strategy emerges with increasing emphasis on worldwide operations, so structures evolve to match. Crucial to the argument is the view that 'change is the consequence of rational analysis' (Stopford and Wells (1972) p. 79), although change is also seen to be a consequence of bargaining between groups of managers. Evidence is produced to show that performance is improved where structure does indeed follow strategy.

The strategy and structure approach has been widely followed. Robock and Simmonds (1983), for instance, emphasize the 'evolutionary' stages of multinational structures. They start from Stopford and Wells and provide a number of examples to support the thesis. The approach has also been criticized on a number of grounds. In particular the 'evolutionary' view has been criticized on both theoretical and empirical grounds.[3] Observations of temporary changes over a limited period in company structures hardly seem to match a concept like evolution which implies gradual change through a process of natural selection over millions of years. In any case the changes recorded in the expansionary 1960s were followed by more dynamic and less predictable changes in the 1970s, as Bartlett has pointed out. The even more competitive atmosphere of the 1980s makes evolutionary views appear less probable still. The evolutionary approach exaggerates the in-company decision process against the pressures of the business environment.

Another criticism is on the grounds of evidence. Studies based largely on published material, albeit supplemented by further research in some cases, hardly support some of the generalizations made. Company reports, for instance, do not necessarily represent the business system as it works in practice. They are drawn up by public relations specialists, not by organization experts. More important is the extent to which the evidence does not support the claim to rationality.

Conflict theory

Greater stress on pressure and negotiation rather than rationality is contained in the *conflict theory* of international organization developed by the present author.[4] This states that change comes about through conflicts of opinion between managers with different priorities and varying responsibilities. In particular, functional interests (worldwide policies for marketing, finance, production and so on), product interests (worldwide policies for particular product lines) and geographical interests (policies for approaching markets other than the domestic) will clash and the organization at any one time will reflect the priority given to one of the interests or a compromise between them.

The results of the conflict are much influenced by changing pressures from outside the company, such as increasing competition in key markets or government interference. From inside the company, factors like the product mix and the relative influence of individual managers will also affect the outcome. Where the Harvard theories derive from economic historians like Chandler, the conflict theory stems from the work of economists like Cyert and sociologists like March.[5] The outcome of the conflicts is one of the following five types of organization:

A type – overall, where managers with overall corporate responsibilities administer the foreign subsidiaries; equivalent to stages 1 and 2 in the Harvard scheme, this means either a single manager in charge of a small company or a central team of chief executive and department heads. This type is much favoured by foreign subsidiaries for which it provides a direct link to the top of the company; it normally breaks down with divisionalization.

B type – geographical, where managers with international or regional remits are responsible for the foreign business. This type is especially relevant when local expertise is important: when the company operates in consumer goods or services, is seeking government contracts or is surrounded by much publicity; it is also used when the products are closely related.

C type – product, where the product divisions manage their businesses worldwide. There is a logic to this approach. If a company has decided to operate through product groups whose managers are held to be profit-responsible, it is not helpful to remove the foreign operation from this responsibility. The logic breaks down when lack of expertise leads to neglect of the foreign markets.

D type – matrix, where managers report along both geographical and product lines. This type (the grid type of the Harvard studies) involves divided loyalties on the part of subsidiary management, but it also implies careful planning. Since the word 'matrix' became fashionable, many companies have been claiming a matrix organization which have only an ambiguous one. There is nothing ambiguous about a true matrix: lines of authority are carefully defined and accounts are made up to match. Profit responsibilites are multiple, not vague. The exact terms vary, but the relationship between the international or regional division and the product groups is often described in terms like landlord and tenant. The geographical division sets up a local subsidiary, organizes the physical arrangements like land and buildings, and establishes a viable framework within which the product groups operate. Agreement has to be reached on a number of matters from investment decisions to the hiring or firing of senior staff. The matrix organization makes heavy demands on its managers, but statements that it has failed appear to be made as a result of investigations into organizations that were not genuinely of the matrix type in the first place.[6] This is not to say that an international matrix is easy to handle. The sharing of authority will often be biased – either as a result of a strong personality or of specific business pressures. Davis has documented some of the difficulties (see Davis and Lawrence (1977)).

E type – project, where flexible and changing groups are set up to manage the foreign subsidiaries. This means that a general manager with a team of specialists is designated to provide both a contact group and a control for specific subsidiaries. The team changes as the business develops. Like the matrix type, this is a generic name for a number of different approaches. Bartlett (see above, note 3) refers to the 'temporary coalition model'. This would seem to refer to an embryonic project system. The main characteristic is the introduction to other sectors of a style of management developed for major contracts in the construction and aircraft industries. The maximum flexibility is provided without tying up resources unnecessarily.

Other options
Other writers describe the options used by companies and their variants without relating them to a theory of change. Examples are Dymsza (1972), who does refer to evolutionary change, and Davis (1979) who provides a series of case studies. The latter also includes some notes on European multinationals (written by Americans) which suggest that they will follow the United States pattern; it also contains some notes on Japanese companies (partly written by Japanese) which anticipate some continuing differences. For further reasons why Japanese companies may be expected to follow a different route, see Sasaki (1981).

Regional centres

A regional organization is the geographical structure of Stopford and Wells and part of the present author's geographical type; but there can also be regional subsidiaries or offices in any of the other types.[7] Even at the first stage of their development abroad, relatively small companies sometimes appoint a national subsidiary to mastermind the business in a region. A regional centre can itself be one of four types.[8]

(1) A national subsidiary with responsibilities outside its own country, including a brief to develop a market plan for the region of which the country is a part.

(2) A regional subsidiary with full line-management responsibility for national organizations in the region, including the consolidation of their accounts. The chief executive for the region normally reports to the chief executive at head office or someone deputed by him.

(3) A regional centre with staff responsibility only – to advise the national subsidiaries in the region and to coordinate their activities.

(4) A mixture of (2) and (3). The regional centre may, for instance, have staff responsibilities towards the more successful national subsidiaries and take over line management for those that are in trouble.

6.10.2   Decision-making – centralization and decentralization

A number of controversies surrounds the understanding of centralization and decentralization; although inseparable, the issues can be examined under four headings: (1) the nature of the concepts; (2) the nature of relevant evidence; (3) the method of measurement; and (4) the implications of conclusions derived from numbers (1) to (3).

The nature of the concepts

The distinction is between those who refer to a *locus* of decision and those who use terms like 'influencing factors'. Between these views there is often a lack of comprehension. On the one hand, it is taken for granted that decisions are either taken at head office or in a foreign subsidiary. If a majority of decisions regarded as significant are delegated to a subsidiary, the company is described as decentralized; if not it is centralized. The opposing view affirms that this is not how important decisions are taken. On the contrary, they are taken as a result of a dialogue between a subsidiary and head office, with messages and often people passing to and fro. Who formally says yes or no at the end of the process is irrelevant – a company is decentralized if a subsidiary brings more influence to bear on the results than head office, and there are a number of criteria for judging the degree of influence. For instance, where was the process leading up to the decision initiated? Where was most of the evidence collected? How independently are the necessary arrangements made? If the answer to all those questions is in the subsidiary and head office rubber stamps the result, the company is decentralized. An example is a decision about an investment whose value is outside the subsidiary's discretion limits – is the response in practice determined in the subsidiary, relying on a consent that is little more than a formality? Most authors refer to a locus or location of decision-making,[9] but an increasing number are looking to influencing factors. The underlying distinction can be traced back to a sustained discussion among sociologists and social psychologists, although management writings often fail to acknowledge this.[10]

Whichever view is taken on the controversy over locus or influence, there are a number of other considerations that need bringing into focus. Are we, for instance, talking about some kind of objective reality – this unit of company X always takes this decision – or are we more concerned with perception? In the latter case, an individual manager may assert that he has taken a decision, whether or not he has done so. Researchers find it is not unusual for different managers to claim they have taken the same decision (see Brooke (1984) Chapter 15). Since the examination of decentralization is often undertaken to see whether there is any relation to motivation, perception is arguably more important than any alleged objective reality. Nevertheless, if there is a discrepancy between the two, that fact is itself an illuminating contribution to the understanding of organization behaviour.

Another issue is whether the concepts are capable of being understood along a relatively straightforward one-dimensional scale, or whether such a view is completely unrealistic. Otterbeck (1981, p. 4) writes: 'It may not even be a question of a zero-sum game where the parent and the affiliate in some way share a given amount of power. Maybe some companies have found effective ways of handling the relationships that do not easily lend themselves to an interpretation on a one dimensional scale. We may recall the concepts of ethnocentric, polycentric and regiocentric companies introduced by Perlmutter (1965) or the open versus closed relationships by Brooke and Remmers (1978) as alternative concepts.'

This point is answered in Brooke (1984) pp. 297–8 on the grounds that there is not an either/or alternative. For purposes of investigation a one-dimensional concept can be assumed; only by doing so can a viable method of measurement be devised. At the same time the measurement is not just to be applied to head-office subsidiary relationships; governments as well as inter-subsidiary influences also have to be considered.

The nature of relevant evidence

A glance at the question of evidence brings back the question of perception. A question like: 'Is this company centralized?' will bring up a number of thoughts in a respondent's mind. Uppermost is likely to be delegation of responsibility to a division. Executives (as well as business journalists) refer to a company as 'decentralized' when this delegation has been carried out. They find it difficult to answer questions about how this affects foreign subsidiaries. Observation often suggests that a so-called decentralized company can appear very centralized to the foreign subsidiary.[11] The reverse is also found. To be convincing, studies of the subject require comparable evidence from subsidiaries as well as from head office.

Another issue under this heading is whether evidence can be legitimately assembled for a company as a whole: in other words, whether it is unrealistic to generalize across a range of functions or whether finance, marketing, production and personnel must not be examined separately. This issue is discussed in Brooke (1984, pp. 270–5) where the conclusion is drawn that companies are generally 'all of a piece'. In other words, one department may well delegate more than another; but, in comparing companies, the variations in delegation are similar (more or less constant) across the sample. A more substantial criticism of the search for a general index of centralization is that head office may have different relationships with different subsidiaries. Even here the evidence is ambiguous. In one research, for instance, an assertion that more 'mature' subsidiaries, and those in industrial countries, were granted greater autonomy was refuted after in-depth investigation.[12]

The method of measurement

Clearly the method favoured will depend on the answers given to the questions that have been outlined. One method is the use of the *normal line* concept.[13] In this case, a line is drawn from high centralization at one end to high decentralization at the other and questions asked at interviews to determine where a company stands at any given time. This method has the advantage that it is not static. It can be used to observe a process of change and, at the same time, a positioning can be made more precise as fresh evidence is collected. One disadvantage of this method has already been suggested: that it is one-dimensional and inadequately subtle to handle complex influences.

Another method asks questions about the degree of influence a subsidiary has on a given decision. The results are then coded from one (very little influence) to five (very high influence) and an average derived. An advantage is that a zero-sum is not presupposed. Thus both head office and a foreign subsidiary may claim a high influence on a given decision. The method uses perceptions and, like other methods, its validity is heavily dependent on the choice of questions. Some decisions, like a major new investment, are too important ever to be left to subsidiaries; others are too trivial for head office to intervene. Between these some will be more efficient discriminators than others.

The implications of conclusions derived from the studies of centralization

Company executives normally assume some relationship between centralization and performance. This is expressed in statements like: 'We have improved our return on investment since we decentralized.' Such statements are difficult to prove or disprove: they presuppose a complex chain of causation as well as a measurement of centralization. If, indeed, performance improves – or deteriorates – when a company delegates more to its foreign subsidiaries, the evidence proves elusive. Most researchers either accept simple measurements or find that the ambiguities of the evidence make a judgement impossible. Another issue is the relationship with culture. Otterbeck (1981) pp. 338–41 raises the question of the consequences of cultural differences. He shows how 'the pattern of HQ-subsidiary relations ... for every home country closely resembles that of the US'; but that departures from the pattern reflect local traditions.[14]

An important implication concerns relationships with the subsidiary's country and government. One writer argues that a main influence on centralization is the tension a subsidiary has to live with between the two environments – its country and its company. It has to operate and to compete in both.[15] Another argues that the controversies between companies and governments have had a paradoxical effect. A government demand is for greater autonomy for the local subsidiary, but a consequence of the controversy is tighter central control. Companies are frightened that local subsidiaries will exacerbate the problem. An example is the long-running Nestlé controversy (see also Chapter 3.1) in which some subsidiaries in developing countries engaged in marketing policies which brought the company into disrepute worldwide. As a result, the company adopted much stricter international rules.

A sub-heading, as it were, of company government relations is the Vredeling directive of the European Community, which is still under discussion. An enforced measure of decentralization gives trade unions the right to bypass local management and go to head office if they are denied information and consultation.[16]

Yet another issue has been called 'inverted centralization' (Brooke (1984) pp. 218, 220 and 293–4). This arises from the discovery that there are frequently pressures in subsidiaries towards *centralization* rather than always to the reverse, as is often assumed. One of those pressures derives from what may be called an alliance of expertise as opposed to that of nationality. This arises from the following situation. A company has been *conciously* decentralized which means that decisions are delegated as a matter of policy; to make this delegation a reality, all communication between the subsidiary and head office is channelled through the top management of the subsidiary. This arrangement proves unsatisfactory to some specialists in a subsidiary when it is found that their local head office does not contain relevant expertise. As a result they will make strong endeavors to bypass the system and communicate direct with their fellow experts. If they succeed, this can ultimately produce a relationship which is more centralized than corporate headquarters intended.

This brief review of the decision-making process demonstrates a complex relationship in which not all of the elements have yet been identified. Although an organization is made up of the two systems – a structure and a decision-making process – the relationship between the two is ambiguous. Any of the structural systems can accompany centralized or decentralized decision-making. There is a suspicion, to put it no higher, that the more elaborate matrix or project organizations are also more decentralized: they assume more sophisticated management. There is also some evidence that the product group worldwide (type C) structure is the most centralized. The greater international expertise positioned in the geographical organization leads to a greater confidence which often also produces more delegation. But these are only tentative hypotheses for which more evidence is required.

6.10.3   Multi-centre structures

After this book went to press, the author learnt of some research conducted in the University of Uppsala that is vital to the subject of this chapter. The concept of *second-degree internationalization* is outlined in two papers read at the 1990 Annual Meeting of the British Chapter of the Academy of International Business: 'Internationalization of the second-degree' by M. Forsgren, U. Holm and J. Johanson and 'The management of headquarter-subsidiary relationships in Swedish multinationals' by P.N. Ghauri.

'Second-degree' is a phrase that refers to a shift in power away from one centre (headquarters) to several centres, a situation in which certain subsidiaries acquire authority over decisions previously reserved for head office. The hierarchical view of international companies becomes irrelevant when this multi-centre structure means that powerful subsidiaries are determining corporate strategies. The author cautions that he has only found these structures in large companies with a very high proportion of their business outside the home country. They may not be of general application, although, in the terms of this chapter, they may turn out to be new forms of regional centres with much enhanced powers.

Notes

1. Much export literature stresses this point; see Chapter 6.2, especially the section on pre-export. For an article specifically on organization for export, see Cavusgil, T. (1984): 'Organizational characteristics associated with export activity', *Journal of Management Studies*, Vol. 2, No. 1 January, pp. 3–22.
2. The original statement of this approach was in Chandler (1962). See also Chandler (1977) pp. 1 and 455 in which he makes the intriguing statement that the 'visible hand of management replaced ... the invisible hand of market forces' in some companies in 1918. The former book (Chandler, 1962) became the basis of a series of studies at the Harvard Business School led by R. Vernon (see Vernon and Wells, 1976). The theory is explained in Stopford and Wells (1972) Chapters 1–6. Studies were extended to other countries; see, for instance, Channon (1973) and Delapierre and Michalet (1976) especially Chapters 1–3. See also Davis, S.M. (1988): 'Organization design', Chapter 13 in Walters and Murray.

3. For the theoretical grounds see Brooke (1984) pp. 39–40; for the empirical grounds see Bartlett, C.A. (1981): 'Multinational structural change: evolution versus reorganization', Chapter 6 in Otterbeck. See also Bartlett, C.A. (1983): 'MNCs get off the reorganization merry-go-round', *Harvard Business Review*, pp. 138–46. A discussion of the extent to which American models can, in any case, be applied to other countries is contained in Clark, P. and Tarn, J. (1986): 'Cultures and Corporations: the M-form in the USA and in Britain', paper read to the Academy of International Business. See also Kono, T. (1980): 'Comparative study of strategy, structure and long-range planning in Japan and US, *Management Japan*, Vol. 13, No. 1, Spring, pp. 20–34.

4. This was first stated in Brooke, M.Z. and Remmers, H.L. (1970): *The Strategy of Multinational Enterprise* (1st edn), Chapter 2. Longman. A second edition (1978) developed the theory, as did Brooke (1984). The author is still exploring its implications including the E-type organization, first mentioned in the 1984 book.

5. See Cyert and March (1963), Chapters 1–6.

6. See, for example Pitts, R.A. and Daniels, J.D. (1984): 'Aftermath of the matrix mania', *Columbia Journal of World Business*, Summer, pp. 48–54.

   For other discussions of matrix organizations see Kagono, T. (1981): 'Structural design of headquarters-division relationships and economic performance: an analysis of Japanese firms' and Prahalad, C.K. and Doz, Y.L. (1981): 'Strategic control – the dilemma in headquarters-subsidiary relationship', Chapters 7 and 8 in Otterbeck. A different view to that expressed in the text is to be found in Otterbeck (1981) p. 142 where a caution is placed beside 'formal matrices' although the alternative is not clearly stated. We are told that: 'Most managers find it frustrating and confusing to have two bosses.' Maybe!

7. For an exhaustive study, see: Van den Bulcke, D. and Van Paakterbeke, M.-A. (1984): *European Headquarters of American Multinational Companies in Belgium and Brussels*. Institut Catholique des Hantes Etudes Commerciales. See also Daniels, J.D. (1985): 'Approaches to European Regional Management by large US multinational firms', paper read to the Academy of International Business Annual Conference.

8. See Brooke and Remmers (1978), pp. 39–48.

9. See, for example, Robinson (1984), pp. 299–300.

10. Some of the background is traced out in Brooke (1984), Chapter 9, especially pp. 155–9; Chapter 17 discusses studies of multinational companies. One article that appears to assume the locus of a decision-making view without acknowledging the existence of any other is Gates, S.R. and Egelhoff, E.G. (1986): 'Centralization in headquarters-subsidiary relationships', *Journal of International Business Studies*, Summer, pp. 71–92. This article does, however, track back to a sociological context. It also lists a number of contingent variables, a subject not considered in the text here. The variables used in the article include: size of foreign operation, size of company, foreign product diversity, product modification differences, extent of outside ownership in subsidiaries, extent of foreign acquisitions, industry sector, nationality, age and others.

11. See Brooke and Remmers (1978), pp. 29 and 68.

12. See Dorrell, M.G.: *The Communication of Control in a Multinational Company*. Unpublished Ph.D. thesis, University of Manchester Institute of Science and Technology.

13. The normal line concept is explained in Brooke (1984), pp. 180–2. For an example of the measurement by influence, see Otterbeck (1981), Chapter 3. See also de Bodinat, H. (1975): 'Influence in the multinational corporation: the case of manufacturing', Harvard Business School research paper, July.
14. Another writing on this subject is Jaeger, A.M. (1986): 'Organization development and national culture: Where's the fit?', *Academy of Management Review* Vol. 11, No. 1, January pp. 178–90.
15. See Grunberg, L. (1981): *Failed Multinational Ventures.* Lexington. The issue of company government relations is discussed in Brooke (1984), Chapter 13.
16. See Van den Bulcke, D. (1983): 'Autonomy of decision-making by subsidiaries of multinational enterprises and the proposed Vredeling Directive of the EC-Commission', *Proceedings* of the 9th Annual Conference, European International Business Association, December, Vol II, pp. 173–208.

References

The articles in this list are additional to those listed in the notes; the books are cross-referenced in the notes.

Bartlett, C.A and Ghoshal, S. (1986): 'Tap your Subsidiaries for Global Reach', *Harvard Business Review*, November–December.

Bartlett, C.A. and Ghoshal, S. (1987): 'Managing across borders: new organizational responses', *Sloan Management Review*, Vol. 29, No.1, Fall, pp. 43–53.

Brooke, M.Z. (1984): *Centralization and Autonomy: A Study in Organization Behaviour.* Holt, Rinehart & Winston.

Brooke, M.Z., and Remmers, H.L. (1978): *The Strategy of Multinational Enterprise* (2nd edn). Pitman.

Chandler, A.D. (1962): *Strategy and Structure.* MIT Press.

Chandler, A.D. (1977): *The Visible Hand: The Managerial Revolution in American Business.* Harvard.

Channon, D.F. (1973): *The Strategy and Structure of British Enterprise.* London: Macmillan.

Cyert, R.M. and March, J.G. (1963): *A Behavioural Theory of the Firm.* Prentice-Hall.

Davis, S.M. (1979): *Managing and Organizing Multinational Corporations.* Pergamon Press.

Davis, S.M. and Lawrence, P.R. (1977): *Matrix.* Addison-Wesley.

Delapierre, M. and Michalet, C.-A. (1976): *Les Implantations Entrangères en France: Stratégies et structures.* Callman-Levy.

Doz, Y. and Prahalad, C.K. (1981): 'Headquarter's influence and strategic control in MNCs', *Sloan Management Review*, Fall, pp. 15–29.

Dymsza, W.A. 1972: *Multinational Business Strategy.* McGraw-Hill.

Garnier, G. (1982): 'Context and decision-making autonomy in the foreign affiliates of US Multinational Corporations', *Academy of Management Journal*, No. 25, pp. 893–908.

Garnier, G. (1978): 'Who makes the decisions? The relationships between US Multinational Corporations and their Mexican Affiliates', *Mex-AM Review*, (Review of the US Chamber of Commerce in Mexico), January, pp. 4–11.

Garnier, G. (1978): 'Jusqu' ou va l'autonomie de décision des filiales? Le cas des filiales françaises d'entreprises multinationales americaines', *Revue Francaise de Gestion*, No. 14, January–February, pp. 42–52. Paris. Reprinted in: *Gestion – Revue Internationale de Gestion*. Vol. 3, No. 3. September 1978, pp. 57–66.

Garnier, G. (1978): 'Autonomie decisionnelle des filiales françaises d'enterprises americaines multinationales', *Etudes Internationales*, Vol. 9, No. 2, June, pp. 214–35.

Garnier, G. (1979): 'Autonomy in the Mexican Affiliates for US Multinational Corporations', *Columbia Journal World Business*, Vol. 9, No. 1, Spring, pp. 78–90.

Garnier, G. (1981): 'Context and Decision-making Autonomy in the Foreign Affiliates of US Multinational Corporations', *Academy of Management Journal*, Vol. 25, No. 4, December, pp. 893–908.

Garnier, G. (1981): 'The Anatomy of Autonomy'. Paper presented at the October 1981 meeting of the Academy of International Business, Montreal.

Garnier, G. (1983): 'Autonomy in the Affiliates of Multinational Corporations: a Comparison of Affiliates Located in Mexico and in the United States'. Paper presented at the April International Meeting of the Academy of International Business, Mexico.

Garnier, G. (1984): 'The Autonomy of Foreign Subsidiaries: Environmental and National Influences', *Journal of General Management*, Vol. 10, No. 1, Fall.

Ghoshal, S. (1987): 'Global Strategy: An Organizing Framework', *Strategic Management Journal*, September–October.

Ghoshal, S. and Bartlett, C.A. (1987): 'Organizing for Innovations: Case of the Multinational Corporation', INSEAD Working Paper No. 87/04, February.

Ghoshal, S. and Kim, S.K. (1986): 'Building Effective Intelligence Systems for Competitive Advantage', *Sloan Management Review*, Fall.

Ghoshal, S. and Nohria, N. (1986): 'Multinational Corporations as Differentiated Networks', Working Paper No. 1789–86, Sloan School of Management, MIT.

Otterbeck, L.-G. (ed.) (1981): *The Management of Headquarters-Subsidiary Relationships in Multinational Corporations*. Gower.

Robinson, R.D. (1984): *Internationalization of Business*. Dryden Press.

Robock, S.H. and Simmonds, K. (1983): *International Business and Multinational Enterprise* (3rd edn), Chapter 16.

Sasaki, N. (1981): *Management and Industrial Structure in Japan*. Pergamon.

Starkey, K. and McKinlay, A. (1989): *Organizational Innovation*. Gower.

Stopford, J.M. and Wells, L.T. (1972): *Managing the Multinational Enterprise: Organization of the Firm and Ownership of the Subsidiaries*. Basic Books and Longman.

Vernon, R. and Wells, L.T. (1976): *Manager in the International Economy* (3rd edn). Prentice-Hall.

Tsurumi, Y. (1984): *Multinational Management*. Ballinger.

Walters, I. and Murray, T. (1988): *Handbook of International Management*. Wiley.

6.11

International Human Resource Management

Ensuring an effective utilization of human resources should be a primary objective of any organization. When business crosses national boundaries, the most effective deployment of labour is even more critical. As Duerr (1968) recognized:

virtually any type of international problem, in the final analysis, is either created by people or must be solved by people. Hence, having the right people in the right place at the right time emerges as the key to a company's international growth.

While few would disagree with such a view, its implementation is a complex and difficult task. This is because labour is unlike other factors of production. Labour displays extreme heterogeneity: no two people are exactly the same. Furthermore, the efficiency of labour varies significantly, both between individuals and for an individual over time. Perhaps the crucial characteristic distinguishing labour from other factors is that its effectiveness is not independent of the way in which it is managed. The likely attitudes, cooperativeness, motivation and performance of labour are all, in part at least, a function of the management process. For these reasons international human resource management raises a variety of interesting issues. The purpose of this chapter is to review the principal issues that have been identified and the available evidence pertaining to them.

The chapter is divided into six major sections. Section 6.11.1 examines the impact of internationalization on the human resources function. This is followed by a review of international management of managerial (Section 6.11.2) and non-managerial (Section 6.11.3) employees. Section 6.11.4 identifies a number of emerging issues in international human resources management. Concluding comments are contained in Section 6.11.5.

6.11.1　Internationalization and human resource management

The internationalization of business affects the human resource management function in a number of ways (Enderwick (1985):

1) The management task is complicated by involvement in a more diverse environment which requires awareness of, and sensitivity towards, differences in language, culture, politics and the legal system (Desatnick and Bennett (1977)). These differences affect the acceptability, effectiveness and management of human resources practices.

2) Internationalization creates issues that do not arise in the national context. The international company has to develop policies with regard to nationality composition, international compensation, the selection and management of expatriates and even transnational collective bargaining.

3) Personnel practices are invariably subject to the influence of source-nation values and procedures. Despite the best efforts to respect local values and customs, management in overseas subsidiaries is inevitably influenced by tradition and experiences generated elsewhere in the corporate network. Thus, United States executives often find it hard to accept that the considerable discretionary power they exercise in the United States may be severely curtailed in other nations.

4) The multinational structure of an international company may influence the human resource management process. Where centralization of authority is high, local managers may be ineffectual in a collective bargaining role. From the perspective of employee representatives, this may be interpreted as a deliberate attempt to frustrate the bargaining process. Similarly, multinational operations create the opportunity for cross-national comparisons of performance and the development and possible introduction of best practices.

5) Foreignness may lead to problems in the area of risk and information interpretation in the human relations area. This is because labour market imperfections are likely to be significant as a result of both the locational specificity of labour and the importance of non-economic considerations in the successful management of labour. This hypothesis suggests that labour issues will be a major cause of problems for international companies, particularly the least experienced investors (Newbould, Buckley and Thurwell (1978)); that labour will be one of the most decentralized functional areas (Bomes and Peterson (1977), Hedlund (1981)) and that there is a high probability of the labour function being headed by a local national (Negandhi (1983)).

6) These problems are compounded by the comparative infancy of the area of international human resource management and the paucity of case-study and other experience (Ondrack (1985)). This makes it difficult to draw firm conclusions regarding the likely effectiveness or otherwise of particular practices.

6.11.2 International management of managerial staff

Executive nationality policies

The question of staff deployment within multinational enterprises has attracted considerable research interest. The early work drawing upon the development stages approach of Perlmutter (1969) identified four principal options with respect to executive nationality policies.

The first, an ethnocentric (Heenan and Perlmutter (1979)) or colonialist (Heller (1980)) approach, is characterized by all key staff positions being filled by parent country nationals. This strategy, which is associated with companies in the early stages of internationalization (Franko (1973)), may be adopted because previous experience is deemed to be the primary consideration in executive selection or simply that suitable host country nationals are not available. While facilitating communication flows with corporate headquarters, this option can disadvantage host-country nationals who may become dissatisfied when denied managerial experience. Similarly, a company may find itself in conflict with a host government which places a high value on the localizaion of management. There may also be a cost if expatriates, unfamiliar with the local business environment, fail to perform as well as host-country management could.

The second option, a polycentric (or bilateral) strategy matches local staff to their country's subsidiaries and source-nation personnel to corporate headquarters. Such a policy reduces the need for, and the cost of, an extensive expatriate programme and may be favourably interpreted by a host government. The multinational enterprise is also maximizing the benefits of local knowledge and ensuring a greater degree of continuity to subsidiary management. The major drawbacks, however, are the difficulties of bridging the divide between headquarters and subsidiary staff and the constraint on executive mobility and development. Neither parent nor host-nation staff have the opportunity to gain experience outside their own country. This is unacceptable today for any successful multinational enterprise.

International team building is more likely under the last two options. One is a geocentric (or internationalist) strategy where the most suitable people are deployed to tasks irrespective of nationality. Such a strategy can help create truly international executive teams able to identify with the global corporate well-being. The second, a regionalized variation of internationalism, may be used when regional or area expertise is important. These latter two strategies are associated with the mature multinational capable of assuming a global perspective (Franko (1973)).

This conception of executive nationality policies implies that the human-resources function is closely integrated with overall corporate strategy (Ondrack

(1985)). Unfortunately, the human-resources function appears to be the least-developed within the corporate-planning system of most firms (Lorange and Murphy (1983), Jain and Murray (1984), Rowland and Summers (1981)). At best it is probably only possible to relate principal motives for executive transfer to strategy type (Edstrom and Galbraith (1977)). Thus, within ethnocentric firms, personnel transfers occur primarily for staffing reasons. At the other extreme, regiocentric and geocentric multinational enterprises transfer executives for both management and organization-development reasons (Onto (1987)).

The current international business environment is increasing the incentive for personnel transfers for reasons of organizational development. With the growth of international mergers, joint ventures and alliances there is considerable value in having multinational teams able to operate across a range of cultures. Such teams and their individual members need to acquire skills in negotiation, management and interpretation in a variety of situations (Adler and Ghadar) 1989), Evans, Laurent and Doz (1989)). Progressive multinational enterprises are investing heavily in the development of such teams. More than 80 per cent of Xerox's top 300 managers have had international assignments. A company like IBM which operates in 132 countries has something like 3,500 assignees over-seas at any one time. All IBM managers, regardless of location, receive annual training on the internationlization of IBM's business and the problems of multinational management (Callahan (1989)).

Research has also revealed that there is considerable variation between firms with regard to executive nationality policies. Variation is apparent with regard to size (ILO (1981), multinational maturity (Dowling and Welch (1988)) and nationality (Negandhi (1980), Tung (1982)). Ethnocentric policies appear more likely within small, immature MNEs and, at least in the 1970s, Japanese. While there is definitely a trend towards the increased globalization of executive teams, further research in at least three areas would be worthwhile.

The first is on the likely response of host-country organizations to executive nationality policies. Most host-country officials appear to prefer a considerable localization of senior management (Howard (1971), Zeira and Harari (1979)). Furthermore, the degree of independence expatriates enjoy in decision making appears to be an important factor in their local acceptance. One comparative study found that while United States multinational enterprises had achieved a greater degree of localization of management in developing countries than their European or Japanese competitors, remaining expatriates suffered a lower level of acceptance. Scepticism about the extent to which localization was accompanied by a real devolution of authority served to discredit the perceived authority of US nationals in the country (Negandhi (1980)). Secondly, most of the literature focuses on the problems of overseas assignments of parent-country nationals. Very little work has been done on the selection of third-country nationals. Where individuals are selected for their ability and not nationality such issues deserve more detailed consideration (Ondrack (1985)). Thirdly, more research is needed on the relationship between executive nationality and control policies. It is not clear if an expatriate management team can substitute for a tightly controlled and centralized operating structure or if the two are likely to coincide (Hulbert and Brandt (1980)).

Expatriate selection and failure

The growing importance of international experience means that considerable attention should be paid to expatriate selection and ways of minimizing the problem of executive failure. A number of studies have addressed the question of expatriate selection and the development of reliable selection techniques and training programmes. There is some evidence to suggest that expatriate selection focuses on strong technical skills, a proven track record and the candidate's period of incumbency (Harvey (1985), Tung (1981)). Indeed, a valid criticism of expatriate selection is that it tends to equate domestic success with likely overseas success. For this reason emphasis is placed on easily measurable factors like technical skills and the individual's track record. This myopic approach to selection is perhaps explained by the inadequate level of understanding about the relevant variables of expatriate acculturation (Mendenhall and Oddou (1985)). Because of this lack of understanding, firms are likely to use inappropriate selection and training methods. Research suggests that expatriate acculturation is a multi-dimensional and not a one-dimensional process. Hence, reliance on a single factor such as technical competence is not conducive to success.

Selection processes have had a number of unfortunate effects. First, women are markedly under-represented among expatriates (Adler (1984a), (1984b), Izraeli, Banai and Zeira (1980), Thal and Cateora (1979)). When women are selected for overseas assignments they are more likely to be employees of the largest multinational enterprises and especially those in service industries like banking, publishing and retailing (Adler (1984b)). Secondly, relatively few firms extend the selection process to include the spouse and family (Dowling and Welch (1988), Harvey (1983), (1985), Ondrack (1985), Tung (1984)) despite the fact that they bear a considerable part of the costs of reassignment (Harvey (1985)) and are a major reason for premature returns (Tung (1984)). Thirdly, selection tests focus to a disproportionate extent on technical skills and insufficient attention is given to relational skills (Tung (1981)) which appear to be an important determinant of successful overseas adjustment (Holmes and Piker (1980)).

Inappropriate selection is a major cause of expatriate failure which can be defined as the premature return of an expatriate manager. The direct and indirect costs of such errors can be considerable. Direct costs include training, salary, travel and relocation expenses. Many companies work on a crude ratio of such costs amounting to around three times normal domestic salary. Indirect costs, which are much more difficult to quantify, manifest themselves as possible loss of market share, difficulties in relationships with host-government officials and susceptibility to pressures to replace expatriates with host-country nationals. The magnitude of such costs is likely to be positively related to the level of the position under consideration.

Empirical studies over a considerable period suggest that expatriate failure is a significant and persistent problem with rates ranging between 25 and 40 per cent in the developed countries and as high as 70 per cent in the case of developing countries (Desatrick and Bennett (1978), Holmes and Piker (1980), Mendenhall and Oddou (1985)). These figures suggest that the costs of expatriate failure may be considerable.

Given the magnitude of these costs it is not surprising that considerable research effort has addressed the reasons for expatriate failure. Three main sets of reasons have been identified. The first is poor selection (Harvey (1985)). The significance of this factor is highlighted by Tung's (1982) finding that within United States multinational enterprises adjustment problems of the manager or his family were the most important reasons for failure. Second, inadequate preparation is correlated with a higher failure rate (Armitage and Sagripanti (1984), Bendall and Gibson (1984), Tung (1981), (1982), (1984)). Under-investment in pre-departure training occurs perhaps because the assignment is seen as temporary (Tung (1981)), a feeling, real or otherwise, that preparatory training is largely ineffective (Baker and Ivancevich (1971), Brislin (1979), Schnapper (1973), Zeira (1975)) or because of insufficient time between selection and departure to ensure adequate training. The third major set of reasons for expatriate failure are the stresses associated with expatriation. These include concern over the adequacy of the compensation package, the danger that an overseas assignment will disrupt a logical career path and anxiety created by inadequate notice of posting (Harvey (1985)).

Suggestions for reducing expatriate failure include improved selection procedures, particularly screening for adaptability and potential for acculturation (Harvey (1985), Hays (1971)) although this is by no means straightforward (Mendenhall and Oddou (1985)), improvements in training programmes (Harvey (1983)) and stress reduction by, for example, the appointment of a 'contact person' in the home country as is done by Exxon. More detailed research is also required on the way in which differences in nationality (Merwe and Merwe (1980)), (Ondrack (1985)) or job type (Tung (1982)) affect these procedures.

A number of the concerns contributing to expatriate failure have been affected by the growing regularization of overseas experience as a means of building multinational teams. Assignments can be more carefully planned and integrated within a clear career programme. This in turn helps overcome the related problem of repatriation (Clague and Krupp (1978), Harvey (1982), Howard (1980), Kendall (1981)).

International compensation

The assignment of expatriate managers involves multinational enterprises in the complex area of international compensation. The complexity results in part from the diverse objectives an effective international compensation policy has to achieve. These include the attraction and retention of staff qualified to undertake overseas assignments, the establishment of sufficient staff mobility between affiliates and between headquarters and affiliates, the need for reasonable equity between the compensation of expatriates, host-country nationals and third-country nationals and the provision of adequate compensation in the light of local conditions and competitor levels.

The compensation package for an expatriate comprises several related elements. The first is a base salary. To this may be added an expatriate premium designed to increase the attractiveness of an overseas posting (or to compensate for its disadvantages). Thirdly, a cost-of-living allowance may be offered to take account of higher housing, education or tax rates. Finally, additional fringe benefits (return visits, part-salary payments in a third currency) may also be added.

There are considerable difficulties in calculating the elements of the compensation package. While there are readily available publications showing cost of living comparisons (the United States Department of State Allowances staff publish quarterly figures, for example) and international trends in executive salaries (such as TPF and C consultants, London) account must also be taken of national variations in the compensation package. Taxation and currency-rate fluctuations affect the real value of overseas income levels. In recent years there has been a widespread downward trend in maximum marginal tax rates but they still display considerable variation, ranging, for example, from 72 per cent in The Netherlands to 11.5 per cent in Switzerland. In high-tax areas like Holland and Belgium, companies may offer non-cash items like a car, chauffeur or grocery provision. Japanese companies typically provide a very high level of benefits to employees, including mortgage assistance, expense accounts and club memberships. The considerable salary differences which exist mean that it may be difficult to achieve reasonable equity between expatriate and local salaries. For example, United States executive salaries tend, on average, to be more than three times the levels paid in countries like Mexico or Korea.

Some research has addressed the management of the international compensation function. This suggests that compensation policies and procedures are generally centralized and have remained largely impervious to changes in the external environment (Toyne and Kuhne (1983)).

6.11.3   International management of non-managerial staff

The impact of international human-resource management on non-managerial staff has attracted by far the most research interest (Enderwick (1985)). In part this is the result of the view of organized labour that the human-relations policies of multinational enterprises are a source of friction in labour-management accord. A major concern has been the transplantation overseas of source-nation values and practices in what some see as totally inappropriate circumstances (Enderwick (1989)). The distinctiveness of multinational enterprise human-resources practices is apparent in a number of areas.

Union organization

While the overt anti-union stance of a small group of large United States multinational enterprises has attracted most attention, evidence from a number of studies suggests that foreign-owned firms are more likely to operate an anti-union policy (Greer and Shearer (1981), Hamill (1983), Stopford (1979)). More recently, a trend towards union rationalization (recognition of a single union) has emerged in countries like the United Kingdom. This practice, which is particularly associated with Japanese multinational enterprises (Dunning (1986), Oliver and Wilkinson (1988)) has begun to affect the bargaining position of indigenous companies setting up greenfield ventures (Bassett (1986).) However, when recognition is achieved, union security (as measured by union-density rates) appears to be similar within national and multinational firms (Buckley and Enderwick (1984)).

Bargaining practices

In general, the evidence supports the view that multinational enterprise subsidiaries adopt bargaining arrangements which are compatible with local conditions, through extensive decentralization of responsibility for collective bargaining International Labour Office (1976b)). However, there is some evidence that foreign-owned firms have accelerated the trend towards plant-and company-level bargaining and away from industry-wide arrangements. This preference for unilateral bargaining is reinforced by a higher probability of multinational enterprises' non-membership of employers' associations (Buckley and Enderwick (1984), Hamill (1983)).

Labour relations practices

A recurring concern of labour unions has been the opportunities a multinational structure provides for the centralization of key decision-making processes. Centralization, which is widely held by union officials to have occurred (Blake

(1972)), may lengthen and obfuscate bargaining processes. Empirical evidence reveals that while labour relations is the most decentralized functional area within multinational enterprises (Bomes and Peterson (1977), Hedlund (1981)) the degree of centralization is generally higher within multinational enterprises than multi-plant uninational enterprises (Buckley and Enderwick (1984), Greer and Shearer (1981)) although the position is influenced by nationality (Hershfield (1975)), the issue under consideration (Peccei and Warner (1981)), subsidiary performance (Aslegg (1971), Welge (1981)), and the degree of intra-firm trade (Hamill (1983), Hedlund (1981)).

The information-disclosure practices of multinational enterprises are a further source of concern to labour (Latta and Bellace (1983)). This concern has focused on the level at which information is compiled, the usefulness of the type of information disclosed, the timing of disclosure and the reliability of the information provided (Enderwick (1985)). While information-disclosure provisions have been incorporated into the major codes of conduct (Robinson (1983)) more comprehensive provisions (the 'Vredling Directive') are being considered within the European Community (Blanpain (1983)).

A continuing area of controversy has been the introduction of novel labour-relations practices. While this is not a new phenomenon, United States multinational enterprises pioneered plant- and company-level bargaining and productivity-bargaining practices in the 1960s (McKersie and Hunter (1972)), recent years have seen an acceleration in the range and scope of such innovations (Enderwick (1989)). The focus of innovative practices in the 1980s has switched to Japanese firms and in particular their pursuit of increased flexibility (Rico (1987)). The interest indigenous companies have shown in these practices suggests that their diffusion will be significant.

The bargaining power of multinational enterprises

The international human resources policies pursued by Multinational Enterprises have led to allegations that these companies enjoy an overwhelming bargaining advantage over labour. The sources of this advantage include the Multinational Enterprises' considerable resources, their ability to source globally and switch production locations in the face of rising labour costs or fractious labour relations, their centralization of decision-making authority and their extensive negotiation skills and experience (Kennedy (1980)).

A number of these allegations have been subject to systematic investigation. On balance, the evidence is not consistent with the idea of an overwhelming bargaining advantage on the part of Multinational Enterprises. The trend towards union rationalization, rather than overt opposition, is not indicative of an overwhelming bargaining advantage. Rather, it is consistent with a view that there are both benefits (reduced labour turnover, increased information exchange) and costs (inter-union disputes) with union recognition. Single union agreements represent an attempt to obtain the benefits without the associated costs.

Studies of industrial conflict within multinational enterprise affiliates provide little support for the view that multinational enterprises enjoy an overwhelming bargaining advantage over labour. If such an advantage existed, one would not expect to see an above-average incidence of disputes within foreign-owned firms (Enderwick and Buckley (1982), Kelly and Brannick (1988), Millward (1979), higher than average pay levels offered by such firms (Buckley and Enderwick (1983), International Labour Office (1976a)) or their very considerable investments in procedures for containing and resolving bargaining disagreements (Buckley and Enderwick (1984)). Further work is required to assess more fully the basis of these concerns.

Regulation of international human resources management

Political initiatives to regulate international human-resources policies are the major constraint on international management. While a variety of responses to the power of multinational enterprises have been suggested or implemented (Enderwick (1985), Chapter 6) the most significant regulations are those provided in the codes of conduct of the International Labour Office, the Organisation for Economic Cooperation and Development and the European Community. For labour, the attainment of transnational collective bargaining is probably the preferred long-term solution. However, the considerable impediments to such a development (Enderwick (1984), (1987)) mean that actual cases are extremely rare (Miscimara (1981)), (Northrup, Rowan and Laffer (1977)) and most labour effort concentrates on the necessary prerequisite stages of information collection and identification of areas of mutual concern.

6.11.4 Emerging issues in international human resource management

Recent years have seen the emergence of a number of new issues in the international labour-management function. The most important have been the growth of multinational enterprises in non-manufacturing, particularly the service industries, concern over employee safety and social responsibility and racism at the workplace.

Multinational enterprise employment in the service sector

A number of service industries are rapidly internationalizing and employment is becoming increasingly concentrated within a small group of very large service multinational enterprises (Enderwick (1989b)). Traditionally, many service industries have been characterized by a high proportion of female employment, low levels of unionization and poor wages and working conditions. Recent studies suggest that the penetration of multinational enterprises into industries like cleaning and fast food has done little to alter such conditions (Lamb and Percy (1987), Landor (1986)).

Employee safety and social responsibility

Since the Bhopal tragedy which killed more than 3000 people and injured some 200,000 there has been growing concern about the health and safety provisions of multinational enterprises and their assumption of social responsibility, particularly in the developing countries.

A recent International Labour Office study found that most multinational enterprises' managers felt that health and safety agreements were entirely a management responsibility and should not form part of the collective bargaining process (International Labour Office (1984)). This suggests the possibility of variation between enterprises and establishments in such provisions. Although the report indicated the above average performance of multinational enterprises in the area of health and safety, their over-representation in possibly hazardous industries like chemicals means that the potential costs of inadequate provisions and controls are enormous and may necessitate more stringent regulation.

Racism at the workplace

In the same way that policy concern over health and safety issues is increasing, the growth of anti-discrimination legislation is highlighting the position of large-scale employers like multinational enterprises. In Britain an investigation of the Canadian multinational Massey-Ferguson found that in a city where about 10 per cent of the population are black the firm's workforce percentage was only 0.15. Through a policy of above-average wage levels, vacancies were readily filled through the network of existing employees, perpetuating the imbalance.

There is growing concern over the practices of Japanese multinational enterprises. In the United States a number of leading Japanese multinational enterprises, including Hitachi and Honda, have faced court action over practices which discriminate against women and minority groups. A recently published study of Japanese automobile plants in the United States, while not alleging overt discrimination, does suggest considerable inequality in employment composition and the possibility that avoidance of areas with a significant black population is one factor in the site-location decision (Cole and Deskins (1988)). While multinational enterprises may be no worse than many indigenous employers in such matters, their size and high profile means they need to be particularly careful in the monitoring of racial composition and in the consideration of potentially discriminatory practices.

6.11.5 Conclusion

Our discussion of international human-resources management suggests a number of conclusions:

1) There is clearly a need for more research in a number of areas. In particular, work oriented towards improving procedures for expatriate selection and training and the management of the international compensation function is required (Earley 1987), Onto (1987)).

2) There is a growing need for the integration of the human-resources function within the strategic planning process. The need for such integration is becoming increasingly important with the development of new international operating forms (such as strategic alliances and joint-ventures) and changing motives for overseas assignments (such as multinational team building). Furthermore, as recent cases have demonstrated, the distinction between the human-resources and crisis-management functions is often a very narrow one (McElrath (1988)).

3) Further research on integrating the human-resources function with theoretical conceptualizations of international management would be valuable. In particular, the role that human capital plays in technology transfer and the successful development of competitive advantage through efficient management of hierarchies is under-researched (Buckley and Enderwick (1989), Doz and Prahalad (1981), Picard (1980)). The importance of this type of consideration is likely to increase with the growth of non-equity forms of overseas market servicing.

4) Further work on the contribution of women managers within international operations is important. Again, the trend towards increased competition and novel operating forms may create conditions favourable to the employment of more women in international positions (Adler (1987), Jelinek and Adler (1988)).

In highlighting these areas we may draw some satisfaction from the results of a recent survey of international companies which confirms that these types of issue are currently faced by international human-resource practitioners (Dowling (1989)).

It is difficult to disagree with Duerr's comments at the beginning of this chapter. Successful corporations are distinguished by the effectiveness of their employees. For an international corporation, the management of an international workforce is likely to be a critical determinant of success.

References

Adler, N.J. (1984a): 'Expecting International Success: Female Managers Overseas', *Columbia Journal of World Business*, Vol. 19, No. 3, pp. 79–85.

Adler, N.J. (1984b): 'Women in International Management: Where Are They?', *California Management Review*, Vol. 26, No. 4, pp. 78–89.

Adler, N.J. (1987): 'Women as Androgynous Managers: A Conceptualization of the Potential for American Women in International Management', *International Journal of Intercultural Relations*, pp. 407–36.

Adler, N.J. and Ghadar, F. (1989): Globalization and Human Resource Management' in Rugman, A.M. (ed.): *Research in Global Strategic Management: A Canadian Perspective*. JAI Press.

Armitage, K. and Sagripanti, S. (1984): *The Role of the Expatriate in the MNC: A Study of Four MNCs*. Unpublished research paper, David Syme Business School, Melbourne, Australia.

Aslegg, R.G. (1971): *Control Relationships Between American Corporations and their European Subsidiaries*, AMA Research Study 107: American Management Association.

Baker, J.C. and Ivancevich, J.M. (1971): 'The Assignment of American Executives Abroad: Systematic, Haphazard or Chaotic', *California Management Review*, Vol. 13, No. 3, pp. 39–44.

Bassett, P. (1986): *Strike Free: New Industrial Relations in Britain*. Macmillan.

Bendall, R. and Gibson, S. (1984): *Expatriate Personnel Practices in Four Australian MNCs*. Unpublished research paper, David Syme Business School, Melbourne, Australia.

Blake, D.H. (1972): 'Corporate Structure and International Unionism', *Columbia Journal of World Business*, Vol. 7, pp. 19–26.

Blanpain, R. (1983): *The OECD Guidelines for Multinational Enterprises and Labour Relations 1979–1982: Experience and Mid-Term Report*. Kluwer.

Bomes, G.B.J. and Peterson, R.B. (1977): 'Multinational Corporations and Industrial Relations: the Case of West Germany and The Netherlands', *British Journal of Industrial Relations*, Vol. 15, pp. 45–62.

Brislin, R.W. (1979): 'Orientation Programs for Cross-Cultural Preparation', in Marsella, A.J., Tharp, G. and Ciborowski, T.J. (eds): *Perspectives on Cross-Cultural Psychology*. Academic Press.

Buckley, P.J. and Enderwick, P. (1983): 'Comparative Pay Levels in Domestically-Owned and Foreign-Owned Plants in UK: Manufacturing-Evidence from the 1980 Workplace. Industrial Relations Survey', *British Journal of Industrial Relations*, Vol. 21, pp. 395–400.

Buckley, P.J. and Enderwick, P. (1984): *The Industrial Relations Practices for Foreign-Owned Firms in Britain*. Macmillan.

Buckley, P.J. and Enderwick, P. (1989): 'Manpower Management in the Domestic International Construction Industry', in Hillebrandt, P.M. and Cannon, J. (eds): *The Management of Construction Firms*. Macmillan.

Callahan, M.R. (1989): 'Preparing the New Global Manager', *Training and Development Journal*, Vol. 43, No. 3, pp. 29–32.

Clague, L. and Krupp, N.B. (1978): 'International Personnel: the Repatriation Problem', *The Personnel Administrator*, April, pp. 29–33.

Cole, R.E. and Deskins, D.R. (1988): 'Racial Factors in Site Location and Employment Patterns of Japanese Auto Firms in America', *California Management Review*, Vol. 31, No. 1, pp. 9–22.

Desatrick, R.L. and Bennett, M.L. (1978): *Human Resource Management in the Multinational Company*. Gower Press.

Dowling, P.J. (1989): 'Hot Issues Overseas', *Personnel Administrator*, January, pp. 66–72.

Dowling, P.J. and Welch, D.E. (1988): 'International Human Resource Management: An Australian Perspective', *Asia Pacific Journal of Management*, Vol. 6, No. 1, pp. 39–65.

Doz, Y. and Prahalad, C.K. (1981): 'An Approach to Strategic Control in MNCs', *Sloan Management Review*, Vol. 22, No. 4, pp. 5–13.

Duerr, M.G. (1968): International Business Management: Its Four Tasks', *Conference Board Record*, October, p. 43.

Dunning, J.H. (1986): *Japanese Participation in British Industry*. Croom Helm.

Earley, P.C. (1987): 'Intercultural Training for Managers: A Comparison of Documentary and Interpersonal Methods', *Academy of Management Journal*, Vol. 30, No. 4, pp. 685–98.

Edstrom, A. and Galbraith, J. (1977): 'Alternative Policies for International Transfers of Managers', *Management International Review*, Vol. 17, No. 2, pp. 11–22.

Enderwick, P. (1984): 'The Labour Utilization Practices of Multinationals and Obstacles to Multinational Collective Bargaining', *The Journal of Industrial Relations*, Vol. 24, pp. 345–64.

Enderwick, P. (1985): *Multinational Business and Labour*. Croom Helm.

Enderwick, P. (1987): 'Trends in the Internationalization of Production and the Trade Union Response' in Spyropoulos, G. (ed.): *Trade Unions Today and Tomorrow*, Vol. I, *Trade Unions in a Changing Europe*, PIE.

Enderwick, P. (1989a): 'Multinationals and Labour: A Review of Contemporary Issues and Concerns', *New Zealand Journal of Industrial Relations*, Vol. 14, No. 2, pp. 119–32.

Enderwick, P. (1989b): *Multinational Service Firms*. Routledge.

Enderwick, P. and Buckley, P.J. (1982): 'Strike Activity and Foreign Ownership: an Analysis of British Manufacturing 1971–1973', *British Journal of Industrial Relations*, Vol. 20, pp. 308–21.

Evans, P., Laurent, A. and Doz, Y. (1989): *Human Resource Management in International Firms: Change, Globalization and Innovation*. London: Macmillan.

Franko, L. (1973): 'Who Manages Multinational Enterprise?', *Columbia Journal of World Business*, Vol. 8, No. 2, pp. 30–42.

Greer, C.R. and Shearer, J.C. (1981): 'Do Foreign-Owned Firms Practise Unconventional Labor Relations?', *Monthly Labor Review*, 104, pp. 44–8.

Hamill, J. (1983): 'The Labour Relations Practices of Foreign-Owned and Indigenous Firms', *Employee Relations*, Vol. 5, pp. 14–16.

Harvey, M.G. (1982): 'The Other Side of Foreign Assignments: Dealing with the Repatriation Dilemma', *Columbia Journal of World Business*, Vol. 17, No. 1, pp. 53–9.

Harvey, M.G. (1983): 'The Multinational Corporation's Expatriate Problem: An Application of Murphy's Law', *Business Horizons*, Vol. 26, No. 1, pp. 71–8.

Harvey, M.G. (1985): 'The Executive Family: An Overlooked Variable in International Assignments', *Columbia Journal of World Business*, Vol. 20, No. 1, pp. 84–92.

Hays, R. (1971): 'Expatriate Selection: Insuring Success and Avoiding Failure', *Journal of International Business Studies*, Vol. 2, pp. 40–6.

Hedlund, G. (1981): 'Autonomy of Subsidiaries and Formalization of Headquarters – Subsidiary Relationships in Swedish MNEs' in Otterbeck, L. (ed.): *The Management of Headquarters – Subsidiary Relationships in Multinational Corporations*: Gower.

Heenan, D.A. and Perlmutter, H.V. (1979): *Multinational Organization Development*. Addison-Wesley.

Heller, J.E. (1980): 'Criteria for Selecting an International Manager', *Personnel*, Vol. 57, No. 3, pp. 47–55.

Hershfield, D.C. (1975): *The Multinational Union Faces the Multinational Company*, Conference board report No. 658, Conference Board.

Holmes, W. and Piker, F.K. (1980): 'Expatriate Failure: Prevention Rather than Cure', *Personnel Management*, Vol. 12, No. 12, pp. 30–3.

Howard, C.G. (1971): 'The Extent of "Nativization" of Management in Overseas Affiliates of Multinational Firms: A World-Wide Study', *Indian Management*, Vol. 10, pp. 11–20.

Howard, C.G. (1980): 'How Relocation Abroad Affects Expatriates' Family Life', *The Personnel Administrator*, 11, pp. 71–8.

Hulbert, J.M. and Brandt, V.K. (1980): *Managing the Multinational Subsidiary*. Holt, Rinehart and Winston.

International Labour Organization (1976a): *Multinationals in Western Europe: the Industrial Relations Experience*. International Labour Office.

International Labour Organization (1976b): *Social and Labour Practices of Some European-Based Multinationals in the Metal Trades*. International Labour Office.

International Labour Organization (1981): *Multinational's Training Practices and Development*. International Labour Office.

International Labour Organization (1984): *Safety and Health Practices of Multinational Enterprises*. International Labour Office.

Izraeli, D.N., Banai, M. and Zeira, Y. (1980): 'Women Executives in MNC Subsidiaries', *California Management Review*, Vol. 23, No. 1, pp. 53–63.

Jain, H. and Murray, V. (1984): 'Why the Human Resources Management Function Fails', *California Management Review*, Vol. 26, No. 4, pp. 95–110.

Jelinek, M. and Adler, N.J. (1988): 'Women: World Class Managers for Global Competition', *The Academy of Management Executives*, February, pp. 11–20.

Kelly, A. and Brannick, T. (1988): 'Explaining the Strike-Proneness of British Companies in Ireland', *British Journal of Industrial Relations*, Vol. 26, No. 1, pp. 37–55.

Kendall, D.W. (1981): 'Repatriation: An Ending and a Beginning', *Business Horizons*, Vol. 24, No. 6, pp. 21–5.

Kennedy, T. (1980): *European Labor Relations*. Lexington Books.

Lamb, H. and Percy, S. (1987): *Working for Big Mac*. Transnational Information Centre.

Landor, J. (1986): *Beyond the Pail*. Transnational Information Centre.

Latta, G.W. and Bellace, J.R. (1983): 'Making the Corporation Transparent: Prelude to Multinational Bargaining', *Columbia Journal of World Business*, Vol. 18, No. 2, pp. 73–80.

Lorange, P. and Murphy, D.C. (1983): 'Strategy and Human Resources: Concepts and Practice', *Human Resource Management*, Vol. 22, pp. 111–35.

McElrath, R. (1988): 'Environmental Issues and the Strategies of the International Trade Union Movement', *Columbia Journal of World Business*, Vol. 23, No. 3, pp. 63–8.

McKersie, R.B. and Hunter, L.C. (1972): *Pay, Productivity and Collective Bargaining*. Macmillan.

Mendenhall, M. and Oddou, G. (1985): 'The Dimensions of Expatriate Acculturation: A Review', *Academy of Management Review*, Vol. 10, No. 1, pp. 39–47.

Millward, N. (1979): 'Research Note: The Strike Record of Foreign-Owned Manufacturing Plants in Great Britain', *British Journal of Industrial Relations*, Vol. 17, pp. 99–104.

Miscimara, P.A. (1981): 'The Entertainment Industry: Inroads in Multinational Collective Bargaining', *British Journal of Industrial Relations*, Vol. 19, pp. 49–65.

Negandhi, A.R. (1980): 'Adaptability of American, European, and Japanese Multinational Corporations in Developing Countries', in Negandhi, A.R. (ed.): *Functioning of the Multinational Enterprise: a Global Comparative Study*, Pergamon Press.

Negandhi, A.R. (1983): 'External and Internal Functioning of American, German and Japanese Multinational Corporations: Decision-making and Policy Issues', in Goldberg, W.H. (ed.): *Governments and Multinationals*. Oelgeschlager, Gunn and Hain.

Newbould, G.D., Buckley, P.J. and Thurwell, J. (1978): *Going International – the Experience of Smaller Companies Overseas*. Associated Business Press.

Northrup, H.R., Rowan, R.L. and Laffer, K. (1977): 'Australian Maritime Unions and the International Transport Workers' Federation', *Journal of Industrial Relations*, Vol. 19, pp. 113–32.

Oliver, N. and Wilkinson, B. (1988): *The Japanization of British Industry*. Basil Blackwell.

Ondrack, D. (1985): 'International Transfers of Managers in North American and European MNEs', *Journal of International Business Studies*, Vol. 16, No. 3, pp. 1–19.

Onto, J. (1987): 'Preparing Managers for International Careers: A Strategic Perspective', *Human Resource Management Australia*, Vol. 25, No. 3, pp. 22–3.

Peccei, R. and Warner, M. (1981): 'Industrial Relations, Strategic Importance and Decision-Making', *Relations Industrielles*, Vol. 36, pp. 132–50.

Perlmutter, H.V. (1969): 'The Tortuous Evolution of the Multi-National Corporation', *Columbia Journal of World Business*, Vol. 5, pp. 9–18.

Picard, J. (1980): 'Organization Structures and Integrative Devices in European Multinational Corporations', *Columbia Journal of World Business*, Vol. 15, pp. 30–5.

Rico, L. (1987): 'The New Industrial Relations: British Electricians' New Style Agreements', *Industrial and Labor Relations Review*, Vol. 11, pp. 63–78.

Robinson, J. (1983): *Multinationals and Political Control*. Gower.

Rowland, K.M. and Summers, S.L. (1981): 'Human Resources Planning: A Second Look', *Personnel Administrator*, December, pp. 73–80.

Schnapper, M. (1973): *Resistances to Intercultural Training*. Paper presented at the Thirteenth Annual Conference of the Society for International Development. San José, Costa Rico.

Stopford, J.M. (1979): *Employment Effects of Multinational Enterprises in the United Kingdom*. Geneva: International Labour Office, Multinational Enterprises Programme, Working Paper 5.

Thal, N. and Cateora, P. (1979): 'Opportunities for Women in International Business', *Business Horizons*, Vol. 22, No. 6, pp. 21–7.

Toyne, B. and Kuhne, R.J. (1983): 'The Management of the International Executive Compensation and Benefits Process', *Journal of International Business Studies*, Vol. 14, No. 3, pp. 37–50.

Tung, R.L. (1981): 'Selection and Training of Personnel for Overseas Assignments', *Columbia Journal of World Business*, Vol. 16, No. 1, pp. 68–78.

Tung, R.L. (1982): 'Selection and Training Procedures of US, European and Japanese Multinationals', *California Management Review*, Vol. 25, No. 1, pp. 57–71.

Tung, R.L. (1984): 'Human Resource Planning in Japanese Multinationals: A Model for US Firms?', *Journal of International Business Studies*, Vol. 15, No. 2, pp. 139–49.

Welge, M.K. (1981): 'The Effective Design of Headquarters – Subsidiary Relationships in German MNCs', in Otterbeck, L. (ed.): *The Management of Headquarters – Subsidiary Relationships in Multinational Corporations*.

Zeira, Y. (1975): 'Overlooked Personnel Problems of Multinational Corporations', *Columbia Journal of World Business*, Vol. 10, No. 2, pp. 96–103.

Zeira, Y. and Harari, E. (1979): 'Host-Country Organizations and Expatriate Managers in Europe', *California Management Review*, Vol. 21, No. 3, pp. 40–50.

6.12

Multinational Dimensions of Accounting

Once firms begin to hold assets and liabilities denominated in foreign currencies, they begin to encounter an additional range of accounting and financial management problems. In acquiring funds, investing them and rewarding the funds contributors, the multinational firm ends up holding assets and obligations that are denominated in foreign currency, with the attendant risk that the domestic-currency value of such assets and liabilities changes as exchange rates move.

Foreign-currency translation poses various financial accounting problems in preparing consolidated group accounts that meaningfully indicate the worldwide commercial performance of the group, especially where subsidiaries are located in high-inflation countries. Financial management problems also arise in funding international trade, financing overseas subsidiaries and evaluating overseas investments where exchange-rate considerations intrude and transfer prices need to be established for intra-group transactions. Such financial management problems have to be viewed against the backcloth of different tax regimes in different countries and possible exchange controls, which pose threats to the company, though with some opportunities for tax planning. Finally multinational companies also face particular problems in devising appropriate management-accounting systems that properly measure the performance of the managers of overseas subsidiaries and provide appropriate incentives for them to improve their performance. Choi (1975) summarizes these various issues; the sections that follow are broadly structured in line with Choi's outline.

6.12.1 Financial Accounting and reporting by multinational companies

In essence, accounting is a service activity designed to facilitate the information needs of external investors, lenders and tax authorities as well as internal decision-makers; its utility derives principally from its service to international financial markets, government policy-makers and the managers of enterprise operations. Their minimum information-needs require reports on the assets and liabilities of a group of companies – the balance sheet, and reports on the income of a group over time – the income statement.

In preparing consolidated group-accounts, multinational groups of companies face problems in consolidating the results of various subsidiaries located in various countries, whose accounting records are expressed in terms of local national currencies. Consolidation in such circumstances requires the parent company to translate the accounts of subsidiary companies expressed in various foreign currencies at appropriate exchange rates and express these accounts in terms of the parent company's national currency. Exchange rates between currencies can change dramatically from period to period, so that financial results can differ markedly from operating results since the former also reflect the gains or losses caused by exchange-rate changes. It is therefore hardly surprising that the question of the most appropriate exchange rate to use for translation purposes has been the subject of considerable discussion (Kubin in Holzer (1984)).

Two main currency translation methods have evolved over time: the closing rate or net-investment method and the temporal or historic-rate method. With the closing-rate method all balance-sheet amounts in foreign currencies are translated at the exchange-rate ruling at the date of the balance sheet, while revenue and expense may be translated at the closing rate or at an average rate for the year. By contrast, with the temporal method, fixed assets and long-term liabilities are translated at the exchange-rate ruling at the date of their acquisition, current assets at historic rates and revenue and expense at an average rate for the year. With the closing-rate method, any gains or losses on exchange arising from translation are taken direct to the group balance sheet and dealt with as changes in reserves so as not to affect reported profit. However, with the temporal method any differences arising on translation are taken to the profit-and-loss account when they serve to affect recorded profit.

The closing rate method is generally applied where the foreign enterprises operate as separate businesses in which the parent company has simply made an investment. On the other hand, where the foreign enterprises operate merely as an extension of the parent company's trade then the temporal method may be more appropriate for consolidation purposes since the subsidiaries' results are more dependent on the economic environment in the parent company's domicile than in their local domiciles. Westwick (1986) provides further details of the application of these methodologies, while Buckley (1986) discusses their commercial implications.

The closing-rate method has generally been used by United Kingdom companies; its use was formally recommended in 1983 with the publication of Statement of Standard Accounting Practice number 20 (SSAP20). The United States used to favour the temporal method but in recent years opinion there has moved to favouring the closing-rate method. In 1981 Statement of Federal Accounting Standard number 52 (SFAS52) broadly similar to SSAP20 was published. This preference was generalized with the publication of International Accounting Standard number 21, broadly similar to SSAP20 and SFAS52, securing some harmonization on this issue. Samuels and Piper (1985) outline various studies of the effects of translation methods highlighting their advantages and disadvantages.

Translation problems are not the only financial accounting issues to confront multinational companies, even though they have received the most attention. To illustrate the range of accounting issues that confront multinationals the following paragraphs touch upon a few other problems to be resolved.

Where a multinational group has subsidiaries that operate in countries experiencing high rates of inflation, it has the problem of incorporating the effects of foreign inflation in the consolidated accounts. This boils down to a question of whether to restate a foreign subsidiary's accounts to reflect the effects of local inflation first and then translate the results to the currency of the parent company, or whether it is better to translate the subsidiary's accounts to their parent-company currency equivalents and then adjust them to reflect the affects of inflation. The restate-and-translate or translate-and-restate debate is still unresolved. Some multinational companies prefer the former method, others the latter.

In consolidating the results of subsidiary companies, a multinational may have to contend with problems caused by differences in accounting standards and rules in different subsidiaries. Ideally a country would like all subsidiaries to adopt a single, uniform financial accounting methodology. However, as Chapter 4.6 made clear, there are considerable variations in accounting principles and practices between countries because of legal requirements, professional standards and other differences. Consequently a subsidiary will need to prepare its accounting results following local accounting conventions (statutory reports) and then may need to prepare parallel results following different accounting conventions imposed by its parent company (business reports) in the interests of consistency. Choi and Mueller (1978) outline these different requirements and discuss their implications for accounting practices in multinational companies.

Preparation of consolidated accounts underlines the nature of the multinational company as a single economic unit reporting its group results to parent-company shareholders and tax authorities in the parent's country. However, many other audiences have an interest in a multinational's subsidiaries including minority shareholders in particular subsidiaries and tax authorities in the countries where subsidiaries are located. Consequently as well as providing aggregated results, multinationals can come under pressure to publish segmental-performance reports covering activities in particular countries or regions.

The various financial accounting and reporting issues discussed above are essentially passive, score-keeping issues to be dealt with by company account-ants. Financial managers within a company can also play a more active part in improving company performances through their investment decisions, funds management and control of the company's exposure to exchange-rate risks. The rest of this section touches upon some of these issues.

6.12.2   Financial planning in multinational companies

All companies need to plan their finances, raising funds from the most appropri-ate sources, investing them in long-term, profit-generating assets and managing their working-capital flows to avoid excessive idle balances. Multinational companies face the same financial management problems but with added dimensions arising from their multi-country, multi-currency operations.

In making long-term investments in overseas subsidiaries a multinational company faces various political risks. The subsidiary might be confiscated by the host government or constrained by price freezes or high minimum-wage requirements imposed upon overseas-owned companies that depress the subsidi-ary's profits. It may risk restrictions being imposed upon the repatriation of capital or dividends. However, a company can take steps to counter these threats through its financing strategies. For example, by financing most of the subsidiary through locally raised loans or equity the multinational reduces its net inward investment in its subsidiary and thus the amount at risk of expropriation. Such local investors and lenders also form a useful pressure group constraining their governments in discriminating against overseas-owned companies. Again, by financing most of a subsidiary using long-term parent-company loans or other long-term debt rather than equity, the multinational can counter dividend repatriation restrictions by substituting remittable interest and capital repay-ments for non-remittable dividends and equity. Buckley (1986) elaborates upon the advantages and disadvantages of these financing strategies.

A multinational can also counter restrictions on the repatriation of income and capital by imposing high interest charges, royalty payments and manage-ment-service charges and fees upon affected subsidiary companies and by charging high transfer prices upon any goods and services transferred to the subsidiary. Such devices ensure repatriation of funds though they can restrict the usefulness of managerial accounting data for planning and control purposes.

In the process of trading, a multinational company frequently needs to con-vert currencies – physically exchange one currency unit for another – and this exposes the company to foreign-exchange risk. Foreign-exchange risk refers to the risk of loss due to changes in the international exchange value of national currencies. For example, a British multinational with a French subsidiary whose money balances are held in francs would experience a foreign-currency gain in terms of pounds whenever the exchange rate of the franc appreciates against the pound and a foreign-currency loss in terms of pounds whenever the exchange rate of the franc depreciates against the pound.

In an era of floating exchange rates, where currencies find their own values levels in international currency markets, exchange rates of currencies change daily and currency values can fluctuate dramatically. To minimize financial losses caused by fluctuating exchange rates multinational companies need to plan their international finances. In principle this involves forecasting exchange-rate movements, measuring the company's exposure to the risks of loss occasioned by currency movements and designing strategies to minimize such exchange risks. However, as Choi and Mueller (1978) point out there is some doubt about whether company decision-makers can predict the potential magnitude of exchange-rate changes and thus outperform foreign-currency markets. For however much data companies collect to facilitate currency forecasts, changes in currency parities are still a function of political sentiment; it is difficult to predict whether a government whose currency is under pressure will intervene in currency markets to defend its currency or rely on the market to remedy the disequilibrium.

Whether the firm seeks to forecast exchange rates or not it can still seek to arrange its financial affairs so as to minimize the detrimental effects of exchange-rate charges. Many of these arrangements consist of little more than good working-capital management practices such as persuading customers to pay promptly then arranging to convert their payments into cash as speedily as possible, before exchange rates change. As Shapiro (1982) points out this can involve a number of devices designed to cut down money-transmission times for the multinational such as direct debits, electronic funds transfers or lock-boxes (company postal boxes to which customers remit funds directly), all designed to cut down postal and bank cheque-clearing delays. Payments netting may also be useful, whereby payments among foreign subsidiaries that trade with each other are set off against one another so that only the net amounts need to be transferred across foreign exchanges.

In addition to the above good financial-management practices the multinational firm can take additional precautions against exchange-risk exposure. Lassen (1982) highlights the major precautions that might be taken. One obvious possibility is to practise currency matching: matching assets and liabilities in the same currencies at both parent-company and subsidiary-company level. In an overseas subsidiary this could be facilitated by raising funds in the form of local debt (loans and trade creditors) while at parent-company level a centralized financing strategy would make maximum use of intra-company financing and overseas borrowings to match overseas assets. In principle this could reduce the multinational's exposure to zero.

Alternatively, to hedge against depreciating foreign currencies, the multinational could insist on invoicing all exports in hard currencies that tend to hold their values while invoicing all imports in the foreign currency of the supplier. In this way the risk of exchange loss is shifted to the multinational's customers and suppliers. However, while this device minimizes potential exchange losses to the multinational it will mean sacrificing potential sales, since some customers would be deterred from buying if they cannot pay for their purchases in their own currencies.

Finally a multinational company can resort to forward-exchange markets to hedge against currency risks. The forward-exchange market is an insurance-type market allowing a firm due to receive a sum of money in foreign currency in, say, three months' time to cover the exchange risk on this sum by selling the foreign currency forward so as to receive a known sum in its own currency. The difference between the forward rate of exchange that the firm contracts to exchange for and the current or spot rate represents an insurance-type premium that the firm pays to avoid the risk of exchange losses. The purchase of future-currency options can achieve the same result; DeMaskey and Baker (1987) point out the appeal of such options in limiting downside risk while leaving upside potential open. Heywood (1978) outlines the various ways in which a firm might use the forward foreign-exchange market, using option-data contracts and overlapping options and the advantages and problems associated with the market.

The above strategies would be relevant for a company taking a defensive attitude towards exchange-rate movements and seeking to minimize exchange-rate risks. However, where a multinational group is confident that exchange rates between certain currencies are likely to change in predictable directions then it may adopt a more active, speculative posture. For example, if a multinational had a subsididary in a country whose currency was likely to depreciate then it would minimize the subsidiary's cash balances and convert any excess cash into hard currencies. At the same time the multinational would speed up payments by the subsidiary to overseas creditors and lenders before exchange-rate depreciation increased the domestic currency burden of these debts. In similar vein the multinational would extend these leading and lagging tactics to intracorporate funds flows associated with trade between subsidiaries, slowing payments of money owed by other subsidiaries to the subsidiary whose currency is likely to depreciate and speeding payments of money owed by the subsidiary in the weak currency country to other subsidiaries. Such devices serve to generate capital gains from exchange-rate changes though they distort working capital balances between subsidiaries.

Many of the financial planning strategies outlined in the above paragraphs have been discussed purely in terms of their effect in minimizing exchange-rate risks. However, many of these strategies simultaneously need to take account of differences in national taxation arrangements which can have a significant effect upon financing decisions. To broaden the picture the following section outlines some relevant aspects of taxation planning for multinational companies.

6.12.3 International taxation and multinational businesses

Differences in national tax systems between countries provide scope for multinational companies to exploit these differences in order to minimize their total world-wide tax burden. Tax implications are likely to colour most management decisions regarding where to invest, what form of business organization to employ, when and where to remit liquid funds, how to finance and what transfer prices to charge, as Choi and Mueller (1978) observe.

Ideally the various national tax systems would be neutral in terms of their effects upon multinational businesses, leaving multinationals to make investment and other decisions on the basis of purely commercial considerations with tax aspects having no effect. In principle such tax neutrality would promote world-wide economic efficiency by allowing capital to move freely from countries where the rate of return is low to countries where high rates of return can be earned. With such neutrality a British citizen should be taxed equally on his domestic investments and his overseas investments and the tax burden on the overseas subsidiary of a British firm should equal that imposed on competitors operating in the same country, as Shapiro (1982) points out.

In practice, world-taxation arrangements depart significantly from the principle of neutrality. National tax systems are instruments of national economic policy, reflecting the political and economic philosophies that predominate in various countries, so it is hardly surprising that diverse national tax systems are encountered. Diversity is encountered in terms of both the rates of company taxation adopted and the legal definition of what constitutes taxable income. Some countries levy high rates and take a broad definition of income, giving a high incidence of taxation; other countries have low tax rates and allow generous depreciation and expenses allowances, granting investment credits for capital expenditure that serve to reduce taxable income and lower the effective tax burden.

All countries claim the right to tax all income that originates within their borders, whether earned by their own citizens or by non-residents. Most countries also claim the right to tax income earned outside their national boundaries by their own citizens, including companies with headquarters in their country. This creates the possibility that the income of multinational companies earned overseas could be taxed twice, once in the country where the income is earned and again in the parent-company's country. In order to permit a degree of tax neutrality and mitigate the burden of taxation on the returns on international investment, most countries grant some relief from double taxation through tax treaties and tax-credit systems. Alworth (1988) discusses the effect of such provisions in encouraging the growth of investment by multinational companies.

Where there are overlapping jurisdictions with the possibility of double taxation, the countries concerned could enter into a network of bilateral tax treaties that agree reciprocal reductions in withholding taxes on dividends and the like. Treaties also generally provide for tax credits whereby taxes are levied in both the income-producing country and the recipient country, but with taxes paid overseas qualifying as credits against the taxes charged at home. Invariably the tax credit for taxes paid to a foreign government is limited to the amount of tax that would have been paid if the income had been earned in the home country, so there is no additional credit if the tax rate in the foreign country is higher than that in the home country. Eckford and Lawson (in Holzer (1984)) provide a detailed outline of the scope and nature of double taxation provisions.

Since the credit against home tax for host-country taxes already charged on the incomes of multinational companies is limited to the home or host-country tax burden, whichever is the lower, differences in national tax rates still require tax planning by multinational companies if they are to minimize an element of double taxation. Some countries also offer a variety of tax incentives in order to encourage inward investment and accelerate their economic development; tax planning can take maximum advantage of these incentives. Such incentives take various forms including non-taxable investment grants and various forms of temporary tax relief like tax holidays or temporary reductions in tax rates.

In their tax planning, multinational companies will generally aim to incur most of their expenditure in countries with high tax rates and generous depreciation and expenses allowances in order to gain maximum tax relief on expenditures. At the same time companies will aim to generate most of their revenues in low-tax countries where they attract little tax. Following this principle multinationals will tend to locate their expensive plants and research and development facilities in high-tax countries to take advantage of investment allowances there. They will also tend to siphon-off profits earned in high-tax countries to low-tax countries through inflated interest payments between group companies, high royalty payments between group companies and excessive intra-group management charges and consultancy fees. Furthermore where subsidiaries supply goods and services to one another or are supplied by the parent company, the parent company will have an incentive to adjust the transfer prices at which such transfers are invoiced. By charging a low transfer price for goods or services shipped from a subsidiary located in a high-tax country to another subsidiary located in a low-tax country, taxable profits in the first subsidiary will be reduced and those of the second subsidiary increased, acting to increase post-tax profits of the group as a whole.

To take maximum benefit from such opportunities multinational companies may also use tax havens. These are countries that often have few natural resources and seek to foster commercial development by offering permanent tax inducements. Examples include the Bahamas and the Cayman Islands, which have no taxes at all, and Gibraltar and the Virgin Islands which have low tax rates. Such countries generally have few tax treaties with other countries, so they are not obliged to furnish information about companies to other governments; they operate few exchange controls, making it easy for companies to move funds into or out of these countries; and they generally have liberal incorporation loans making it easy to set up new companies there. Shapiro (1982) provides details of the taxation and other regulations that apply in the major tax havens.

Establishing a foreign holding company or major subsidiary company domiciled in a tax-haven country enables a multinational group to use this shell company to receive tax-free profits earned by operating subsidiaries. Recycling of funds can allow operating subsidiaries to be financed through loans from the tax-haven country, so that interest payments reduce the taxable income of subsidiaries in high-tax countries. Group patents could also be assigned to the haven company, allowing it to collect royalties from operating subsidiaries in high-tax countries that it receives tax free. Management charges and fees could also be levied upon operating subsidiaries and invoiced to the haven company with similar tax-saving effects. Multinationals can even establish their own offshore insurance companies in tax havens to receive insurance premiums paid by operating subsidiaries with the same tax-saving effects. Finally by invoicing goods and services at artificially low transfer prices to the tax-haven company and at artificially high transfer prices from the haven country a portion of the profits earned by subsidiaries located in high-tax countries could be shifted to the haven company without these goods ever physically passing through the tax-haven country.

Governments faced with potential losses of tax revenues from tax-avoidance policies adopted by multinational companies have taken steps to counter such measures. Many expense deductions of the type outlined above are covered by provisions within the double-taxation agreements negotiated between countries or within national tax legislation. If profits are being creamed by way of artificially high interest payments then the interest deduction in the income-producing country can be restricted to an amount that is commercially justified. Again, payments of royalties by operating subsidiaries in excess of a commercial rate can be restricted, like interest payments. In the same way the allocation of head-office management charges and fees to operating subsidiaries may be restricted to what can be commercially justified. Finally in transactions between associated companies concerning the supply of goods and services the taxation authorities can insist upon a transfer price that reflects arm's-length transactions between independent enterprises. This means that tax authorities can substitute their own deemed transfer price where they feel the transfer prices being employed by a multinational are artificially high or low. In their investigations tax authorities tend to look particularly closely at transactions routed via tax havens.

Miller (1979) suggests that in their tax planning multinational companies need to observe two cardinal rules. First, they must recognize that though tax considerations are important, under no circumstances should they serve to relegate business strategy to a minor role. Commercial and business considerations must predominate in any investment and pricing decisions. Secondly, they must recognize that frequent changes in national tax regulations and narrowing of tax differentials restrict the potential benefits of international tax planning. Both these considerations are relevant to the design of management-accounting systems for multinational companies; for investments, royalties, fees and transfer prices designed to minimize total group taxes can distort multinational control systems. Specifically where subsidiaries are evaluated as separate profits centres, tax-orientated policies that result in inequitable performance measures generally lead to conflicts between subsidiary and group goals, as Choi and Mueller (1978) remind us. These issues are explored further in the following section.

6.12.4 Management accounting in multinational companies

Management accounting practices are needed to ensure that company resources are rationally allocated within a organization; to coordinate the activities of different sub-units and functions in the company; to provide an early warning of things going wrong with operations; to assist with evaluating the performance of various sub-units or subsidiaries; to help with evaluating the performance of individual managers; and to provide a means of motivating managers. A management-accounting system for control purposes needs to reflect the authority relationships and organizational structure of a company. Decentralization adds to the difficulties of coordinating the activities of sub-units in order to achieve overall company goals. In delegating responsibility to subordinates, top management needs to define the various responsibility centres that have control over costs, revenues and profits. Cost centres are the simplest form of responsibility centres: they are units where local managers are able to exercise control over inputs of resources and where responsibility reports focus attention on controllable costs. Revenue centres are similarly simple: they are units where local managers can affect output levels and revenues but have no direct control over costs and where responsibility reports focus attention on controllable revenues. By contrast, profit centres are sub-units where local managers have control over both costs and revenues, being free to purchase the resources they need and to market their outputs. Such profit centres are, in effect, independent business units financed by the parent company. Remote from cost and revenue centres are investment centres which are fully independent sub-units with full control over costs and revenues, and with control over the raising of capital and long-term investments.

Few sub-units within large organizations merit investment-centre status: financial matters are usually centralized, with headquarters staff retaining responsibility for raising capital and approving major investment products.

Furthermore, though large organizations often decentralize manufacturing and marketing activities, where there are significant interdependencies between sub-units their profit-centre status may be curtailed. For example, if one sub-unit does not have discretion over its selling prices but must sell some or all of its outputs to the other sub-units at transfer prices established by head-quarters, then the profit performance of the sub-unit will depend not only upon the efforts of local managers in efficiently producing output but also upon the transfer prices set by top management. Such interdependencies complicate the process of evaluating the performance of sub-units and their managers. Further-more, where headquarters staff are responsible for financing and investment decisions the assets employed within a sub-unit are the product of past invest-ment decisions; only some of the assets employed are controllable by sub-unit managers, complicating the evaluation of sub-unit performance in terms of return on assets employed.

The various issues traced above apply to all large companies but they apply with particular force to multinational businesses. Some companies set transfer prices for transfers of goods and services between sub-units and set royalty payments and management fees for sub-units influenced by the need to minimize group taxes or circumvent exchange controls or other restrictions on the repatriation of income. Again, in arranging capital flows to and between subsidiaries and in specifying inter-subsidiary credit arrangements, multinationals may seek to minimize the political risks of expropriation or avoid exchange-rate risks. These considerations distort the profitability and capital base of sub-sidiaries by shifting profits or liquidity from one subsidiary to another. Such considerations make it difficult to evaluate how well a subsidiary is doing as an economic entity. Miller (1979) outlines the various cost- and market-based trans-fer pricing formulae that might be employed and traces their potentially distorting effects.

The effect of these distortions upon management motivation also warrants consideration. It is a fundamental tenet of management-accounting that managers should only be held responsible for cost and revenue items they can control. Yet where the sub-unit managers must buy or sell to other subsidiaries at predetermined transfer prices, it is unreasonable to evaluate and reward these sub-unit managers according to the reported profits of their unit. Some distinc-tion between the performance of the sub-unit and the performance of the managers is needed and managers should be evaluated purely in terms of costs and revenues they can control.

Further problems arise from the multicurrency nature of multinational operations where budgets and performance reports must be translated from the national currencies of sub-units into the currency of the group headquarters. It is unfair, for example, to evaluate and reward overseas managers according to the profits earned by their sub-unit converted into pounds and adjusted for gains and losses due to exchange rate fluctuations, since managers have no influence over the rates. Instead a forecast future exchange rate may be substituted for budgeting purposes. Hosseini and Aggarwal (1983) analysed various foreign-currency translation methods that might be employed according to their suitability for appraising foreign affiliate performance; they found no one translation method yielded significantly superior results in all circumstances. Jacque and Lorange (1985) argue that the methods used to express foreign-subsidiary budgets in parent-currency terms for evaluation purposes can be particularly misleading where the subsidiary operates in a country experiencing rapid inflation.

Geographical and cultural distance provide further problems for multinational companies. Geographic distance precludes frequent personal contacts between headquarters managers and sub-unit managers; it even slows down the transmission of formal written communications, so that prompt feedback about sub-unit performance is hindered. Cultural distance arises from cultural differences and language difficulties between parent-company managers and local sub-unit managers along with possible differences in education standards. Institutional backgrounds also differ with differences in natural economic systems and policies, distribution arrangements and financial institutions. Kollaritsch (in Holzer (1984)) elaborates upon these various cultural, economic, legal and political factors. The combined effect of all these constraints imposes significant demands upon the management-accounting system within a multinational company; it may distort managerial planning and control efforts and affect motivation and morale within the organization. Only through good systems that are sensitive to human motives and cultural differences can a multinational company harness the efforts of its employees worldwide.

6.12.5 Conclusion

Some years ago Plasschaert (1971) sought to identify the key ingredients of an integrated multinational financial management system, which, he argued, would have the following objectives: facilitating external financing; pooling excess liquidity and facilitating intra-subsidiary financing; speeding up money transfers between sub-units; minimizing exchange-risk exposure; minimizing overall tax liabilities, and setting transfer prices that facilitate good planning and control. Such goals are still the essential accounting and financial goals of multinational companies and multinationals continue to make progress in designing accounting systems that foster the realization of these goals. However, as the previous sections have made clear, many fundamental problems remain that are inherent in the large-scale, multicountry, multicurrency operations of multinational corporations.

References

Alworth, J.S. (1988): *The Finance, Investment and Taxation Decisions of Multinationals.* Basil Blackwell.

Buckley, A. (1986): *Multinational Finance.* Philip Allan.

Choi, F.D.S. (1975): 'Multinational Challenges for Managerial Accountants', *Journal of Contemporary Business*, 1975, pp. 51–67. Reproduced in Gray, S.G. (ed.) (1983): *International Accounting and Transnational Decisions.* Butterworth.

Choi, F.D.S. and Mueller, G.G. (1978): *An Introduction to Multinational Accounting.* Prentice Hall.

De Maskey, A. and Baker, J.C. (1987): 'Foreign Currency Options – Their Use by Multinational Corporations and Banks', *Foreign Trade Review*, Vol. 22, No. 3, October, pp. 243–58.

Eckford, J.C. and Lawson, G.H. (1984): 'Aspects of International Corporate Taxation', in Holzer, H.P. (ed.): *International Accounting.* Harper and Row.

Gray, S.G. (ed.) (1983): *International Accounting and Transnational Decisions.* Butterworth.

Heywood, J. (1978): *Foreign Exchange and the Corporate Treasurer.* A. and C. Black.

Holzer, H.P. (ed.) (1984): *International Accounting.* Harper and Row.

Hosseini, A. and Aggarwal, R. (1983): 'Evaluating Foreign Affiliates: The Impact of Alternative Foreign Currency Translation Methods', *The International Journal of Accounting*, Vol. 19, No. 1, pp. 63–87.

Jacque, L.L. and Lorange, P. (1985): 'The International Control Conundrum: The case of "Hyperinflationary" Subsidiaries', *Journal of International Business Studies*, Fall, pp. 185–201. Reproduced in Choi, F.D.S. and Mueller, G.G. (eds): 1985: *Frontiers of International Accounting: An Anthology.* UMI Research Press.

Kollaritsch, F.P. (1984): 'Managerial Accounting Problems of Multinational Corporations' in Holzer, H.P. (ed.): *International Accounting.* Harper and Row.

Kubin, K.W. (1984): 'Financial Accounting and Reporting for International Business Operations' in Holzer, H.P. (ed.): *International Accounting.* Harper and Row.

Lassen, R. (1982): *Currency Management.* Woodhead-Faulkner.

Miller, E.L. (1979): *Accounting Problems of Multinational Enterprises.* Lexington Books.

Plasschaert, S. (1971): 'Emerging Patterns of Financial Management in Multinational Companies', *Economisch en Sociaal Tijoschrift*, Vol. 25, No. 6, pp. 561–81.

Samuels, J.M. and Piper, A.G. (1985): *International Accounting: A Survey.* Croom Helm.

Shapiro, A.C. *Multinational Financial Management* (2nd edn) (1986). Allyn and Bacon.

Westwick, C.A. (1986): *Accounting for Overseas Operations.* Arthur Anderson and Co.

Part 7

International Business Teaching
and Research

Contents

7.1

Research in International Business

A recent article by Leavitt (1989) raises the issue: what role can international business play in general business education? It raises a number of key issues and provides a focus to a discussion of developments in the teaching of international business.

Leavitt raises several key issues, notably the following. How is creativity or vision (pathfinding) to be incorporated into teaching? Can values be included in courses? Can drive or determination to succeed be encouraged, or at least not suppressed? For faculty, what is the correct relationship between teaching and research? The view presented, by implication, in Jorde and Teece (1989) is that United States business has a lot to learn by observing business practices outside the United States of America. This can be generalized by arguing that all countries have much to learn from the rest of the world. This leads to a view of the importance of comparative research which is the essence of studies of competitiveness, a comparative concept *par excellence* (Buckley, Pass and Prescott (1988)). The argument presented here is that international business is evolving in teaching and research as a vehicle that can begin to answer some of Leavitt's queries.

Four themes in international business studies suggest it is capable of beginning to meet Leavitt's challenges – its attention to comparative studies across national frontiers, its interdisciplinarity, its innovativeness as illustrated by progress in the study of competitive dynamics and its role in integrating functional areas and academic study with the real world.

7.1.1 Comparative Studies

Many of today's key issues require analysis in a comparative framework. One primary example is competitiveness that carries within itself the notion of comparability: Competitiveness relative to whom? There are three potential bases of comparison: (i) with a different historical period, thus giving the idea of a loss of competitiveness; (ii) with another spatial location, usually another country; and (iii) with a well-defined counterfactual position such as: what would be the case if a key event had not taken place? Of these three choices, the most illuminating and often the most intractable is the international comparison (Buckley (1989)).

The intractability of comparative studies arises from the immense amount of data required and the fact that in amassing this information it is often difficult to avoid secondary sources. This also means it is often difficult to separate the raw information from the implicit analysis. It therefore requires judgement – even vision – to separate out the key indicators.

The great strength of comparative research is that it provides a carefully specified 'counterfactual' – comparing two or more actual cases. The method of comparative work is precise. It requires judgement of precisely the kind for which Leavitt calls.

There is far more to judgements of this kind than simple analytics. Because behaviour will be influenced by cultural background, teachers and students utilizing comparative research methods will eventually be confronted with ethical judgements. For instance, in considering competitiveness, a frequent judgement is that welfare-spending is inimical to competitive performance. Such researchers have put the two dimensions of performance and welfare on orthogonal axes (Scott and Lodge (1985)). No one can pretend this analysis is devoid of ethical content. Comparative research can point to differences in the two dimensions, points in two dimensional space, but this is only the beginning of a debate that includes normative content. Simply, different countries and people do things differently.

A further twist to this issue is that each individual brings a different set of cultural baggage in approaching such issues. Recognition of our own prejudices and the confrontation of our own beliefs can be an important step in advancing new solutions to old problems.

7.1.2 Interdisciplinarity

International business has grown as an interdisciplinary subject. Integration of the disciplines has been imperfectly achieved and many teachers of international business still owe their primary loyalty to their core discipline, be it marketing, finance, organizational behaviour or economics. However, there have recently been a spate of articles advocating a greater degree of interdisciplinarity (or transdisciplinarity): (Toyne (1989), Dunning (1989), Casson (1988)) and some that actually attempt to use interdisciplinary tools to tackle problems (Buckley and Casson (1989), Boddewyn (1988)).

One of Leavitt's primary complaints arises because students are able to hide within disciplinary mores, particularly the 'number crunching' ones, which enable results to be achieved without any spark of originality or drive from the individual student. Removal of such monodisciplinary armour renders the student (and the teacher) open to the chill winds of doubt and uncertainty that are the mother of invention.

7.1.3 Innovation

The study of international business has been innovative in many dimensions. Notably, it has included many variables that are not conventionally covered in the functional areas of business studies. Most notable is the embracing nature of 'culture'. It is clear that this variable must be more carefully specified than hitherto has been the case; but an awareness that values in different countries are different and that international business operations must transcend such culture-and-value differences requires teachers, practitioners and students to question their own values. This is exemplified by differences in gift-giving behaviour in different cultures and the value boundary between a gift and a bribe. Thus a philosophical issue is transformed into a question of everyday business operation.

The study of competitive dynamics

International business researchers and teachers have created something of a niche in the study of competitive dynamics. Guises such as globalization, internationalization and global competition cannot obscure the fact that much of core international business theory concerns competitive strategies in the (changing) world economy (Buckley (1990)). The entry of Japan as a world economic power has focused attention on the particular roots and attributes of that nation's success.

Part of the attention has focused on the (presumed) differing nature of competition and cooperation in Japan versus 'the West', particularly the United States of America. This has moved on to a questioning of the optimum amount of competition and, indeed, the actual amount of competition in Western economies. There has been a rediscovery of writers who point to non-competitive modes of coordination of economic activity, notably Richardson (1960), (1972)). The review by Jorde and Teece (1989) is a useful element in this reappraisal, although it is surprisingly narrow in its sources – one notable omission being the volume on cooperative strategy edited by Contractor and Lorange (1988).

7.1.4 Integration

The study of international business can play a major integrative role in two dimensions: (i) integrating the core functional areas of business teaching; and (ii) integrating business theory and practice.

The integration of functional aspects of business into a coherent role is an essential aspect of good business-school practice. Traditionally this has been achieved by 'capstone' courses such as business policy that attempt to focus different analytical frameworks on the totality of business operations. Many courses in international business have developed in this way with international business as an (often voluntary) integrative component taken towards the end of a business education course. The inadequacy of this approach – the view that international issues are separate and separable from other aspects – has led to an alternative mode of internationalizing the curriculum by internationalizing each functional-based module. This has the danger that international issues are swamped, or treated as a residual in functionally based courses. No 'big push' on international issues takes place and no career ladder exists for specialists on international aspects of business. However, it is only by embedding international issues deeply into what is taught that the integrative role can be achieved. This still leaves room for specialist courses or electives in international business *per se* in order to address as a central issue international competition and the way it impinges upon even the most recalcitrant firm and nation.

The integration of business theory and practice is a role that international business studies can perform. Case-studies with an international dimension are perforce rooted in real-world situations where similarities and contrasts of business conditions require the rethinking of standard approaches and where not all the nuances of business operations can be encompassed in balance-sheet entries, much less in simple equations. The fact that more than one solution may be feasible, or that no one solution can meet all the requirements of acceptability in conventional terms, may be startling, even unsettling, to students used to 'pat' textbook answers. What international business cases show is that while careful analysis from many viewpoints using all the techniques derived from the functional areas is necessary, it may not be sufficient. What is further required is innovative thinking, lateral approaches to difficulties and even rigorous self-analysis. The variety of solutions that can be thought up by students of different cultural backgrounds is illuminating and is, in itself, sufficient reason for mixing nationalities on business courses. Students who call for professional consultants to be brought in to recruit a chief executive for a new foreign subsidiary may be startled to find that students from a culture based much more on extended family links suggest the best solution is to send the chief executive's brother-in-law! An evaluation of the two approaches in an international context is not a simple problem; attention needs to be paid to detailed environmental differences requiring knowledge of real-world business conditions and a display of creative intuition.

In the course of achieving this integration, international business researchers have not been afraid of confronting 'the big issues'. Questions of the growth and development of (rival) nations, the cultural basis of growth, the dynamics of global competition, the tension between competition and cooperation in firms and nations and the determinants of the changing structure of the world economy have been among those directly tackled by researchers. The crisis confronting many other social science disciplines – for example, economic history (Gray (1989) – that they confront only trivial, easily researchable, unimportant questions cannot be levelled at researchers in international business. This approach to research enlivens teaching and forces students to lift their sights away from micro, immediate, easily solvable trivia to the real challenges they will have to face as businesspeople, and indeed as people, in the real world.

7.1.5 Conclusion

The potential of international business studies in meeting Leavitt's challenges is immense. Not all these challenges are currently being met, confronted or even recognized. One of the key shortages is skilled individuals with the motivation to put in place the necessary changes. Neither are all decision-makers equipped with the vision to encompass the changes in the external environment that create the necessity to change business education. Until the increasing interdependence of the world economy is fully recognized, the potential of new avenues of teaching will not be achieved.

References

Boddewyn, Jean J. (1988): 'Political Aspects of MNE Theory', *Journal of International Business Studies*, Fall, 3, pp. 341–64.

Buckley, Peter J. (1989): *The Frontiers of International Business Research*. University of Bradford mimeo.

Buckley, Peter J. (1990): 'Problems and Developments in the Core Theory of International Business', *Journal of International Business Studies*, Vol. 21, No. 4, pp. 657–65.

Buckley, Peter J. and Casson, Mark (1988): 'A Theory of Cooperation in International Business', in Contractor, Farok J. and Lorange, Peter (eds): *Co-operative Strategies in International Business*. Lexington MA: Lexington Books.

Buckley, Peter J. and Casson, Mark (1989): 'Multinational Enterprises in Less Developed Countries: Cultural and Economic Interaction', University of Reading Discussion Papers in *International Investment and Business Studies*, No. 126, January (in Buckley and Clegg, 1990, op. cit.).

Buckley, Peter J. and Clegg, Jeremy (eds) (1990): *Multinational Enterprises in Less Developed Countries*. London: Macmillan.

Buckley, Peter J., Pass, C.L. and Prescott, Kate (1988): 'Measures of International Competitiveness: A Critical Survey', *Journal of Marketing Management*, Vol. 4, No. 2, Winter, pp. 175–200.

Casson, Mark (1988): 'The Theory of International Business as a Unified Social Science', University of Reading Discussion Papers in *International Investment and Business Studies*, No. 123, November.

Dunning, John H. (1989): 'The Study of International Business: A Plea For a More Interdisciplinary Approach', University of Reading Discussion Papers in *International Investment and Business Studies*, No. 127, February.

Gray, Mark (1989): 'Marginal Obsessions', *Times Higher Education Supplement*, 28, July, p. 9.

Jorde, Thomas M. and Teece, David J. (1989): 'Competition and Cooperation: Striking the Right Balance', *California Management Review*, Vol. 31, No. 3, Spring, pp. 25–37.

Leavitt, Harold J. (1989): 'Educating our MBAs: On Teaching What We Haven't Taught', *California Management Review*, Vol. 31, No. 3, Spring, pp. 38–50.

Richardson, G.B. (1960): *Information and Investment*. Oxford: Oxford University Press.

Richardson, G.B. (1972): 'The Organization of Industry', *Economic Journal*, 82, pp. 883–96.

Scott, B.R. and Lodge, G.C. (1985): *US Competitiveness in the World Economy*. Boston, Mass: Harvard Business School Press.

Toyne, Brian (1989): 'International Exchange: A Foundation for Theory Building in International Business', *Journal of International Business Studies*, Spring, pp. 1–18.

7.2

Teaching in International Business

7.2.1 Overview

At both undergraduate and postgraduate level there are many different types of international business course. For example, some concentrate on one specific topic such as Negotiating International Contracts, or concentrate on a specific geographical area such as Pacific Rim countries. Others offer a relatively large number of topics in a wide international context but view these from the perspective of single discipline or management function, such as marketing or economics. Indeed, much of the international business taught in Europe (and to a lesser extent in the United States) has been introduced as an extension of functional subjects such as marketing, finance, organization and behaviour. In some cases the specifically international content of these courses has increased to such an extent and has embraced so many diverse topics that the original functional specialism is no longer in clear focus. A recent report[1] points out that there is often no sufficiently clear distinction between what is taught under the title of International Marketing and that of International Business.

As often as not, international business appears to have evolved from the International Economics component of more general economics courses; this explains why, in Europe at least, most courses were originally economics based. However, following the pioneering work done in teaching and research, much of which is covered in this volume, international business has now clearly emerged as a subject in its own right and one which is best approached from a multi-disciplinary perspective. Within Europe, many of the more recently devised courses seek to provide an overview of the subject and how it relates to the other main management functions. Consequently, they are largely, although not entirely, centred on the firm. They are nevertheless much broader in scope than the 'how-to' courses that predominate in the United States. It is sometimes suggested that because American courses tend to concentrate on explaining how managers and executives ought to conduct international business, and are strong on techniques, their courses are more practical and vocational than those in Europe and elsewhere. This point needs to be qualified. Students who undertake management or business studies courses are not all destined to work for private-sector firms; at least some will work in the public sector, in the media or in academia. Also, while the 'how-to' approach has its merits and serves a specific market, it is important that those who are going to work in the private sector have some knowledge of how business activities affect national economies, international trade and the natural environment. Topics that were considered external or marginal to the main subject have a habit of becoming matters of central concern in a short period of time. Many, sometimes all, of these wider issues are omitted from the 'how-to' courses, presumably because they often lie outside the scope of existing techniques.

It is becoming increasingly common for undergraduate degree courses in business and management subjects to include international business either as a compulsory or an elective component. This is often in addition to internationalizing other functional areas such as finance and marketing. It is exceptional these days for a Masters in Business Administration degree not to include at least one elective in the subject and there are often several. In Europe, Masters in Business Administration students who choose the international business route often take a general overview elective (concentrating on multinational companies as mentioned above) followed by a more specialized course such as International Business and International Law, Managing the Multinational Enterprise, The European Economic Community and the World Economy, Japan and the Asian Newly Industrialized Countries, or International Business Negotiations. International business has proven to be popular with students, and employers have indicated they have an urgent and growing need for more staff with knowledge of this subject. For these reasons the 1990s will see an increase in the amount taught on existing business courses and the introduction of new degree courses, especially at advanced levels, entirely devoted to this subject.

The move towards greater standardization of teaching will gather pace, at least in Europe, over the next few years. There is already sufficient evidence to suggest that Continental Europe is to a significant extent following the British model in that the subject is largely presented from the firm's point of view. It would help if those European institutions that have evolved their courses from a particular functional specialism would recognize and acknowledge this development; in some cases almost identical courses covering the main international business topics appear as International Marketing, International Economics and International Business Strategy. The first two course titles should be reserved for those cases where the functional specialism (Marketing and Economics) is being presented in an international context. Meanwhile, prospective students need to exercise care when selecting courses; where possible they should study the syllabus before reaching a decision, as course titles and even brochures can be misleading.

It is too early to specify with any great degree of confidence what the more standardized European international business course will be like. However, virtually all European courses at present contain something on the theory and practice of the firm and the methods by which the firm can become internationalized. It would be surprising therefore if this were not a component of international business courses in the future. More controversial will be the question of whether the subject should be taught with a single, specific functional bias such as marketing or economics, or whether it should be presented as a multidisciplinary subject which incorporates both these specialisms and several others too. The trend appears to be towards the latter, at least in Europe. It is increasingly common for the subject to integrate many of the traditional managerial specialisms, as well as more recent topics such as the influence of national culture and history on business practice and the challenges this presents to those operating in the international domain. The challenges presented to the teachers are obviously considerable; how many different national cultures can one person really master, and when culturally determined values conflict how is the conflict to be resolved?

There is also a trend in many educational institutions towards a structure comprising an initial overview of the subject and the several different courses that focus on a specific aspect of international business such as marketing or negotiations, or a particular geographic or economic region. While this structure provides teachers and students with the opportunity for some measure of specialization, in practice it seems that the existence of specialist courses itself stimulates the demand for yet further courses in related topics or geographical areas not currently on offer. The future of international business teaching shares with research a serious constraint: the shortage of appropriately qualified and motivated people. Those currently teaching this subject are among the best placed to identify and encourage new talent.

Note

1. *The European Teaching of International Business: Prospects for Collaboration and Exchange*. Report submitted to the Erasmus Bureau, November 1989 by Hafiz Mirza and Peter J. Buckley.

7.2.2 List of institutions offering courses in international business

Constraints of space and time make it impossible to list here all those institutions that offer courses in international business of one type of another. Such a list would be several hundred pages longer than the one we have provided. Instead we have concentrated on those institutions that provide courses on international business as such; we have omitted those which offer 'only' internationalized functional specialisms such as international finance or international marketing. The list has been compiled from most of the major institutional reference books and, in particular, *International Business Curricula: A Global Survey*, compiled and edited by John Thanopoulos with the assistance of Joseph W. Leonard, Academy of International Business, 1986. We wrote to a further three hundred institutions around the world and contacted many more by telephone. In this way we are able to add to and revise the data derived from the various published sources. This list also differs from others in that it includes institutions whose courses are current as opposed to merely featured in brochures. We cannot claim the list is completely accurate and comprehensive. It has not been possible to check every entry derived from published sources, and in our efforts to reflect the position in 1990, we are not suggesting that we have traced every institution offering a course that meets our criteria. Nevertheless it is probably the most comprehensive and up-to-date list of its kind at the time of publication. We hope that scholars and students alike will find it useful.

Key to the terms in brackets after each entry
U = undergraduate
P = postgraduate
D = doctorate
When a term is underlined e.g. (U P D) it means that institution
allows some specialization in international business at this level.
In the case of American institutions, underlining signifies that
international business is a major at this level.

ARGENTINA

Universidad Nacional de la Plata, Facultad de Ciencias Economicas, Dr Anibla Barrenda, 48 No555.–1990 La Plata, Argentina. 021–43985/211466. Liliana C. Galan. (UP)

AUSTRALIA

University of Adelaide, Faculty of Economics, Mr N.J. Thompson, Dean, Box 498, G.P.O. Adelaide S.A. 5001, Australia. (08) 228–5523. Mr R.L. Newman. (UPD)

Ballarat College of Advanced Education, Dean Patrick Hope, Box 663, Ballarat, Victoria 3350, Australia. (053) 301–800. (UPD)

Bendigo College of Advanced Education, Faculty of Business Studies, R.B. Howland, Dean, P.O. Box 199, Bendigo, Vict. 3550, Australia. (054) 403–249, Mr L.T. Lourens. (U)

Canberra College of Advanced Education, School of Administrative Studies, Dr R.L. Wettenhall, P.O. Box 1, Belconnen A.C.T., Australia 2616. (062) 52–2061. (UP)

Chrisholm Institute of Technology, David Syme Business School, Dr Ken Tucker, 900, Dandenong Road, Caulfield, Vict. 3145, Australia. (03) 573–2222. (UP)

Darling Downs Institute of Advanced Education, School of Business Studies, Ian Langoon, Darling Heights Post Office, Toowoomba, Queensland 4350, Australia. 301300 (076). (U)

Darwin Institute of Technology, Mr L.H. Greenwood, P.O. Box 40146, Casuarina N.T., Australia 5792. (089) 20–4449. (U)

Deakin University, School of Management, Professor David Lethbridge, Waurn Ponds, Geelong, Vict. 3217, Australia. (UPD)

Gippsland Institute of Advanced Education, Head of School of Business, Mr Eric L. Thorne, Switchback Road, Churchill, Vict. 3842, Australia. (07) 051– 220–321. (UP)

Griffith University, School of Social and Industrial Administration, Dr Peter Coaldrake, Kessels Road, Nathan, Queensland 4111, Australia. (07) 275–7145. (U)

Monash University, Faculty of Economics and Politics, Professor W. Sinclair, Clayton, Victoria 3168, Australia. (03) 541–9711. Dr L.S. Welsh. (UP)

University of Newcastle, Department of Management, Professor Alan J. Williams, N.S.W. 2308, Australia. (049) 685–742. (UPD)

University of New England, Faculty of Economics Studies, B.J. Philips, Dean, Armidale, N.S.W. 2351, Australia. 06773–2200. J. Trueman. (UPD)

New South Wales Institute of Technology, Faculty of Business, David Fraser, Dean, P.O. Box 123, Broadway 2007, Australia. (02) 218–9739. (UP)

University of New South Wales, Faculty of Commerce, Professor J.W. Neule, Kesington 2033, Australia. 697–3190. (UPD)

Philip Institute of Technology, Brian Sheedon, Dean, Plenty Road, Bundoora, Vict. 3083, Australia. (613) 468–2295 [350, 35, E, UM].

Riverina-Murray Institute of Higher Education, Edwin Brooks, Dean, P.O. Box 588, Wagga Wagga, N.S.W. 2650, Australia. (069) 23–2484. (UP)

School of Business Brisbane Cae, Dr W.D. McCarthy, P.O. Box 117, Kedron 4931 Q, Australia. (07) 577077. (UP)

South Australia College of Advanced Education, Dr Jillian ailing, 46 Kintore Avenue, Adelaide, South Australia 5000, Australia. (08) 2281611. (U)

South Australian Institute of Technology, School of Accountancy, Professor Ian Scarman, North Ice, Adelaide, Australia. 2280–309. (UP)

University of Sydney, Faculty of Economics, Stephen M. Salisbury, Dean, N.S.W. 2006, Australia. 692–2222. (UPD)

University of Tasmania, Faculty of Economics and Commerce, P.C. Molhuysen, Dean, P.O. Box 252C, Hobart, Tasmania 7001, Australia. (002) 202101. S. Rucinski. (UPD)

Western Australian College of Advanced Education, Head of School of Business, P.O. Box 217, Doubleview, Western Australia, Australia 6018. 3879371. Dr Valentine Pervan. (U)

University of Western Australia, Faculty of Economics and Commerce, Dr John Jackson, Perth, Australia. 380–2930. (UPD)

Western Australia Institute of Technology, Division of Business Administration, Dr. K. Hall, Bently, Western Australia 6102. 3507553. S E Bovdville. (UP)

AUSTRIA

Universitaet Graz, Sozial-Und Wirtschaftswissenschaftliche Fakultaet, Dr Karl Acham, Universitaetsplatz 3, A-8010 Graz, Austria. (01143/316) 380–3260. (PD)

University of Innsbruck, Faculty of Social and Economic Sciences, Professor Hans Lexa, Innrain 52, A-6020 Innsbuck, Austria. 0043–5222–7240. Professor Hans Hinterhuber. (PD)

Universitat Wien, Professor Gerhart Bruckmann, Dr Karl Lueger, Ring 1, A-1010 Vienna, Austria. 4300–2131. Dr Rudolph Vetschera. (PD)

Wirschaftuniversitat Wein, Rektor Herbert Matis, Augasse 2–6, 1090 Vienna, Austria. 34–05–25. (PD)

BAHAMAS

College of the Bahamas, Business and Administrative Studies Division, Peter L. Daniels, P.O. Box N4912, Nassau, Bahamas. (809) 32–60730.

BARBADOS

Barbados Community College, Principal Alvin F.E. Barnett, Howell's Cross Road, St Michael, Barbados. 809–426–3186. Norma Holder.

European University, Amerikalei 131, 2000 Antwerp, Belgium. John P. Wells, Assistant to the President. (32–3) 218–81–82. (P̲)

State University of Ghent, Faculty of Economics, Dr Jos Van Acker, Hoveniers Berg 4, 9000 Belgium. (091) 233821 ext. 2037. (UPD)

I.C.H.E.C., P. Dupriez, Boulevard Brand Whitlock 2, 1150 Bruxelles, Belgium. 02–735–91–44. (P)

Katholieke Universiteit Leuven, Department of Applied Economics Sciences, Dr D. Van de Bulcke, Dekenstraat 2, 3000 Leuven, Belgium. 016–227517. (P)

Ecole des Hautes Etudes Commerciales de Liège, Mr Marcel Aldenhoff, 21 rue Sohet, 4000 Belgium. 041–52–36–78. (U̲)

Université de Liège, Ecole d'Administration des Affaires, President Dister Guy, Blvd. DU Rectorat 7, Sart Tilman 4000 Liège, Belgium. 41562726. Professor L. Braggard. (U̲)

Université Catholique De Louvain, Institut D'Administration et de Gestion, Professor Jacques T. Lehmann, 16 Ave. De L'Epinette, 1348 Louvain La Nueve, Belgium. 70–433022. (UPD)

University of Botswana, School of Accounting and Management Studies, Professor K.P. Varghese, P/Bag 0022, Gaborone, Botswana. (U)

Pontificia Universidade Catolica de Campinas, Faculty of Economics, Candido Ferreira de Silva, Rodovia D. Pedro I, Km 12, Campinas, Sao Paulo, Brazil. 52.0899 Ramal 199. (U)

Universidade Federal De Juiz De Fora, Faculdade De Economia, Alfredo Alencar Saggioro, Martelos-Juiz De Fora – Estado De Minas Gerais, Minas Gerais, Brazil. (U̲)

Federal University of Minas Gerais, Faculdade De Ciencias Economicas, Jacques Schwartzman, R. Writiba 832, Belo Horizonte, MG, Brazil. (UP)

Universidade Federal Do Parana, Faculdade Catolica De Administracaeo, E. Economia, Dr Heriberto Arns, Rua 24 De Maio, 135-Cx. Postal 6045, 80000 Curitiba-Parana, Brazil. (041) 233–4222. (U)

Universidade Metodista de Piracicaba, Dr Davi Ferreira Barros, Caixa Postal 68, 13.400 Piracicaba (SP), Brazil. (0194) 335011. (U)

Universidade De Sao Paulo, Faculdade De Economia E. Administracaeo, Jacques Marcovitch, Av. Prof. Luciano Gualberto 908 – Cidade-Universitaria 05499, Sao Paulo, Brazil. (011) 211–04–11. (UPD)

Higher Institute of Finances and Economics, Professor M. Kounev, Svishtov, Bulgaria. 2–27–22. Professor Svetlozar Kalchev Tsonev. (UPD)

Acadia University, School of Business Administration, Walter E. Isenor, Dean, Wolfville, Nova Scotia, BOP 1XO, Canada. (902) 542–2201 ext. 216. Pearl H. Dodds. (U)

University of Alberta, Dean Roger Smith, Room 4–40 Faculty of Business Building, University of Alberta, Edmonton, Alberta T6 2R6, Canada. (403) 432–3901. (UPD)

University of Athabasca, Administrative Studies, Alan Meech, Box 10000, Athabasca, Alberta TOG 2RO, Canada. (403) 675–6197. (U)

University of British Columbia, Faculty of Commerce and Business Administration, Peter Lusetig, Dean, Vancouver, BC V6T 1Y8, Canada. (604) 228–3222. (UPD)

University of Calgary, Faculty of Management, Michael Maher, Dean, 2500 University Drive N. W., Calgary, Canada. (403) 284–5685. (UP)

The MMS Program, School of Business, Carleton University, Ottawa, Ontario, Canada K15 5B6. The Supervisor, 613–564–4373. (P)

Dalhousie University, School of Business Administration, 6152 Coburg Road, Halifax, NS., B3H 125, Canada. Philip Rosson, Acting Director, Centre for International Business Studies. (902) 424–6553. (U)

Université Laval, Faculté des sciences de l'administration, Monsieur Jean-Louis Malouin, Quebec G1K 7P4, Canada. 656–2216. Monsieur Macel Roberge. (UPD)

McGill University, Faculty of Management, Laurent Picard, Dean, 1001 Sherbrooke West, Montreal, Canada. 392–5877. (UPD)

University of Manitoba, Roland G. Grandore, Dean, Faculty of Administrative Studies, Winnipeg, Manitoba, Canada R3T 2N2. (204) 474–9711. (UP)

Memorial University of Newfoundland, Faculty of Business Administration, Dr James Barnes, St John's, Newfoundland AB 1J9, Canada. (709) 737–8854. Carol Doody. (UP)

Université De Moncton, Faculté d'Administration, Rene Didier Doyen, Moncton N.B., Canada E1A 3E9. 1–506–858–4205. (UP)

University of New Brunswick, Faculty of Administration, K.P. Nair, Dean, Fredericton, E3B 5AS, Canada. (506) 543–4549. (UP)

University of Ottawa, Faculty of Administration, Gilles Paquet, Dean, 275 Nicholas St., Ottawa, Ontario KIN 6N5, Canada. (613) 231–4918. Neri Johnston. (UP)

Université du Quebec, Gilles Boulet, Dean, 2875 Laurier Boulevard, Ste-foy, Quebec G1V 2M3, Canada. (418) 657–3551. Grant Regalbuto. (UPD)

Queen's University, Dr John Gordon, School of Business, Kingston, Ontario K7L 3N6, Canada. (613) 547–3230. (UPD)

University of Regina, Faculty of Administration, Murray R. Hutchings, 4th Floor, Education Building, Wascana Parkway Regina, Saskatchewan S4S OA2, Canada. (306) 584–4724. Hally Levesque. (UP)

University of Saskatchewan, College of Commerce, W. John Brennan, Dean, Saskatoon, Saskatchewan S7N OWO, Canada. (306) 966–4786. (UP)

University of Sherbrooke, Faculty of Commerce, Jean-Pierre Garant, 2500 University Blvd, Sherbrooke, Quebec J1K 2R1, Canada. (819) 821–7311. Jacques Lavallee. (UP)

University of Toronto, Faculty of Management Studies, T.J. Tigert, Dean, 246 Bloor St West, Toronto, Ontario M5S 1V4, Canada. (416) 978–3422. (PD)

University of Victoria, P.O. Box 1700, Victoria B.C., CanadaV8W 2YW. (604) 721–7002.

University of Waterloo, Department of Management Sciences, Michael Magazine, Chairman, Waterloo, Ontario N21 3G1, Canada. (519) 885–1211. (UPD)

University of Western Ontario, School of Business Administration, C.B. Johnston, Dean, London, Ontario N6A 3K7, Canada. (519) 679–3206. Lynne Lesko. (UPD)

Wilfrid Laurier University, School of Business and Economics, J. Alex Murray, 75 University Ave West, Waterloo, Ontario, Canada. (519) 884–1970. (UP)

University of Windsor, Faculty of Business Administration, Eric West, Dean, 401 Sunset Avenue, Windsor, Ontario, Canada. (519) 253–4232. (UP)

York University, Faculty of Administrative Studies, Alan Hockin, Dean, 4700 Keele St, North York, Ontario M3J 2R6, Canada. 667–2210. (UPD)

CHILE

Universidad Austral de Chile, Faculty of Economics and Administrative Sciences, Dean Guido Meller Mayr, Cassilla 567, Valdivia, Chile, Professor David W. Hedrick. (UP)

Catholic University of Valparaiso, School of Commercial Engineering (Business Administration), Director Claudio Elortegui R., Casilla 4059, Valparaiso, Chile. 251024 ext. 3293. (U)

University of Chile, School of Selume Economics and Business Administration, Jorge Selure, Dean, Diagonal Paraguay 257, Santiago, Chile. 2228521. (UP)

Pontificia Universidad Catolica de Chile, Facultad de Ciencias Economicas y Administrative, Juan Ignacio Varas Castellon, Vicuna Mackenna 4860, Santiago, Chile Cassilla 274–V, Correo 21, Santiago, Chile. 511077. (UP)

Universidad De Santiago De Chile, Facultad de Administracion Y Economia, Luiz Arturo Fuenzalida, Dean, Avda. Libertador Bernardo O'Higgins 3389, Santiago, Chile. 761184. [2300, 50, S, UA].

Universidad Federico Santa Maria, Escuela de Negocios de Valparaiso, Fund. Adolfo Ibanez, Gustavo Fonck, Dean, Balmaceda 1625, Recreo Vina Del Mar, Chile. 660211. (U)

CHINA

The Chinese University of Hong Kong, Faculty of Business Administration, Y. T. Chung, Dean, Shatin N.T., Hong Kong. 0–6352778. (UP)

COLOMBIA

University of Bogota, Jorge Tadeo Lozano, Dean Augusto Alvarez, Calle 23 No. 4047, Bogota, Colombia. 243–61–01. (U)

Universidad Externado de Colombia, Facultad de Ciencias Economicas, Enrique Low Murtra, Apartado Aereo 034141, Calle #12 1–17 Este, Bogota, Colombia. (U)

Universidad Nacional de Colombia, Departmento de Administracion de Empresas, Administrador Mauricio Avella Gomez, Ciudad Universitaria, Apartado Aereo 14.490, Bogota, Colombia. 2691700 ext. 567. (U)

Pontificia Universidad Javeriana, School of Economics and Business Administration, Luiz Kose Tarazano, Dean, Carrera Za. No. 40–90 Piso 5, Bogota, Colombia. 232–0246. (UP)

Universidad del Valle, Faculty of Administration, Ruben Dario Echeverry, Dean, P.O. Box 25360, Cali, Colombia. 586680. [645, 37, S, UMA].

CZECHOSLOVAKIA

Graduate School of Economics, Faculty of Trade, Dr Vitazoslav Balhar, 832 20 Bratislava, Odbojarov 10, Czechoslovakia. 68842. Dr Jaroslav Tesarek. (PD)

DOMINICAN REPUBLIC

Universidad Catolica Madre y Maestra, Jose Luiz Aleman, Dean, Apdo. 822, Autop. Duarte Km. 1 1/2, Santiago de los Caballeros, Dominican Republic. (UP)

ECUADOR

Pontificia Universidad Catolica del Ecuador, Facultad de Ciencias Administrativas, Mr Fabian Raza Davila, Av. 12 de Octubre y Ladron de Guevara, Quito, Ecuador. 231–691. (U)

EGYPT

American University in Cairo, Center for Middle-East Management Studies, Mr Farouk El-Hitami, 113 Kasr Al-Aini St., Cairo, Egypt. 22969. (UP)

University of Mansoura, Faculty of Commerce, Professor Mohamed E. Zayed, Al-Gomhoria St., Mansoura, Egypt. 050–327826. (UP)

Menoufia University, Faculty of Commerce, Dr Seddik Moh. Affifi, Sheebem El-Kom, Egypt. 048–21027. (UPD)

Tanta University, Faculty of Commerce, Dr Mohamed Adel Elhamy, Tanta, Gharbia, Egypt. (040) 326612. (UPD)

ETHIOPIA

Addis Ababa University, College of Social Sciences, Dr Seyoum G. Sellassie, P.O. Box 1176, Addis Ababa, Ethiopia. (UP)

FIJI

University of the South Pacific, School of Social and Economic Development, Dr R.R. Thaman, P.O. Box 1168, Suva, Fiji. Suva-313900. L.H. Lyons. (UP)

FINLAND

University of Helsinki, Aleksanterinkatu 7 A, 00100 Helsinki 10, Finland. 358– 0–1912550. Professor Paavo Seppanen.

FRANCE

Bordeaux I, Institut D'Administration Des Entreprises, Jean-Guy Merigot, 35, place Pey-Berland, 33076 Bordeaux Cedex, France. (56) 52–99–80. Robert Bloch. (PD)

Centre d'Enseignement et de Recherche de Statistique Appliquée, Jean-Pierre Therme, 10 rue Berlin Poiree, 75001 Paris. 233–97–14.

Centre de Perfectionnement Aux Affaires, Richard Zisswiller, 108 bd. Malesherbes, 75017 Paris, France. (1) 7665134.

Ecole Superieure de Commerce et d'Administration des Entreprises, Directeur Gabriel Murat, Case 911, Comaine de Luminy, 13288 Hanella Cedex 9, France. (91) 410160. (P)

Ecole Superieure de Commerce – Clermont, Director Henri Verdier, 4 Blvd. Trudaine, 63037 Clermont Ferrand, France. 73923871. (P)

Ecole Superieure de Commerce, Jean-Christophe Clerget, 8 Route de la Janeliere, 4403 Nantes Cedex, France. (40) 294455. (P)

EAP – European School of Management, Dr Bruno Leblanc, 108 Blvd. Malessherbes, 75017 Paris, France. (1) 7665134. (P)

Institut Européen d'Administration des Affairs, Boulevard de Constance, 77305 Fontainebleau Cedex, France. Sumantra Ghoshal, Assistant Professor of Business Policy, France 60 72 42 56. (P)

Institut Superieur des Sciences Techniques Economie Commerciale, Directeur C.J. Gourdain, 24 rue Hamelin, 75116 Paris, France. (1) 7278870. (P)

Lyon Graduate School of Business Administration Yves Reale, 23 Ave Guy de Collonque, 69130 Ecully, France. (7) 8338122. (PD)

Université de Nancy II, Institut Commercial de Nancy, Director Jean Lacombe, 4 rue de la Ravinelle 54037 Nancy, France. (8) 335–22–52. (P)

Université de Nice, Institut d'Administration des Entreprises, Director J. Lebraty, Avenue Emile Herriot, 06050 Nice Cedex, France. (33) 970506. (PD)

Université Paris IX, UER Gestion et Economie Appliques, Professor Claude Gauvin, 75775 Paris Cedex 16, France. (U)

Université Paris 13, Faculté de Gestion, Professeur Jean-Richard Sulzer, Avenue J.B. Clement, 93430 Villetaneuse, France. (1) 8216170. (PD)

Parix XII – Val de Marne, V.E.R. de Sciences Economiques et de Gestion, Dr B. Marchal, 58 Ave. Didier, 94210 La Varenne St Hillaire, France. 886–1179 poste 623. (UPD)

Université de Rouben, Faculté de Droit, Professeur Gelard, Bd. A. Siegfried, 76130 Mont-Saint-Algnan, France. (35) 98–5885. Professeur Lehmann. (PD)

Université des Sciences Sociales, Institut D'Administration des Entreprises, Director Claude Echevin, BP 47X, 38040 Grenoble Cedex, France. 54–81–78. (D)

Université des Sciences et Techniqeus de Lille, Institut De Preparation Aux Affaires – Institut D'Administration des Entreprises, Henri Le Marois, 1 Bis Rue Georges Lefevre, 59043 Lille Cedex, France. (20) 52–32–65. Mlle Carole Dumoulin. (PD)

Université Strasbourg III, Institut d'Administration des Entreprises, Jean Muller, 61 Ave. des Vosges, 670000 Strasbourg, France. (88) 35–0382. (P)

University of Toulouse-Social Sciences, I.B.A., Dr Pierre Spiteri, 2 Rue Albert Lautman, 31000 Toulouse, France. (61) 215518. (D)

GERMANY

Universität Augsburg, Wiso Fakultat, Dr O. Opitz, Memmingerstr. 14, D 89 Augsburg, Germany. 0821–598–385. Dr O. Neuberger. (PD)

Christian-Albrechts Universität zu Kiel, Wirtschafts and Sozialwissenschaftsliche Fakultät, Institut fur Betriebswirtschaftslehre, Olshausenstr. 40, D–2300, West Germany. (0431) 880–03991. Dr K. Dellmann. (PD)

University Dortmund, School of Business Administration, Dr Berg, 46 Dortmund 50, Germany. 0231–155–3182. Dr H.G. Meissuer. (UPD)

University of Duisburg, Faculty of Economics, Dr Guenter Heiduk, Lotharstrabe 65, 4100 Duisburg, Germany. 0203–379–2521. (PD)

Universität Essen, FB 5 Wirtschaftswissenchaften, Dr Martin K. Welge, Postfach 103 764, 4300 Essen 1, Deutschland, Germany. (P)

Fernuniversität Gesamthochschule Hagen, Fachbereich Wirtschaftswissenschaft, Klaus Anderseck, Dean, Postfach 940. D-5800 Hagen 1, Germany. 02334/804–2425. (PD)

Friedrich-Alexander Universität, Institut Exporforschung, Dr Berekoven, Lange Gasse 20, 85 Nuernberg 1, West Germany. (0911) 5302214. Thomas Heidecker. (PD)

University of Giessen, College of Business Administration, Licher Strasse 74, D6300 Giessen, Germany. (0641) 702–5100. Dr Karl Weber. (UD)

Julius-Maximillians-Universität Wurzburg, Wirschaftswissenschaftliche Fakultät, Dr Gunter Petermann, Sanderring 2, D–8700 Wurzburg, Germany. (0931) 31900. (PD)

Ludwig-Maximillians-Universität München, Institüt fur Finanzwirtschaft, Dr K.V. Wysocki, Ludwigstr. 28, 8000 Munchen 22, West Germany. (089) 2180–3284. (U)

Universität Manheim, Fakultät für Betriebswirtschaftslehre, Dr Peter Eichron, Schloss D-6800 Mannheim, Germany. (0621) 292–5428. Dr Alfred Keiser. (UPD)

University of Paderborn, Department of Economics and Business Administration, Dr Gunter Steinmann, P.O. Box 1621, D-4790 Paderborn, F.R. Germany. (5251) 602113. (UPD)

Ruprecht-Karls Universität Heidelberg, Wirtchaftswissenschaftliche Fakultaï, Dr Manfred Rose, Grabengasse 14, 6900 Heidelberg, West Germany. (06221) 542915. (UPD)

Schiller International University (Germany, Spain, France, UK). Friedreich-Ebert-Anlage 4, 6900 Heidelberg, West Germany. J.G. Eggert, Academic Dean. (0622) 12046. (UP)

GREECE

American College of Greece, Deree College, Theodore Lyras, 6 Gravias St, GR 153–42 Ag. Paraskevi, Greece. 6593250 ext. 345. (U)

Pantios School of Political Science, Rector George Contogeorgis, 136 Syngrou Ave., 17671 Athens, Greece. 922–0100.

Piraeus Graduate School of Industrial Studies, Rector Theodore Gamaletsos, 40 Karaoli-Dimitriou, Pireaus, Greece. 4120751. Professor B. Metakas. (U)

GUATEMALA

Universidad de San Carlos, Escuela de Administracion de Empresas, Licenciado Alvaro Enrique Salguero, Ciudad Universitaria, zona 12, Guatemala City. 760790–94 ext. 426. (U)

HONDURAS

National University of Honduras, Business Administration Department, Lic. Roman Valladares R., Carretera a Suyapa, Tegusigalpa, Honduras. 32–55–42. Lic. Carlos Perdomo. (UP)

HONG KONG

University of Hong Kong, Department of Management Studies, Head of Department, Professor S.G. Redding, Pokfulam Road, Hong Kong. – 58592266. (UP)

Wuhan University, Department of Economic Management, Director Fan Ming, Wuchang, Hubei, China. (UP)

College for Foreign Trade, Karoly Ivanyi, Principal, 3 Ecseri Street, 1476 Budapest, Hungary. 573–166.

Aligarh Muslim University, Faculty of Commerce, Professor Ishrat H. Farooqi, Aligarh, India. 5674. (UPD)

Banares Hindu University, Faculty of Commerce, Professor R.A. Singh, Old-b 2/1 Jodhpur Colony, 221005 Uttar Pradesh, India. 54291 ext. 368. (UPD)

Bangalore University, Department of Commerce and Management, Dr O.R. Krishnaswami, Bangalore 560001, India. 258419. (PD)

University of Bombay, Department of Commerce, Dr B.D. Ghonasgi, Ranade Bhavan, Vidyanagari Campus, Kalina, Bombay 400098, India. 6127021. Professor Malati Anagol. (PD)

Department of Commerce, Delhi School of Economics, University of Delhi, Delhi-110007, S. Kumar, Head of Department, India. 2521521 ext. 385. (P)

University of Jodhpur, Department of Commerce, Professor V.N. Hukku, Jodhpur, India. 23840. (UPD)

Karnatak University Dharwad-3, Faculty of Commerce, K.R. Mallikarjunappa, Dean, Dharwad-3, India. 8194/36. (UPD)

Kumaun University Nainital, Almora Campus Almora, Dr R.M. Saksena, Faculty of Commerce, Almora, Uttar Pradesh 263601, India. 2183. (UPD)

Marathwada University, Aurangabad, Post Department of Commerce, Dr S. Mishra, 19 Ranchankar Colony, Station Road, Aurangabad, India. 443. (UPD)

Punjabi University, Department of Management, Dr B.S. Bhatia, Patiala, India. (P)

Saurashtra University, College of Arts and Commerce, N.N. Sheth, Dean, 20 New Jagnath Plot, Rajkot 360001, India. 26248. (U)

South Kujarat University, College of Commerce, A.V. Patel, Principal, Bjlimora, India. (UPD)

Sukhadia University, College of Commerce and Management Studies, R.B.L. Agarwal, Dean, Udaipur, India. Dr. K.R. Sharma. (UPD)

Utkal University, Department of Commerce and Business Administration, Dr R.K. Jena, Vani-Vihar, Bhubaneswar 751, Puri Orissa, India. 52520 PBX-45 ext. (PD)

Gadjah Mada University, Faculty of Economics, Dr Sukanto Reksohadiprodja, Bukalsumur, Yogyakarta, Indonesia. 88688 ext. 243. (UPD)

University of Indonesia, Faculty of Economics, Dr Wagiono Ismangil, Jalan Salemba Raya, Jakarta, Indonesia. 882413. (UP)

Sriwijaya University, Faculty of Economics, Dr Soebedjo Pardjan, Jalan Srijayanegara, Bukit Besar, Palembang, Indonesia. 26172. (U)

Universitas Sumatra Utara, Fakultas Ekonomi, O.K. Harmaini, Medan, Indonesia. 23210 ext. 275. (UP)

Al-Mustensiriyeh University, College of Administration and Economy, Mothanna Al-Hoori, Dean, Baghdad, Iraq. Dr Fakri Jassim. (UP)

University of Dublin, Trinity College, Professor Charles McCarthy, Faculty of Economics and Social Studies, Dublin 2, Ireland. 772941. (UP)

Universita degli Studi di PISA, Facolta de Economia e Commercio, Riccardo Varalda, Dean, Via Ridolfi, 10 56100 Pisa, Italia. (050) 598031. Monica Tangheroni. (UD)

Pontifical Gregorian University, Faculty of Social Sciences, Dr Johannes Schasching, Piazza della Pilotta 4, I–00187, Rome, Italy. 67011. (UPD)

Kobe University, School of Business Administration, Akio Mori, Dean, 657 Rokko, Nada, Kobe, Japan. 078–881–1212. (UPD)

Nagoya University, School of Economics, Dr Eiji Ogawa, Furo-cho, Chikusa-ku, Nagoya 464, Japan. (052) 781–5111 ext. 2355. (UPD)

Rikkyo University, Faculty of Economics, Shozo Takahashi, Dean, Nishi-Ikebukoro, Toshima-ku, Tokyo, Japan. 03–985–2349. (UPD)

Ryukoku University, Business Administration, Professor Akira Kayashi, Fukakusa, Fashimi-ku, Kyoto, Japan. 075–642–1111. Kesaji Kobayashi. (UPD)

Senshu University, Dr Masayoshi Deushi, 3–8 Kanda-jimbocho, Chiyoda-ku, Tokyo 101, Japan. 03–265–6211. (UPD)

Tokyo Keizai University, Department of Business Administration, Professor Akitoshi Iki, 1–7 Minami-cho, Kokubunji City, Tokyo, Japan. 0423–21–1941. Mr Yoshihiro Nagajima. (UPD)

University of Tsukuba, Chairman of the Master's program in Management Sciences Public Policy Studies, 1–1–1 Tennodai, Sakura-mura, Niihari, Ibaraki, Japan. 0298–53–5178. (P)

Waseda University, Graduate School of Commerce, Mr Kiyomitsu Arai, 6–1 Nishiwaseda 1-chome, Shinjukuku, Tokyo 160, Japan. 03–203–4141 ext. 3153. Osamu, Nishisawa. (PD)

JORDAN

Yarmouk University, Faculty of Economics and Administrative Sciences, Dr Hesham Gharaibeh, Irbid, Jordan. (6) 27111 ext. 2271/72/73. (UP)

KENYA

University of Nairobi, Faculty of Commerce, Dr Francis N. Kibera, P.O. Box 30197, Nairobi, Kenya. 334244 ext. 2177. (UPD)

KOREA

Kon-Kuk University, College of Commerce and Economics, Dean Yong-kuk Kim, 93–1 Mojin-dong, Seongdong-gu, Seoul, Korea 133. 445–0061/70. (UPD)

Kyungpook National University, Graduate School of Business, Dr Kim Yung-Soo, 1370 Sangyuk-dong, Bukyu, Taegu 635, Korea. 94–5116. (P)

Pusan National University, Graduate School of Management, Dean Byong-in Suh, 30 Jangjun-dong, Dongnae-ku, Pusan, Korea. 56–1164. (P)

Won Kuang University, College of Business Administration, Park Byung Hong, 344–2 Sim-Ryang-Dong, Iri, Jedlabukdo, Republic of Korea. 52–2111–9. (UPD)

Yeungnam University, College of Commerce and Economics, Professor Ryu Chang Ou, Gyungbuk, Gyongsan 632, Taegu, Seoul, Korea. (UPD)

Yonsei University, College of Business and Economics, Boong Ro Yoo, Dean, 134 Shinchon-Dong, Sudaemoon-ku, Seoul-120, Korea. 3920131. (UPD)

LEBANON

Université Saint Joseph, Faculté De Gestion et de Management, Fayek Abillama, Dean, rue Hunekin Beyrouth, Lebanon BP 293. 326636. (UP)

MALAYSIA

University of Malaya, Faculty of Economics and Administration, Dr Fong Chan Onn, Kuala Lumpur 22–11, Malaysia. (03) 554111. Professor Gregory Thong. (UP)

MEXICO

Universidad Nacional Autonoma de Mexico, Facultad de Contaduria y Administracion, C.P. Alfredo Adam, Circuito Exterior, Ciudad Universitaria Delegacion, Coyoacan, C.P. 04510 Mexico, D.F. 5–48–19–54. Pedro Gomez Flores-Verdad. (UPD)

NEPAL

Tribhovan University, Institute of Management, Mohan Prasad Upadhyay, Dean, P.O. Box 1246, Kirtipur, Kathmandu, Nepal. (2) 13076. (UPD)

THE NETHERLANDS

University of Amsterdam, Faculty of Economics, Professor C.A. Boukema, Jodenbreestraat 23, 1011 NH Amsterdam, Holland. (020) 5254128. (UPD)

Universidat Di Aruba, Dr C. Browne, Aruba, Holland. 2–2811. (UPD)

Netherlands School of Business, A. G. van Vijfeijken, Dean, Straatweg 25, 3621 BG Breukelen, Holland. (0) 3462–61044. Miss Maria Meyer. (UP)

NEW ZEALAND

University of Auckland, Faculty of Commerce, Professor A. Maccormick, Private Bag, Auckland, New Zealand. 737–964. (UPD)

University of Canterbury, Faculty of Commerce, Dr J. A. George, Private Bag, Christchurch, New Zealand. 482009. (UPD)

Massey University, Faculty of Business Studies, Dr Ralph Love, Private Bag, Palmerston North, New Zealand. 69099 ext. 8671. (UPD)

University of Otago, Mr Michael Fay, Faculty of Commerce, P.O. Box 56, Dunedin, New Zealand, 740–411. (UPD)

Victoria University of Wellington, Faculty of Commerce and Administration, Professor F. Jackson, Private Bag, Wellington, New Zealand. 721–000. (UPD)

University of Waikato, School of Management Studies, J.T. Ward, Dean, Hamilton, New Zealand. 62889. (UPD)

NIGER

Université de Niamey, Faculté des Sciences Econiques et Juridiques, Mamadou Dagra, Dean, B.P. 12, 442 Niamey, Niger. 732494. [30, 1, F, MD].

NIGERIA

University of Nigeria, Enugu Campus, Faculty of Business Administration, Pita N.O. Ejiofor, Dean, Nigeria. (UPD)

NORWAY

Norges Handels Hoysuole, School of Economics and Business Administration, Rector Arne Kinserdal, Helleveten 30, 5035 Bergen, Norway. (05) 256500. (UPD)

Uppsala Universitet, Foretagsekonomiska Institutionen, Box 513, S-751 20 Uppsala. 46–18–15–5400.

PAKISTAN

University of Karachi, Institute of Business Administration, Dr Abdul Wahab, Karachi-32, Pakistan. 460121. (UPD)

University of Peshawar, College of Commerce and Business Administration, Principal Abdul Malik Hashmi, Peshawar, Pakistan. (UP)

Punjab University, Hailey College of Commerce, Professor Anis Ahmad Siddiqui, New Campus, Lahore, Pakistan. 850381. (UP)

PERU

ESAN, Casilla Postal 1846, Lima 100, Peru, South America. Jorge Talavera, Dean. 360140. (P)

Universidad Nacional de la Amazonia Peruana, College of Administration and Accountancy, Eco. Jose Luis Antinori, Apartado 496, Iquitos, Peru. (094) 234364. (U)

PHILIPPINES

Adamson University, College of Commerce, Jose Ma R. Quintos, Dean, 900 San Marcelino St., Ermita Manila, Philippines. 58–96–25 local 312. (U)

Arellano University, College of Commerce, Francisco Cayco, Dean, 2600 Legarda, Sampaloc, Manila, Philippines. 60–74–41. (UP)

Ateneo de Manila University, Graduate School of Business, Professor Alfredo M. Tengco, H.V. de la Costa, S.J. Street, Salcedo Village, Makati, Metro Manila, Philippines. 817–8491. (P)

University of Baguio, College of Commerce, I.V. Dacones, Dean, Gen. Luna St, Baguio City, Philippines. 442–3071. Dr Felipe L de Gyzman. (UP)

Centro Escolar University, College of Commerce and Secretarial Administration, Dr Violeta A. Llanes, Mendiola, Manila, Philippines. 741–0912. (UP)

Divine Word University of Tacloban, College of Commerce, Mrs Conrita T. Tudtud, Sagkanhan Old Road, Tacloban City, Philippines. 321–2667. (U)

Mindanao State University, College of Business, Dean Marlene Hofer-Tamano, Marawi City, Lanao del sur Province, Philippines. Criselda Zerna. (UP)

University of Negros Occidental Recoletos, College of Commerce, Dr Edgar Grino, Bacolod City, Philippines. 2–3342. (UP)

Notre Dame University, College of Commerce, Dean Myrna B. Lim, Cotabato City, Philippines. 26–98. (UP)

Saint Louis University, School of Commerce and Business Administration, Gabino L Garoy, Dean, Bonifacio St., Baguio City 0216, Philippines. 442–2793. (U)

University of San Carlos, College of Commerce and Business Administration, Victoria Satorre, Dean, 78 Bonifacio St., Cebu City, Philippines. 61552. (UP)

POLAND

Academy of Economics, Faculty of Management and Computer Science, Dr Stanislawa Bartosiewicz, 53–345 Wroclaw, ul. Komandorska 118/120, Poland. 65–11–55. (PD)

Karol Adamiecki Academy of Economics in Katowice, Faculty of Trade, Dr Franciszek Piontek, 40–287 Katowice 1 Maja 50, Poland. 59–8421. Asst. Professor Leszek Zabinski. (UPD)

Krakow Academy of Economics, Faculty of Economics, Dr Jerzy Altkorn, 27 Rakowicka St., 31–510 Krakow, Poland. 21–0099.
University of Lodz, College of Economics, Dr Zdzistaw Prochowski, 90–131 Lodz, Narutonicza 65, Poland. 57–2075. (P)

PORTUGAL

Universidade de Coimbra, Faculdade de Economia, Professor Joaquim Romero Magalhaes, Av. Dias da Silva 165, 3000 Coimbra, Portugal. 714886.

ROMANIA

University of Cluj-Napoca, Faculty of Economic Sciences, Professor Gheorghe Postelnicu, Piata Stefan cel Mare nr. 1, 3400-cluj Napoca, Romania. 15616. (PD)

Academy of Economics Studies, Professor Illie Vaduva, 70167 Bucharest, Piata Romana 6, Romania. 11–59–60. Dr Valentine Nicolea. (UD)

SAUDI ARABIA

King Saud University, College of Administrative Sciences, Riyadh, P.O. Box 2459, Saudi Arabia. 467–4351. Dr Hussein Alawi. (UP)

SINGAPORE

National University of Singapare, School of Management, Head Associate Professor Tan Chin Tiong, Kent Ridge, Singapore 0511. (065) 775–6666 ext. 3002. Professor Lee Soon Ann. (UP)

SOUTH AFRICA

University of Cape Town, Graduate School of Business, John Simpson, Dean, Private Bag, Rondebosch, Cape, South Africa. 69–5382. Dr David Beaty. (UPD)

University of Durban, Graduate School of Business, Professor Joop Venter, Private Bag X54001, Durban 2000, Rep. of South Africa. (031) 82–1211 ext. 197. (P)

University of Natal, Professor B.M. Gourley, King George V Avenue, Durban 4001, South Africa. (031) 816–2651. (UPD)

University of the O.F.S., Professor P.C. Fourie, P.O. Box 339, Bloemfontein, South Africa. (301) 70711. Mr A.J. Schoonwinkel. (UPD)

Potchefstroom University for Christian Higher Education, Post Graduate School of Management, Professor N.P. Du Preez, Potchefstroom 2520, Transvaal. (01481) 22112 ext. 2132. (PD)

University of Stellenbosch Business School, H.P. Muller, Director, Box 610 Bellville 7530, South Africa. (021) 975761. (PD)

Technikon RSA, W.F.C. Kockemoer, Director, Private Bag 7, Braansfontein, Johannesburg 2017, South Africa. 725–1030. (U)

University of the Western Cape, Faculty of Economics and Management Sciences, Dr A.D. Muller, Private Bag X17, Belloville 7530, South Africa. 951–2301. (UPD)

University of Zululand, Department of Business Economics, Professor S.J. Zondi, Private Bag X1001, Kwa-Dlangezwa 3886, Natal, South Africa. 93–911. (UPD)

Universidad de Deusto, Faculty of Economic Sciences and Business, Antonio Freije, Dean, Spain. (UPD)

ESADE (Escuela Superior de Administracion y Direccion de Empresas), Avda. Pedrables 60–62, 08034 Barcelona, Spain. Lluis M. Puges, Dean. (34–3) 203–78–00. (UP).

Universidad Nacional de Educacion a Distancia, Facultad de Ciencias Economicas y Empresariales, Rafael Catejon Montijano, Dean, Ciudad Universitaria, Apartado 50487, 28040 Madrid, Spain. 243–8653. Professor Luiz T. Diez. (P)

University of Navarra, Instituto de Estudios Superiores de la Empressa, IESE, Professor Carlos Cavalle, Avda. Pearson, 21 08034 Barcelona, Spain. (93) 204–4000. Ramon Nubiola. (PD)

Universidad Politecnica de Barcelona, ESADE, Director General Dr Xavier Adroer, Avda. Pedralbes 60–62, 08034 Barcelona, Spain. (343) 203–7800. (UP)

Valladolid, Facultad de Ciencias Economicas y Entresariales, Fernando R Artigas, Avda. del Valle Esgueva 6, 47011 Valladolid, Spain. (PD)

Open University of Sri Lanka, P.O. Box 21, Nawala, Nugegoda, Sri Lanka.

Lunds University, Department of Business Administration, Dr Gosta Wijk, Box 5136, s-22005 Lunds 5, Sweden. (046) 107822. (UPD)

University of Geneva, Faculty of Social and Economic Sciences, Professor Peter Tschopp, 3 place de l'Université, 1211 Geneva 4, Switzerland. (022) 209333. (UPD)

University of Damascus, College of Economics and Commerce, Dr Akram Shakra, Chairman of the Business Administration Department, Damaseur, Syria. 223–855. (UPD)

National Taiwan University, College of Lan, James Yang, Chairman, Department of Graduate Institute of Business Administration, Taipei, Taiwan R.O.C. (UP)

Soochow University, School of Business, Chia-lin Cheng, 56 Kuei Yang St. Sec. 1, Taipei, Taiwan. (02) 3111531–54. (UP)

Tunghai University, College of Management, Dean Yin Wu Li, Box 974, Taichung, Taiwan 400. (04) 2560271. (UP)

University of Daar Es Salaam, Faculty of Commerce and Management, Associate Professor Keu L. Edwards, P.O. Box 35046, Dar es Salaam, Tanzania. (UPD)

Chulalongkorn University, Faculty of Commerce and Accountancy, Suthi Ekahitanonda, Dean, Bangkok 10500, Thailand. 251–5988. (UP)

Kasetsart University, Faculty of Economics and Business Administration, Chamnein Boonma, Dean, Bangkok 10900, Thailand. (02) 579–8547. (UP)

National Institute of Development Administration, School of Business Administration, Dr Nikorn Wattanapanom, Sukapiban II Road, Bangkapi, Klongchan, Bangkok 10240, Thailand. 377–7417. (P)

Sukhothai Thammathirat Open University, School of Management Sciences, Professor Kulthon Thanapongsthorn, Bangphood, Pakkred, Nonthaburi 11120, Thailand. 5735840–1. (U)

University of Tunis, Faculty of Economics and Management, Abdellatif Khemakhem, Dean, Campus Universitaire, route de l'aerodrome, B.P. 69, 3028 Sfax, Tunisia. (UP)

Bogazici University, School of Economics and Administrative Sciences, Dr Murat Sertel, Bebek, Istanbul, Turkey. 163–1500. (UPD)

University of Istanbul, Faculty of Business Administration, Dr Kemal Kurtulus, Rumelihisarvstu, Istanbul, Turkey. 165–9765. (UPD)

Mamara University, Faculty of Economics and Administrative Sciences, Professor Omer Faruk Batirel, Ressam Namik Ismail Sok. No 1, Bahcelievler, Istanbul, Turkey. 5759664. (UPD)

Middle East Technical University, Department of Management, Dr Atilla Dicle, Chairman, Ankara, Turkey. 237–100/2004. (UP)

UNITED KINGDOM

Aston Business School, Aston University Aston Triangle, Birmingham, B4 7ET, England. Dr A. Cox (undergraduate programme), Alan J. Bennet, Director of Postgraduate Studies. UK 021–359–3011. (UP)

University of Bath, School of Management, Professor C.R. Tomkins, Clavertown Down, Bath BA2 7AY Avon, England. (0225) 61244. (UPD)

Birkbeck College, Faculty of Economics, Professor D.W. Rhind, Malet Street, London WC1E 7HX, England. (01) 580–6622. (PD)

City of Birmingham Polytechnic, Faculty of Business Studies and Law, D.F. Murray, Perrybarr, Birmingham B42 2SU, England. (UP)

University of Birmingham, Professor G.E. Cherry, Faculty of Commerce and Social Sciences, Birmingham, B15 2TT, England. (021) 412–1301 ext. 3534. (UPD)

University of Bradford, Management Centre,, Professor David T. Weir, Emm Lane, Bradford BD9 4JL, West Yorkshire, England. 0274 384370. (UPD)

University of Cambridge, Vice Chancellor Sir John Butterfield, The Old Schools, Cambridge CB2 1TN, United Kingdom. 0223–358933. G.B. Skelsky.

Polytechnic of Central London, Faculty of Management Studies, W.A. Westgate, Dean, 35 Marylebone Road, London NW1, England. 071 486–5811. (P)

City University, School of Business, Professor B. Griffiths, Frobisher Crescent, Barbican Center, London EC2Y 84B, England. 071–920–0111. G.E. Moulton. (UPD)

Coventry Clamchester Polytechnic, Faculty of Business, Prior Street, Coventry CV1 5FB, England. 0203–24166. (U)

Cranfield School of Management, Cranfield Institute of Technology, Cranfield, Bedford MK43 OAL, England, UK. J.G. Nelks, MBA Programme Director. UK 0234–751122. (UPD)

Dundee College of Commerce, Craig M. Brown, 30 Constitution Road Dundee, Scotland. (0382) 29151. Assistant Principal: Gordon Laird. (UP)

Dundee College of Technology, Dr W.S. Howe, Head of Department of Business Studies, Bell Street, Dundee DD1 1HG, Scotland. (0382) 27225. (U)

University of East Anglia, School of Economics and Social Studies, Professor J. M. Hollis, University Plain, Norwich NR4 7TJ, Norfolk, United Kingdom. (0603) 56161. (UPD)

University of Edinburgh, Simon Coke, Dean, Head of Department, William Robertson Building, Department of Business Studies, 50 George Square, Edinburgh, Scotland. (031) 667 1011 ext. 6577. (UPD)

University of Essex, Department of Economics, A.N.D. McAuley, Wirknhoe Park, Colchester CO4 3SQ, Essex, United Kingdom. 862286. J. Richmond. (UPD)

Exeter University, Faculty of Social Sciences, B.A. Turner, Dean, Amory Building, Rennes Drive, Exeter EX4 4RJ, United Kingdom. 0392–236236. (UPD)

Glasgow Business School, Department of Management Studies, University of Glasgow, 53–59 Southpark Avenue, Glasgow G12 8LF, Scotland, UK. Douglas Briggs, Director. 041–339–8855. (UPD)

Glasglow College of Technology, N.G. Meadows, Director, Low Gardens Road, Glasgow G4 OBA, Scotland. (041) 332–7040. Mr P.B. Finch. (U)

Hatfield Polytechnic, School of Business and Social Sciences, Mr J.M. Oliver, Balls Park, Hertford, Herts SG13 8QF, England. (0992) 558451. (UP)

Henley The Management College, Greenlands, Henley-On-Thames, Oxon RG9 3AU, England, UK. W.L. Weirstein, Professor of International Business. United Kingdom 0491–571454. (UP)

Heriot-Watt Business School, Heriot-Watt University, MBA Suite, Chambers Street, Edinburgh EH1 1HX, Scotland, UK. Dr T. Clarkoon. Tel 031–449 5111 (U)

Polytechnic of Huddersfield, Faculty of Business, P.S. Halls, Dean, Queensgate, Huddersfield HA1 3DH, England. (UP)

University of Hull, Department of Management Systems and Sciences, Cottingham Road, Hull, England. 0482–46311. Mr P.W. Maclagan. (UPD)

Imperial College, Manchester Science Department, Professor Samuel Eilon, Exhibition Road, London SW7, England. (071) 589–3111. Anne Benjamin. (PD)

University of Kent at Canterbury, Dean of Social Sciences, David Morgan, The Registry, Canterbury, United Kingdom. 0227 66822. (UPD)

Kingston Polytechnic, Kingston Business School, Kingston Hill, Kingston-Upon-Thames, Surrey KT2 7LB, England, UK. David Miles, Dean, 01–549–1141. (UP)

Lancashire Polytechnic, Faculty of Business 'and Management, Director Eric Robinson, Preston PR1 2TQ, England. 0772–22141. (UP)

London University, Queen Mary College, Registrar David Joyne, Mile End Road, London E1 4NS, England. 081–980–4811. Mr R.J. Allard.

University of Technology, Loughborough, Leicestershire, LE11 3TU, England. Professor G. Gregory, Department of Management Studies. 0509–263171. (U)

Manchester Polytechnic, Faculty of Management and Business, J.H. Hepburn, Dean, Aytoun Street, Manchester M1 3EH, United Kingdom. 061–23806177. (UPD)

University of Manchester, Manchester Business School, R. Telfer, Director, Booth Street West, Manchester M15 6PB, England. 061–273–8228. Barbara Kennerley. (PD)

Manchester School of Management, University of Manchester Institute of Science and Technology, P.O. Box 88, Manchester M60 1QD, England, UK. Professor J. Goodman. 061–200–3418. (UPD)

Middlesex Polytechnic, Middlesex Business School, D.G. Harper, Dean, The Burroughs, Hendon NW4 4BT, United Kingdom. (01) 204–6545. (UPD)

University of Newcastle Upon Tyne, Department of Economics, Dr C.G. Hanson, NE1 7RU, England. 328511. (P)

Polytechnic of North London, The Business School, Neil Dorward, Dean, Stapleton House, Holloway, London N7 8DB, England. (071) 607–2789 ext. 2465. (UPD)

Open University, European and International Office, Mr Glyn Martin, Director, Walton Hall, Milton Keynes, United Kingdom. 0908 653052. (P)

School of Oriental and African Studies, Professor C.D. Cowan, Malet Street, London WC1E 7HP, England. (01) 637–2388. Registrar J.P. Bishop. (UPD)

Plymouth Polytechnic, Plymouth Business School, D.W. Cowell, Dean, Drake Circus, Plymouth, Devon, England. (0752) 264666. (UPD)

Portsmouth Polytechnic, Business School, Head of School, G. Oliver, Locksway Road, Portsmouth PO4 8JF, England. (0705) 735241. (UPD)

Reading University, Department of Economics, Professor John Dunning, Whiteknights, Reading, Berkshire RG6 2AA, United Kingdom. 0734–875123. (UPD)

University of St Andrews, Department of Economics, P. McKiernan, Director, St Andrews, Scotland. 0334–76161. (UPD)

Sheffield City Polytechnic, Business School, Dyson House, Sheffield S1 1BW England. Dr A.H. Fowler, Head of International Business and Languages. 0742 533647. (UPD)

University of Sheffield, Division of Economics Studies, E.A. Lowe, Chairman, Sheffield SLO 2TN, England. 0742–78555. (UPD)

South Bank Polytechnic, Faculty of Administrative Studies, 103 Borough Road, London SE1 OAA, England, UK. 071–928–8989. (U)

University of Strathclyde, Strathclyde Business School, Professor C.B. Burns, 130 Rottenrow, Glasgow, Scotland. (041) 552–7141. R. Armour. (UP)

Surrey University, Department of Management Studies, Dr A. Kelley, Guildford GU2 5XH, United Kingdom. (0483) 571281. Professor Reeves. (UPD)

Trent Polytechnic, Trent Business School, Professor P.J.C. Seneque, Burton Street, Nottingham NG1 4BU, United Kingdom. 418248. (UP)

University of Ulster at Jordanstown, Newtownabbey, Co. Antrim BT37 OQB, Northern Ireland, UK. Patrick B. McNamee, Professor of International Business. United Kingdom 0232–365131. (UP)

Polytechnic of Wales, Faculty of Professional Studies, P. Hawkins, Dean, Pentymidd, Wales, United Kingdom. (0443) 405133. Dr R. Roberts. (UP)

University College of Wales Aberystwyth, Mr J.R. Edwards, Faculty Office, Llandimam, VCW Aberystwyth, Dyfed, United Kingdom. (0970) 3111. Dr C.R. Emanuel. (UP)

University of Wales, Institute of Science and Technology, Centre for Graduate Management Studies, Roger Mansfield, Director, Aberconway Building, Colum Drive, Cardiff CF1 3EU, United Kingdom. 425888 ext. 2100. (UPD)

University of Warwick, School of Industrial and Business Studies, Professor Yao Su Hu, Coventry CV4 7AL, England. 0203–523523 ext. 2845. (UPD)

UNITED STATES OF AMERICA

Adelphi University, Schools of Business, Garden City, NY 11530. Carol H. Schwartz, Acting Dean. (516) 663–1176. (UP)

University of Alabama, College of Commerce and Business Administration, P.O. Box J, University, AL 35486 Edward M. Smith. (205) 348–4537. (UP)

Alabama A&M University, 215 CCN, Normal, AL 35762. Herman Mixon, Chairman, Business Administration. (205) 859-7400. (UP)

Alabama State University, 915 So. Jackson St., Montgomery, AL 36195. (205) 293-4124. (U)

American Graduate School of International Management – Thunderbird, Glendale, AZ 85306. Marshall Geer, Academic Vice President. (602) 978-7250. (UP)

American International College, 1000 State Street, Springfield, MA 01109. Charles F. Maher, Acting Academic Dean, School of Business Administration. (413) 737-7000 ext. 230. (U)

American University, Kogod College of Business Administration, 4400 Mass. Ave., N.W., Washington, D.C. 20016. James H. Sood, Director, International Business Center. (202) 885-1953. (UP)

Arizona State University, College of Business, Tempe, AZ 85287. (602) 965-6757. (UP)

University of Arkansas at Fayetteville, Fayetteville, AR 72701. Tracy Murray, Phillips Petroleum Company Distinguished Professor. (501) 575-6225. (P)

Boston University SMG, Boston, MA 02215. Professor David J. Ashton. (617) 353-2679. (UP)

Brigham Young University, School of Management, Provo, UT 84602. Paul H. Thompson, Dean. (801) 378-4121. (U)

University of California at Berkeley, Berkeley, CA 94720. Professor Richard H. Holton. (415) 642-1424. (UP)

California Polytechnic State University at San Luis Obispo, San Luis Obispo, CA. Kenneth D. Walters, Dean. (805) 546-2704. (U)

California State University Dominguey Hills (CSUDH), Carson, CA 90747. Carol Lopilato, Director, International Business Program. (213) 516-3582. (U)

California State University at Los Angeles, 5151 State University Drive, Los Angeles, CA 90032. Moonson David, Director, International Business Programs. (213) 224-2811. (U)

California State University at Stanislaus, Turlock, CA 95380. D.A. Ball, Dean. (209) 667-3287. (UP)

Central Washington University, Ellensburg, WA 98926. Lawrence A. Danton, Dean, School of Business and Economics. (509) 963-1955. (U)

Cleveland State University, 430 University Center, Cleveland, OH 44115. Edward G. Thomas, Associate Dean. (216) 687-3786. (U)

University of Dallas, Graduate School of Management, University of Dallas Station, Irving, TX 75061. Robert G. Lynch, Director, MBA-International. (214) 721–5326. (P)

East Central Oklahoma State University, Ada, OK 74820. David Alexander, Chairman, Business Administration. (405) 332–8000. (U)

Eastern Washington University, School of Business, Cheney, WA 99004. Phillip L. Beukema, Dean. (509) 458–6396. (U)

Fairleigh Dickinson University, 1000 River Road, Teaneck, NJ 07666. Alexander Garcia, Director, International Business Programs. (201) 692–2142. (UP)

Florida International University, Tamiami Campus, Miami, FL 33199. William R. Beaton, Associate Dean, College of Business Administration. (305) 554–3282. (UP)

Fordham University, Graduate School of Business Administration, New York NY10023. Victor M. Borun, Finance Area Coordinator. (212) 841–5461. (UP)

George Mason University, 4400 University Drive, Fairfax, VA 22030. Lloyd M. DeBoer, Dean. (703) 323–2760. (UP)

George Washington University, School of Government and Business Administration, Washington, D.C. 20052. Adel I. El-Ansary, Chairman, Business Administration. (202) 676–6115. (UD)

Georgia College, Milledgeville, GA 31061. Donald Thompson. (921) 453–5772. (U)

Georgia State University, University Plaza, Atlanta, GA 30303. Arthur F. Schreiber, Associate Dean. (404) 658–2600. (U)

Golden Gate University, 536 Mission Street, San Francisco, CA 94105. A.G. Homan, Dean. Graduate School of International Management. (415) 442–7225. (P)

Gonzaga University, 502 E Boon, WA 94258. (U)

Harvard Business School, Soldiers Field, Boston, MA 02163. Thomas Piper, Senior Associate Dean. (617) 495–6370. (PD)

Hofstra University, School of Business, 1000 Fulton Avenue, Hempstead, NY 11550. Russell M. Moore, Associate Dean. (516) 560–5676. (U)

Holy Family College, Grant & Frankford Aves, Philadelphia, PA 19114. Bette Tokar, Chairman, Business Administration. (215) 637–7700. Home 357–4516. (U)

University of Houston, University Park CBA, Houston, TX 77004. Professor Robert R. Miller. (713) 749–7605. (P)

College of Idaho, J.A. Albertson School of Business, 2112 Cleveland Blvd, Caldwell, ID 83605. John Kilpatrick, Associate Professor. Management and International Business. (208) 459–5224. (U)

Illinois Benedictine College, 5700 College Road, Lisle, IL 60532. John E. Eber, Dean. (312) 960–1500. (U)

Illinois Institute of Technology, Chicago, IL 60616. J.S. Chung, Professor of Economics. (312) 567–5122. (P)

University of Iowa, College of Business Administration, Iowa City, IA 52242. W.P. Albrecht, Associate Dean. (319) 353–4334. (UPD)

Ithaca College, School of Business, Danby Road, Ithaca, NY 14850. David L. Long, Dean. (607) 274–3341. (U)

University of Kansas, School of Business, Lawrence, KS 66045. John Garland, Assistant Professor of International Business. (913) 864–3157. (UP)

La Salle University, 20th & Olney Ave., Philadelphia, PA 19141. Joshua Buch, Director of International Studies. (215) 951–1030. (P)

Lebanon Valley College, Annville, PA 17003. Alan Heffner, Chairman, Department of Management. (717) 867–4411 ext. 301. (U)

University of Lowell, Lowell, MA 01854. Braxton Hinchey, Chairman, Management. (617) 452–5000 ext. 2304. (U)

Lynchburg College, School of Business, Lynchburg, VA 24501. Kamal Abouzeid, Dean. (804) 522–8257. (UP)

University of Maine at Orono, College of Business Administration, 8 South Stevens Hall (CBA), Orono, ME 04469. Dean W. Stanley Devino. (207) 581–1968. (P)

Manhattan College, Riverdale, NY 10471. Emily Sun, Professor of Economics. (212) 920–0463. (U)

University of Miami, School of Business Administration, P.O. Box 249145, Coral Gables, FL 33124. Duane Kujawa, Director, International Business and Banking Institute. (305) 284–5484. (U)

Middle Tennessee State University, P.O. Box 101, Murfreesboro, TN 37132. Ben McNew, Dean. (615) 898–2300. (U)

Millsaps College, Jackson, MS 39210. Jerry Whitt, Dean, School of Management. (601) 35405201. (U)

University of North Carolina at Chapel Hill, School of Business Administration, Chapel Hill, NC 27514. Edward M. Graham, Associate Professor. (919) 962–3160. (UPD)

University of North Carolina at Greensboro, School of Business and Economics, 1000 Spring Garden St., Greensboro, NC 27412. Phil Friedman, Dean. (919) 379–5051. (UP)

Northeastern University, 360 Huntington Ave., Boston, MA 02115. Philip McDonald, Dean of Staff. (617) 437–3239. (UP)

Northwest Missouri State University, 214 Colden Hall, Maryville, MO 64468. Sharon Browning, Chairman of Maketing and International Business. (816) 562–1282. (U)

Ohio State University, College of Business Administration, Hagerty Hall, Columbus, OH 43210. Lee Nehrt. (614) 422–5288. (UP)

Oregon State University, College of Business, Corvallis, OR 97331. Stephen J. Lawton, International Business Coordinator. (505) 754–4033. (U)

University of Pittsburgh, Graduate School of Business, Pittsburgh, PA 15260. Josephine E. Olson, Associate Professsor of Business Administration; Coordinator of International Interest Group. (412) 624–6670. (P)

Queens College, 1900 Selwyn, Charlotte, NC 28012. Claire Vonk Brooks, Chairman, Business Division. (704) 337–2310. (UP)

Radford University, Radford, VA 24142. Allen L. Bures, Chairman. (703) 731–5481. (UP)

Rice University, Jesse H. Jones Graduate School of Administration, P.O. Box 1892, Houston, TX 77251. Francis D. Tuggle, Dean. (713) 527–4838. (P)

Rutgers, The State School of New Jersey, Graduate School of Management, 92 New St., Newark, NJ 07102. David H. Blake, Dean. (201) 648–5128. (P)

St John Fisher College, Graduate School of Management, Rochester, NY 14618. Selim Ilter. (716) 385–8082. (UP)

University of South Alabama, College of Business and Management Studies, Mobile, AL 36688. Julius M. Blum, Professor of International Business. (205) 460–6411. (UP)

University of South Carolina, College of Business Administration, Columbia, SC 29208. W.R. Folks, Jr, Program Director of International Business. (803) 777–7435. (UP)

Southeastern Louisiana University, Hammond, LA 70402. Joseph H. Miller, Jr, Dean. (504) 549–2258. (U)

Southern Methodist University, Dallas, TX 75275. R.R. Ferris, Associate Dean for Academic Affairs. (214) 692–3163. (UP)

Leonard N. Stern School of Business, New York University, 100 Trinity Place, New York, NY 10006–1594, USA. Undergraduate Programme, New York 998–4102; MBA Programme, New York 285–8827; PhD Programme, New York 285–8911. (UPD)

Suffolk University, School of Management, 8 Ashburton Place, Boston, MA 02108. Ronald E. Sundberg, Assistant Dean. (617) 723–4700 ext. 307. (U)

SUNY at Binghamton, School of Management, Vestal Parkway East, Birmingham, BY 13901. George Westacott, Associate Professor of International Business. (607) 777–2552. (UP)

University of Tennessee-Knoxville, 716 Stokely Management Center, UTK, Knoxville, TN 37996–0570. John R. Moore, Associate Dean. (615) 974–5061. (U)

University of Texas at Austin, Austin, TX 78712. Robert T. Green, Professor of International Business. (512) 471–1128. (UPD)

University of Toledo, Bancroft St, Toledo, OH 43606. James K. Weekly, Professor of International Business. (419) 537–2093. (U)

Utah State University, College of Business, Logan, UT. Keith L. Taylor, Assistant Professor of Business Administration. (801) 750–2363. (U)

Vanderbilt University, Owen Graduate School of Management, Nashville, TN 37203. David W. Stewart, Associate Dean. (615) 322–2534. (P)

Villanova University, Villanova, PA 19805. John J. Dugan, Assistant Professor (215) 645–4395. (UP)

University of Virginia, Colgate Darden Graduate School of Business, North Grounds, Box 6550, Charlottesville, VA 22906. Charles R. Kennedy, Jr, Assistant Professor. (804) 924–3208. (P)

Wake Forest University, Babcock Graduate School of Management, Winston-Salem, NC 27109. James M. Clapper, Associate Dean. (919) 761–5038. (P)

Washburn University, School of Business, Topeka, KS 66621. Richard E. Olson, Dean. (913) 295–6307. (P)

Wayne State University, School of Business Administration, Detroit, MI 48202. Attila Yaprak, Assistant Professor of Marketing. (313) 577–4493. (P)

Weber State College, 3750 Harrison, Ogden, UT 84408. Sterling Sessions. (801) 626–6812. (U)

Western Carolina University, Cullowhee, NC 28723. John F. McCreary, Dean of School of Business. (704) 227–7401. (U)

Wichita State University, 1845 Fairmount, Wichita, KS 67208. Douglas Sharp, Dean. (316) 689–3200. (U)

William Paterson College of New Jersey, 300 Pompton Road, Wayne, NJ 07470. Berch Haroian, Dean, School of Management. (201) 595–2731. (U)

University of Wisconsin at Madison, School of Business, Madison, WI 53706. R.T. Aubey. (608) 263–1169. (UP)

University of Wisconsin at Milwaukee, P.O. Box 742, Milwaukee, WI 53201. U. Kanti Prasad, Associate Dean. (414) 963–4238. (PD)

Xavier University, Cincinnati, OH 45207. Harold L. Bryant, Professor of Economics. (513) 745–3051.

VENEZUELA

Universidad Nacional Abierta, Coordinator Maria Angelina de Kolstar, Avda. Gamboa No. 18, San Bernardino, Caracas, Venezuela. 02–514824. (U)

Universidad Catolica Andres Bello, School of Business and Accounting, Pedro Linares, Director, La Vega-Montalban, Apartado 29068, Caracas, Venezuela. 475111 al 19. Gustavo Sucre, Dean. (UP)

Universidad Centrooccidental 'Lisandro Alvarado', Escuela de Administracion y Contaduria, Lic. Francesco Leone, Apartado 400 – Barquisimeto – Edo. Lara, Venezuela. 514383. Pedro A. Leal. (UP)

Universidad de Los Andes, School of Administration and Public Accounting, Mr Oscar E. Parrar, Merida, Venezuela. (074) 49722. (U)

YUGOSLAVIA

'Djuro Pucar Stari' Banjaluka, Faculty of Economics, Dr Sabahudin Osmancevic, Danka Mitrova bb, 78000 Banjaluka, Yugoslavia. 078–46097.

Edvard Kardelj University of Ljubljana, Boris Kidric Faculty of Economics, Professor Viljem Merhar, Kardeljeva ploscad 17, 61000 Ljubljana, Yugoslavia. (061) 345–669. (UPD)

University of Split, Faculty of Economics at Split, Dr Drazen Stambuk, Radovanova 13, 58000 Split, Yugoslavia. 958–581–644. Sliskovuc Davor. (UPD)

ZAMBIA

University of Zambia, School of Humanities and Social Sciences, C.J.J. Mphaisha, Dean, P.O. Box 32379, Lusaka, Zambia. (01) 253827. (UP)

ZIMBABWE

University of Zimbabwe, Department of Accountancy, M.R. Hove, Chairman, P.O. Box MP167, Mount Pleasant, Harare, Zimbabwe. 303211 ext. 198. (U)

Index of Names

(Names of authors cited. On principle these are only referenced to pages which provide details of their publications.)

Index of Subjects

(The word 'international' is assumed in the following headings and is not repeated.)